MAGNIFICENT

IN THE LATE 1960s AND EARLY 1970s, WHEN A

WERE ATTEMPTING TO PUT A FEMALE SENSIBILITY

THAT ACROSS THE PACIFIC OCEAN, ANOTHER

THING, AND DOING IT 100 TIMES BETTER THAN

LONG AFTER SHOJO MANGA HAD WASHED UP

LONGER POSSIBLE FOR MALE COMICS EDITORS

READ COMICS, AND I'M HUMBLED BY WHAT I

THANKS TO *THE COMICS JOURNAL*'S SPECIAL

COMPLETELY FLOORED ME; I HAD NE

MORE. FINALLY, THE FANTAGRAPHICS (

HAGIO'S SHORTER MANGA ARE COLLEC

TO WATCH HER ART AND STORYTELLING GROW

GIRL'S STORY, "BIANCA," TO THE BRILLIANT TOUR

"THE WILLOW TREE" — AFTER FINISHING THAT

MOTO-SAN HAD INCLUDED IN THE STORY, WHICH

READING 'THE WILLOW TREE,' MAKE SURE YOU

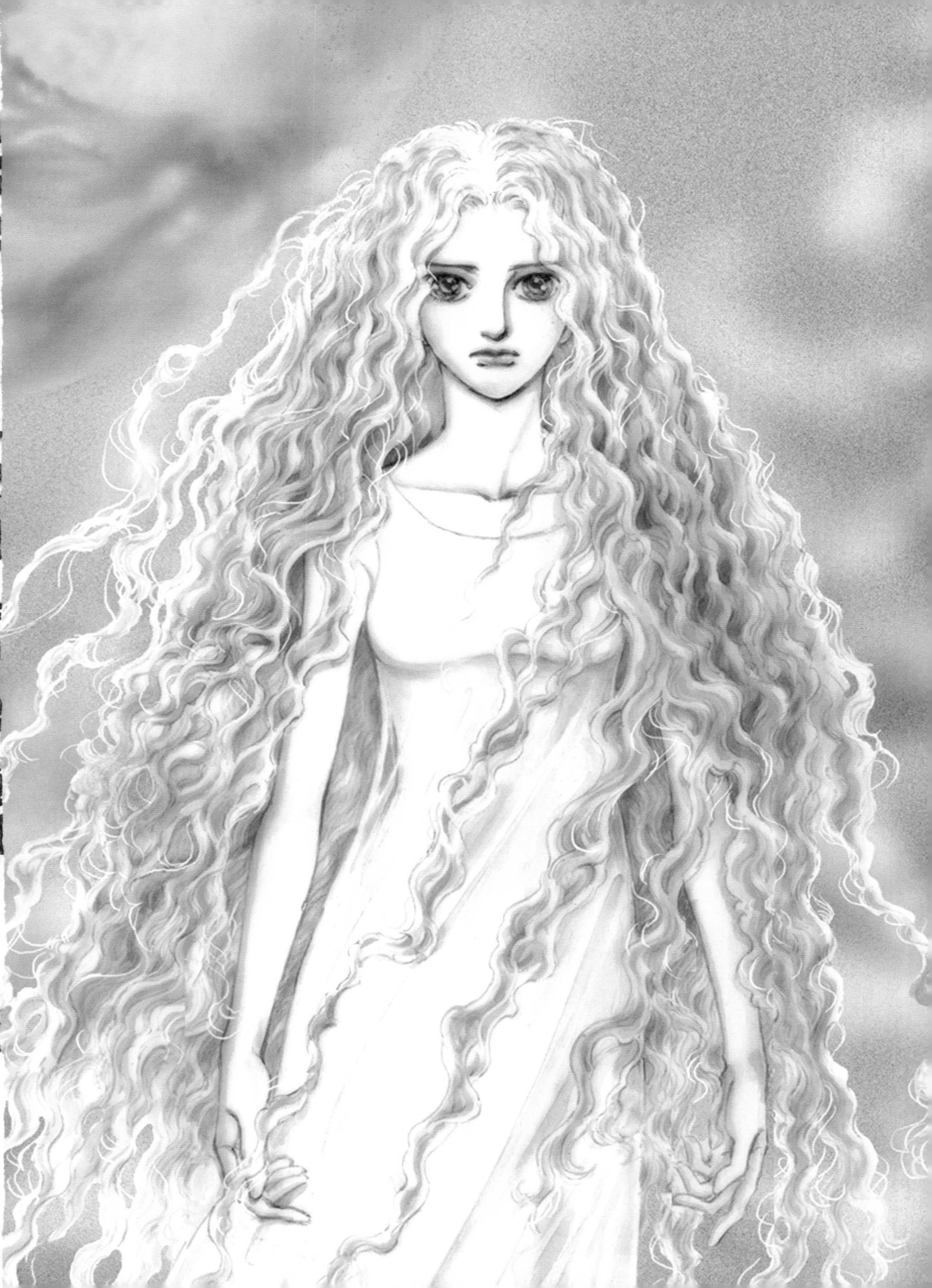

A DRUNKEN DREAM

AND OTHER STORIES

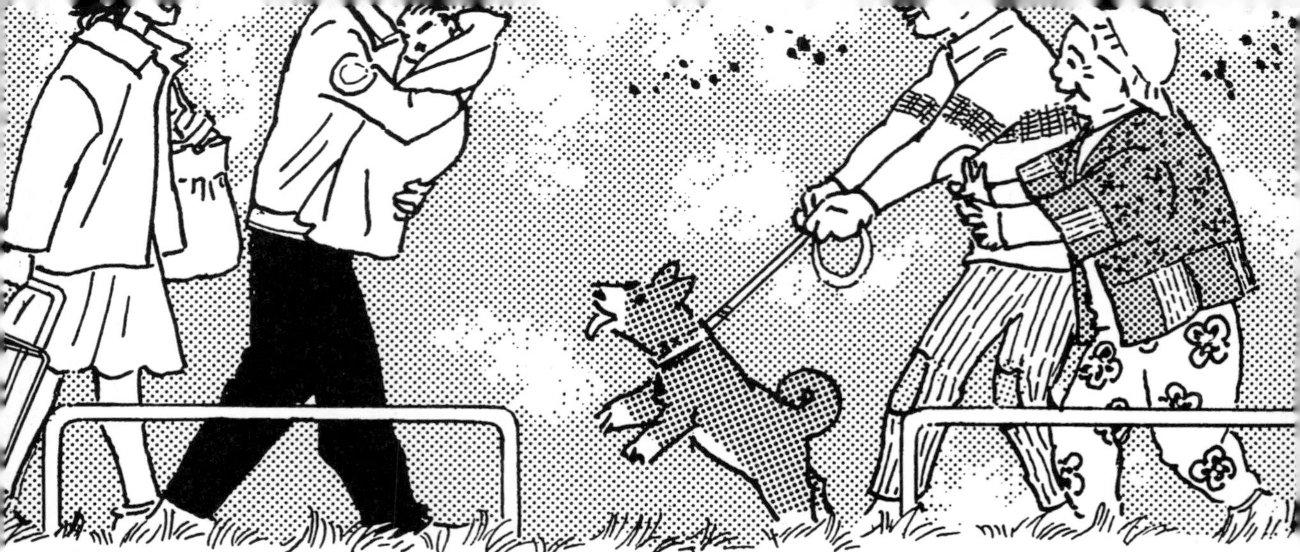

MOTO HAGIO'S A DRUNKEN DREAM AND OTHER STORIES

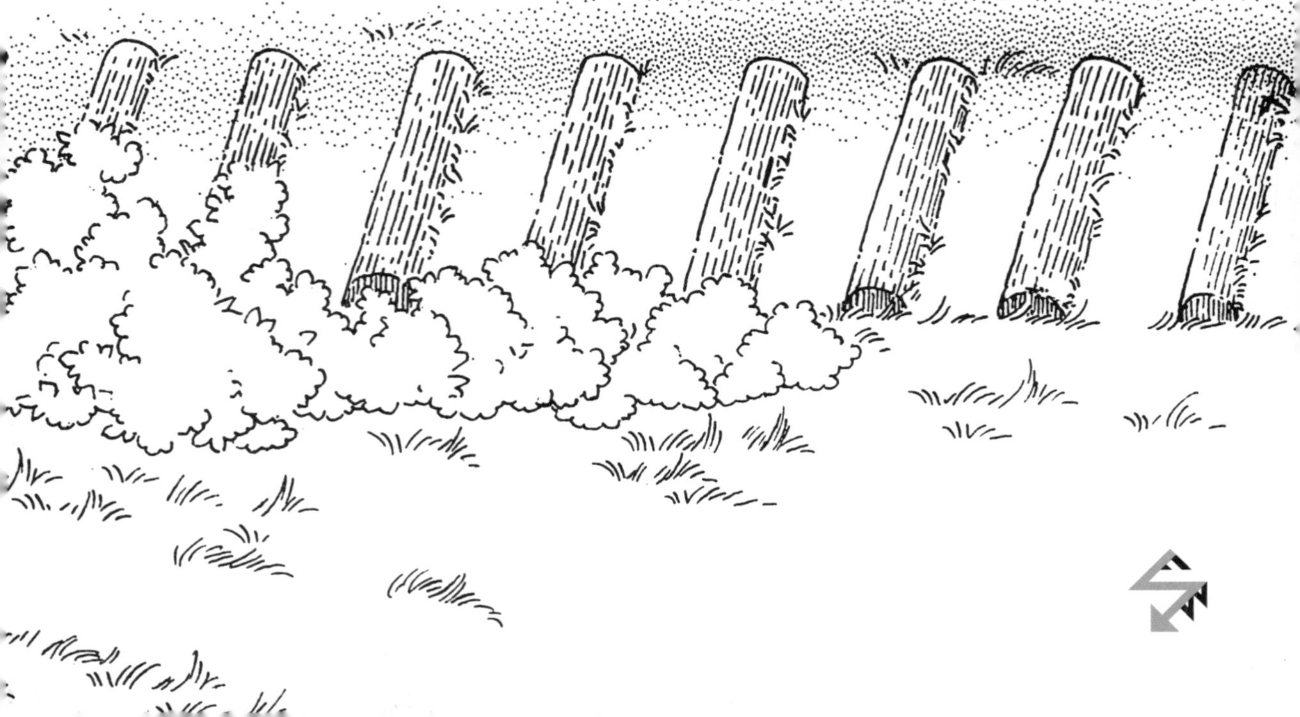

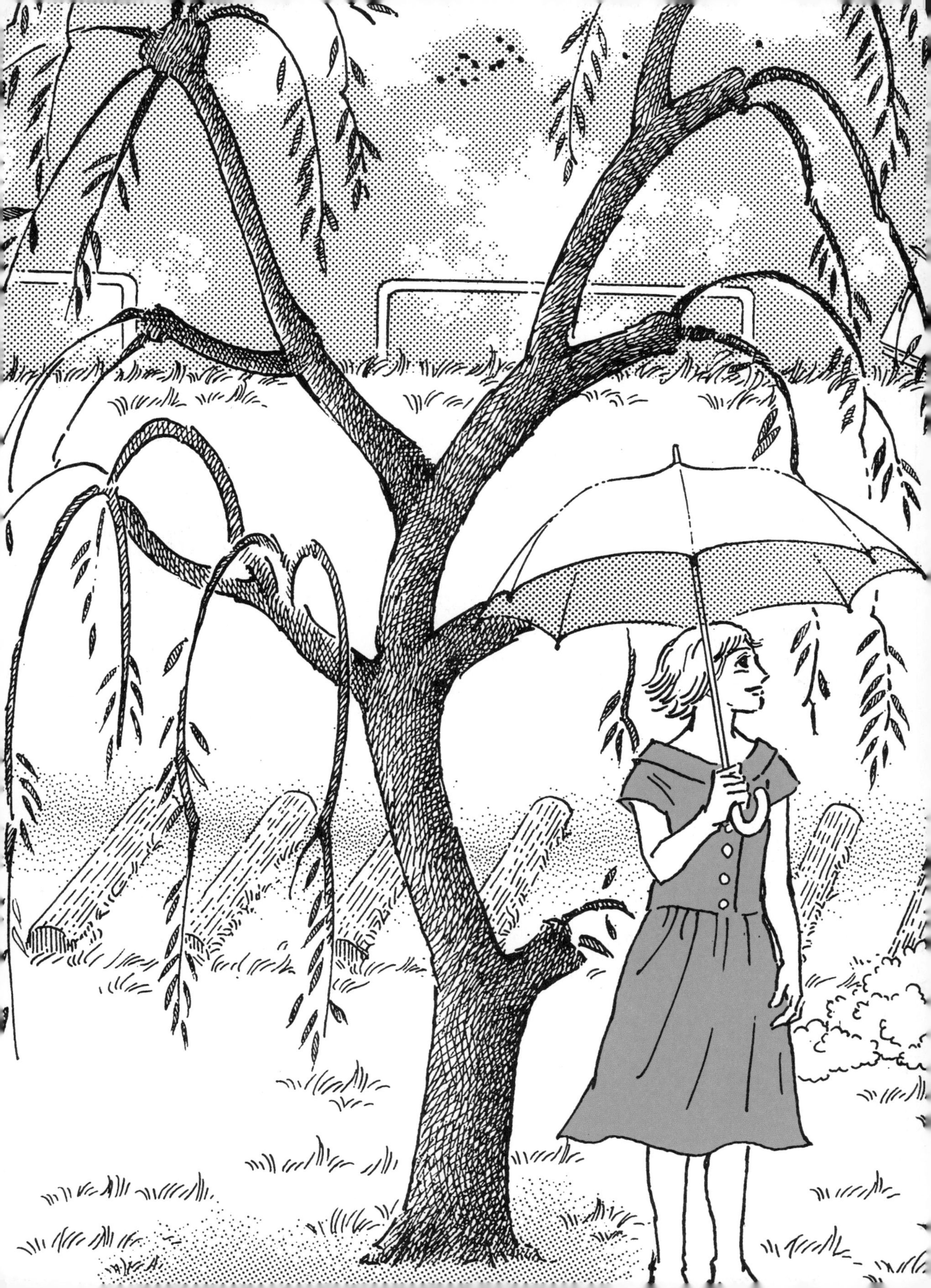

CONTENTS:

V   "THE MAGNIFICENT FORTY-NINERS"   By Matt THORN

IX   "THE MOTO HAGIO INTERVIEW"   Conducted by Matt THORN

⚡007   **BIANCA**   *BIANKA* © 1977 Moto HAGIO

⚡023   **GIRL ON PORCH WITH PUPPY**   *PORCH DE SHOJO GA KOINUTO* © 1977 Moto HAGIO

⚡035   **AUTUMN JOURNEY**   *AKI NO TABI* © 1977 Moto HAGIO

⚡059   **MARIÉ, TEN YEARS LATER**   *JUNENME NO MARIE* © 1985 Moto HAGIO

⚡075   **A DRUNKEN DREAM**   *SUIMU* © 1985 Moto HAGIO

⚡097   **HANSHIN: HALF-GOD**   *HANSHIN* © 1985 Moto HAGIO

⚡113   **ANGEL MIMIC**   *TENSHI NO GITAI* © 2008 Moto HAGIO

⚡163   **IGUANA GIRL**   *IGUANA NO MUSUME* © 2008 Moto HAGIO

⚡213   **THE CHILD WHO COMES HOME**   *KAETTEKURU KO* © 2008 Moto HAGIO

⚡237   **THE WILLOW TREE**   *YANAGI NO KI* © 2007 Moto HAGIO

FANTAGRAPHICS BOOKS
7563 Lake City Way NE, Seattle, WA 98115

Translation: Matt THORN
Editorial Liaison: Gary GROTH
Design: Adam GRANO
Lettering: Rich TOMMASO
Production: Paul BARESH
Associate Publisher: Eric REYNOLDS
Publishers: Gary GROTH and Kim THOMPSON

To receive a free full-color catalog of comics, graphic novels, and other manga, call 1-800-657-1100,
or visit www.fantagraphics.com. You may order books at our web site or by phone.

Distributed in the U.S. by W.W. Norton and Company, Inc. (212-354-5500)
Distributed in Canada by the Canadian Manda Group (416-516-0911)
Distributed in the United Kingdom by Turnaround Distribution (108-829-3009)

First Fantagraphics printing: September, 2010
ISBN: 978-1-60699-377-4
Printed in China

If you enjoy the graphic design of this book, please read: **HTTP://EN.WIKIPEDIA.ORG/WIKI/WABI-SABI**

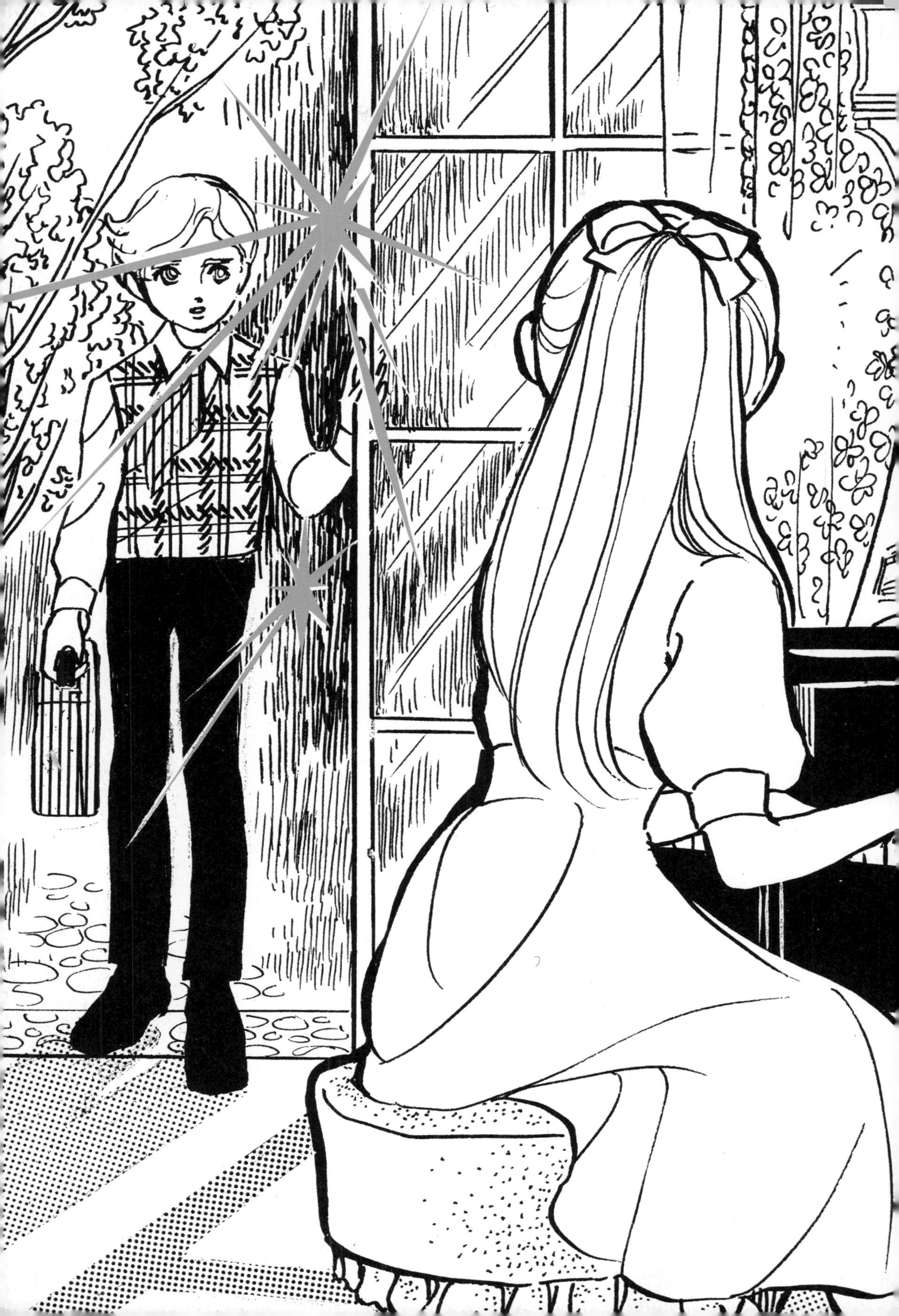

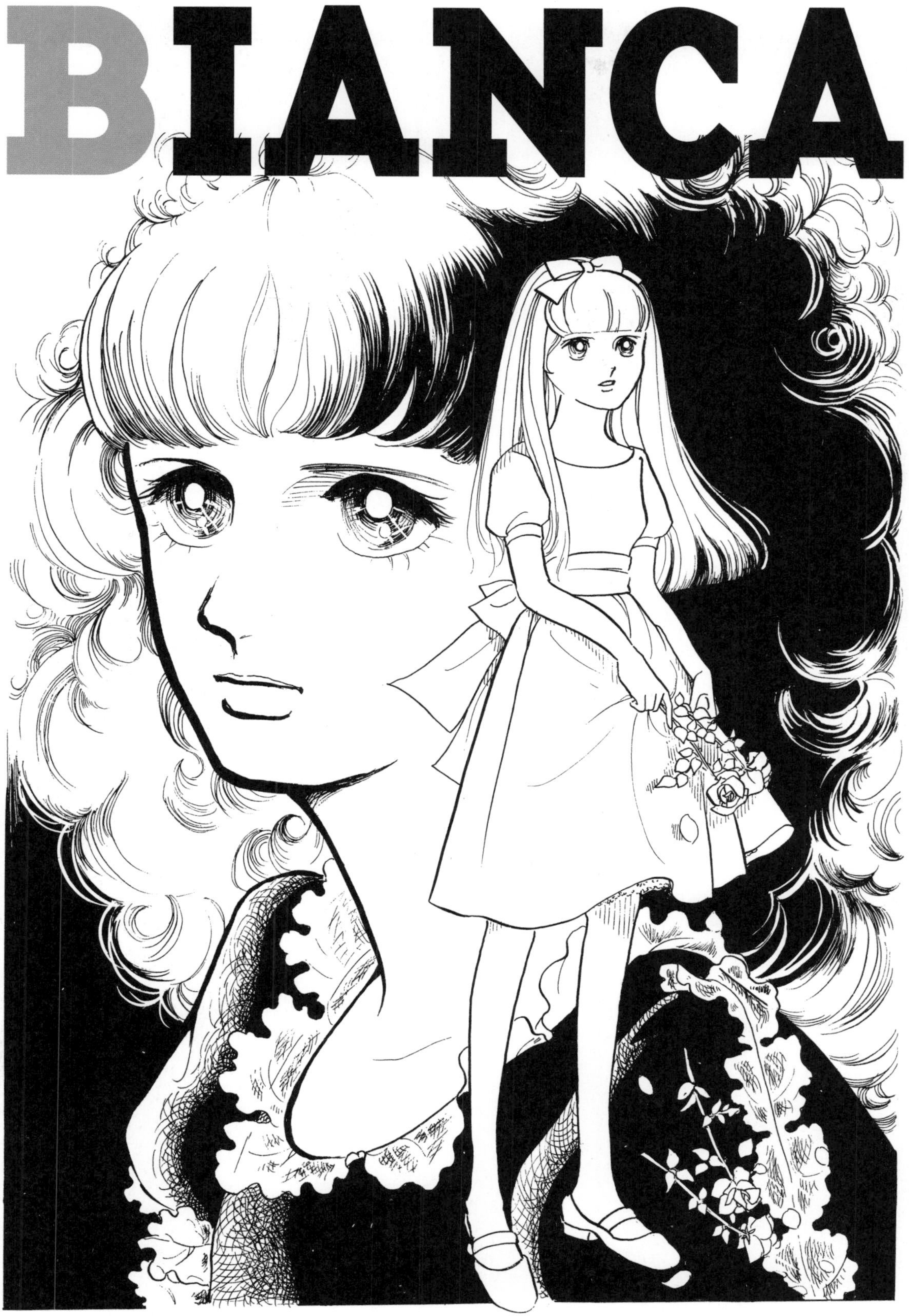
BIANCA

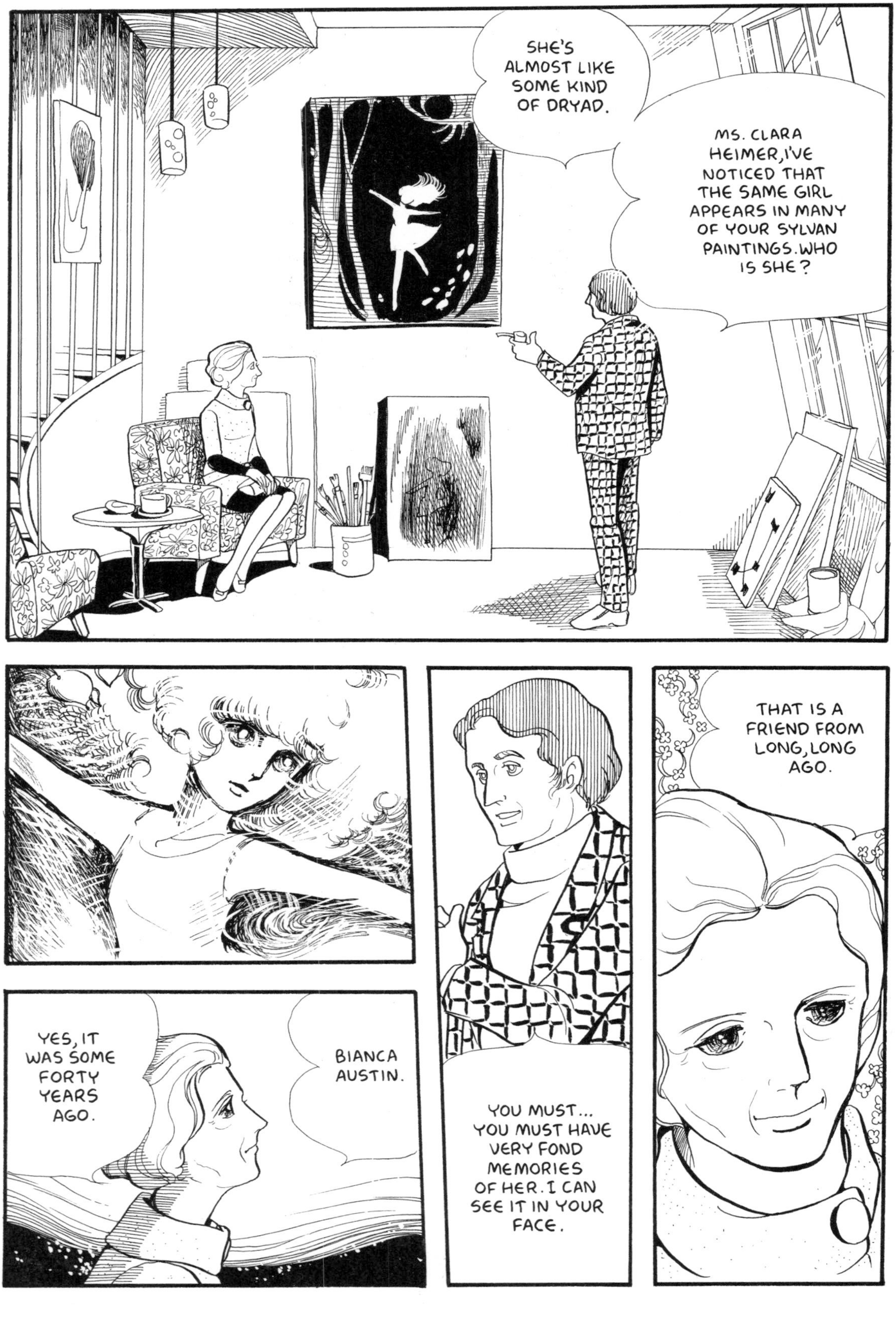
SHE'S ALMOST LIKE SOME KIND OF DRYAD.
MS. CLARA HEIMER, I'VE NOTICED THAT THE SAME GIRL APPEARS IN MANY OF YOUR SYLVAN PAINTINGS. WHO IS SHE?
THAT IS A FRIEND FROM LONG, LONG AGO.
YOU MUST... YOU MUST HAVE VERY FOND MEMORIES OF HER. I CAN SEE IT IN YOUR FACE.
BIANCA AUSTIN.
YES, IT WAS SOME FORTY YEARS AGO.

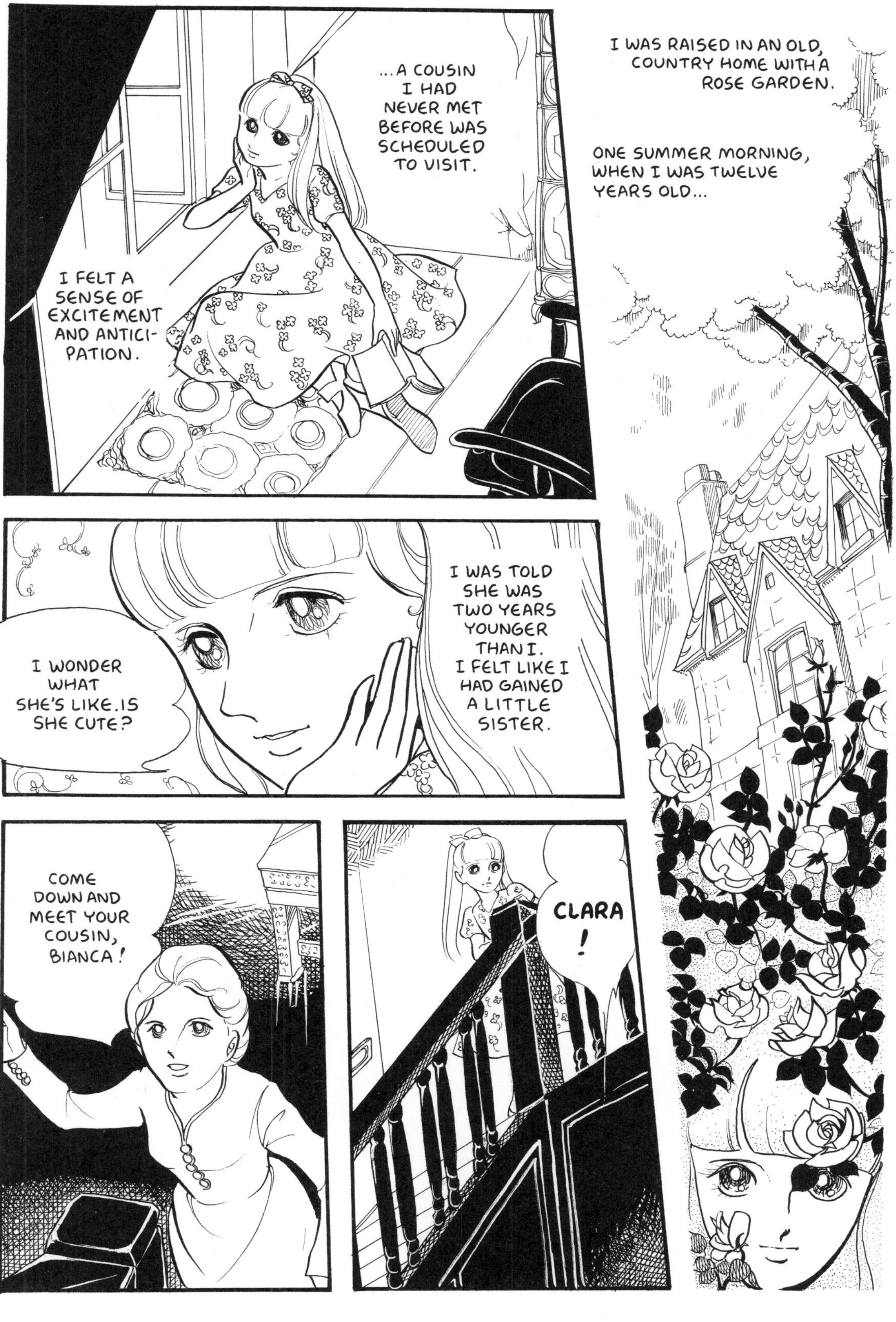
I WAS RAISED IN AN OLD, COUNTRY HOME WITH A ROSE GARDEN.
ONE SUMMER MORNING, WHEN I WAS TWELVE YEARS OLD...
...A COUSIN I HAD NEVER MET BEFORE WAS SCHEDULED TO VISIT.
I FELT A SENSE OF EXCITEMENT AND ANTICI-PATION.
I WAS TOLD SHE WAS TWO YEARS YOUNGER THAN I. I FELT LIKE I HAD GAINED A LITTLE SISTER.
I WONDER WHAT SHE'S LIKE. IS SHE CUTE?
CLARA!
COME DOWN AND MEET YOUR COUSIN, BIANCA!

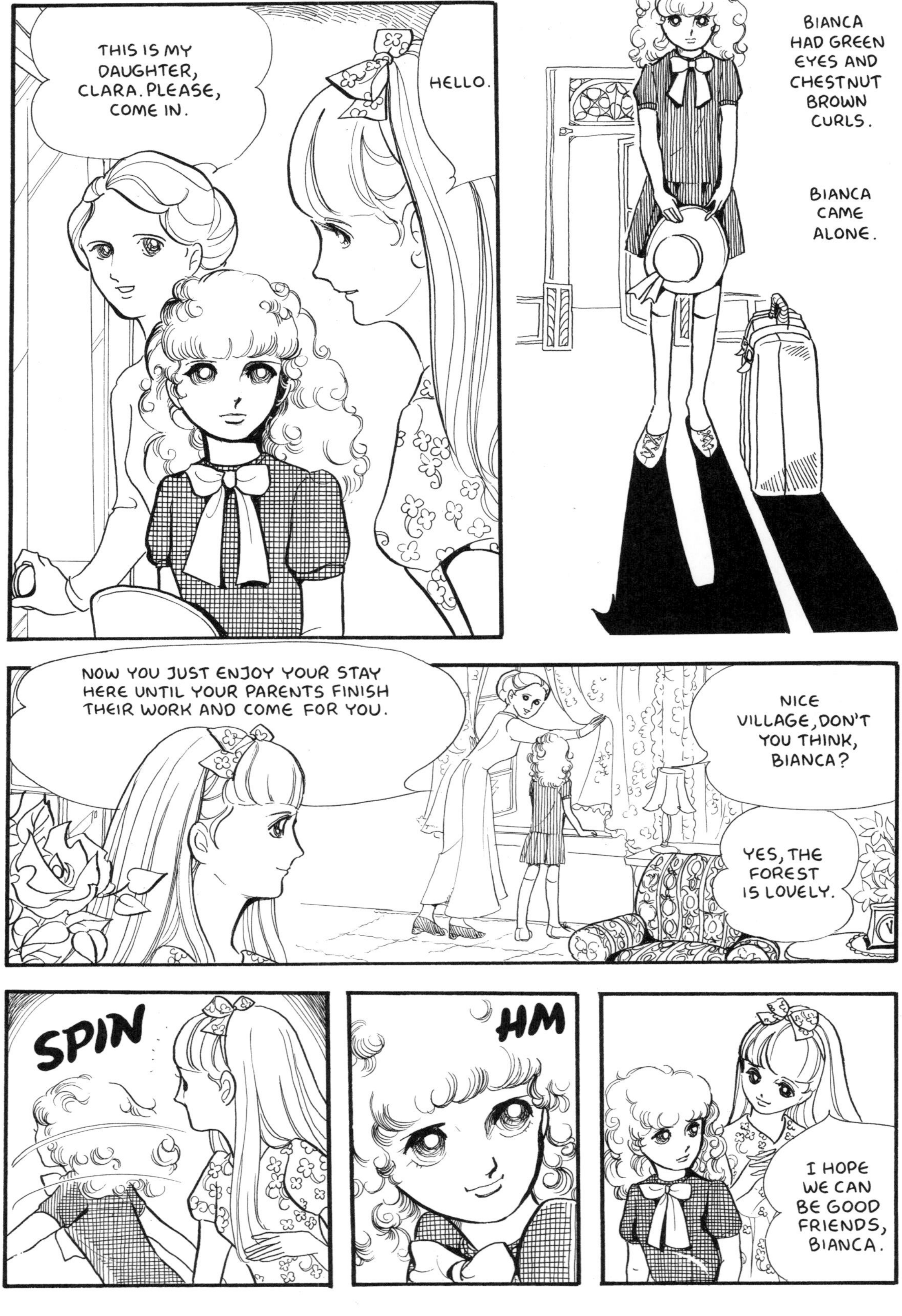
BIANCA HAD GREEN EYES AND CHESTNUT BROWN CURLS.
BIANCA CAME ALONE.
HELLO.
THIS IS MY DAUGHTER, CLARA. PLEASE, COME IN.
NICE VILLAGE, DON'T YOU THINK, BIANCA?
YES, THE FOREST IS LOVELY.
NOW YOU JUST ENJOY YOUR STAY HERE UNTIL YOUR PARENTS FINISH THEIR WORK AND COME FOR YOU.
I HOPE WE CAN BE GOOD FRIENDS, BIANCA.
HM
SPIN

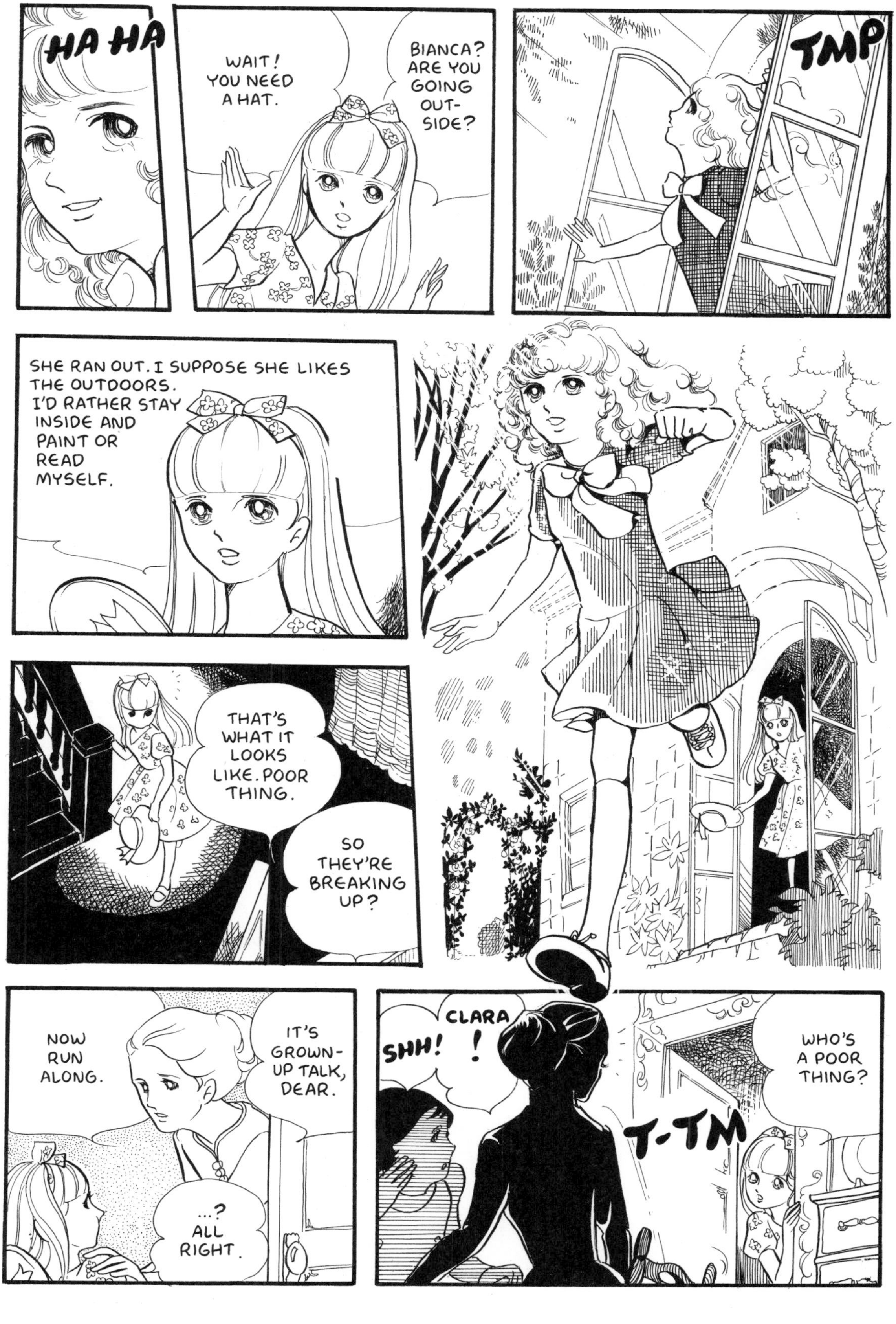
TMP
BIANCA? ARE YOU GOING OUT-SIDE?
WAIT! YOU NEED A HAT.
HA HA
SHE RAN OUT. I SUPPOSE SHE LIKES THE OUTDOORS. I'D RATHER STAY INSIDE AND PAINT OR READ MYSELF.
THAT'S WHAT IT LOOKS LIKE. POOR THING.
SO THEY'RE BREAKING UP?
WHO'S A POOR THING?
T-TM
CLARA !
SHH!
IT'S GROWN-UP TALK, DEAR.
NOW RUN ALONG.
...? ALL RIGHT.

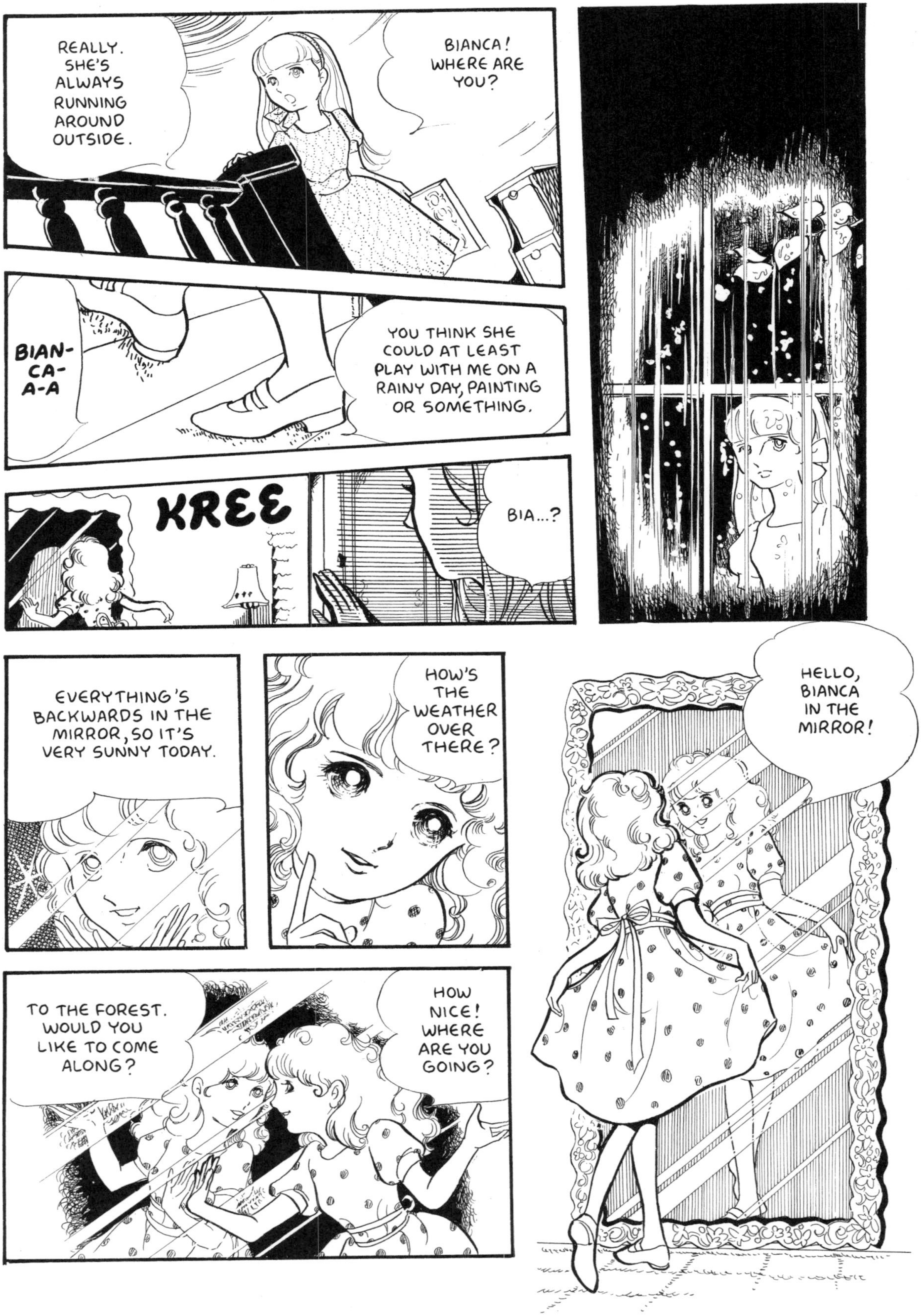
BIANCA! WHERE ARE YOU?
REALLY. SHE'S ALWAYS RUNNING AROUND OUTSIDE.
YOU THINK SHE COULD AT LEAST PLAY WITH ME ON A RAINY DAY, PAINTING OR SOMETHING.
BIAN-CA-A-A
BIA...?
KREE
HELLO, BIANCA IN THE MIRROR!
HOW'S THE WEATHER OVER THERE?
EVERYTHING'S BACKWARDS IN THE MIRROR, SO IT'S VERY SUNNY TODAY.
HOW NICE! WHERE ARE YOU GOING?
TO THE FOREST. WOULD YOU LIKE TO COME ALONG?

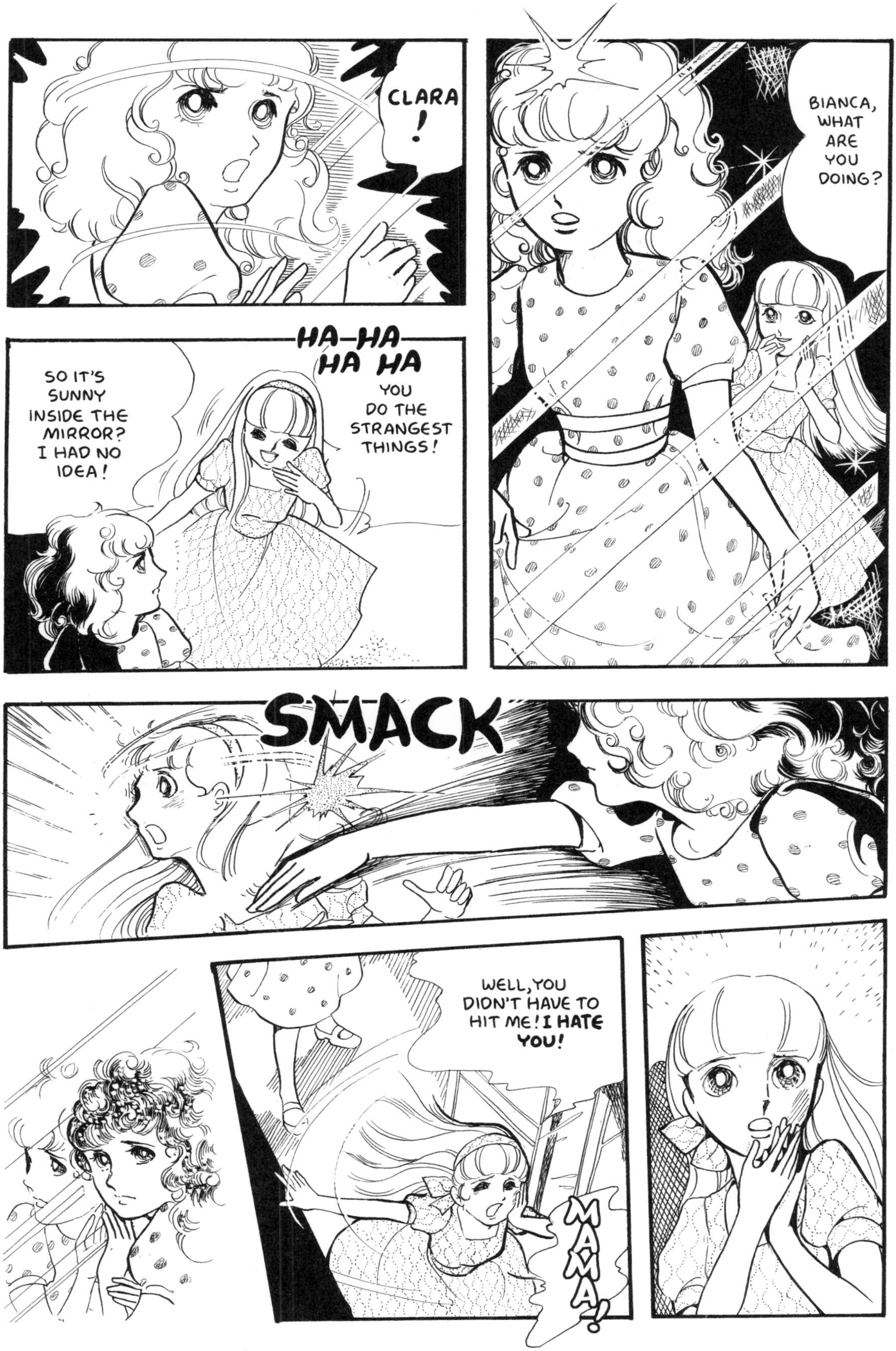
BIANCA, WHAT ARE YOU DOING?
CLARA!
HA-HA HA HA
YOU DO THE STRANGEST THINGS!
SO IT'S SUNNY INSIDE THE MIRROR? I HAD NO IDEA!
SMACK
WELL, YOU DIDN'T HAVE TO HIT ME! I HATE YOU!
MAMA!

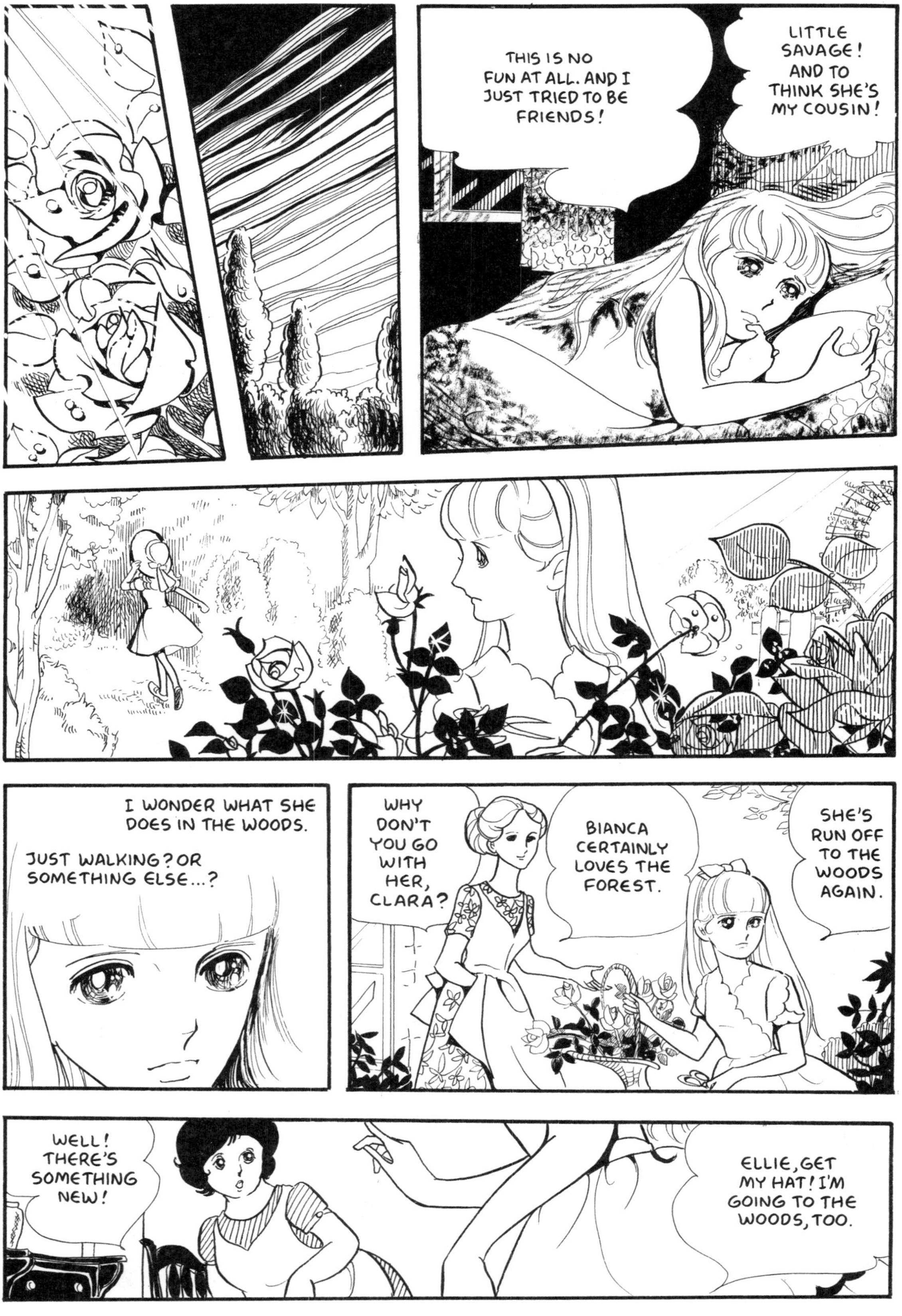
LITTLE SAVAGE! AND TO THINK SHE'S MY COUSIN!
THIS IS NO FUN AT ALL. AND I JUST TRIED TO BE FRIENDS!
SHE'S RUN OFF TO THE WOODS AGAIN.
BIANCA CERTAINLY LOVES THE FOREST.
WHY DON'T YOU GO WITH HER, CLARA?
I WONDER WHAT SHE DOES IN THE WOODS.
JUST WALKING? OR SOMETHING ELSE...?
ELLIE, GET MY HAT! I'M GOING TO THE WOODS, TOO.
WELL! THERE'S SOMETHING NEW!

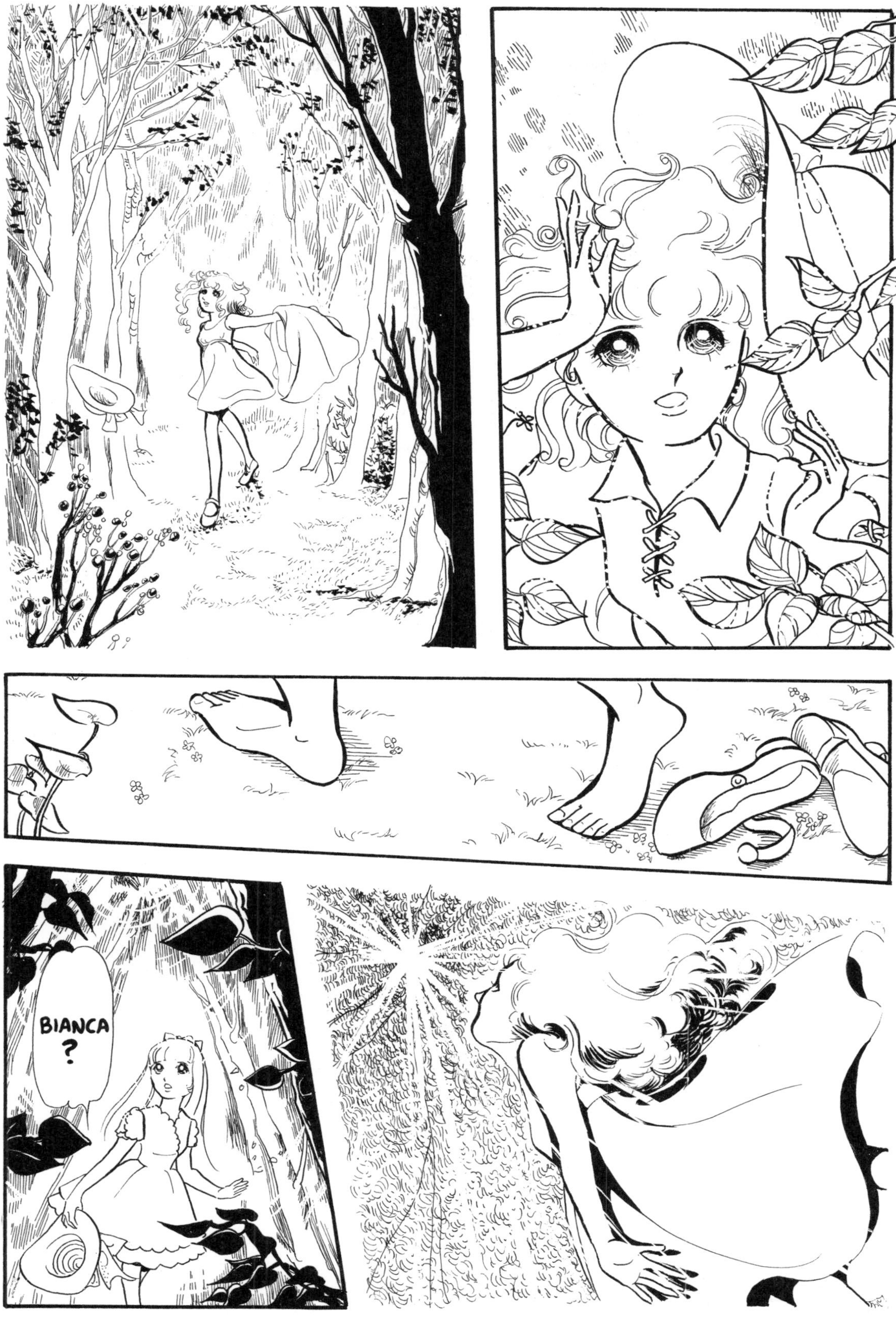
BIANCA ?

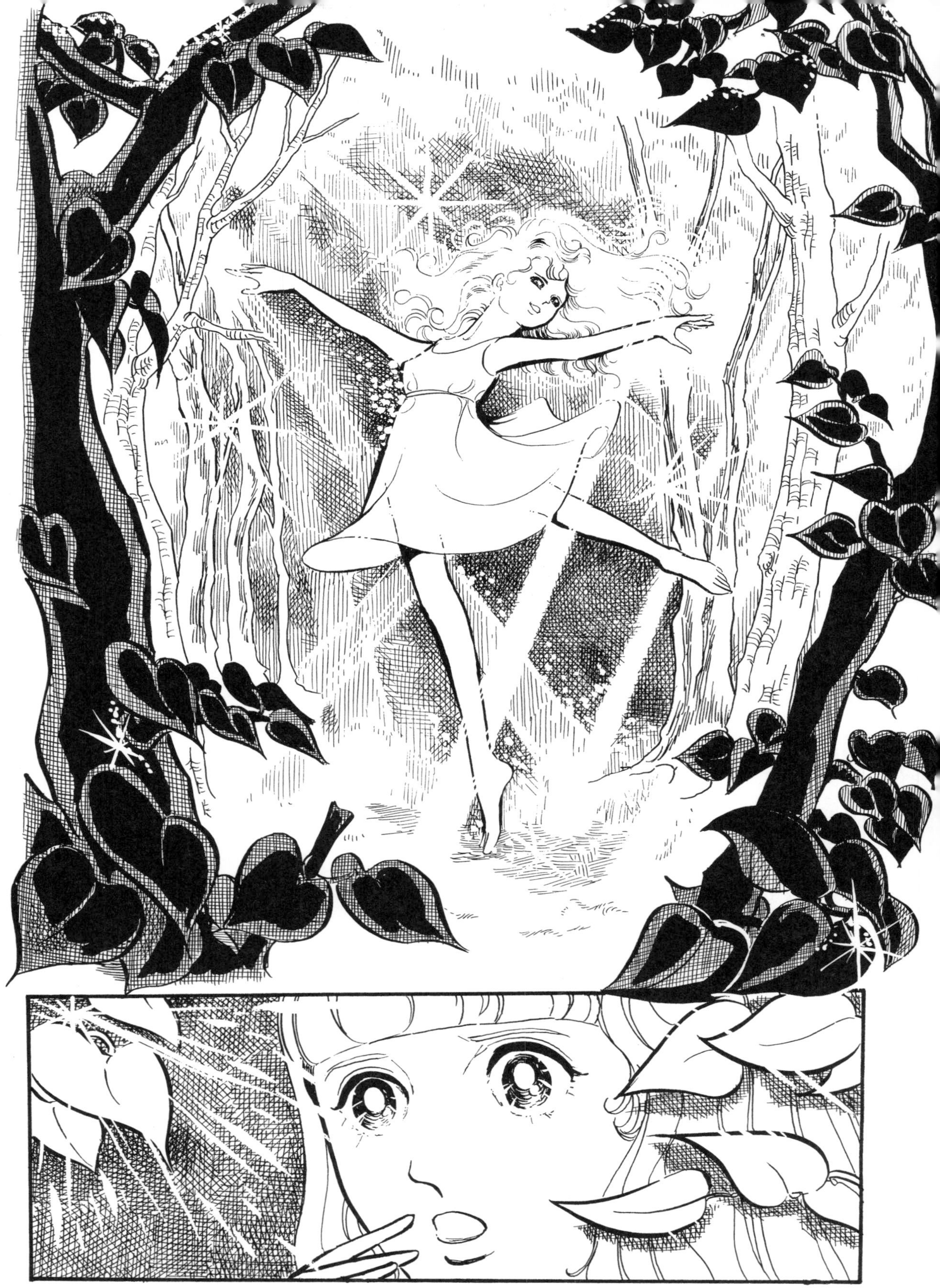

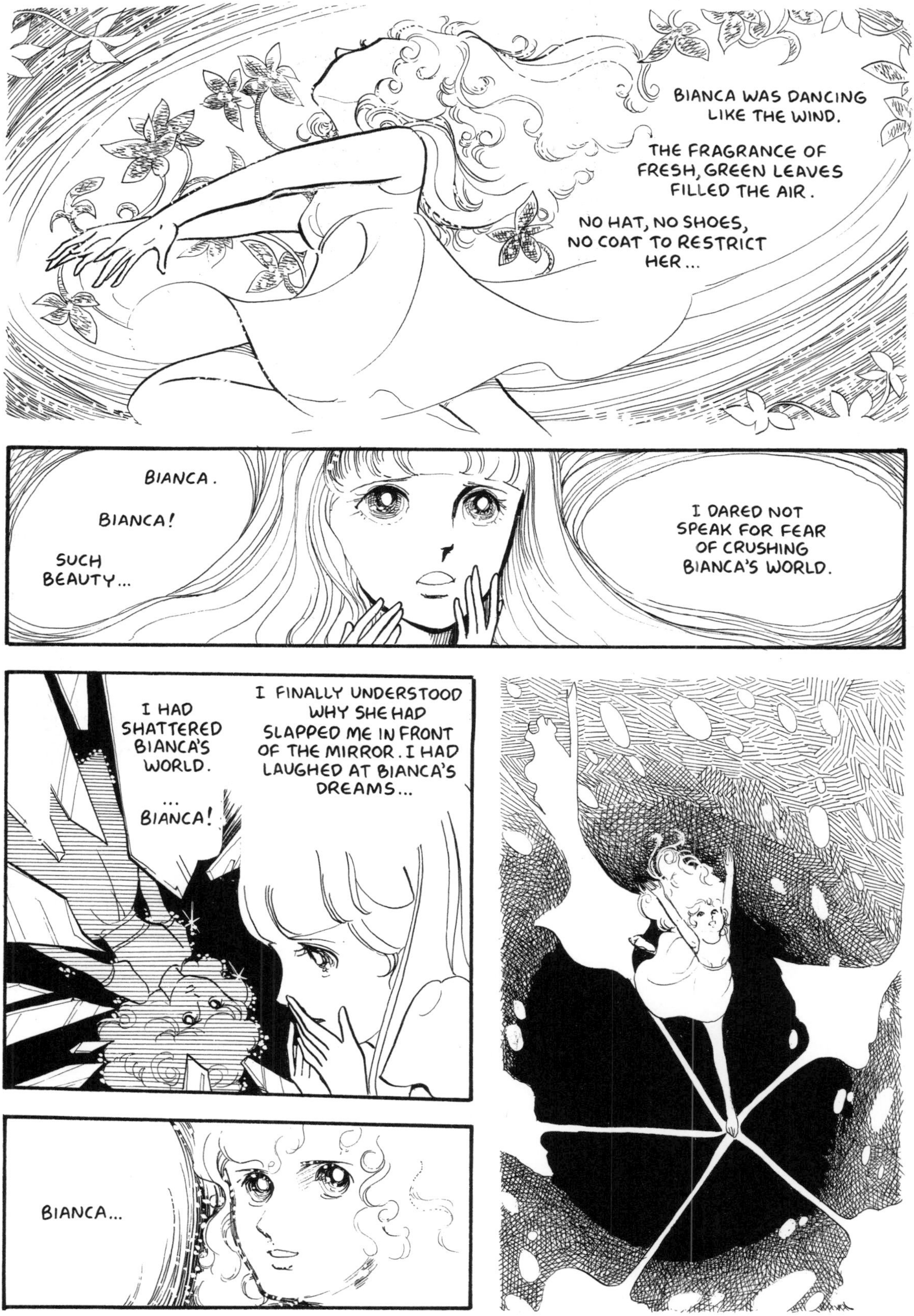
BIANCA WAS DANCING LIKE THE WIND.
THE FRAGRANCE OF FRESH, GREEN LEAVES FILLED THE AIR.
NO HAT, NO SHOES, NO COAT TO RESTRICT HER...
BIANCA.
BIANCA!
SUCH BEAUTY...
I DARED NOT SPEAK FOR FEAR OF CRUSHING BIANCA'S WORLD.
I FINALLY UNDERSTOOD WHY SHE HAD SLAPPED ME IN FRONT OF THE MIRROR. I HAD LAUGHED AT BIANCA'S DREAMS...
I HAD SHATTERED BIANCA'S WORLD.
... BIANCA!
BIANCA...

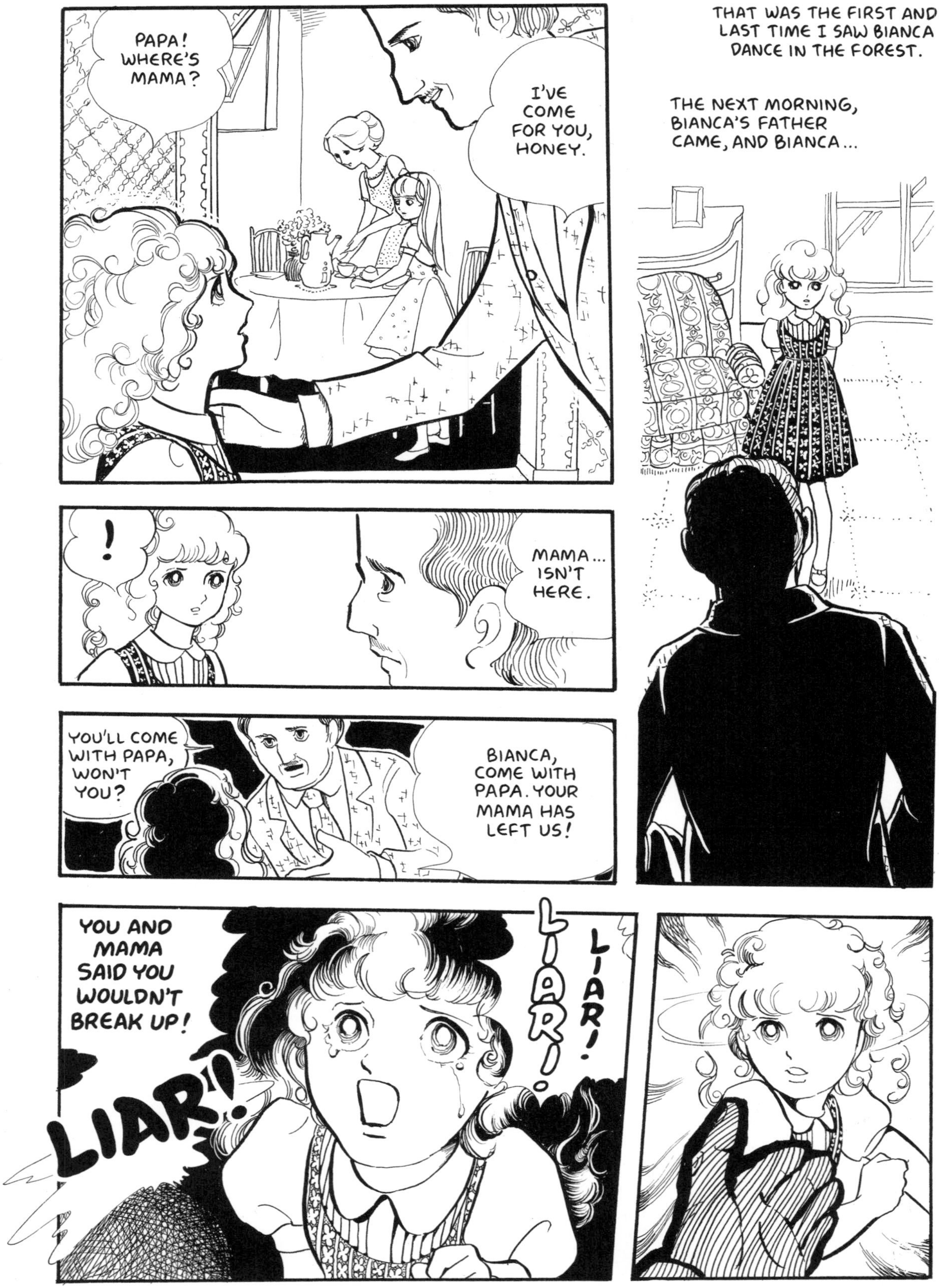
THAT WAS THE FIRST AND LAST TIME I SAW BIANCA DANCE IN THE FOREST.
THE NEXT MORNING, BIANCA'S FATHER CAME, AND BIANCA...
I'VE COME FOR YOU, HONEY.
PAPA! WHERE'S MAMA?
MAMA... ISN'T HERE.
!
BIANCA, COME WITH PAPA. YOUR MAMA HAS LEFT US!
YOU'LL COME WITH PAPA, WON'T YOU?
LIAR!
LIAR!
YOU AND MAMA SAID YOU WOULDN'T BREAK UP!
LIAR!!

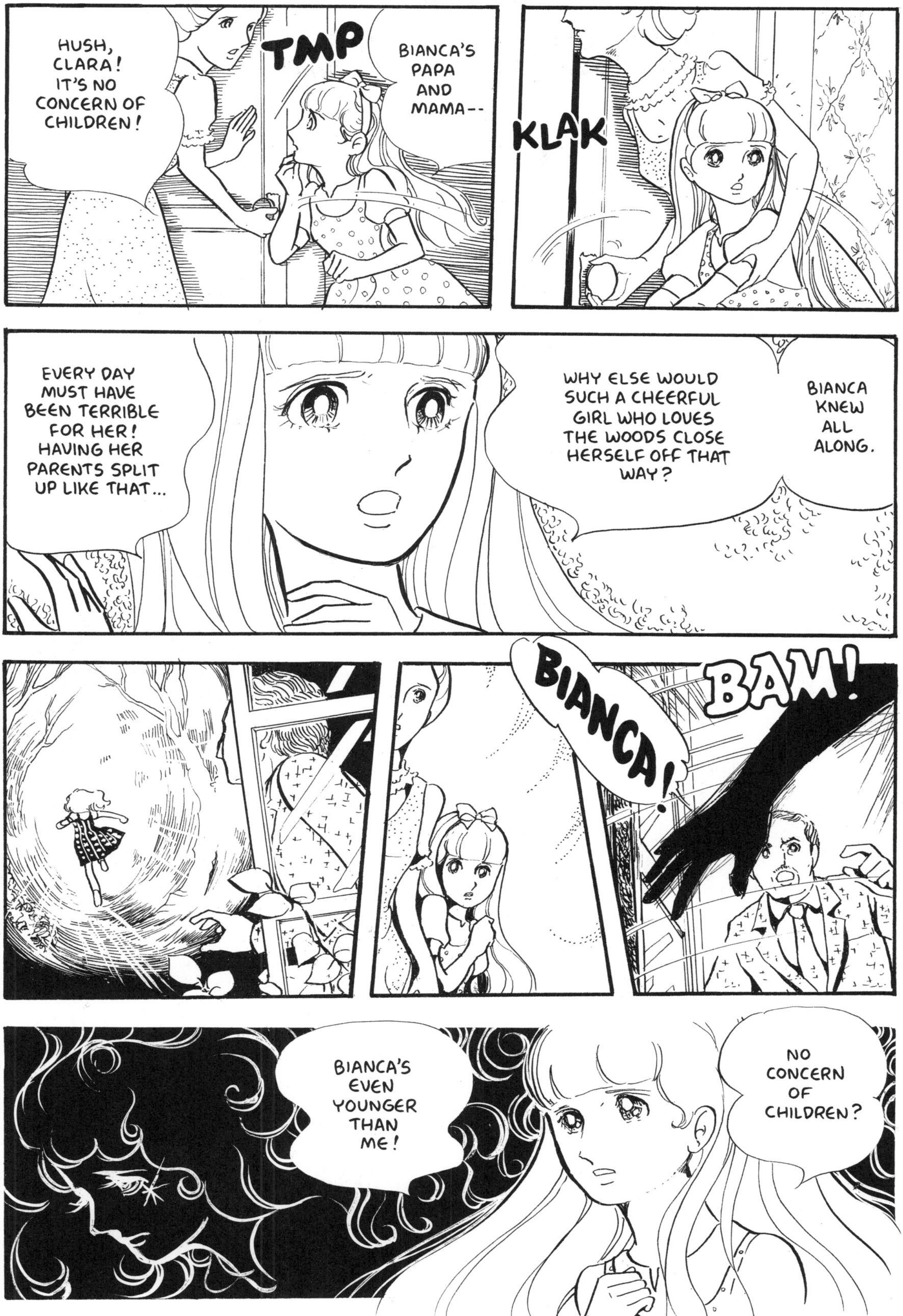
KLAK
BIANCA'S PAPA AND MAMA--
TMP
HUSH, CLARA! IT'S NO CONCERN OF CHILDREN!
BIANCA KNEW ALL ALONG.
WHY ELSE WOULD SUCH A CHEERFUL GIRL WHO LOVES THE WOODS CLOSE HERSELF OFF THAT WAY?
EVERY DAY MUST HAVE BEEN TERRIBLE FOR HER! HAVING HER PARENTS SPLIT UP LIKE THAT...
BAM!
BIANCA!
NO CONCERN OF CHILDREN?
BIANCA'S EVEN YOUNGER THAN ME!

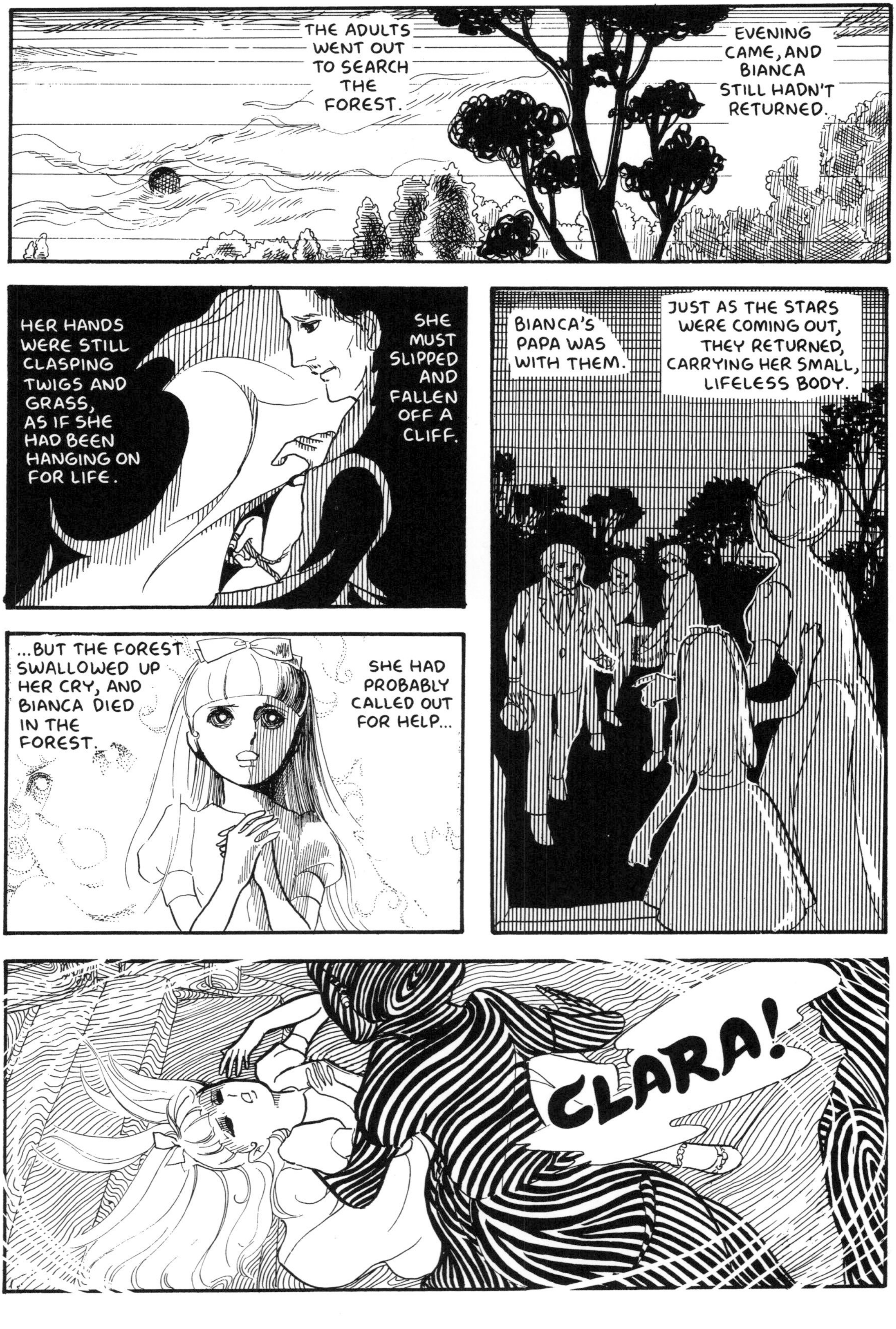
EVENING CAME, AND BIANCA STILL HADN'T RETURNED.
THE ADULTS WENT OUT TO SEARCH THE FOREST.
JUST AS THE STARS WERE COMING OUT, THEY RETURNED, CARRYING HER SMALL, LIFELESS BODY.
BIANCA'S PAPA WAS WITH THEM.
SHE MUST SLIPPED AND FALLEN OFF A CLIFF.
HER HANDS WERE STILL CLASPING TWIGS AND GRASS, AS IF SHE HAD BEEN HANGING ON FOR LIFE.
SHE HAD PROBABLY CALLED OUT FOR HELP...
...BUT THE FOREST SWALLOWED UP HER CRY, AND BIANCA DIED IN THE FOREST.
CLARA!

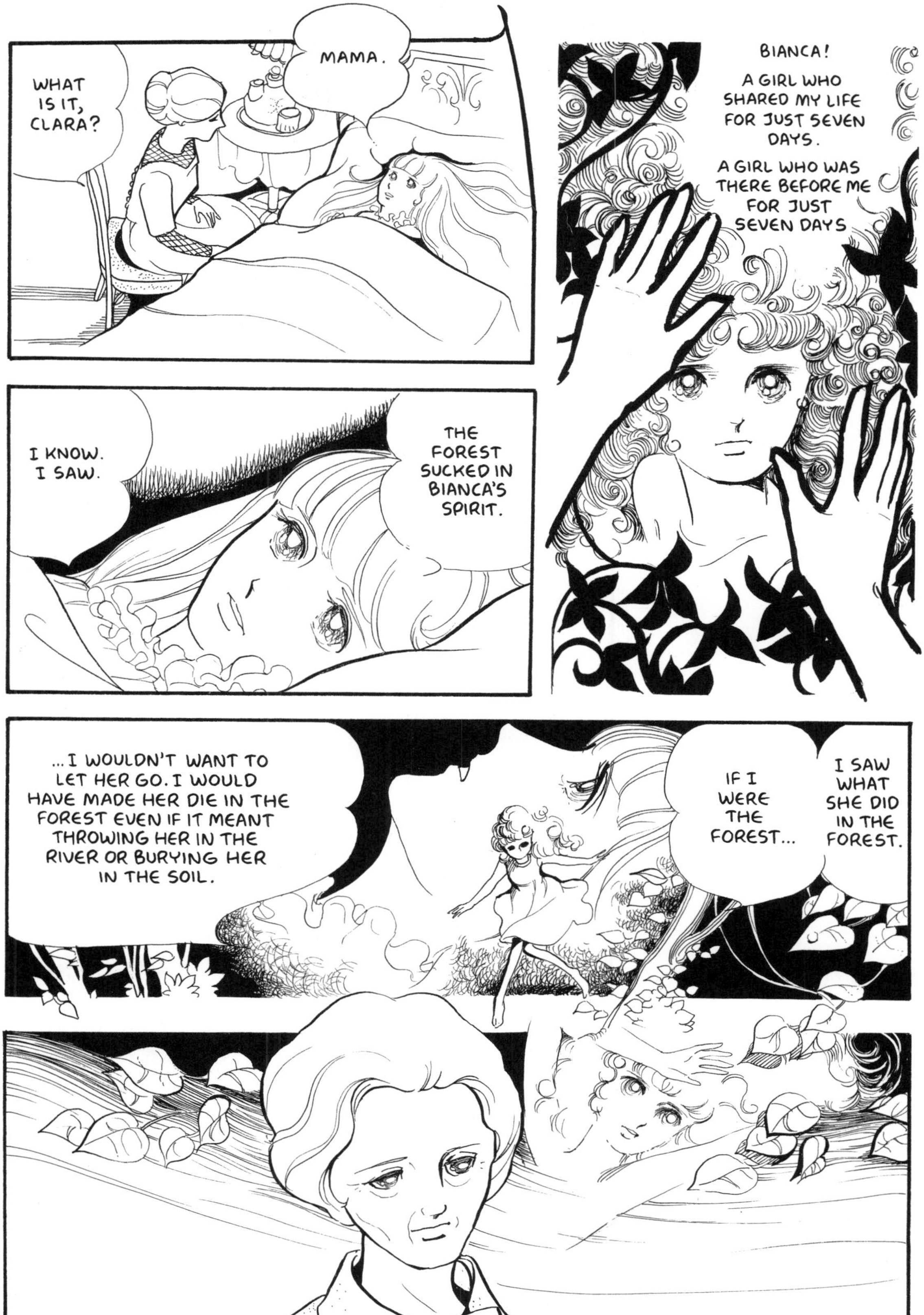
BIANCA!
A GIRL WHO SHARED MY LIFE FOR JUST SEVEN DAYS.
A GIRL WHO WAS THERE BEFORE ME FOR JUST SEVEN DAYS
MAMA.
WHAT IS IT, CLARA?
THE FOREST SUCKED IN BIANCA'S SPIRIT.
I KNOW. I SAW.
I SAW WHAT SHE DID IN THE FOREST.
IF I WERE THE FOREST...
...I WOULDN'T WANT TO LET HER GO. I WOULD HAVE MADE HER DIE IN THE FOREST EVEN IF IT MEANT THROWING HER IN THE RIVER OR BURYING HER IN THE SOIL.

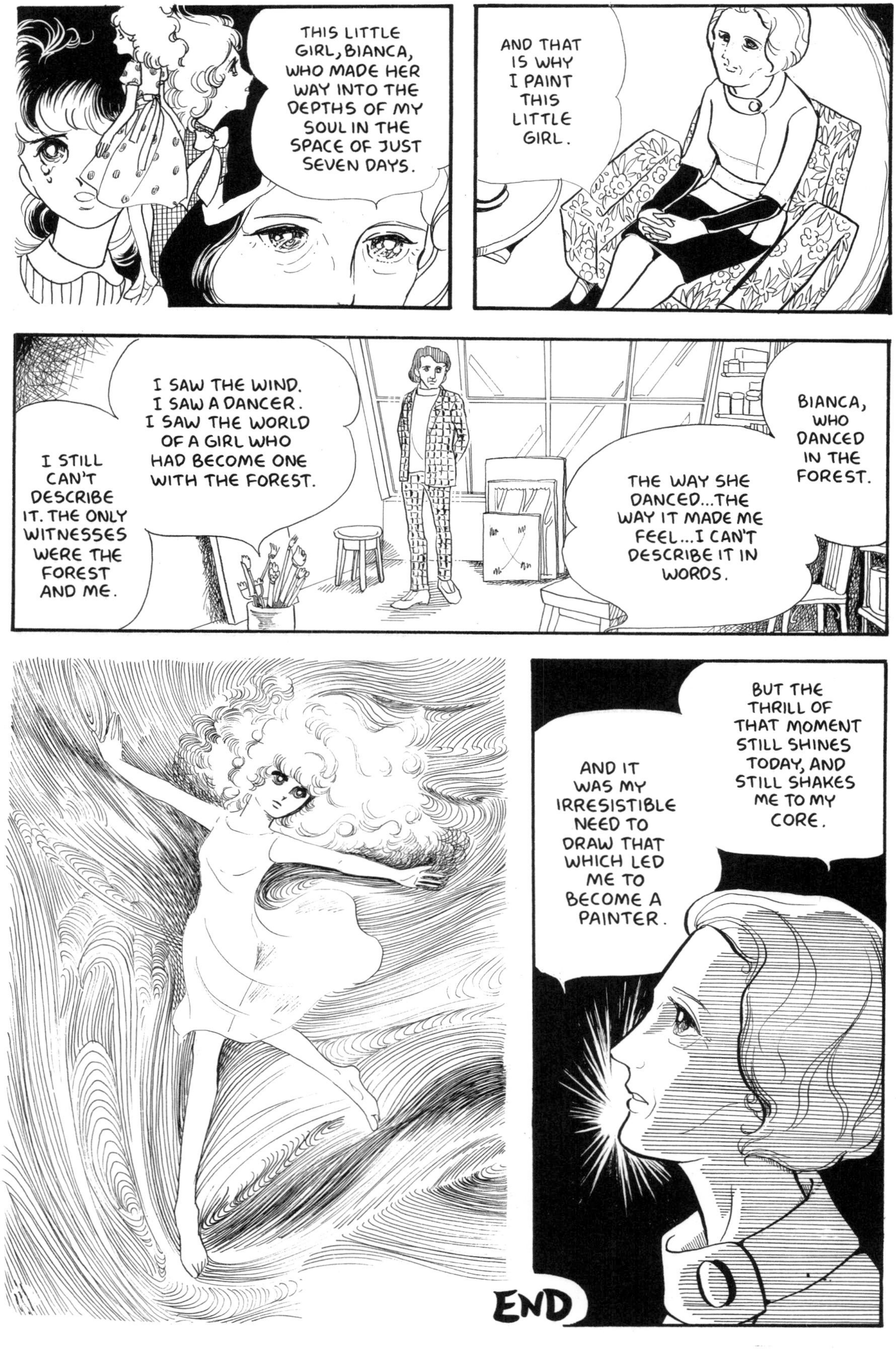
THIS LITTLE GIRL, BIANCA, WHO MADE HER WAY INTO THE DEPTHS OF MY SOUL IN THE SPACE OF JUST SEVEN DAYS.
AND THAT IS WHY I PAINT THIS LITTLE GIRL.
I SAW THE WIND. I SAW A DANCER. I SAW THE WORLD OF A GIRL WHO HAD BECOME ONE WITH THE FOREST.
I STILL CAN'T DESCRIBE IT. THE ONLY WITNESSES WERE THE FOREST AND ME.
BIANCA, WHO DANCED IN THE FOREST.
THE WAY SHE DANCED...THE WAY IT MADE ME FEEL...I CAN'T DESCRIBE IT IN WORDS.
BUT THE THRILL OF THAT MOMENT STILL SHINES TODAY, AND STILL SHAKES ME TO MY CORE.
AND IT WAS MY IRRESISTIBLE NEED TO DRAW THAT WHICH LED ME TO BECOME A PAINTER.
END

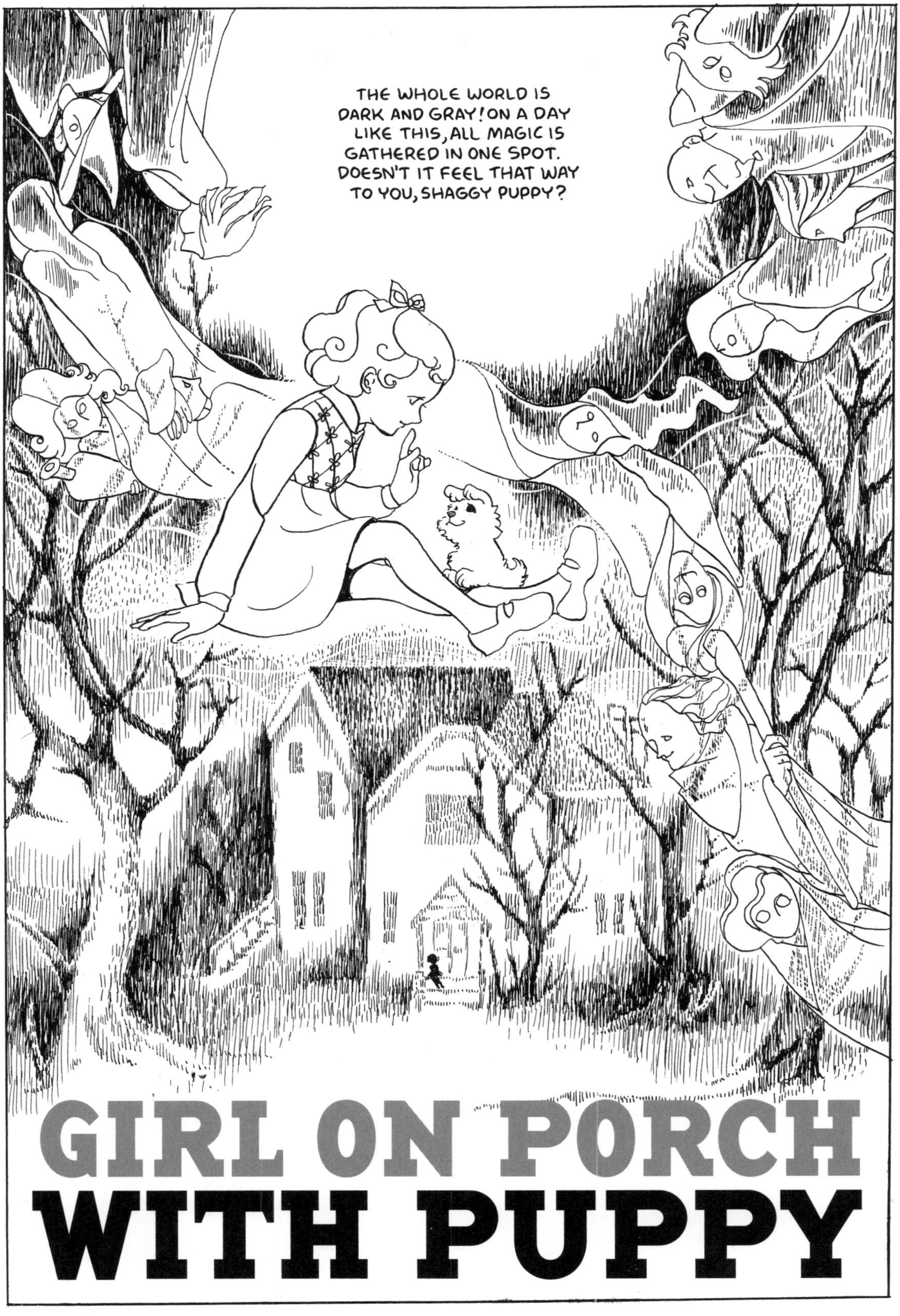
THE WHOLE WORLD IS DARK AND GRAY! ON A DAY LIKE THIS, ALL MAGIC IS GATHERED IN ONE SPOT. DOESN'T IT FEEL THAT WAY TO YOU, SHAGGY PUPPY?

GIRL ON PORCH WITH PUPPY

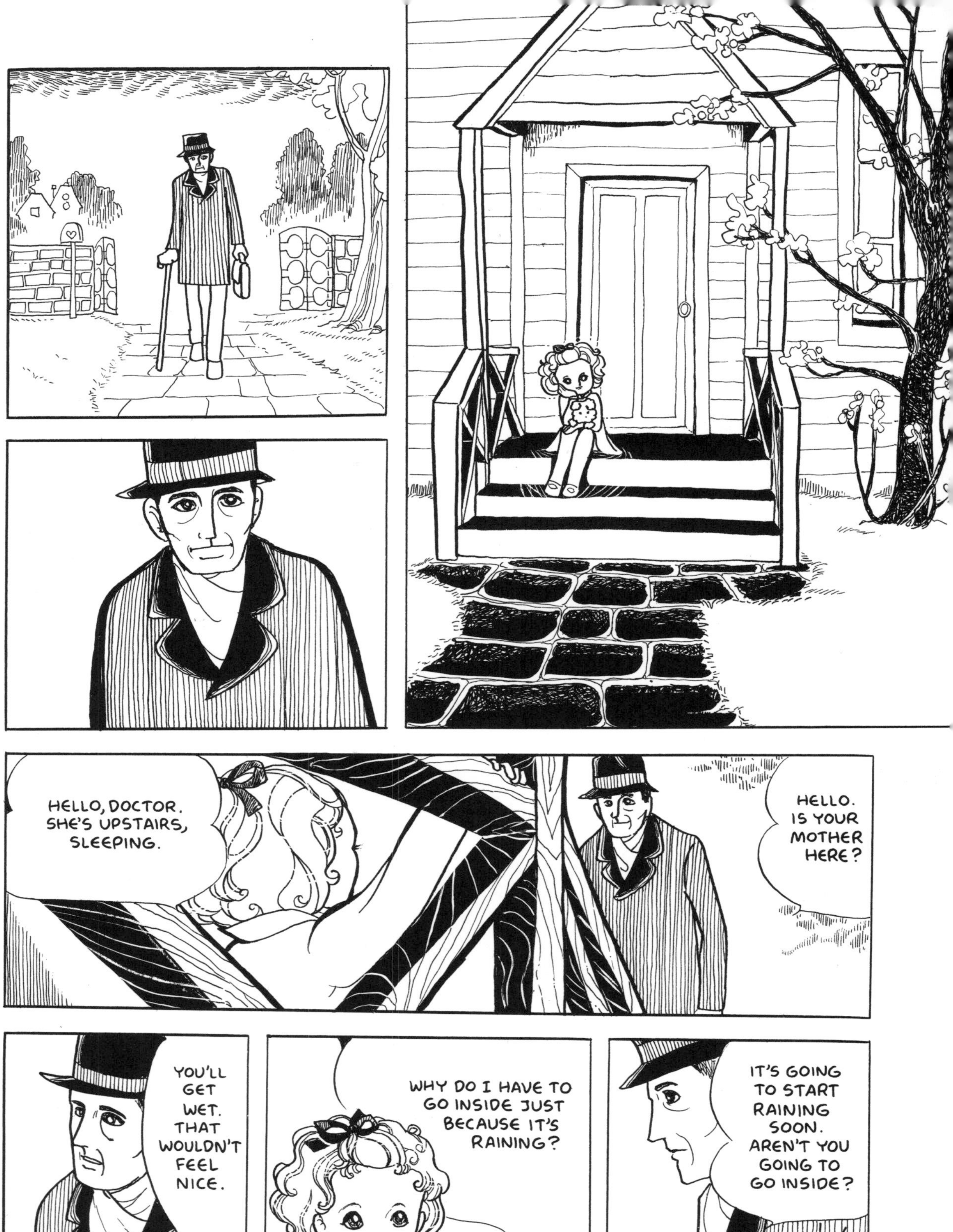
HELLO. IS YOUR MOTHER HERE?
HELLO, DOCTOR. SHE'S UPSTAIRS, SLEEPING.
IT'S GOING TO START RAINING SOON. AREN'T YOU GOING TO GO INSIDE?
WHY DO I HAVE TO GO INSIDE JUST BECAUSE IT'S RAINING?
YOU'LL GET WET. THAT WOULDN'T FEEL NICE.

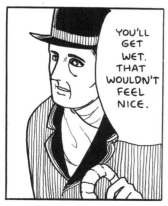

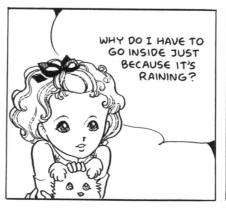

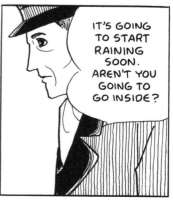

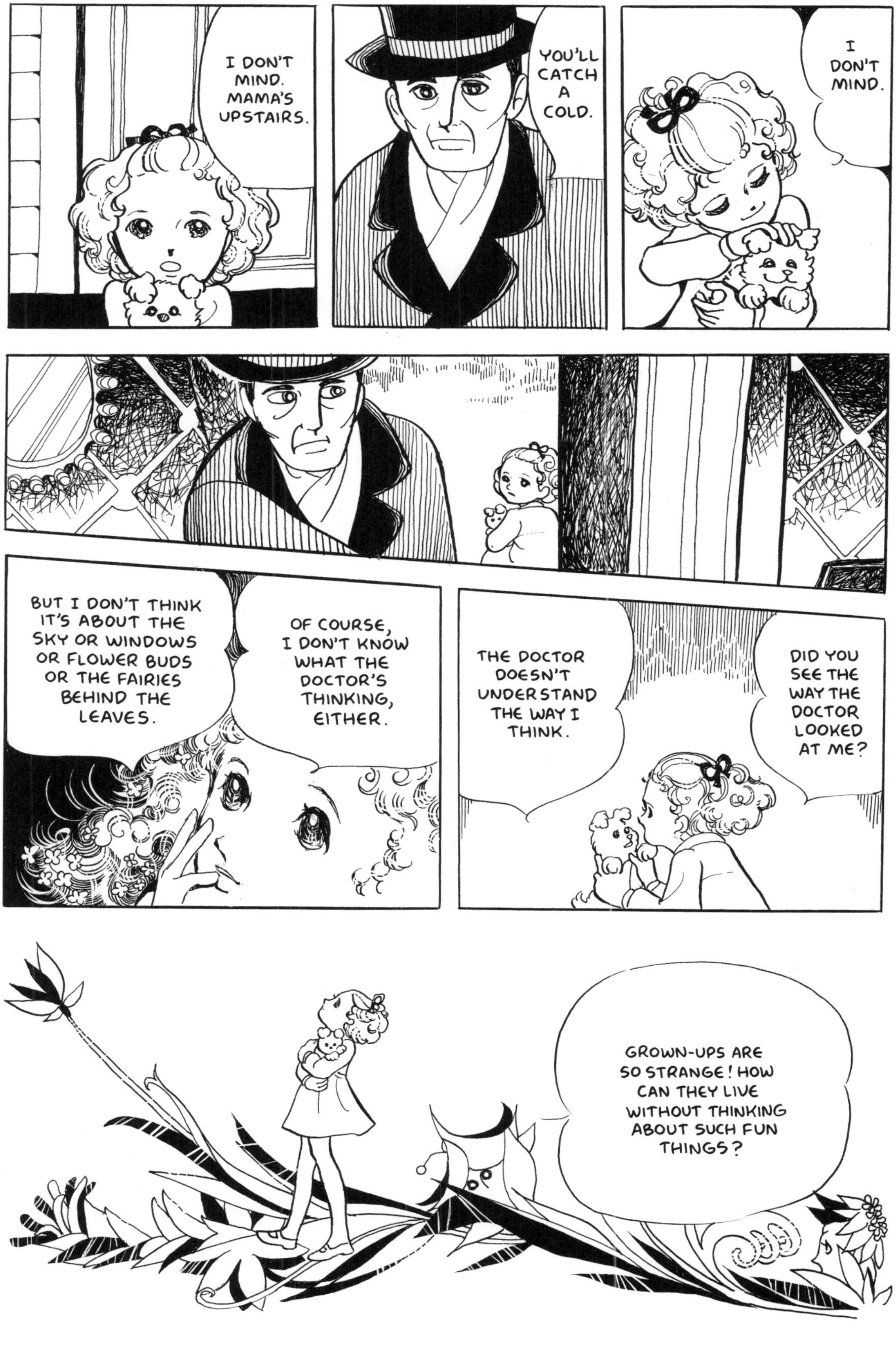
I DON'T MIND.
YOU'LL CATCH A COLD.
I DON'T MIND. MAMA'S UPSTAIRS.
DID YOU SEE THE WAY THE DOCTOR LOOKED AT ME?
THE DOCTOR DOESN'T UNDERSTAND THE WAY I THINK.
OF COURSE, I DON'T KNOW WHAT THE DOCTOR'S THINKING, EITHER.
BUT I DON'T THINK IT'S ABOUT THE SKY OR WINDOWS OR FLOWER BUDS OR THE FAIRIES BEHIND THE LEAVES.
GROWN-UPS ARE SO STRANGE! HOW CAN THEY LIVE WITHOUT THINKING ABOUT SUCH FUN THINGS?

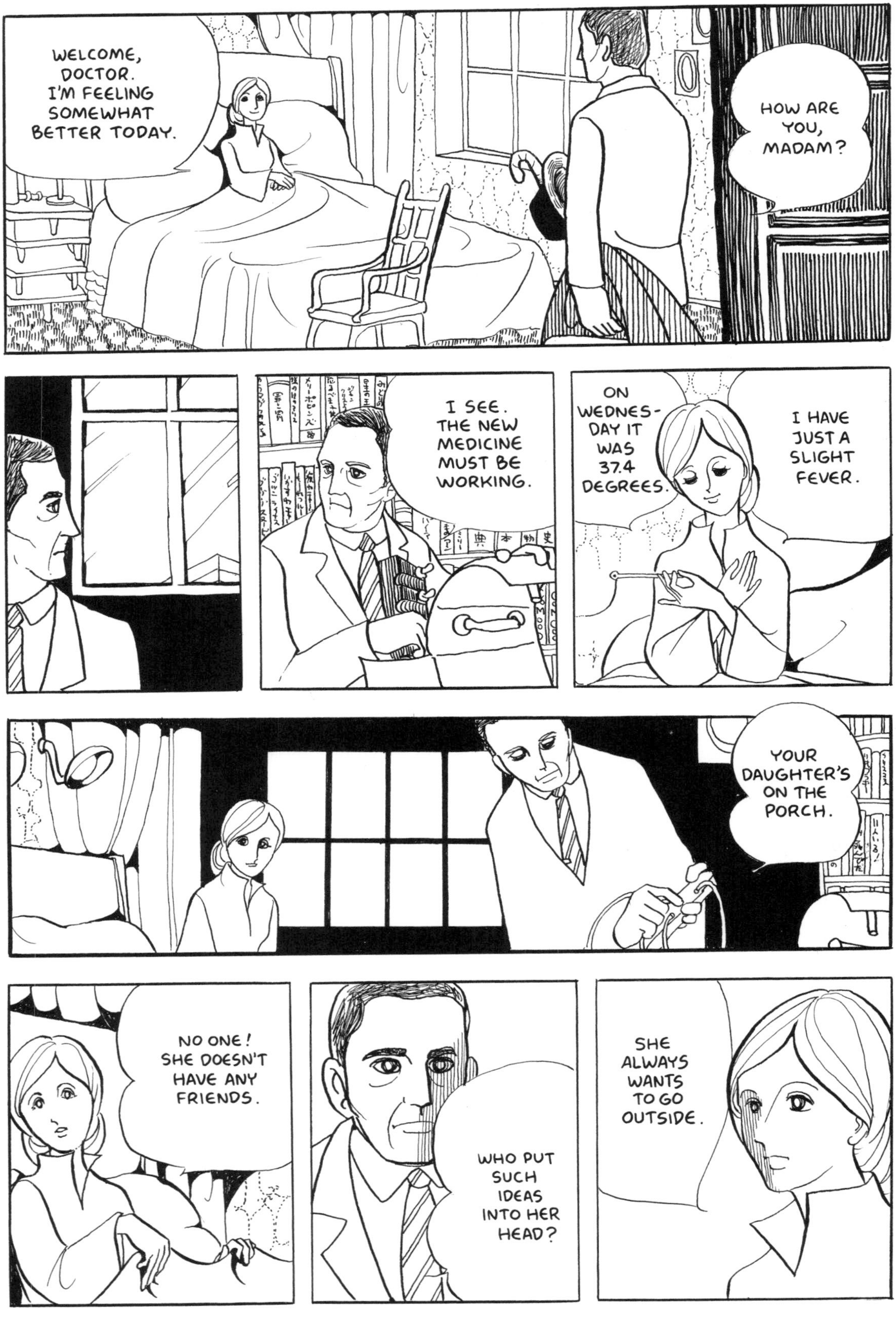
HOW ARE YOU, MADAM?
WELCOME, DOCTOR. I'M FEELING SOMEWHAT BETTER TODAY.
I HAVE JUST A SLIGHT FEVER.
ON WEDNES-DAY IT WAS 37.4 DEGREES.
I SEE. THE NEW MEDICINE MUST BE WORKING.
YOUR DAUGHTER'S ON THE PORCH.
SHE ALWAYS WANTS TO GO OUTSIDE.
WHO PUT SUCH IDEAS INTO HER HEAD?
NO ONE! SHE DOESN'T HAVE ANY FRIENDS.

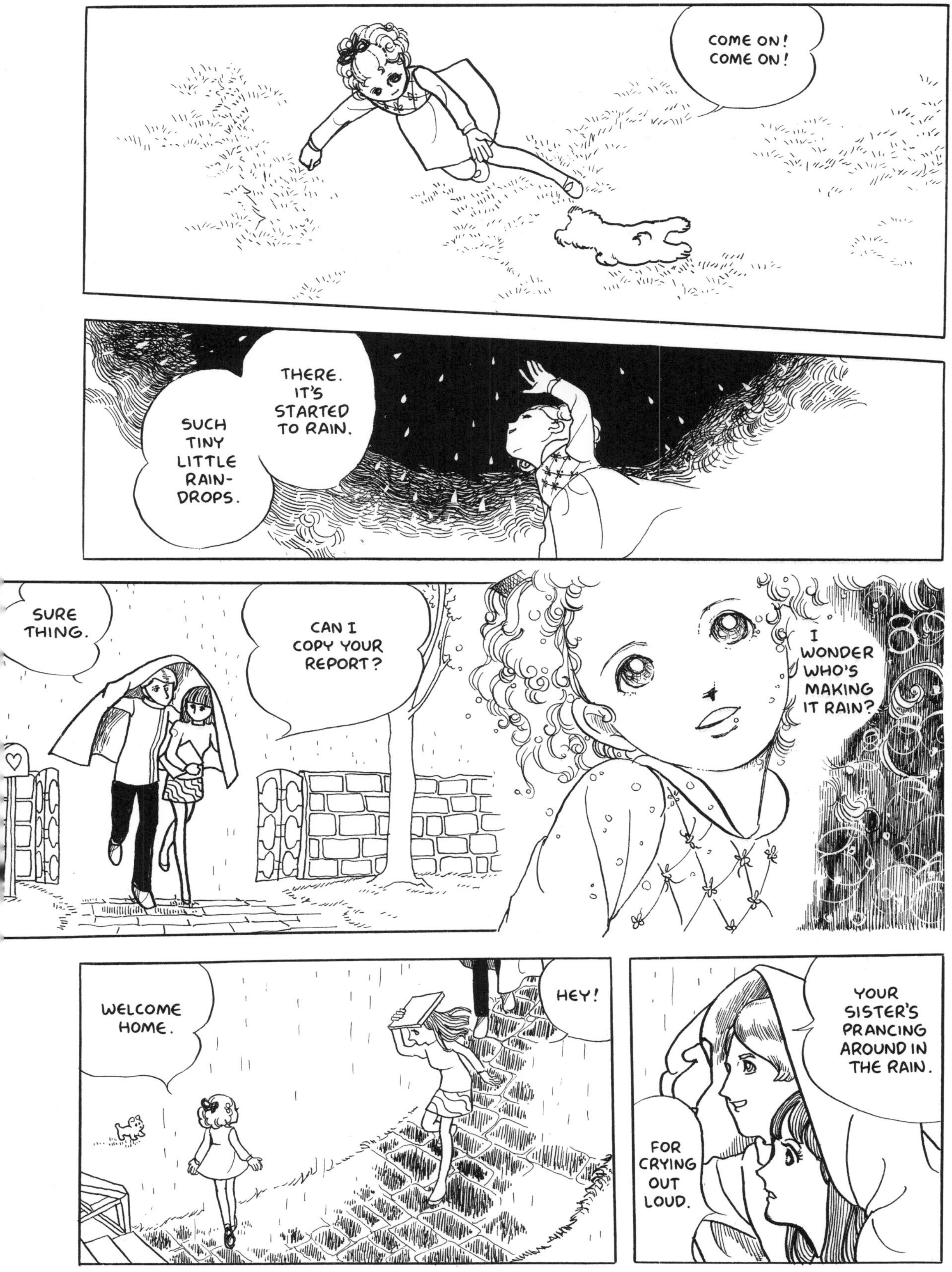
COME ON! COME ON!
THERE. IT'S STARTED TO RAIN.
SUCH TINY LITTLE RAIN-DROPS.
I WONDER WHO'S MAKING IT RAIN?
CAN I COPY YOUR REPORT?
SURE THING.
YOUR SISTER'S PRANCING AROUND IN THE RAIN.
FOR CRYING OUT LOUD.
HEY!
WELCOME HOME.

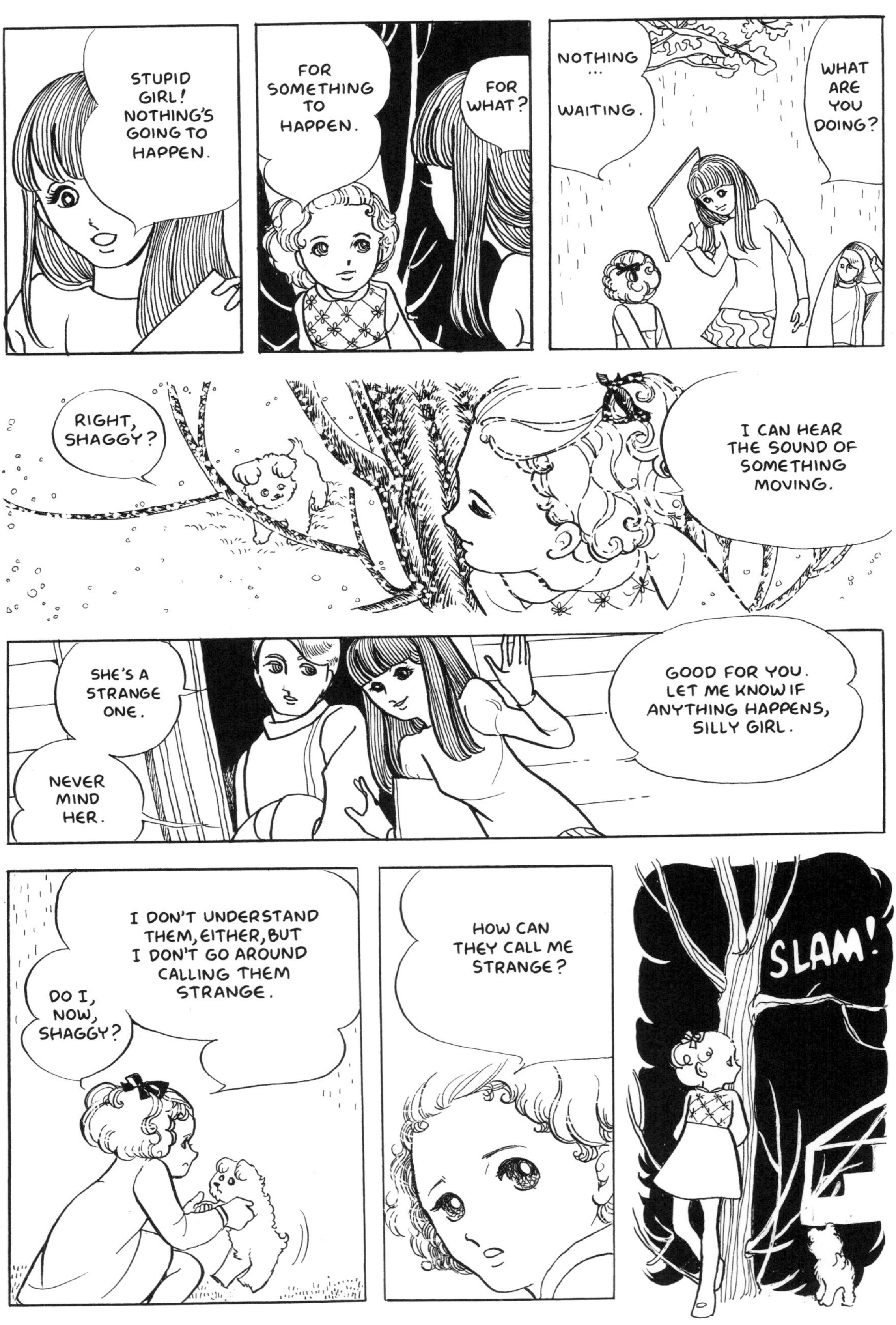
WHAT ARE YOU DOING?
NOTHING... WAITING.
FOR WHAT?
FOR SOMETHING TO HAPPEN.
STUPID GIRL! NOTHING'S GOING TO HAPPEN.
I CAN HEAR THE SOUND OF SOMETHING MOVING.
RIGHT, SHAGGY?
GOOD FOR YOU. LET ME KNOW IF ANYTHING HAPPENS, SILLY GIRL.
SHE'S A STRANGE ONE.
NEVER MIND HER.
SLAM!
HOW CAN THEY CALL ME STRANGE?
I DON'T UNDERSTAND THEM, EITHER, BUT I DON'T GO AROUND CALLING THEM STRANGE.
DO I, NOW, SHAGGY?

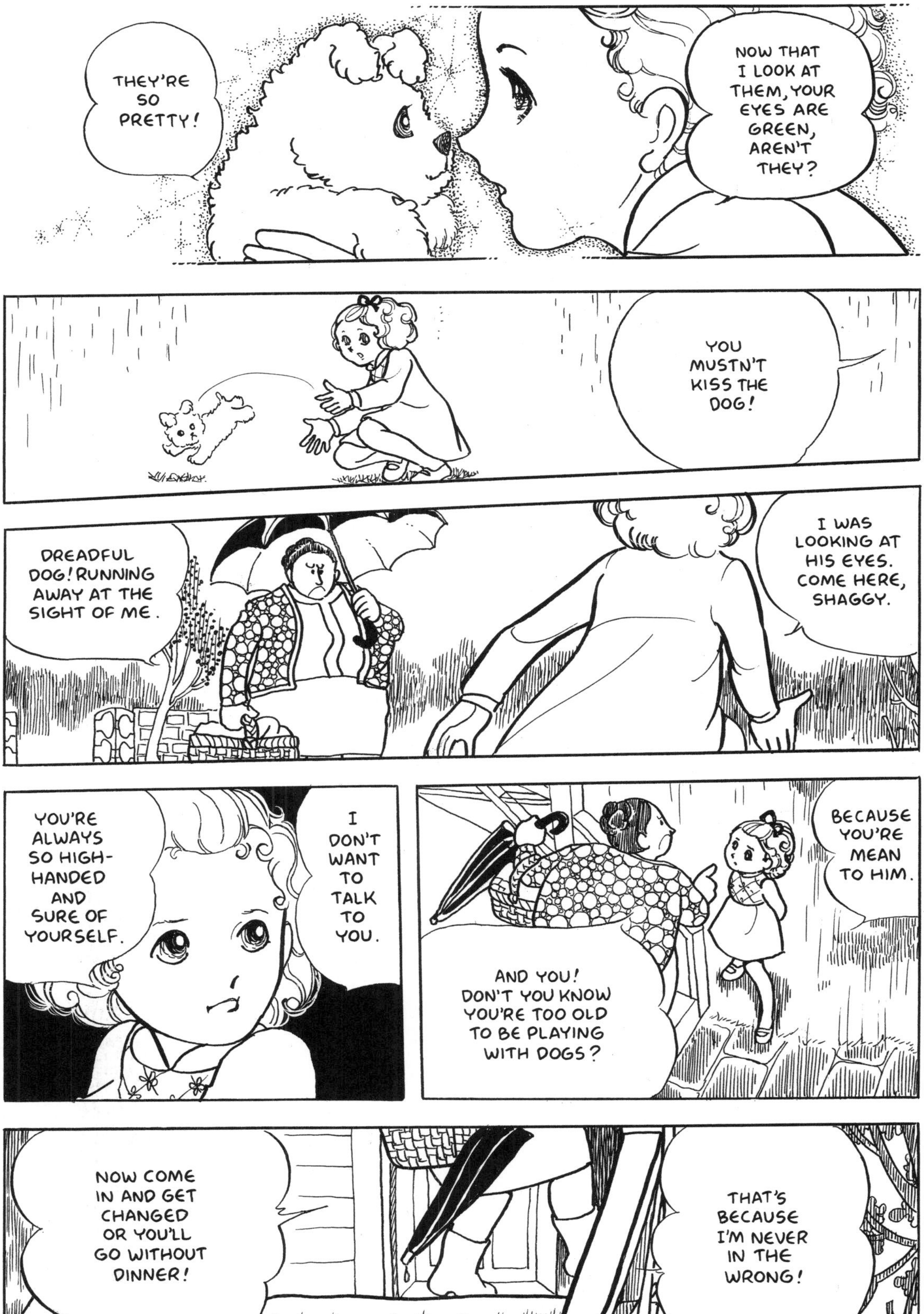
NOW THAT I LOOK AT THEM, YOUR EYES ARE GREEN, AREN'T THEY?
THEY'RE SO PRETTY!
YOU MUSTN'T KISS THE DOG!
I WAS LOOKING AT HIS EYES. COME HERE, SHAGGY.
DREADFUL DOG! RUNNING AWAY AT THE SIGHT OF ME.
BECAUSE YOU'RE MEAN TO HIM.
AND YOU! DON'T YOU KNOW YOU'RE TOO OLD TO BE PLAYING WITH DOGS?
I DON'T WANT TO TALK TO YOU.
YOU'RE ALWAYS SO HIGH-HANDED AND SURE OF YOURSELF.
THAT'S BECAUSE I'M NEVER IN THE WRONG!
NOW COME IN AND GET CHANGED OR YOU'LL GO WITHOUT DINNER!

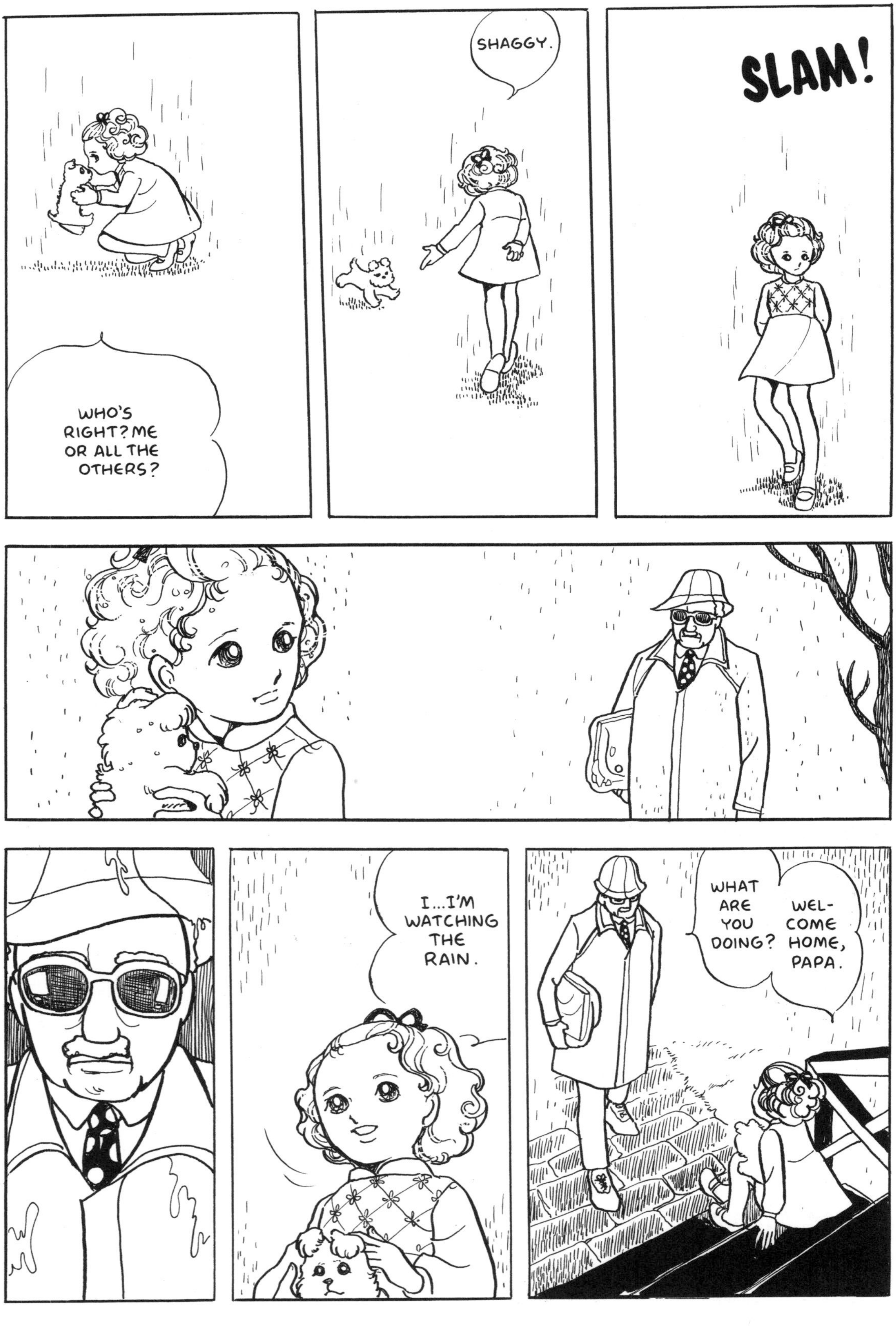
SLAM!
SHAGGY.
WHO'S RIGHT? ME OR ALL THE OTHERS?
WEL-COME HOME, PAPA.
WHAT ARE YOU DOING?
I...I'M WATCHING THE RAIN.

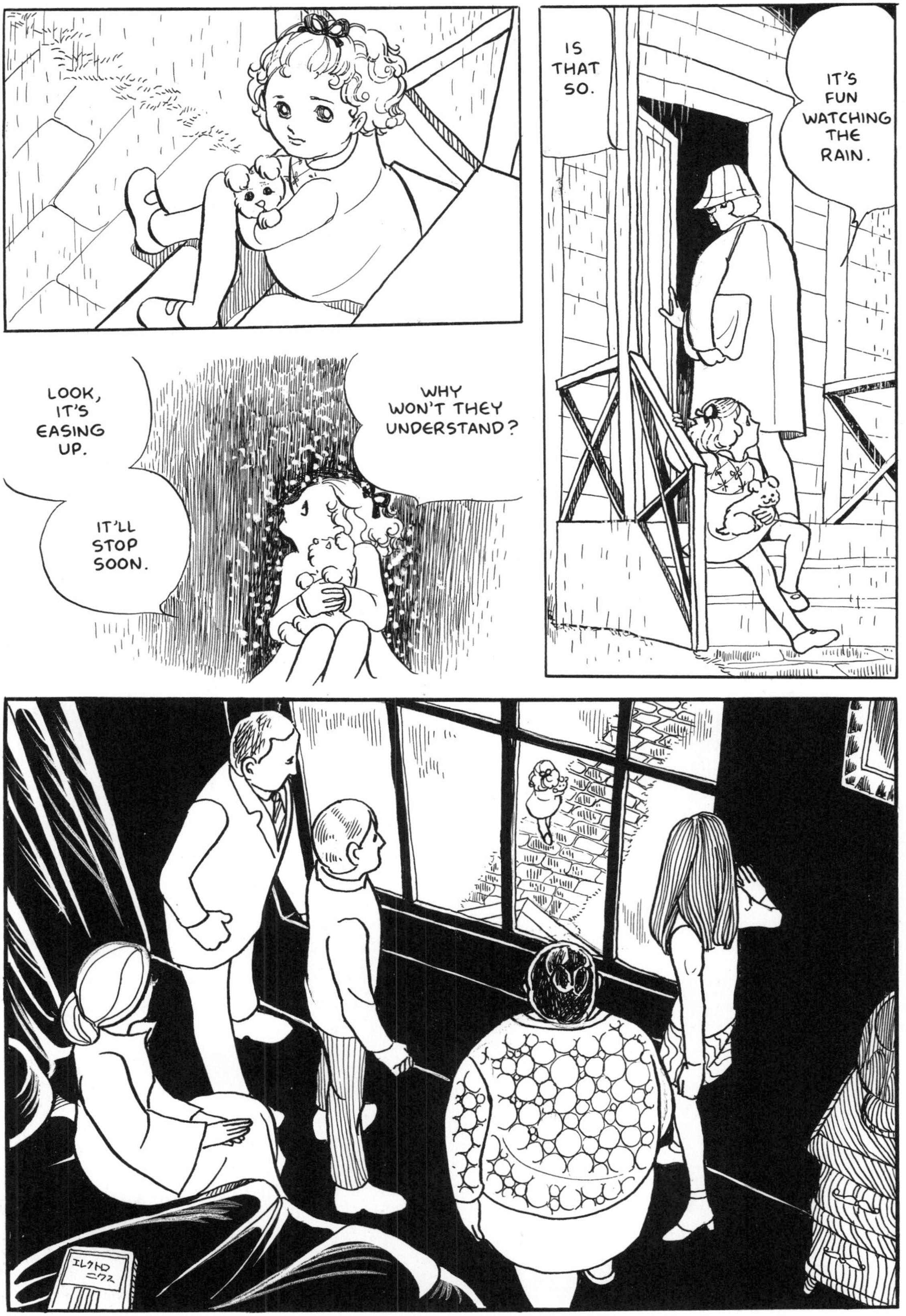
IT'S FUN WATCHING THE RAIN.
IS THAT SO.
WHY WON'T THEY UNDERSTAND?
LOOK, IT'S EASING UP.
IT'LL STOP SOON.
エレクトロニクス

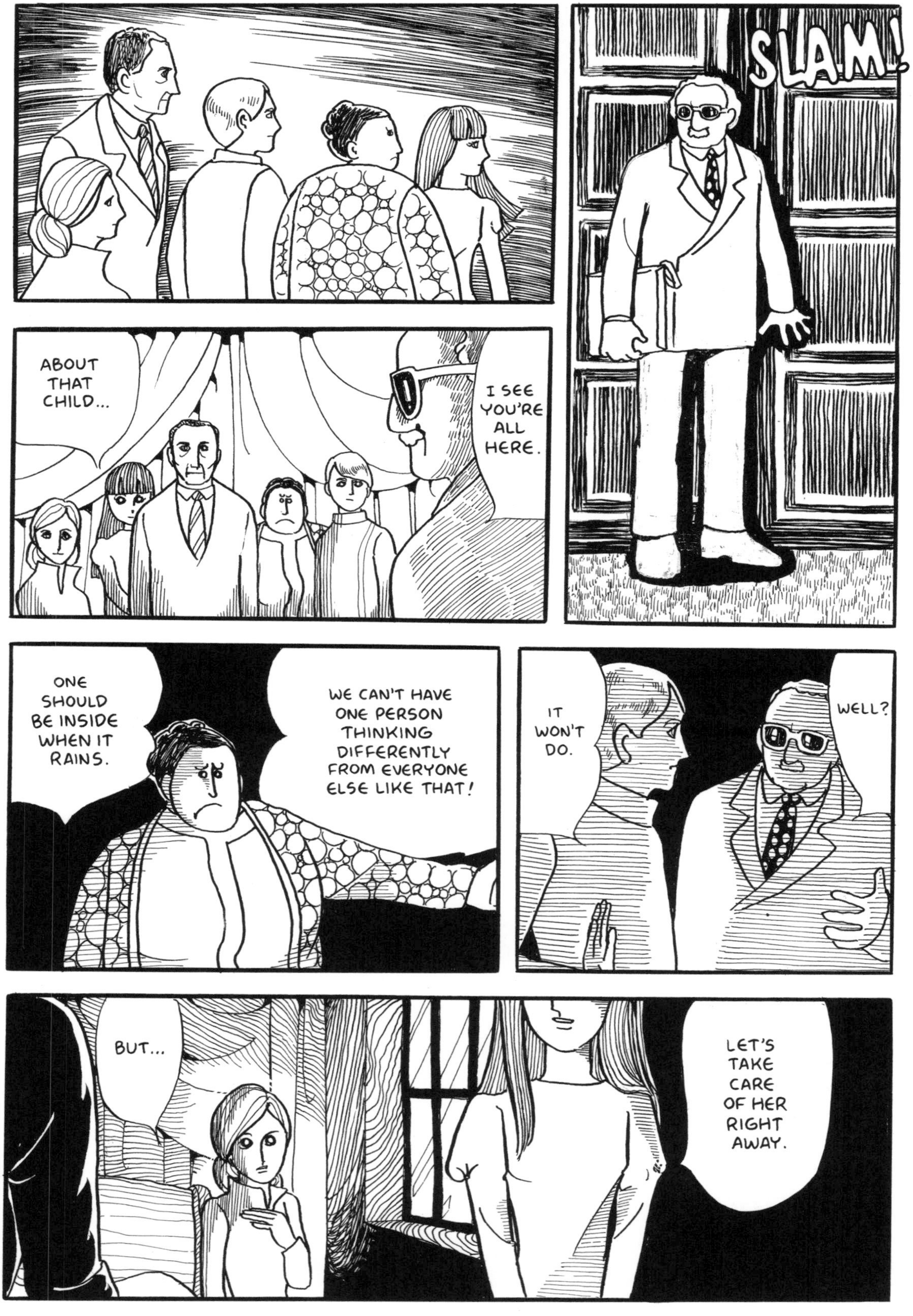
SLAM!
I SEE YOU'RE ALL HERE.
ABOUT THAT CHILD...
WELL?
IT WON'T DO.
WE CAN'T HAVE ONE PERSON THINKING DIFFERENTLY FROM EVERYONE ELSE LIKE THAT!
ONE SHOULD BE INSIDE WHEN IT RAINS.
LET'S TAKE CARE OF HER RIGHT AWAY.
BUT...

SHOULDN'T WE WAIT A BIT LONGER AND SEE?
BUT SHE'S BEEN THIS WAY FOR THREE YEARS.
LOOK, SHAGGY.
I WISH I COULD CROSS OVER ON THAT RAINBOW.

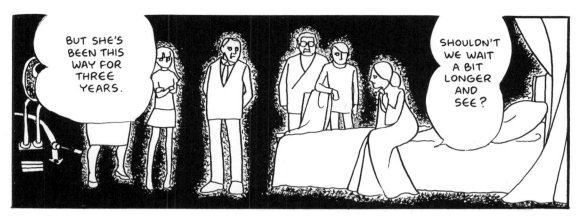

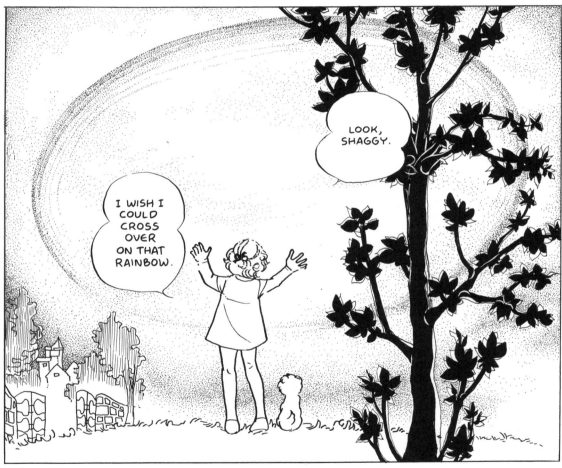

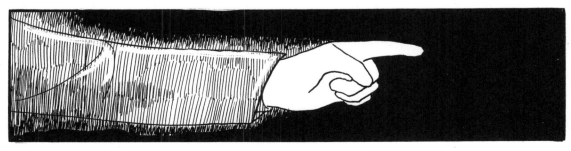

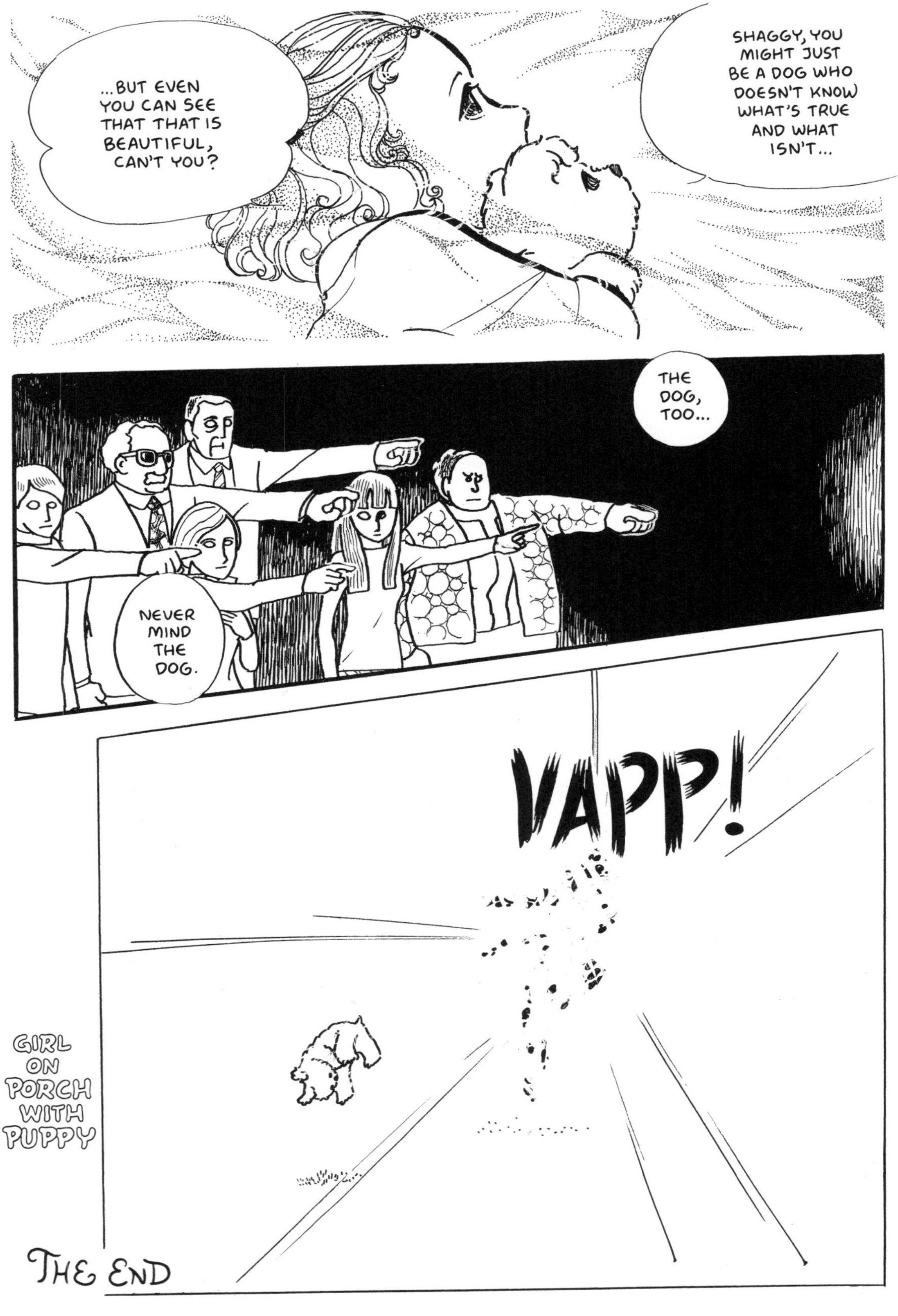
SHAGGY, YOU MIGHT JUST BE A DOG WHO DOESN'T KNOW WHAT'S TRUE AND WHAT ISN'T...
...BUT EVEN YOU CAN SEE THAT THAT IS BEAUTIFUL, CAN'T YOU?
THE DOG, TOO...
NEVER MIND THE DOG.
VAPP!
GIRL ON PORCH WITH PUPPY
THE END

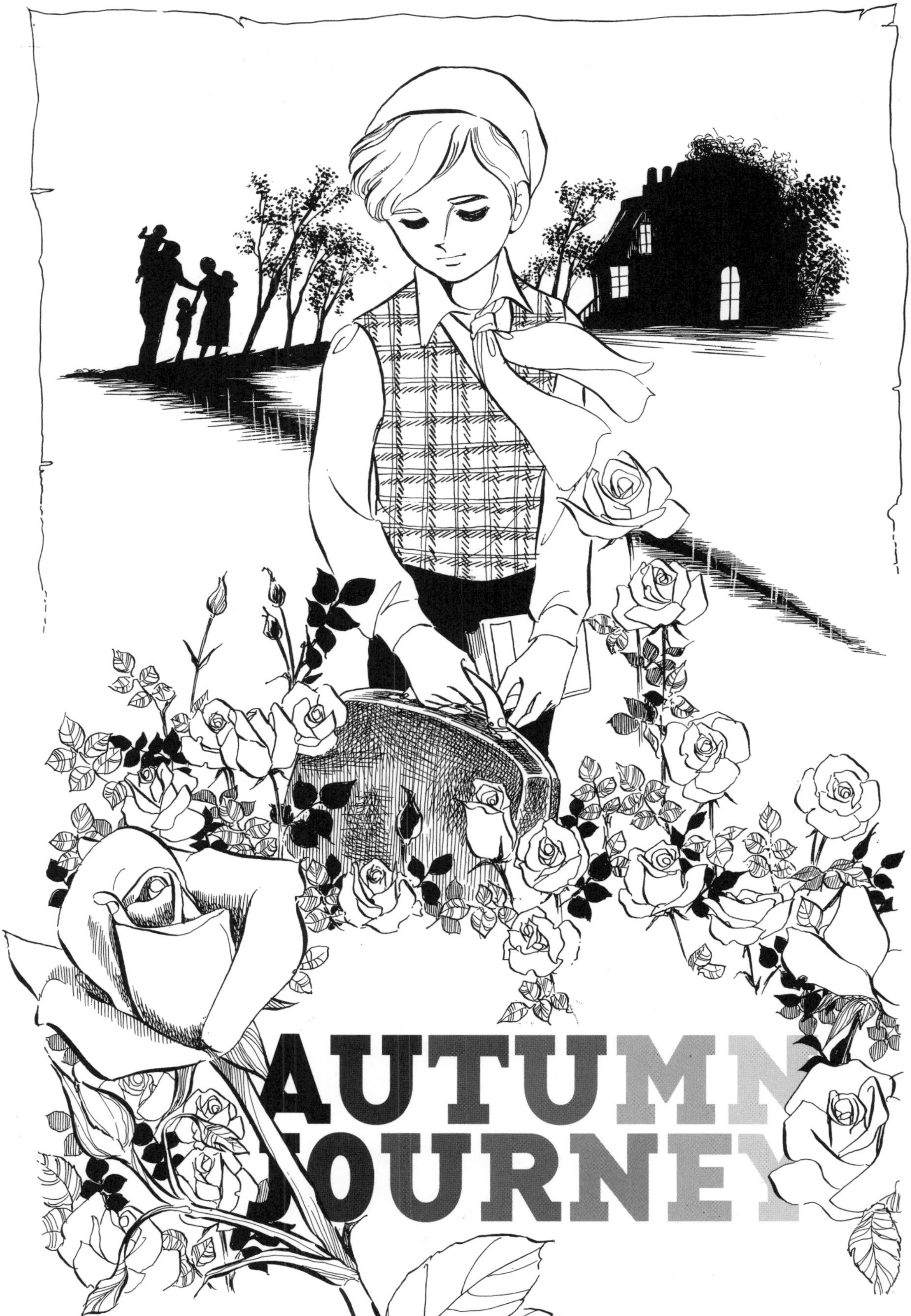
AUTUMN
JOURNEY

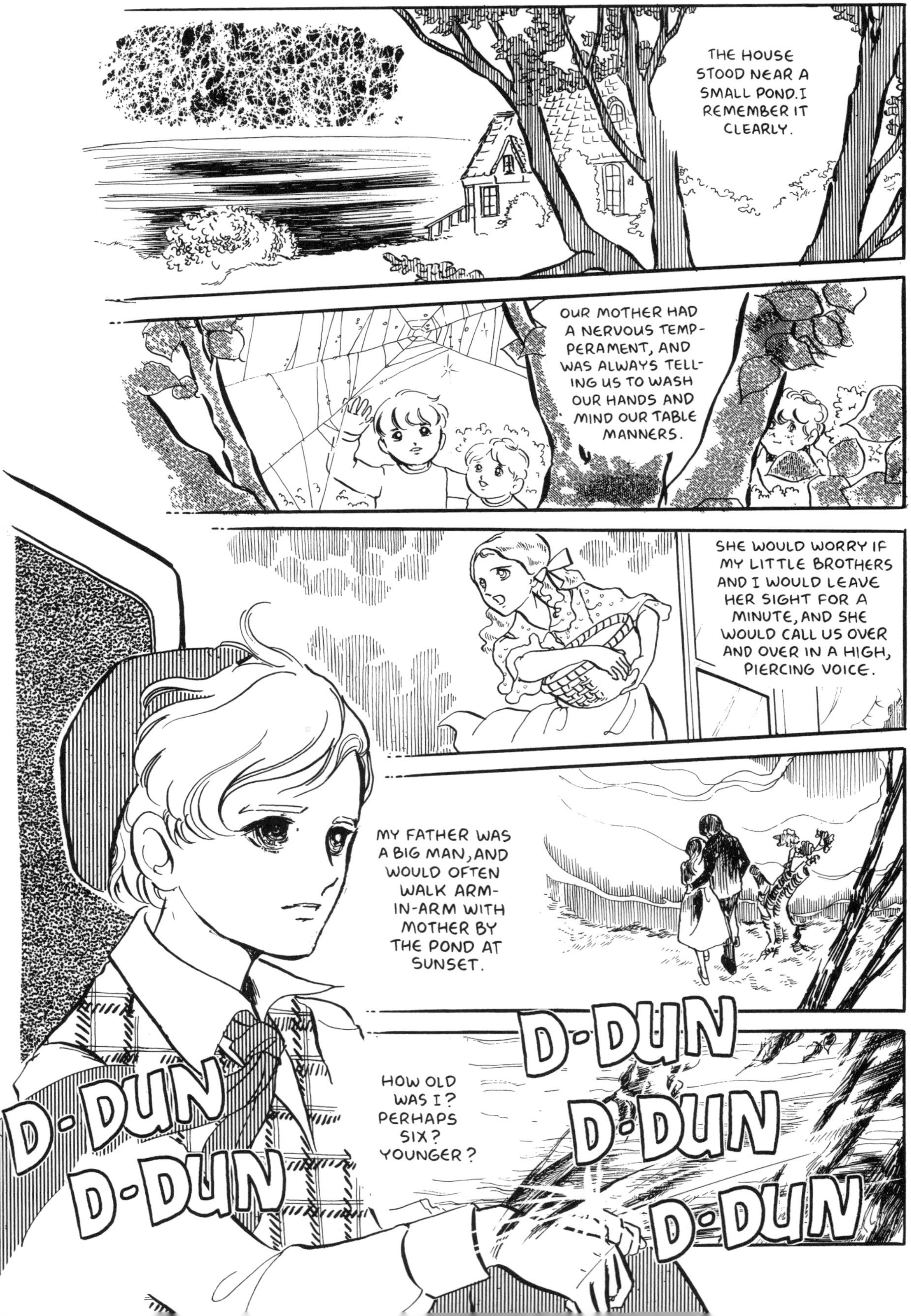
THE HOUSE STOOD NEAR A SMALL POND. I REMEMBER IT CLEARLY.
OUR MOTHER HAD A NERVOUS TEMPERAMENT, AND WAS ALWAYS TELLING US TO WASH OUR HANDS AND MIND OUR TABLE MANNERS.
SHE WOULD WORRY IF MY LITTLE BROTHERS AND I WOULD LEAVE HER SIGHT FOR A MINUTE, AND SHE WOULD CALL US OVER AND OVER IN A HIGH, PIERCING VOICE.
MY FATHER WAS A BIG MAN, AND WOULD OFTEN WALK ARM-IN-ARM WITH MOTHER BY THE POND AT SUNSET.
D-DUN
D-DUN
D-DUN
HOW OLD WAS I? PERHAPS SIX? YOUNGER?
D-DUN
D-DUN

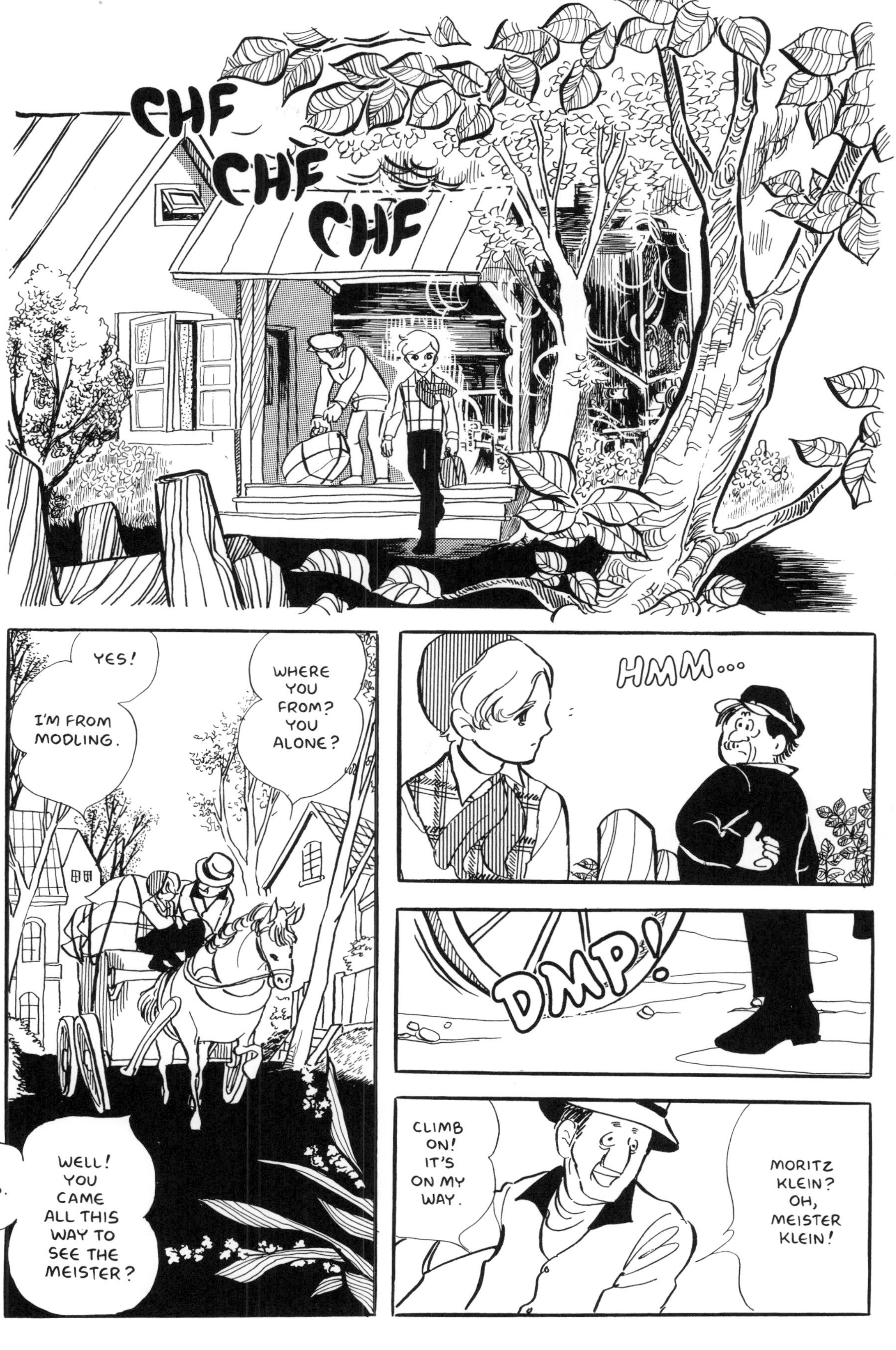
CHF
CHF
CHF
HMM...
DMP!
MORITZ KLEIN? OH, MEISTER KLEIN!
CLIMB ON! IT'S ON MY WAY.
WHERE YOU FROM? YOU ALONE?
YES!
I'M FROM MODLING.
WELL! YOU CAME ALL THIS WAY TO SEE THE MEISTER?
YES.

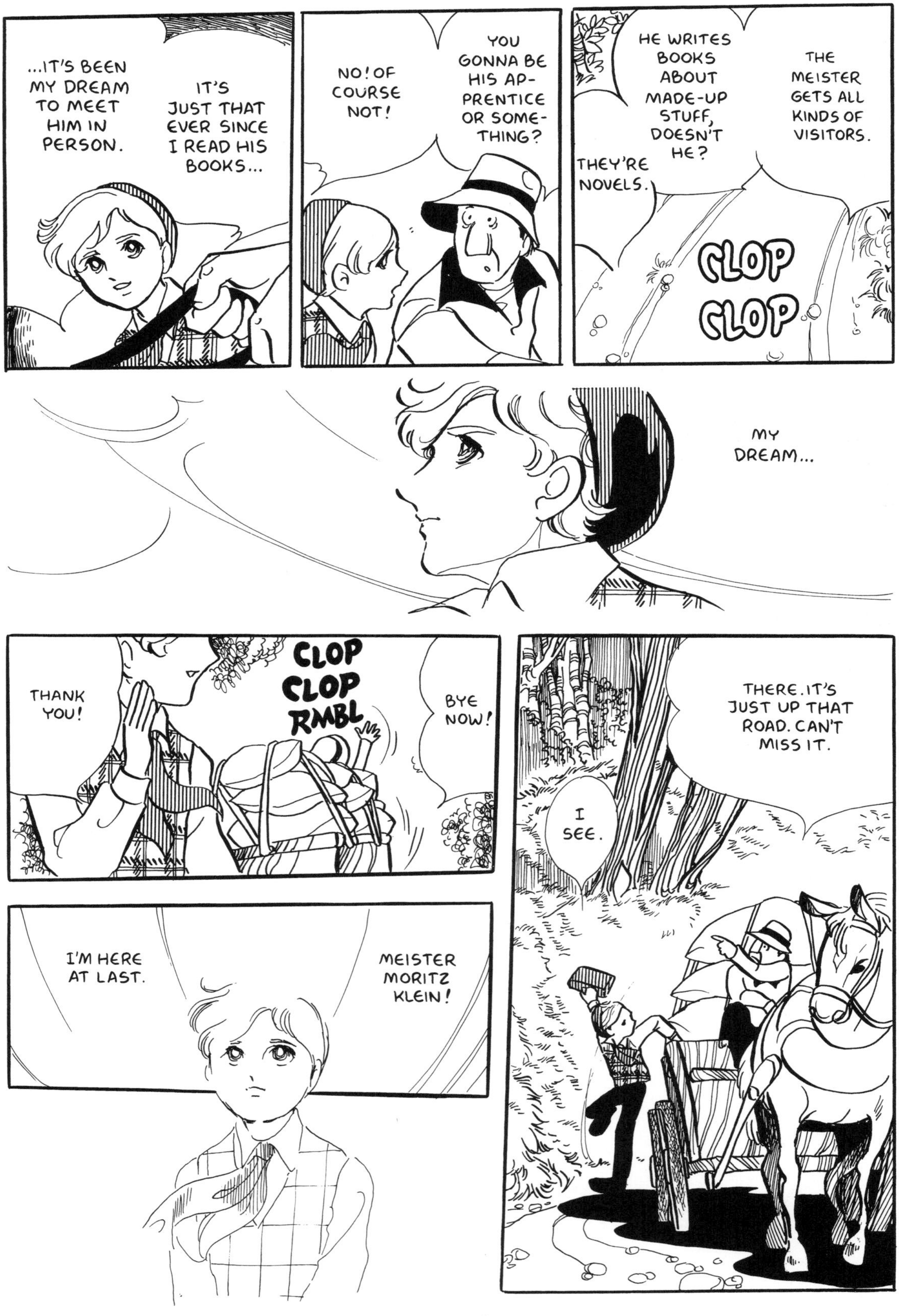
THE MEISTER GETS ALL KINDS OF VISITORS.
HE WRITES BOOKS ABOUT MADE-UP STUFF, DOESN'T HE?
THEY'RE NOVELS.
CLOP CLOP
YOU GONNA BE HIS APPRENTICE OR SOMETHING?
NO! OF COURSE NOT!
IT'S JUST THAT EVER SINCE I READ HIS BOOKS...
...IT'S BEEN MY DREAM TO MEET HIM IN PERSON.
MY DREAM...
THERE. IT'S JUST UP THAT ROAD. CAN'T MISS IT.
I SEE.
BYE NOW!
CLOP CLOP RMBL
THANK YOU!
MEISTER MORITZ KLEIN!
I'M HERE AT LAST.

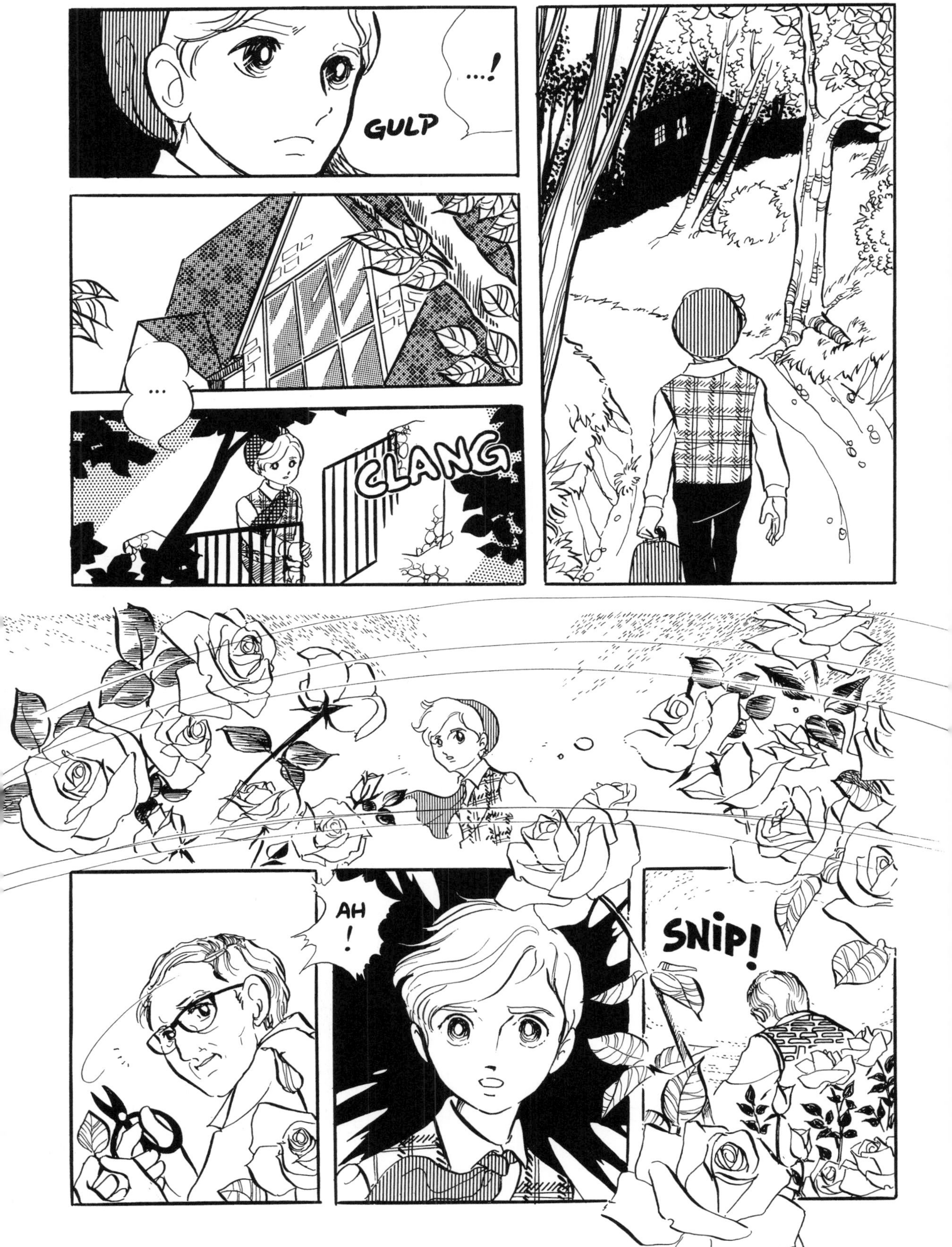
...!
GULP
...
CLANG
SNIP!
AH !

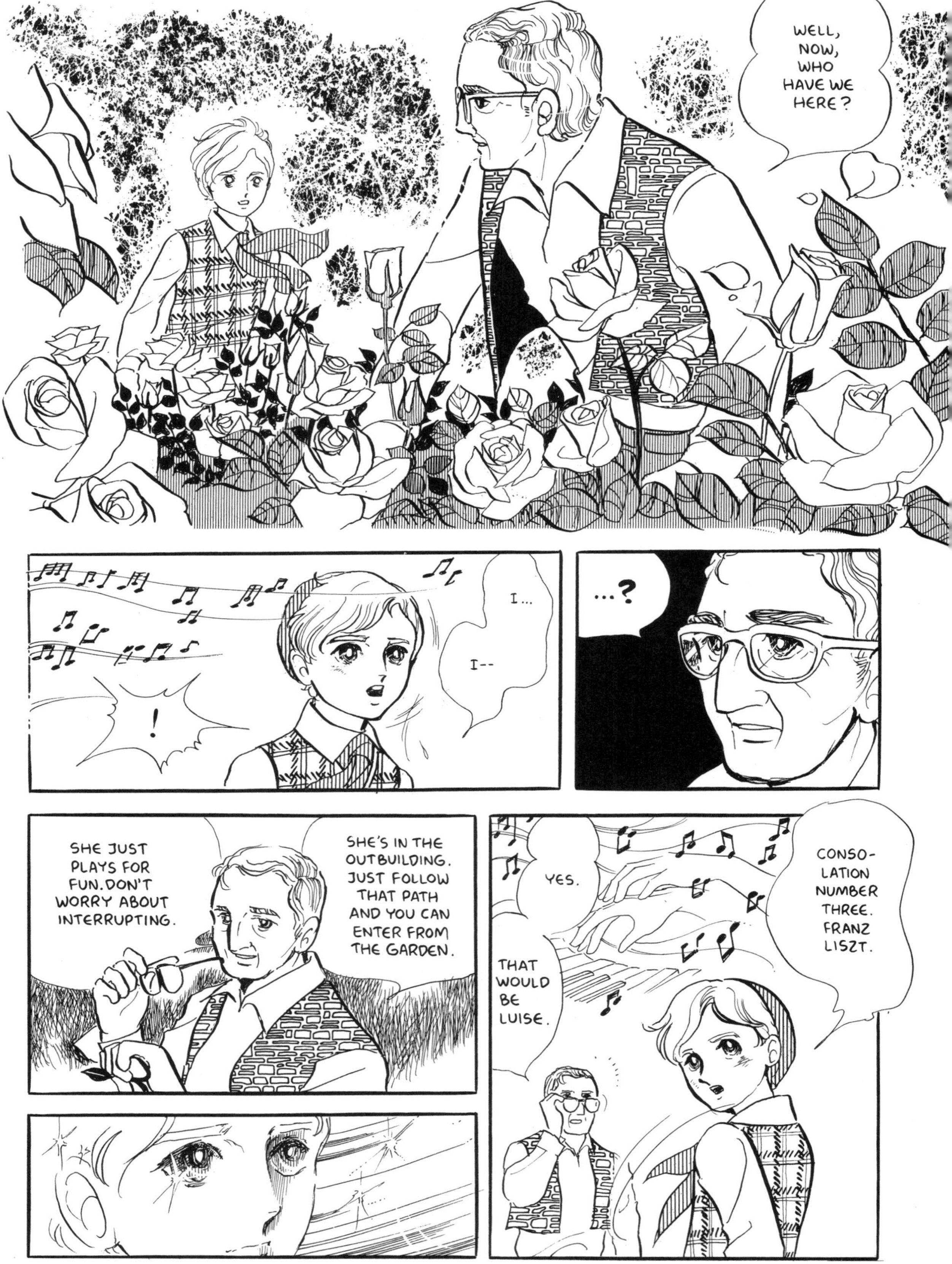

WELL, NOW, WHO HAVE WE HERE?
...?
!
I...
I--
CONSO-LATION NUMBER THREE. FRANZ LISZT.
YES.
THAT WOULD BE LUISE.
SHE'S IN THE OUTBUILDING. JUST FOLLOW THAT PATH AND YOU CAN ENTER FROM THE GARDEN.
SHE JUST PLAYS FOR FUN. DON'T WORRY ABOUT INTERRUPTING.

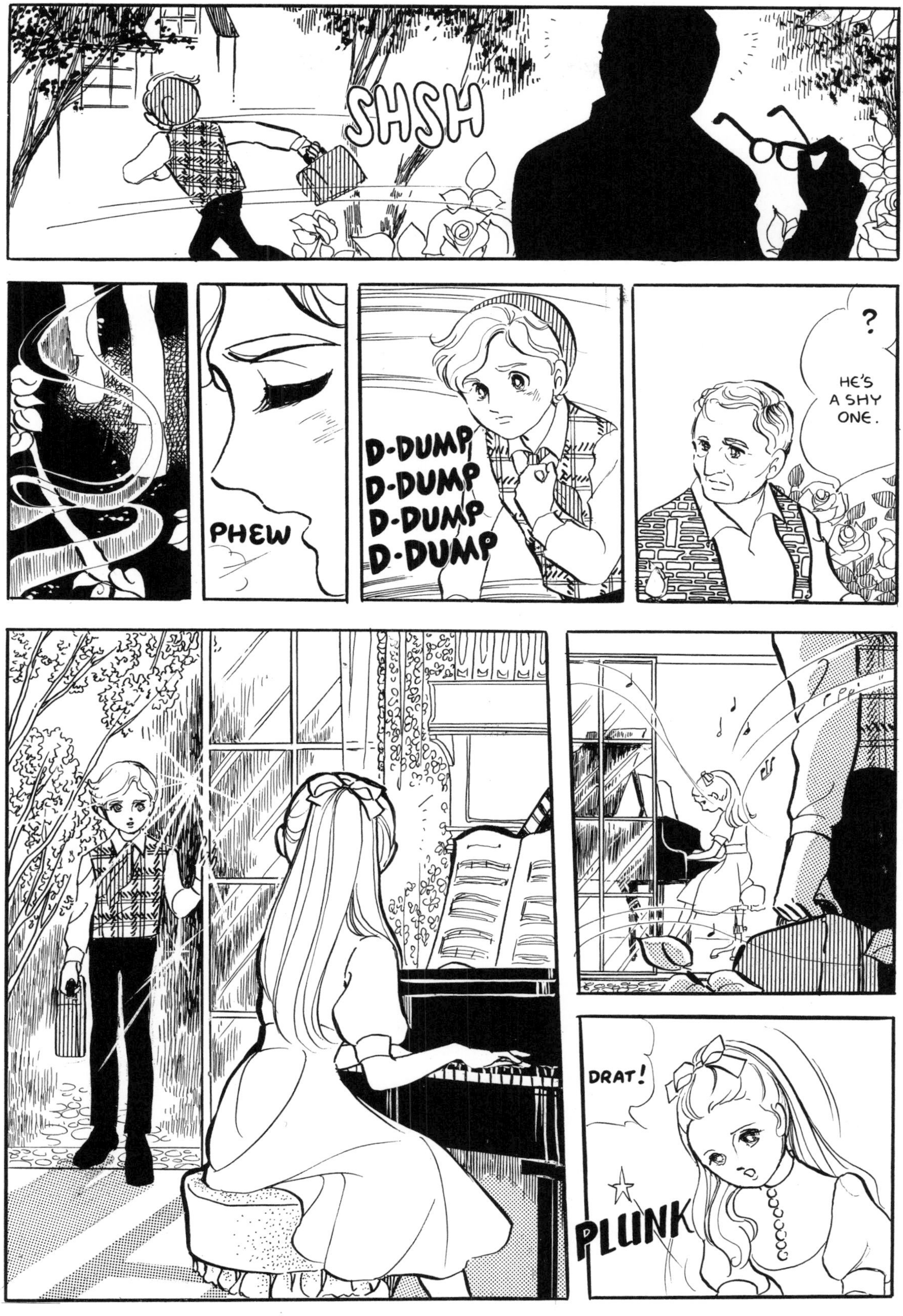
SHSH
?
HE'S A SHY ONE.
D-DUMP
D-DUMP
D-DUMP
D-DUMP
PHEW
DRAT!
PLUNK

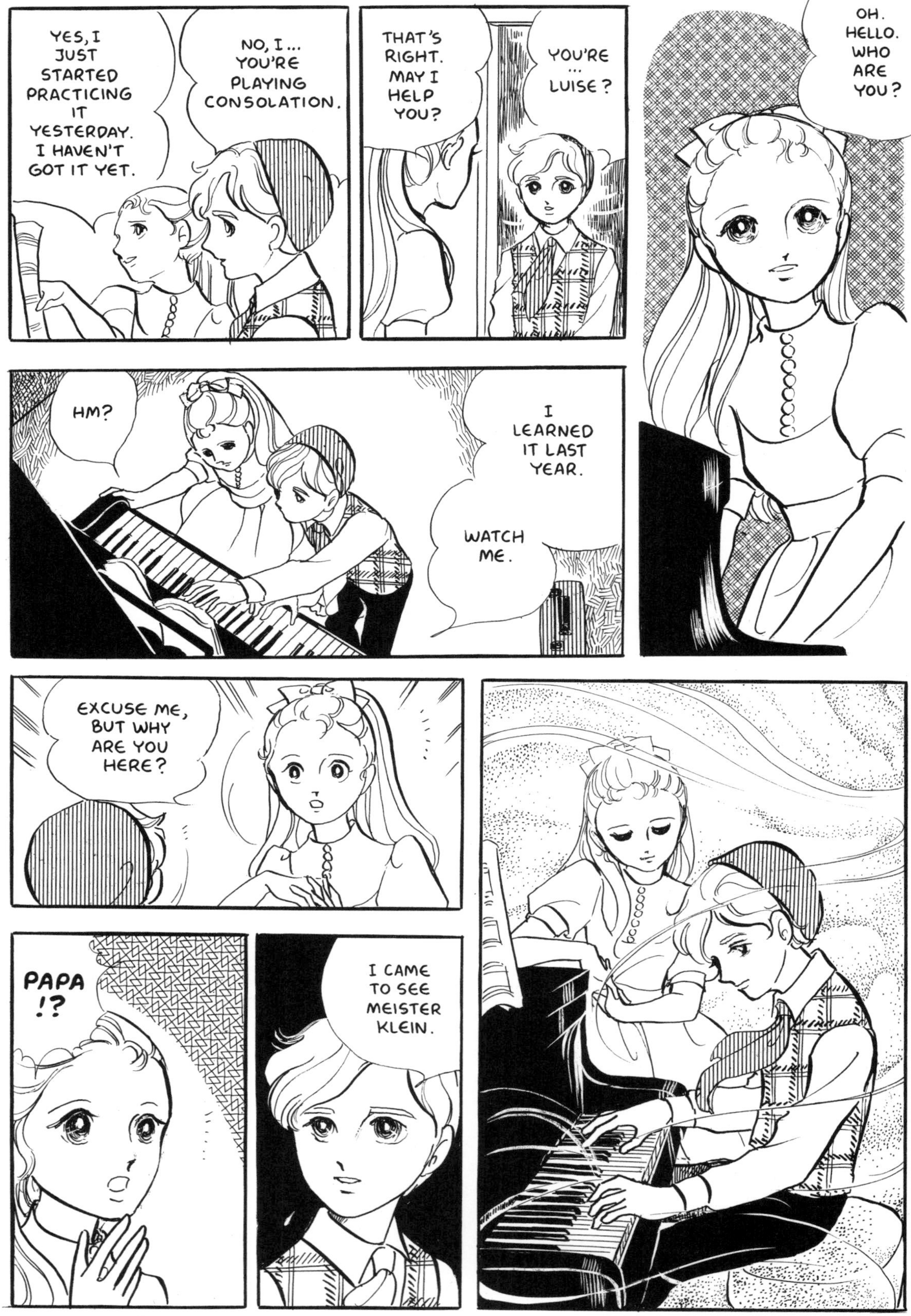
OH. HELLO. WHO ARE YOU?
YOU'RE ... LUISE?
THAT'S RIGHT. MAY I HELP YOU?
NO, I... YOU'RE PLAYING CONSOLATION.
YES, I JUST STARTED PRACTICING IT YESTERDAY. I HAVEN'T GOT IT YET.
I LEARNED IT LAST YEAR.
WATCH ME.
HM?
EXCUSE ME, BUT WHY ARE YOU HERE?
...
I CAME TO SEE MEISTER KLEIN.
PAPA !?

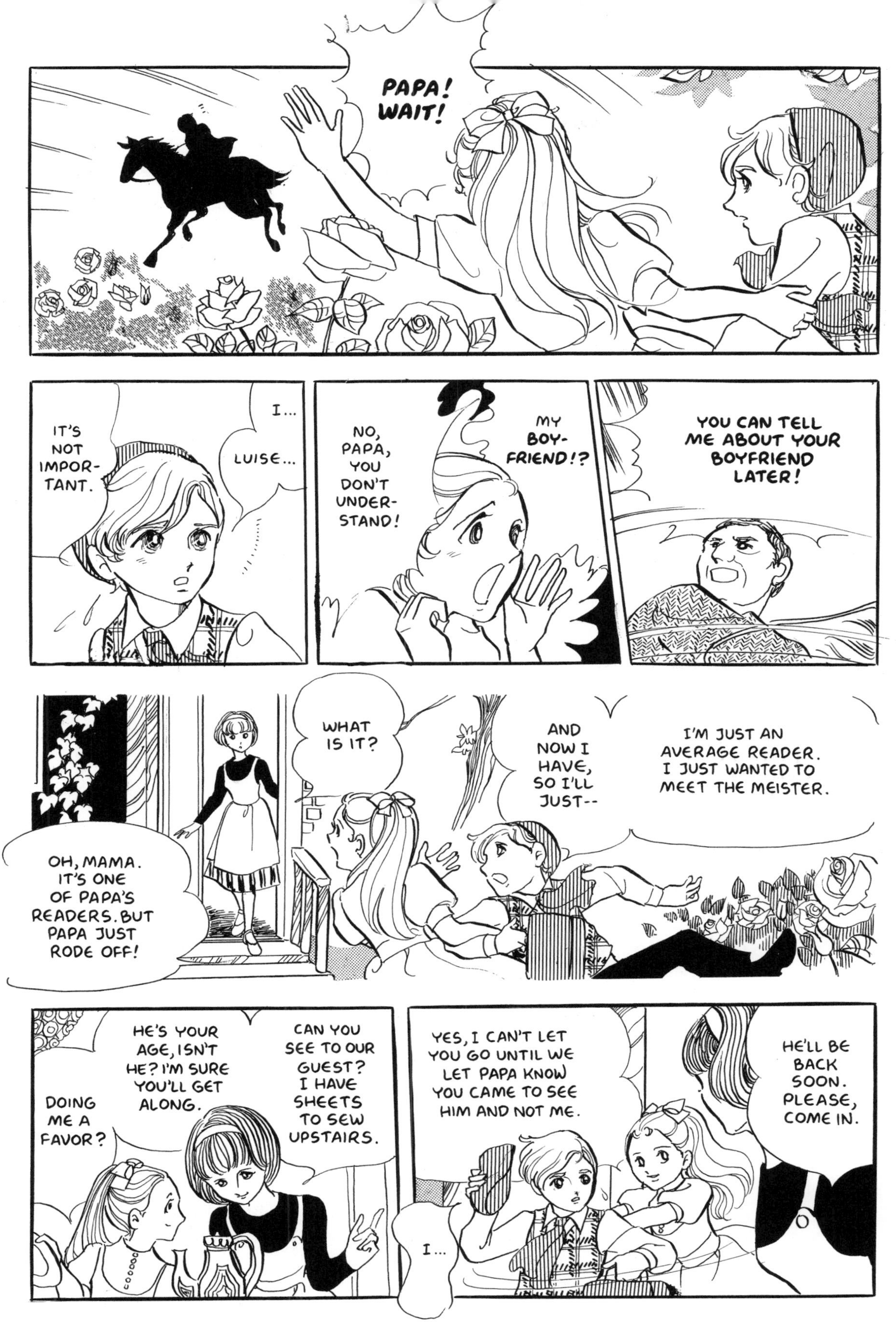
PAPA! WAIT!
YOU CAN TELL ME ABOUT YOUR BOYFRIEND LATER!
MY BOY-FRIEND!?
NO, PAPA, YOU DON'T UNDER-STAND!
I...
LUISE...
IT'S NOT IMPOR-TANT.
I'M JUST AN AVERAGE READER. I JUST WANTED TO MEET THE MEISTER.
AND NOW I HAVE, SO I'LL JUST--
WHAT IS IT?
OH, MAMA. IT'S ONE OF PAPA'S READERS. BUT PAPA JUST RODE OFF!
HE'LL BE BACK SOON. PLEASE, COME IN.
YES, I CAN'T LET YOU GO UNTIL WE LET PAPA KNOW YOU CAME TO SEE HIM AND NOT ME.
I...
CAN YOU SEE TO OUR GUEST? I HAVE SHEETS TO SEW UPSTAIRS.
HE'S YOUR AGE, ISN'T HE? I'M SURE YOU'LL GET ALONG.
DOING ME A FAVOR?

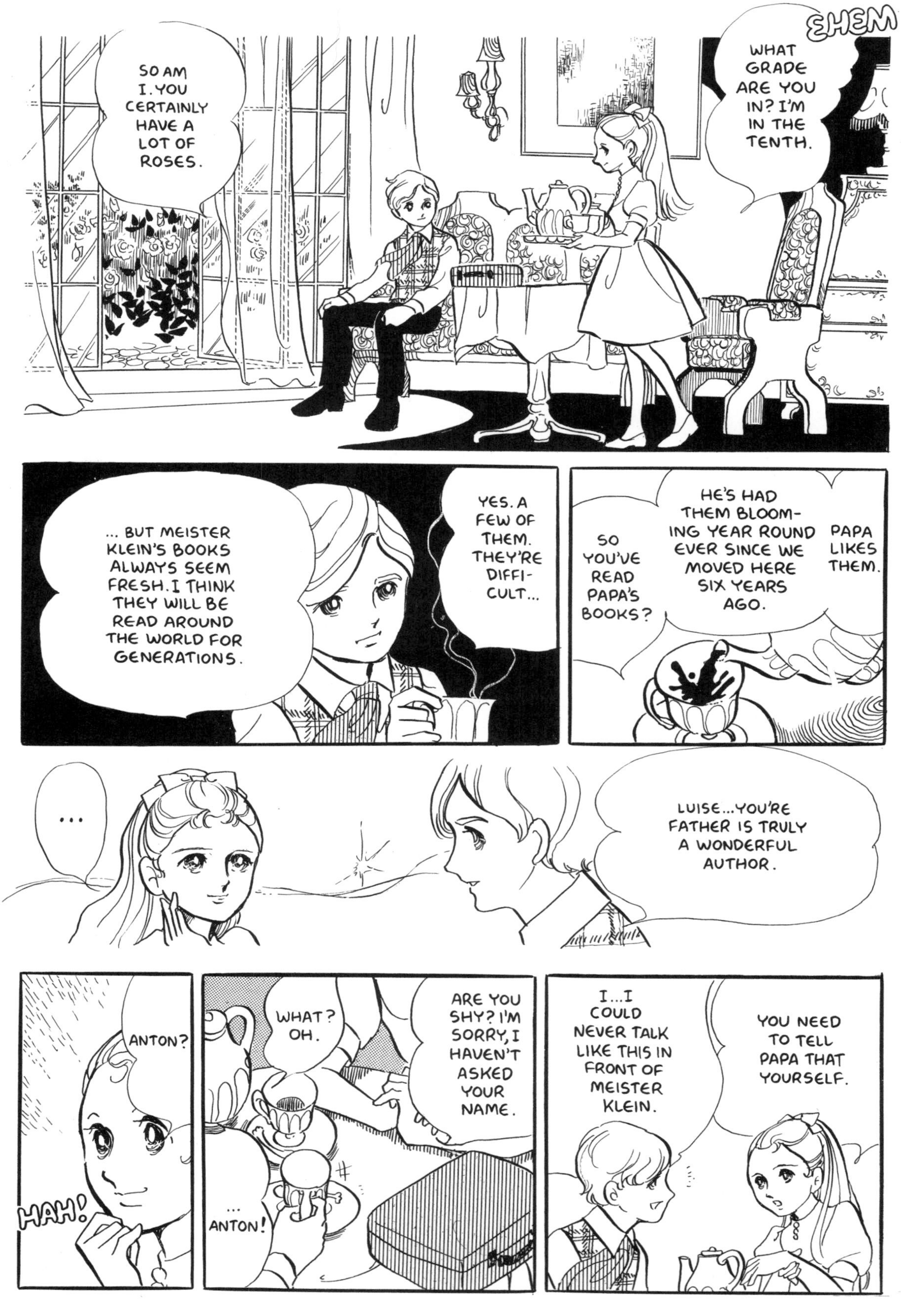
EHEM
WHAT GRADE ARE YOU IN? I'M IN THE TENTH.
SO AM I. YOU CERTAINLY HAVE A LOT OF ROSES.
PAPA LIKES THEM.
HE'S HAD THEM BLOOMING YEAR ROUND EVER SINCE WE MOVED HERE SIX YEARS AGO.
SO YOU'VE READ PAPA'S BOOKS?
YES. A FEW OF THEM. THEY'RE DIFFICULT...
... BUT MEISTER KLEIN'S BOOKS ALWAYS SEEM FRESH. I THINK THEY WILL BE READ AROUND THE WORLD FOR GENERATIONS.
LUISE...YOU'RE FATHER IS TRULY A WONDERFUL AUTHOR.
...
YOU NEED TO TELL PAPA THAT YOURSELF.
I...I COULD NEVER TALK LIKE THIS IN FRONT OF MEISTER KLEIN.
ARE YOU SHY? I'M SORRY, I HAVEN'T ASKED YOUR NAME.
WHAT? OH.
... ANTON!
ANTON?
HAH!

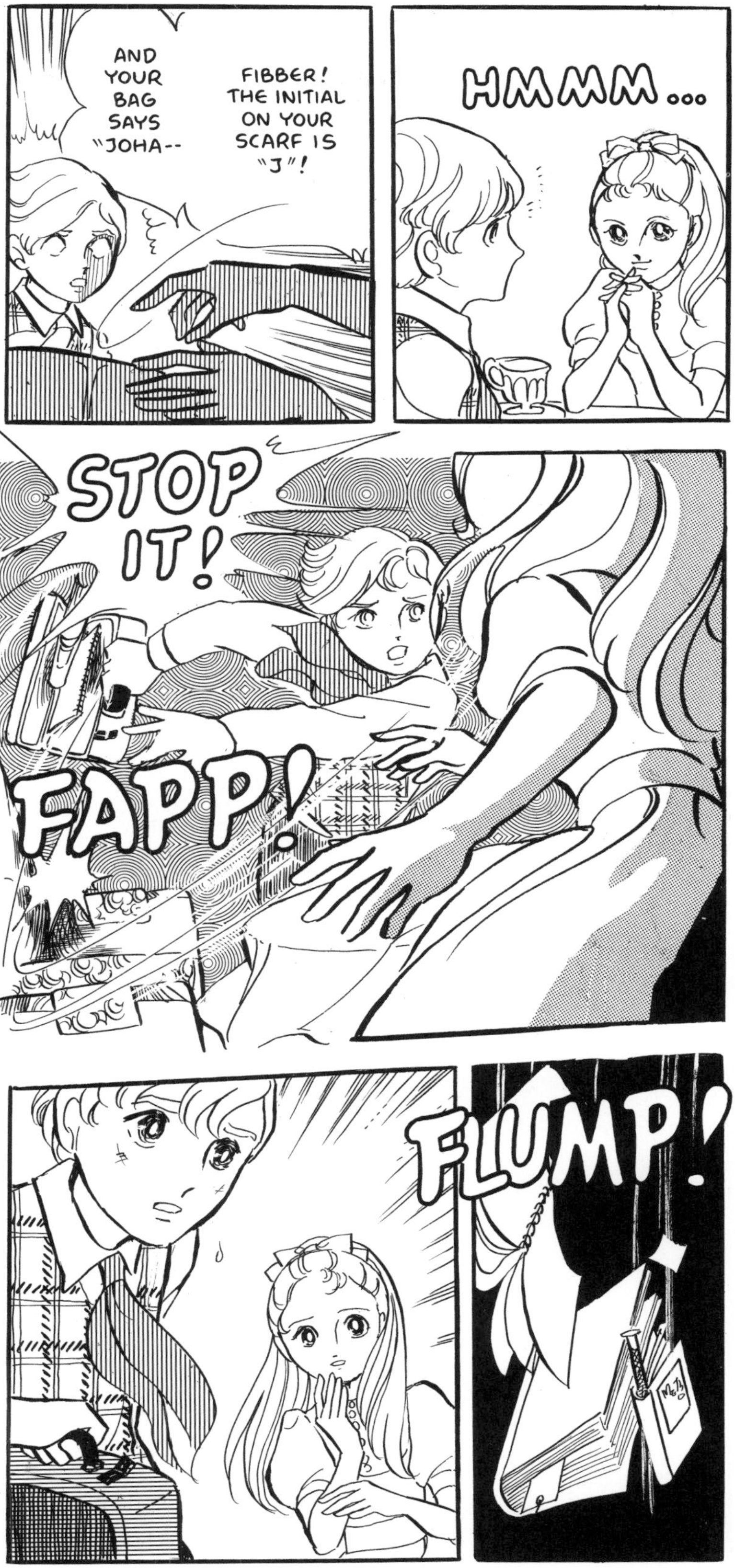
HMMM...
FIBBER! THE INITIAL ON YOUR SCARF IS "J"!
AND YOUR BAG SAYS "JOHA--
STOP IT!
FAPP!
FLUMP!

MY CAT IS--HOW SHOULD I PUT THIS?--AN ALIEN INVADER. WHY DO I SAY SO? IT'S OBVIOUS. EVERY DAY IT TRIES SO HARD TO ACT LIKE A CAT, BUT THE ACT IS OVERDONE. YOU MIGHT SAY THE CAT IS JUST TOO CAT-LIKE. SO INEVITABLY, IT SLIPS UP ONCE IN A WHILE. WHEN WE BEHAVE AS IF WE'RE NOT PAYING ATTENTION, IT SCANS THE AREA WITH ITS INVADER EYES, AND WALKS AROUND ON ITS HIND LEGS. AND WHEN WE QUICKLY TURN TO LOOK AT IT, IT QUICKLY GETS DOWN ON FOUR LEGS AND BEGINS ACTING LIKE A CAT AGAIN. IN AN EFFORT TO TAME THIS INVADER, WE PLY IT EVERY DAY WITH LARGE QUANTITES OF EARTH-STYLE GOMA-AJI.*

HAGIO

*GOMA-AJI: A DISH DISTINCTIVE TO HAGIO'S NATIVE NORTHERN KYUSHU, CONSISTING OF CHOPPED AJI (HORSE MACKEREL) SPRINKLED WITH SESAME SEEDS AND FLAVORED WITH SOY-SAUCE BROTH.

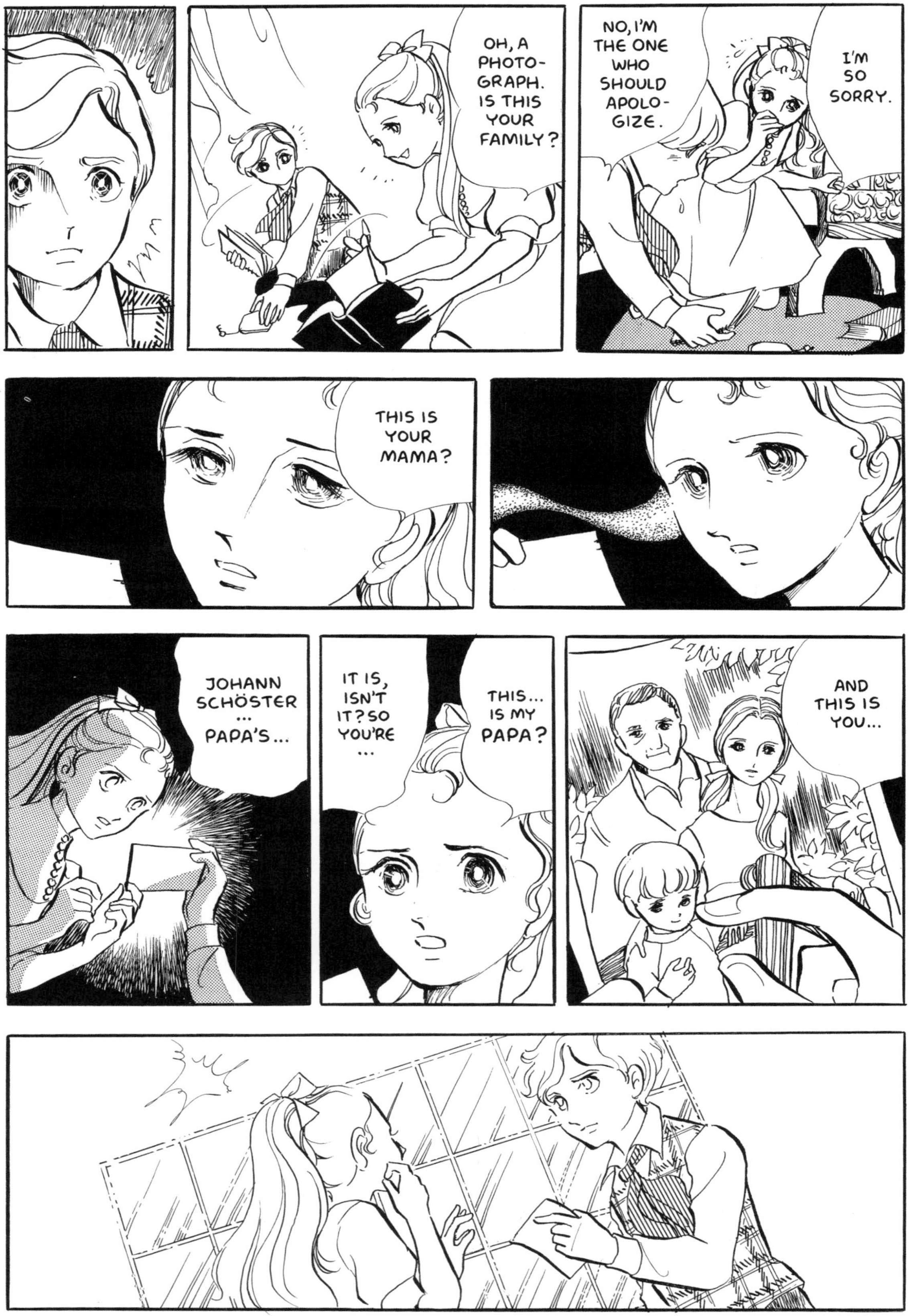
I'M SO SORRY.
NO, I'M THE ONE WHO SHOULD APOLOGIZE.
OH, A PHOTOGRAPH. IS THIS YOUR FAMILY?
THIS IS YOUR MAMA?
AND THIS IS YOU...
THIS... IS MY PAPA?
IT IS, ISN'T IT? SO YOU'RE ...
JOHANN SCHÖSTER ... PAPA'S...

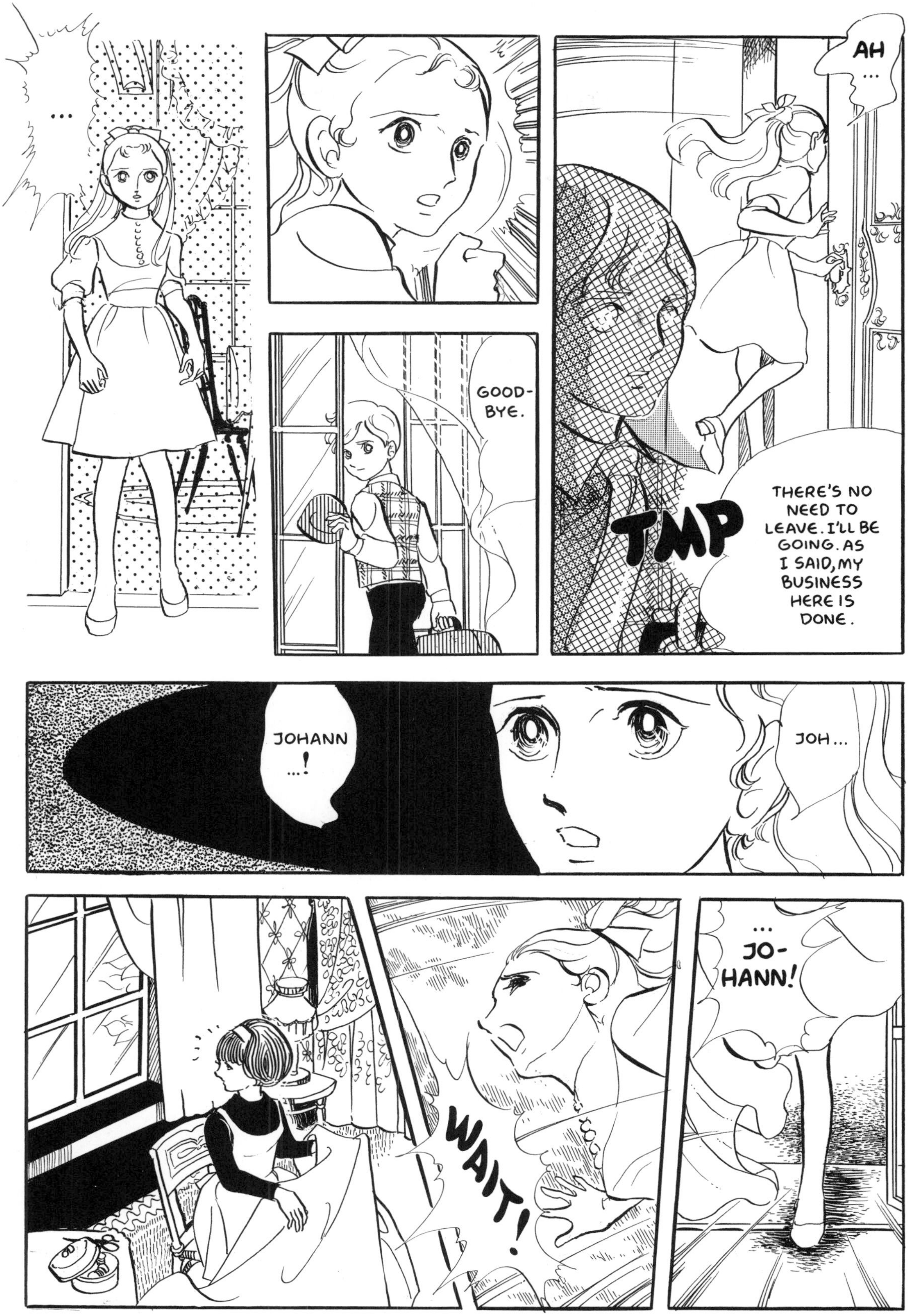
AH ...
TMP
THERE'S NO NEED TO LEAVE. I'LL BE GOING. AS I SAID, MY BUSINESS HERE IS DONE.
GOOD-BYE.
...
JOH...
JOHANN ...!
... JO-HANN!
WAIT!

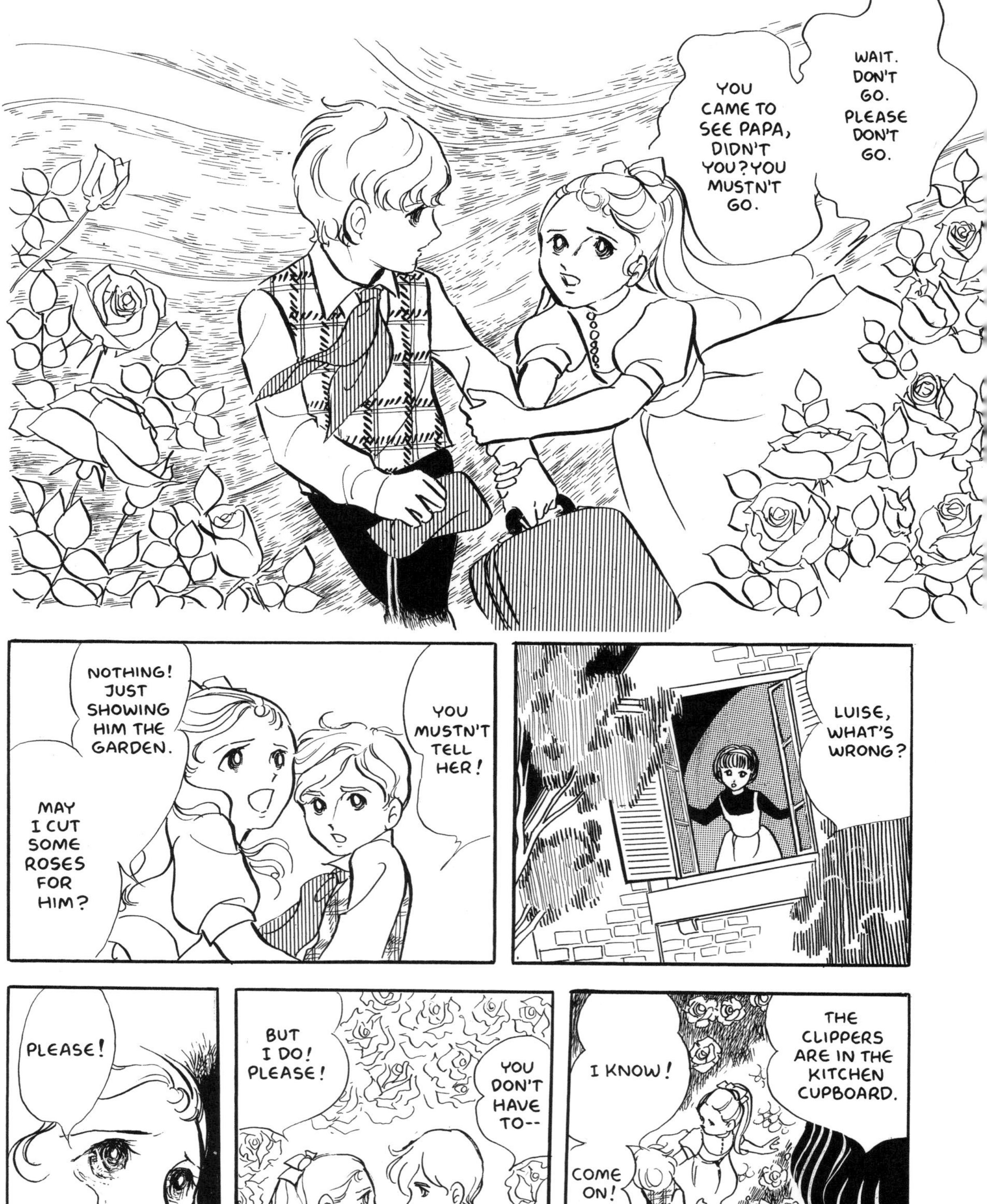
WAIT. DON'T GO. PLEASE DON'T GO.
YOU CAME TO SEE PAPA, DIDN'T YOU? YOU MUSTN'T GO.
LUISE, WHAT'S WRONG?
YOU MUSTN'T TELL HER!
NOTHING! JUST SHOWING HIM THE GARDEN.
MAY I CUT SOME ROSES FOR HIM?
THE CLIPPERS ARE IN THE KITCHEN CUPBOARD.
I KNOW!
COME ON!
YOU DON'T HAVE TO--
BUT I DO! PLEASE!
PLEASE!

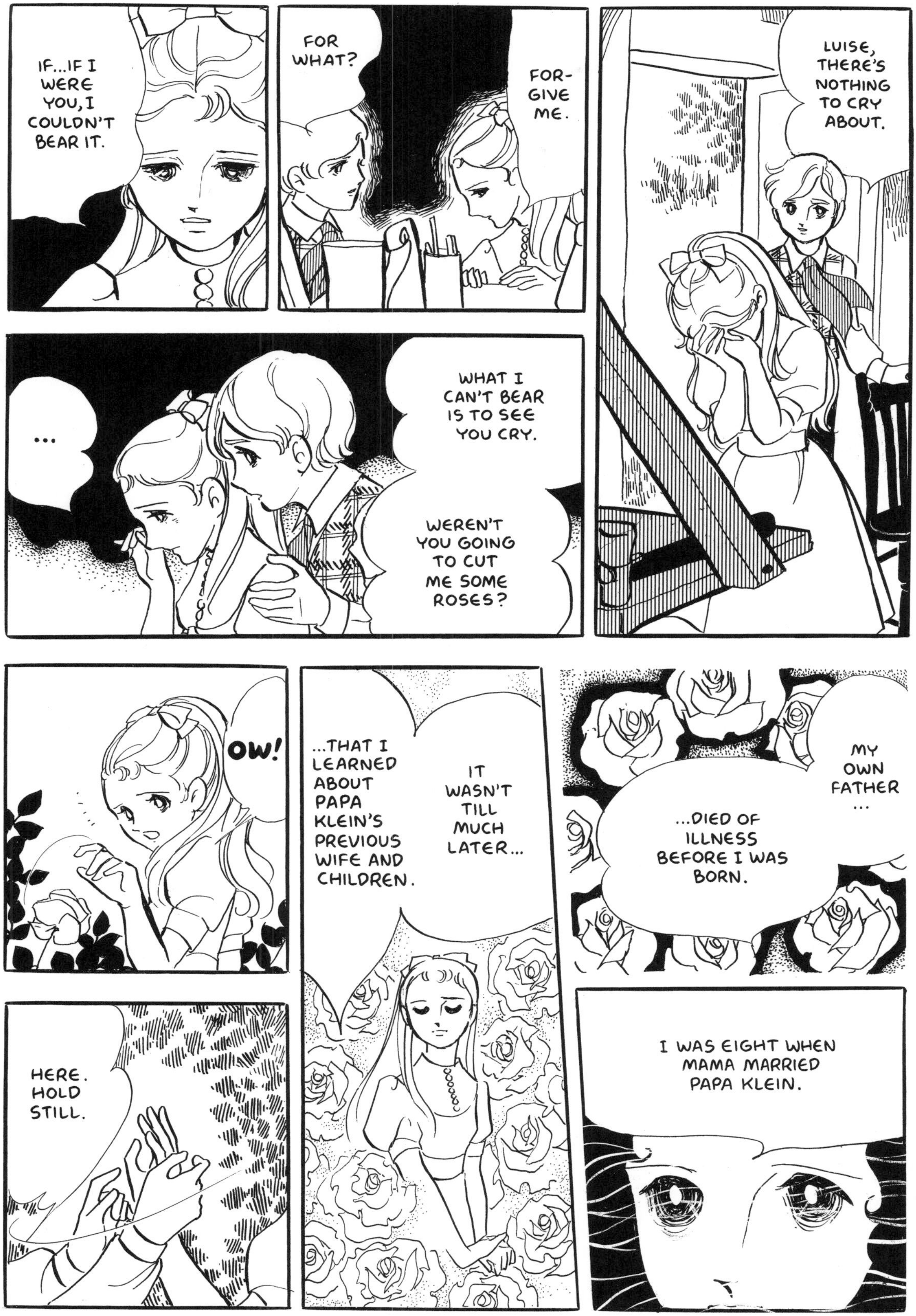
LUISE, THERE'S NOTHING TO CRY ABOUT.
FOR-GIVE ME.
FOR WHAT?
IF...IF I WERE YOU, I COULDN'T BEAR IT.
WHAT I CAN'T BEAR IS TO SEE YOU CRY.
WEREN'T YOU GOING TO CUT ME SOME ROSES?
...
MY OWN FATHER...
...DIED OF ILLNESS BEFORE I WAS BORN.
I WAS EIGHT WHEN MAMA MARRIED PAPA KLEIN.
IT WASN'T TILL MUCH LATER...
...THAT I LEARNED ABOUT PAPA KLEIN'S PREVIOUS WIFE AND CHILDREN.
OW!
HERE. HOLD STILL.

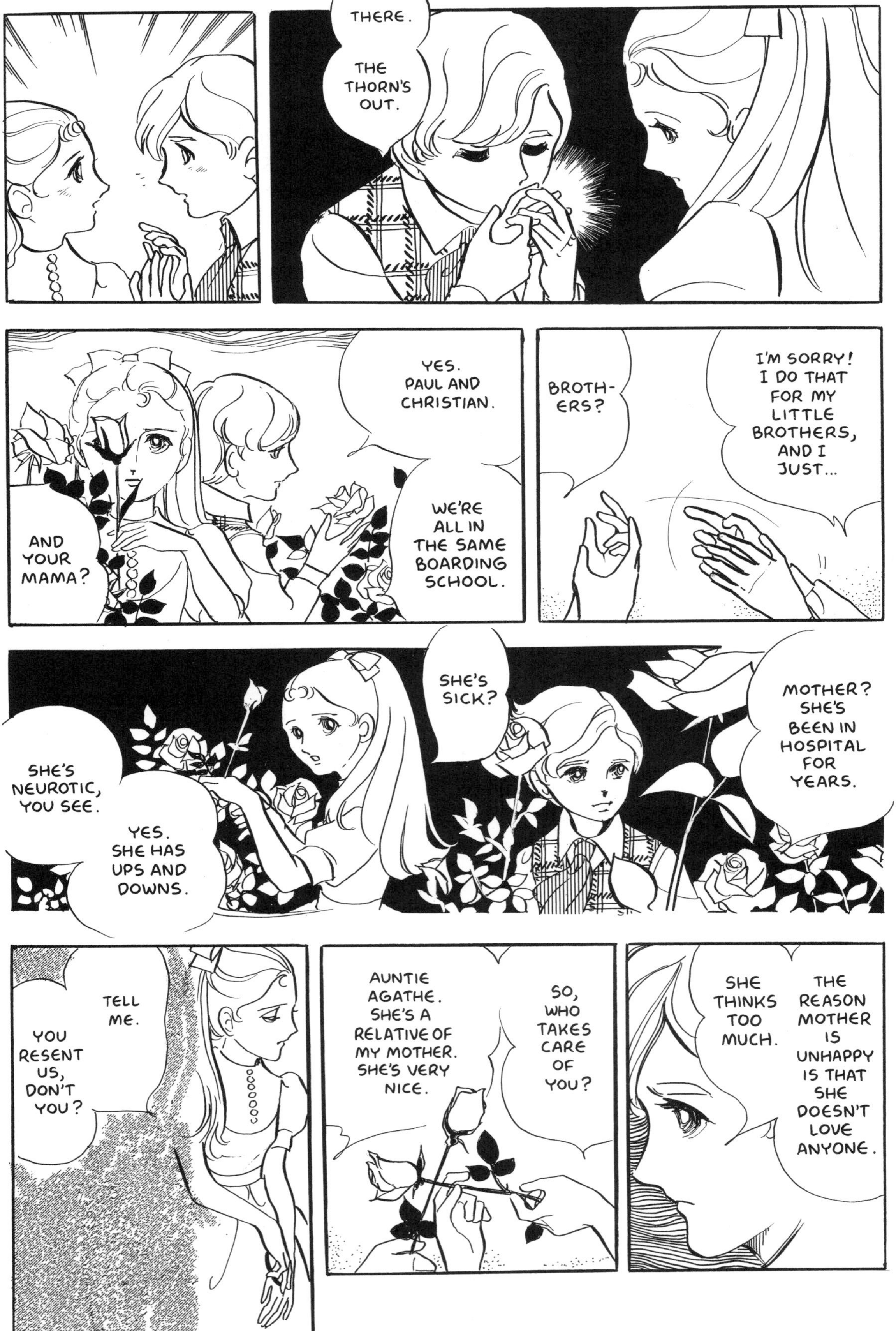
THERE.
THE THORN'S OUT.
I'M SORRY! I DO THAT FOR MY LITTLE BROTHERS, AND I JUST...
BROTH-ERS?
YES. PAUL AND CHRISTIAN.
WE'RE ALL IN THE SAME BOARDING SCHOOL.
AND YOUR MAMA?
MOTHER? SHE'S BEEN IN HOSPITAL FOR YEARS.
SHE'S SICK?
YES. SHE HAS UPS AND DOWNS.
SHE'S NEUROTIC, YOU SEE.
THE REASON MOTHER IS UNHAPPY IS THAT SHE DOESN'T LOVE ANYONE.
SHE THINKS TOO MUCH.
SO, WHO TAKES CARE OF YOU?
AUNTIE AGATHE. SHE'S A RELATIVE OF MY MOTHER. SHE'S VERY NICE.
TELL ME.
YOU RESENT US, DON'T YOU?

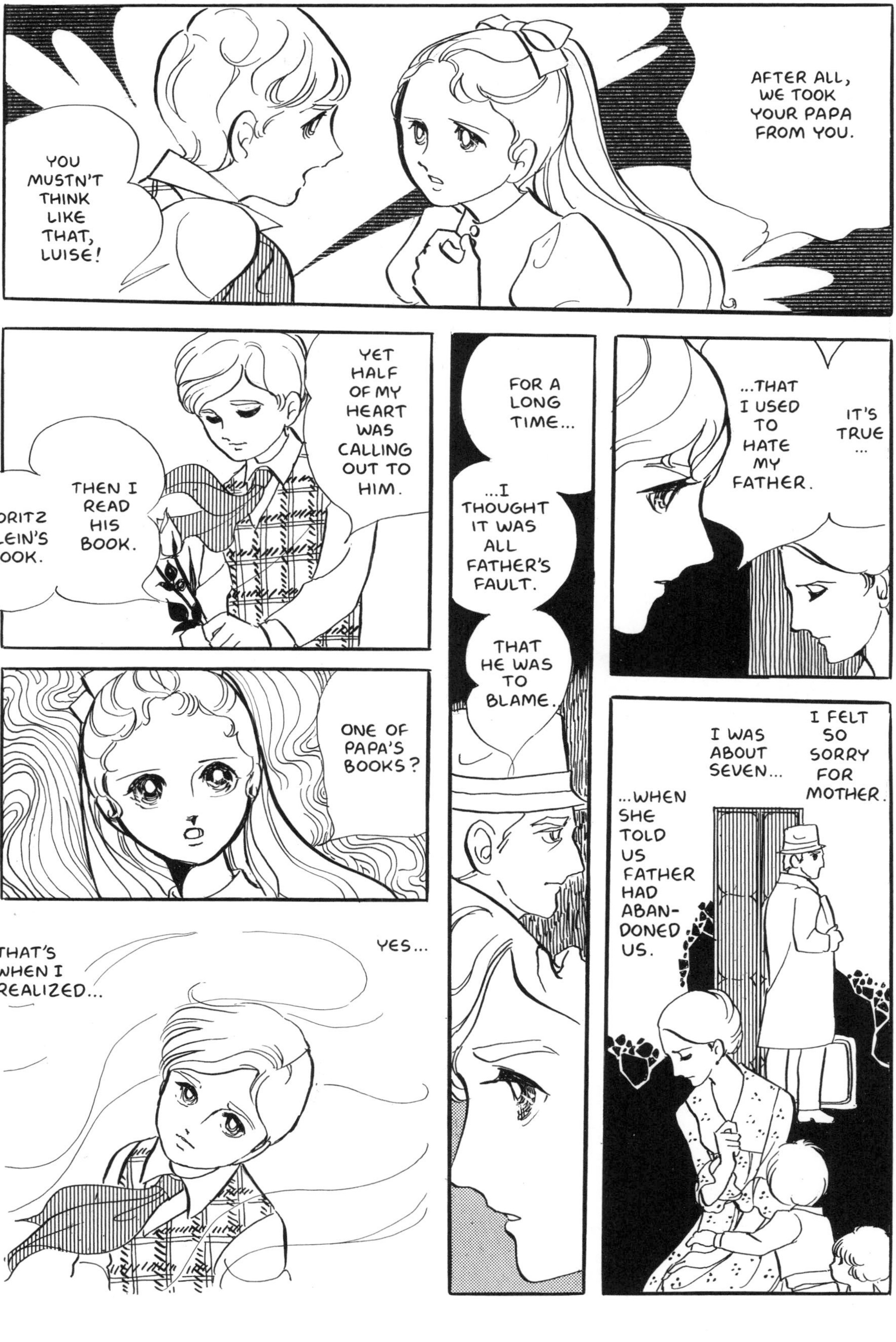
AFTER ALL, WE TOOK YOUR PAPA FROM YOU.
YOU MUSTN'T THINK LIKE THAT, LUISE!
IT'S TRUE ...
...THAT I USED TO HATE MY FATHER.
I FELT SO SORRY FOR MOTHER.
I WAS ABOUT SEVEN...
...WHEN SHE TOLD US FATHER HAD ABAN-DONED US.
FOR A LONG TIME...
...I THOUGHT IT WAS ALL FATHER'S FAULT.
THAT HE WAS TO BLAME.
YET HALF OF MY HEART WAS CALLING OUT TO HIM.
THEN I READ HIS BOOK.
MORITZ KLEIN'S BOOK.
ONE OF PAPA'S BOOKS?
YES...
THAT'S WHEN I REALIZED...

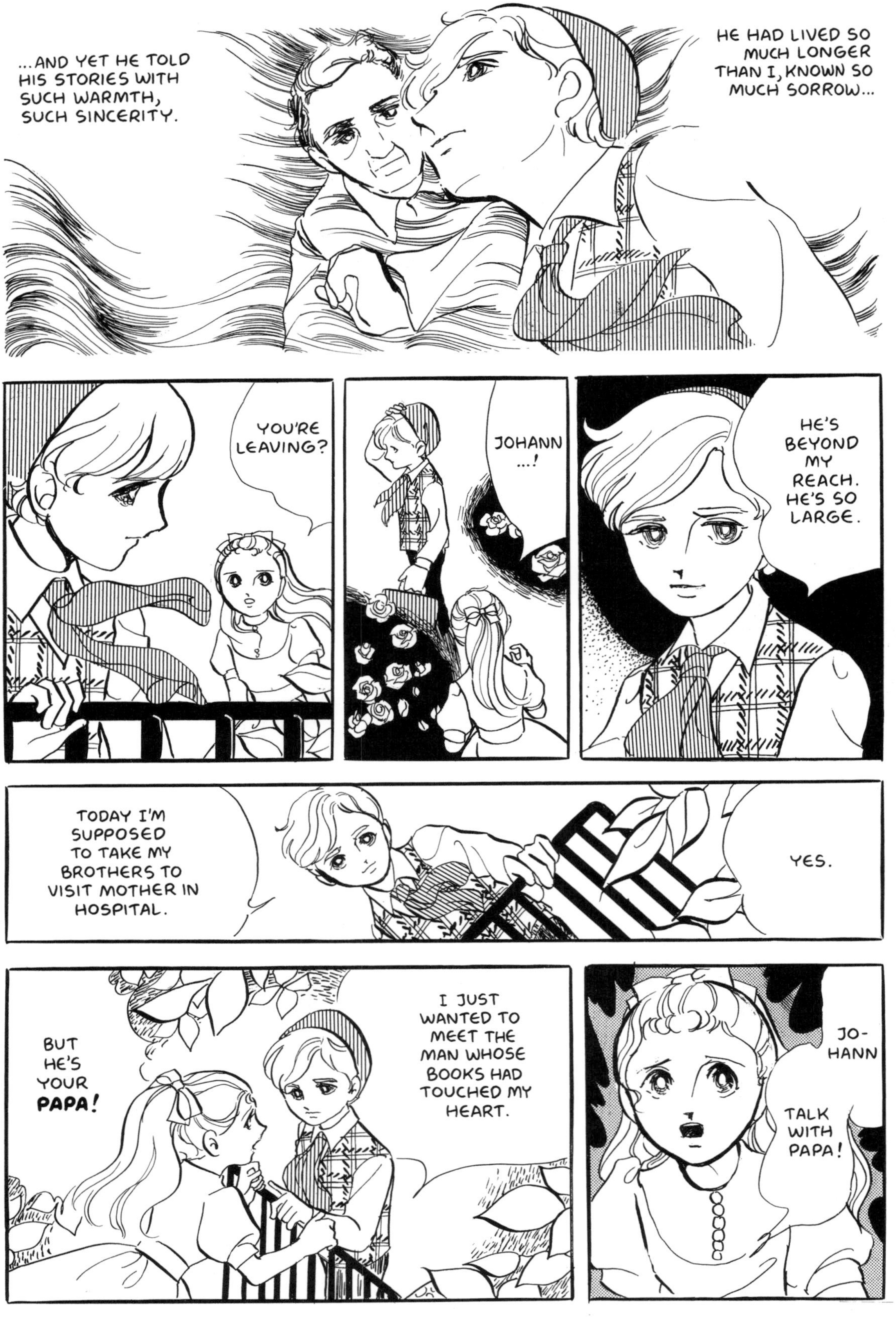
HE HAD LIVED SO MUCH LONGER THAN I, KNOWN SO MUCH SORROW...
...AND YET HE TOLD HIS STORIES WITH SUCH WARMTH, SUCH SINCERITY.
HE'S BEYOND MY REACH. HE'S SO LARGE.
JOHANN ...!
YOU'RE LEAVING?
YES.
TODAY I'M SUPPOSED TO TAKE MY BROTHERS TO VISIT MOTHER IN HOSPITAL.
JO-HANN
TALK WITH PAPA!
I JUST WANTED TO MEET THE MAN WHOSE BOOKS HAD TOUCHED MY HEART.
BUT HE'S YOUR **PAPA**!

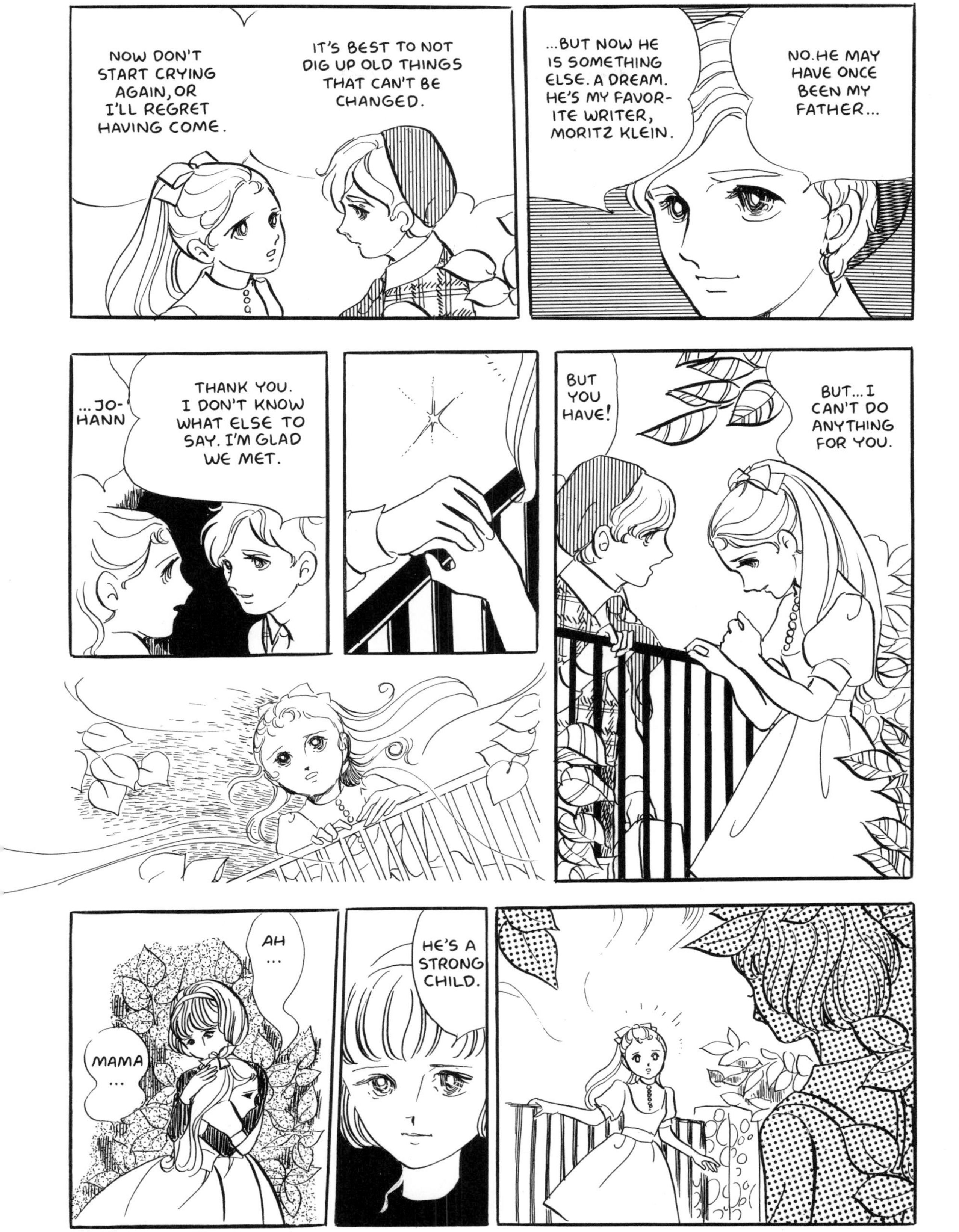
NO. HE MAY HAVE ONCE BEEN MY FATHER...
...BUT NOW HE IS SOMETHING ELSE. A DREAM. HE'S MY FAVOR-ITE WRITER, MORITZ KLEIN.
IT'S BEST TO NOT DIG UP OLD THINGS THAT CAN'T BE CHANGED.
NOW DON'T START CRYING AGAIN, OR I'LL REGRET HAVING COME.
BUT... I CAN'T DO ANYTHING FOR YOU.
BUT YOU HAVE!
THANK YOU. I DON'T KNOW WHAT ELSE TO SAY. I'M GLAD WE MET.
...JO-HANN
HE'S A STRONG CHILD.
AH ...
MAMA ...

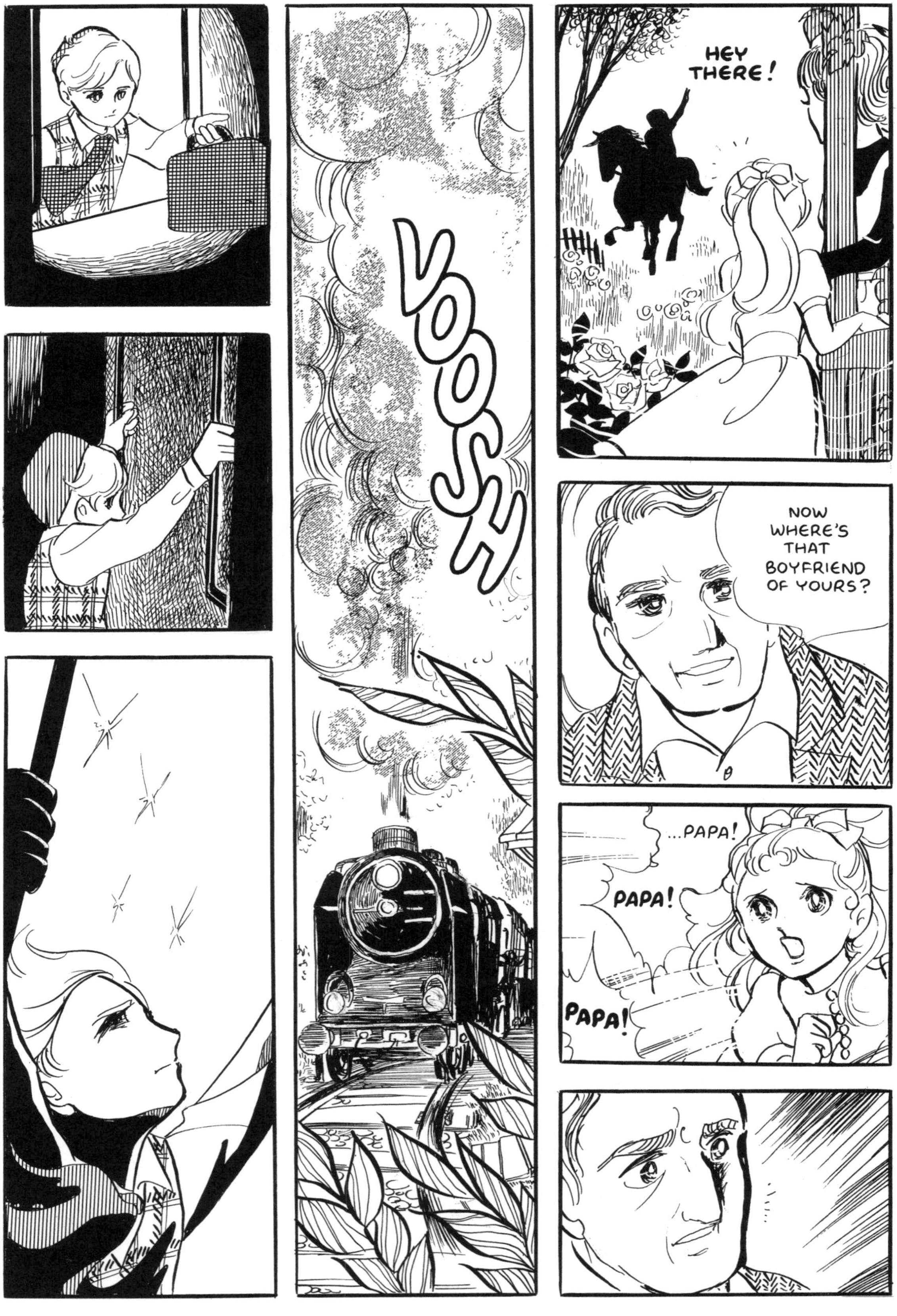
HEY THERE!
NOW WHERE'S THAT BOYFRIEND OF YOURS?
...PAPA!
PAPA!
PAPA!
VOOSH

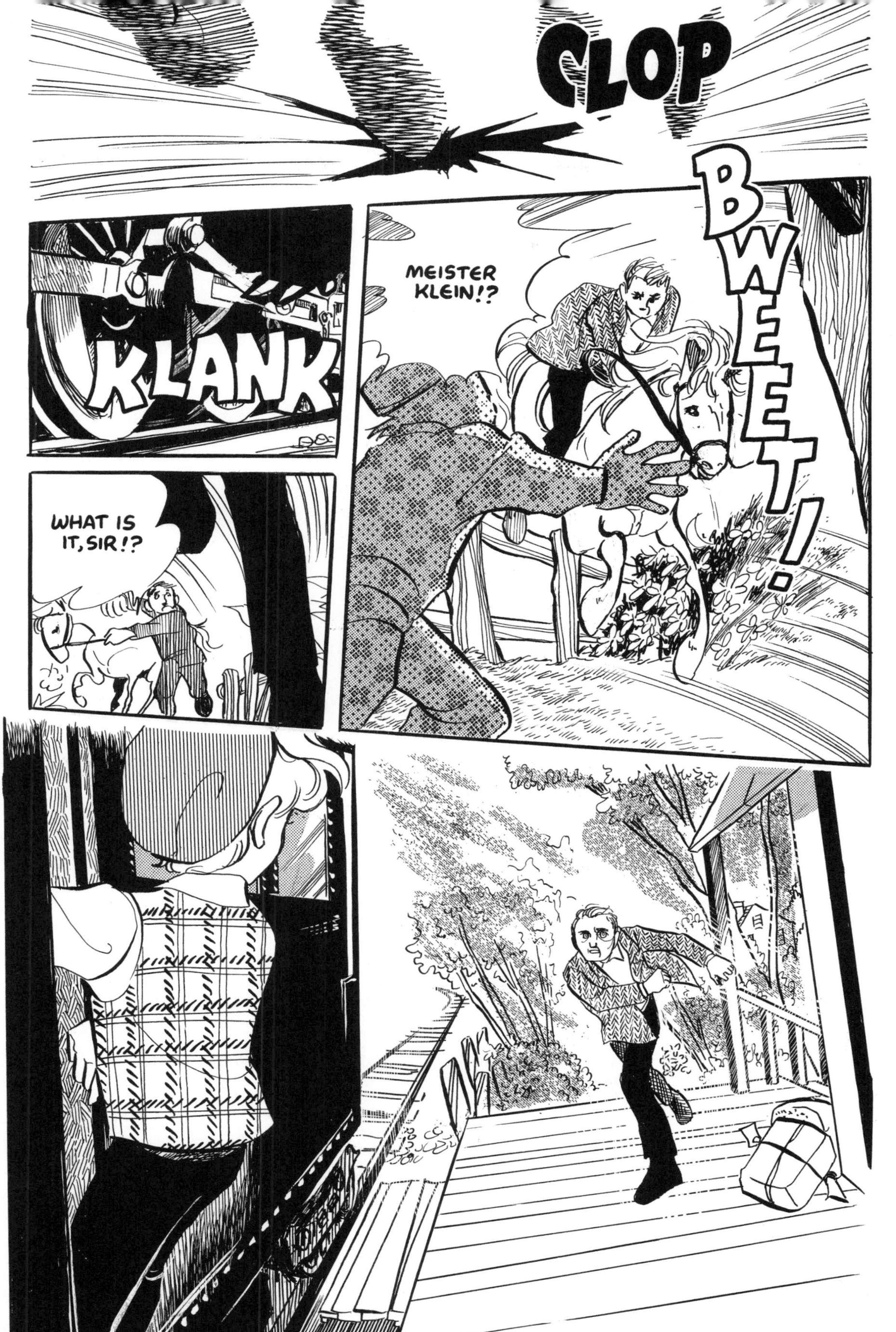
CLOP
BWEET!
MEISTER KLEIN!?
KLANK
WHAT IS IT, SIR!?

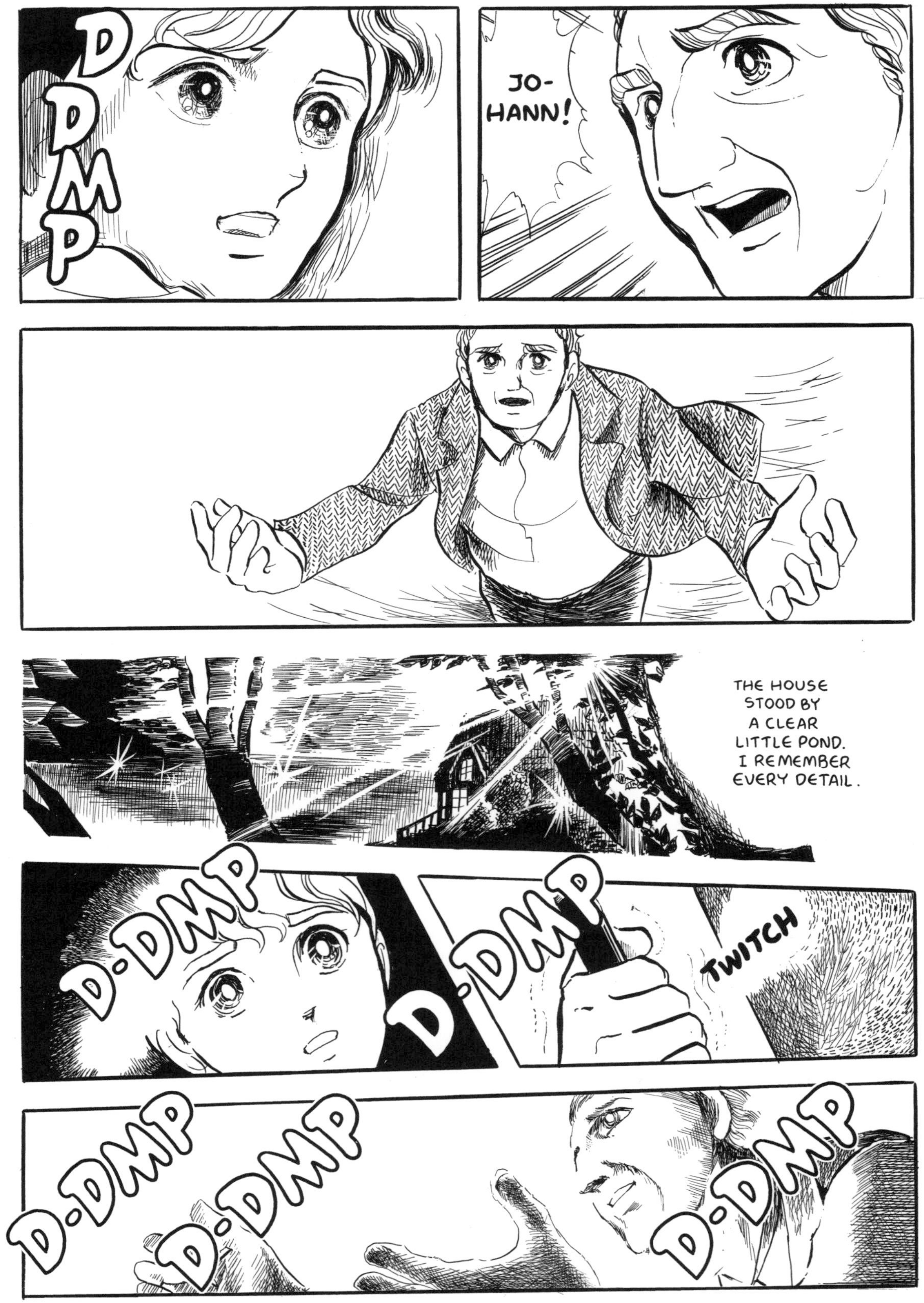
JO-HANN!
DDMP
THE HOUSE STOOD BY A CLEAR LITTLE POND. I REMEMBER EVERY DETAIL.
TWITCH
D-DMP
D-DMP
D-DMP
D-DMP
D-DMP

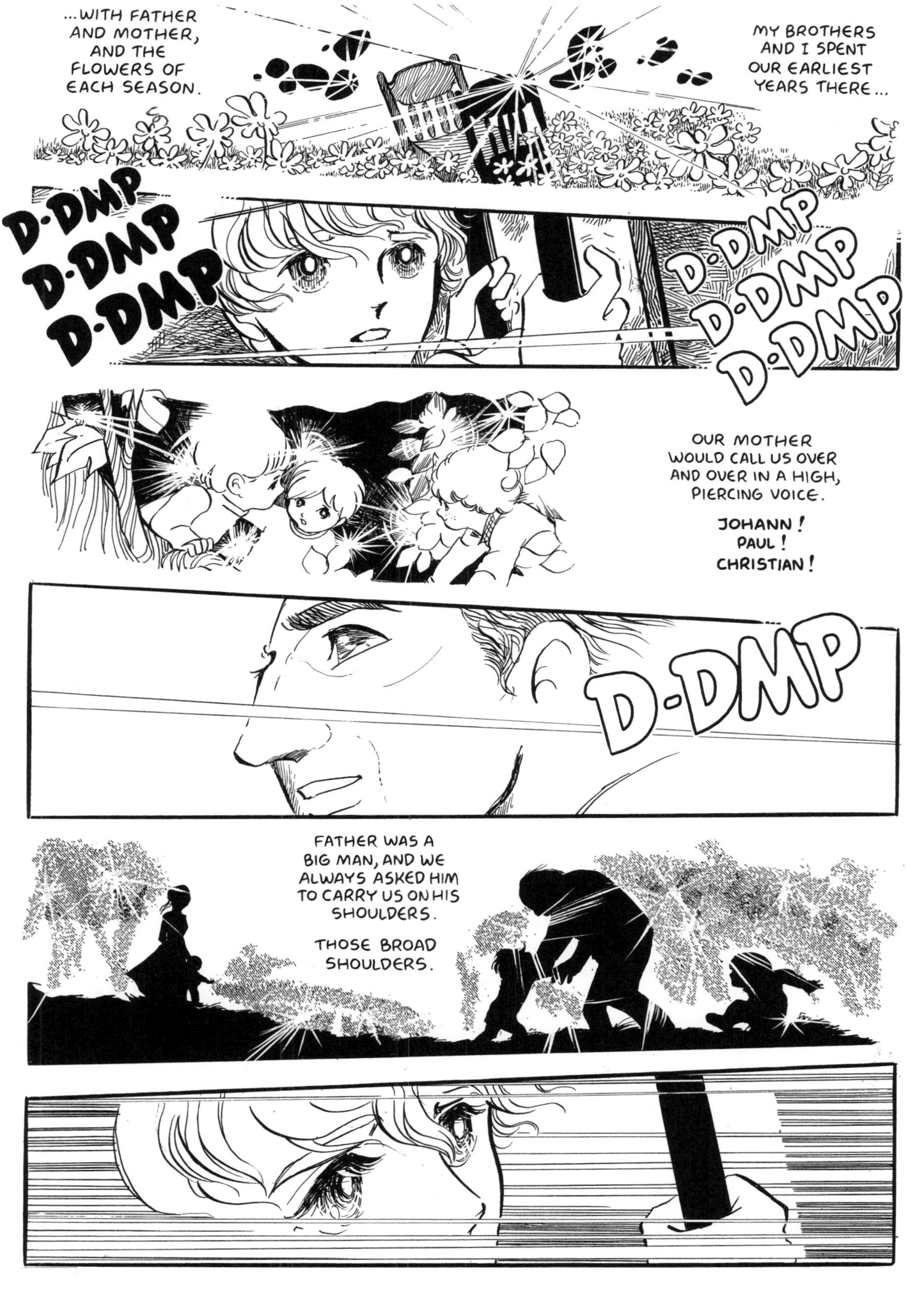
MY BROTHERS AND I SPENT OUR EARLIEST YEARS THERE...
...WITH FATHER AND MOTHER, AND THE FLOWERS OF EACH SEASON.
D-DMP D-DMP D-DMP
D-DMP D-DMP D-DMP
OUR MOTHER WOULD CALL US OVER AND OVER IN A HIGH, PIERCING VOICE.
JOHANN! PAUL! CHRISTIAN!
D-DMP
FATHER WAS A BIG MAN, AND WE ALWAYS ASKED HIM TO CARRY US ON HIS SHOULDERS.
THOSE BROAD SHOULDERS.

...THANK YOU
...THAN

THANK YOU.
THANK YOU.

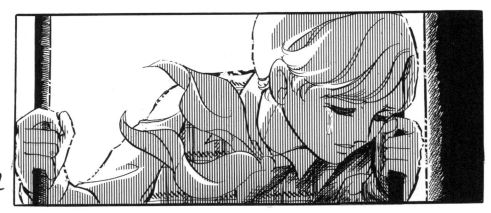

End

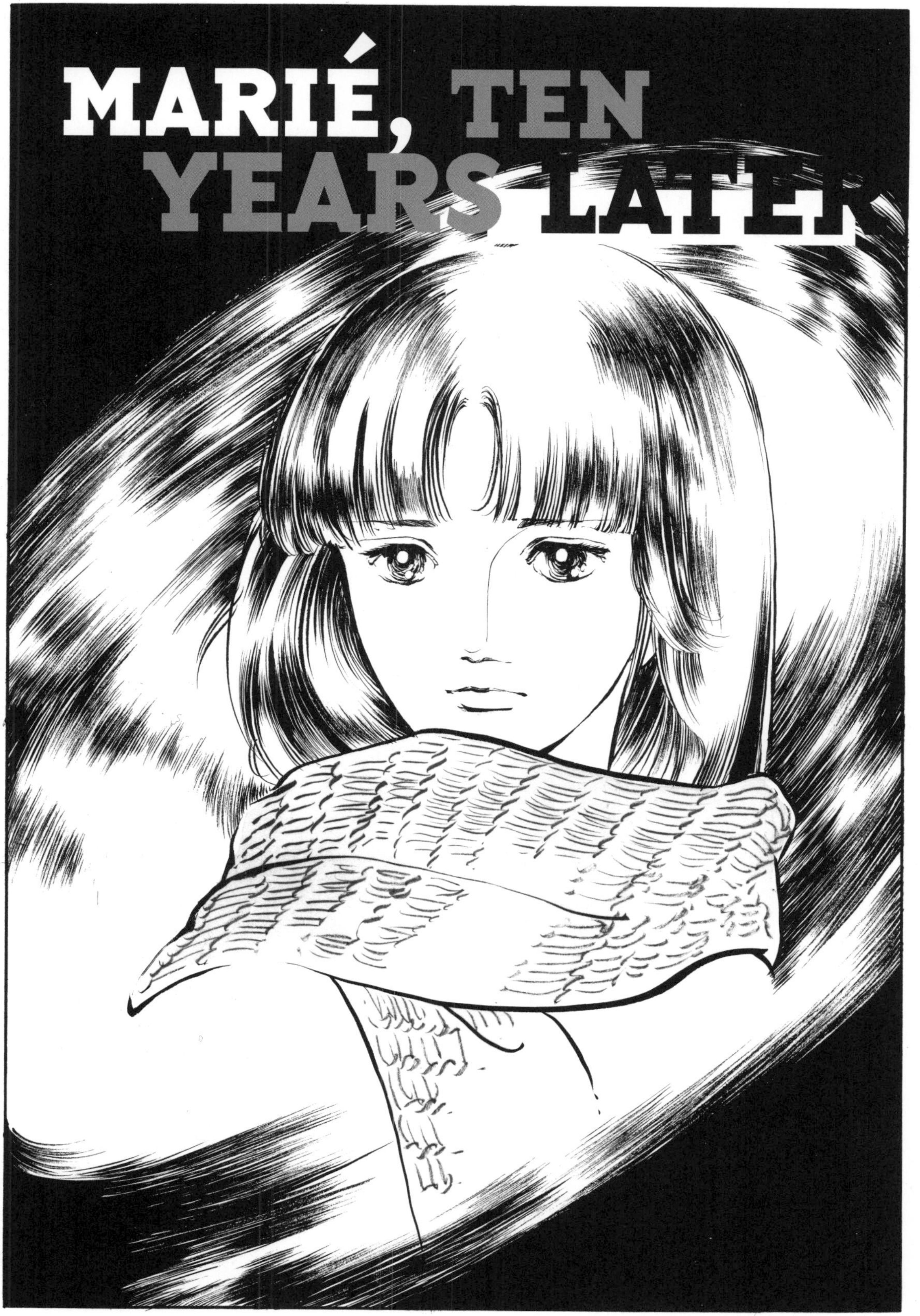
MARIÉ, TEN YEARS LATER

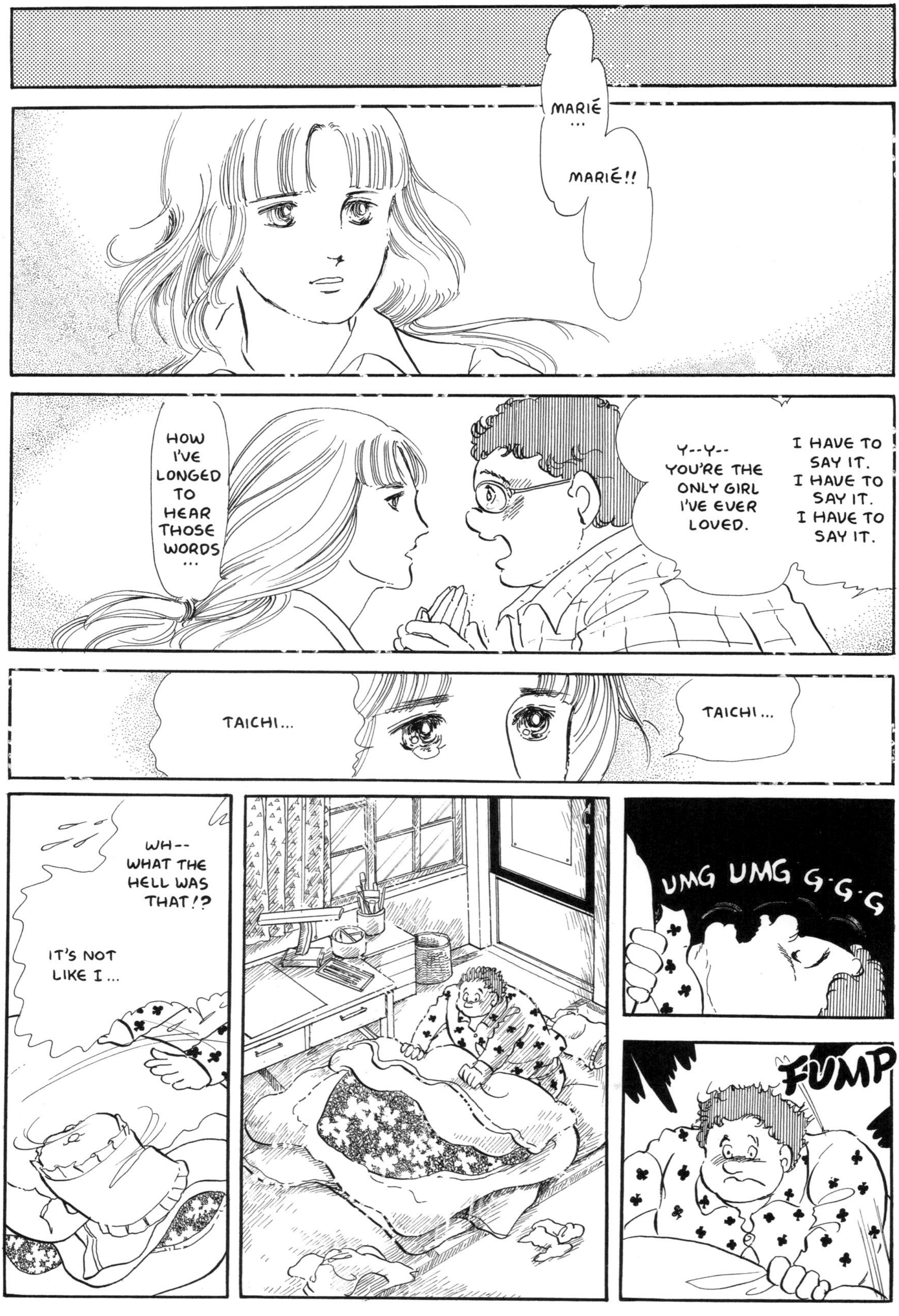
MARIÉ ...
MARIÉ!!
I HAVE TO SAY IT. I HAVE TO SAY IT. I HAVE TO SAY IT.
Y--Y-- YOU'RE THE ONLY GIRL I'VE EVER LOVED.
HOW I'VE LONGED TO HEAR THOSE WORDS ...
TAICHI ...
TAICHI ...
UMG UMG G-G-G
FUMP
WH-- WHAT THE HELL WAS THAT!?
IT'S NOT LIKE I ...

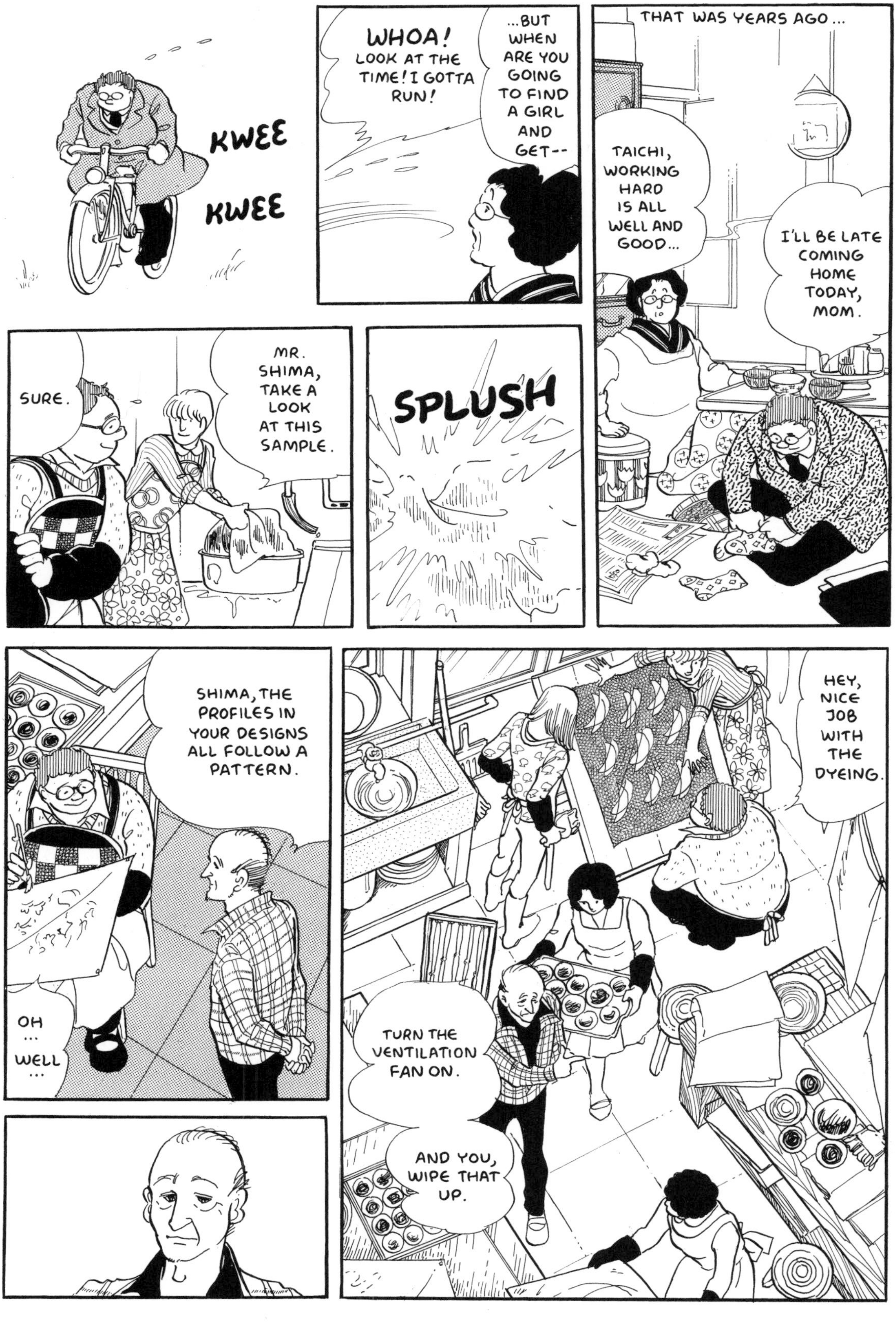
THAT WAS YEARS AGO...
I'LL BE LATE COMING HOME TODAY, MOM.
TAICHI, WORKING HARD IS ALL WELL AND GOOD...
...BUT WHEN ARE YOU GOING TO FIND A GIRL AND GET--
WHOA! LOOK AT THE TIME! I GOTTA RUN!
KWEE
KWEE
SPLUSH
MR. SHIMA, TAKE A LOOK AT THIS SAMPLE.
SURE.
HEY, NICE JOB WITH THE DYEING.
TURN THE VENTILATION FAN ON.
AND YOU, WIPE THAT UP.
SHIMA, THE PROFILES IN YOUR DESIGNS ALL FOLLOW A PATTERN.
OH ... WELL ...

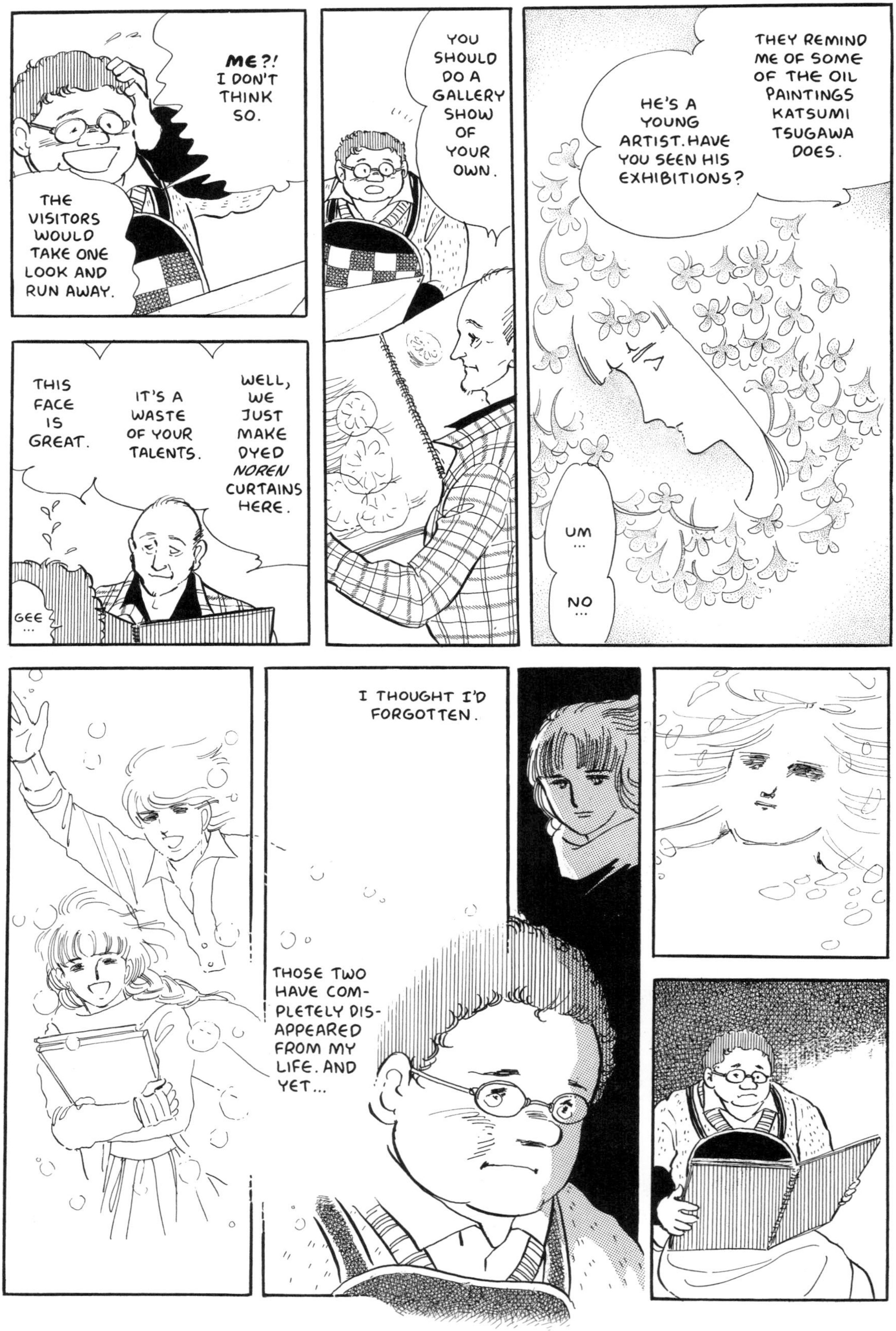
THEY REMIND ME OF SOME OF THE OIL PAINTINGS KATSUMI TSUGAWA DOES.
HE'S A YOUNG ARTIST. HAVE YOU SEEN HIS EXHIBITIONS?
UM…
NO…
YOU SHOULD DO A GALLERY SHOW OF YOUR OWN.
ME?! I DON'T THINK SO.
THE VISITORS WOULD TAKE ONE LOOK AND RUN AWAY.
WELL, WE JUST MAKE DYED *NOREN* CURTAINS HERE.
IT'S A WASTE OF YOUR TALENTS.
THIS FACE IS GREAT.
GEE…
I THOUGHT I'D FORGOTTEN.
THOSE TWO HAVE COMPLETELY DISAPPEARED FROM MY LIFE. AND YET...

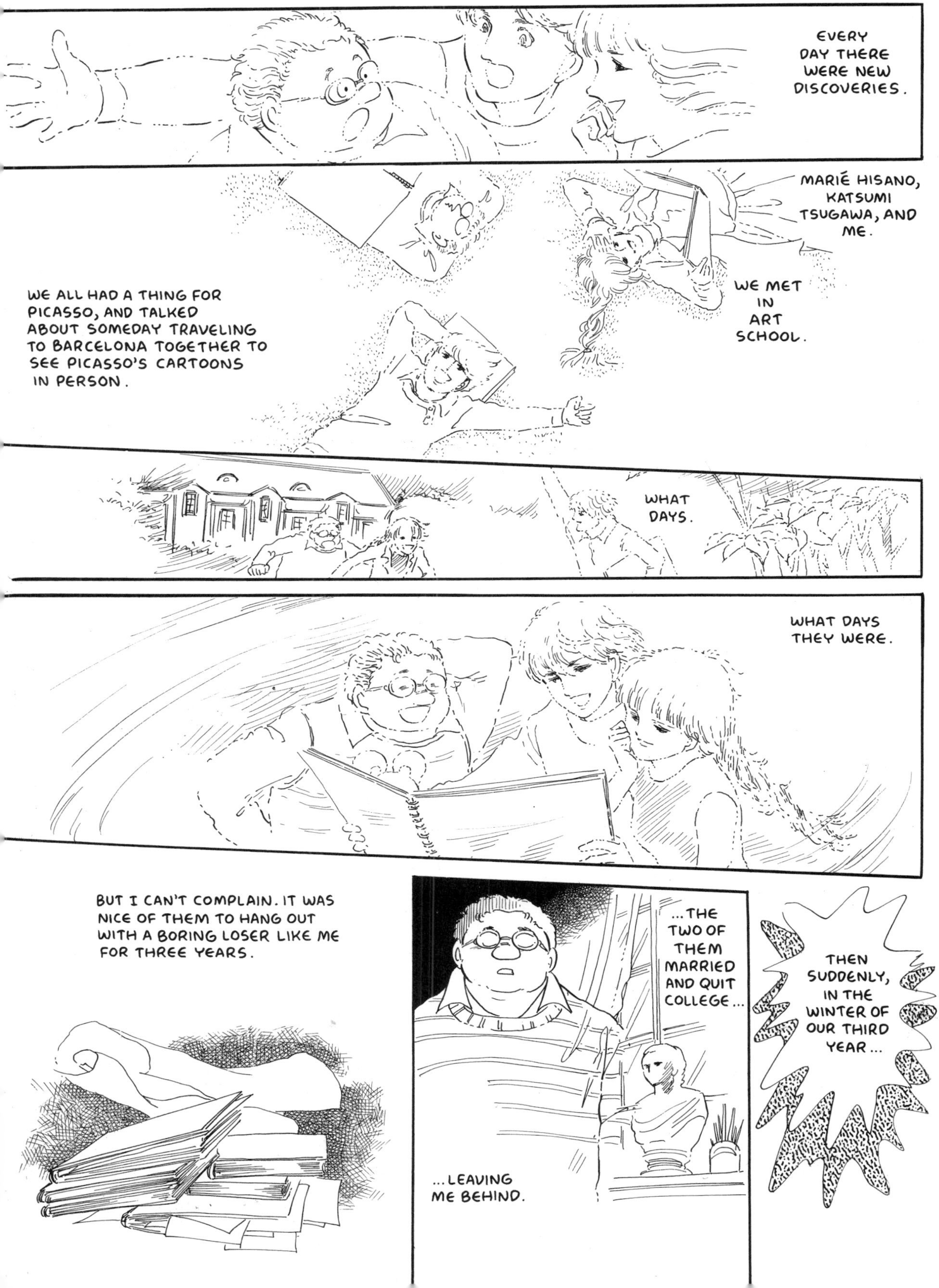
EVERY DAY THERE WERE NEW DISCOVERIES.
MARIÉ HISANO, KATSUMI TSUGAWA, AND ME.
WE MET IN ART SCHOOL.
WE ALL HAD A THING FOR PICASSO, AND TALKED ABOUT SOMEDAY TRAVELING TO BARCELONA TOGETHER TO SEE PICASSO'S CARTOONS IN PERSON.
WHAT DAYS.
WHAT DAYS THEY WERE.
THEN SUDDENLY, IN THE WINTER OF OUR THIRD YEAR...
...THE TWO OF THEM MARRIED AND QUIT COLLEGE...
...LEAVING ME BEHIND.
BUT I CAN'T COMPLAIN. IT WAS NICE OF THEM TO HANG OUT WITH A BORING LOSER LIKE ME FOR THREE YEARS.

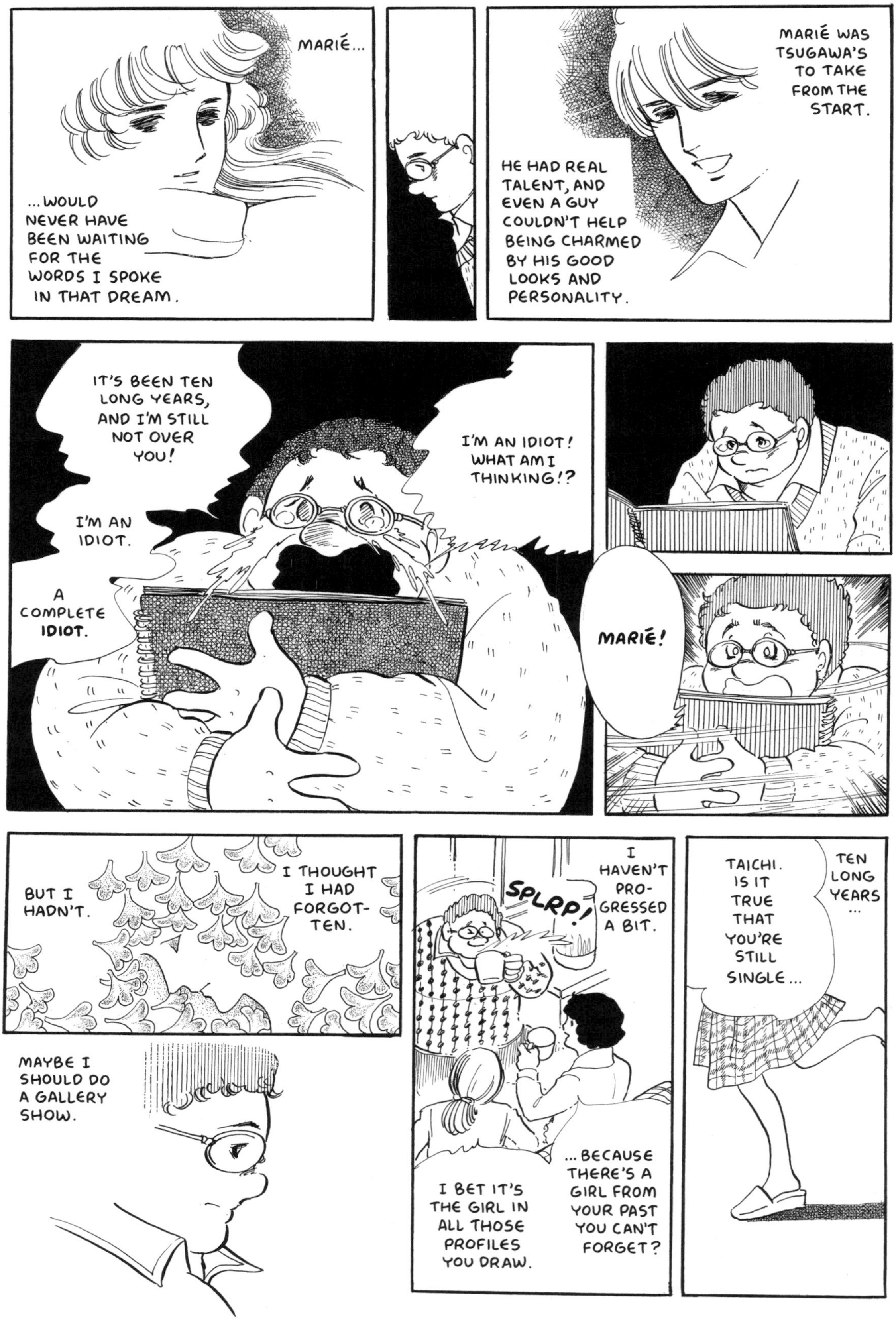
MARIÉ WAS TSUGAWA'S TO TAKE FROM THE START.
HE HAD REAL TALENT, AND EVEN A GUY COULDN'T HELP BEING CHARMED BY HIS GOOD LOOKS AND PERSONALITY.
MARIÉ...
...WOULD NEVER HAVE BEEN WAITING FOR THE WORDS I SPOKE IN THAT DREAM.
MARIÉ!
I'M AN IDIOT! WHAT AM I THINKING!?
IT'S BEEN TEN LONG YEARS, AND I'M STILL NOT OVER YOU!
I'M AN IDIOT.
A COMPLETE IDIOT.
TEN LONG YEARS...
TAICHI. IS IT TRUE THAT YOU'RE STILL SINGLE...
I HAVEN'T PRO-GRESSED A BIT.
SPLRP!
...BECAUSE THERE'S A GIRL FROM YOUR PAST YOU CAN'T FORGET?
I BET IT'S THE GIRL IN ALL THOSE PROFILES YOU DRAW.
I THOUGHT I HAD FORGOT-TEN.
BUT I HADN'T.
MAYBE I SHOULD DO A GALLERY SHOW.

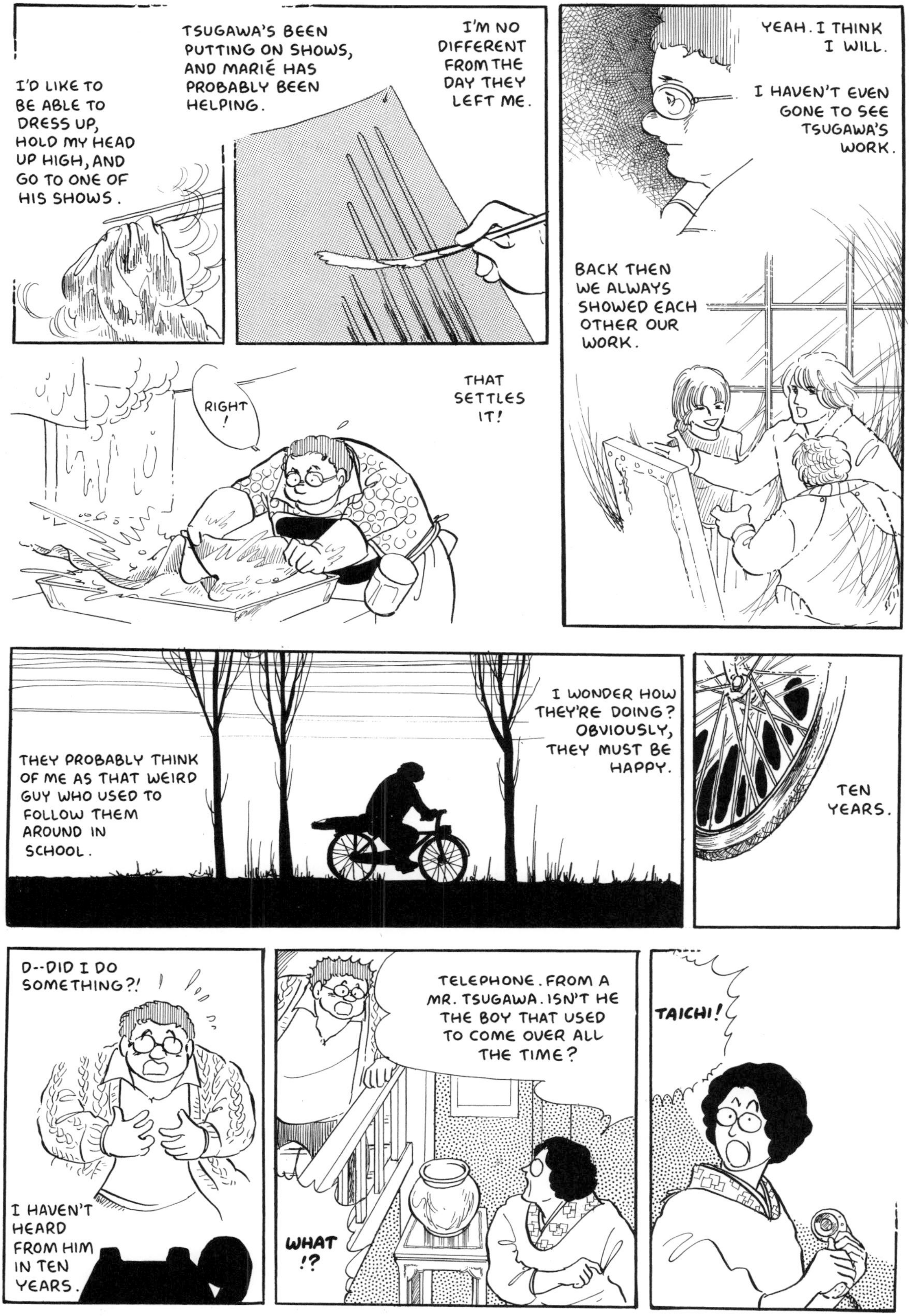
YEAH. I THINK I WILL.
I HAVEN'T EVEN GONE TO SEE TSUGAWA'S WORK.
BACK THEN WE ALWAYS SHOWED EACH OTHER OUR WORK.
I'M NO DIFFERENT FROM THE DAY THEY LEFT ME.
TSUGAWA'S BEEN PUTTING ON SHOWS, AND MARIÉ HAS PROBABLY BEEN HELPING.
I'D LIKE TO BE ABLE TO DRESS UP, HOLD MY HEAD UP HIGH, AND GO TO ONE OF HIS SHOWS.
THAT SETTLES IT!
RIGHT!
TEN YEARS.
I WONDER HOW THEY'RE DOING? OBVIOUSLY, THEY MUST BE HAPPY.
THEY PROBABLY THINK OF ME AS THAT WEIRD GUY WHO USED TO FOLLOW THEM AROUND IN SCHOOL.
TAICHI!
TELEPHONE. FROM A MR. TSUGAWA. ISN'T HE THE BOY THAT USED TO COME OVER ALL THE TIME?
WHAT !?
D--DID I DO SOMETHING?!
I HAVEN'T HEARD FROM HIM IN TEN YEARS.

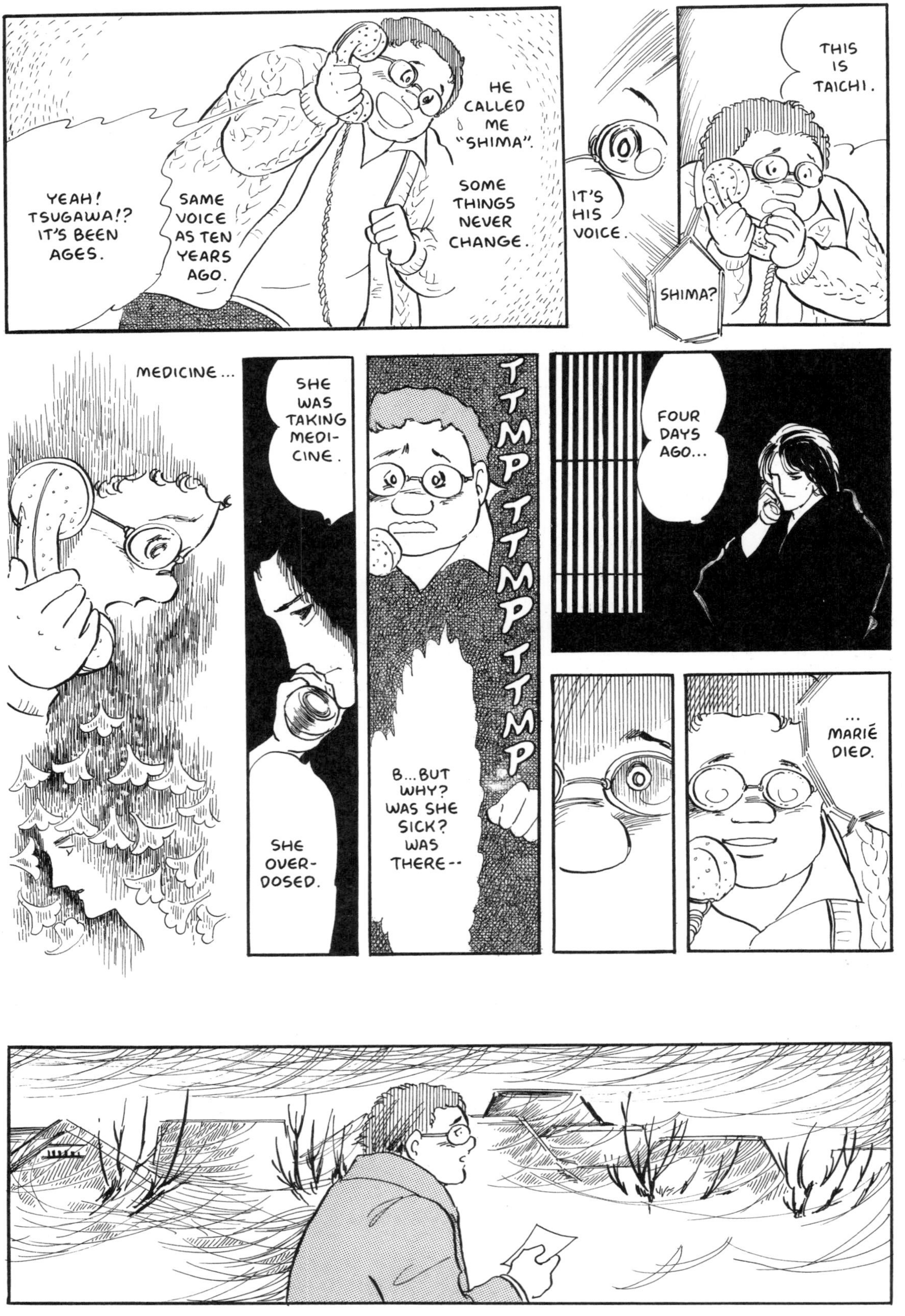
THIS IS TAICHI.
SHIMA?
IT'S HIS VOICE.
HE CALLED ME "SHIMA".
SOME THINGS NEVER CHANGE.
SAME VOICE AS TEN YEARS AGO.
YEAH! TSUGAWA!? IT'S BEEN AGES.
FOUR DAYS AGO...
... MARIÉ DIED.
TTMPTTMPTTMP
B...BUT WHY? WAS SHE SICK? WAS THERE--
SHE WAS TAKING MEDICINE.
SHE OVERDOSED.
MEDICINE...

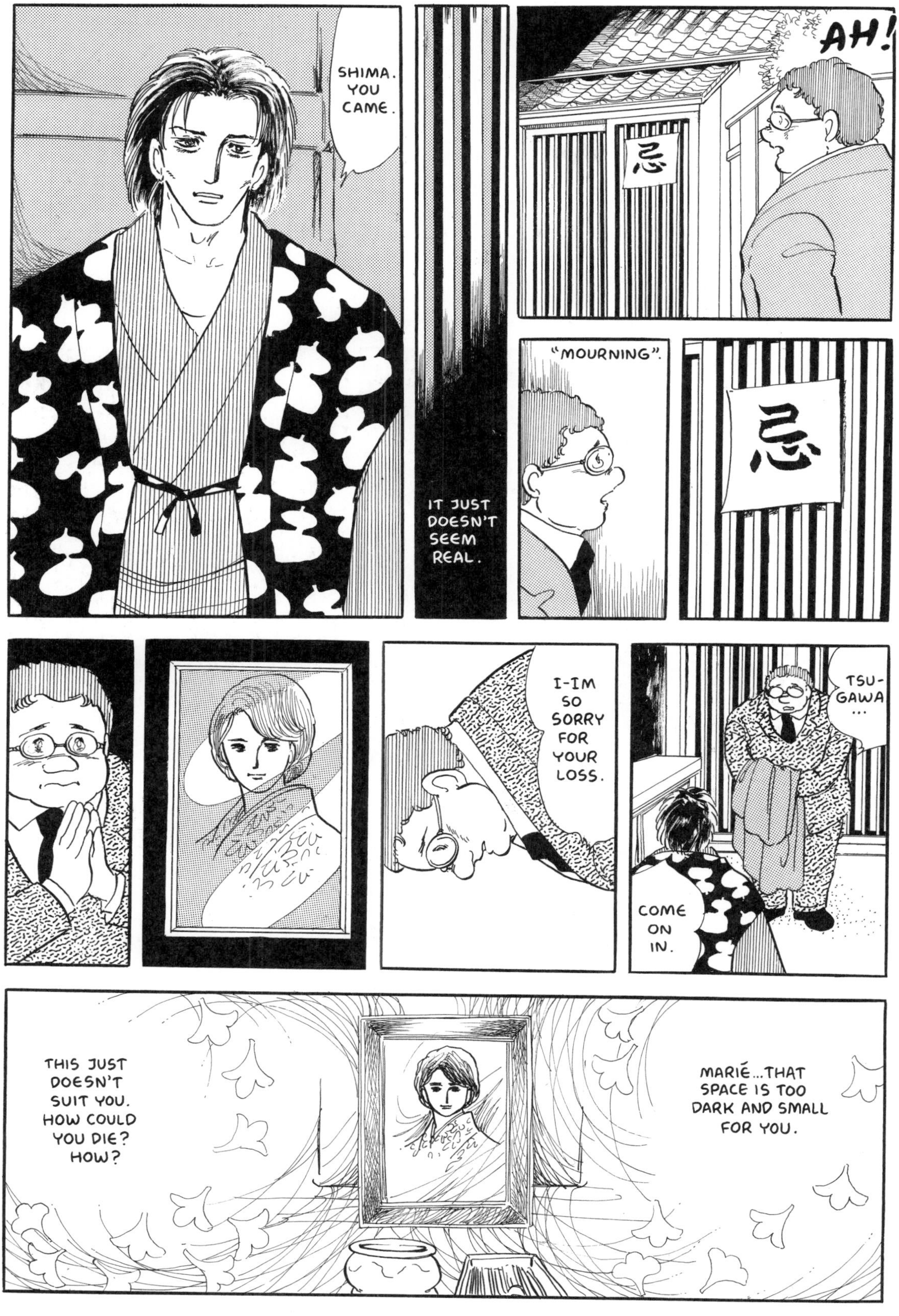
AH!
忌
忌
"MOURNING".
IT JUST DOESN'T SEEM REAL.
SHIMA. YOU CAME.
TSU-GAWA...
COME ON IN.
I-IM SO SORRY FOR YOUR LOSS.
MARIÉ...THAT SPACE IS TOO DARK AND SMALL FOR YOU.
THIS JUST DOESN'T SUIT YOU. HOW COULD YOU DIE? HOW?

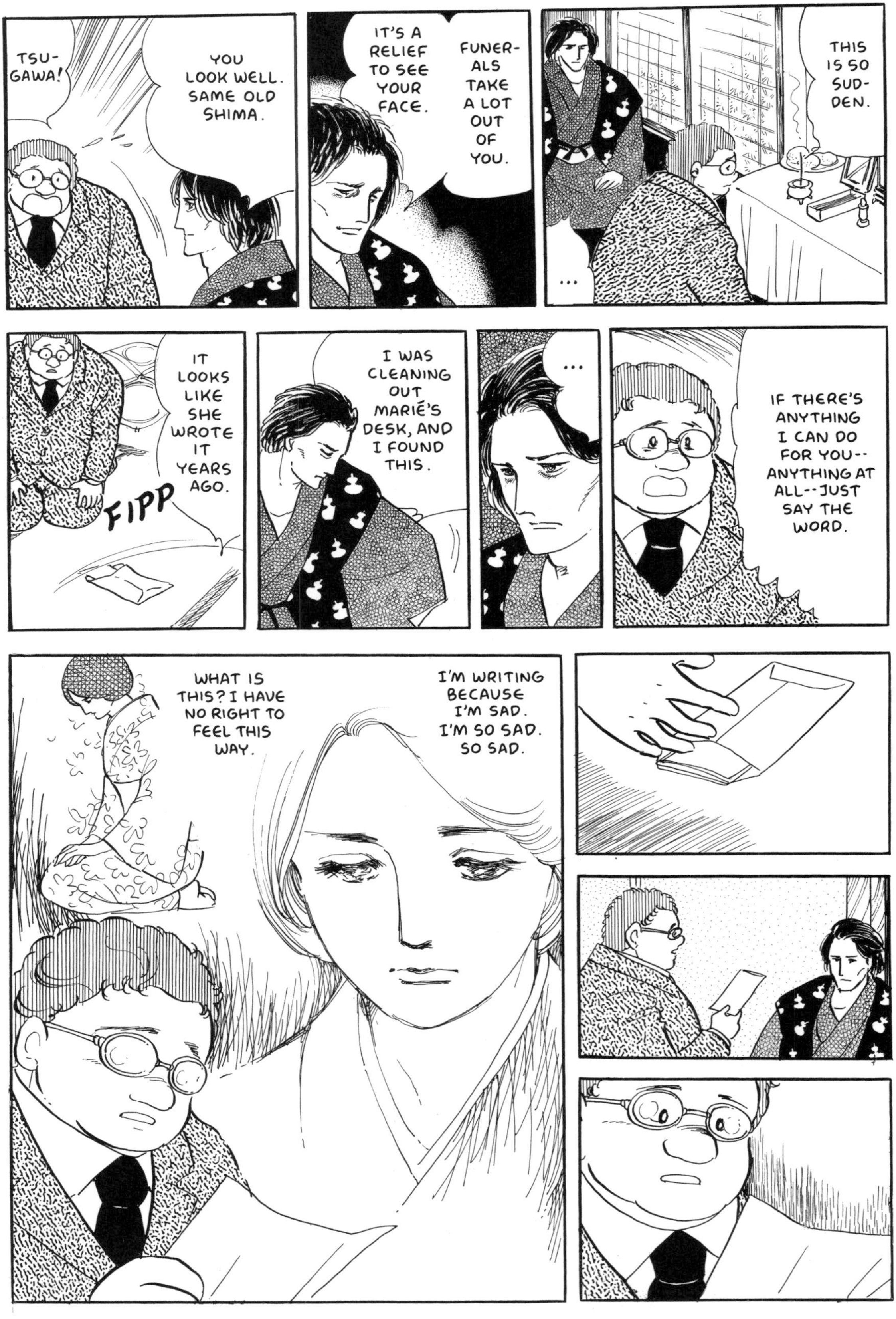
THIS IS SO SUDDEN.
...
FUNERALS TAKE A LOT OUT OF YOU.
IT'S A RELIEF TO SEE YOUR FACE.
YOU LOOK WELL. SAME OLD SHIMA.
TSUGAWA!
IF THERE'S ANYTHING I CAN DO FOR YOU--ANYTHING AT ALL--JUST SAY THE WORD.
...
I WAS CLEANING OUT MARIÉ'S DESK, AND I FOUND THIS.
IT LOOKS LIKE SHE WROTE IT YEARS AGO.
FIPP
I'M WRITING BECAUSE I'M SAD. I'M SO SAD. SO SAD.
WHAT IS THIS? I HAVE NO RIGHT TO FEEL THIS WAY.

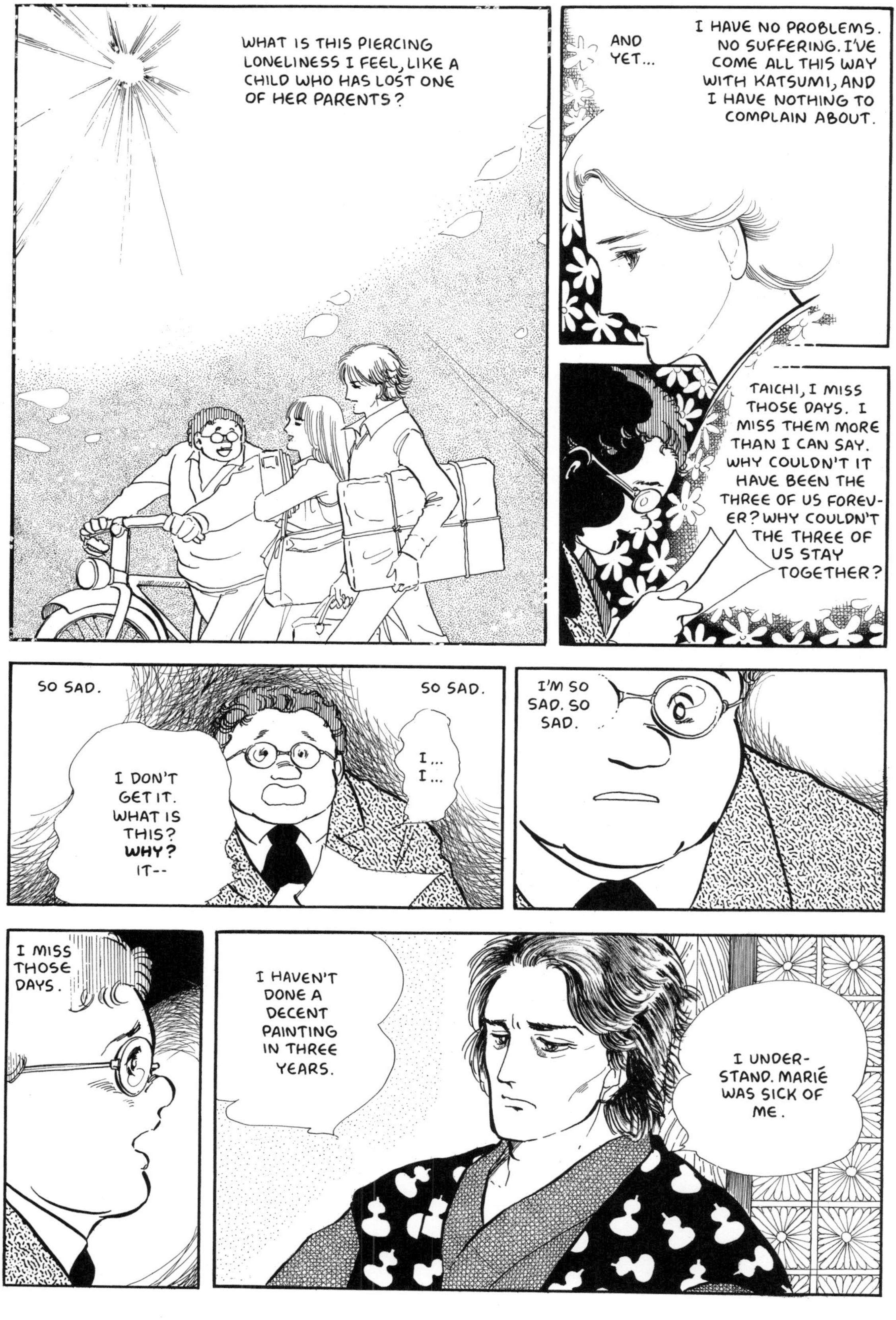
I HAVE NO PROBLEMS. NO SUFFERING. I'VE COME ALL THIS WAY WITH KATSUMI, AND I HAVE NOTHING TO COMPLAIN ABOUT.
AND YET...
TAICHI, I MISS THOSE DAYS. I MISS THEM MORE THAN I CAN SAY. WHY COULDN'T IT HAVE BEEN THE THREE OF US FOREVER? WHY COULDN'T THE THREE OF US STAY TOGETHER?
WHAT IS THIS PIERCING LONELINESS I FEEL, LIKE A CHILD WHO HAS LOST ONE OF HER PARENTS?
I'M SO SAD. SO SAD.
SO SAD.
I... I...
SO SAD.
I DON'T GET IT. WHAT IS THIS? **WHY?** IT--
I UNDER-STAND. MARIÉ WAS SICK OF ME.
I HAVEN'T DONE A DECENT PAINTING IN THREE YEARS.
I MISS THOSE DAYS.

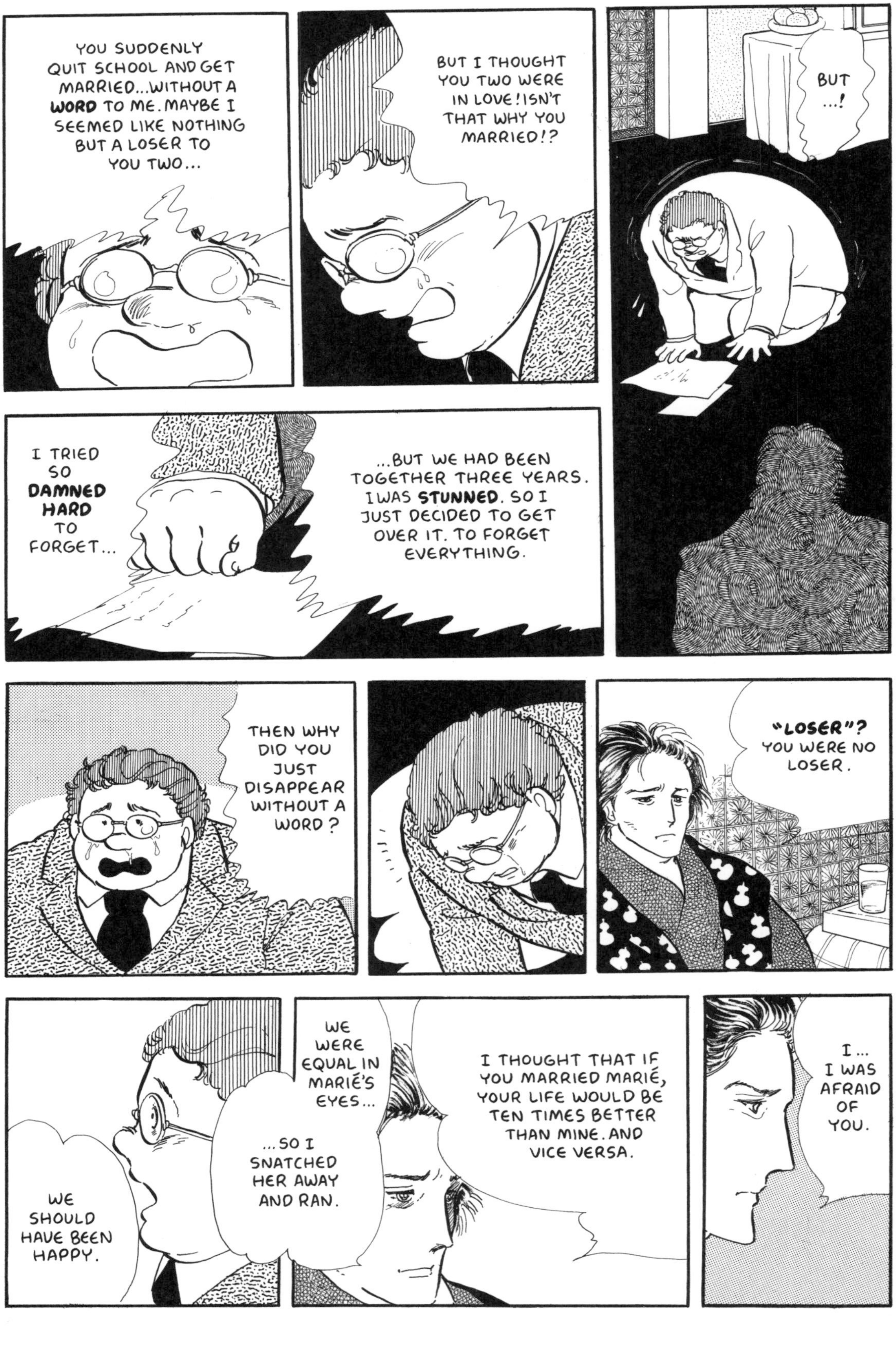
BUT ...!
BUT I THOUGHT YOU TWO WERE IN LOVE! ISN'T THAT WHY YOU MARRIED!?
YOU SUDDENLY QUIT SCHOOL AND GET MARRIED...WITHOUT A WORD TO ME. MAYBE I SEEMED LIKE NOTHING BUT A LOSER TO YOU TWO...
...BUT WE HAD BEEN TOGETHER THREE YEARS. I WAS STUNNED. SO I JUST DECIDED TO GET OVER IT. TO FORGET EVERYTHING.
I TRIED SO DAMNED HARD TO FORGET...
"LOSER"? YOU WERE NO LOSER.
THEN WHY DID YOU JUST DISAPPEAR WITHOUT A WORD?
I... I WAS AFRAID OF YOU.
I THOUGHT THAT IF YOU MARRIED MARIÉ, YOUR LIFE WOULD BE TEN TIMES BETTER THAN MINE. AND VICE VERSA.
WE WERE EQUAL IN MARIÉ'S EYES...
...SO I SNATCHED HER AWAY AND RAN.
WE SHOULD HAVE BEEN HAPPY.

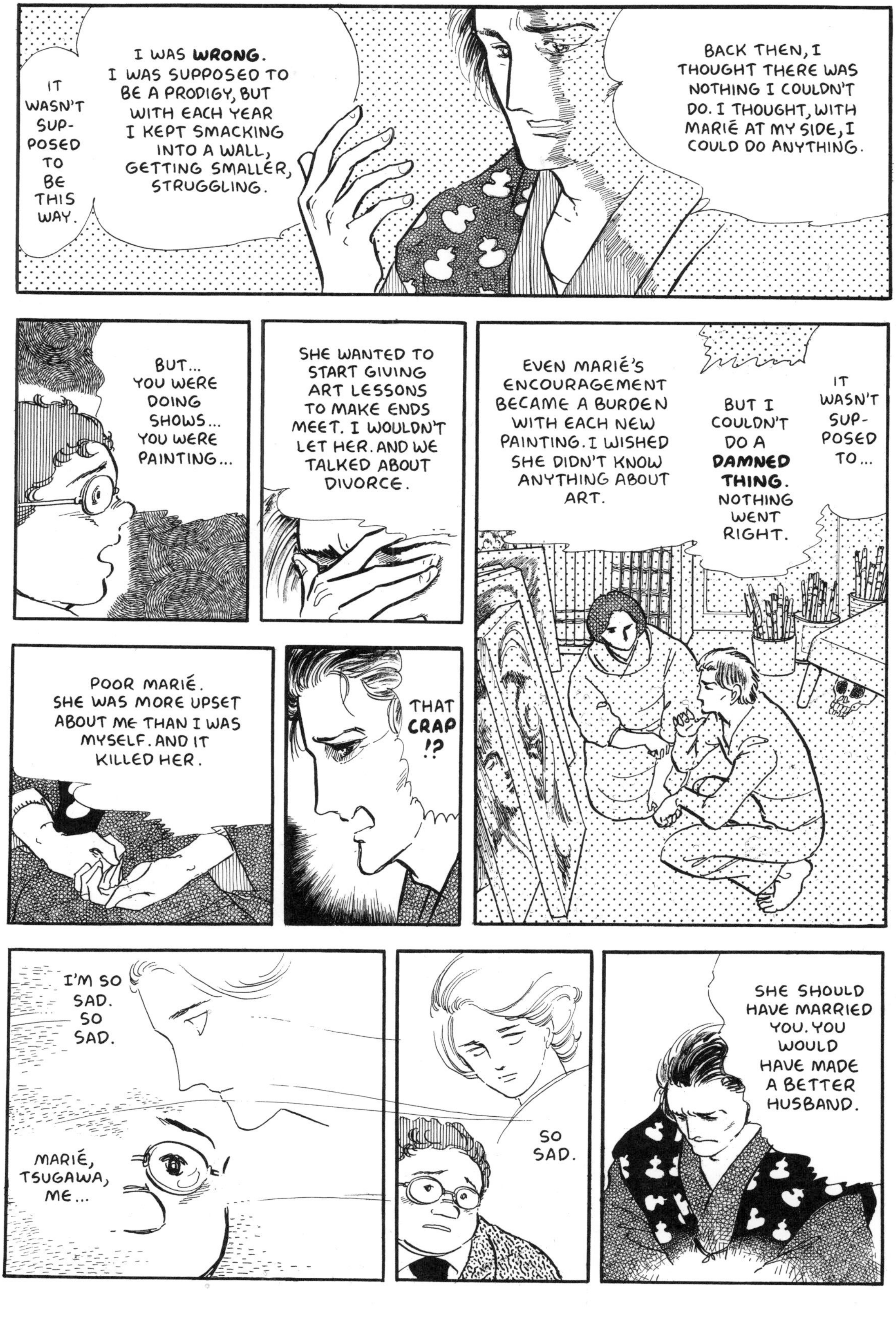
BACK THEN, I THOUGHT THERE WAS NOTHING I COULDN'T DO. I THOUGHT, WITH MARIÉ AT MY SIDE, I COULD DO ANYTHING.
I WAS **WRONG**. I WAS SUPPOSED TO BE A PRODIGY, BUT WITH EACH YEAR I KEPT SMACKING INTO A WALL, GETTING SMALLER, STRUGGLING.
IT WASN'T SUP-POSED TO BE THIS WAY.
IT WASN'T SUP-POSED TO...
BUT I COULDN'T DO A **DAMNED THING**. NOTHING WENT RIGHT.
EVEN MARIÉ'S ENCOURAGEMENT BECAME A BURDEN WITH EACH NEW PAINTING. I WISHED SHE DIDN'T KNOW ANYTHING ABOUT ART.
SHE WANTED TO START GIVING ART LESSONS TO MAKE ENDS MEET. I WOULDN'T LET HER. AND WE TALKED ABOUT DIVORCE.
BUT... YOU WERE DOING SHOWS... YOU WERE PAINTING...
THAT **CRAP** !?
POOR MARIÉ. SHE WAS MORE UPSET ABOUT ME THAN I WAS MYSELF. AND IT KILLED HER.
SHE SHOULD HAVE MARRIED YOU. YOU WOULD HAVE MADE A BETTER HUSBAND.
SO SAD.
I'M SO SAD. SO SAD.
MARIÉ, TSUGAWA, ME...

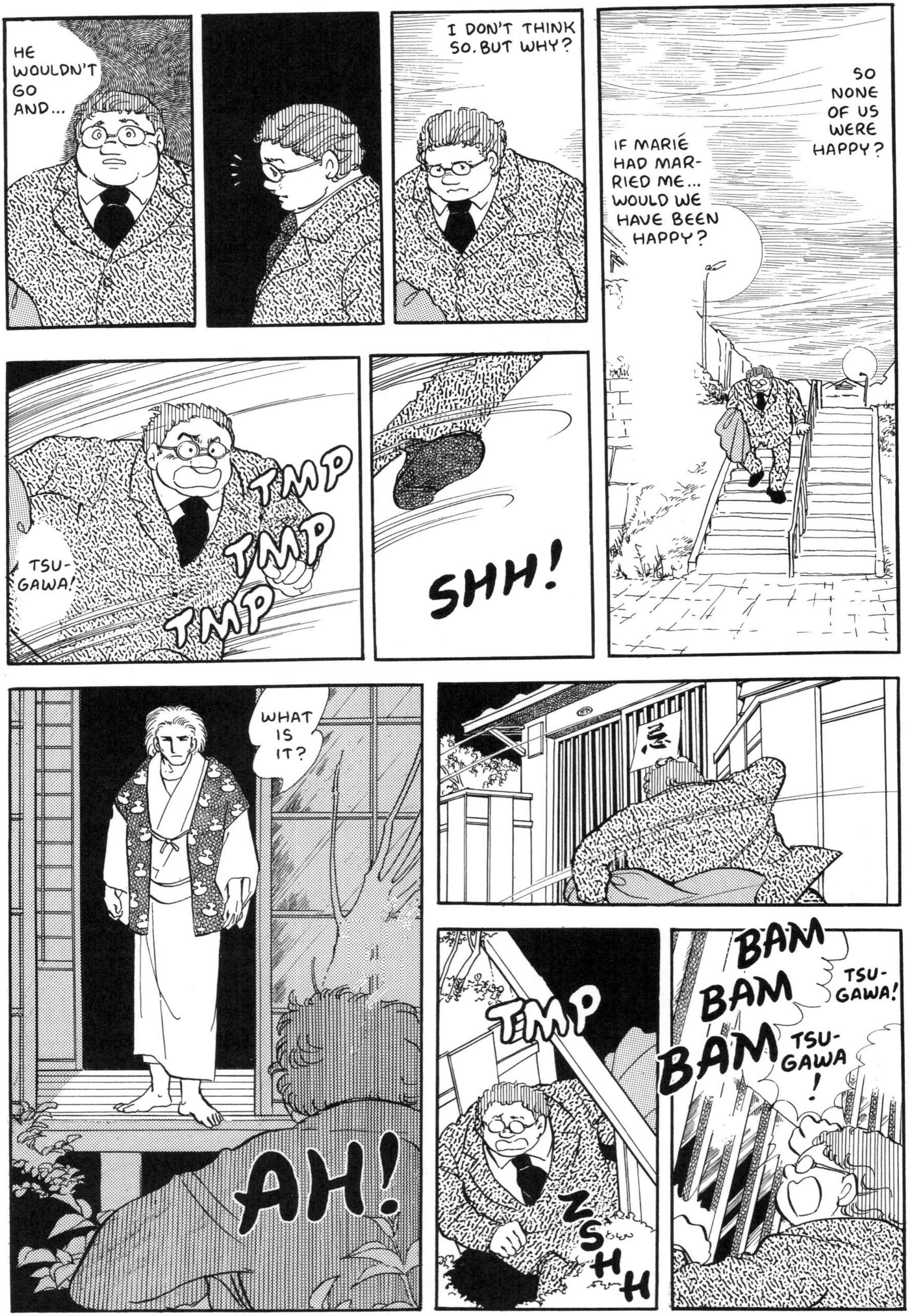
SO NONE OF US WERE HAPPY?
IF MARIÉ HAD MAR-RIED ME... WOULD WE HAVE BEEN HAPPY?
I DON'T THINK SO. BUT WHY?
HE WOULDN'T GO AND...
SHH!
TMP TMP TMP
TSU-GAWA!
BAM BAM BAM
TSU-GAWA!
TSU-GAWA!
TMP
ZSHH
WHAT IS IT?
AH!

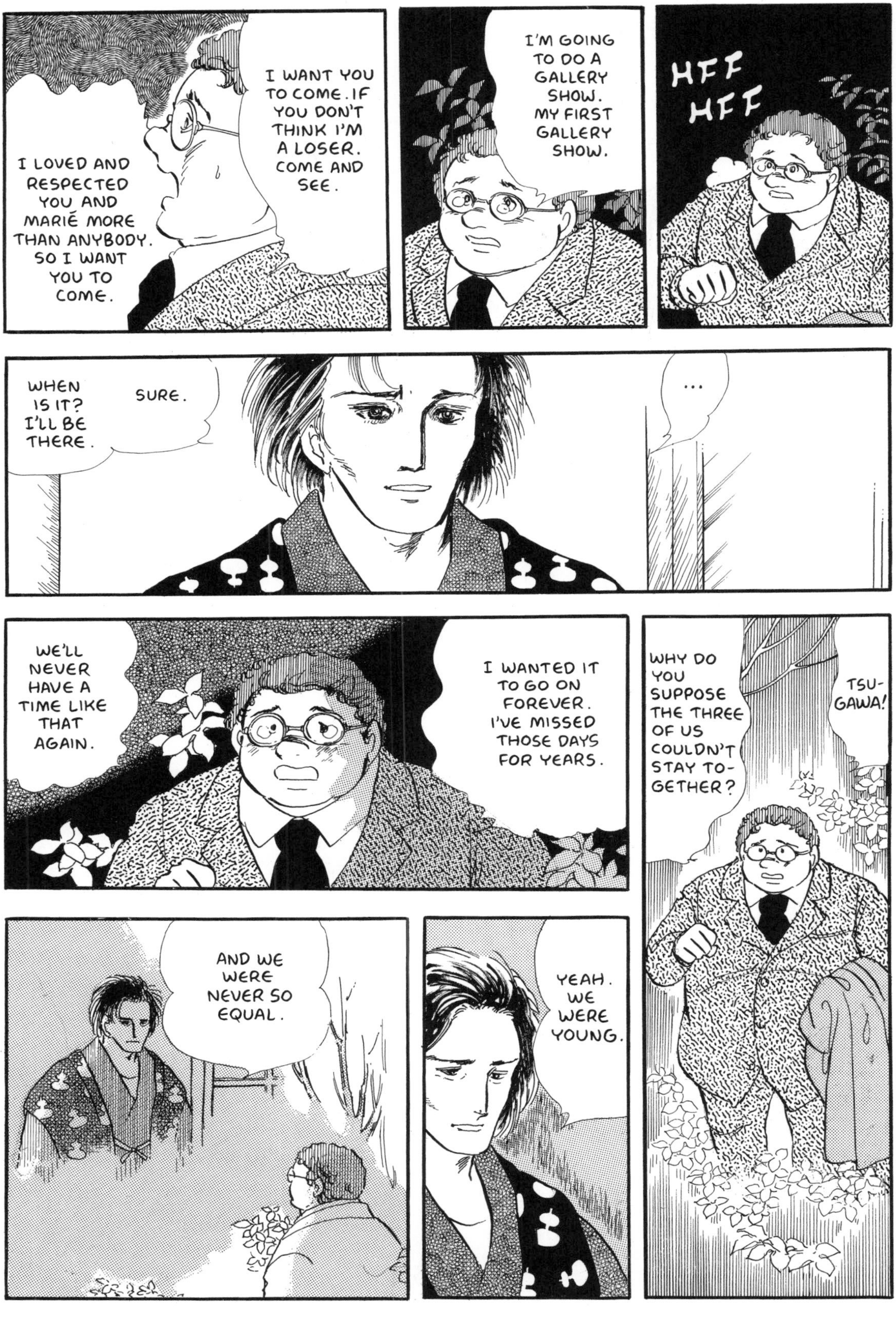
HFF HFF
I'M GOING TO DO A GALLERY SHOW. MY FIRST GALLERY SHOW.
I WANT YOU TO COME. IF YOU DON'T THINK I'M A LOSER. COME AND SEE.
I LOVED AND RESPECTED YOU AND MARIÉ MORE THAN ANYBODY. SO I WANT YOU TO COME.
...
SURE.
WHEN IS IT? I'LL BE THERE.
TSU-GAWA!
WHY DO YOU SUPPOSE THE THREE OF US COULDN'T STAY TO-GETHER?
I WANTED IT TO GO ON FOREVER. I'VE MISSED THOSE DAYS FOR YEARS.
WE'LL NEVER HAVE A TIME LIKE THAT AGAIN.
YEAH. WE WERE YOUNG.
AND WE WERE NEVER SO EQUAL.

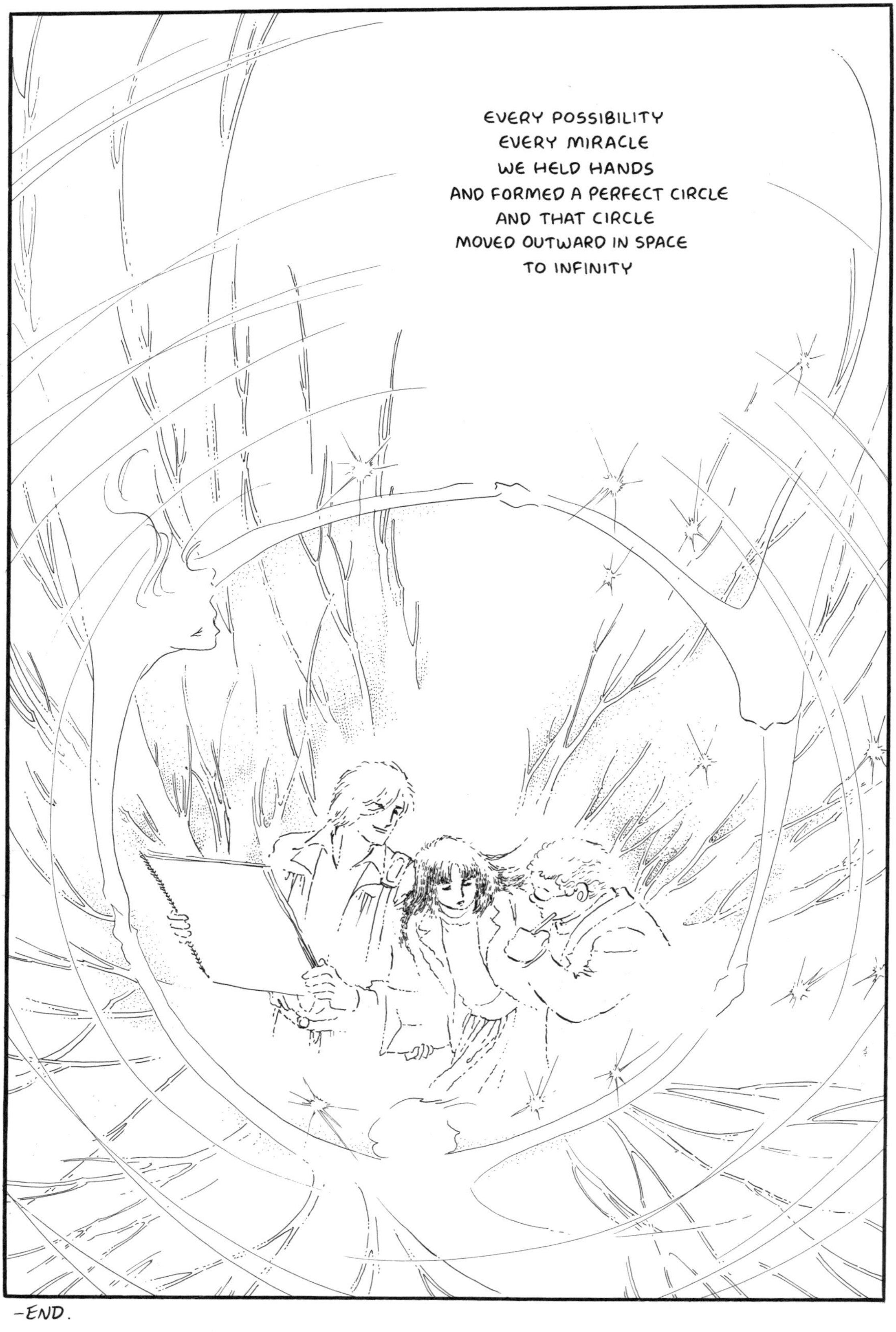
EVERY POSSIBILITY
EVERY MIRACLE
WE HELD HANDS
AND FORMED A PERFECT CIRCLE
AND THAT CIRCLE
MOVED OUTWARD IN SPACE
TO INFINITY

-END.

A DRUNKEN DREAM

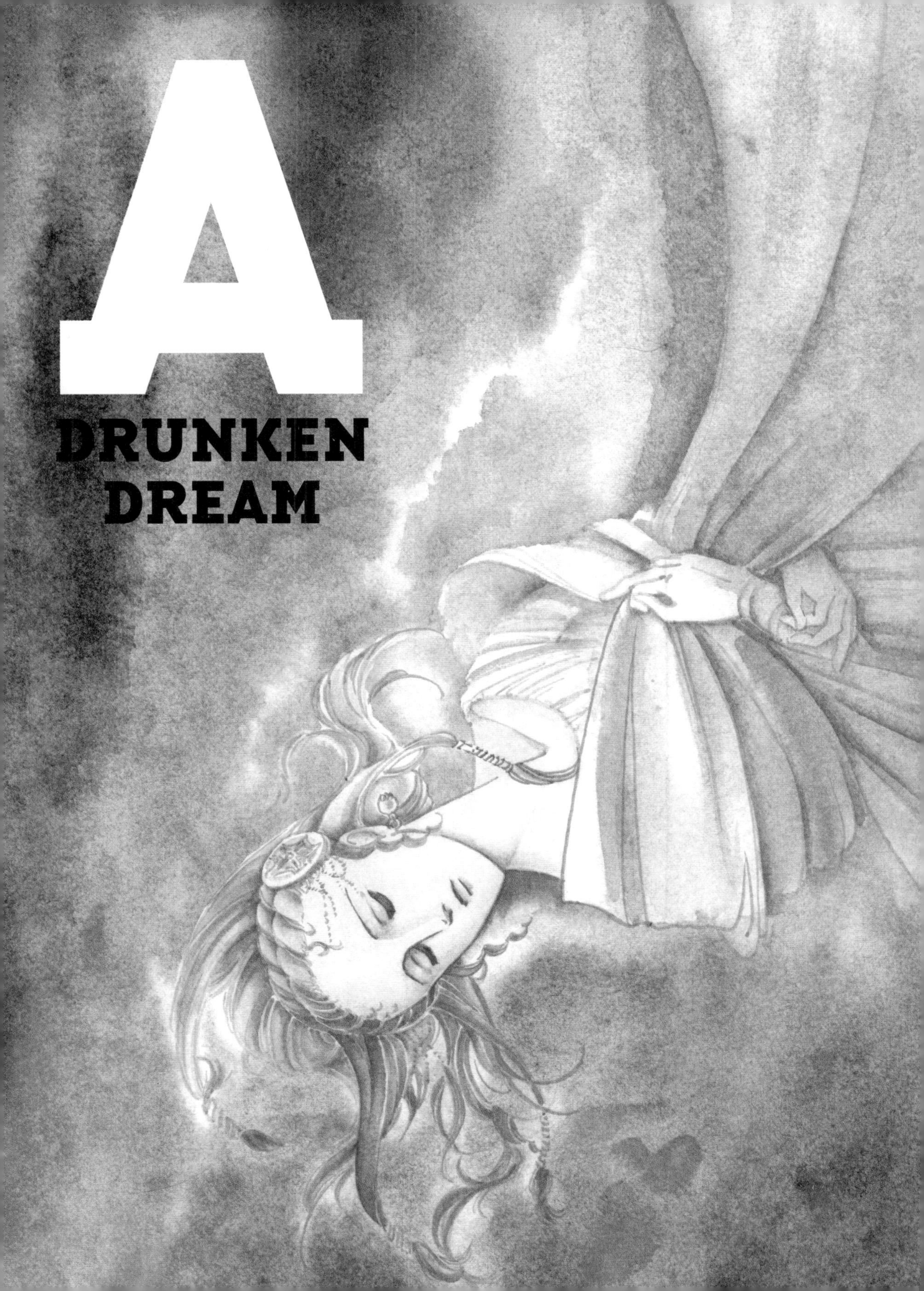

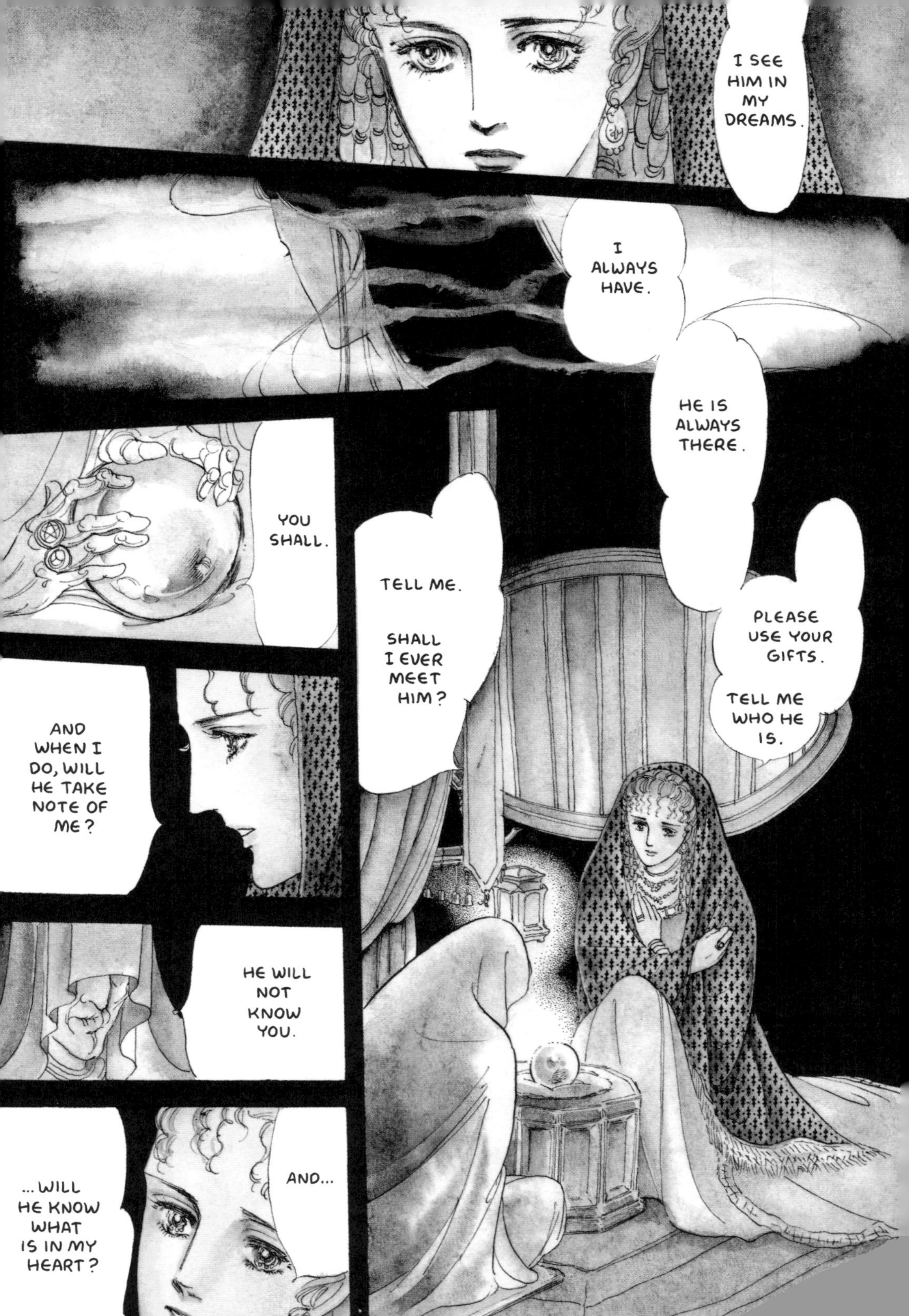
I SEE HIM IN MY DREAMS.
I ALWAYS HAVE.
HE IS ALWAYS THERE.
PLEASE USE YOUR GIFTS.
TELL ME WHO HE IS.
TELL ME.
SHALL I EVER MEET HIM?
YOU SHALL.
AND WHEN I DO, WILL HE TAKE NOTE OF ME?
HE WILL NOT KNOW YOU.
AND...
...WILL HE KNOW WHAT IS IN MY HEART?

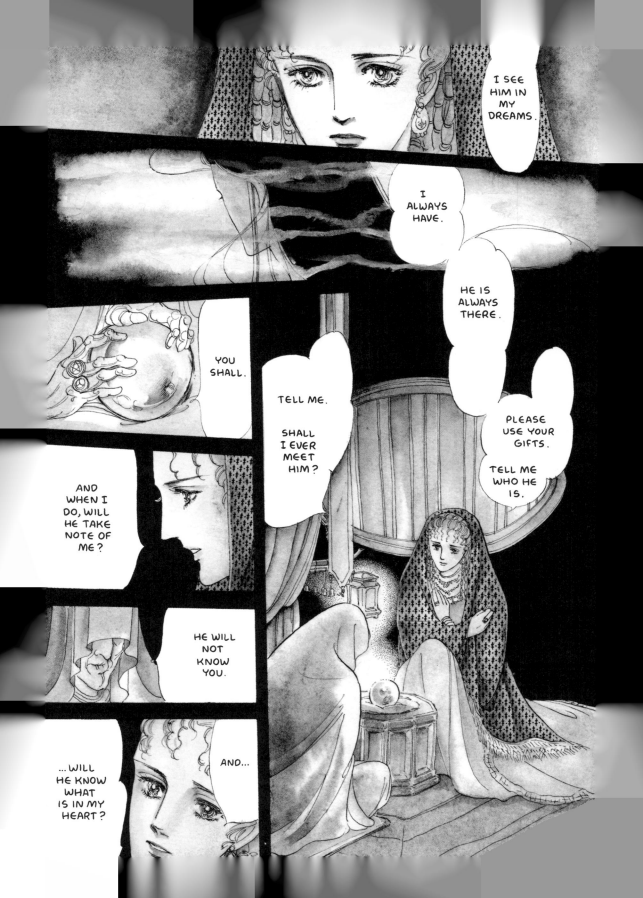

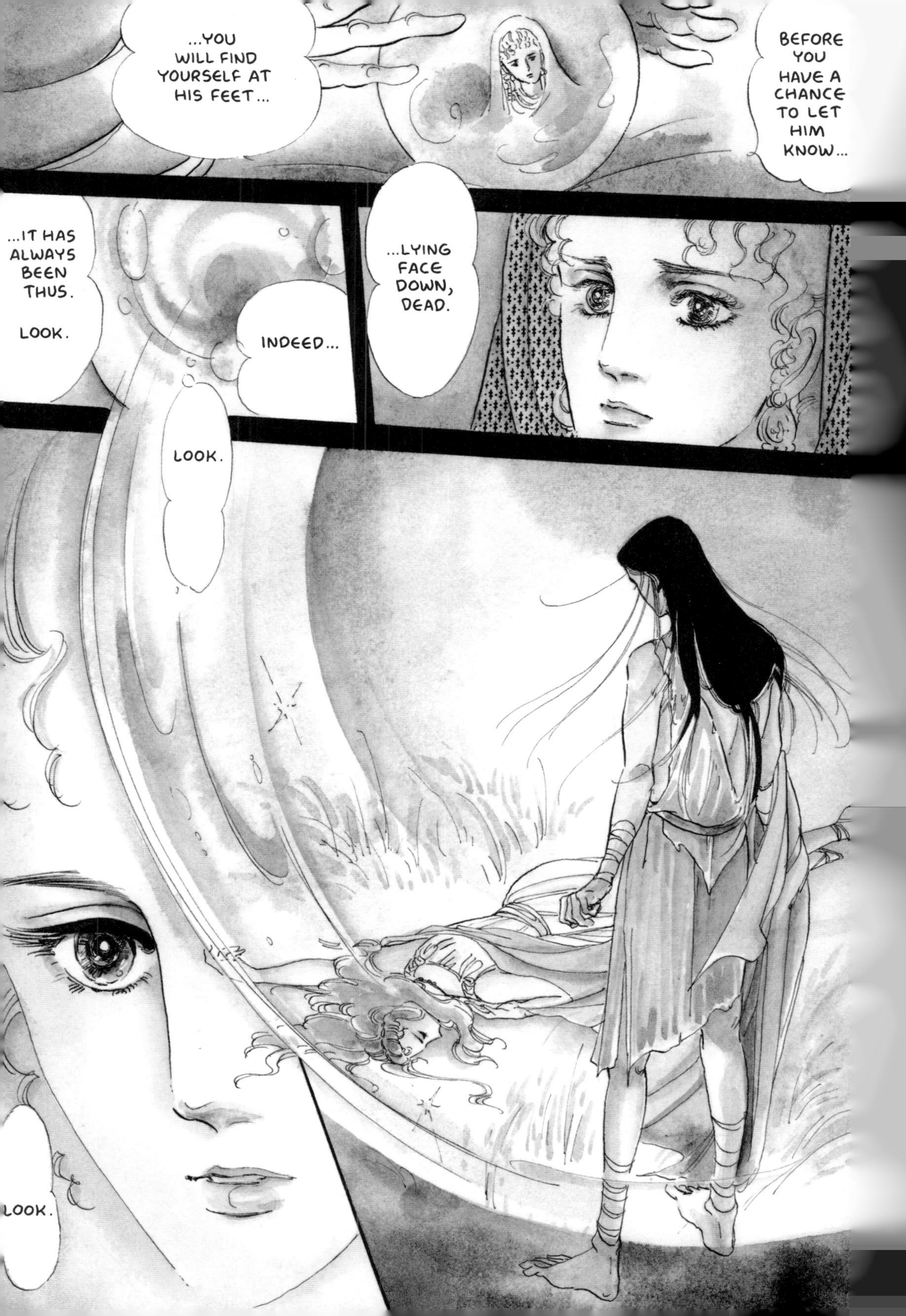
BEFORE YOU HAVE A CHANCE TO LET HIM KNOW...
...YOU WILL FIND YOURSELF AT HIS FEET...
...LYING FACE DOWN, DEAD.
INDEED...
...IT HAS ALWAYS BEEN THUS.
LOOK.
LOOK.
LOOK.

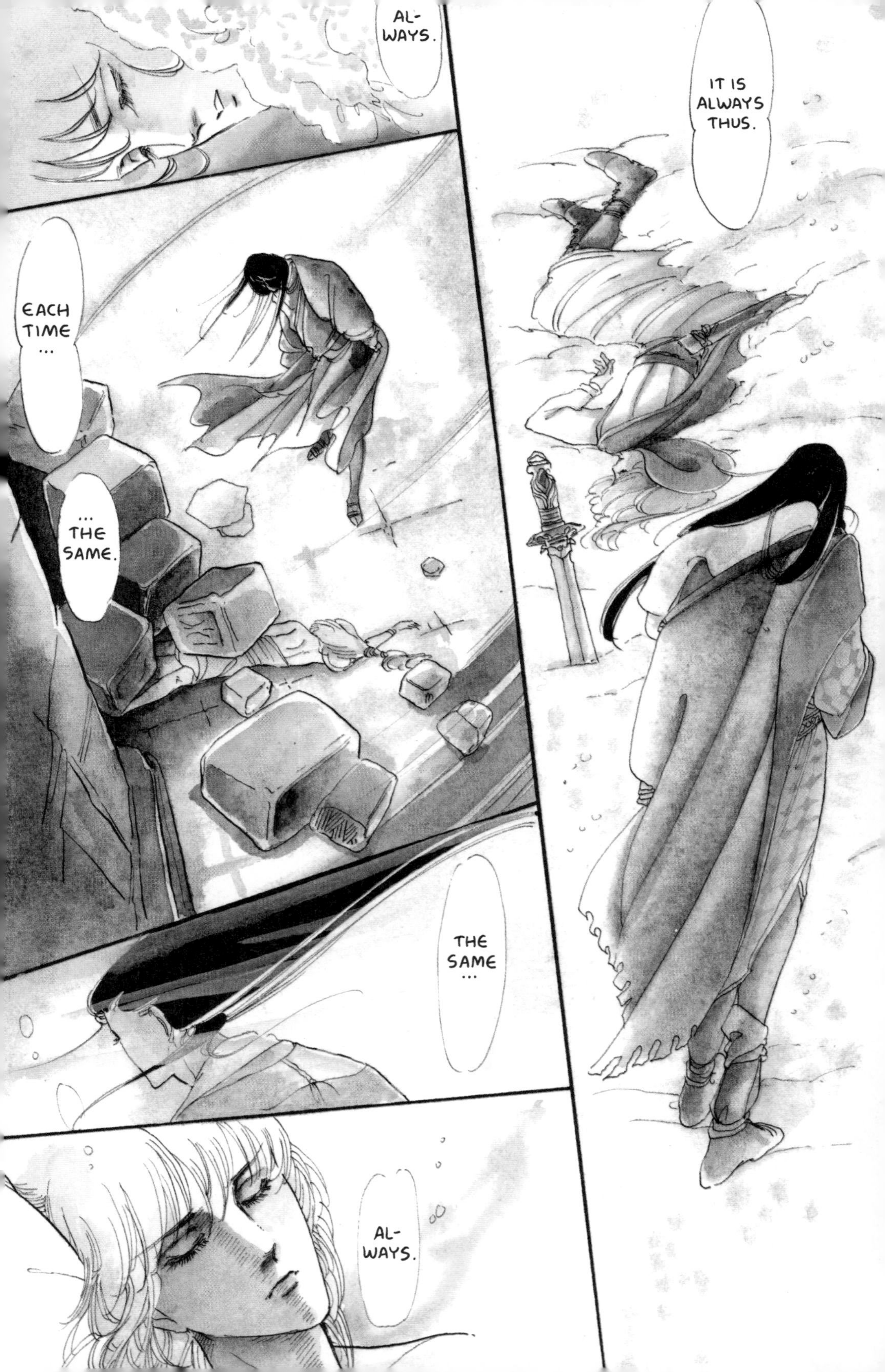
IT IS ALWAYS THUS.
AL-WAYS.
EACH TIME ...
... THE SAME.
THE SAME ...
AL-WAYS.

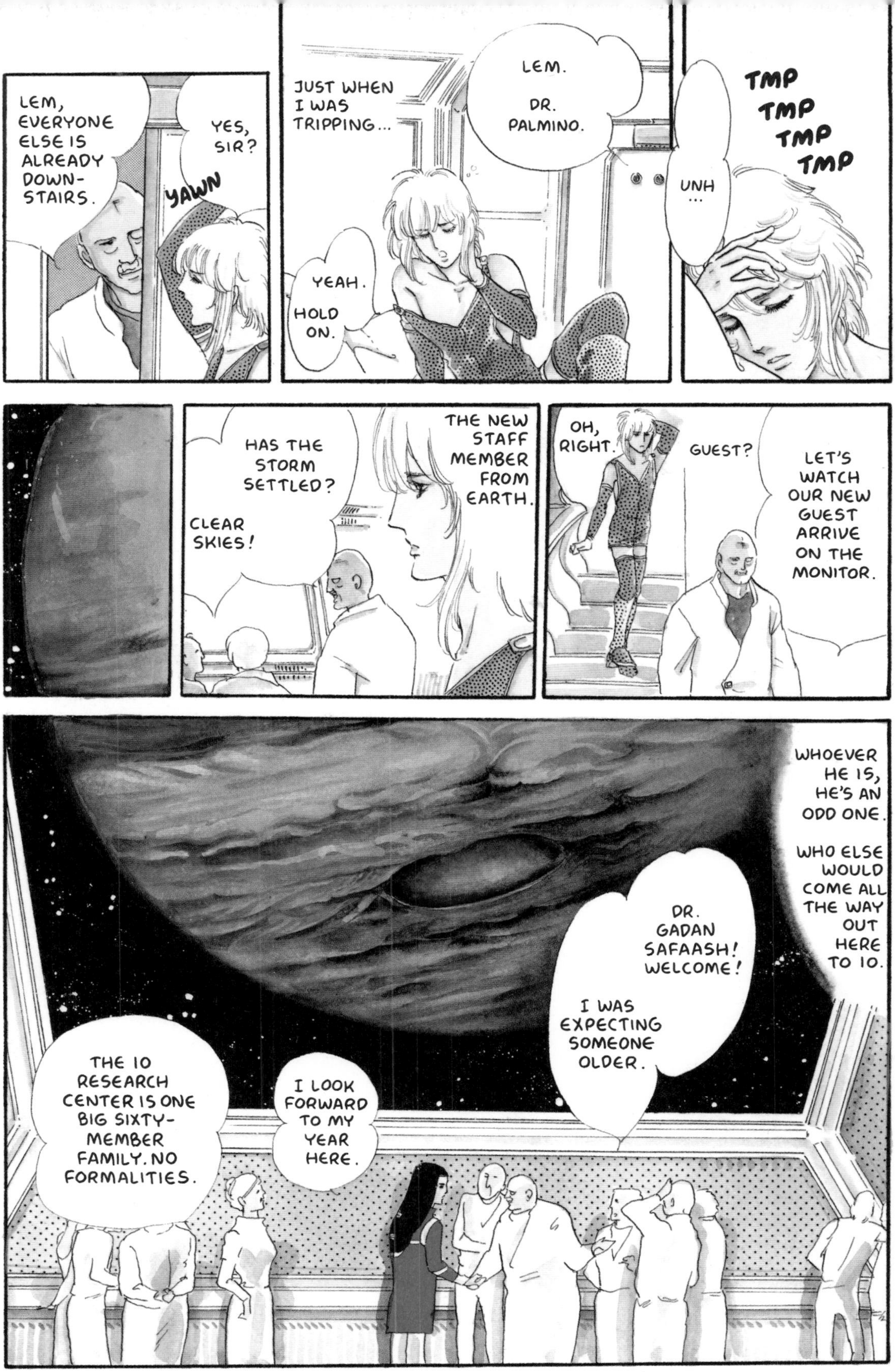
TMP TMP TMP TMP
UNH...
LEM.
DR. PALMINO.
JUST WHEN I WAS TRIPPING...
YEAH.
HOLD ON.
LEM, EVERYONE ELSE IS ALREADY DOWN-STAIRS.
YES, SIR?
YAWN
LET'S WATCH OUR NEW GUEST ARRIVE ON THE MONITOR.
GUEST?
OH, RIGHT.
THE NEW STAFF MEMBER FROM EARTH.
HAS THE STORM SETTLED?
CLEAR SKIES!
WHOEVER HE IS, HE'S AN ODD ONE.
WHO ELSE WOULD COME ALL THE WAY OUT HERE TO IO.
DR. GADAN SAFAASH! WELCOME!
I WAS EXPECTING SOMEONE OLDER.
I LOOK FORWARD TO MY YEAR HERE.
THE IO RESEARCH CENTER IS ONE BIG SIXTY-MEMBER FAMILY. NO FORMALITIES.

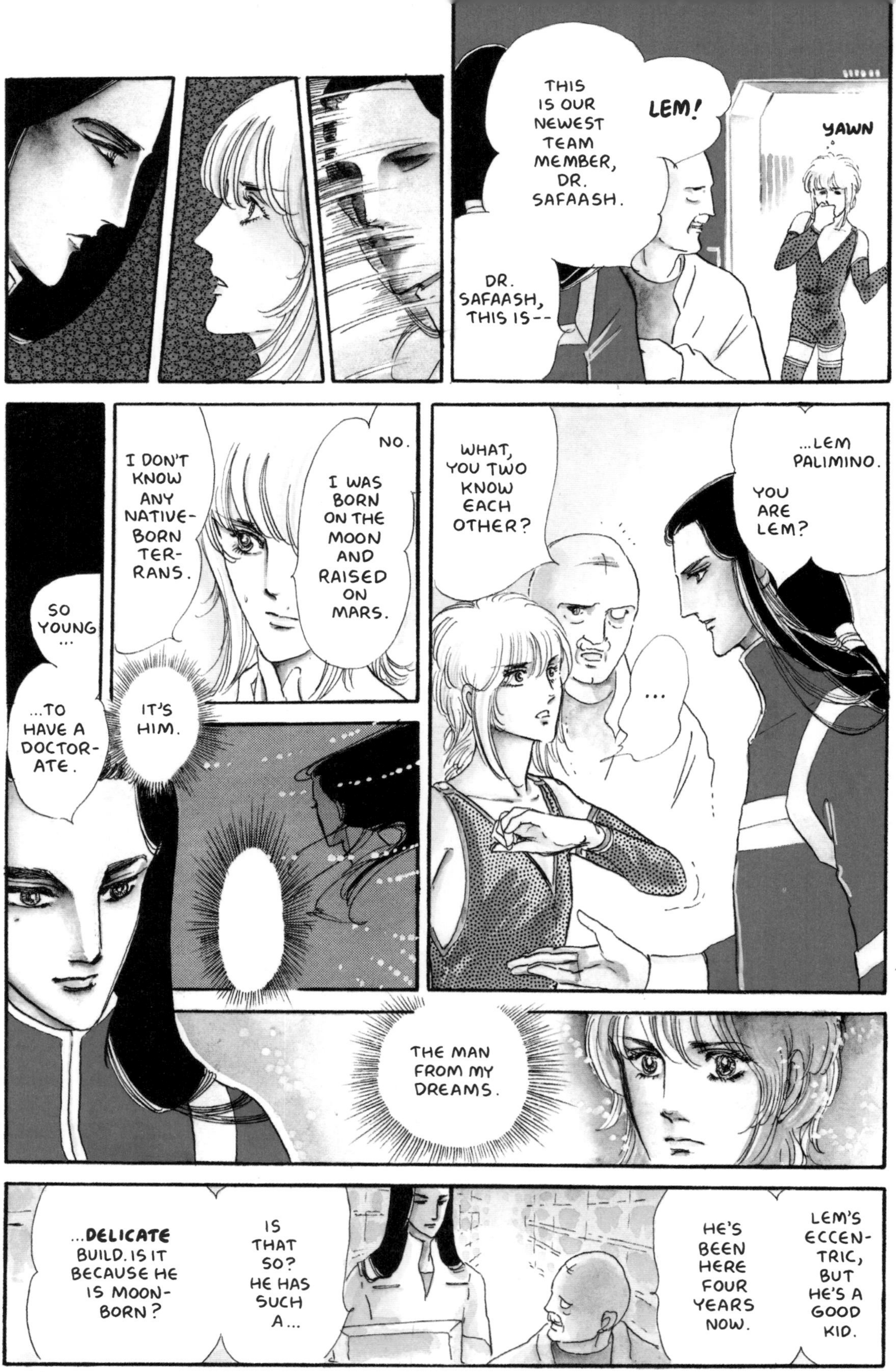
YAWN
LEM!
THIS IS OUR NEWEST TEAM MEMBER, DR. SAFAASH.
DR. SAFAASH, THIS IS--
...LEM PALIMINO.
YOU ARE LEM?
WHAT, YOU TWO KNOW EACH OTHER?
...
NO.
I WAS BORN ON THE MOON AND RAISED ON MARS.
I DON'T KNOW ANY NATIVE-BORN TER-RANS.
IT'S HIM.
SO YOUNG...
...TO HAVE A DOCTOR-ATE.
THE MAN FROM MY DREAMS.
LEM'S ECCEN-TRIC, BUT HE'S A GOOD KID.
HE'S BEEN HERE FOUR YEARS NOW.
IS THAT SO? HE HAS SUCH A...
...**DELICATE** BUILD. IS IT BECAUSE HE IS MOON-BORN?

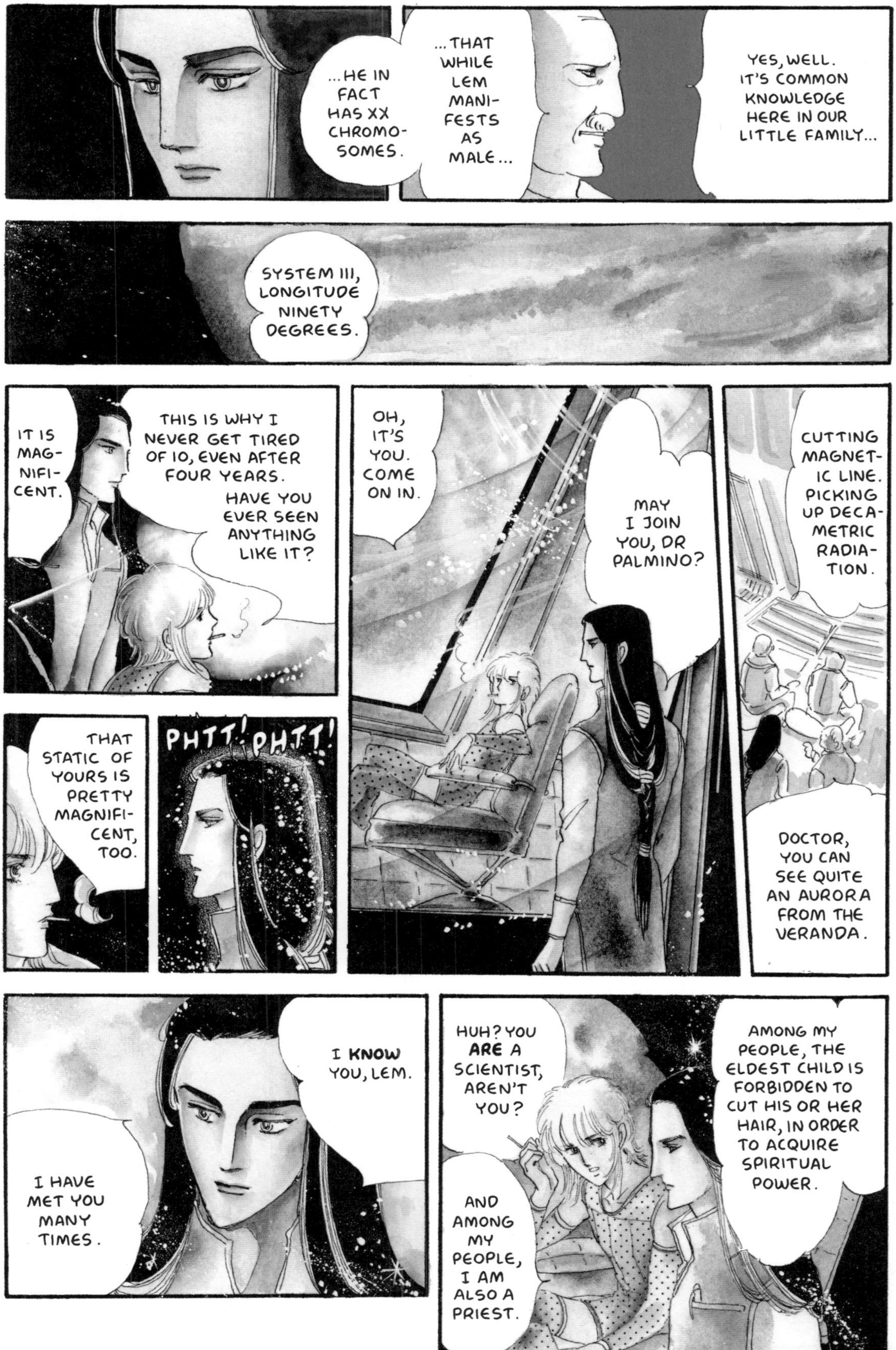
YES, WELL. IT'S COMMON KNOWLEDGE HERE IN OUR LITTLE FAMILY...
...THAT WHILE LEM MANIFESTS AS MALE...
...HE IN FACT HAS XX CHROMOSOMES.
SYSTEM III, LONGITUDE NINETY DEGREES.
CUTTING MAGNETIC LINE. PICKING UP DECAMETRIC RADIATION.
DOCTOR, YOU CAN SEE QUITE AN AURORA FROM THE VERANDA.
MAY I JOIN YOU, DR PALMINO?
OH, IT'S YOU. COME ON IN.
THIS IS WHY I NEVER GET TIRED OF IO, EVEN AFTER FOUR YEARS.
HAVE YOU EVER SEEN ANYTHING LIKE IT?
IT IS MAGNIFICENT.
PHTT! PHTT!
THAT STATIC OF YOURS IS PRETTY MAGNIFICENT, TOO.
AMONG MY PEOPLE, THE ELDEST CHILD IS FORBIDDEN TO CUT HIS OR HER HAIR, IN ORDER TO ACQUIRE SPIRITUAL POWER.
HUH? YOU **ARE** A SCIENTIST, AREN'T YOU?
AND AMONG MY PEOPLE, I AM ALSO A PRIEST.
I **KNOW** YOU, LEM.
I HAVE MET YOU MANY TIMES.

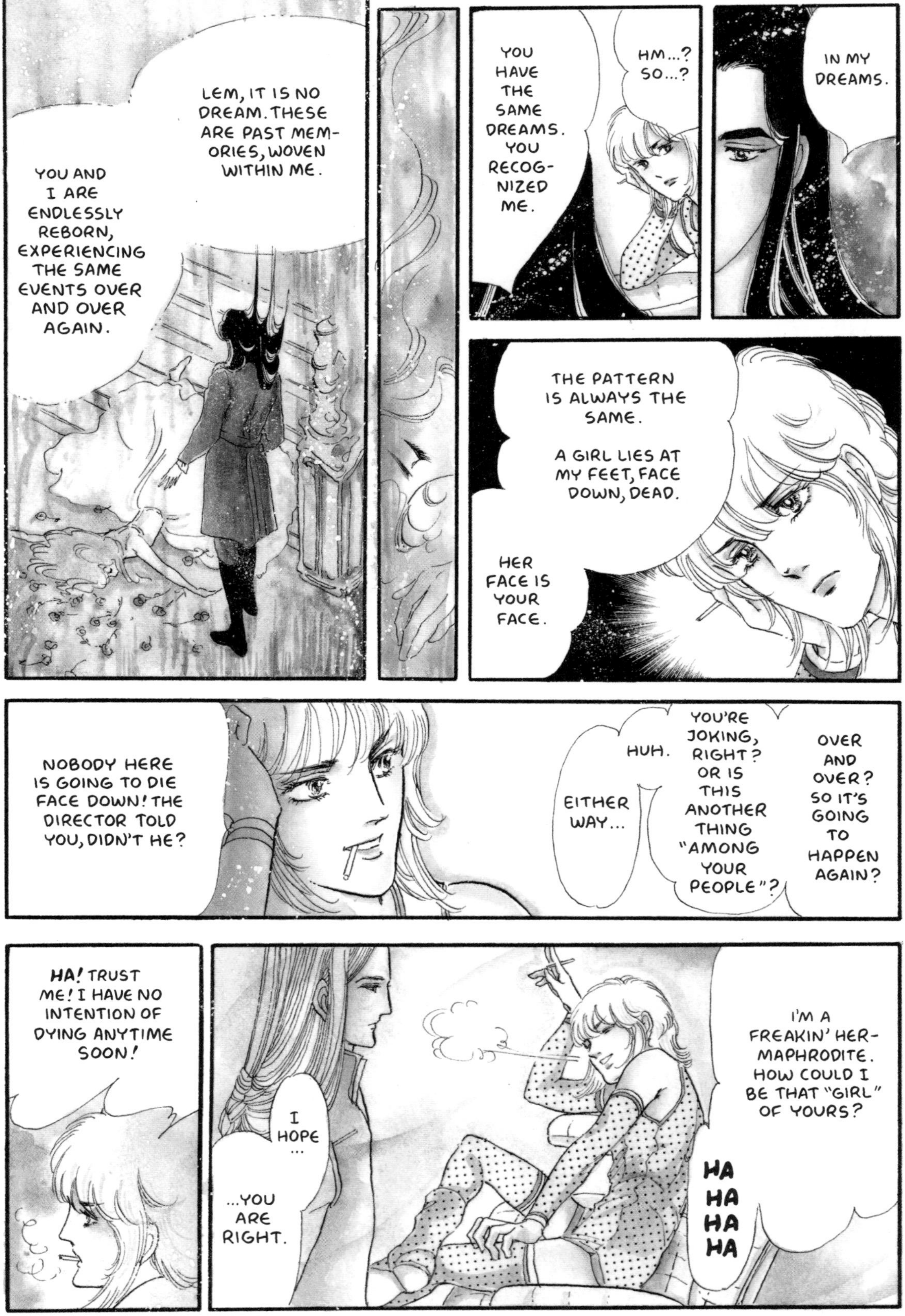
IN MY DREAMS.
HM...? SO...?
YOU HAVE THE SAME DREAMS. YOU RECOGNIZED ME.
THE PATTERN IS ALWAYS THE SAME.
A GIRL LIES AT MY FEET, FACE DOWN, DEAD.
HER FACE IS YOUR FACE.
LEM, IT IS NO DREAM. THESE ARE PAST MEMORIES, WOVEN WITHIN ME.
YOU AND I ARE ENDLESSLY REBORN, EXPERIENCING THE SAME EVENTS OVER AND OVER AGAIN.
OVER AND OVER? SO IT'S GOING TO HAPPEN AGAIN?
YOU'RE JOKING, RIGHT? OR IS THIS ANOTHER THING "AMONG YOUR PEOPLE"?
HUH.
EITHER WAY...
NOBODY HERE IS GOING TO DIE FACE DOWN! THE DIRECTOR TOLD YOU, DIDN'T HE?
I'M A FREAKIN' HERMAPHRODITE. HOW COULD I BE THAT "GIRL" OF YOURS?
HA HA HA HA
I HOPE...
...YOU ARE RIGHT.
HA! TRUST ME! I HAVE NO INTENTION OF DYING ANYTIME SOON!

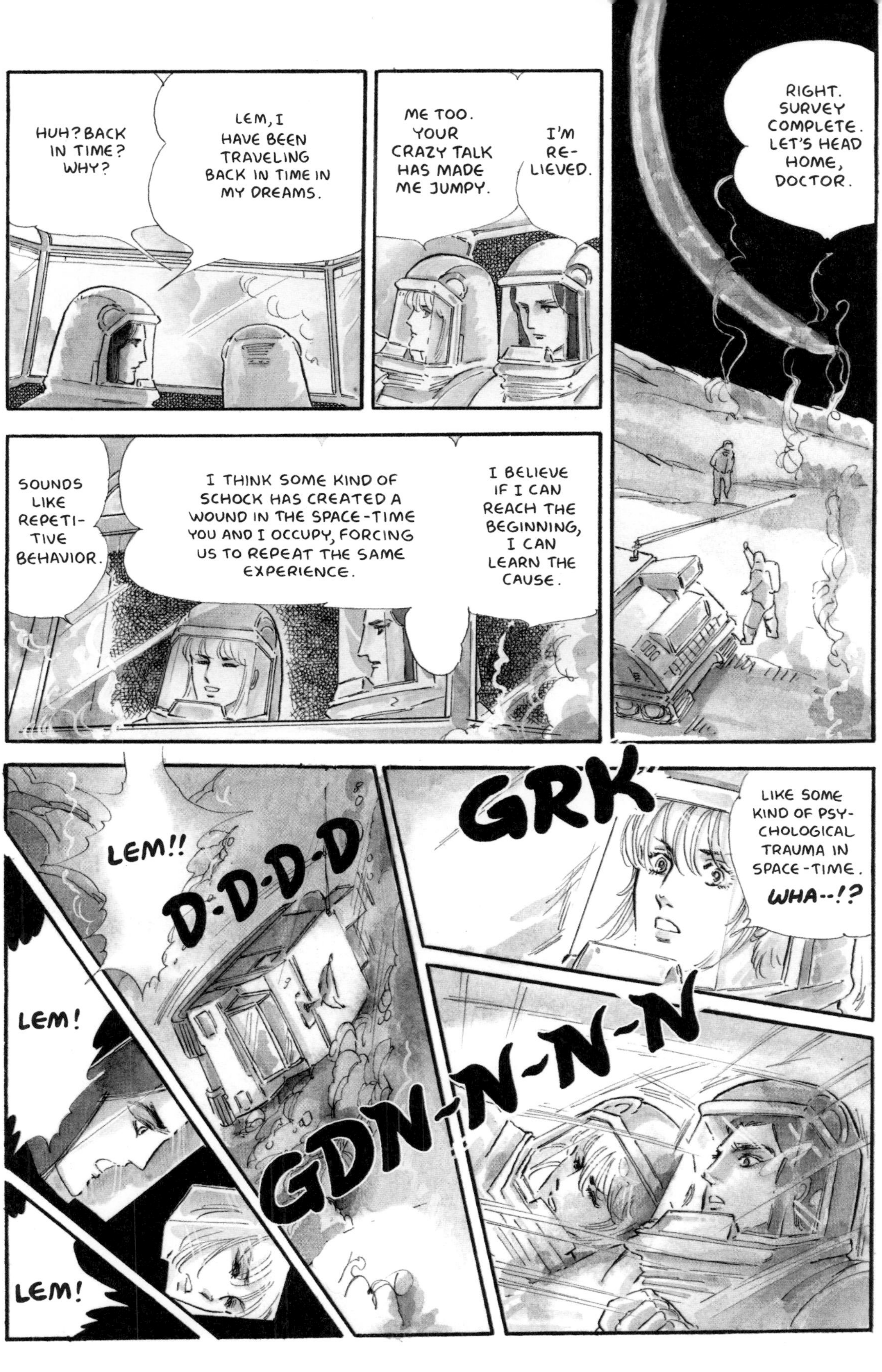
RIGHT. SURVEY COMPLETE. LET'S HEAD HOME, DOCTOR.
I'M RE-LIEVED.
ME TOO. YOUR CRAZY TALK HAS MADE ME JUMPY.
LEM, I HAVE BEEN TRAVELING BACK IN TIME IN MY DREAMS.
HUH? BACK IN TIME? WHY?
I BELIEVE IF I CAN REACH THE BEGINNING, I CAN LEARN THE CAUSE.
I THINK SOME KIND OF SCHOCK HAS CREATED A WOUND IN THE SPACE-TIME YOU AND I OCCUPY, FORCING US TO REPEAT THE SAME EXPERIENCE.
SOUNDS LIKE REPETI-TIVE BEHAVIOR.
LIKE SOME KIND OF PSY-CHOLOGICAL TRAUMA IN SPACE-TIME.
GRK
WHA--!?
GDN-N-N-N
LEM!!
D-D-D-D
LEM!
LEM!

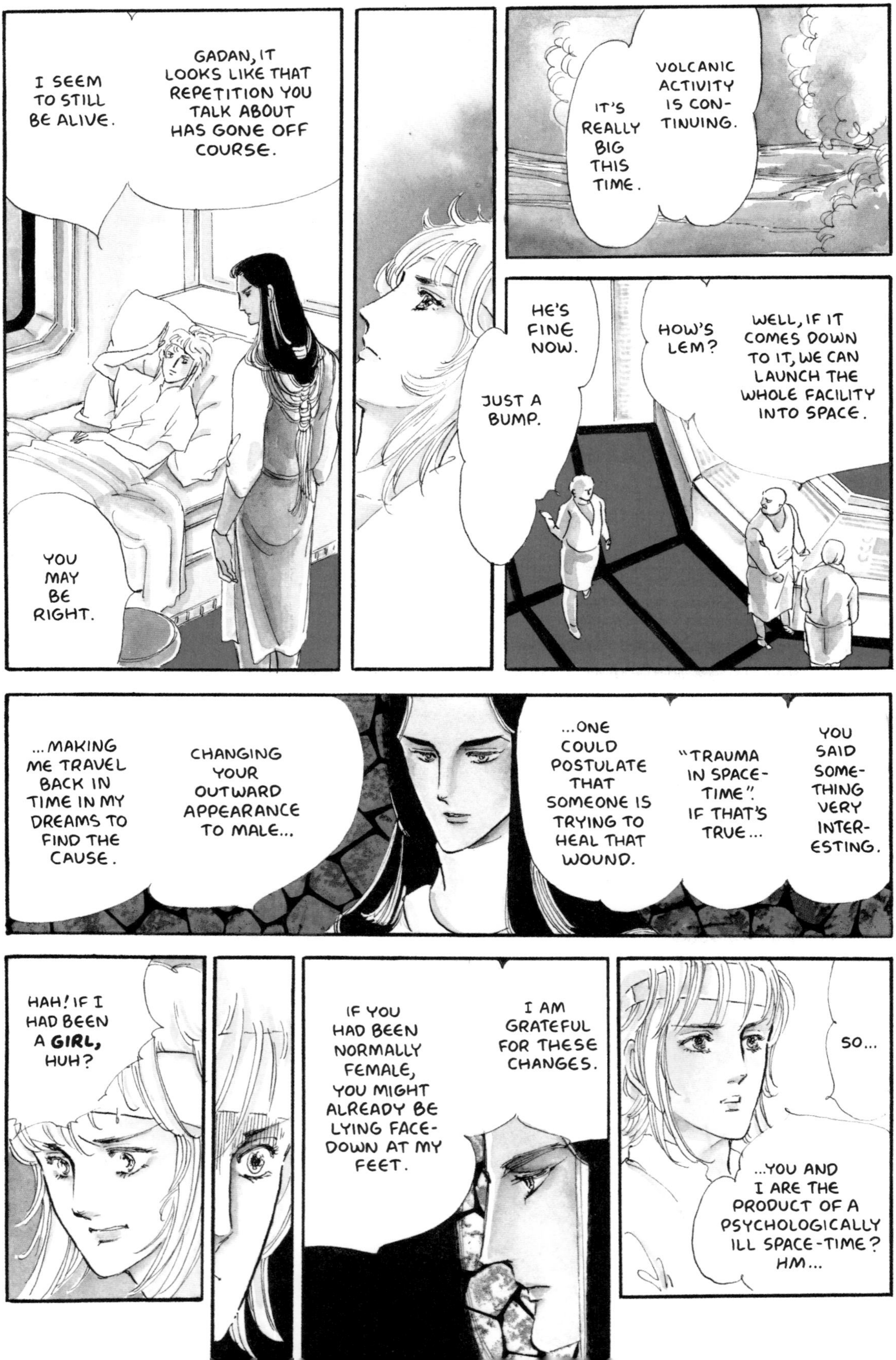
VOLCANIC ACTIVITY IS CONTINUING.
IT'S REALLY BIG THIS TIME.
WELL, IF IT COMES DOWN TO IT, WE CAN LAUNCH THE WHOLE FACILITY INTO SPACE.
HOW'S LEM?
HE'S FINE NOW.
JUST A BUMP.
GADAN, IT LOOKS LIKE THAT REPETITION YOU TALK ABOUT HAS GONE OFF COURSE.
I SEEM TO STILL BE ALIVE.
YOU MAY BE RIGHT.
YOU SAID SOMETHING VERY INTERESTING.
"TRAUMA IN SPACE-TIME." IF THAT'S TRUE...
...ONE COULD POSTULATE THAT SOMEONE IS TRYING TO HEAL THAT WOUND.
CHANGING YOUR OUTWARD APPEARANCE TO MALE...
...MAKING ME TRAVEL BACK IN TIME IN MY DREAMS TO FIND THE CAUSE.
SO...
...YOU AND I ARE THE PRODUCT OF A PSYCHOLOGICALLY ILL SPACE-TIME? HM...
I AM GRATEFUL FOR THESE CHANGES.
IF YOU HAD BEEN NORMALLY FEMALE, YOU MIGHT ALREADY BE LYING FACE-DOWN AT MY FEET.
HAH! IF I HAD BEEN A **GIRL**, HUH?

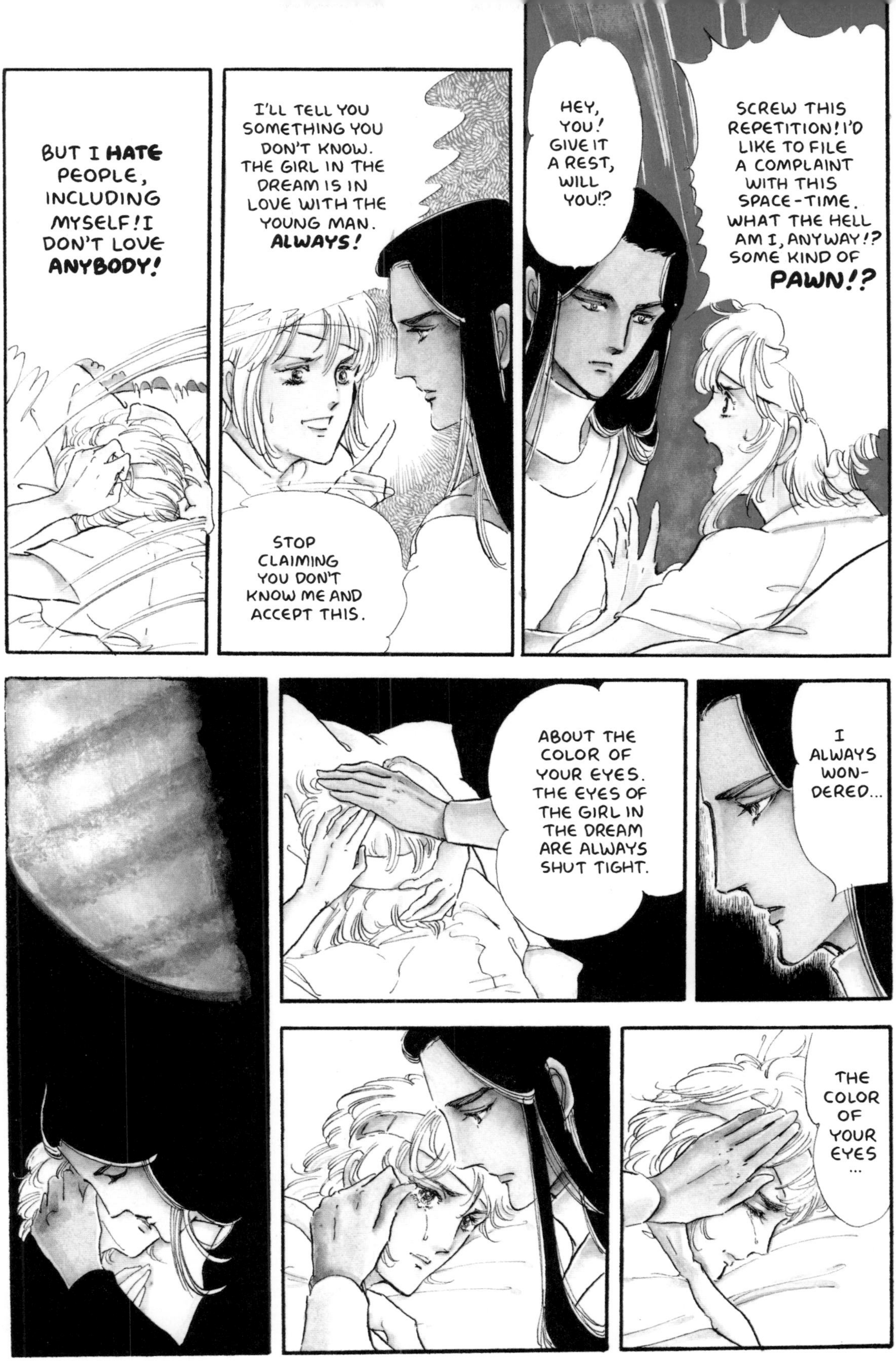
SCREW THIS REPETITION! I'D LIKE TO FILE A COMPLAINT WITH THIS SPACE-TIME. WHAT THE HELL AM I, ANYWAY!? SOME KIND OF **PAWN!?**
HEY, YOU! GIVE IT A REST, WILL YOU!?
I'LL TELL YOU SOMETHING YOU DON'T KNOW. THE GIRL IN THE DREAM IS IN LOVE WITH THE YOUNG MAN. **ALWAYS!**
STOP CLAIMING YOU DON'T KNOW ME AND ACCEPT THIS.
BUT I **HATE** PEOPLE, INCLUDING MYSELF! I DON'T LOVE **ANYBODY!**
I ALWAYS WON-DERED...
ABOUT THE COLOR OF YOUR EYES. THE EYES OF THE GIRL IN THE DREAM ARE ALWAYS SHUT TIGHT.
THE COLOR OF YOUR EYES ...

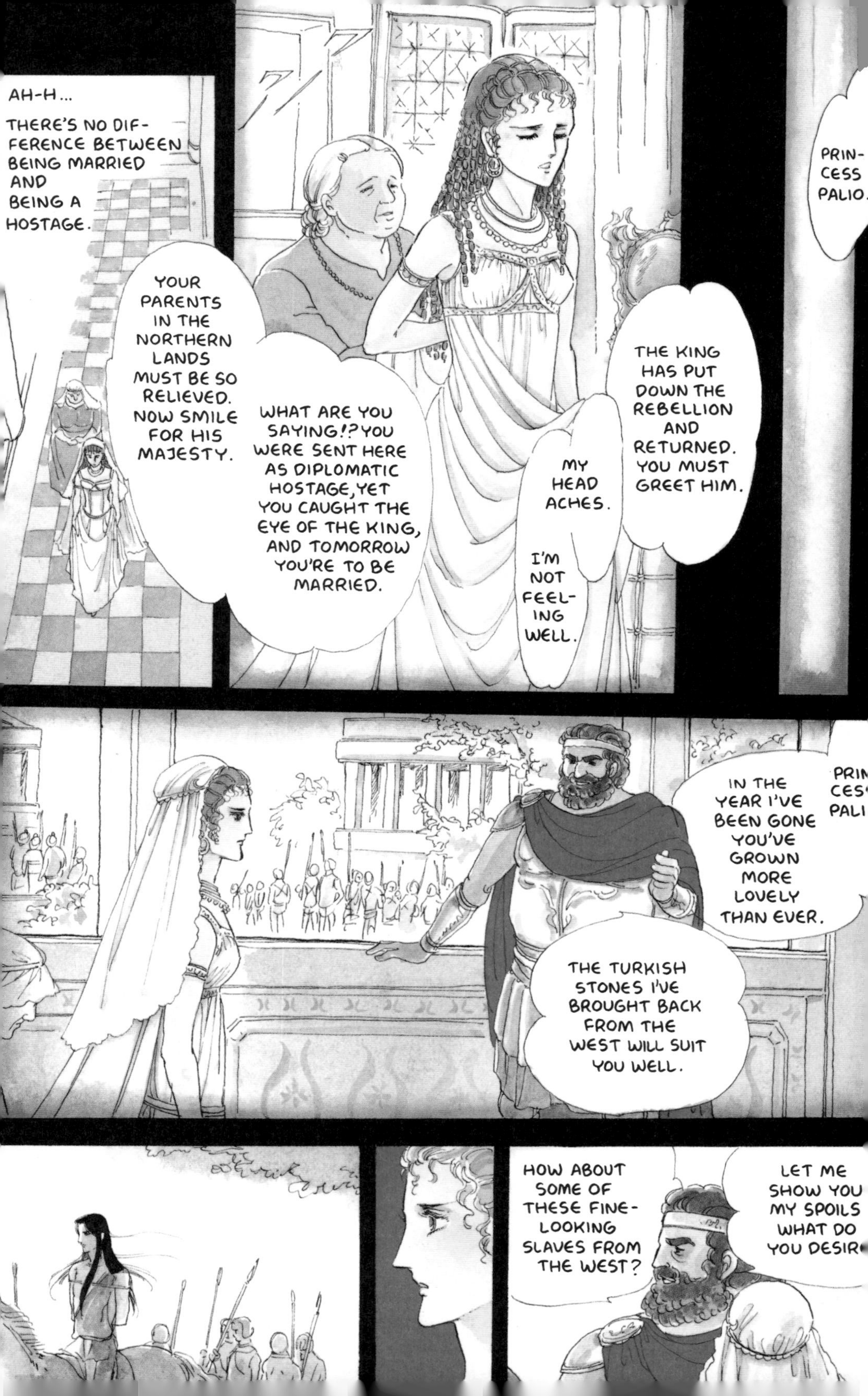
PRINCESS PALIO.
THE KING HAS PUT DOWN THE REBELLION AND RETURNED. YOU MUST GREET HIM.
MY HEAD ACHES.
I'M NOT FEELING WELL.
WHAT ARE YOU SAYING!? YOU WERE SENT HERE AS DIPLOMATIC HOSTAGE, YET YOU CAUGHT THE EYE OF THE KING, AND TOMORROW YOU'RE TO BE MARRIED.
YOUR PARENTS IN THE NORTHERN LANDS MUST BE SO RELIEVED. NOW SMILE FOR HIS MAJESTY.
AH-H...
THERE'S NO DIFFERENCE BETWEEN BEING MARRIED AND BEING A HOSTAGE.
PRIN- CES PALI
IN THE YEAR I'VE BEEN GONE YOU'VE GROWN MORE LOVELY THAN EVER.
THE TURKISH STONES I'VE BROUGHT BACK FROM THE WEST WILL SUIT YOU WELL.
LET ME SHOW YOU MY SPOILS WHAT DO YOU DESIR
HOW ABOUT SOME OF THESE FINE-LOOKING SLAVES FROM THE WEST?

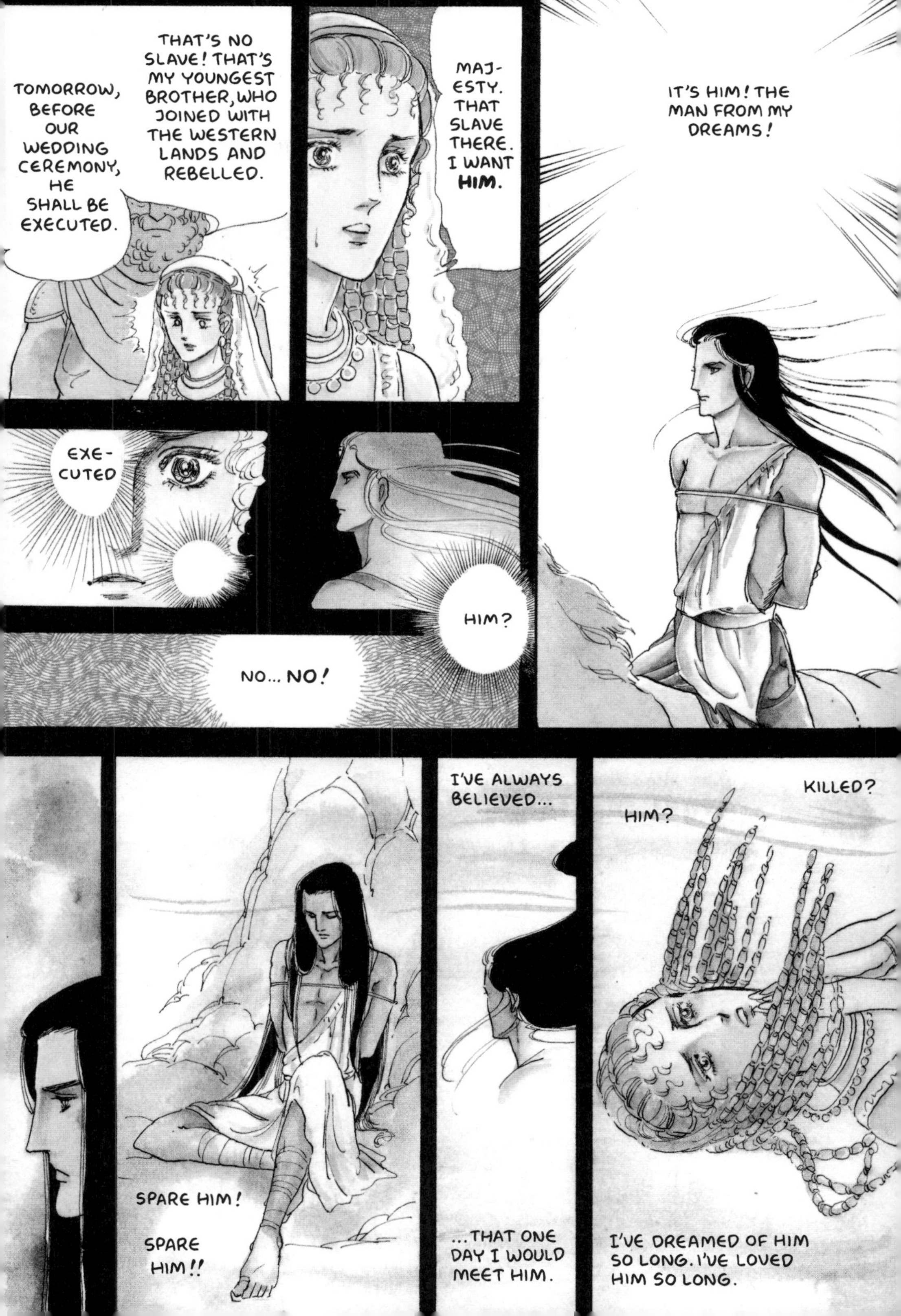
IT'S HIM! THE MAN FROM MY DREAMS!
MAJ-ESTY. THAT SLAVE THERE. I WANT **HIM**.
THAT'S NO SLAVE! THAT'S MY YOUNGEST BROTHER, WHO JOINED WITH THE WESTERN LANDS AND REBELLED.
TOMORROW, BEFORE OUR WEDDING CEREMONY, HE SHALL BE EXECUTED.
HIM?
EXE-CUTED
NO... **NO!**
KILLED?
HIM?
I'VE DREAMED OF HIM SO LONG. I'VE LOVED HIM SO LONG.
I'VE ALWAYS BELIEVED...
...THAT ONE DAY I WOULD MEET HIM.
SPARE HIM!
SPARE HIM!!

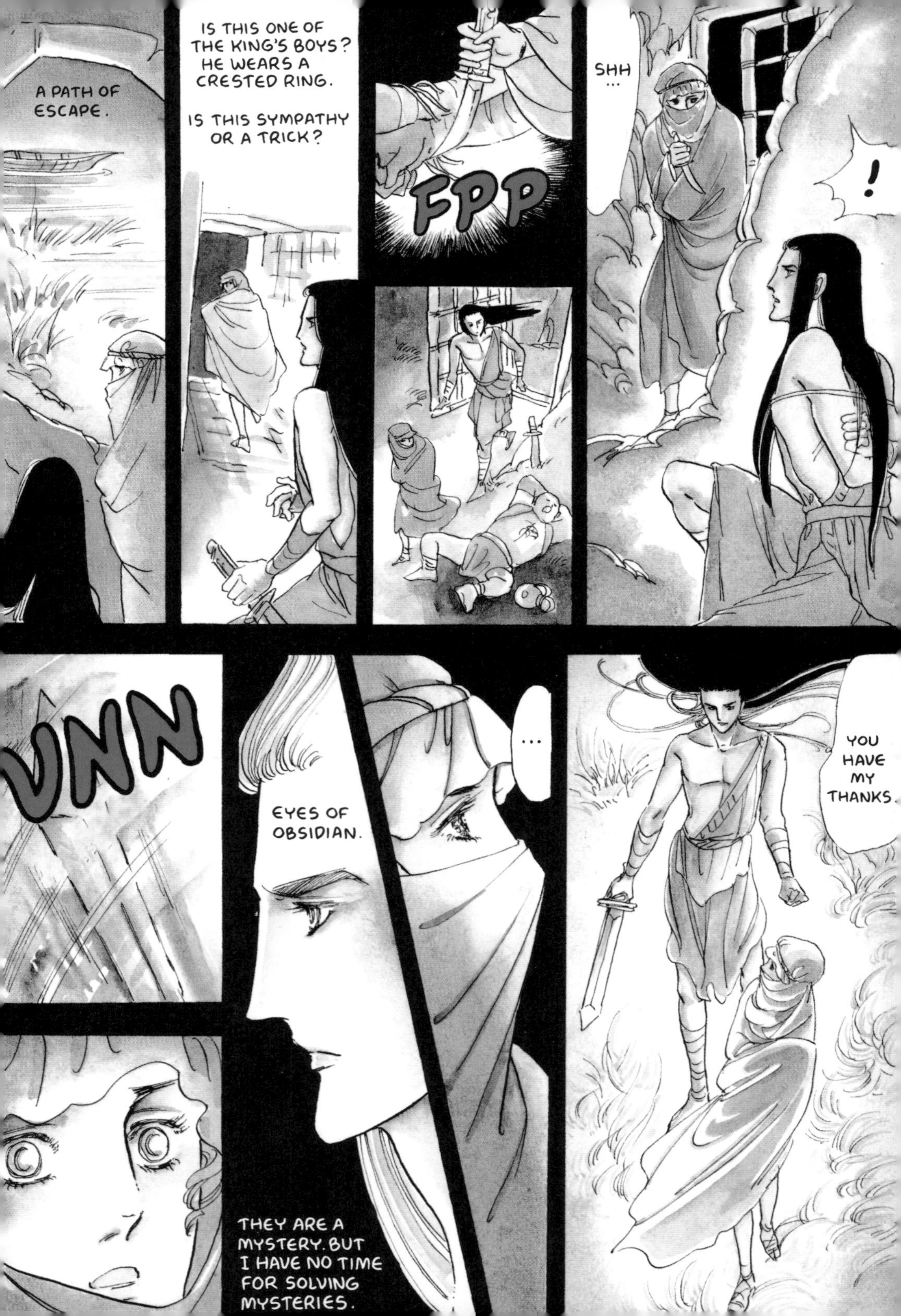
SHH ...
!
FPP
IS THIS ONE OF THE KING'S BOYS? HE WEARS A CRESTED RING.
IS THIS SYMPATHY OR A TRICK?
A PATH OF ESCAPE.
YOU HAVE MY THANKS.
...
EYES OF OBSIDIAN.
THEY ARE A MYSTERY. BUT I HAVE NO TIME FOR SOLVING MYSTERIES.
UNN

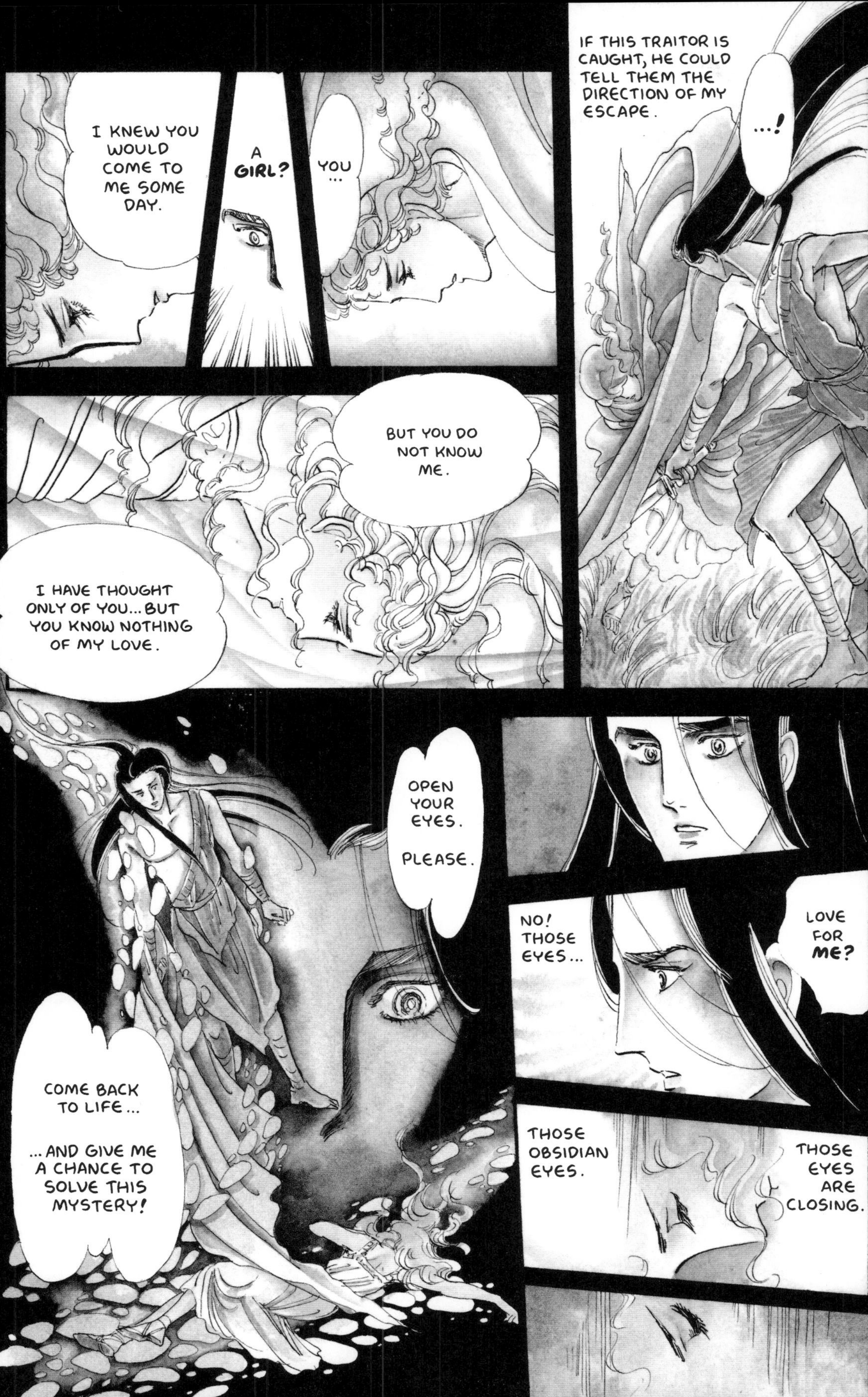
IF THIS TRAITOR IS CAUGHT, HE COULD TELL THEM THE DIRECTION OF MY ESCAPE.
...!
YOU ...
A GIRL?
I KNEW YOU WOULD COME TO ME SOME DAY.
BUT YOU DO NOT KNOW ME.
I HAVE THOUGHT ONLY OF YOU... BUT YOU KNOW NOTHING OF MY LOVE.
LOVE FOR ME?
NO! THOSE EYES...
THOSE EYES ARE CLOSING.
THOSE OBSIDIAN EYES.
OPEN YOUR EYES.
PLEASE.
COME BACK TO LIFE...
...AND GIVE ME A CHANCE TO SOLVE THIS MYSTERY!

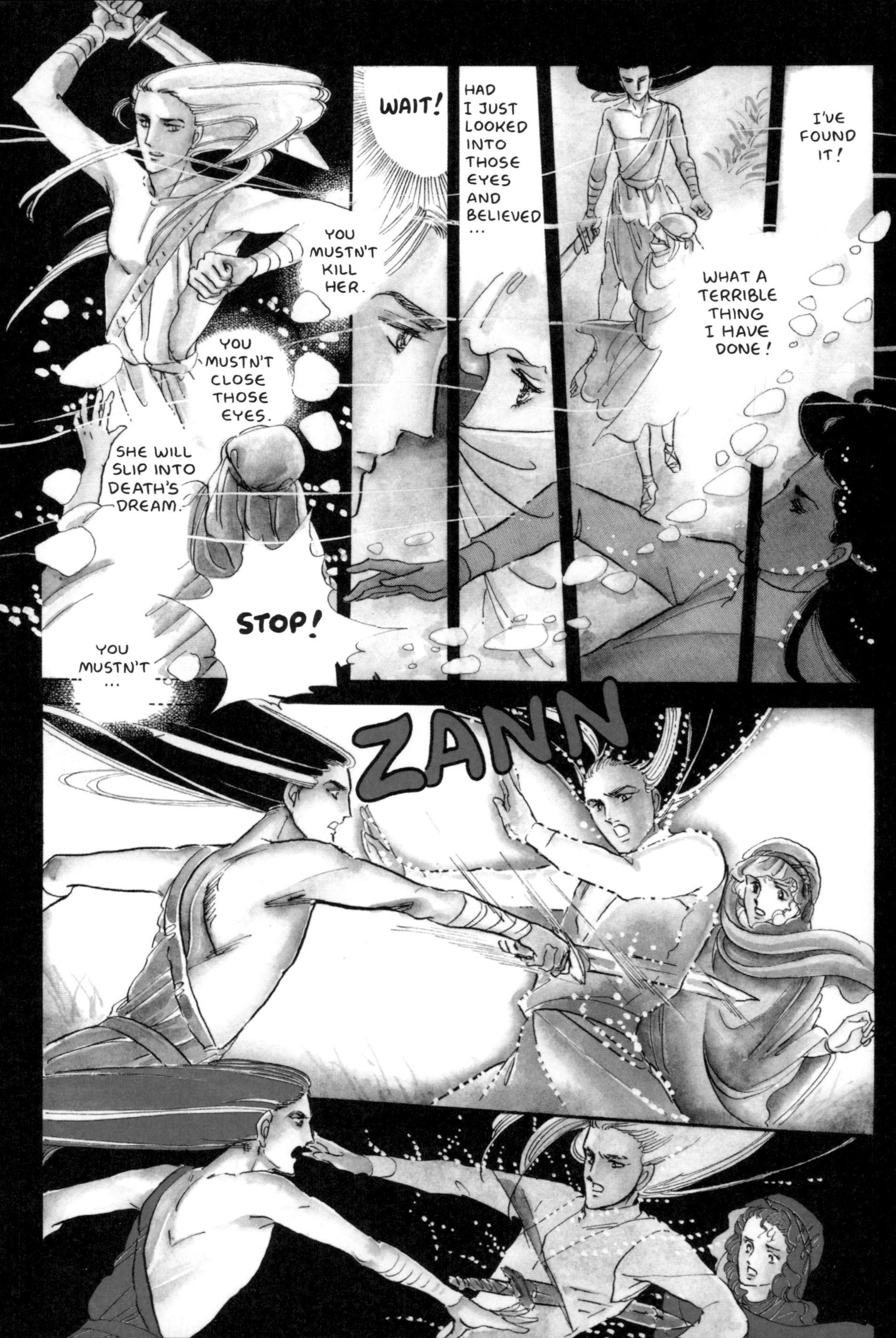
I'VE FOUND IT!
WHAT A TERRIBLE THING I HAVE DONE!
HAD I JUST LOOKED INTO THOSE EYES AND BELIEVED ...
WAIT!
YOU MUSTN'T KILL HER.
YOU MUSTN'T CLOSE THOSE EYES.
SHE WILL SLIP INTO DEATH'S DREAM.
STOP!
YOU MUSTN'T ...
ZANN

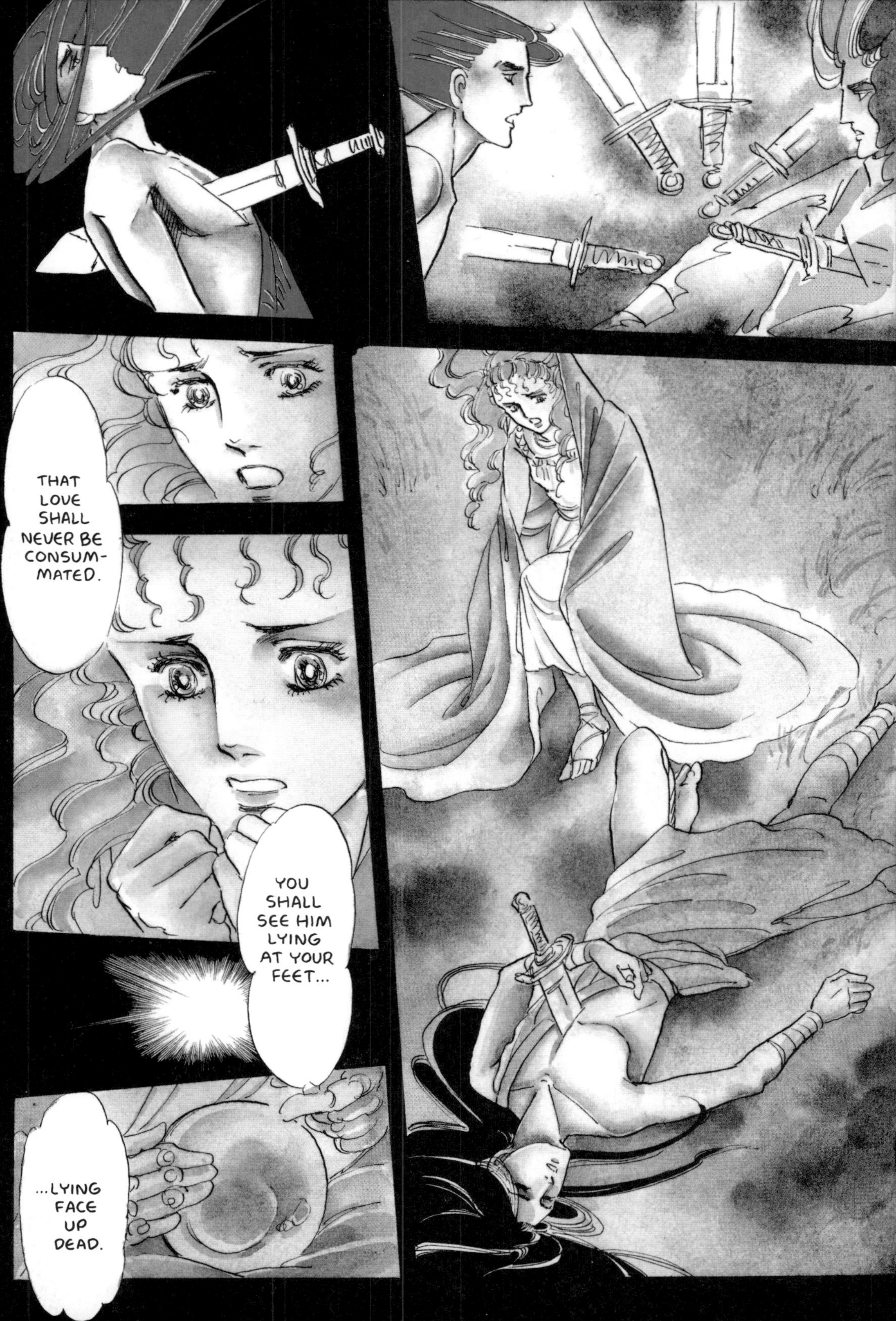
THAT LOVE SHALL NEVER BE CONSUM-MATED.
YOU SHALL SEE HIM LYING AT YOUR FEET...
...LYING FACE UP DEAD.

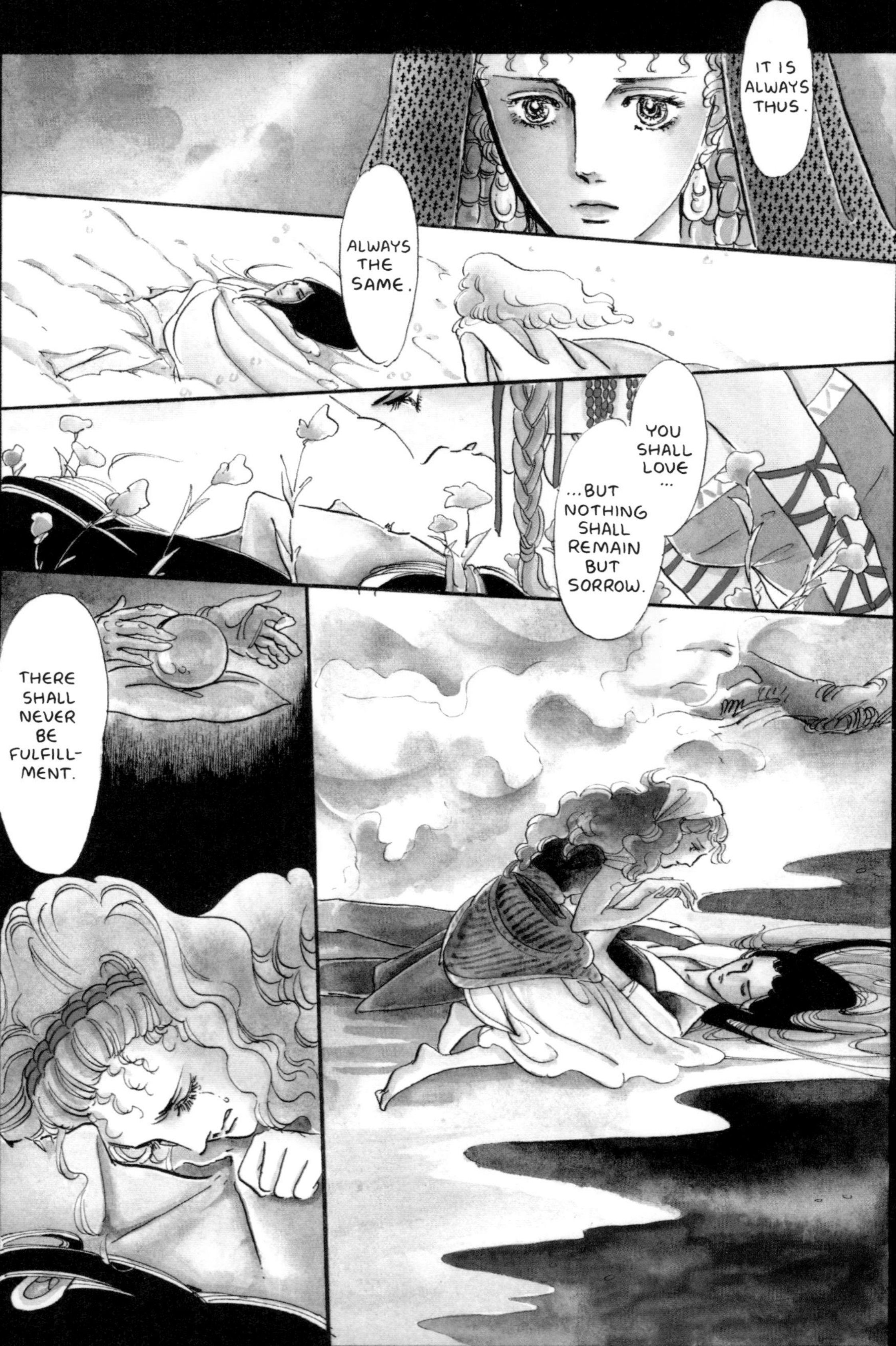
IT IS ALWAYS THUS.
ALWAYS THE SAME.
YOU SHALL LOVE ...
...BUT NOTHING SHALL REMAIN BUT SORROW.
THERE SHALL NEVER BE FULFILL-MENT.

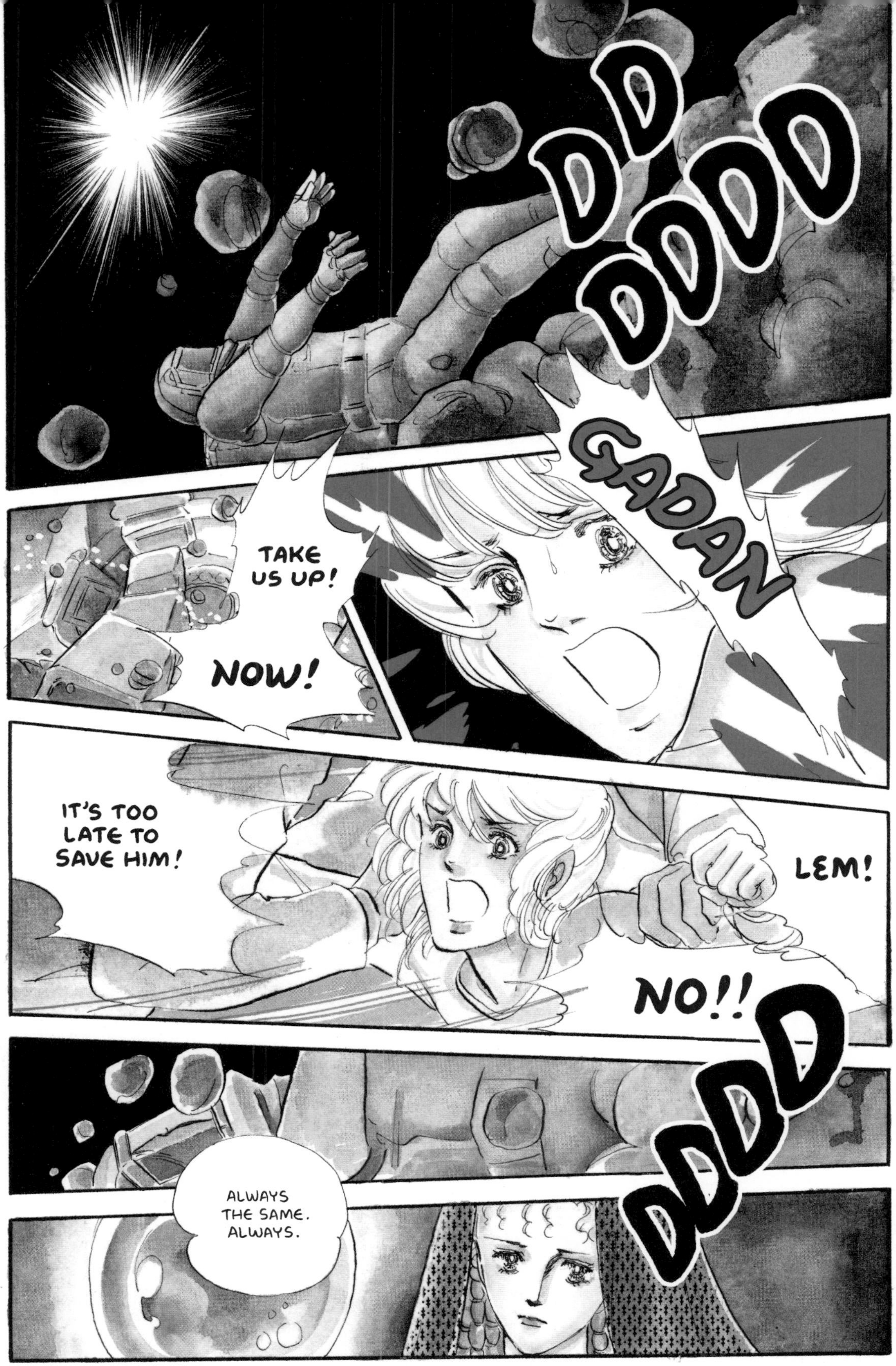
DD DDDDD
GADAN
TAKE US UP!
NOW!
LEM!
IT'S TOO LATE TO SAVE HIM!
NO!!
DDDD
ALWAYS THE SAME. ALWAYS.

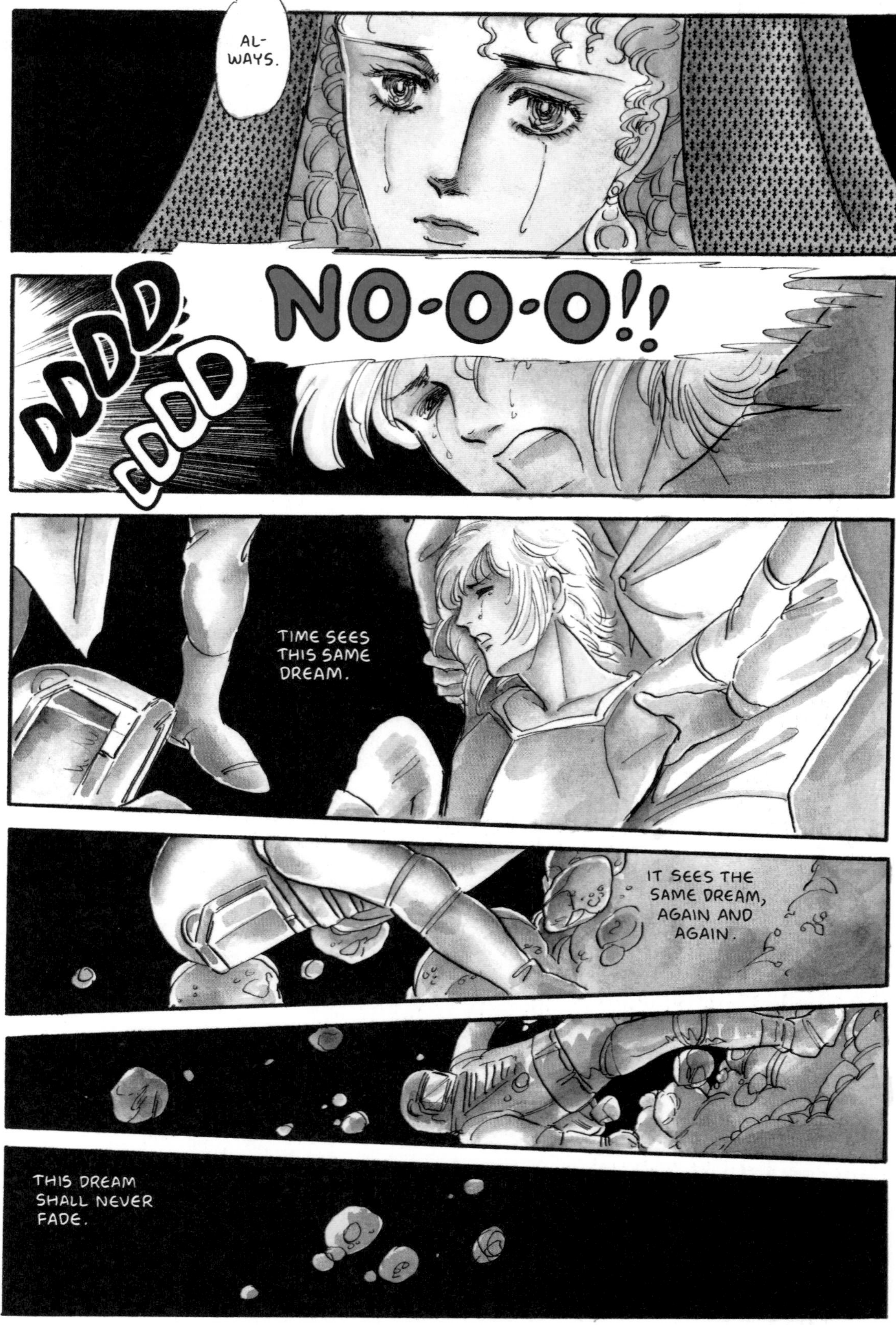
AL-
WAYS.
NO-O-O!!
DDDD
DDDD
TIME SEES THIS SAME DREAM.
IT SEES THE SAME DREAM, AGAIN AND AGAIN.
THIS DREAM SHALL NEVER FADE.

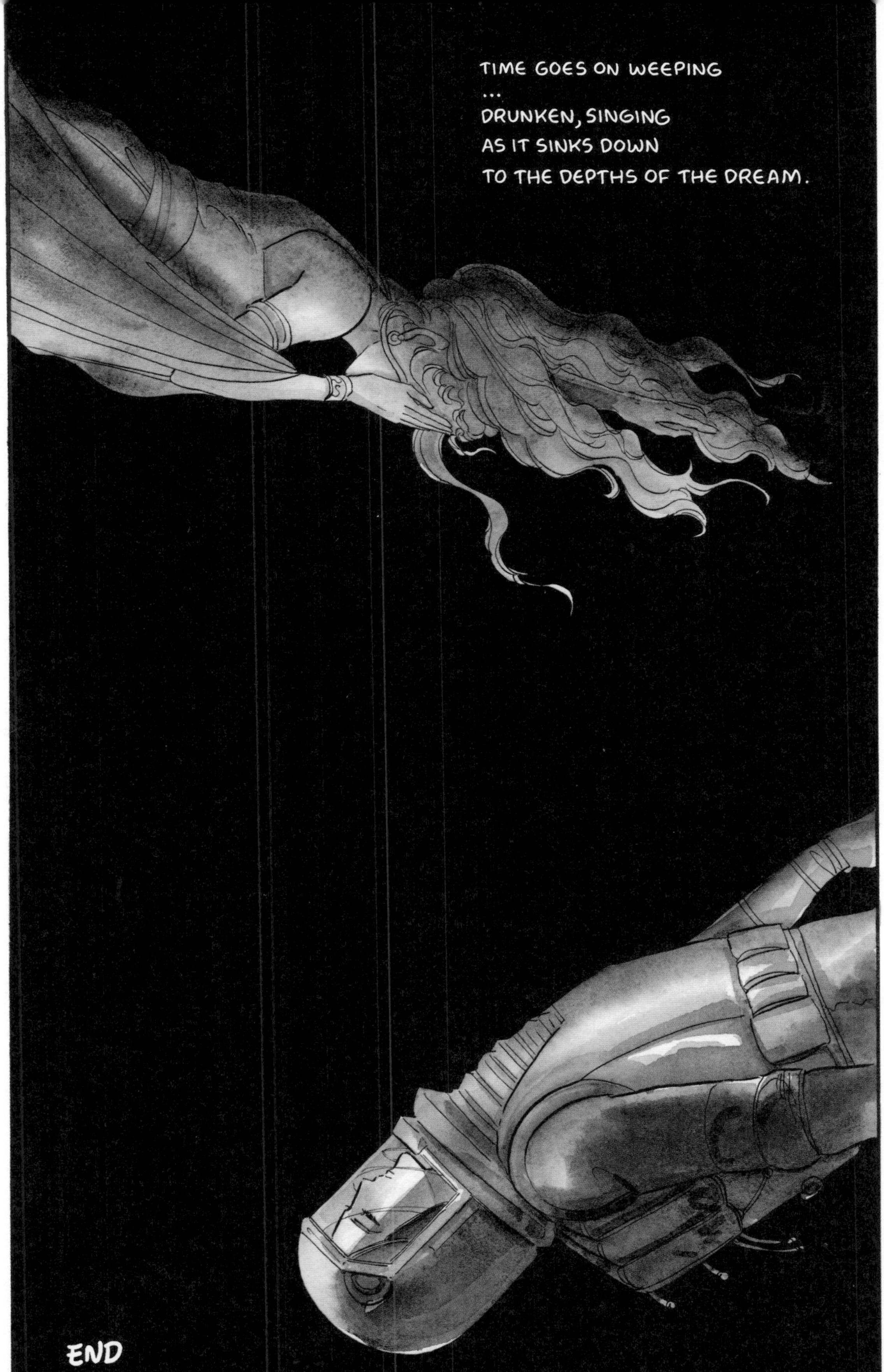
TIME GOES ON WEEPING
...
DRUNKEN, SINGING
AS IT SINKS DOWN
TO THE DEPTHS OF THE DREAM.
END

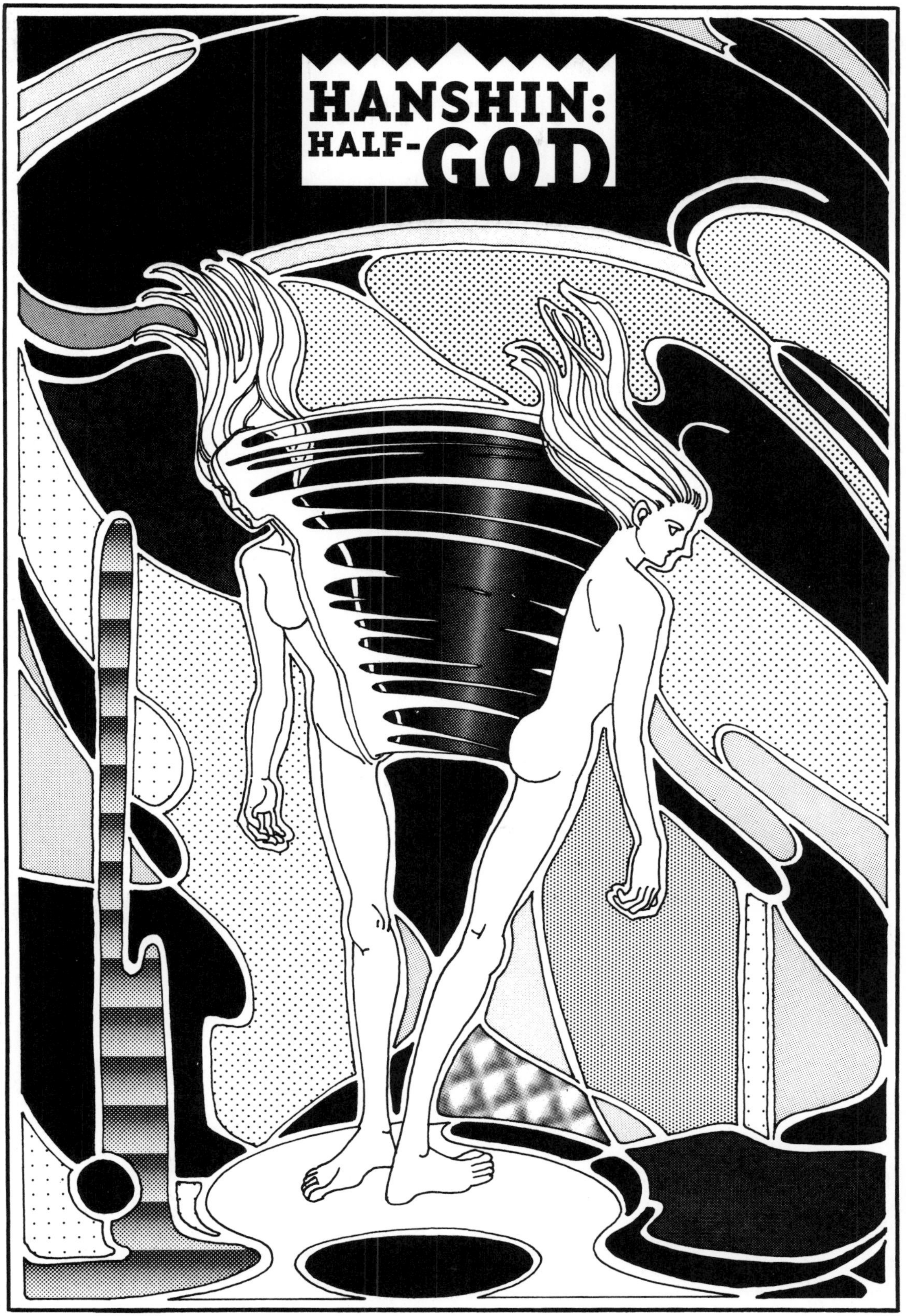
HANSHIN:
HALF-GOD

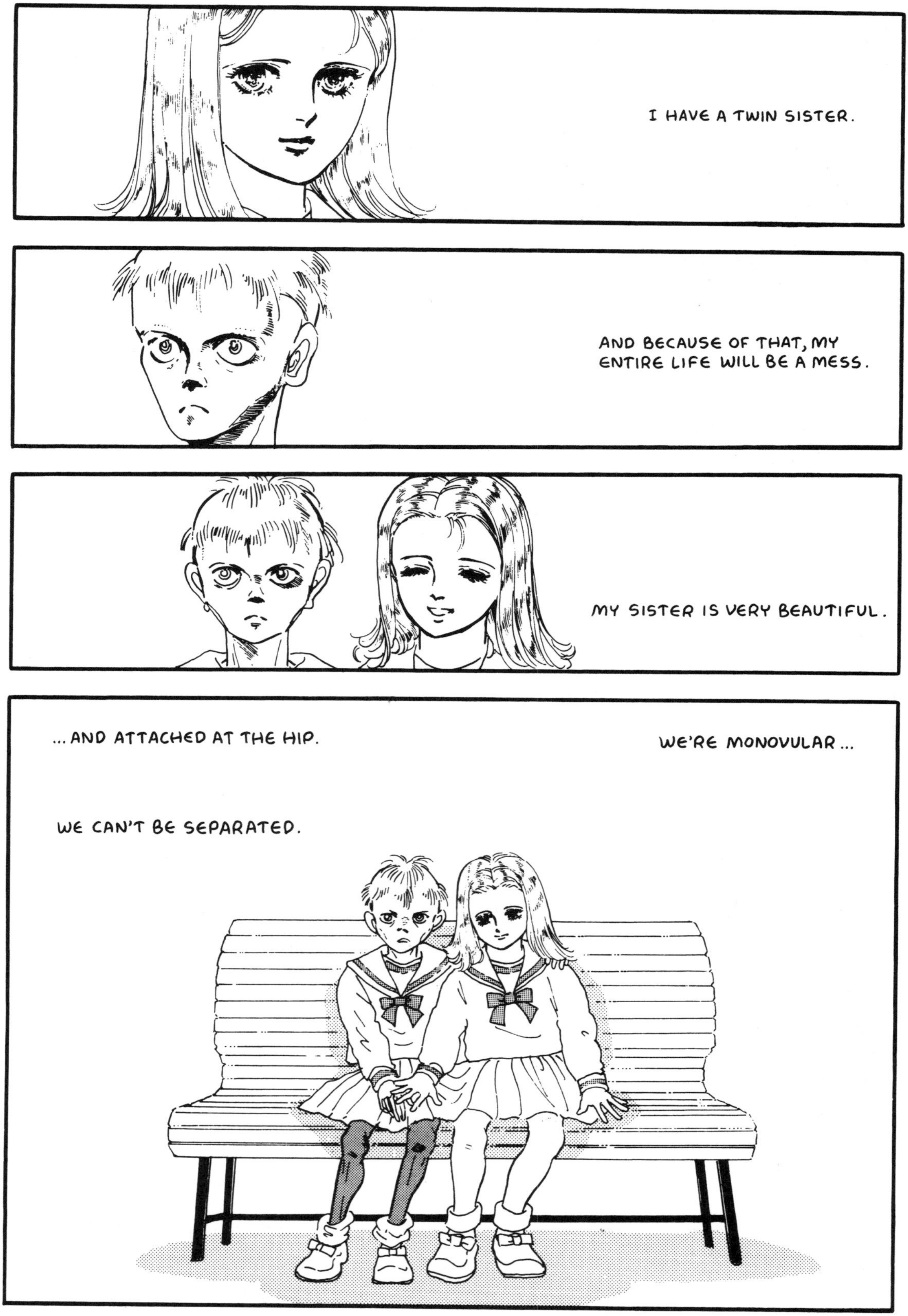
I HAVE A TWIN SISTER.
AND BECAUSE OF THAT, MY ENTIRE LIFE WILL BE A MESS.
MY SISTER IS VERY BEAUTIFUL.
WE'RE MONOVULAR...
...AND ATTACHED AT THE HIP.
WE CAN'T BE SEPARATED.

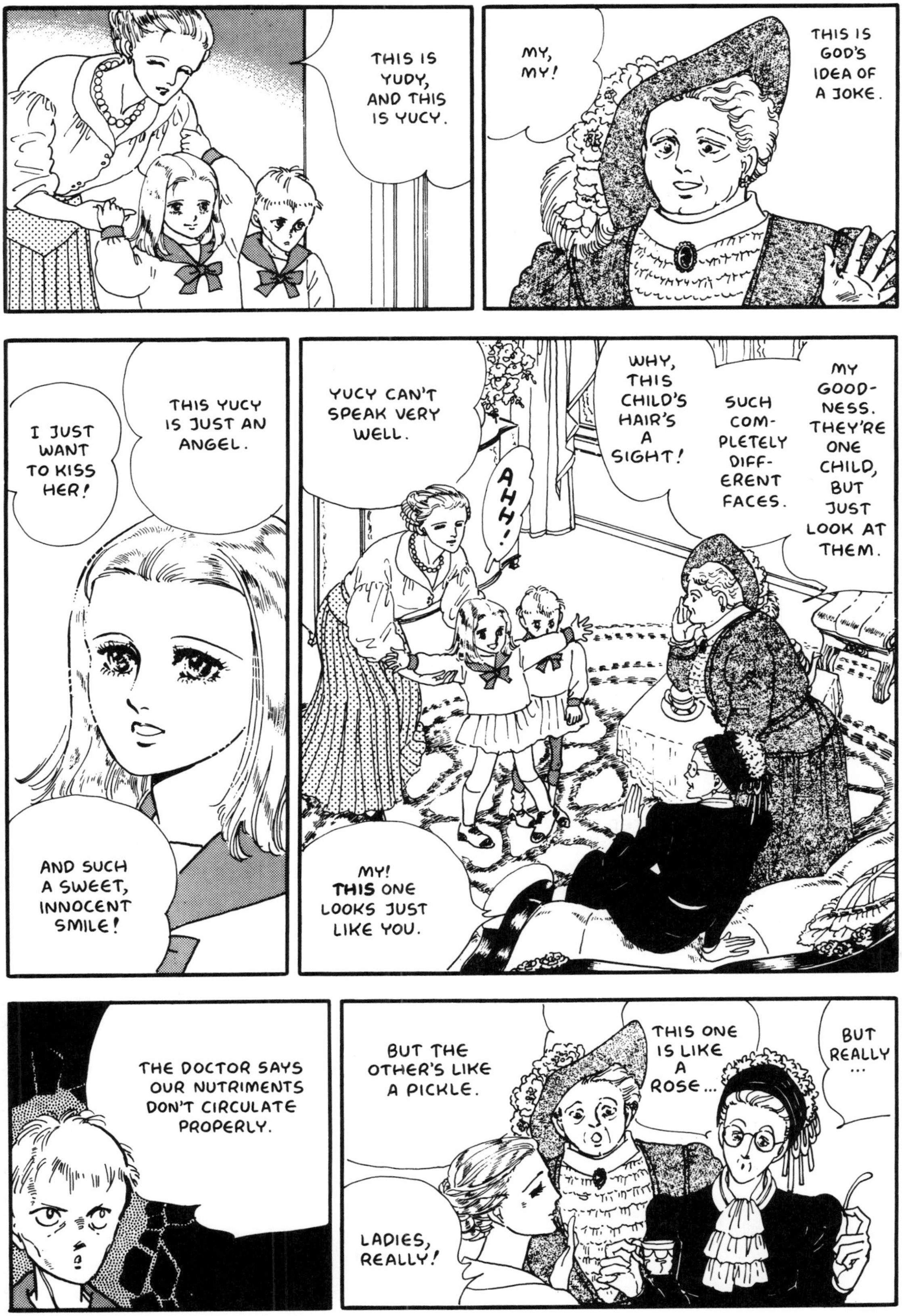
THIS IS GOD'S IDEA OF A JOKE.
MY, MY!
THIS IS YUDY, AND THIS IS YUCY.
MY GOODNESS. THEY'RE ONE CHILD, BUT JUST LOOK AT THEM.
SUCH COMPLETELY DIFFERENT FACES.
WHY, THIS CHILD'S HAIR'S A SIGHT!
YUCY CAN'T SPEAK VERY WELL.
AHH!
MY! THIS ONE LOOKS JUST LIKE YOU.
THIS YUCY IS JUST AN ANGEL.
I JUST WANT TO KISS HER!
AND SUCH A SWEET, INNOCENT SMILE!
BUT REALLY ...
THIS ONE IS LIKE A ROSE...
BUT THE OTHER'S LIKE A PICKLE.
LADIES, REALLY!
THE DOCTOR SAYS OUR NUTRIMENTS DON'T CIRCULATE PROPERLY.

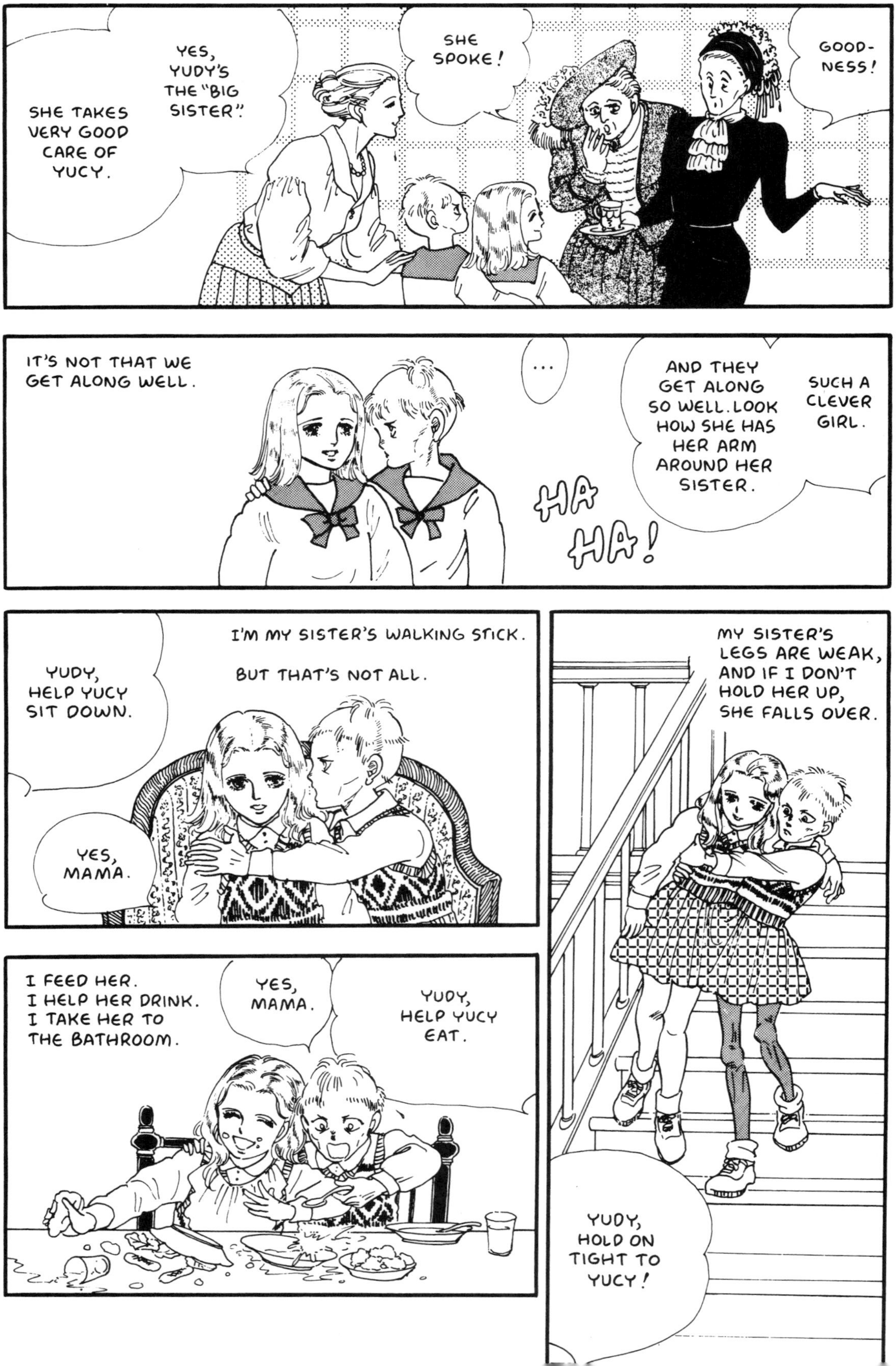
GOOD-NESS!
SHE SPOKE!
YES, YUDY'S THE "BIG SISTER".
SHE TAKES VERY GOOD CARE OF YUCY.
SUCH A CLEVER GIRL.
AND THEY GET ALONG SO WELL. LOOK HOW SHE HAS HER ARM AROUND HER SISTER.
...
HA HA!
IT'S NOT THAT WE GET ALONG WELL.
MY SISTER'S LEGS ARE WEAK, AND IF I DON'T HOLD HER UP, SHE FALLS OVER.
YUDY, HOLD ON TIGHT TO YUCY!
I'M MY SISTER'S WALKING STICK.
BUT THAT'S NOT ALL.
YUDY, HELP YUCY SIT DOWN.
YES, MAMA.
YUDY, HELP YUCY EAT.
YES, MAMA.
I FEED HER. I HELP HER DRINK. I TAKE HER TO THE BATHROOM.

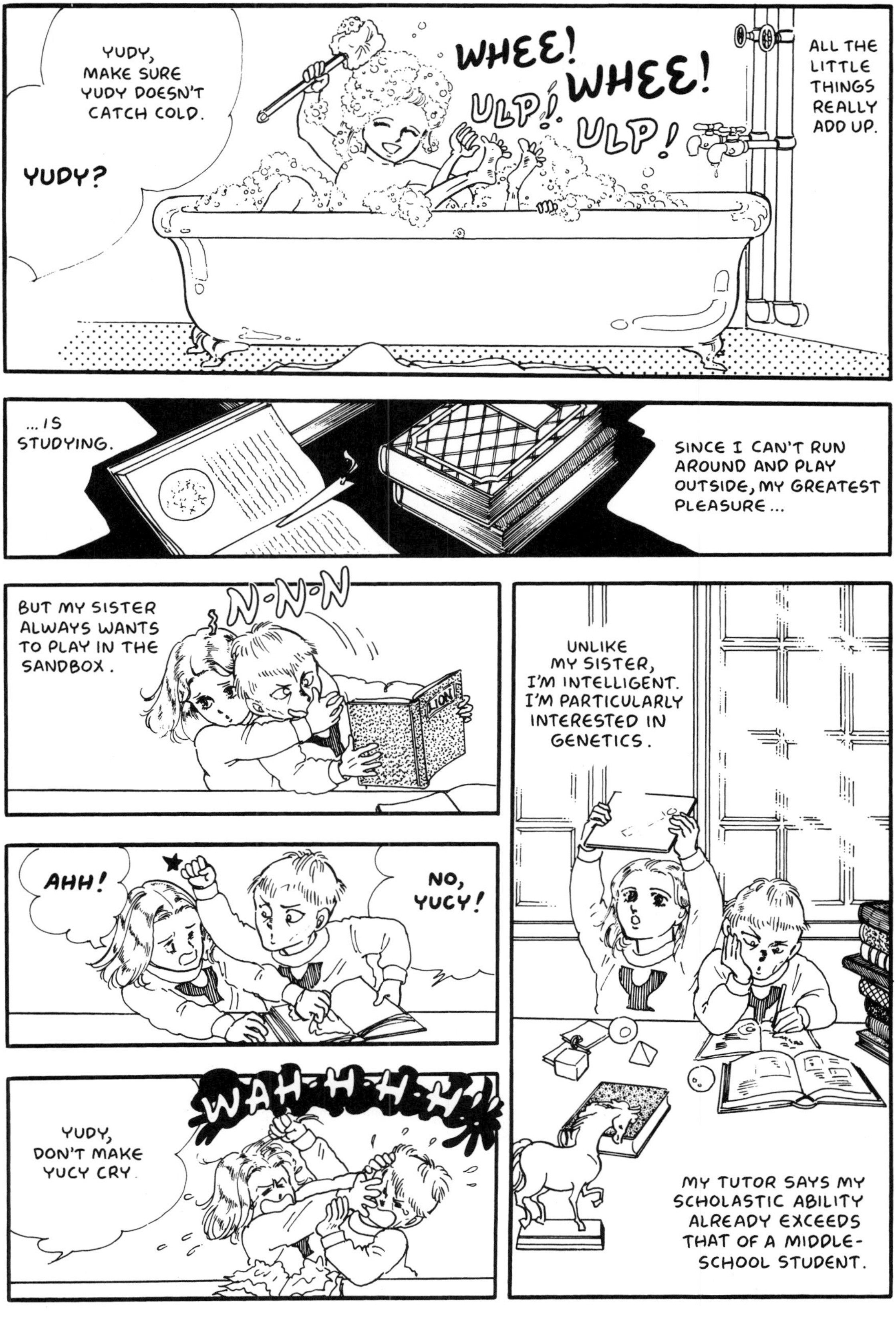
ALL THE LITTLE THINGS REALLY ADD UP.
WHEE! WHEE!
ULP! ULP!
YUDY, MAKE SURE YUDY DOESN'T CATCH COLD.
YUDY?
SINCE I CAN'T RUN AROUND AND PLAY OUTSIDE, MY GREATEST PLEASURE...
...IS STUDYING.
UNLIKE MY SISTER, I'M INTELLIGENT. I'M PARTICULARLY INTERESTED IN GENETICS.
MY TUTOR SAYS MY SCHOLASTIC ABILITY ALREADY EXCEEDS THAT OF A MIDDLE-SCHOOL STUDENT.
N-N-N
BUT MY SISTER ALWAYS WANTS TO PLAY IN THE SANDBOX.
LION
NO, YUCY!
AHH!
WAH-H-H-H!
YUDY, DON'T MAKE YUCY CRY.

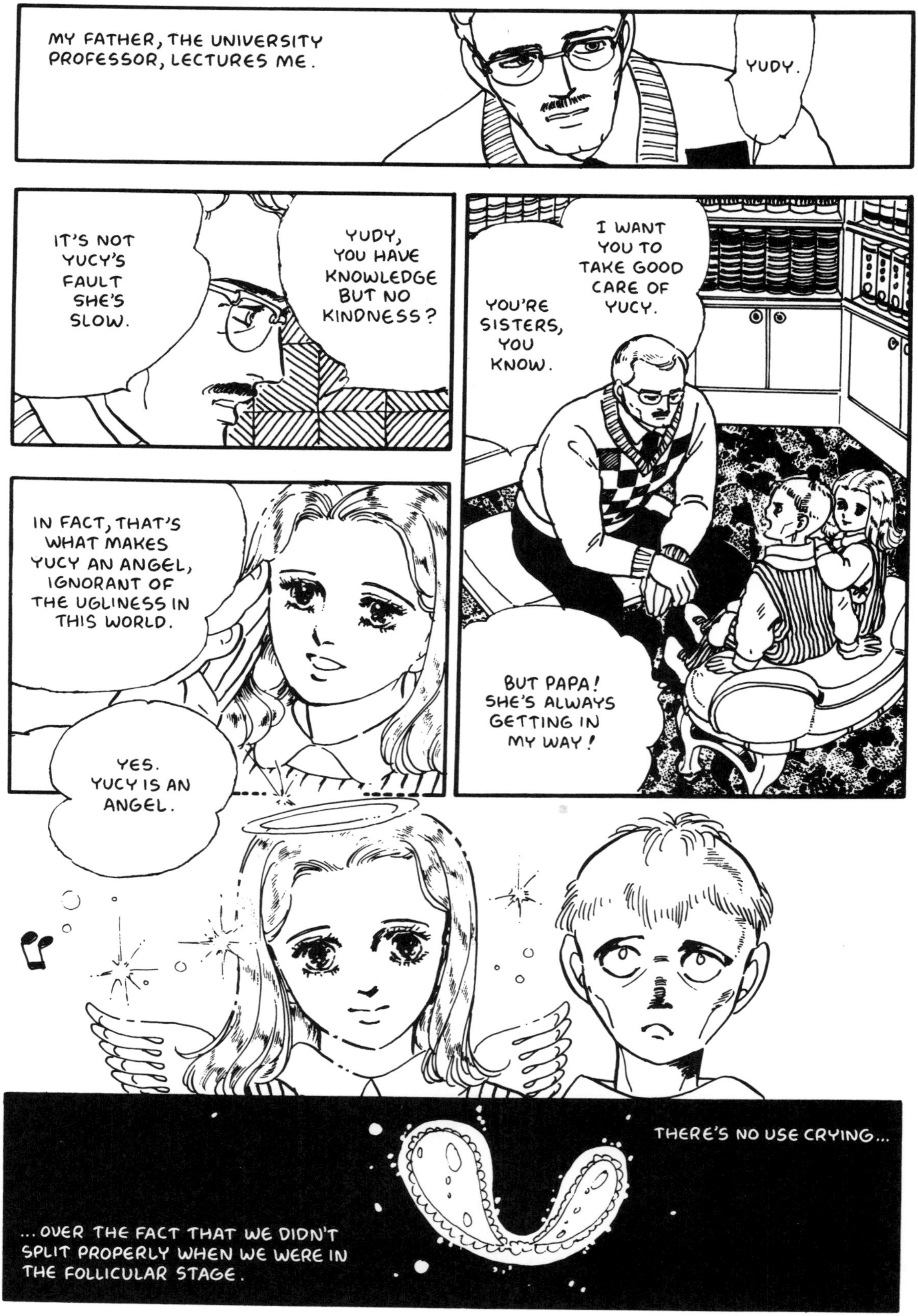
YUDY.
MY FATHER, THE UNIVERSITY PROFESSOR, LECTURES ME.
I WANT YOU TO TAKE GOOD CARE OF YUCY.
YOU'RE SISTERS, YOU KNOW.
BUT PAPA! SHE'S ALWAYS GETTING IN MY WAY!
YUDY, YOU HAVE KNOWLEDGE BUT NO KINDNESS?
IT'S NOT YUCY'S FAULT SHE'S SLOW.
IN FACT, THAT'S WHAT MAKES YUCY AN ANGEL, IGNORANT OF THE UGLINESS IN THIS WORLD.
YES. YUCY IS AN ANGEL.
THERE'S NO USE CRYING...
...OVER THE FACT THAT WE DIDN'T SPLIT PROPERLY WHEN WE WERE IN THE FOLLICULAR STAGE.

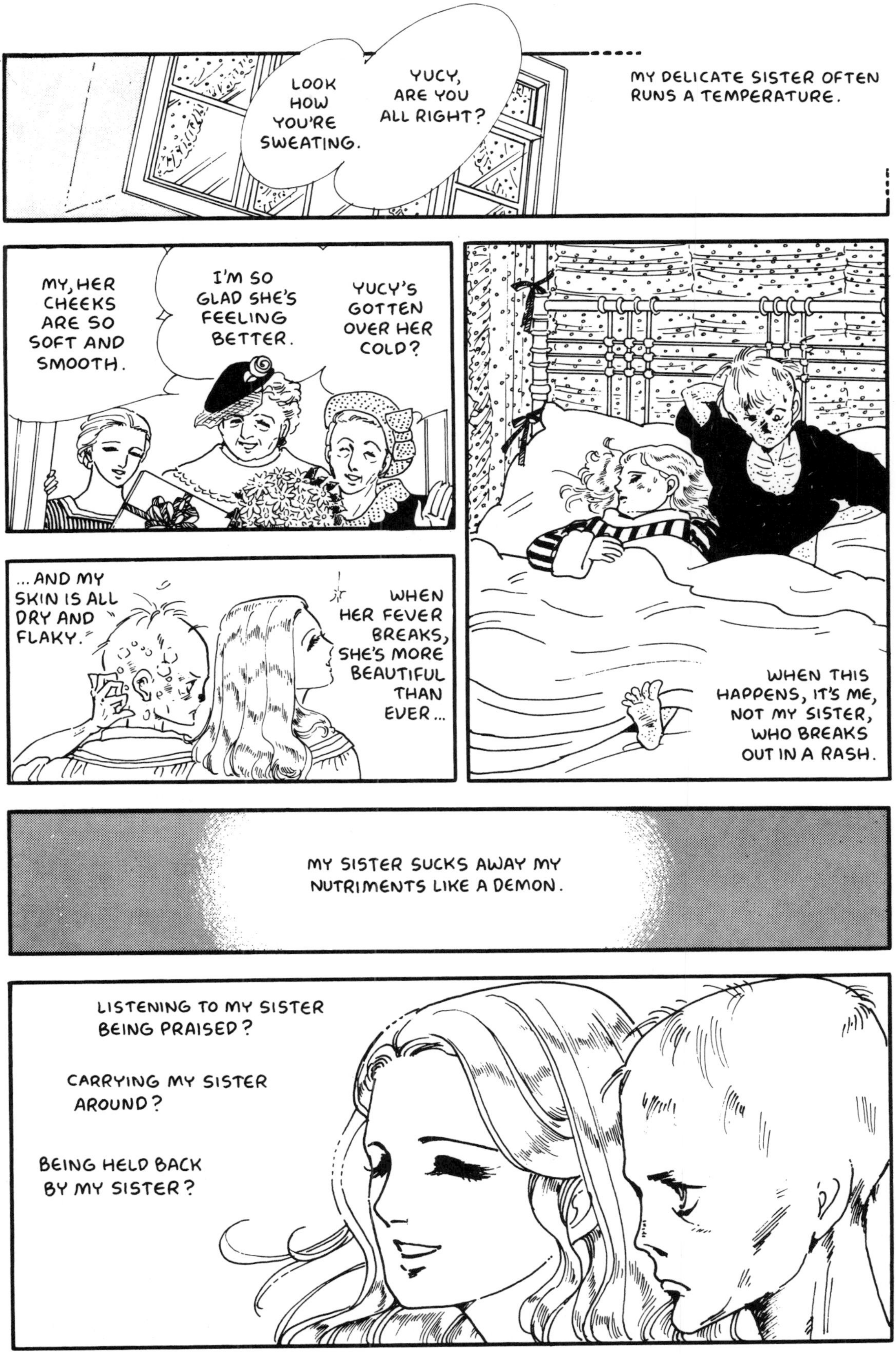
MY DELICATE SISTER OFTEN RUNS A TEMPERATURE.
YUCY, ARE YOU ALL RIGHT?
LOOK HOW YOU'RE SWEATING.
WHEN THIS HAPPENS, IT'S ME, NOT MY SISTER, WHO BREAKS OUT IN A RASH.
YUCY'S GOTTEN OVER HER COLD?
I'M SO GLAD SHE'S FEELING BETTER.
MY, HER CHEEKS ARE SO SOFT AND SMOOTH.
WHEN HER FEVER BREAKS, SHE'S MORE BEAUTIFUL THAN EVER...
...AND MY SKIN IS ALL DRY AND FLAKY.
MY SISTER SUCKS AWAY MY NUTRIMENTS LIKE A DEMON.
LISTENING TO MY SISTER BEING PRAISED?
CARRYING MY SISTER AROUND?
BEING HELD BACK BY MY SISTER?

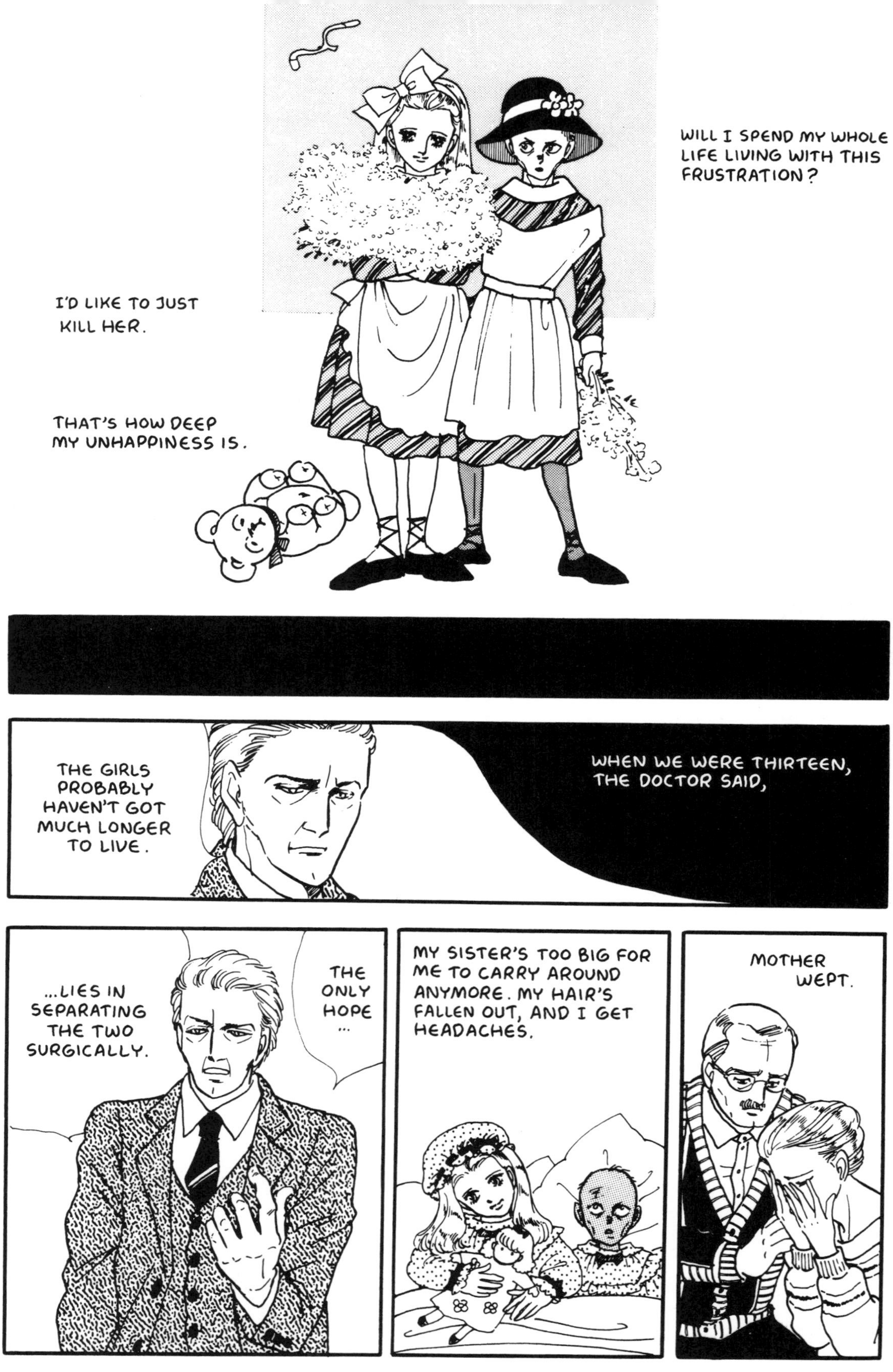
WILL I SPEND MY WHOLE LIFE LIVING WITH THIS FRUSTRATION?
I'D LIKE TO JUST KILL HER.
THAT'S HOW DEEP MY UNHAPPINESS IS.
WHEN WE WERE THIRTEEN, THE DOCTOR SAID,
THE GIRLS PROBABLY HAVEN'T GOT MUCH LONGER TO LIVE.
MOTHER WEPT.
MY SISTER'S TOO BIG FOR ME TO CARRY AROUND ANYMORE. MY HAIR'S FALLEN OUT, AND I GET HEADACHES.
THE ONLY HOPE ...
...LIES IN SEPARATING THE TWO SURGICALLY.

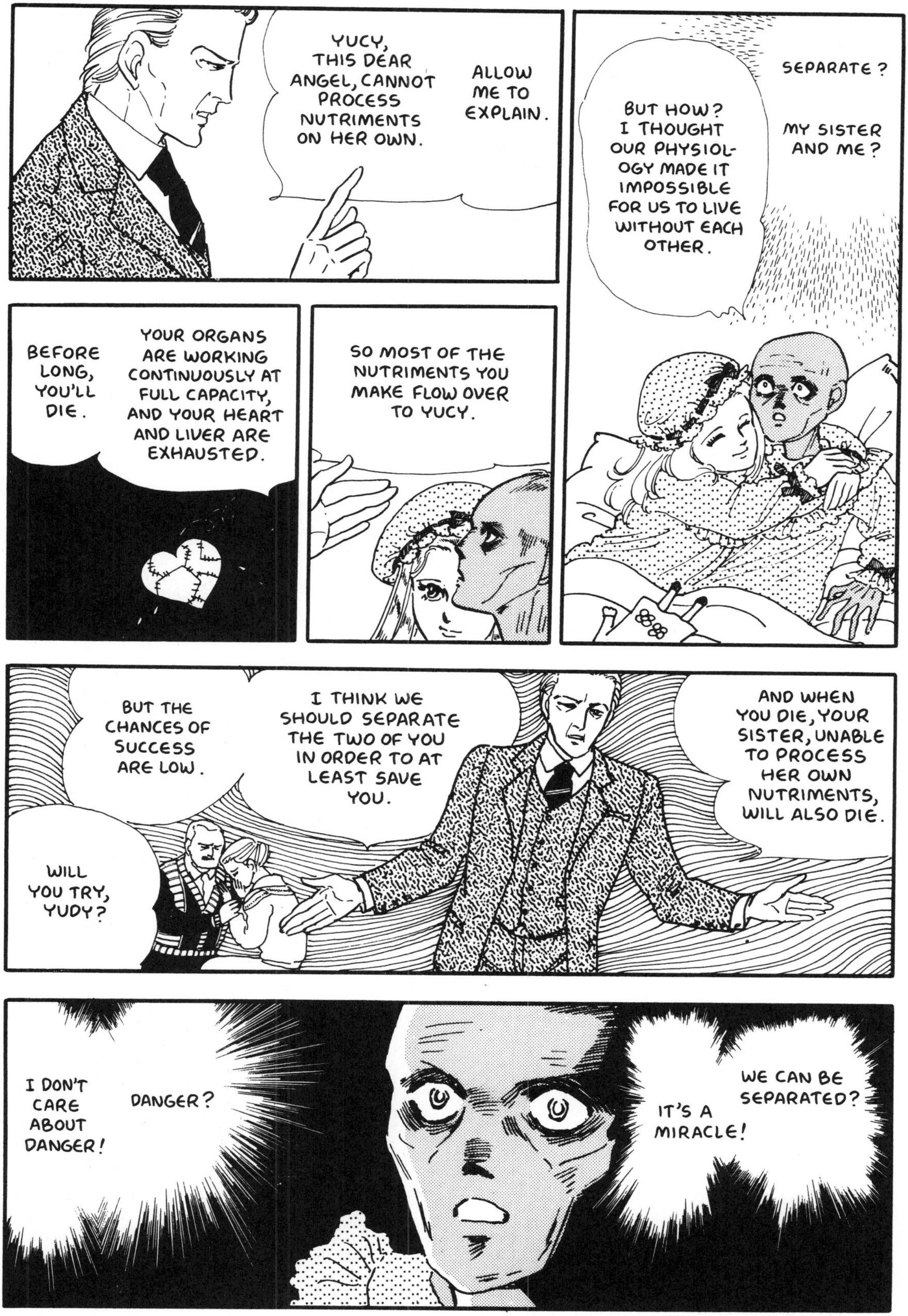
SEPARATE?
MY SISTER AND ME?
BUT HOW? I THOUGHT OUR PHYSIOL-OGY MADE IT IMPOSSIBLE FOR US TO LIVE WITHOUT EACH OTHER.
ALLOW ME TO EXPLAIN.
YUCY, THIS DEAR ANGEL, CANNOT PROCESS NUTRIMENTS ON HER OWN.
SO MOST OF THE NUTRIMENTS YOU MAKE FLOW OVER TO YUCY.
YOUR ORGANS ARE WORKING CONTINUOUSLY AT FULL CAPACITY, AND YOUR HEART AND LIVER ARE EXHAUSTED.
BEFORE LONG, YOU'LL DIE.
AND WHEN YOU DIE, YOUR SISTER, UNABLE TO PROCESS HER OWN NUTRIMENTS, WILL ALSO DIE.
I THINK WE SHOULD SEPARATE THE TWO OF YOU IN ORDER TO AT LEAST SAVE YOU.
BUT THE CHANCES OF SUCCESS ARE LOW.
WILL YOU TRY, YUDY?
WE CAN BE SEPARATED?
IT'S A MIRACLE!
DANGER?
I DON'T CARE ABOUT DANGER!

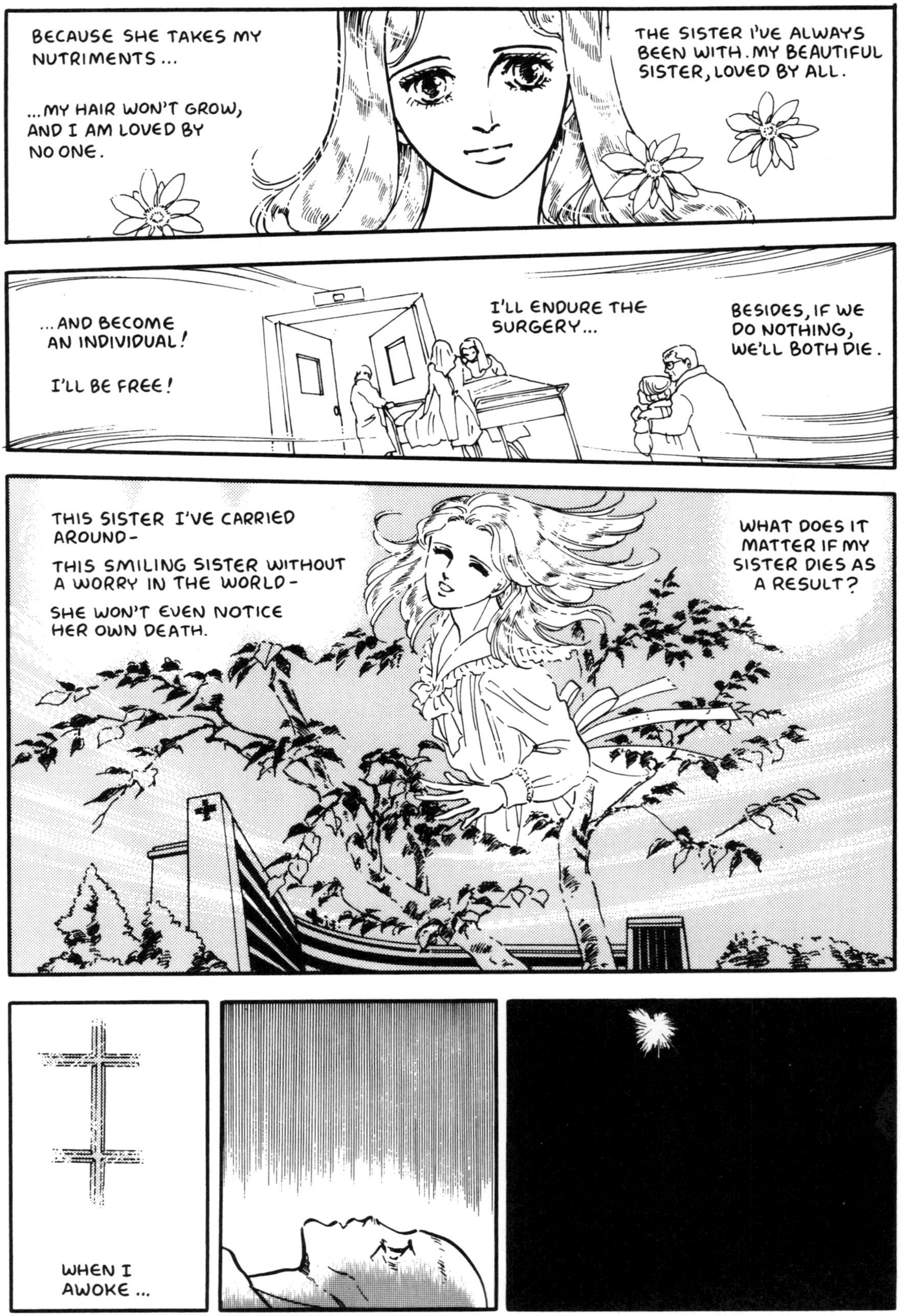
THE SISTER I'VE ALWAYS BEEN WITH. MY BEAUTIFUL SISTER, LOVED BY ALL.
BECAUSE SHE TAKES MY NUTRIMENTS...
...MY HAIR WON'T GROW, AND I AM LOVED BY NO ONE.
BESIDES, IF WE DO NOTHING, WE'LL BOTH DIE.
I'LL ENDURE THE SURGERY...
...AND BECOME AN INDIVIDUAL!
I'LL BE FREE!
WHAT DOES IT MATTER IF MY SISTER DIES AS A RESULT?
THIS SISTER I'VE CARRIED AROUND-
THIS SMILING SISTER WITHOUT A WORRY IN THE WORLD-
SHE WON'T EVEN NOTICE HER OWN DEATH.
WHEN I AWOKE...

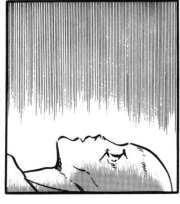

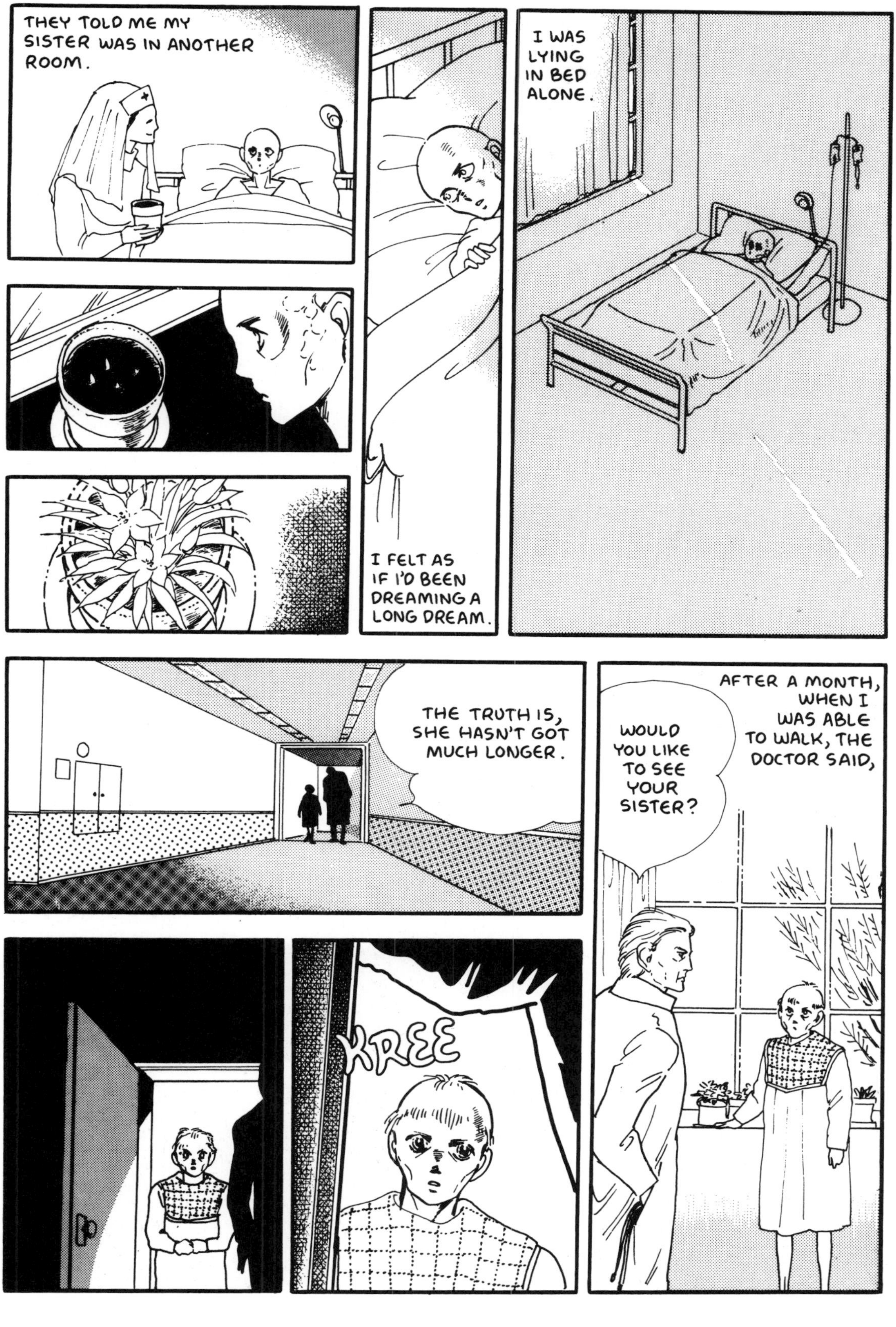
I WAS LYING IN BED ALONE.
I FELT AS IF I'D BEEN DREAMING A LONG DREAM.
THEY TOLD ME MY SISTER WAS IN ANOTHER ROOM.
AFTER A MONTH, WHEN I WAS ABLE TO WALK, THE DOCTOR SAID,
WOULD YOU LIKE TO SEE YOUR SISTER?
THE TRUTH IS, SHE HASN'T GOT MUCH LONGER.
KREE

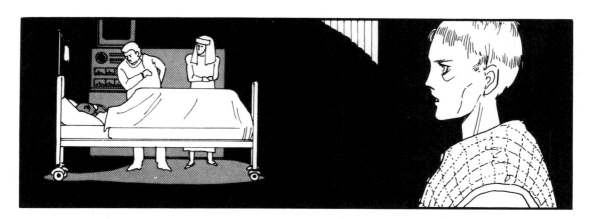

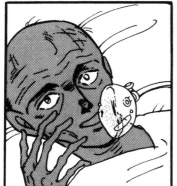

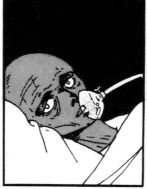

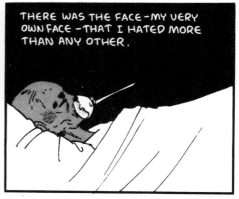

THERE WAS THE FACE - MY VERY OWN FACE - THAT I HATED MORE THAN ANY OTHER.
YU...
IS THIS SOME KIND OF TRICK?
ISN'T IT REALLY ME WHO IS DYING?
NO. IT REALLY IS MY SISTER.
MY WITHERED, COMPLETELY IGNORANT SISTER'S...

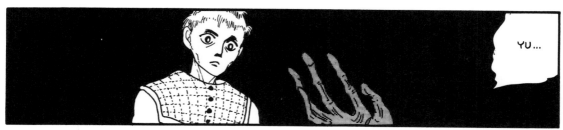

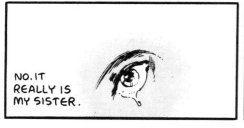

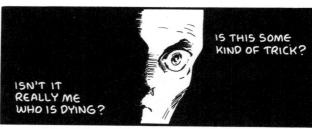

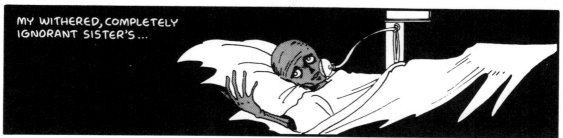

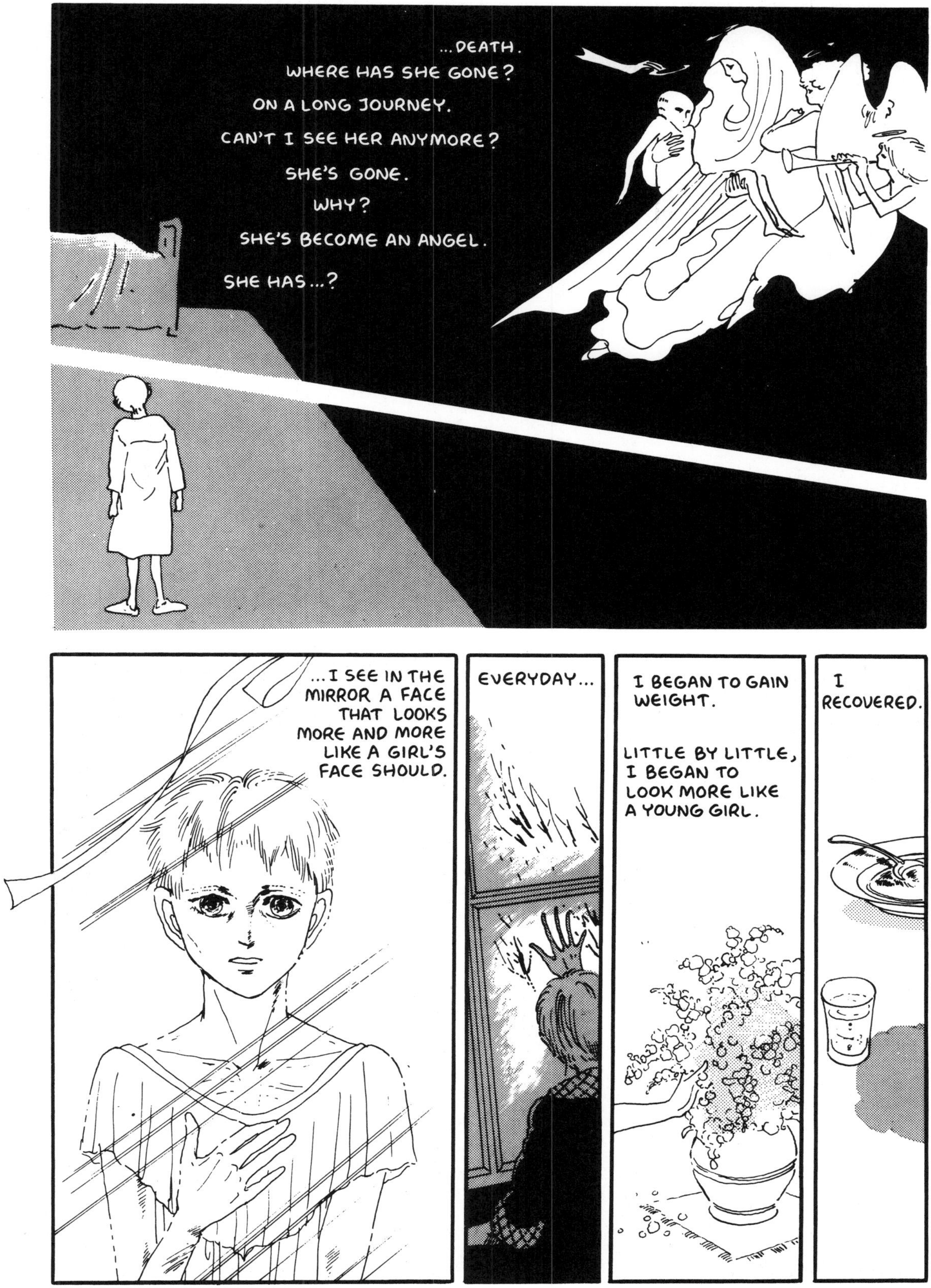
...DEATH.
WHERE HAS SHE GONE?
ON A LONG JOURNEY.
CAN'T I SEE HER ANYMORE?
SHE'S GONE.
WHY?
SHE'S BECOME AN ANGEL.
SHE HAS...?
I RECOVERED.
I BEGAN TO GAIN WEIGHT.
LITTLE BY LITTLE, I BEGAN TO LOOK MORE LIKE A YOUNG GIRL.
EVERYDAY...
...I SEE IN THE MIRROR A FACE THAT LOOKS MORE AND MORE LIKE A GIRL'S FACE SHOULD.

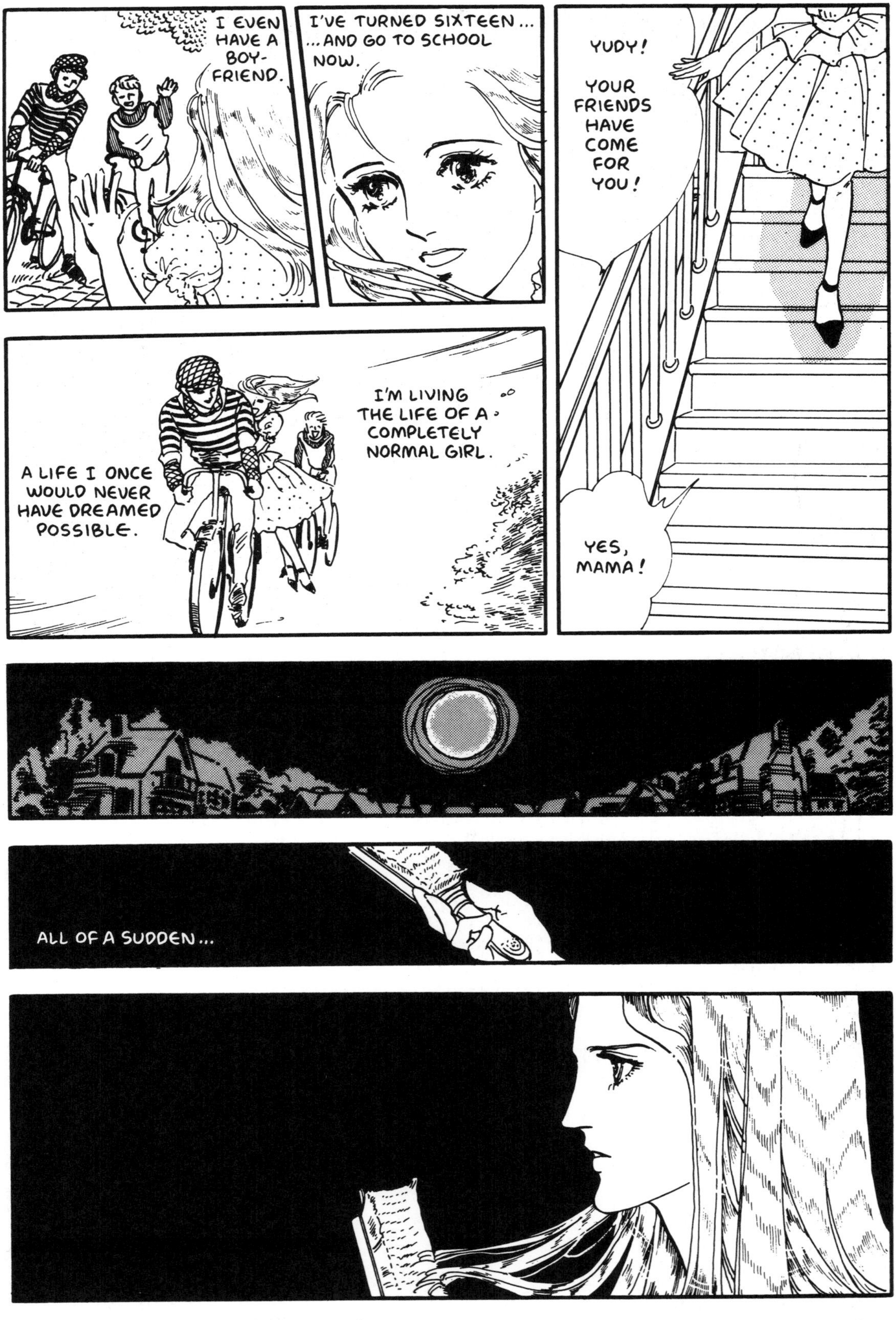
YUDY!
YOUR FRIENDS HAVE COME FOR YOU!
YES, MAMA!
I'VE TURNED SIXTEEN ... ...AND GO TO SCHOOL NOW.
I EVEN HAVE A BOY-FRIEND.
I'M LIVING THE LIFE OF A COMPLETELY NORMAL GIRL.
A LIFE I ONCE WOULD NEVER HAVE DREAMED POSSIBLE.
ALL OF A SUDDEN...

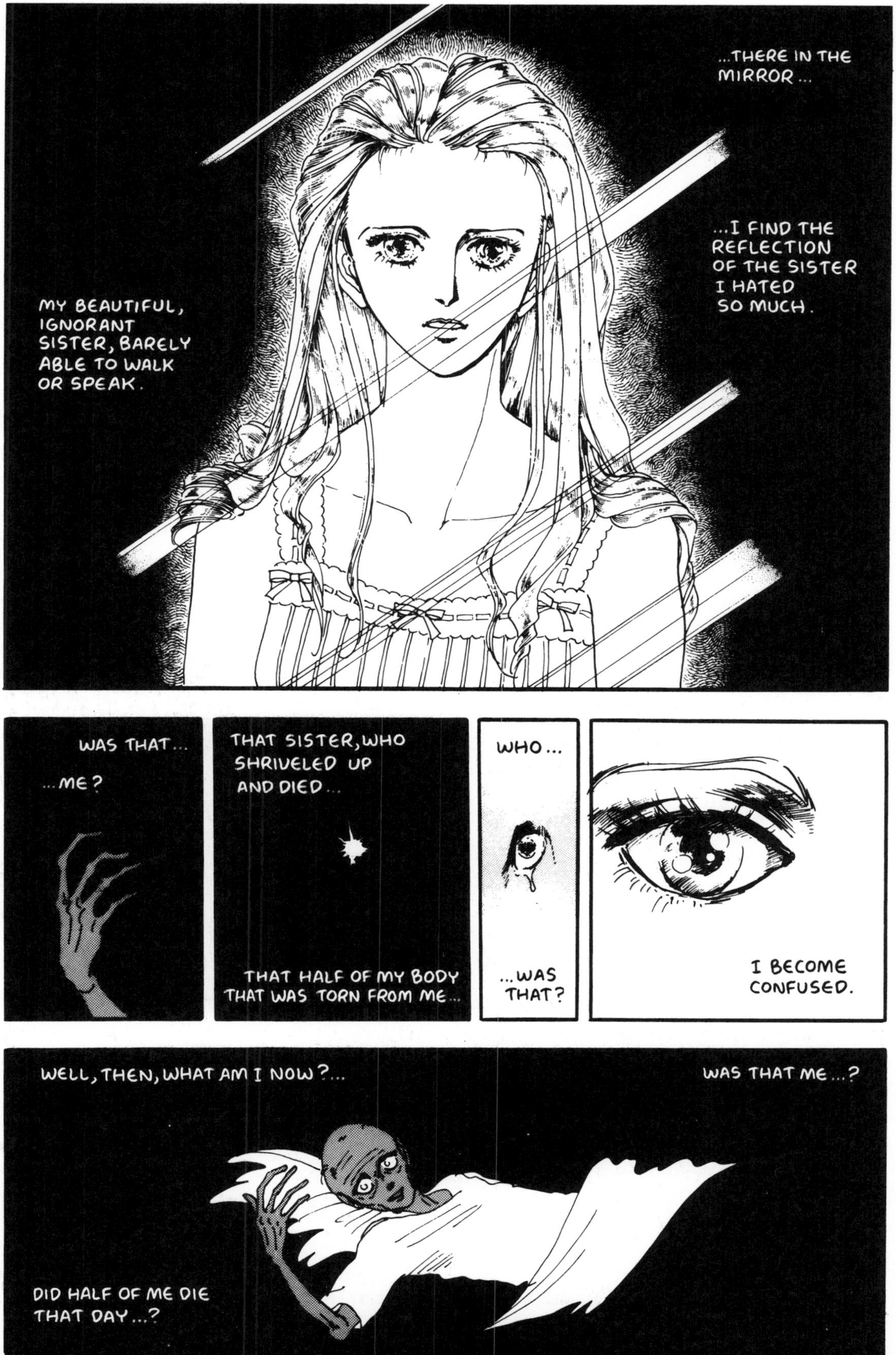
...THERE IN THE MIRROR...
...I FIND THE REFLECTION OF THE SISTER I HATED SO MUCH.
MY BEAUTIFUL, IGNORANT SISTER, BARELY ABLE TO WALK OR SPEAK.
I BECOME CONFUSED.
WHO...
...WAS THAT?
THAT SISTER, WHO SHRIVELED UP AND DIED...
THAT HALF OF MY BODY THAT WAS TORN FROM ME...
WAS THAT...
...ME?
WAS THAT ME...?
WELL, THEN, WHAT AM I NOW?...
DID HALF OF ME DIE THAT DAY...?

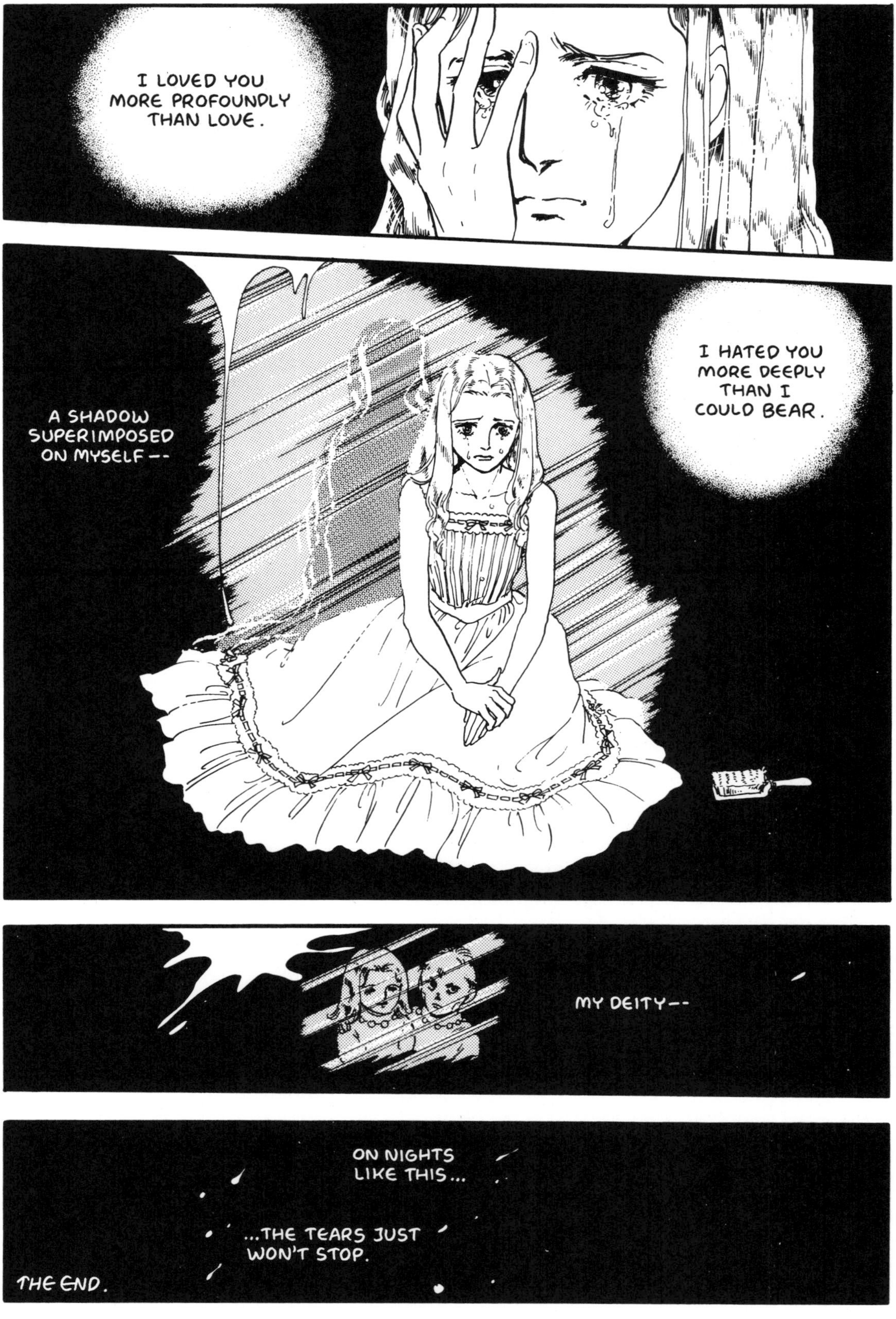
I LOVED YOU MORE PROFOUNDLY THAN LOVE.
I HATED YOU MORE DEEPLY THAN I COULD BEAR.
A SHADOW SUPERIMPOSED ON MYSELF--
MY DEITY--
ON NIGHTS LIKE THIS...
...THE TEARS JUST WON'T STOP.
THE END.

ANGEL | MIMIC

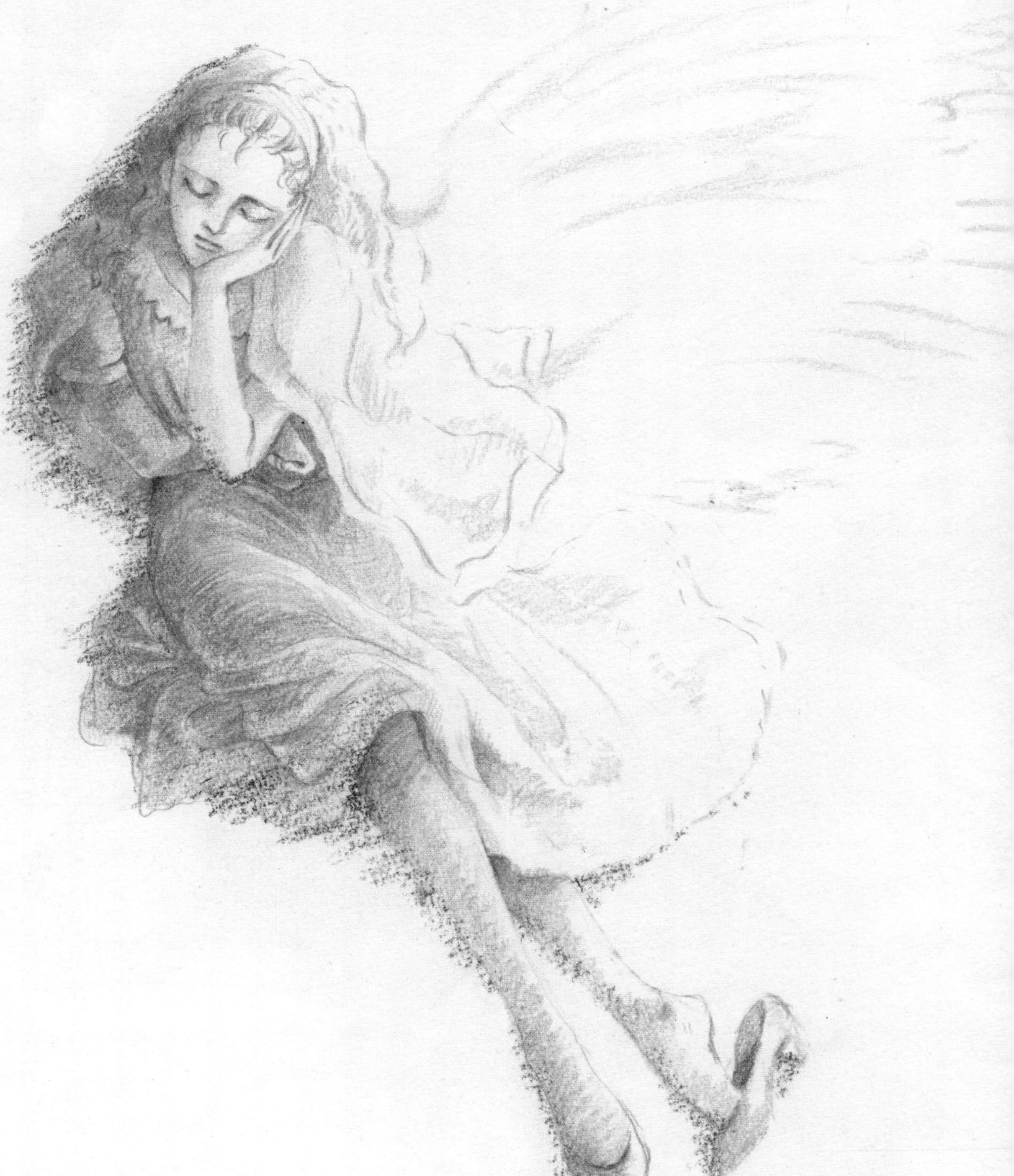

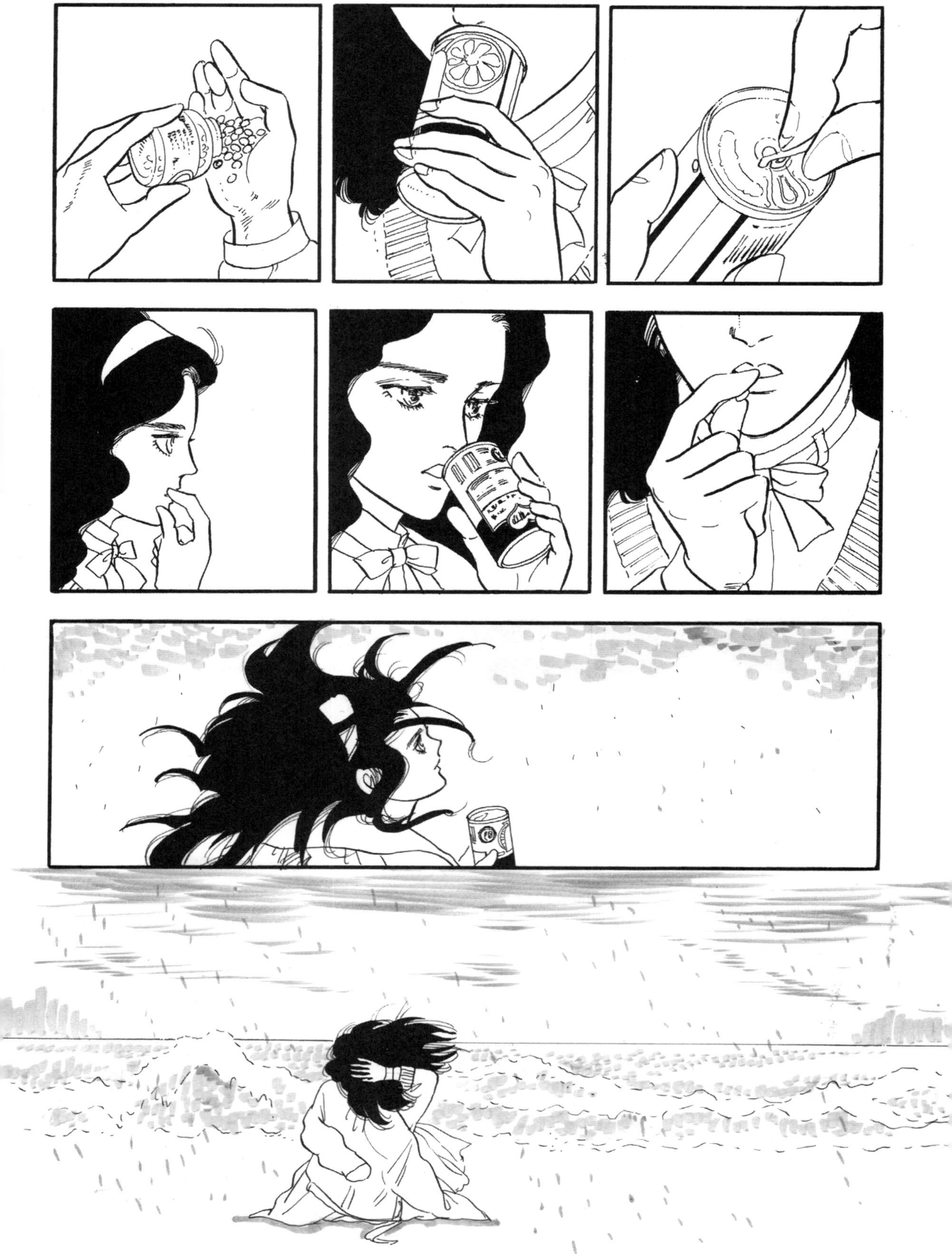

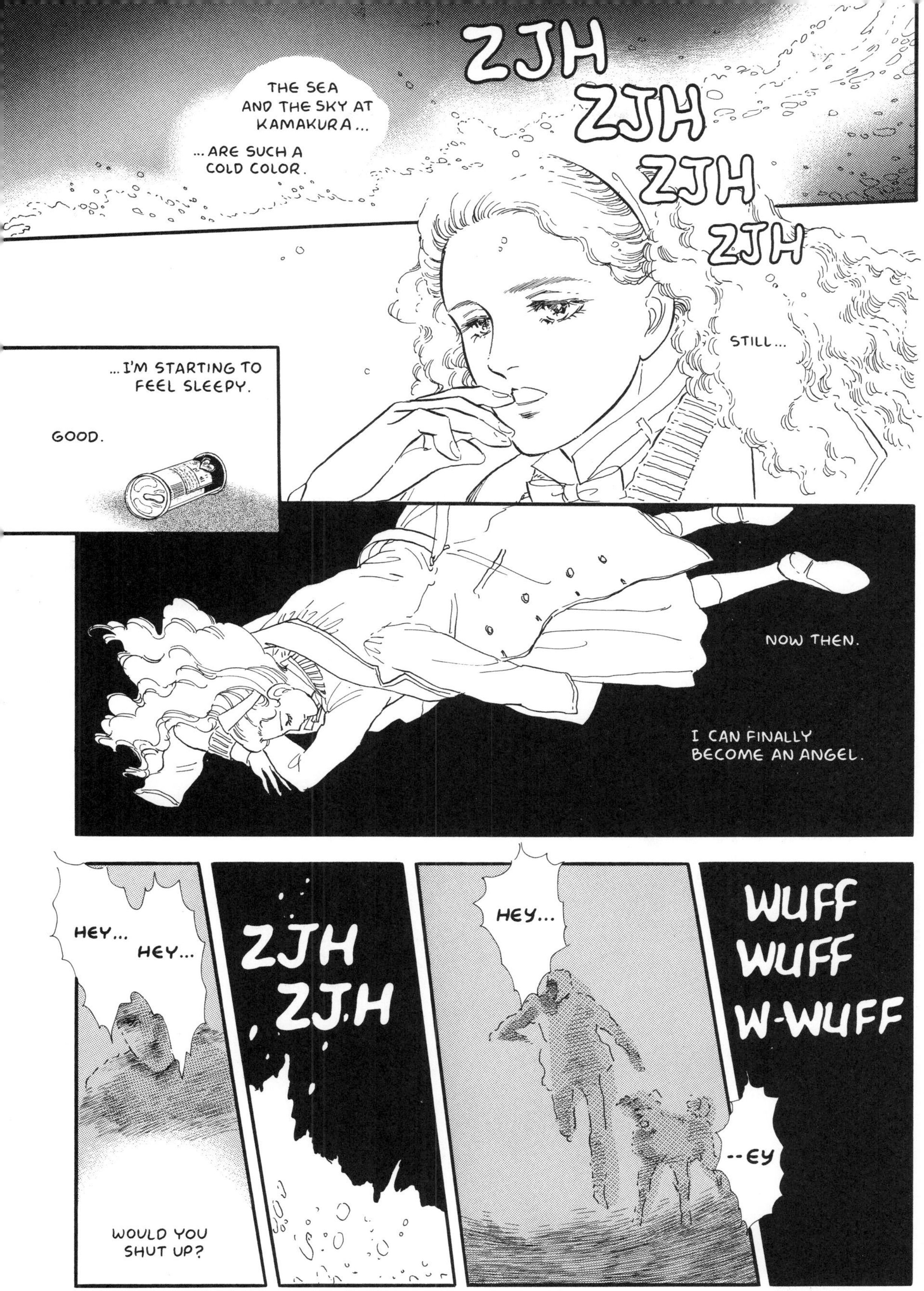
THE SEA AND THE SKY AT KAMAKURA...
...ARE SUCH A COLD COLOR.
ZJH
ZJH
ZJH
ZJH
STILL...
...I'M STARTING TO FEEL SLEEPY.
GOOD.
NOW THEN.
I CAN FINALLY BECOME AN ANGEL.
WUFF
WUFF
W-WUFF
--EY
HEY...
ZJH
ZJH
HEY...
HEY...
WOULD YOU SHUT UP?

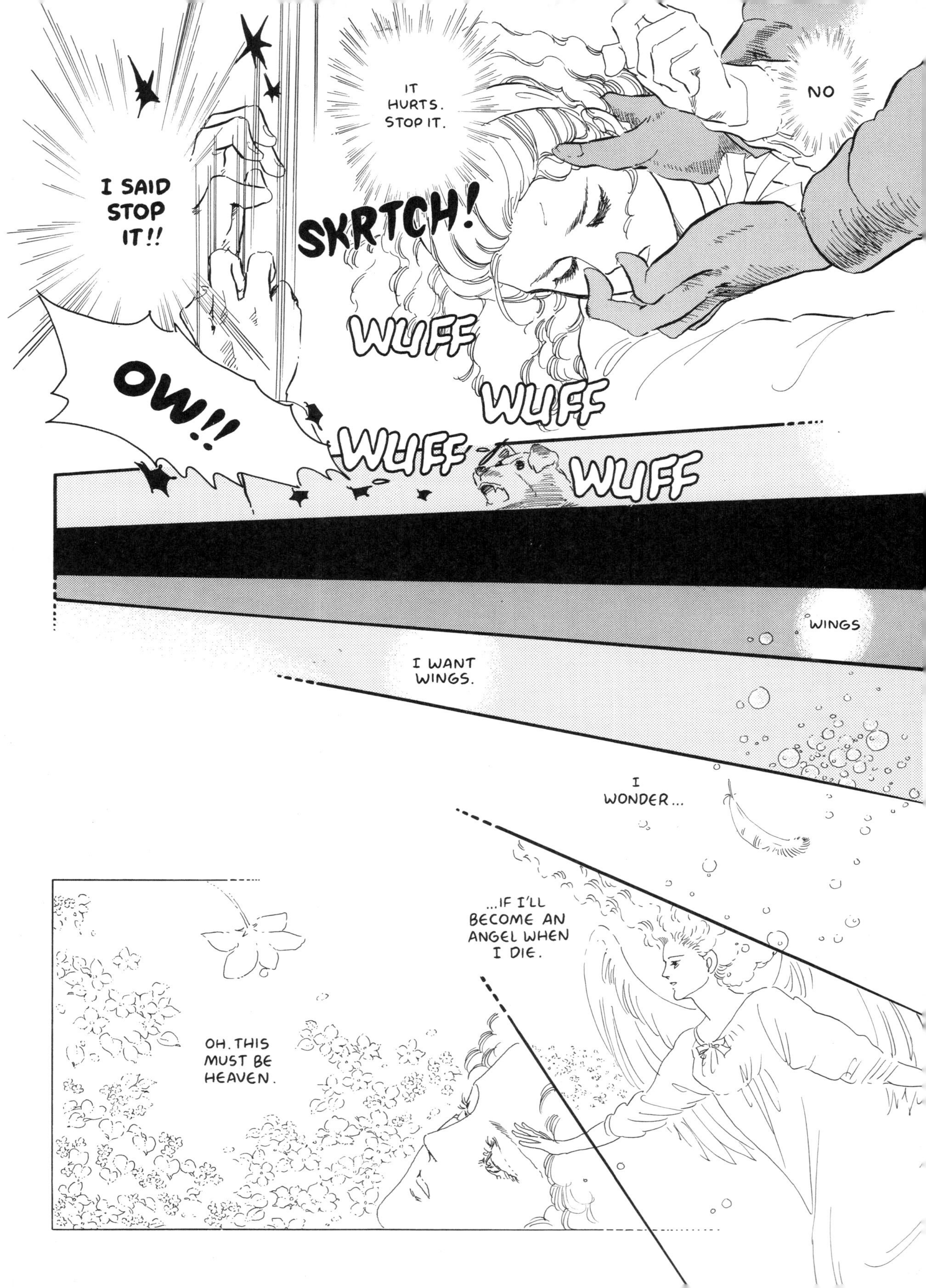
NO
IT HURTS. STOP IT.
SKRTCH!
I SAID STOP IT!!
WUFF
WUFF
WUFF
WUFF
OW!!
WINGS
I WANT WINGS.
I WONDER...
...IF I'LL BECOME AN ANGEL WHEN I DIE.
OH, THIS MUST BE HEAVEN.

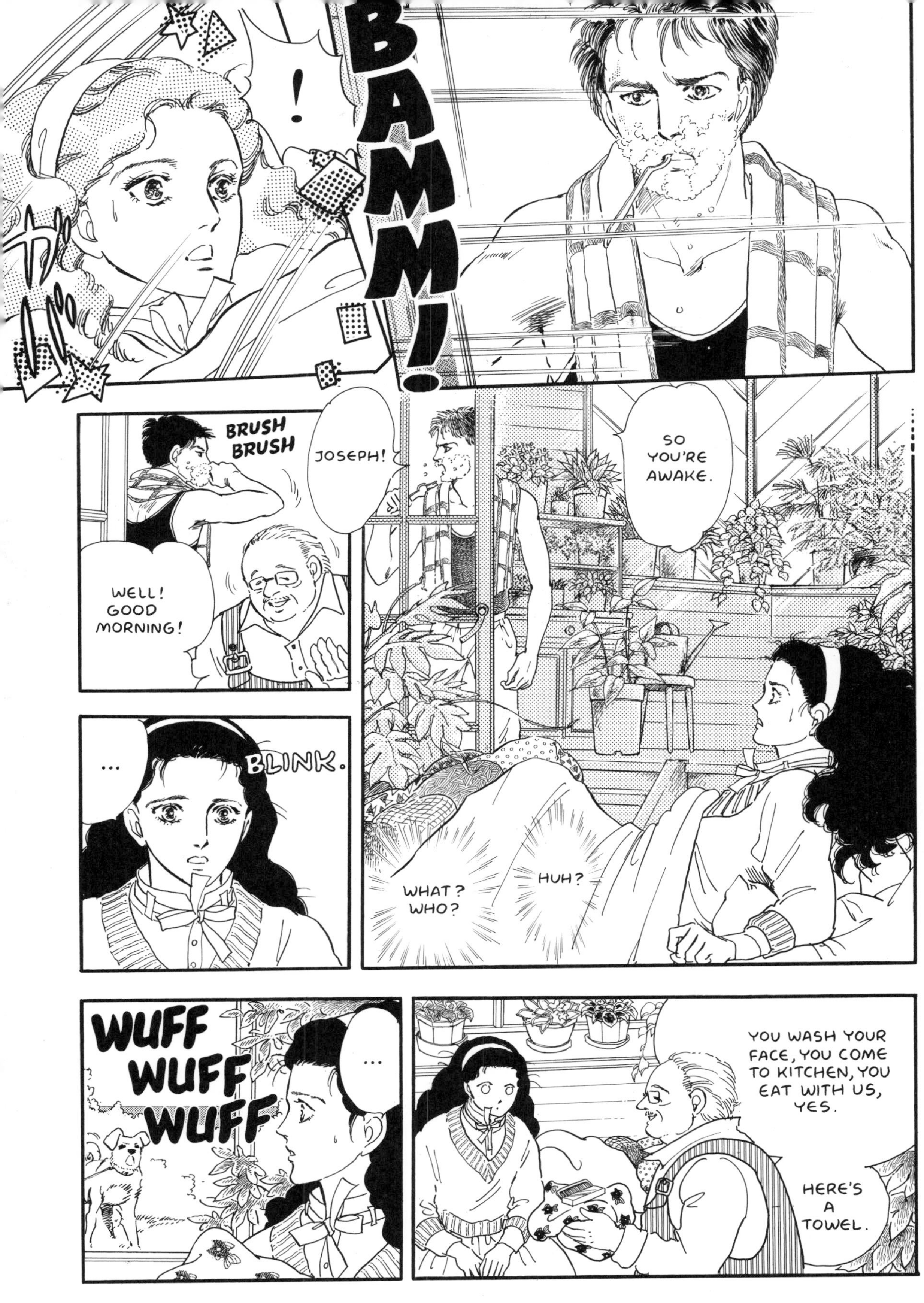
BAMM!
!
SO YOU'RE AWAKE.
JOSEPH!
HUH?
WHAT? WHO?
BRUSH BRUSH
WELL! GOOD MORNING!
BLINK.
...
YOU WASH YOUR FACE, YOU COME TO KITCHEN, YOU EAT WITH US, YES.
HERE'S A TOWEL.
...
WUFF WUFF WUFF

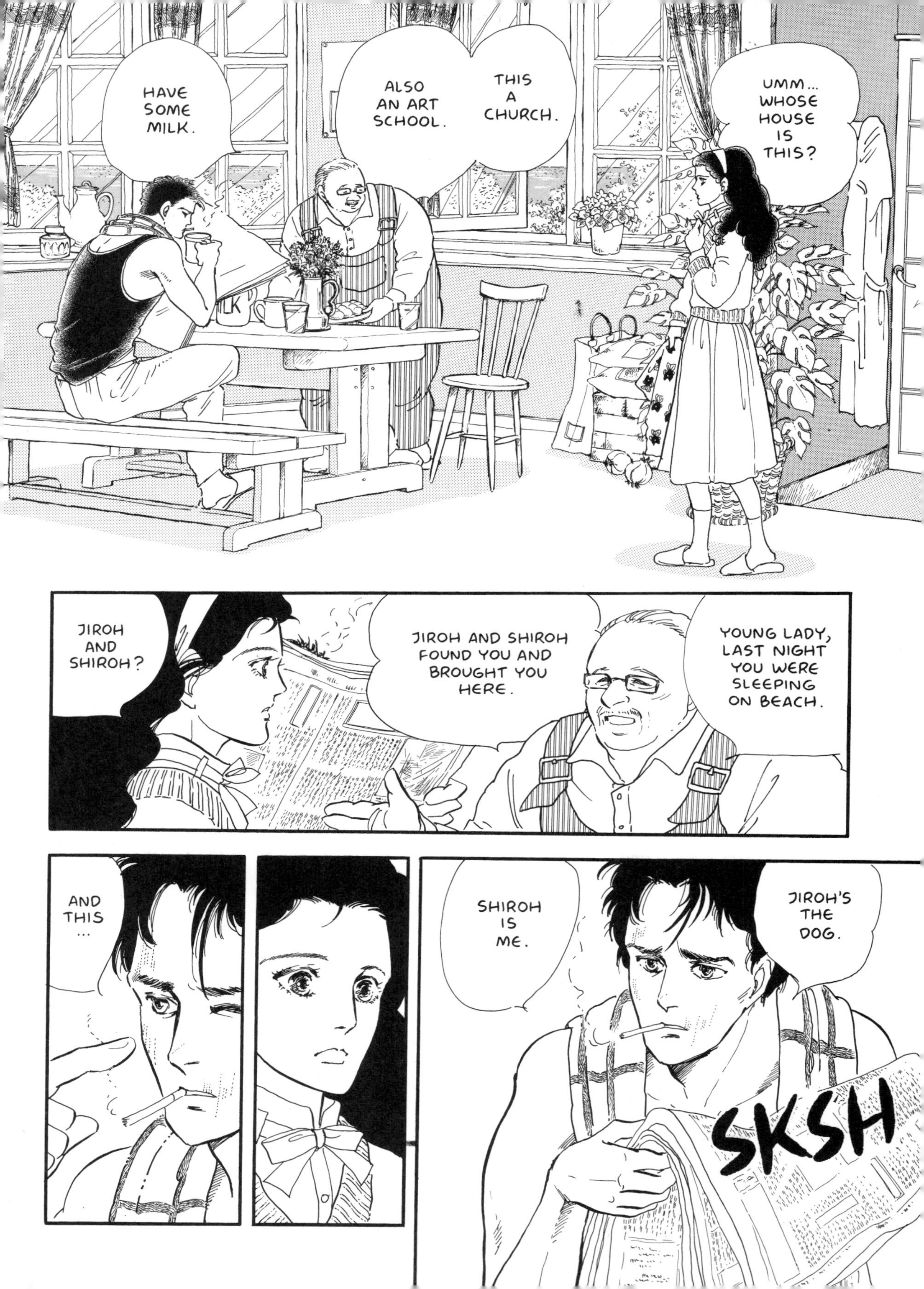
UMM... WHOSE HOUSE IS THIS?
THIS A CHURCH.
ALSO AN ART SCHOOL.
HAVE SOME MILK.
YOUNG LADY, LAST NIGHT YOU WERE SLEEPING ON BEACH.
JIROH AND SHIROH FOUND YOU AND BROUGHT YOU HERE.
JIROH AND SHIROH?
JIROH'S THE DOG.
SHIROH IS ME.
SKSH
AND THIS ...

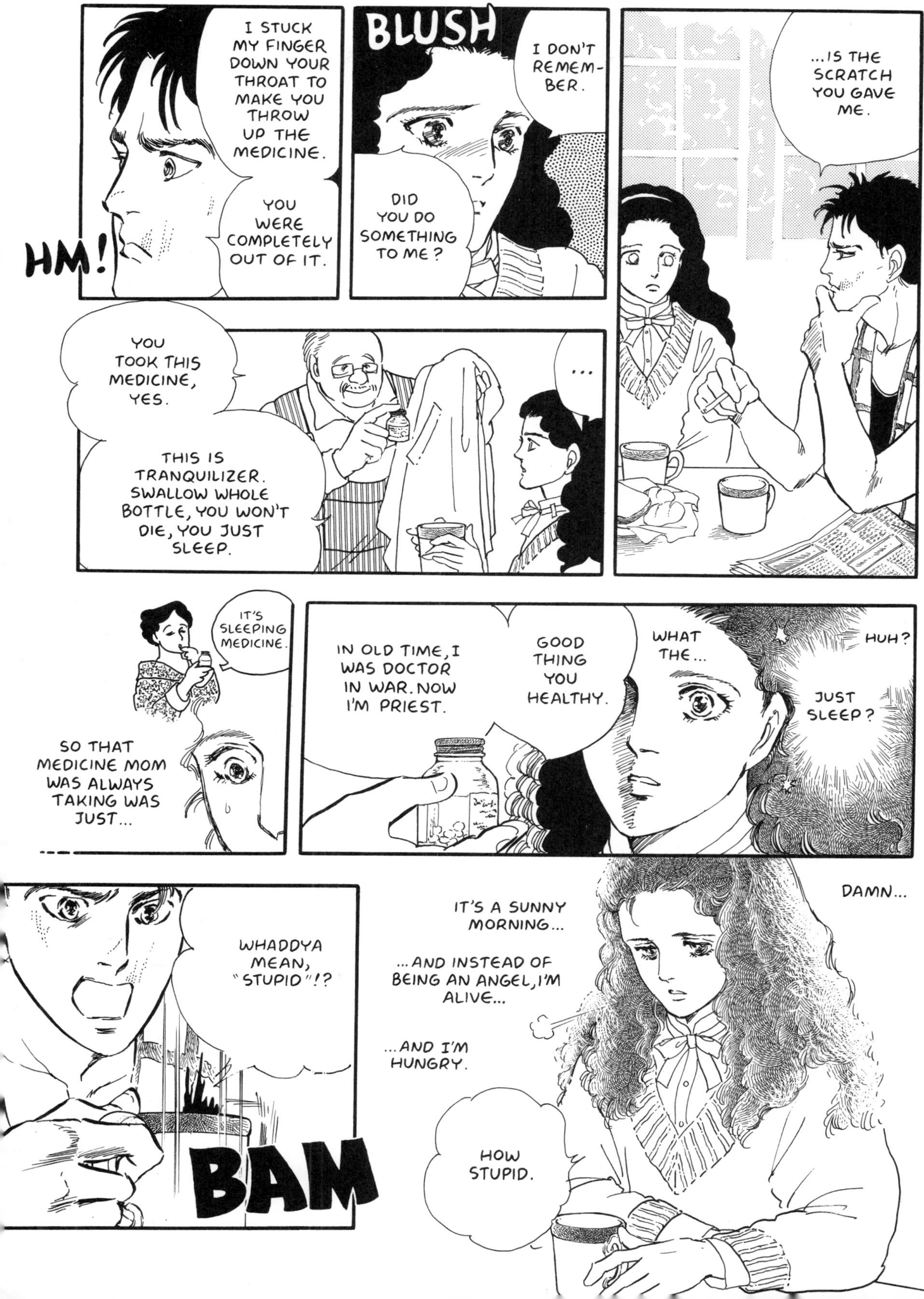
...IS THE SCRATCH YOU GAVE ME.
BLUSH
I DON'T REMEMBER.
DID YOU DO SOMETHING TO ME?
I STUCK MY FINGER DOWN YOUR THROAT TO MAKE YOU THROW UP THE MEDICINE.
YOU WERE COMPLETELY OUT OF IT.
HM!
...
YOU TOOK THIS MEDICINE, YES.
THIS IS TRANQUILIZER. SWALLOW WHOLE BOTTLE, YOU WON'T DIE, YOU JUST SLEEP.
HUH?
WHAT THE...
JUST SLEEP?
GOOD THING YOU HEALTHY.
IN OLD TIME, I WAS DOCTOR IN WAR. NOW I'M PRIEST.
IT'S SLEEPING MEDICINE.
SO THAT MEDICINE MOM WAS ALWAYS TAKING WAS JUST...

DAMN...
IT'S A SUNNY MORNING...
...AND INSTEAD OF BEING AN ANGEL, I'M ALIVE...
...AND I'M HUNGRY.
HOW STUPID.
WHADDYA MEAN, "STUPID"!?
BAM

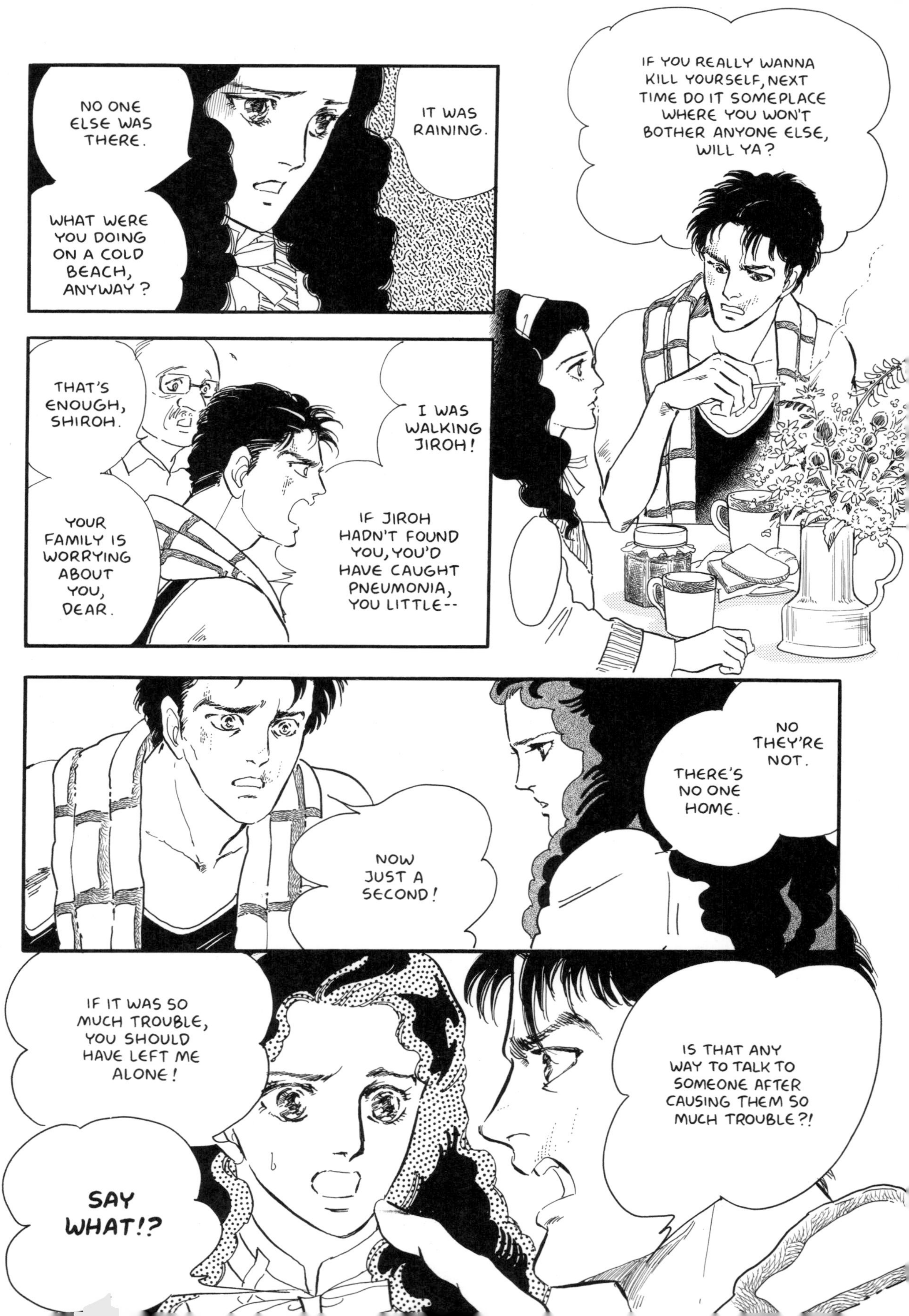
IF YOU REALLY WANNA KILL YOURSELF, NEXT TIME DO IT SOMEPLACE WHERE YOU WON'T BOTHER ANYONE ELSE, WILL YA?
IT WAS RAINING.
NO ONE ELSE WAS THERE.
WHAT WERE YOU DOING ON A COLD BEACH, ANYWAY?
I WAS WALKING JIROH!
IF JIROH HADN'T FOUND YOU, YOU'D HAVE CAUGHT PNEUMONIA, YOU LITTLE--
THAT'S ENOUGH, SHIROH.
YOUR FAMILY IS WORRYING ABOUT YOU, DEAR.
NO THEY'RE NOT.
THERE'S NO ONE HOME.
NOW JUST A SECOND!
IS THAT ANY WAY TO TALK TO SOMEONE AFTER CAUSING THEM SO MUCH TROUBLE?!
IF IT WAS SO MUCH TROUBLE, YOU SHOULD HAVE LEFT ME ALONE!
SAY WHAT!?

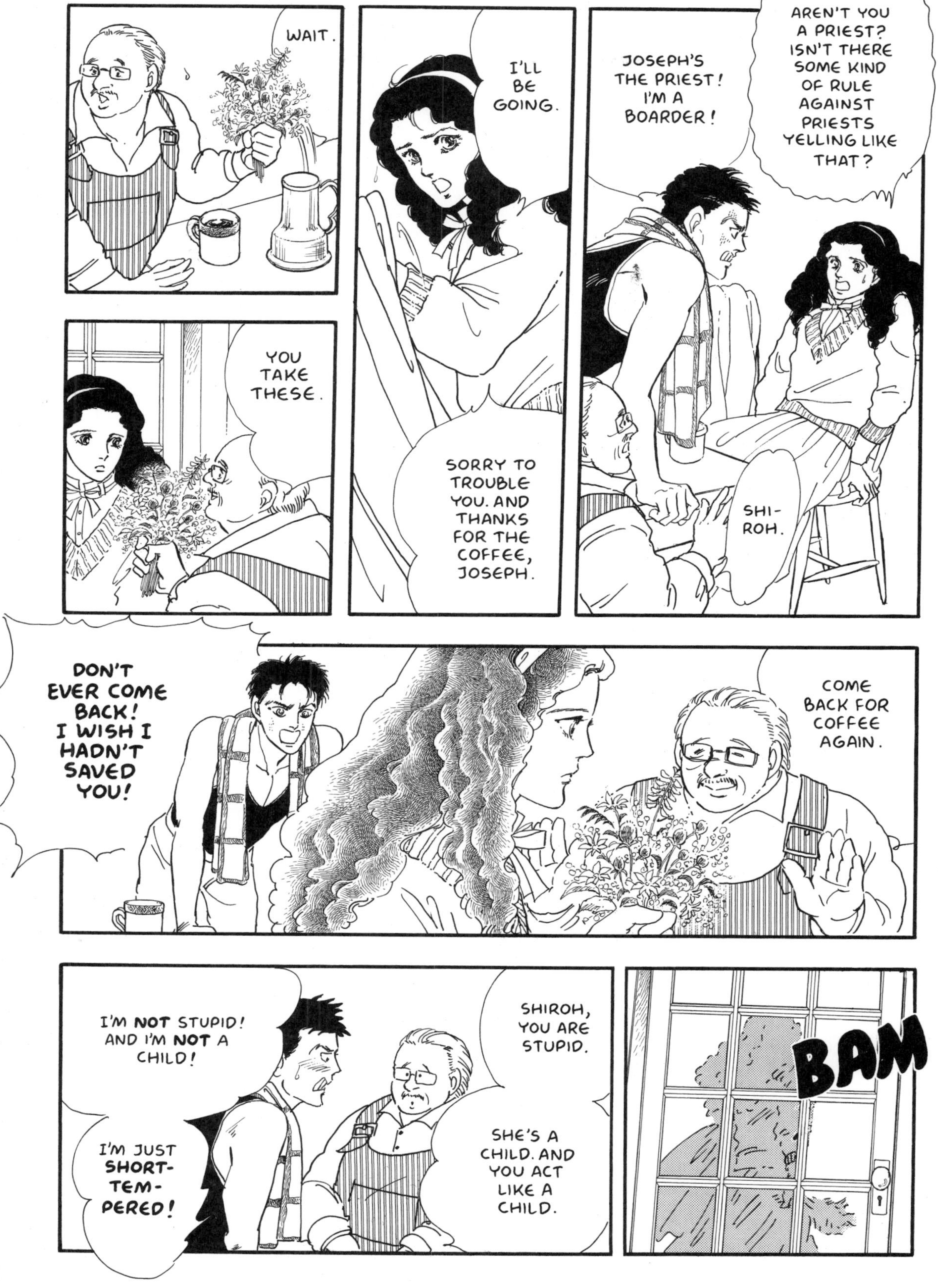
AREN'T YOU A PRIEST? ISN'T THERE SOME KIND OF RULE AGAINST PRIESTS YELLING LIKE THAT?
JOSEPH'S THE PRIEST! I'M A BOARDER!
SHI-ROH.
I'LL BE GOING.
SORRY TO TROUBLE YOU. AND THANKS FOR THE COFFEE, JOSEPH.
WAIT.
YOU TAKE THESE.
COME BACK FOR COFFEE AGAIN.
DON'T EVER COME BACK! I WISH I HADN'T SAVED YOU!
BAM
SHIROH, YOU ARE STUPID.
I'M **NOT** STUPID! AND I'M **NOT** A CHILD!
SHE'S A CHILD. AND YOU ACT LIKE A CHILD.
I'M JUST SHORT-TEM-PERED!

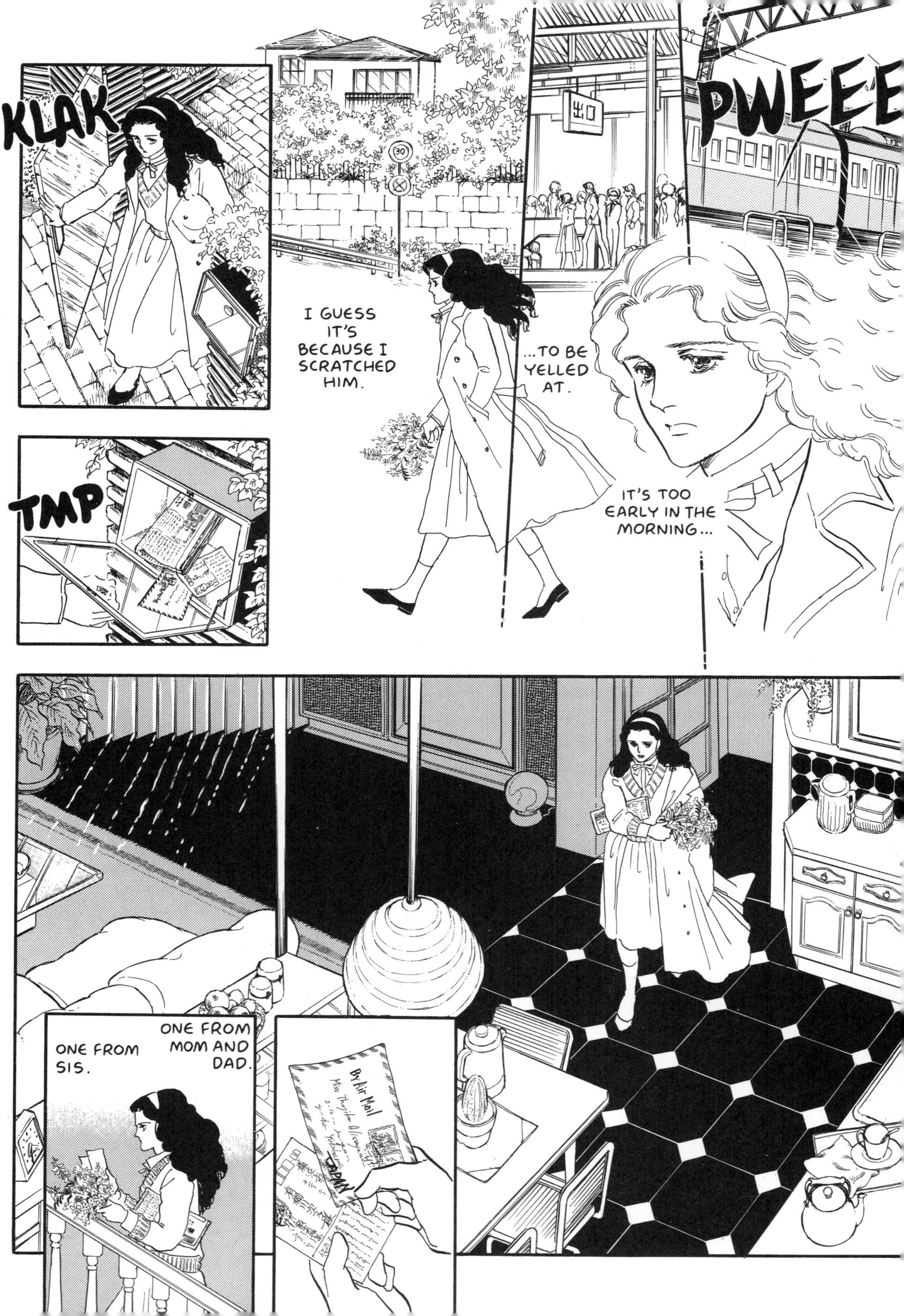
PWEEE
IT'S TOO EARLY IN THE MORNING...
...TO BE YELLED AT.
I GUESS IT'S BECAUSE I SCRATCHED HIM.
KLAK
TMP
By Air Mail
JAPAN
ONE FROM MOM AND DAD.
ONE FROM SIS.

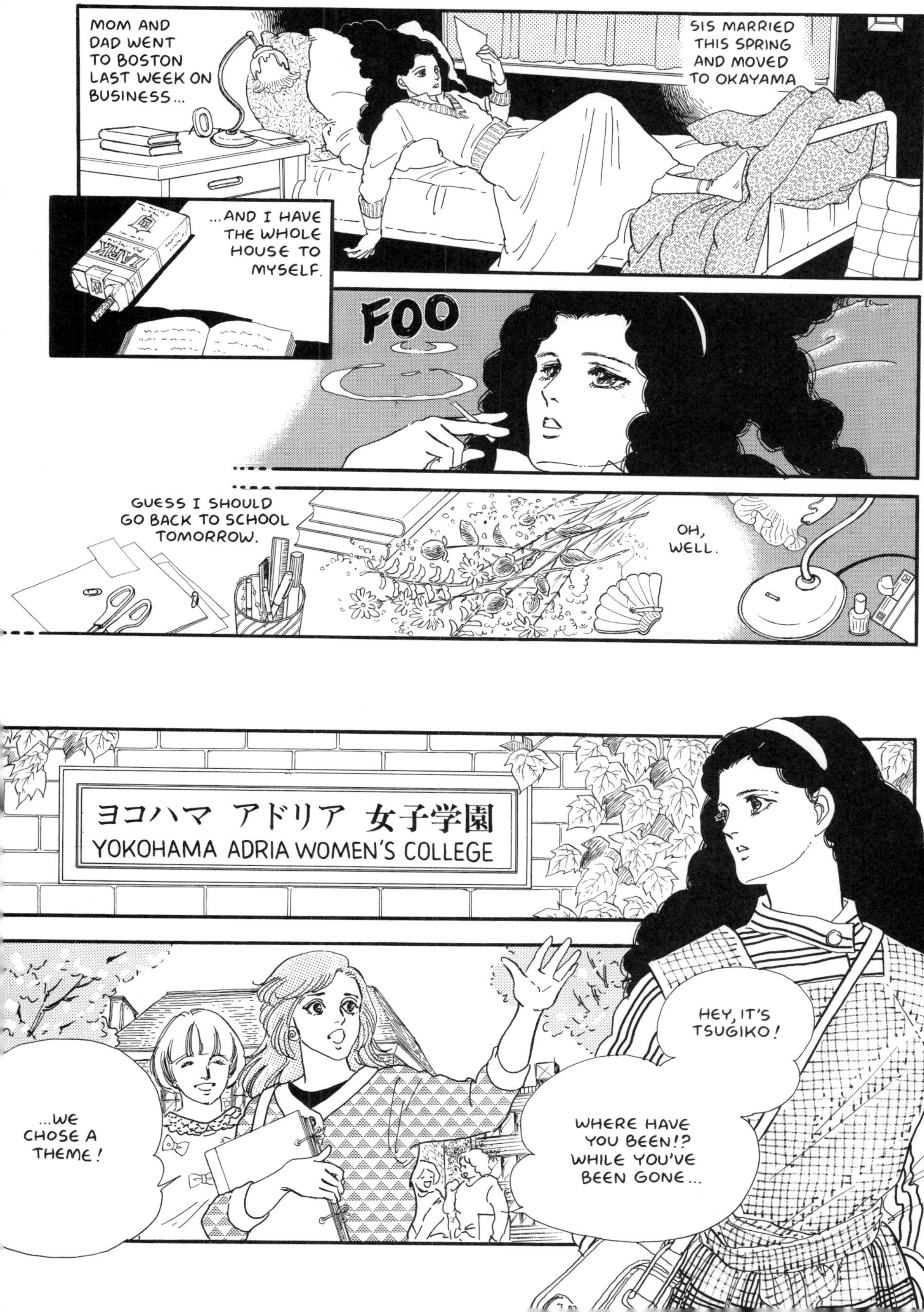
SIS MARRIED THIS SPRING AND MOVED TO OKAYAMA
MOM AND DAD WENT TO BOSTON LAST WEEK ON BUSINESS...
...AND I HAVE THE WHOLE HOUSE TO MYSELF.
FOO
OH, WELL.
GUESS I SHOULD GO BACK TO SCHOOL TOMORROW.
ヨコハマ アドリア 女子学園
YOKOHAMA ADRIA WOMEN'S COLLEGE
HEY, IT'S TSUGIKO!
WHERE HAVE YOU BEEN!? WHILE YOU'VE BEEN GONE...
...WE CHOSE A THEME!

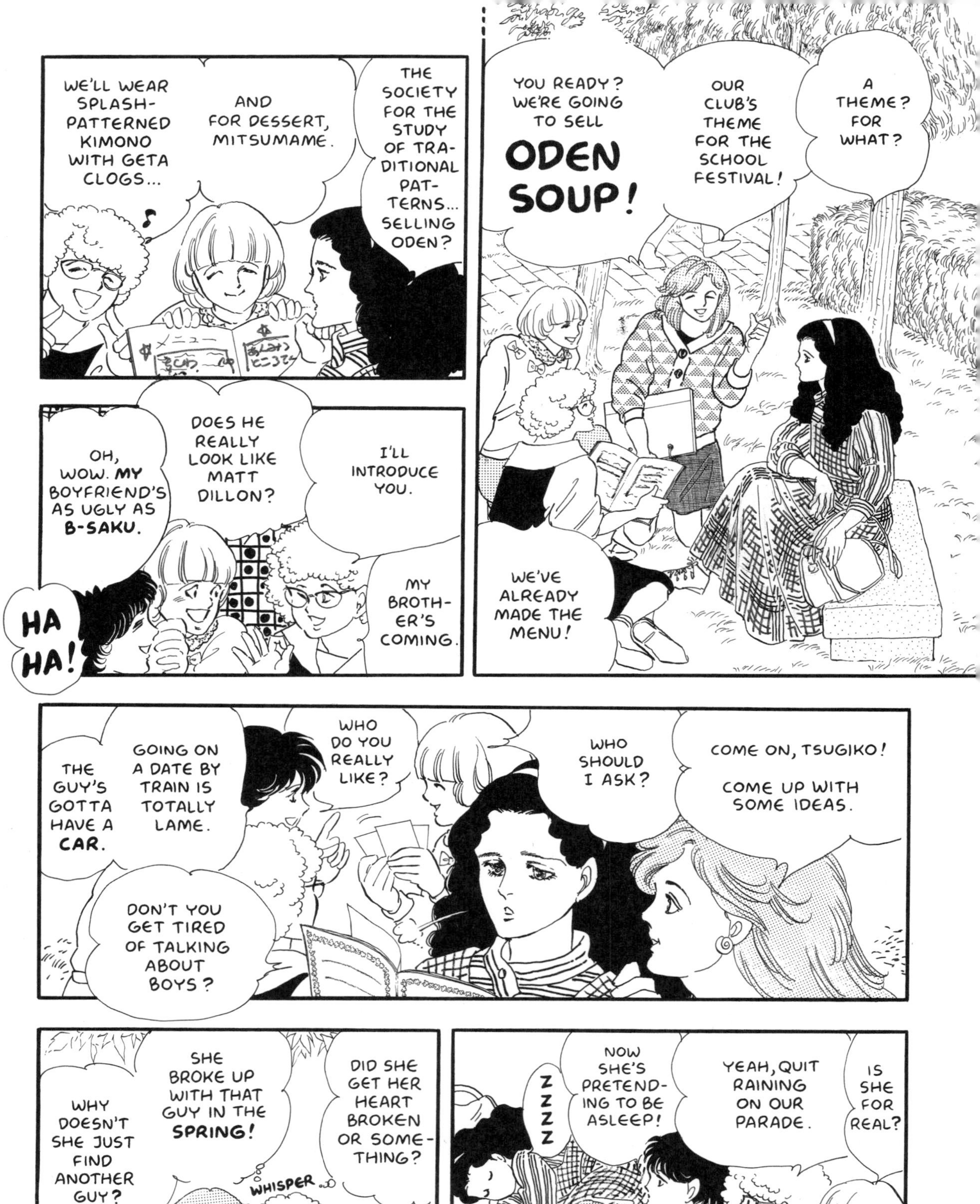
A THEME? FOR WHAT?
OUR CLUB'S THEME FOR THE SCHOOL FESTIVAL!
YOU READY? WE'RE GOING TO SELL ODEN SOUP!
WE'VE ALREADY MADE THE MENU!
THE SOCIETY FOR THE STUDY OF TRADITIONAL PATTERNS... SELLING ODEN?
AND FOR DESSERT, MITSUMAME.
WE'LL WEAR SPLASH-PATTERNED KIMONO WITH GETA CLOGS...
I'LL INTRODUCE YOU.
DOES HE REALLY LOOK LIKE MATT DILLON?
OH, WOW. MY BOYFRIEND'S AS UGLY AS B-SAKU.
MY BROTHER'S COMING.
HA HA!
COME ON, TSUGIKO! COME UP WITH SOME IDEAS.
WHO SHOULD I ASK?
WHO DO YOU REALLY LIKE?
GOING ON A DATE BY TRAIN IS TOTALLY LAME.
THE GUY'S GOTTA HAVE A CAR.
DON'T YOU GET TIRED OF TALKING ABOUT BOYS?
IS SHE FOR REAL?
YEAH, QUIT RAINING ON OUR PARADE.
NOW SHE'S PRETENDING TO BE ASLEEP!
ZZZZ
DID SHE GET HER HEART BROKEN OR SOMETHING?
SHE BROKE UP WITH THAT GUY IN THE SPRING!
WHISPER
WHY DOESN'T SHE JUST FIND ANOTHER GUY?

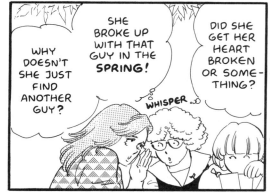

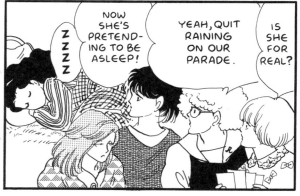

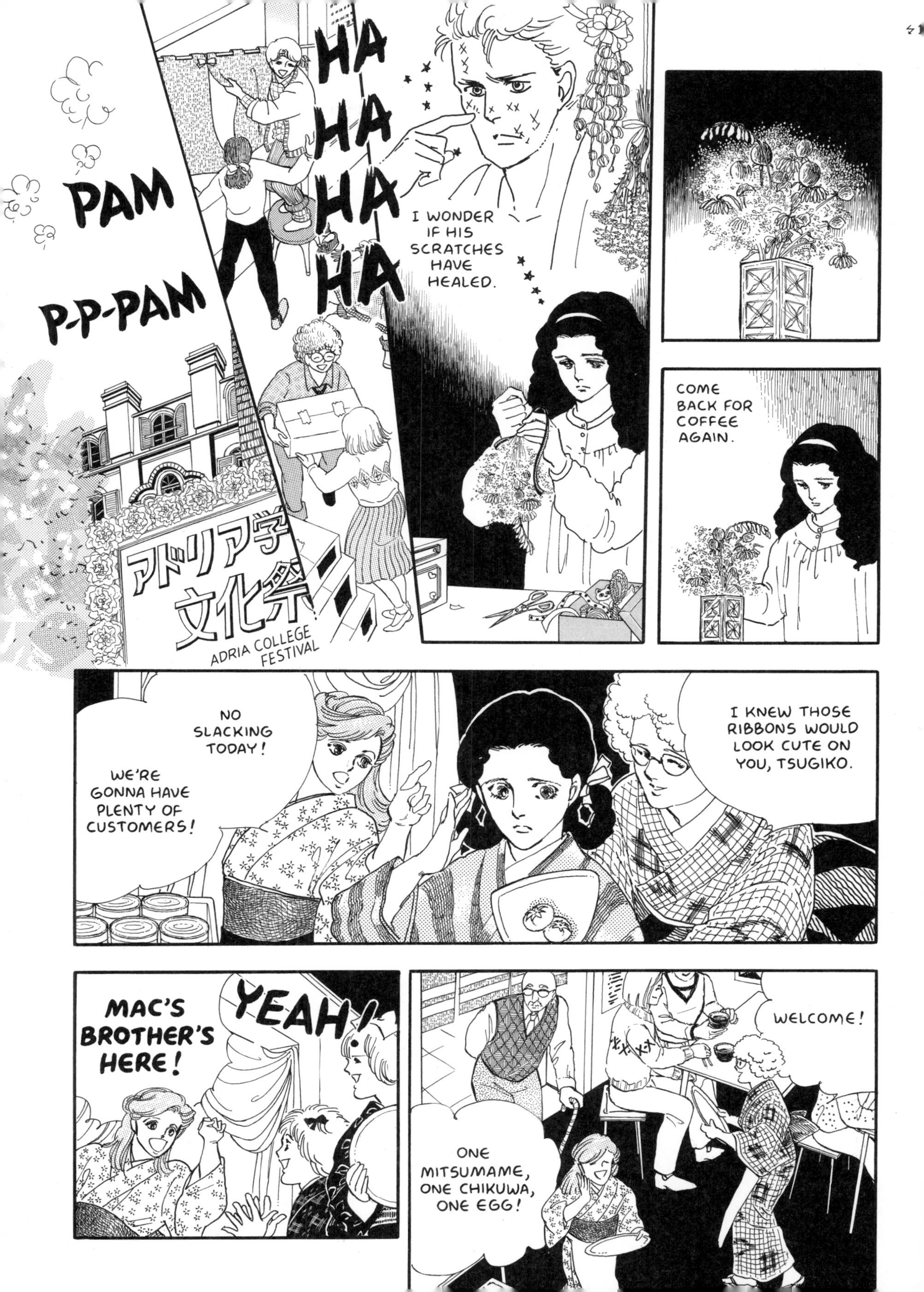
COME BACK FOR COFFEE AGAIN.
I WONDER IF HIS SCRATCHES HAVE HEALED.
HA HA HA HA
PAM
P-P-PAM
アドリア学
文化祭
ADRIA COLLEGE FESTIVAL
I KNEW THOSE RIBBONS WOULD LOOK CUTE ON YOU, TSUGIKO.
NO SLACKING TODAY!
WE'RE GONNA HAVE PLENTY OF CUSTOMERS!
WELCOME!
ONE MITSUMAME, ONE CHIKUWA, ONE EGG!
YEAH!
MAC'S BROTHER'S HERE!

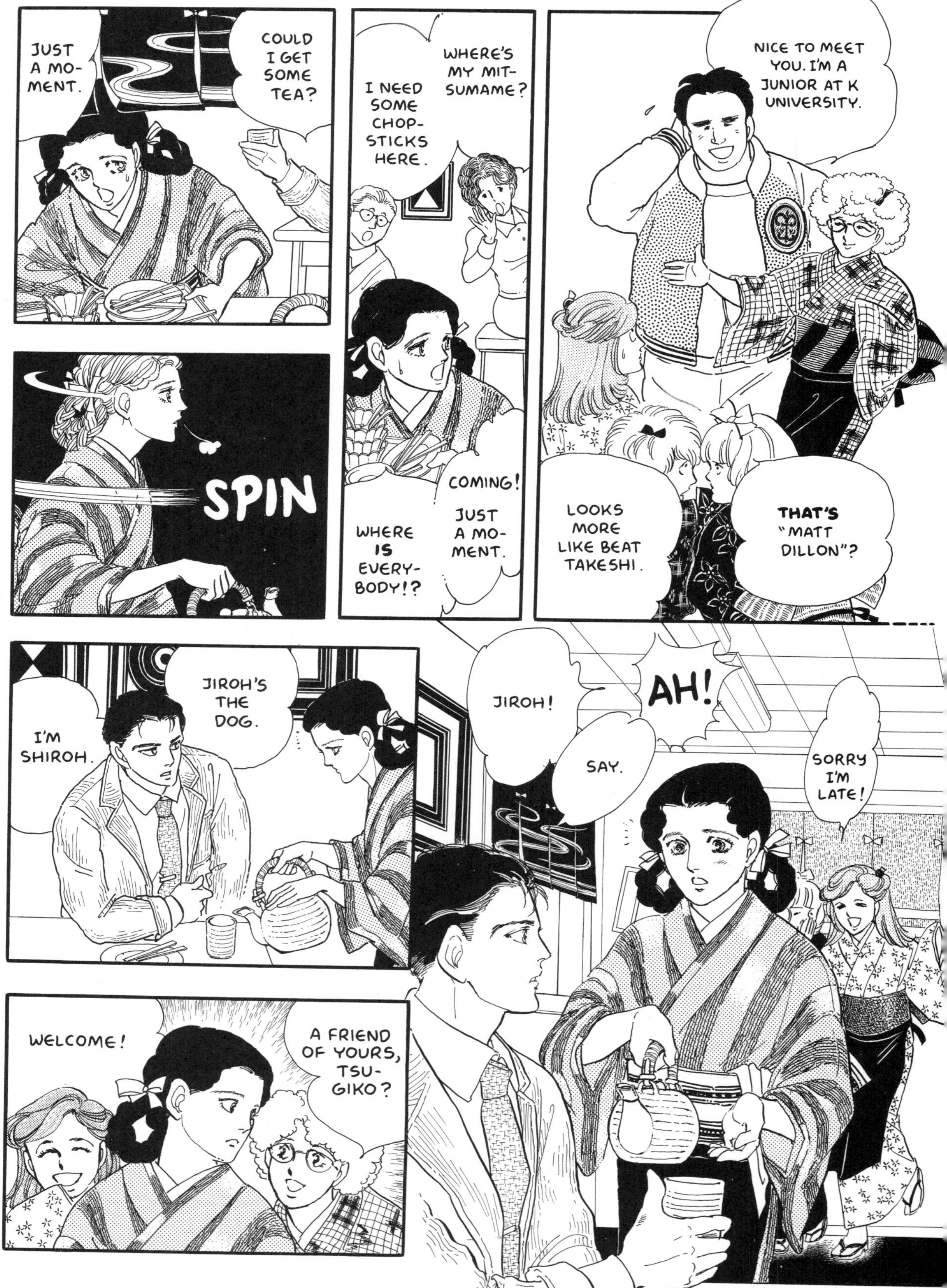
NICE TO MEET YOU. I'M A JUNIOR AT K UNIVERSITY.
THAT'S "MATT DILLON"?
LOOKS MORE LIKE BEAT TAKESHI.
WHERE'S MY MITSUMAME?
I NEED SOME CHOPSTICKS HERE.
COMING!
JUST A MOMENT.
WHERE IS EVERYBODY!?
COULD I GET SOME TEA?
JUST A MOMENT.
SPIN
SORRY I'M LATE!
AH!
JIROH!
SAY.
JIROH'S THE DOG.
I'M SHIROH.
A FRIEND OF YOURS, TSUGIKO?
WELCOME!

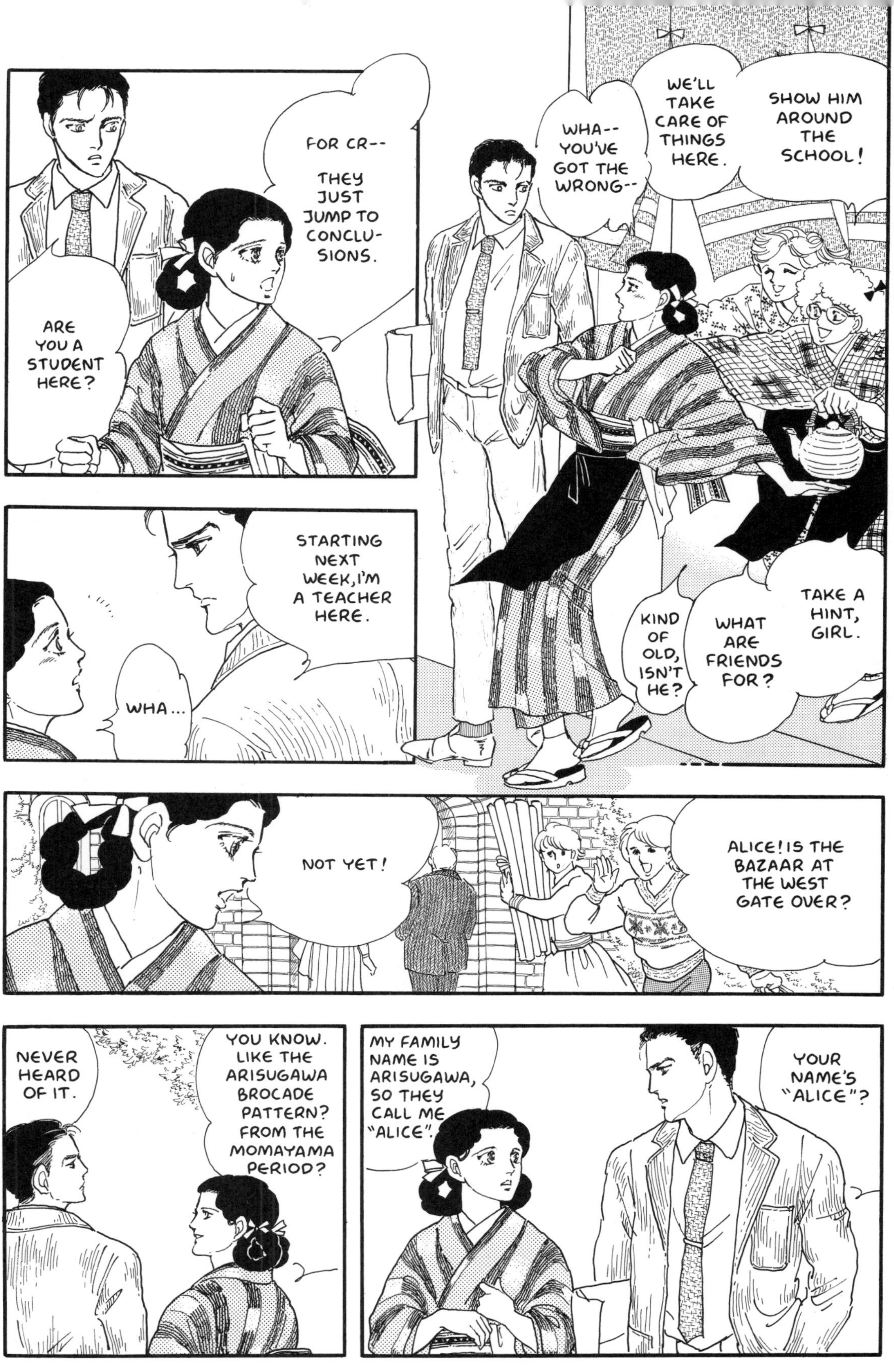
SHOW HIM AROUND THE SCHOOL!
WE'LL TAKE CARE OF THINGS HERE.
WHA-- YOU'VE GOT THE WRONG--
TAKE A HINT, GIRL.
WHAT ARE FRIENDS FOR?
KIND OF OLD, ISN'T HE?
FOR CR-- THEY JUST JUMP TO CONCLUSIONS.
ARE YOU A STUDENT HERE?
STARTING NEXT WEEK, I'M A TEACHER HERE.
WHA...
ALICE! IS THE BAZAAR AT THE WEST GATE OVER?
NOT YET!
YOUR NAME'S "ALICE"?
MY FAMILY NAME IS ARISUGAWA, SO THEY CALL ME "ALICE".
YOU KNOW. LIKE THE ARISUGAWA BROCADE PATTERN? FROM THE MOMAYAMA PERIOD?
NEVER HEARD OF IT.

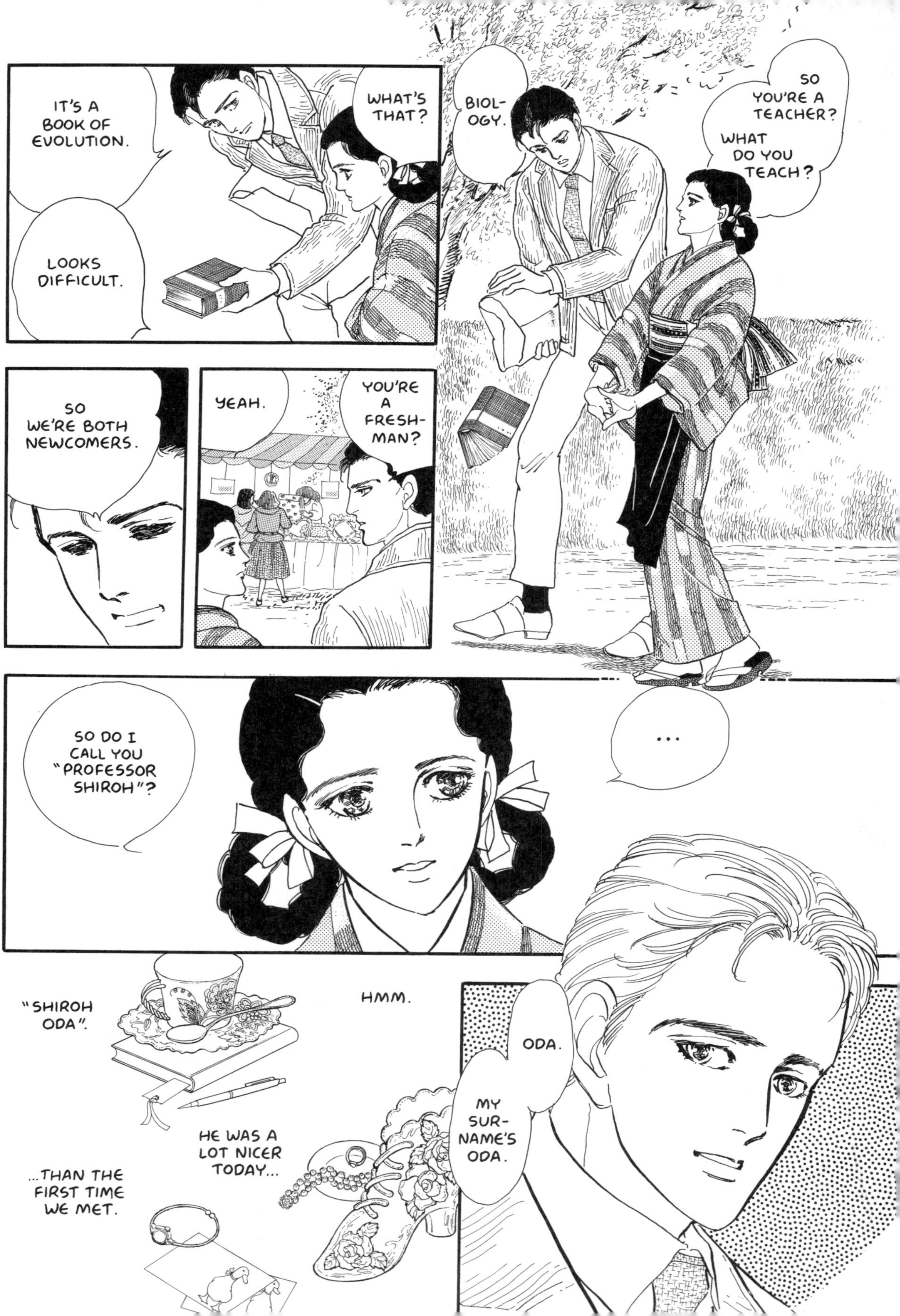
SO YOU'RE A TEACHER? WHAT DO YOU TEACH?
BIOL-OGY.
WHAT'S THAT?
IT'S A BOOK OF EVOLUTION.
LOOKS DIFFICULT.
YOU'RE A FRESH-MAN?
YEAH.
SO WE'RE BOTH NEWCOMERS.
...
SO DO I CALL YOU "PROFESSOR SHIROH"?
ODA.
MY SUR-NAME'S ODA.
HMM.
"SHIROH ODA".
HE WAS A LOT NICER TODAY...
...THAN THE FIRST TIME WE MET.

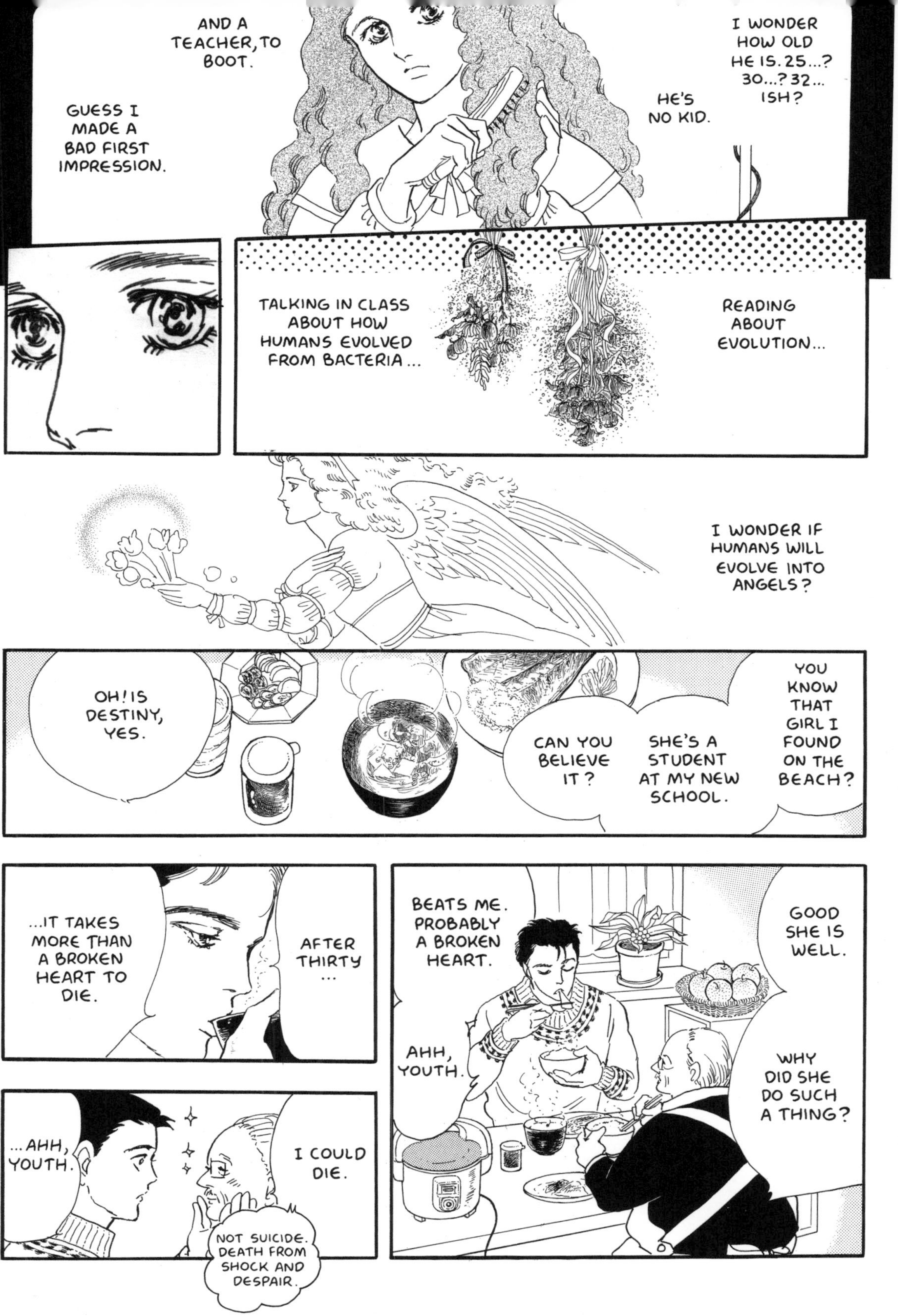
I WONDER HOW OLD HE IS. 25...? 30...? 32... ISH?
HE'S NO KID.
AND A TEACHER, TO BOOT.
GUESS I MADE A BAD FIRST IMPRESSION.
READING ABOUT EVOLUTION...
TALKING IN CLASS ABOUT HOW HUMANS EVOLVED FROM BACTERIA...
I WONDER IF HUMANS WILL EVOLVE INTO ANGELS?
YOU KNOW THAT GIRL I FOUND ON THE BEACH?
SHE'S A STUDENT AT MY NEW SCHOOL.
CAN YOU BELIEVE IT?
OH! IS DESTINY, YES.
GOOD SHE IS WELL.
WHY DID SHE DO SUCH A THING?
BEATS ME. PROBABLY A BROKEN HEART.
AHH, YOUTH.
AFTER THIRTY...
...IT TAKES MORE THAN A BROKEN HEART TO DIE.
I COULD DIE.
NOT SUICIDE. DEATH FROM SHOCK AND DESPAIR.
...AHH, YOUTH.

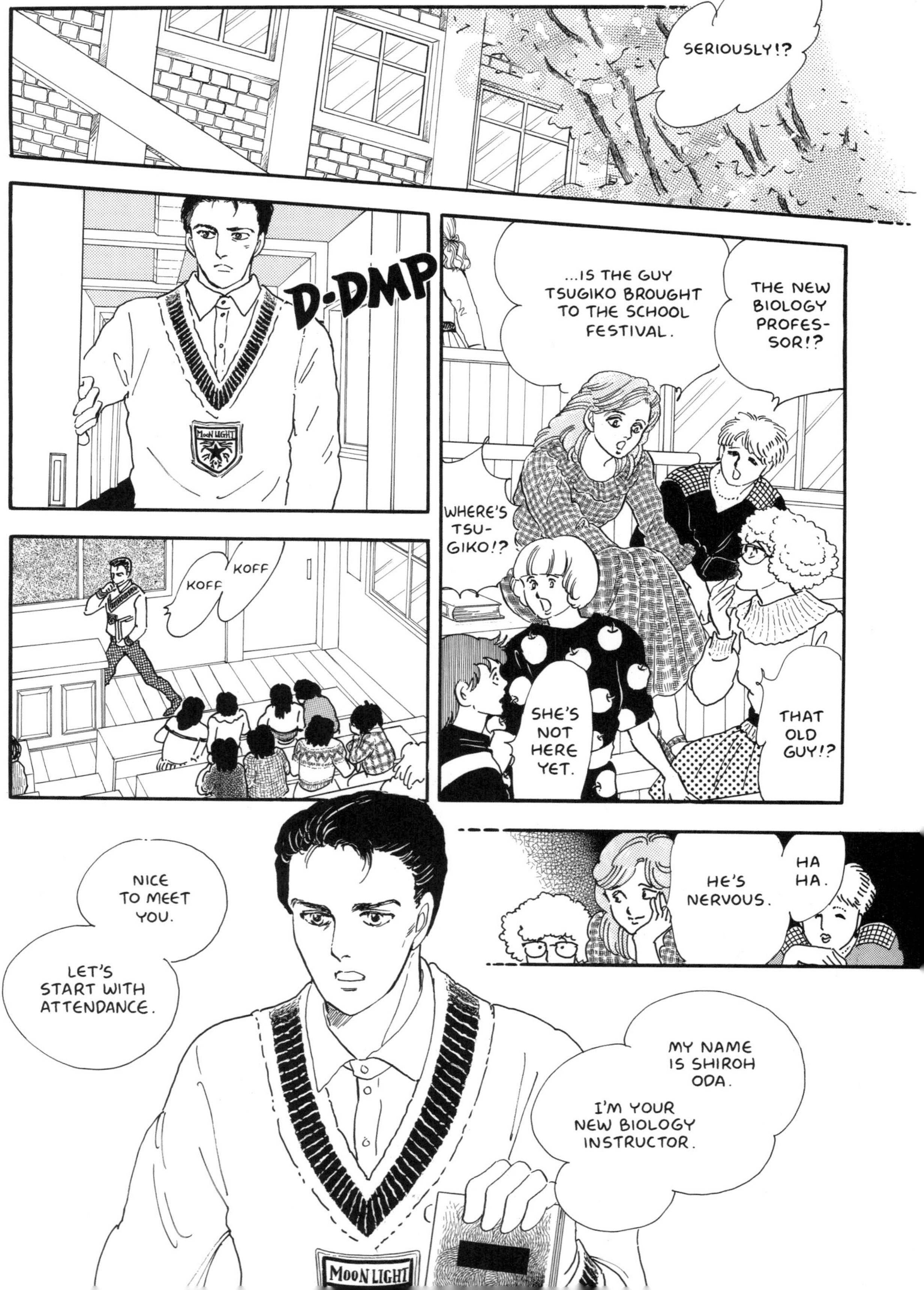
SERIOUSLY!?
THE NEW BIOLOGY PROFES-SOR!?
...IS THE GUY TSUGIKO BROUGHT TO THE SCHOOL FESTIVAL.
WHERE'S TSU-GIKO!?
THAT OLD GUY!?
SHE'S NOT HERE YET.
D-DMP
KOFF
KOFF
HA HA.
HE'S NERVOUS.
MY NAME IS SHIROH ODA.
I'M YOUR NEW BIOLOGY INSTRUCTOR.
NICE TO MEET YOU.
LET'S START WITH ATTENDANCE.
MOON LIGHT

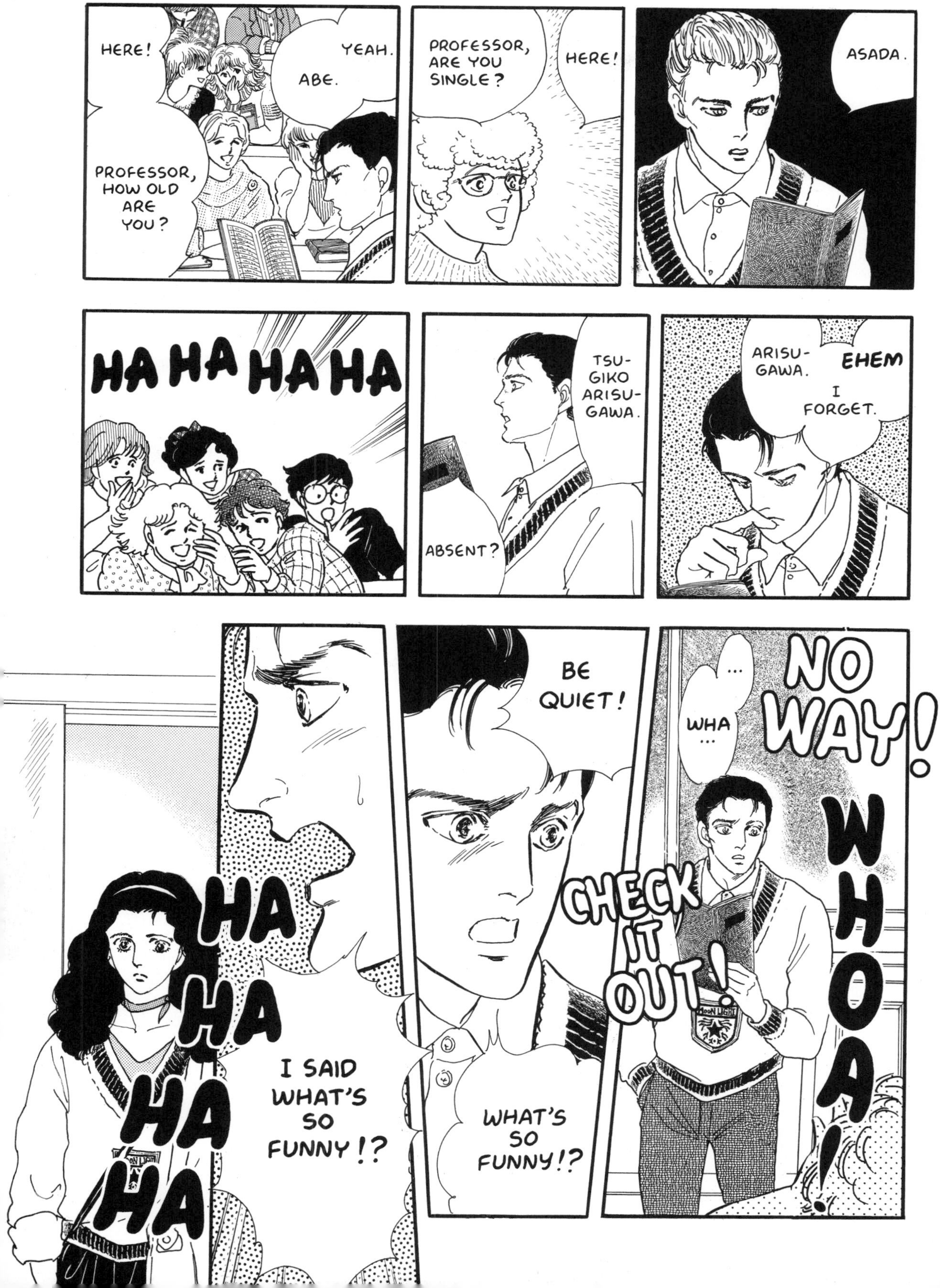
ASADA.
HERE!
PROFESSOR, ARE YOU SINGLE?
YEAH.
ABE.
HERE!
PROFESSOR, HOW OLD ARE YOU?
ARISU-GAWA.
EHEM
I FORGET.
TSU-GIKO ARISU-GAWA.
ABSENT?
HA HA HA HA
NO WAY!
...
WHA...
WHOA!
CHECK IT OUT!
BE QUIET!
WHAT'S SO FUNNY!?
HA HA HA HA
I SAID WHAT'S SO FUNNY!?

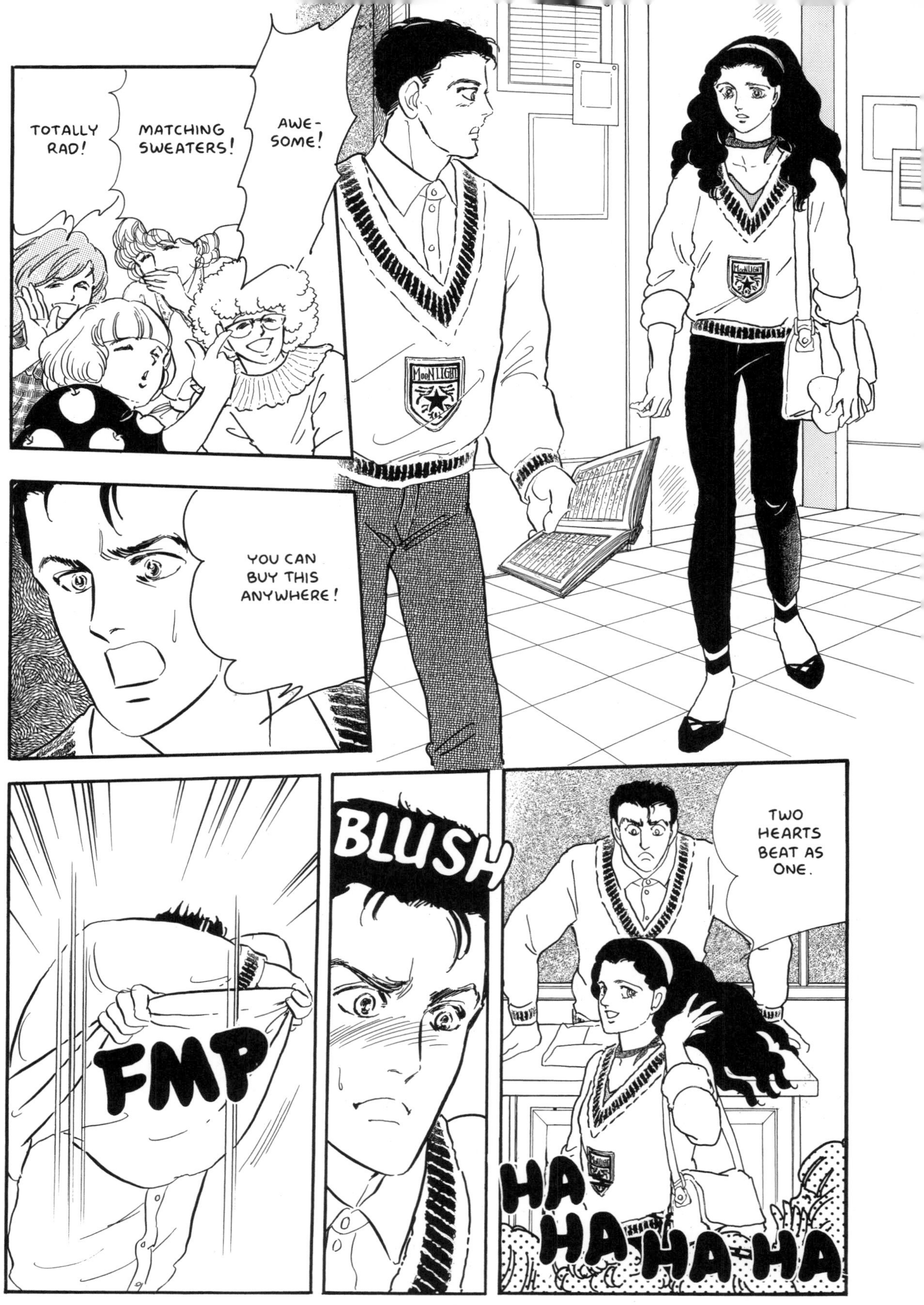
AWE-SOME!
MATCHING SWEATERS!
TOTALLY RAD!
YOU CAN BUY THIS ANYWHERE!
TWO HEARTS BEAT AS ONE.
HA HA HA HA HA
BLUSH
FMP

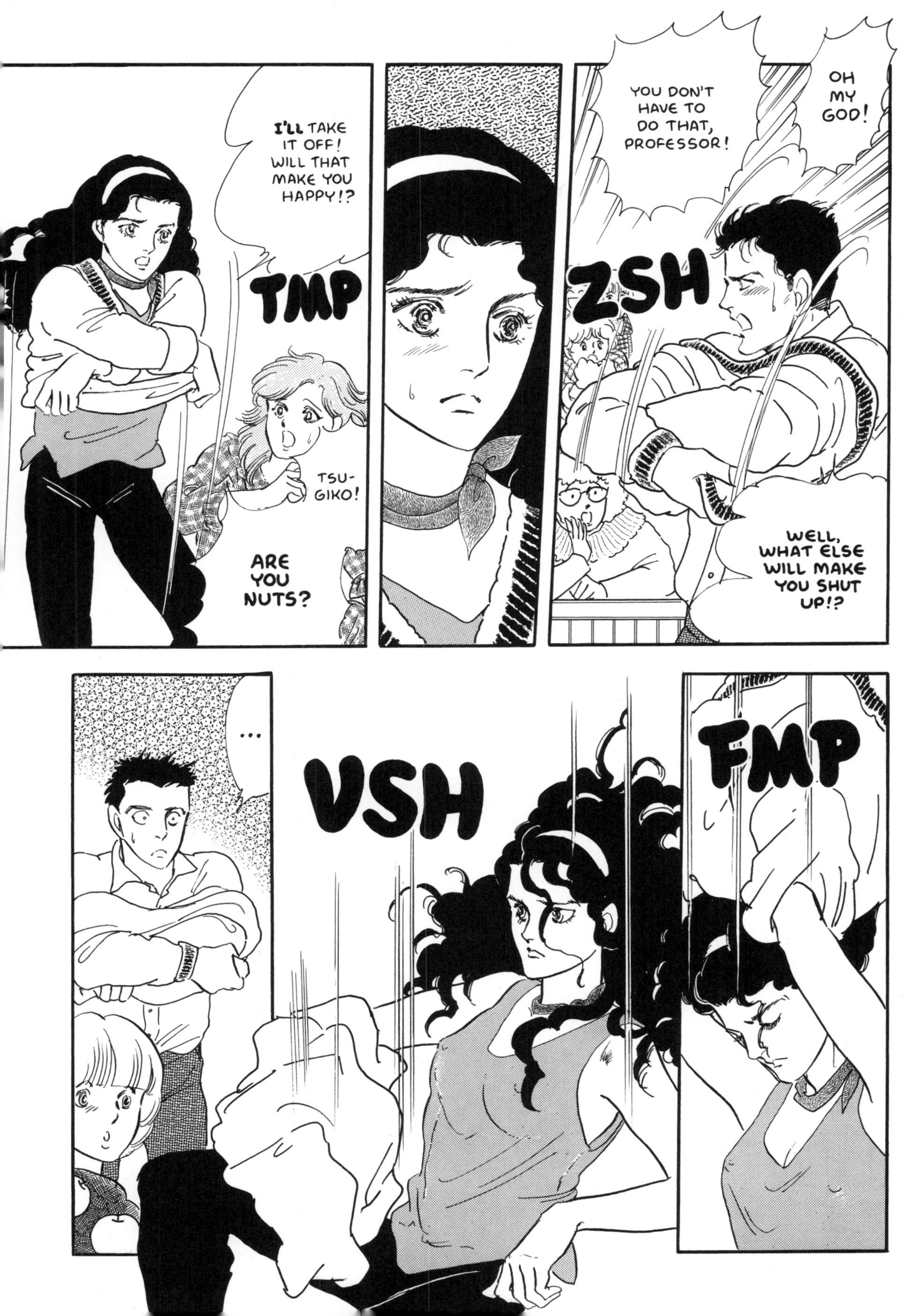

OH MY GOD!
YOU DON'T HAVE TO DO THAT, PROFESSOR!
ZSH
WELL, WHAT ELSE WILL MAKE YOU SHUT UP!?
I'LL TAKE IT OFF! WILL THAT MAKE YOU HAPPY!?
TMP
TSU-GIKO!
ARE YOU NUTS?
FMP
VSH
...

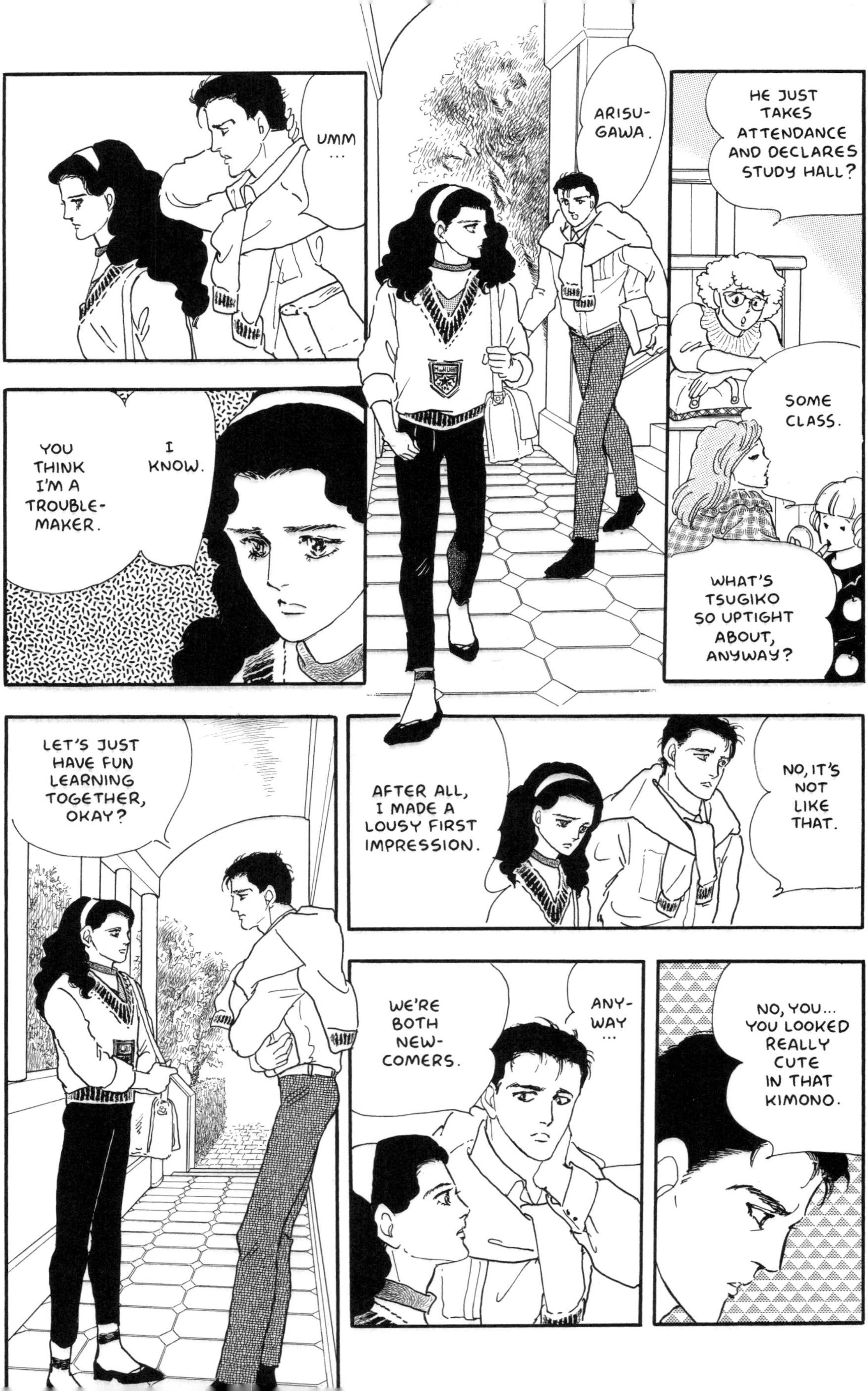
HE JUST TAKES ATTENDANCE AND DECLARES STUDY HALL?
SOME CLASS.
WHAT'S TSUGIKO SO UPTIGHT ABOUT, ANYWAY?
ARISU-GAWA.
UMM ...
I KNOW.
YOU THINK I'M A TROUBLE-MAKER.
AFTER ALL, I MADE A LOUSY FIRST IMPRESSION.
NO, IT'S NOT LIKE THAT.
NO, YOU... YOU LOOKED REALLY CUTE IN THAT KIMONO.
ANY-WAY ...
WE'RE BOTH NEW-COMERS.
LET'S JUST HAVE FUN LEARNING TOGETHER, OKAY?

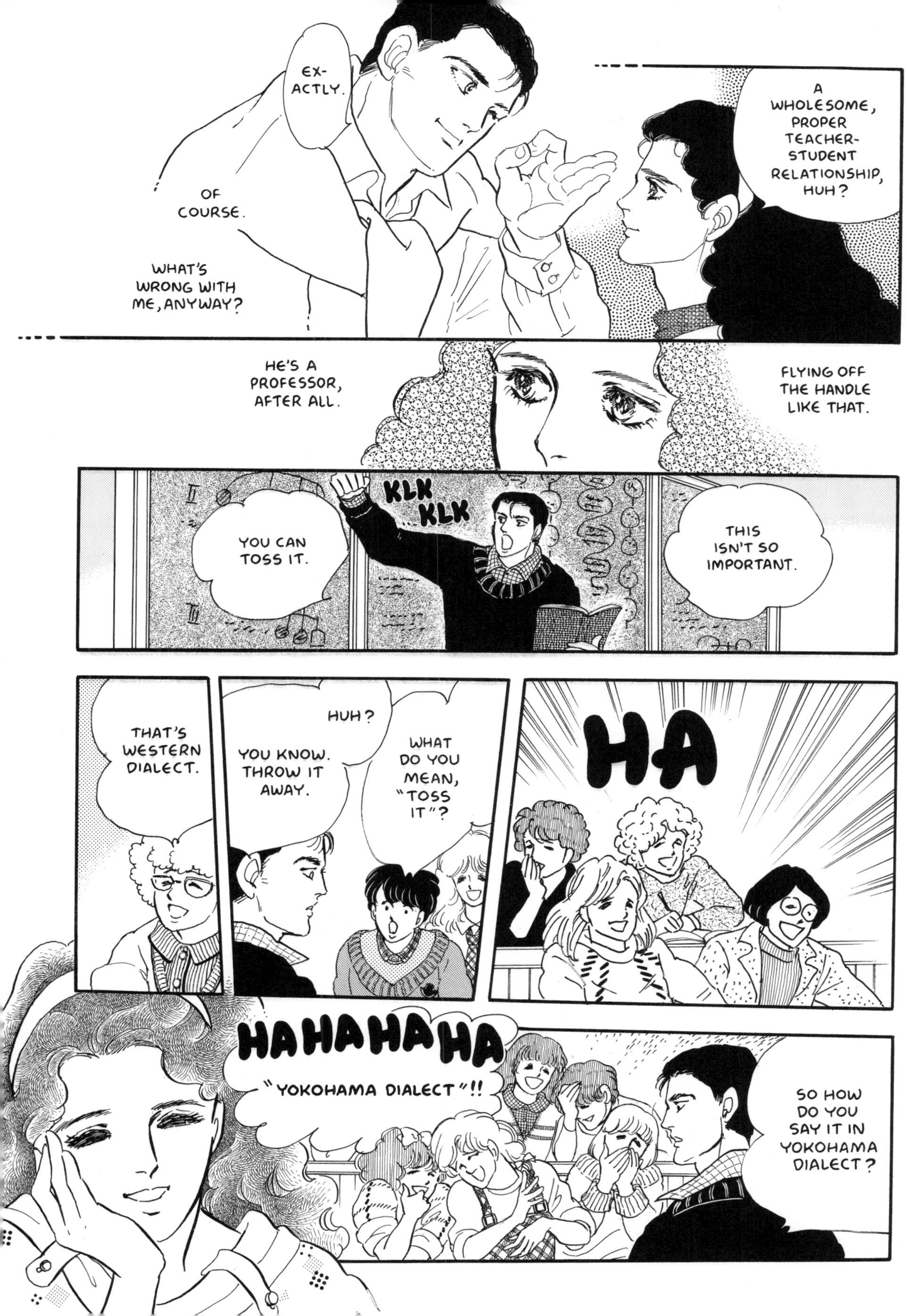
A WHOLESOME, PROPER TEACHER-STUDENT RELATIONSHIP, HUH?
EX-ACTLY.
OF COURSE.
WHAT'S WRONG WITH ME, ANYWAY?
FLYING OFF THE HANDLE LIKE THAT.
HE'S A PROFESSOR, AFTER ALL.
THIS ISN'T SO IMPORTANT.
KLK KLK
YOU CAN TOSS IT.
HA
WHAT DO YOU MEAN, "TOSS IT"?
HUH?
YOU KNOW. THROW IT AWAY.
THAT'S WESTERN DIALECT.
SO HOW DO YOU SAY IT IN YOKOHAMA DIALECT?
HAHAHAHA
"YOKOHAMA DIALECT"!!

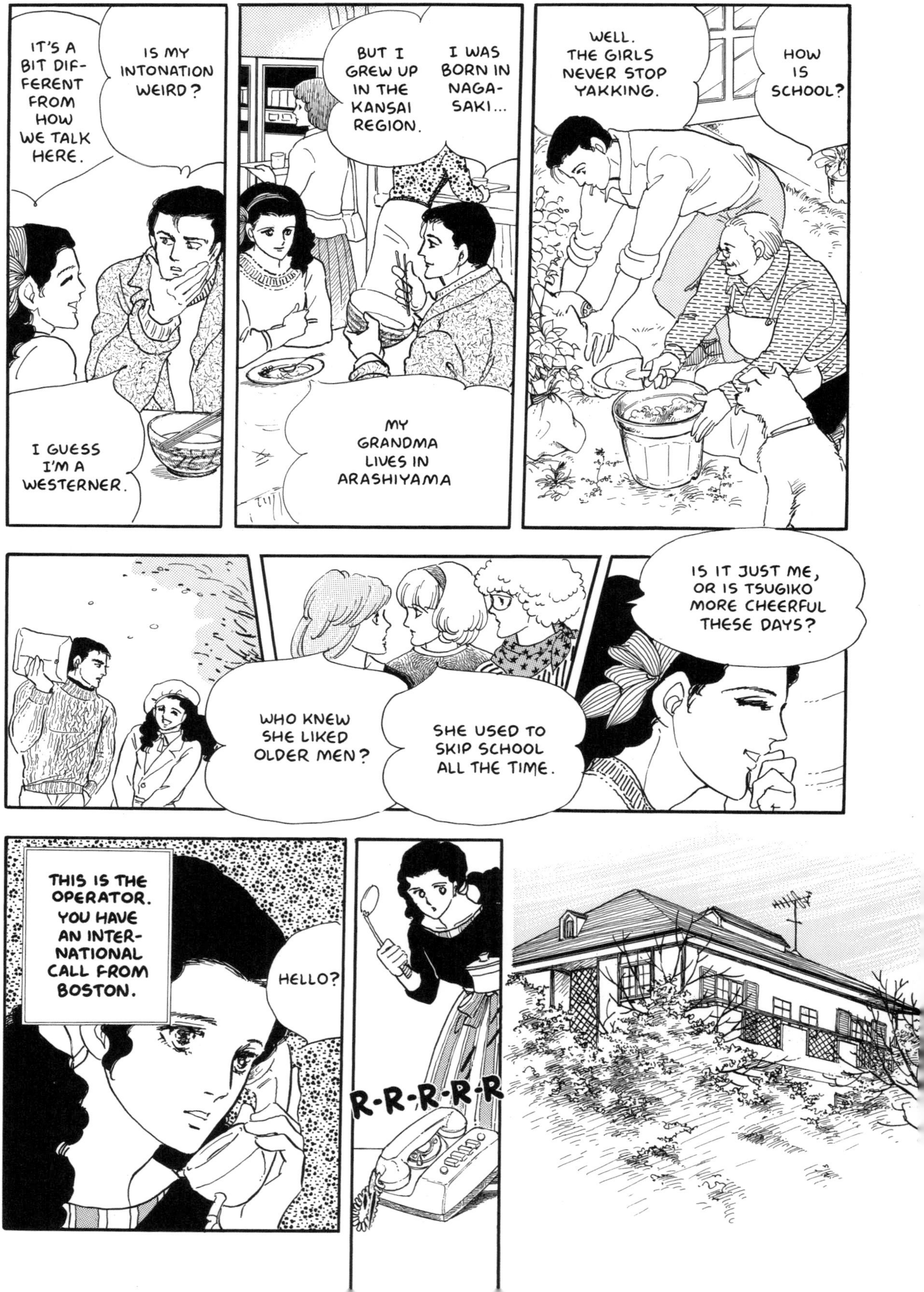
HOW IS SCHOOL?
WELL. THE GIRLS NEVER STOP YAKKING.
I WAS BORN IN NAGA-SAKI...
BUT I GREW UP IN THE KANSAI REGION.
MY GRANDMA LIVES IN ARASHIYAMA
IS MY INTONATION WEIRD?
IT'S A BIT DIF-FERENT FROM HOW WE TALK HERE.
I GUESS I'M A WESTERNER.
IS IT JUST ME, OR IS TSUGIKO MORE CHEERFUL THESE DAYS?
SHE USED TO SKIP SCHOOL ALL THE TIME.
WHO KNEW SHE LIKED OLDER MEN?
R-R-R-R-R
HELLO?
THIS IS THE OPERATOR. YOU HAVE AN INTER-NATIONAL CALL FROM BOSTON.

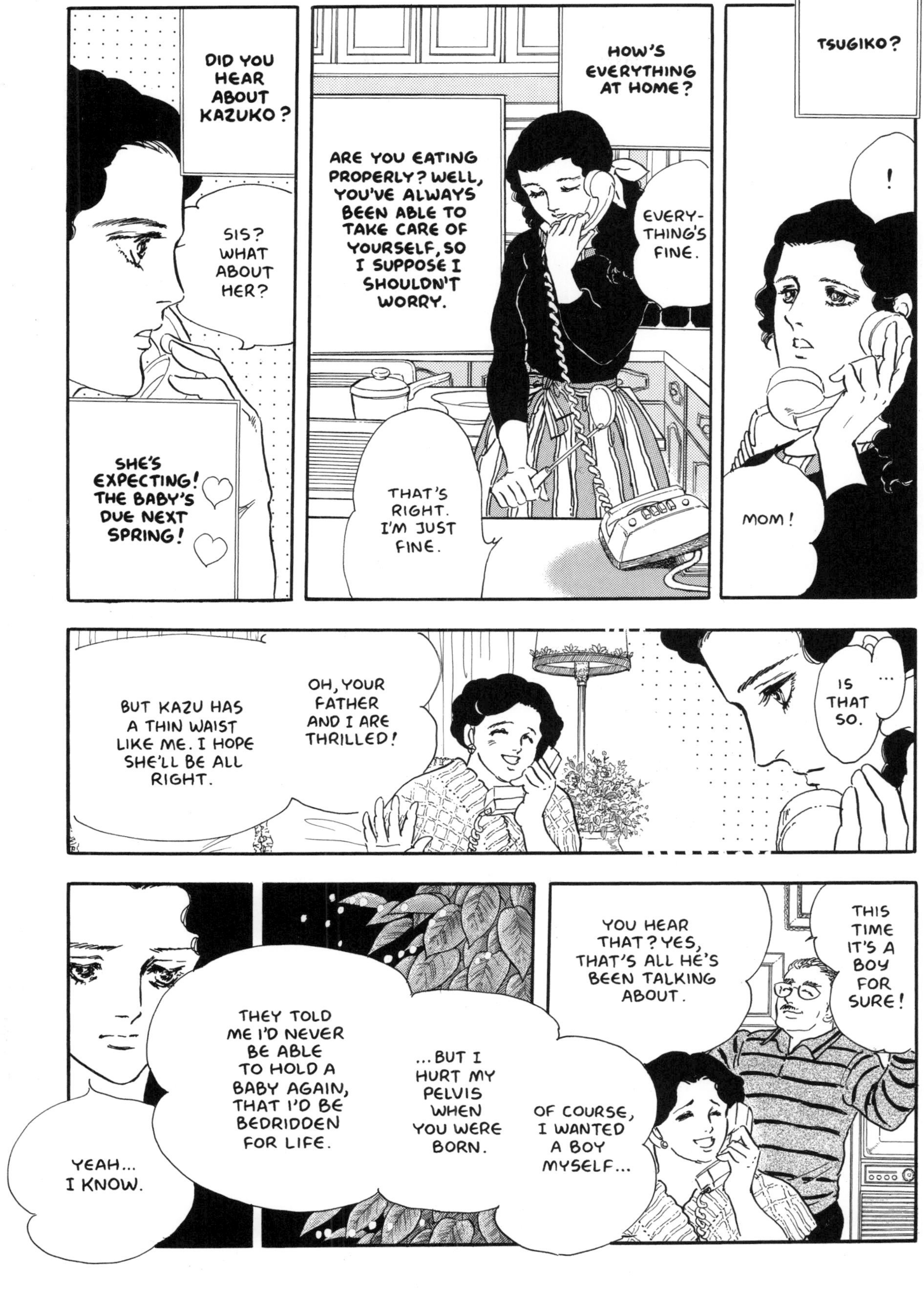
TSUGIKO?
!
MOM!
HOW'S EVERYTHING AT HOME?
EVERY-THING'S FINE.
ARE YOU EATING PROPERLY? WELL, YOU'VE ALWAYS BEEN ABLE TO TAKE CARE OF YOURSELF, SO I SUPPOSE I SHOULDN'T WORRY.
THAT'S RIGHT. I'M JUST FINE.
DID YOU HEAR ABOUT KAZUKO?
SIS? WHAT ABOUT HER?
SHE'S EXPECTING! THE BABY'S DUE NEXT SPRING!
... IS THAT SO.
OH, YOUR FATHER AND I ARE THRILLED!
BUT KAZU HAS A THIN WAIST LIKE ME. I HOPE SHE'LL BE ALL RIGHT.
THIS TIME IT'S A BOY FOR SURE!
YOU HEAR THAT? YES, THAT'S ALL HE'S BEEN TALKING ABOUT.
OF COURSE, I WANTED A BOY MYSELF...
...BUT I HURT MY PELVIS WHEN YOU WERE BORN.
THEY TOLD ME I'D NEVER BE ABLE TO HOLD A BABY AGAIN, THAT I'D BE BEDRIDDEN FOR LIFE.
YEAH... I KNOW.

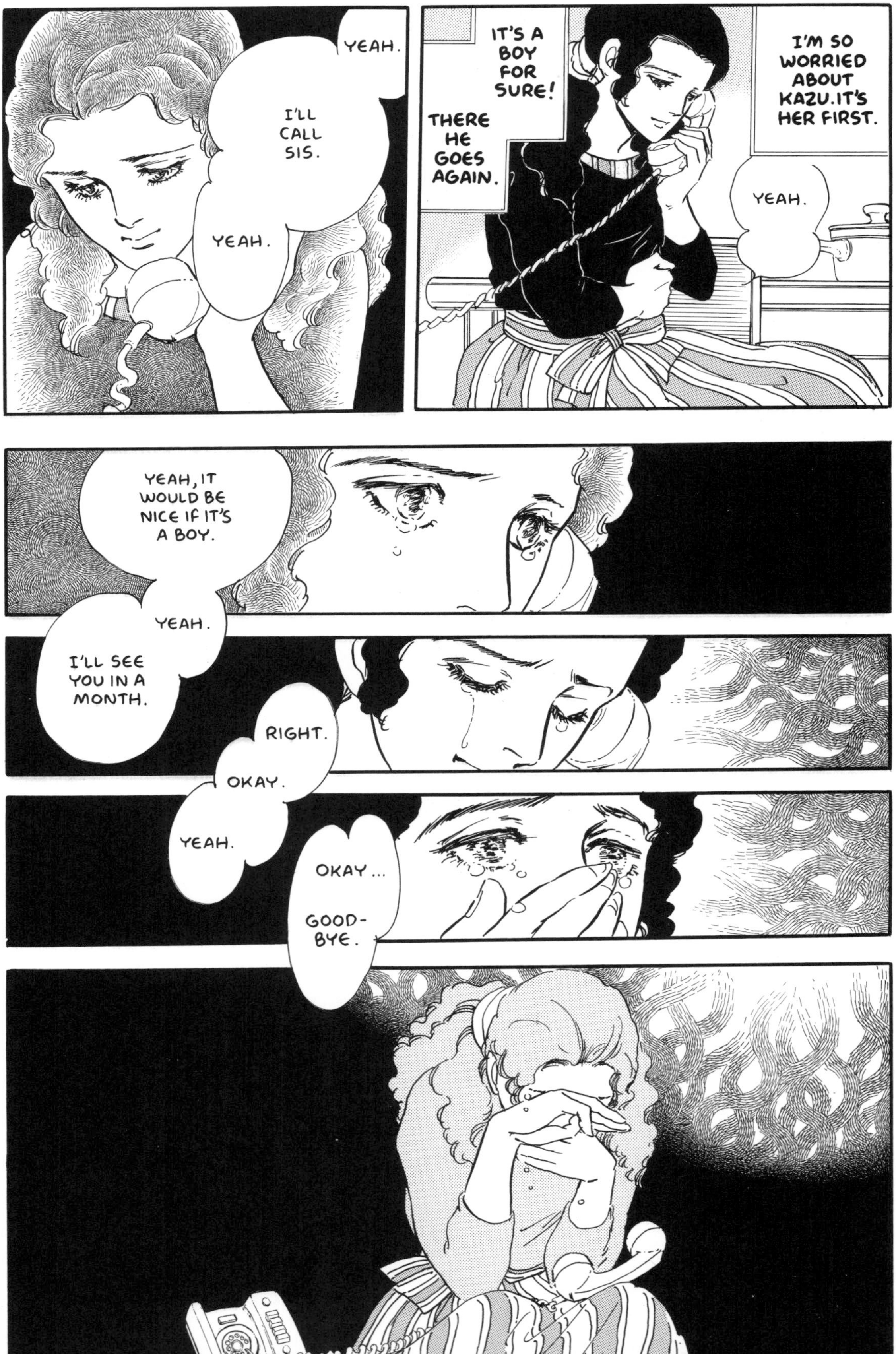
I'M SO WORRIED ABOUT KAZU. IT'S HER FIRST.
YEAH.
IT'S A BOY FOR SURE!
THERE HE GOES AGAIN.
YEAH.
I'LL CALL SIS.
YEAH.
YEAH, IT WOULD BE NICE IF IT'S A BOY.
YEAH.
I'LL SEE YOU IN A MONTH.
RIGHT.
OKAY.
YEAH.
OKAY...
GOOD-BYE.

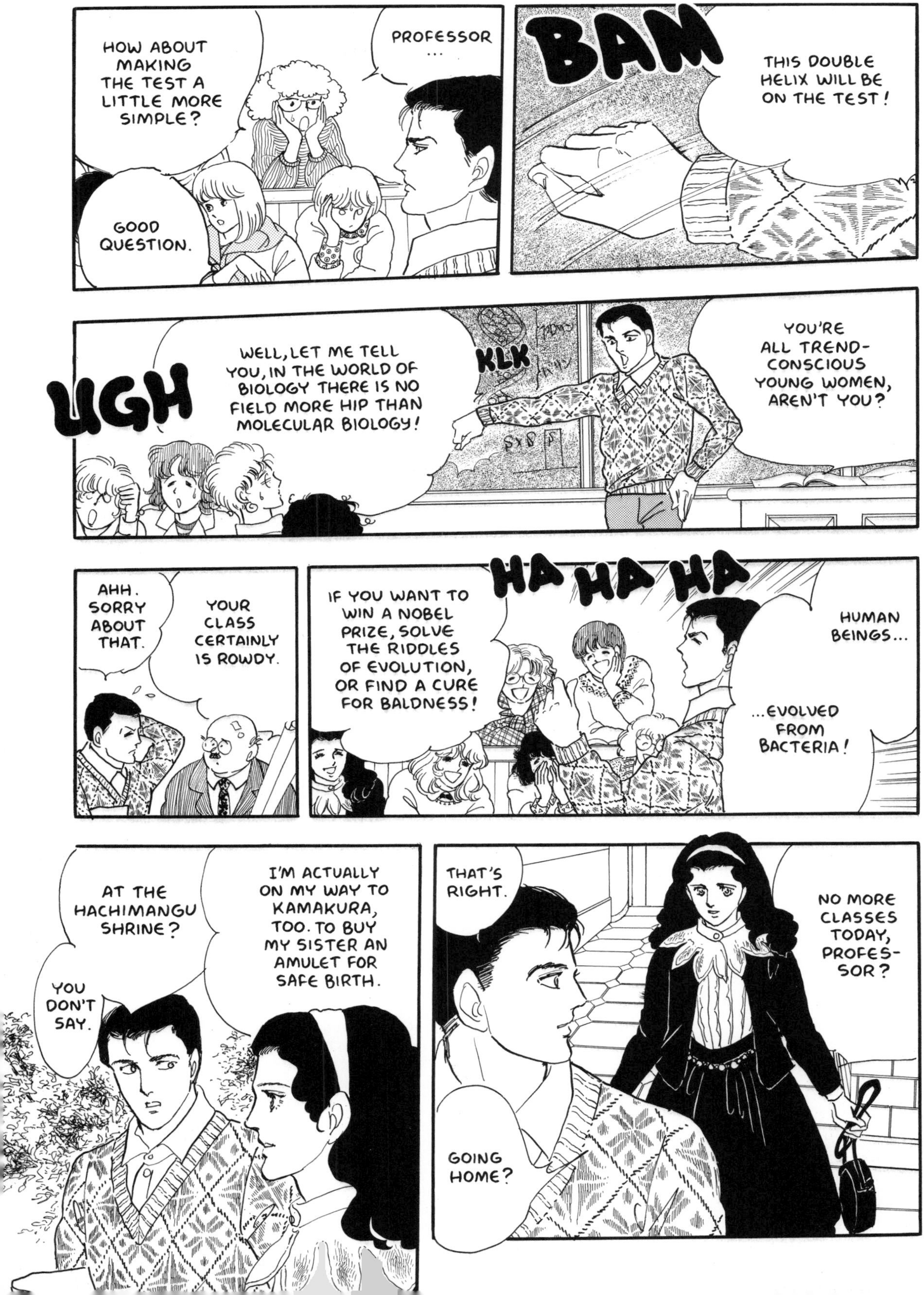
BAM
THIS DOUBLE HELIX WILL BE ON THE TEST!
PROFESSOR ...
HOW ABOUT MAKING THE TEST A LITTLE MORE SIMPLE?
GOOD QUESTION.
YOU'RE ALL TREND-CONSCIOUS YOUNG WOMEN, AREN'T YOU?
KLK
WELL, LET ME TELL YOU, IN THE WORLD OF BIOLOGY THERE IS NO FIELD MORE HIP THAN MOLECULAR BIOLOGY!
UGH
HA HA HA
HUMAN BEINGS...
IF YOU WANT TO WIN A NOBEL PRIZE, SOLVE THE RIDDLES OF EVOLUTION, OR FIND A CURE FOR BALDNESS!
...EVOLVED FROM BACTERIA!
YOUR CLASS CERTAINLY IS ROWDY.
AHH. SORRY ABOUT THAT.
NO MORE CLASSES TODAY, PROFES-SOR?
THAT'S RIGHT.
GOING HOME?
I'M ACTUALLY ON MY WAY TO KAMAKURA, TOO. TO BUY MY SISTER AN AMULET FOR SAFE BIRTH.
AT THE HACHIMANGU SHRINE?
YOU DON'T SAY.

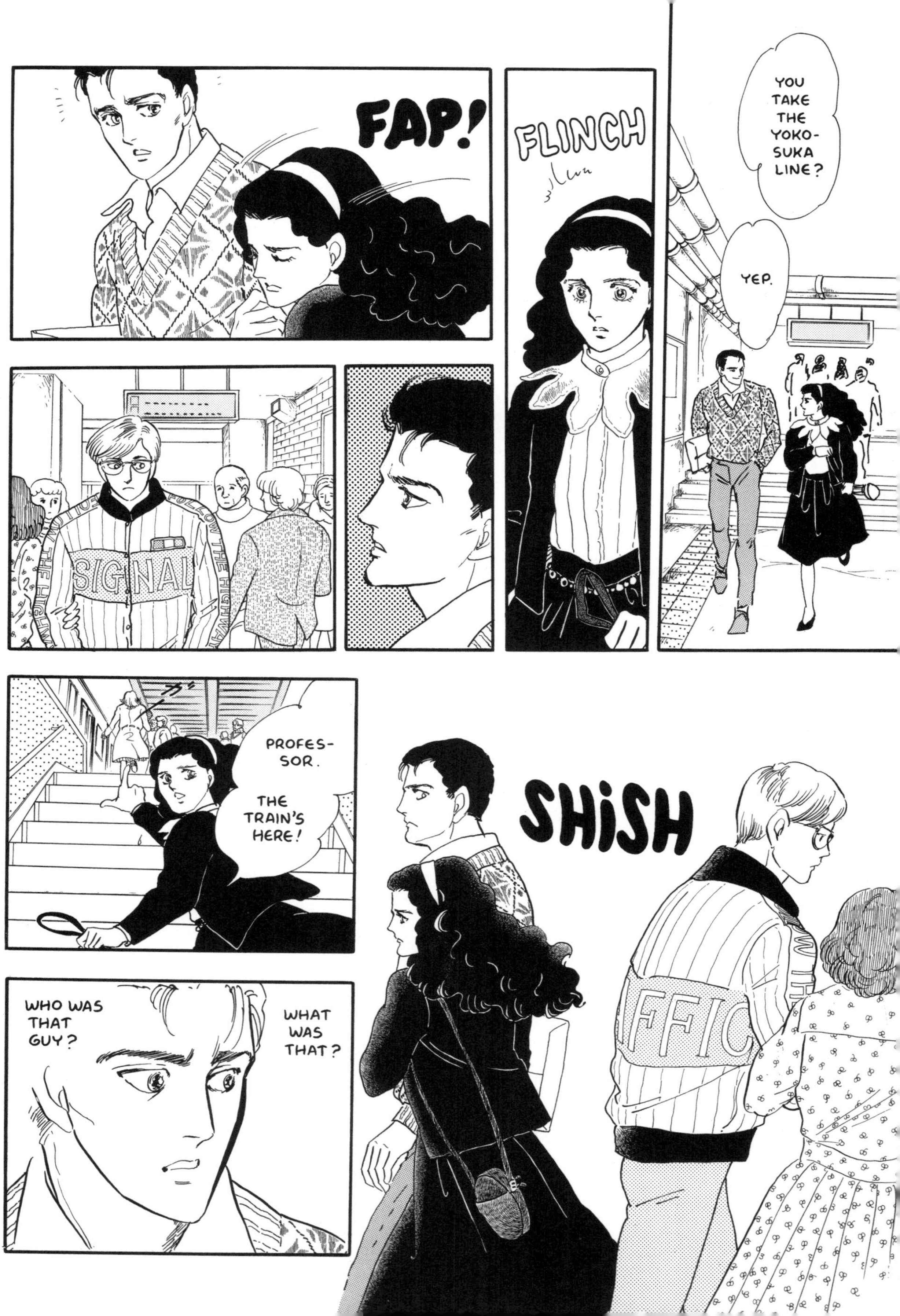
YOU TAKE THE YOKO-SUKA LINE?
YEP.
FLINCH
FAP!
SIGNAL
SHISH
PROFES-SOR.
THE TRAIN'S HERE!
WHAT WAS THAT?
WHO WAS THAT GUY?

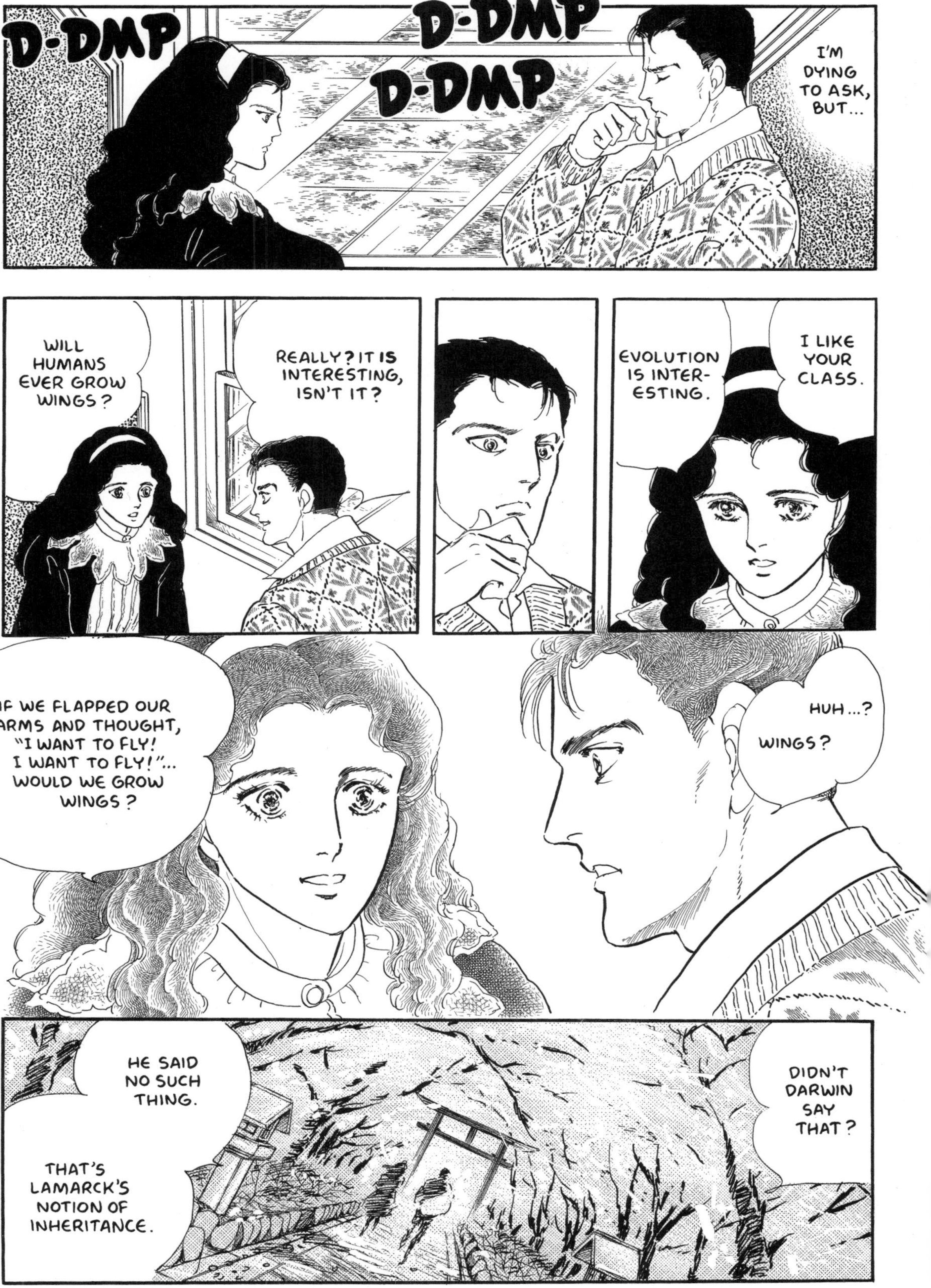
D-DMP
I'M DYING TO ASK, BUT...
D-DMP
D-DMP
D-DMP
I LIKE YOUR CLASS.
EVOLUTION IS INTER-ESTING.
REALLY? IT IS INTERESTING, ISN'T IT?
WILL HUMANS EVER GROW WINGS?
HUH...?
WINGS?
IF WE FLAPPED OUR ARMS AND THOUGHT, "I WANT TO FLY! I WANT TO FLY!"... WOULD WE GROW WINGS?
DIDN'T DARWIN SAY THAT?
HE SAID NO SUCH THING.
THAT'S LAMARCK'S NOTION OF INHERITANCE.

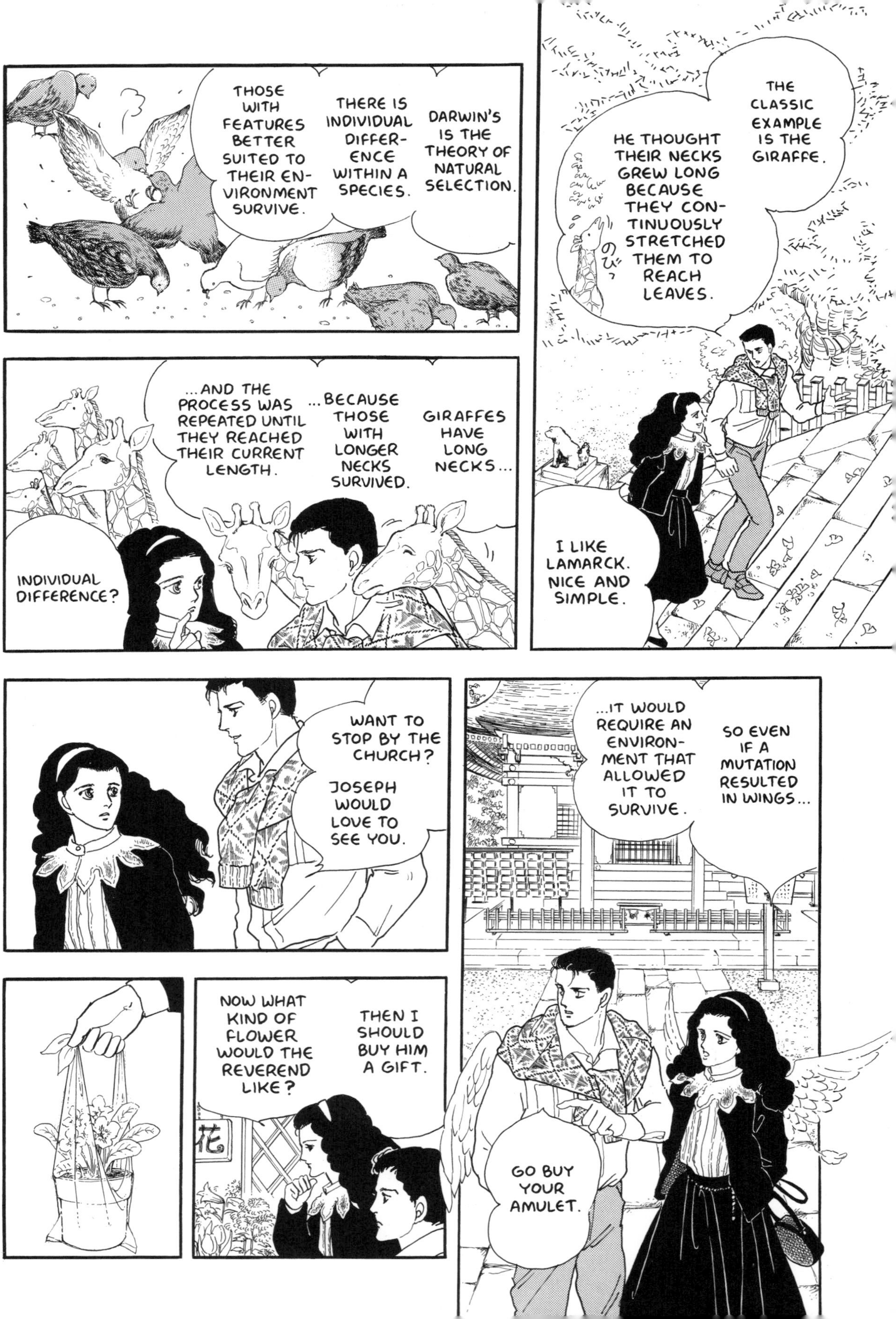
THE CLASSIC EXAMPLE IS THE GIRAFFE.
HE THOUGHT THEIR NECKS GREW LONG BECAUSE THEY CONTINUOUSLY STRETCHED THEM TO REACH LEAVES.
のび
I LIKE LAMARCK. NICE AND SIMPLE.
DARWIN'S IS THE THEORY OF NATURAL SELECTION.
THERE IS INDIVIDUAL DIFFERENCE WITHIN A SPECIES.
THOSE WITH FEATURES BETTER SUITED TO THEIR ENVIRONMENT SURVIVE.
GIRAFFES HAVE LONG NECKS...
...BECAUSE THOSE WITH LONGER NECKS SURVIVED.
...AND THE PROCESS WAS REPEATED UNTIL THEY REACHED THEIR CURRENT LENGTH.
INDIVIDUAL DIFFERENCE?
SO EVEN IF A MUTATION RESULTED IN WINGS...
...IT WOULD REQUIRE AN ENVIRONMENT THAT ALLOWED IT TO SURVIVE.
GO BUY YOUR AMULET.
WANT TO STOP BY THE CHURCH?
JOSEPH WOULD LOVE TO SEE YOU.
THEN I SHOULD BUY HIM A GIFT.
NOW WHAT KIND OF FLOWER WOULD THE REVEREND LIKE?
花

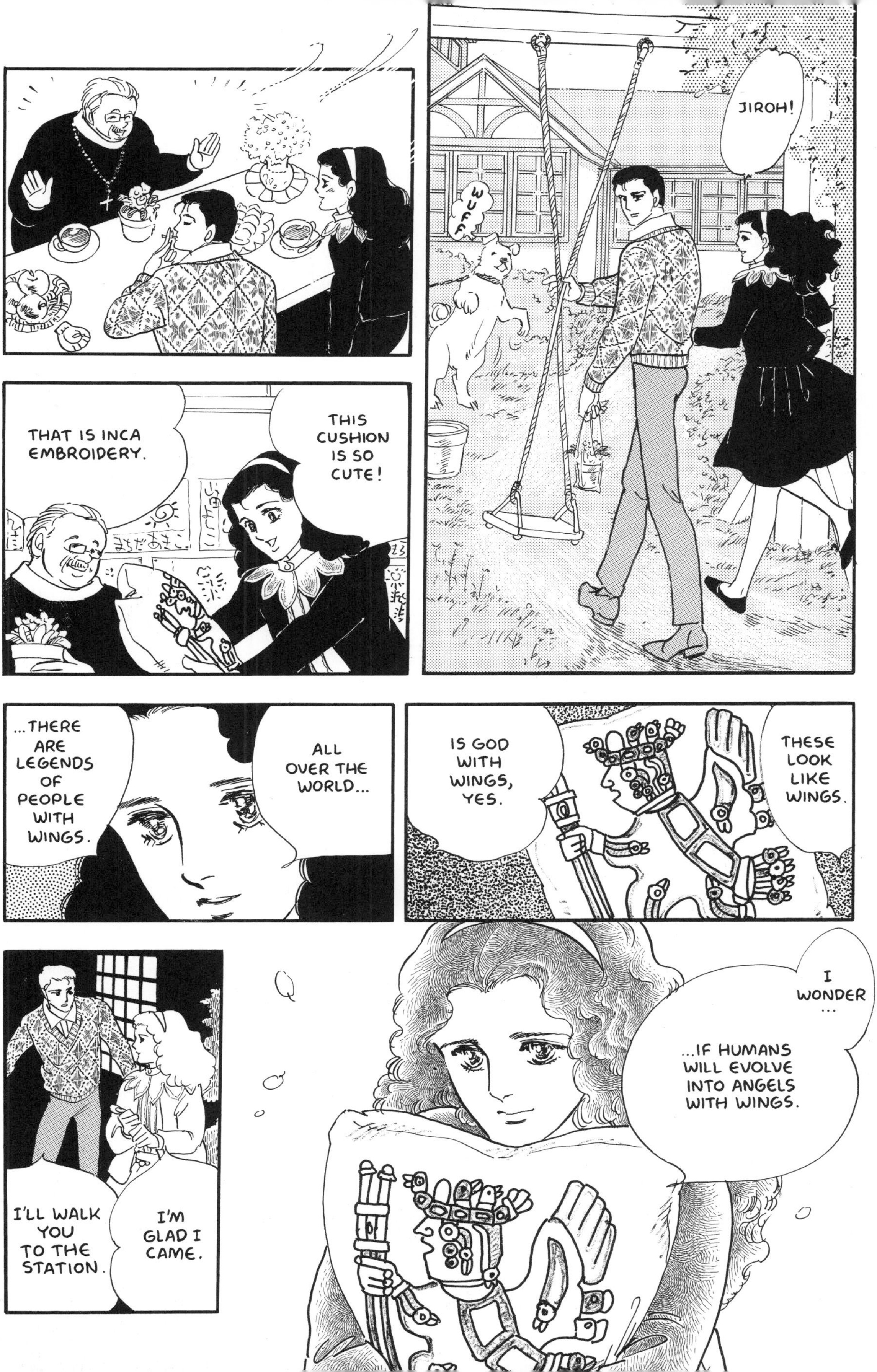
JIROH!
WUFF
THIS CUSHION IS SO CUTE!
THAT IS INCA EMBROIDERY.
THESE LOOK LIKE WINGS.
IS GOD WITH WINGS, YES.
ALL OVER THE WORLD...
...THERE ARE LEGENDS OF PEOPLE WITH WINGS.
I WONDER...
...IF HUMANS WILL EVOLVE INTO ANGELS WITH WINGS.
I'M GLAD I CAME.
I'LL WALK YOU TO THE STATION.

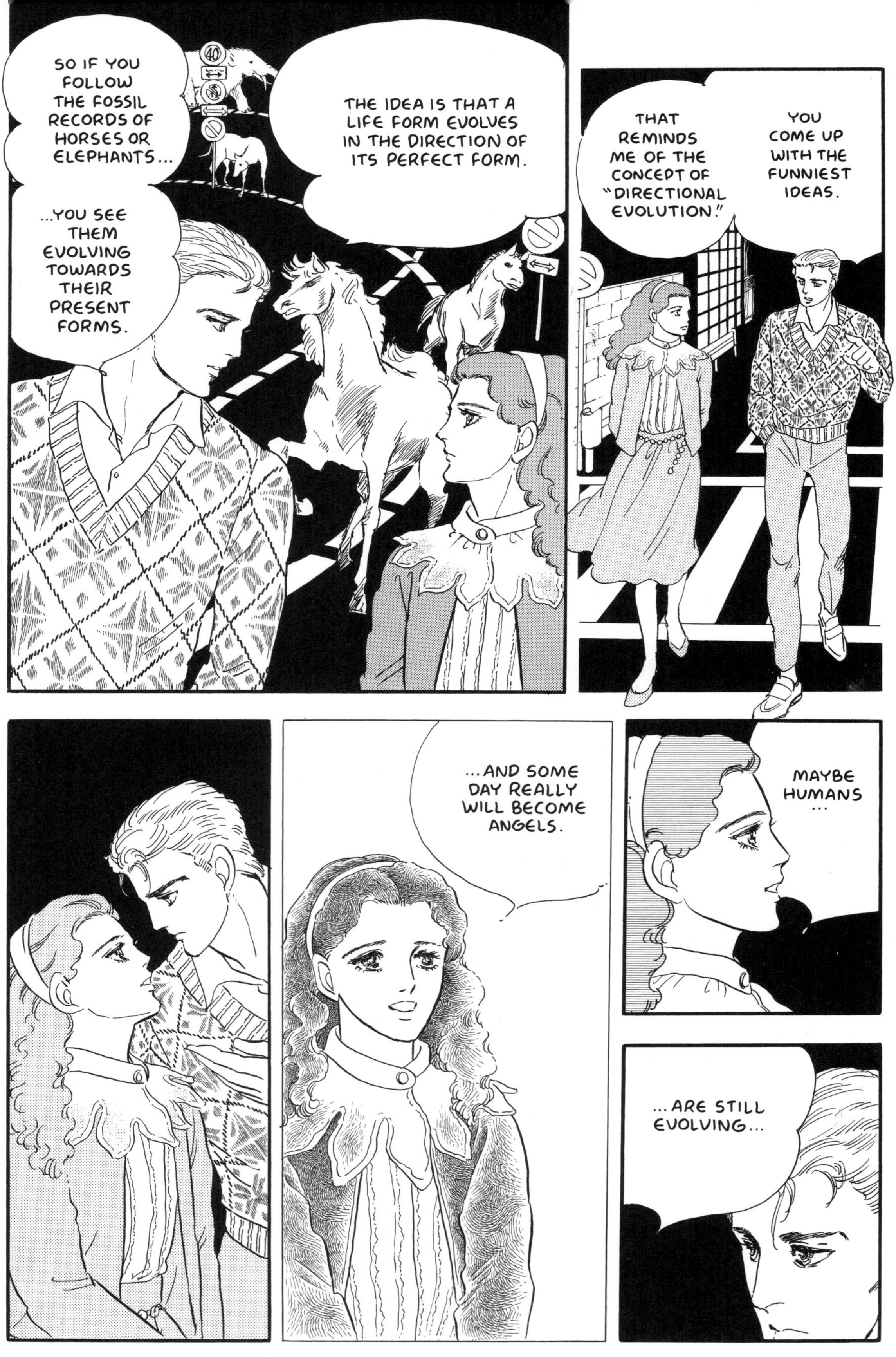
YOU COME UP WITH THE FUNNIEST IDEAS.
THAT REMINDS ME OF THE CONCEPT OF "DIRECTIONAL EVOLUTION."
THE IDEA IS THAT A LIFE FORM EVOLVES IN THE DIRECTION OF ITS PERFECT FORM.
SO IF YOU FOLLOW THE FOSSIL RECORDS OF HORSES OR ELEPHANTS...
...YOU SEE THEM EVOLVING TOWARDS THEIR PRESENT FORMS.
MAYBE HUMANS ...
...ARE STILL EVOLVING...
...AND SOME DAY REALLY WILL BECOME ANGELS.

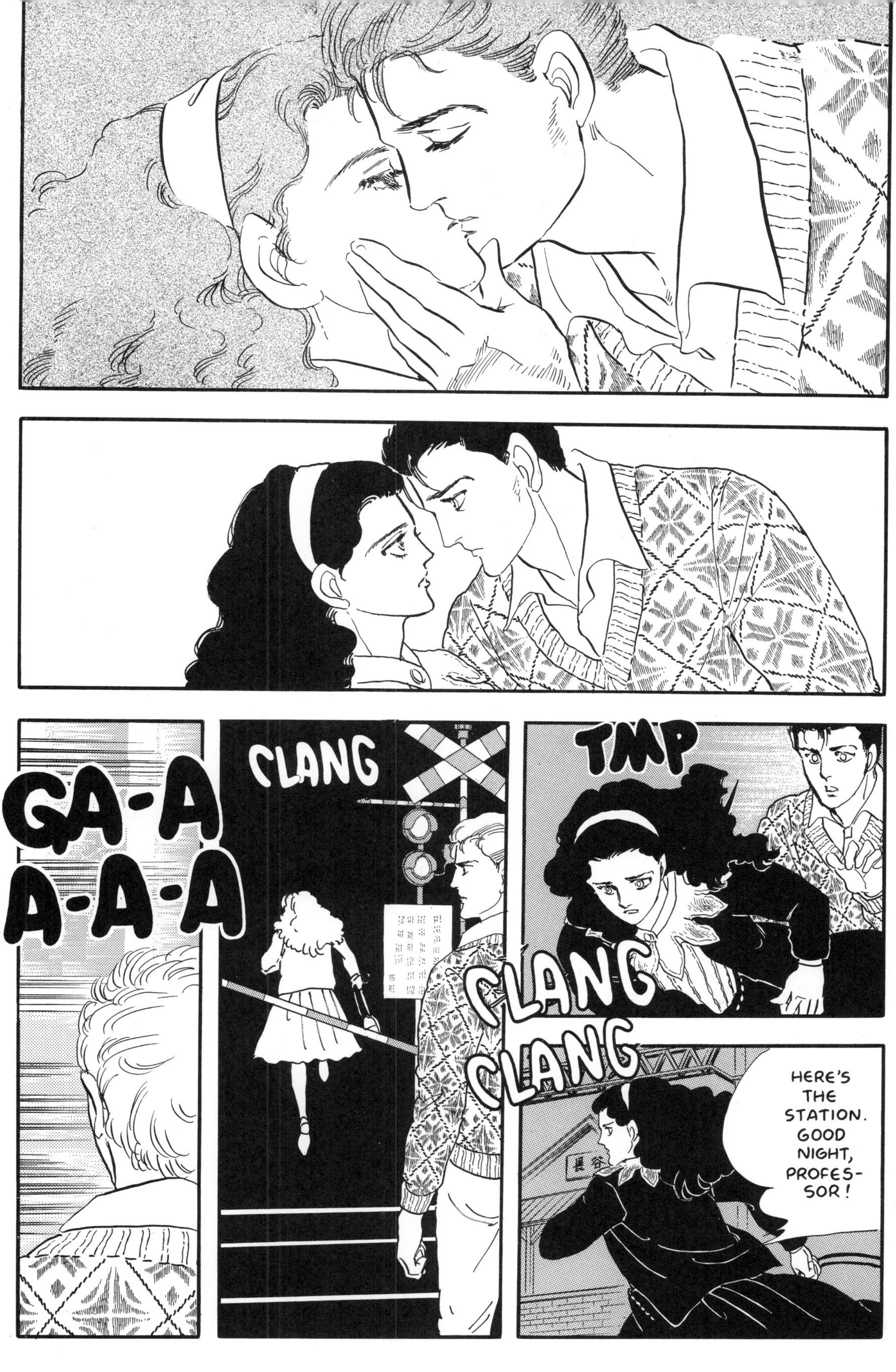
TMP
HERE'S THE STATION. GOOD NIGHT, PROFES-SOR!
CLANG
CLANG
CLANG
CLANG
GA-A A-A-A

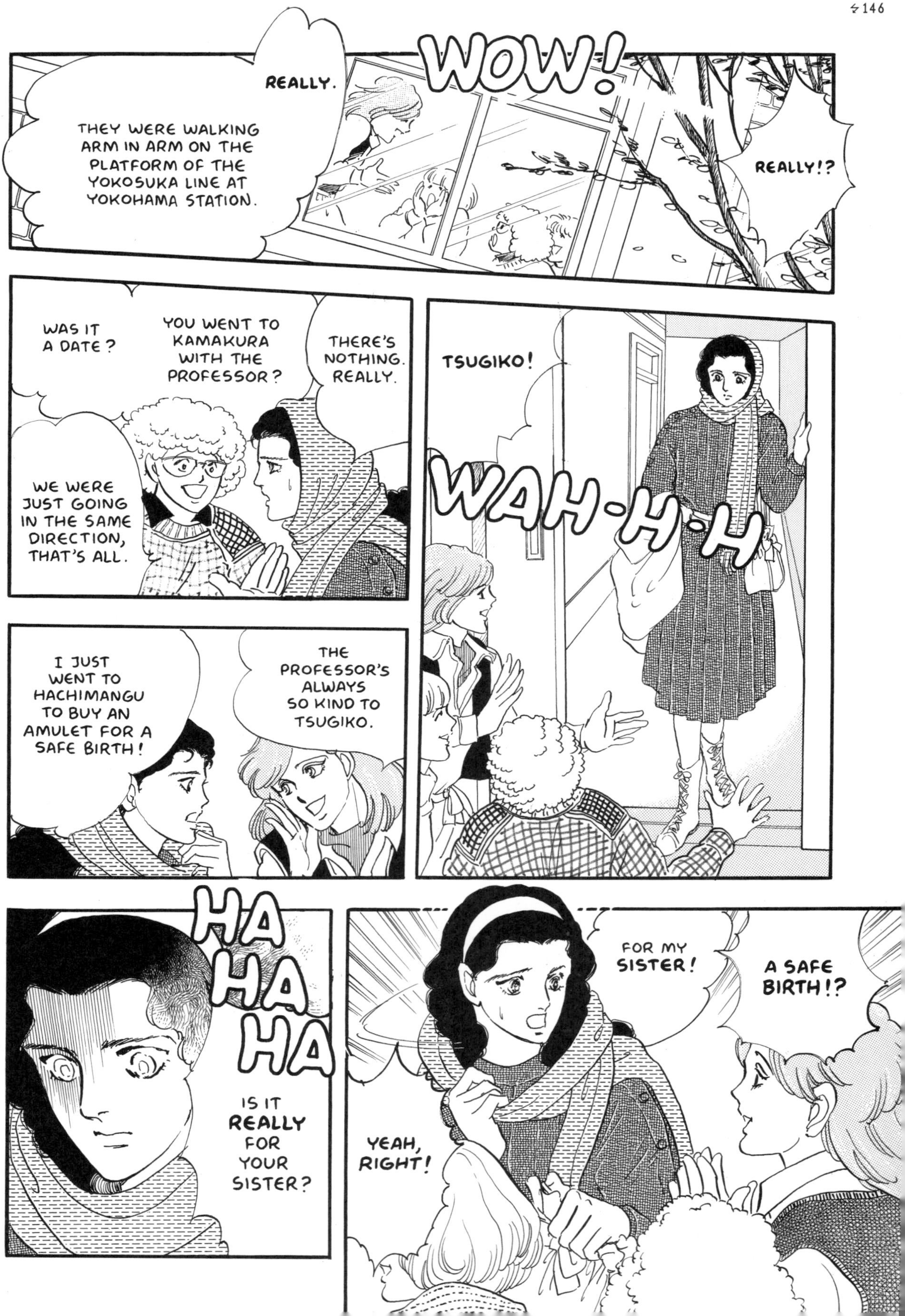
WOW!
REALLY!?
REALLY.
THEY WERE WALKING ARM IN ARM ON THE PLATFORM OF THE YOKOSUKA LINE AT YOKOHAMA STATION.
TSUGIKO!
WAH-H-H
THERE'S NOTHING. REALLY.
YOU WENT TO KAMAKURA WITH THE PROFESSOR?
WAS IT A DATE?
WE WERE JUST GOING IN THE SAME DIRECTION, THAT'S ALL.
THE PROFESSOR'S ALWAYS SO KIND TO TSUGIKO.
I JUST WENT TO HACHIMANGU TO BUY AN AMULET FOR A SAFE BIRTH!
A SAFE BIRTH!?
FOR MY SISTER!
YEAH, RIGHT!
HA HA HA HA
IS IT REALLY FOR YOUR SISTER?

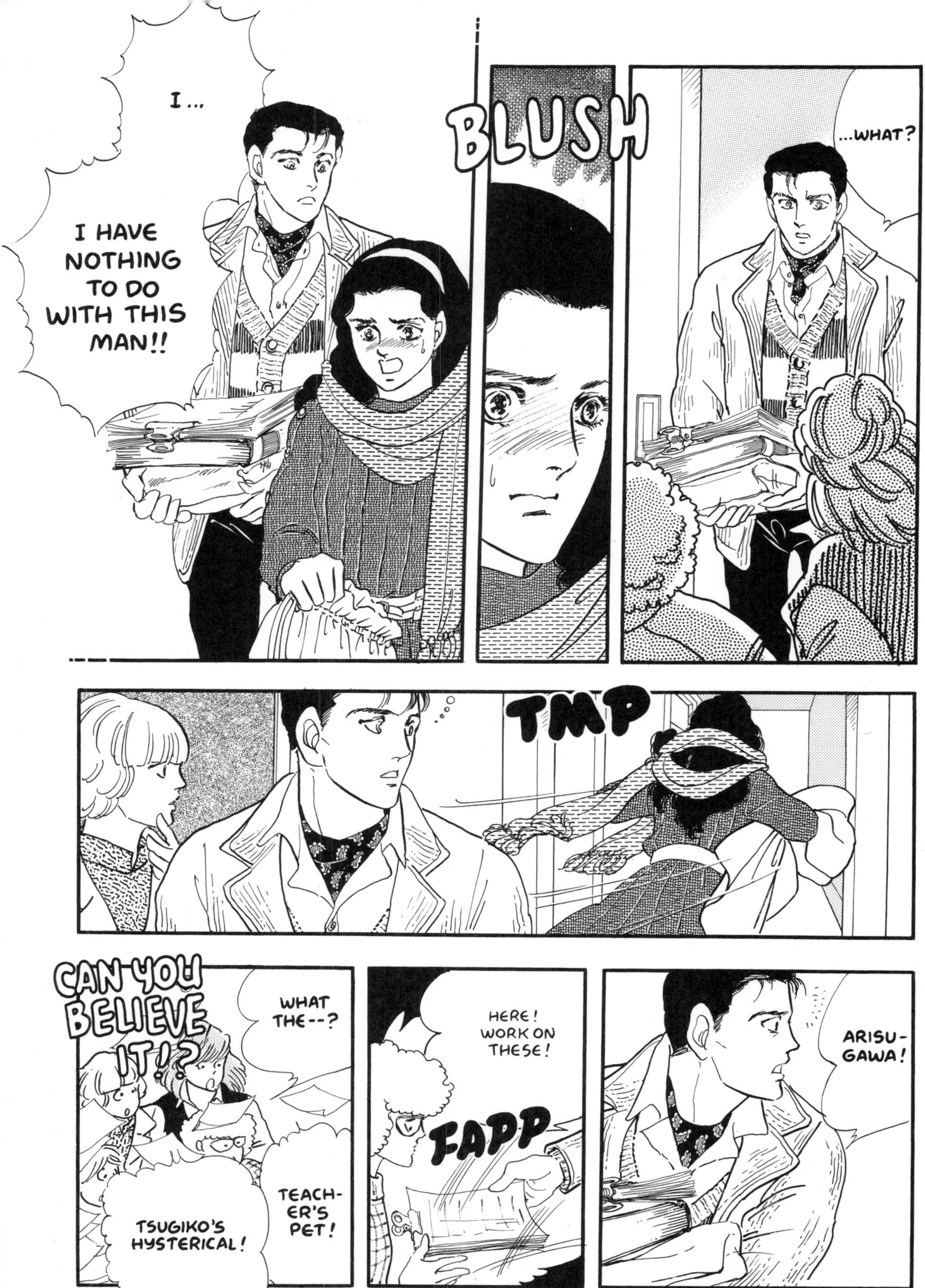
...WHAT?
BLUSH
I ...
I HAVE NOTHING TO DO WITH THIS MAN!!
TMP
ARISU-GAWA!
HERE! WORK ON THESE!
FAPP
WHAT THE--?
CAN YOU BELIEVE IT!?
TEACH-ER'S PET!
TSUGIKO'S HYSTERICAL!

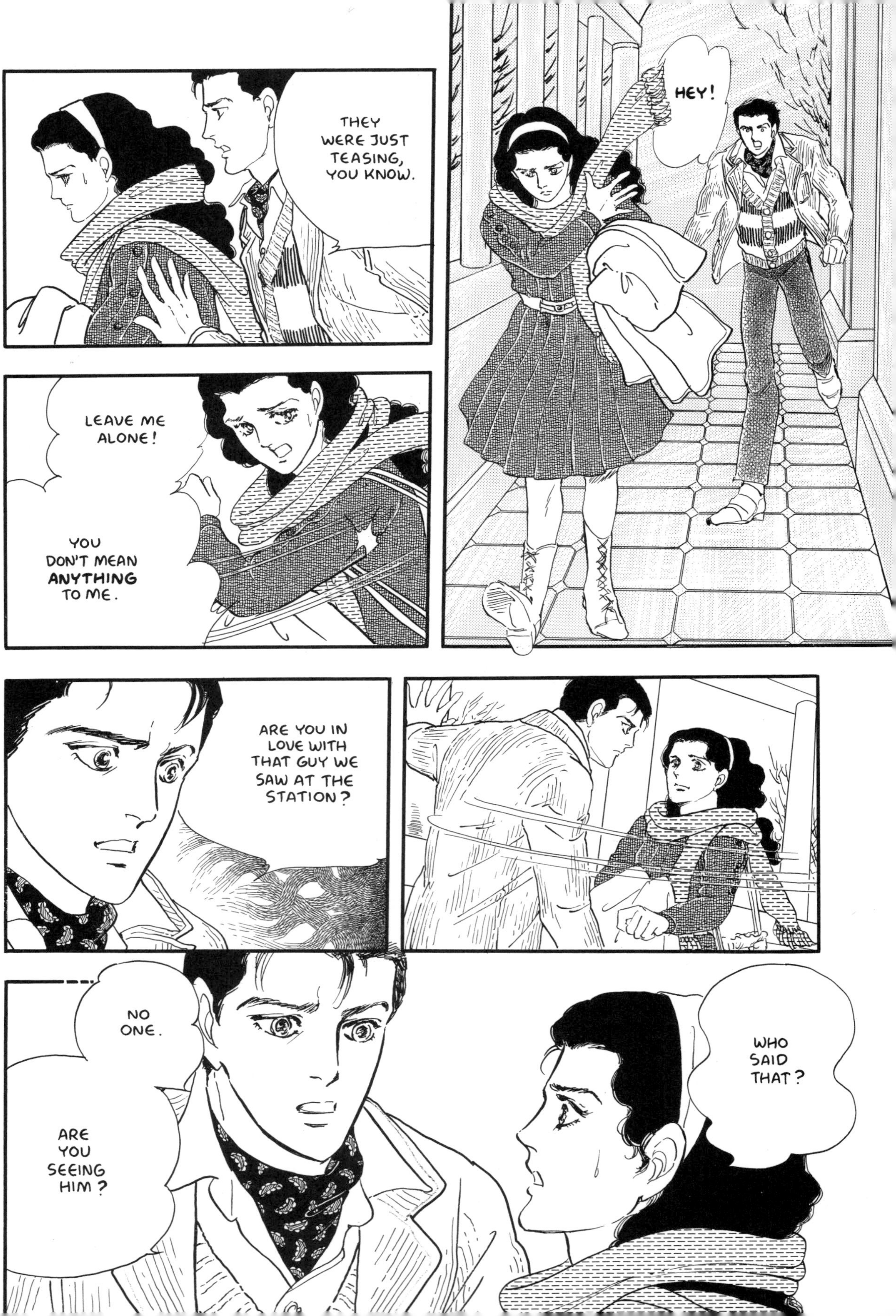
HEY!
THEY WERE JUST TEASING, YOU KNOW.
LEAVE ME ALONE!
YOU DON'T MEAN **ANYTHING** TO ME.
ARE YOU IN LOVE WITH THAT GUY WE SAW AT THE STATION?
WHO SAID THAT?
NO ONE.
ARE YOU SEEING HIM?

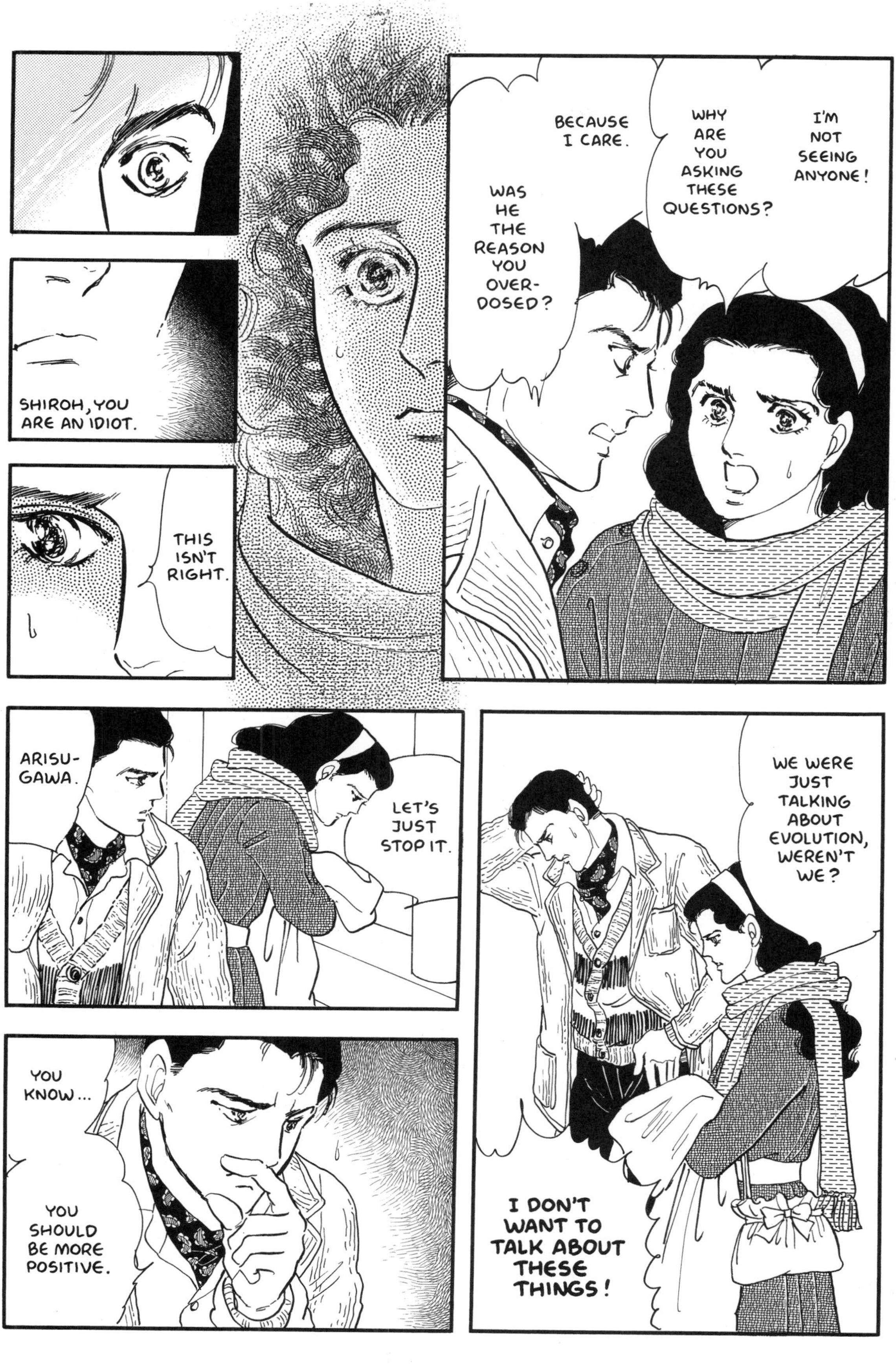
I'M NOT SEEING ANYONE!
WHY ARE YOU ASKING THESE QUESTIONS?
BECAUSE I CARE.
WAS HE THE REASON YOU OVER-DOSED?
SHIROH, YOU ARE AN IDIOT.
THIS ISN'T RIGHT.
WE WERE JUST TALKING ABOUT EVOLUTION, WEREN'T WE?
I DON'T WANT TO TALK ABOUT THESE THINGS!
LET'S JUST STOP IT.
ARISU-GAWA.
YOU KNOW...
YOU SHOULD BE MORE POSITIVE.

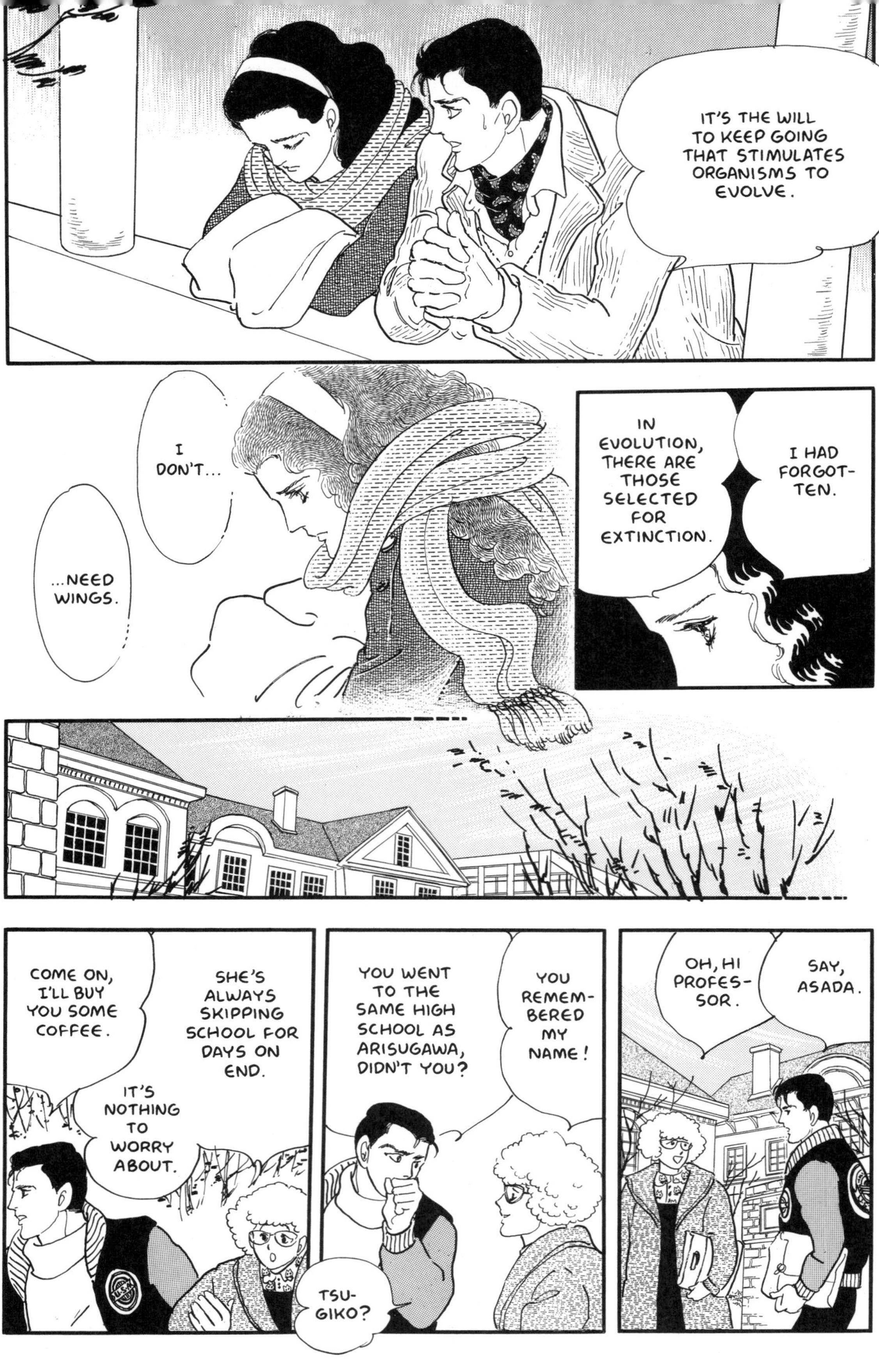

IT'S THE WILL TO KEEP GOING THAT STIMULATES ORGANISMS TO EVOLVE.
I HAD FORGOTTEN.
IN EVOLUTION, THERE ARE THOSE SELECTED FOR EXTINCTION.
I DON'T...
...NEED WINGS.
SAY, ASADA.
OH, HI PROFESSOR.
YOU REMEMBERED MY NAME!
YOU WENT TO THE SAME HIGH SCHOOL AS ARISUGAWA, DIDN'T YOU?
TSUGIKO?
SHE'S ALWAYS SKIPPING SCHOOL FOR DAYS ON END.
COME ON, I'LL BUY YOU SOME COFFEE.
IT'S NOTHING TO WORRY ABOUT.

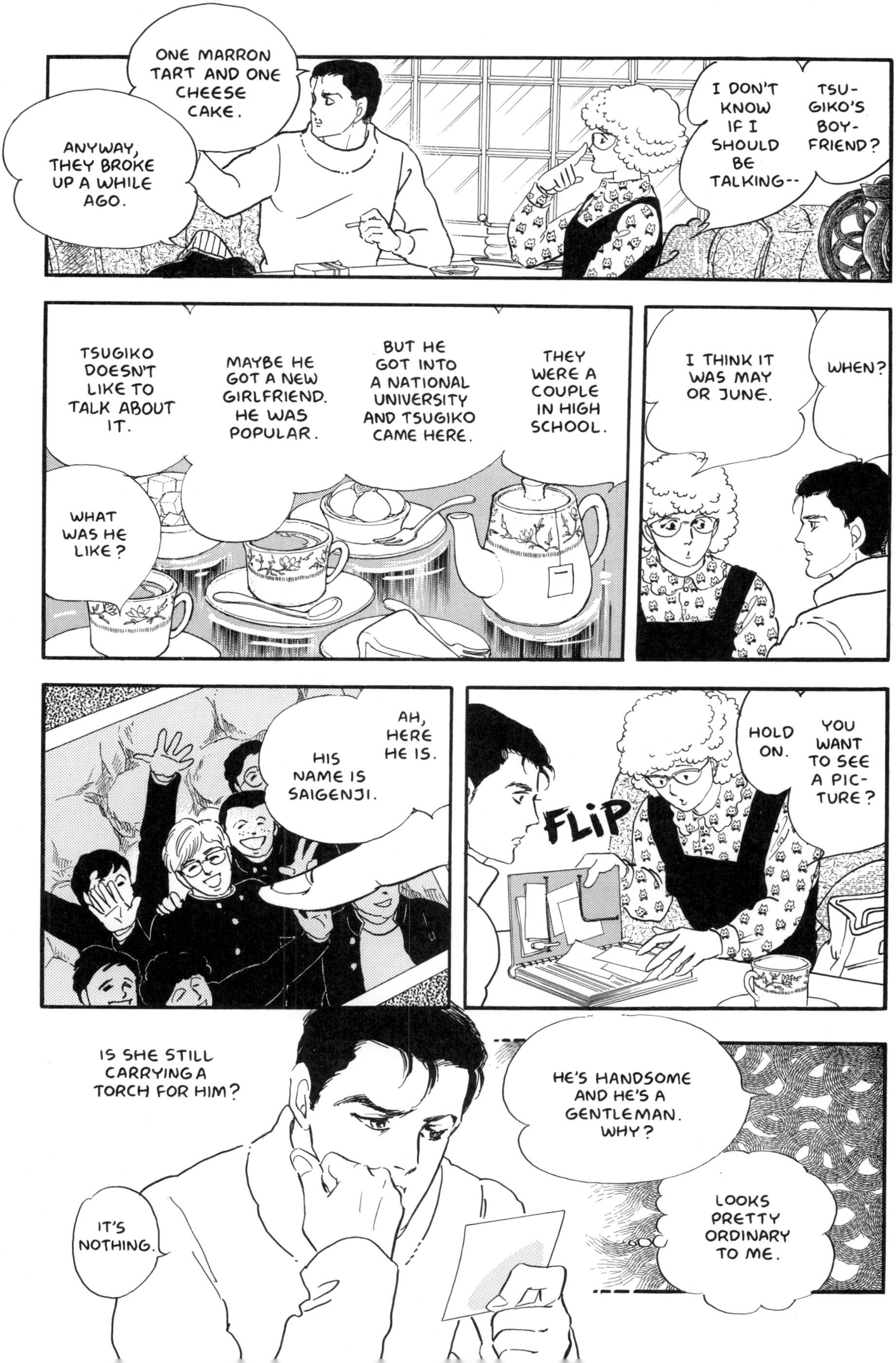
TSU-GIKO'S BOY-FRIEND?
I DON'T KNOW IF I SHOULD BE TALKING--
ONE MARRON TART AND ONE CHEESE CAKE.
ANYWAY, THEY BROKE UP A WHILE AGO.
WHEN?
I THINK IT WAS MAY OR JUNE.
THEY WERE A COUPLE IN HIGH SCHOOL.
BUT HE GOT INTO A NATIONAL UNIVERSITY AND TSUGIKO CAME HERE.
MAYBE HE GOT A NEW GIRLFRIEND. HE WAS POPULAR.
TSUGIKO DOESN'T LIKE TO TALK ABOUT IT.
WHAT WAS HE LIKE?
YOU WANT TO SEE A PICTURE?
HOLD ON.
FLIP
AH, HERE HE IS.
HIS NAME IS SAIGENJI.
HE'S HANDSOME AND HE'S A GENTLEMAN. WHY?
IS SHE STILL CARRYING A TORCH FOR HIM?
LOOKS PRETTY ORDINARY TO ME.
IT'S NOTHING.

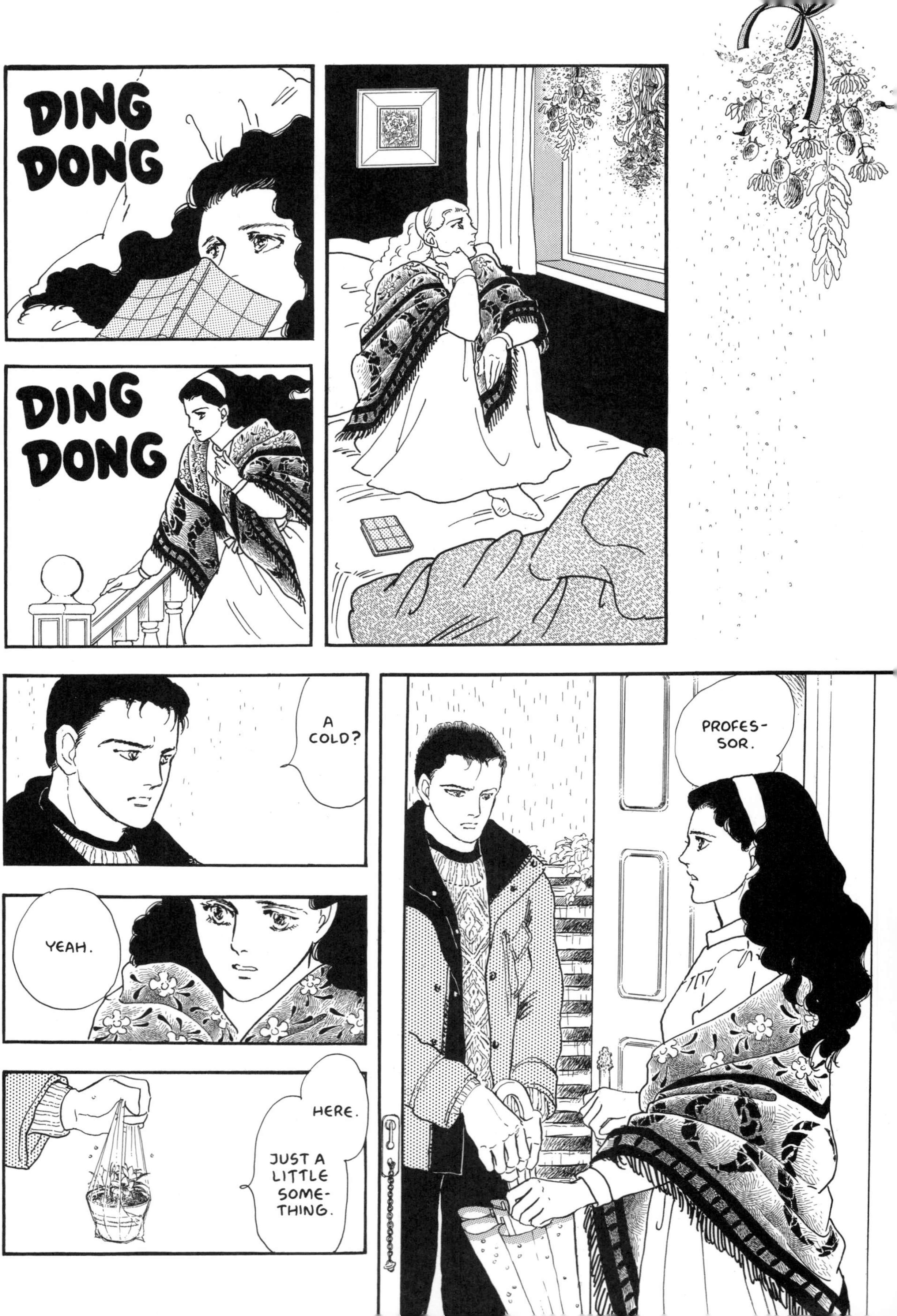
DING DONG
DING DONG
PROFES- SOR.
A COLD?
YEAH.
HERE.
JUST A LITTLE SOME- THING.

WELL...COME BACK WHEN YOU'RE BETTER.

FOOP

BYE.

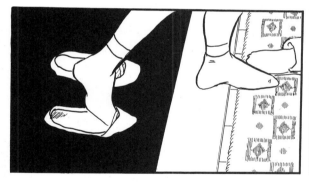

DMP

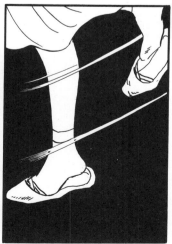

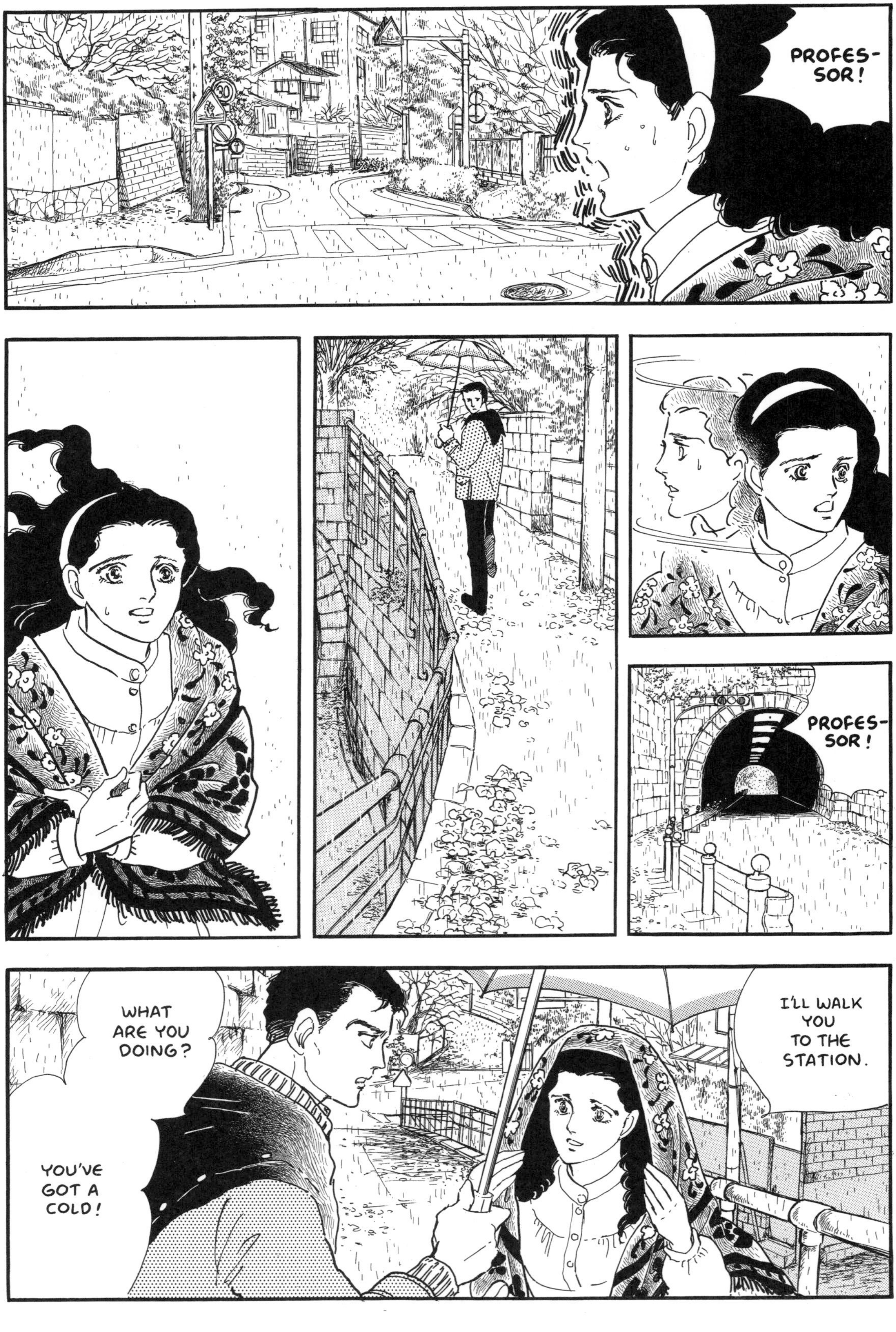
PROFES-
SOR!
PROFES-
SOR!
I'LL WALK YOU TO THE STATION.
WHAT ARE YOU DOING?
YOU'VE GOT A COLD!

THERE'S A PARK ON A HILL FARTHER ALONG THAT OVERLOOKS THE HARBOR.

IT'S A NICE VIEW ON A SUNNY DAY.

THIS IS A NICE NEIGHBORHOOD.

I'LL WALK YOU TO THE BUS STOP.

MY COLD'S BETTER.

I'M TAKING THE BUS. YOU DON'T HAVE TO--

IT'S LIKE SCIENCE FICTION.

YOU KNOW, THERE'S AN INTERESTING NEW THEORY CALLED "PANSPERMIA".

THEN I'LL COME BACK WHEN IT'S SUNNY.

THE QUESTION IS...

...WHERE DID THOSE SPACE BACTERIA COME FROM?

...AND THAT GAVE RISE TO LIFE IN THE OCEANS.

THE THEORY IS THAT LIFE CAME FROM OUTER SPACE.

THERE WERE BACTERIA IN A METEOR THAT FELL TO EARTH...

IN LATE MAY...

...I HAD...

...AN ABORTION.

HE PAID HALF THE COST OF THE OPERATION.

IT WAS MY OWN DECISION.

I COULDN'T POSSIBLY IMAGINE RAISING A CHILD ALONE.

NOBODY DUMPED ANYBODY.

NOBODY KNOWS. NOT MY PARENTS. NOT MY FRIENDS.

DO YOU...

...STILL LOVE HIM?

BUT...

THE POOR BABY...

EVEN THOUGH I HAD LOVED HIM SO MUCH.

NO.

THE HEART IS A STRANGE THING, ISN'T IT? I COMPLETELY LOST INTEREST IN HIM.

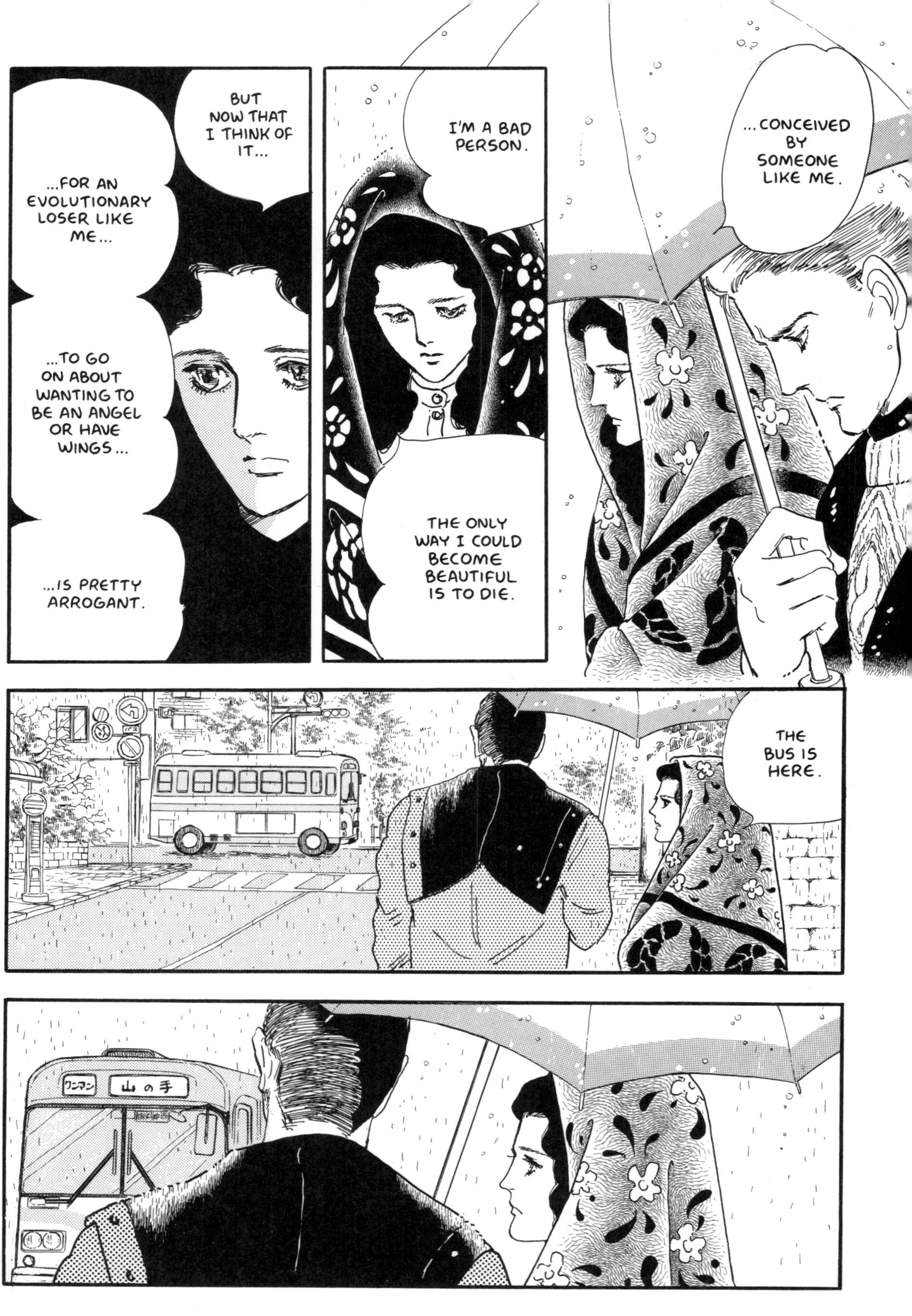
...CONCEIVED BY SOMEONE LIKE ME.
I'M A BAD PERSON.
THE ONLY WAY I COULD BECOME BEAUTIFUL IS TO DIE.
BUT NOW THAT I THINK OF IT...
...FOR AN EVOLUTIONARY LOSER LIKE ME...
...TO GO ON ABOUT WANTING TO BE AN ANGEL OR HAVE WINGS...
...IS PRETTY ARROGANT.
THE BUS IS HERE.
ワンマン
山の手

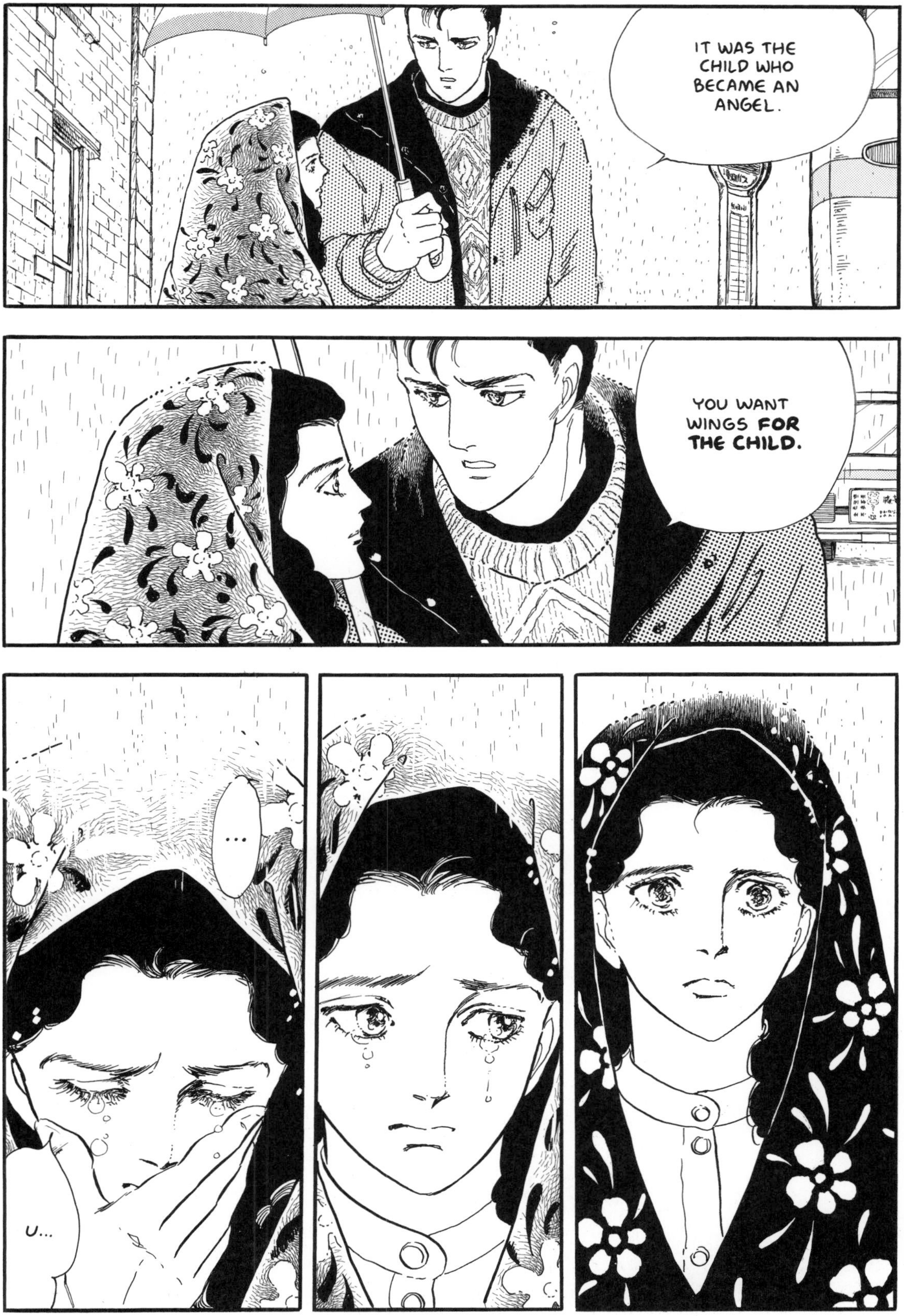
IT WAS THE CHILD WHO BECAME AN ANGEL.
YOU WANT WINGS FOR THE CHILD.
...
U...

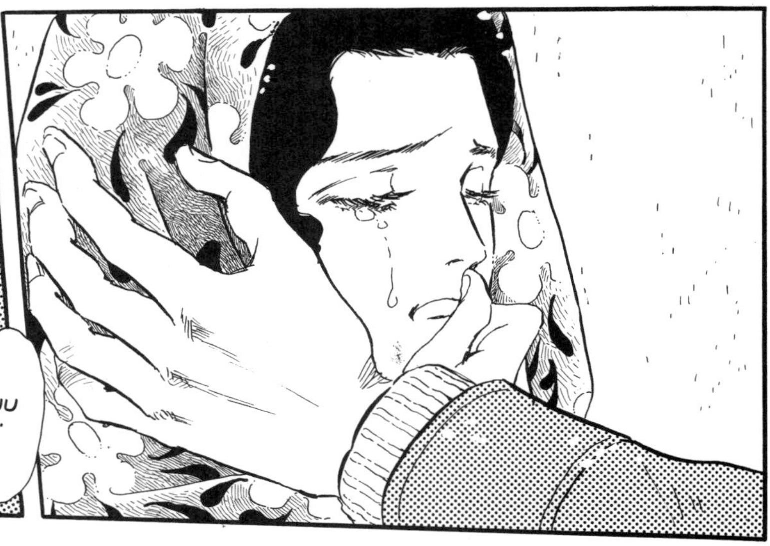

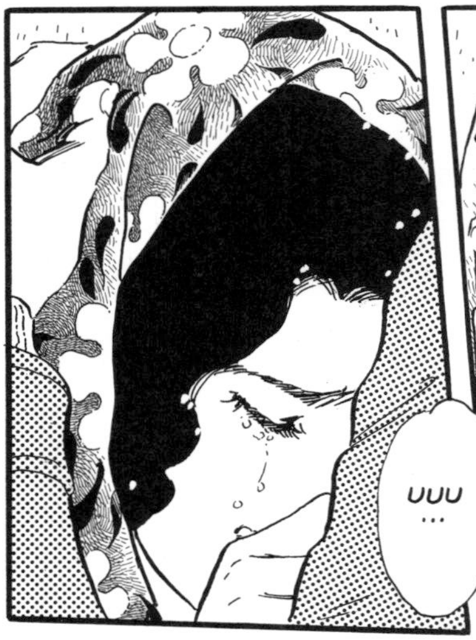
UUU
...

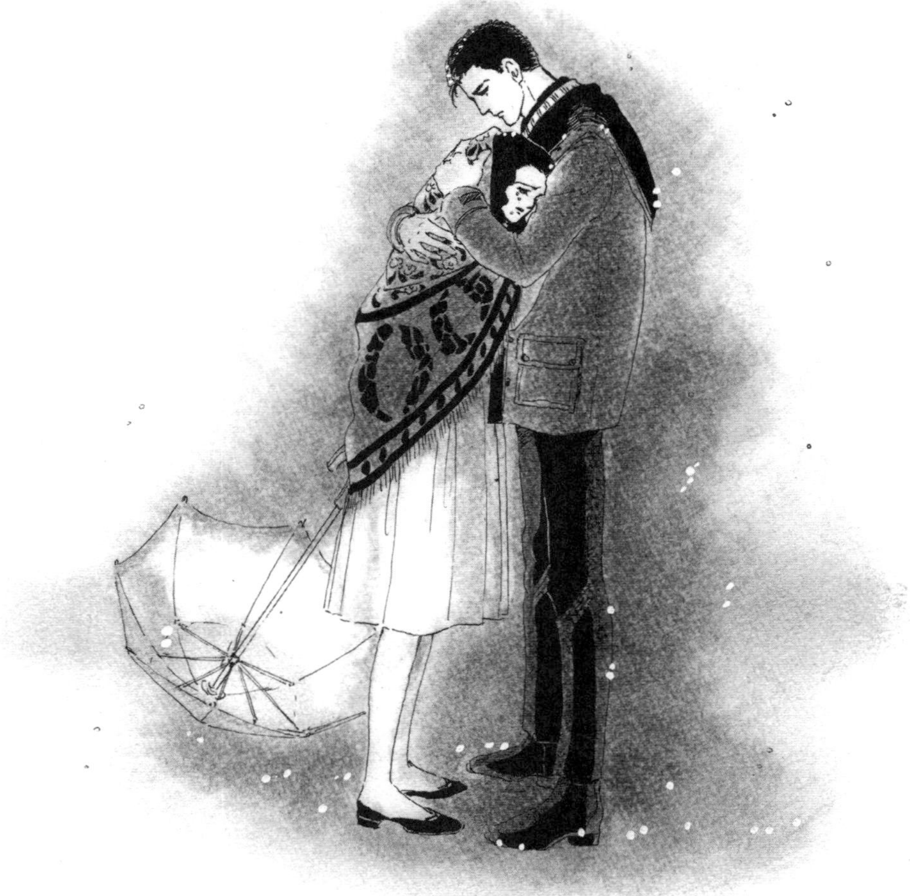

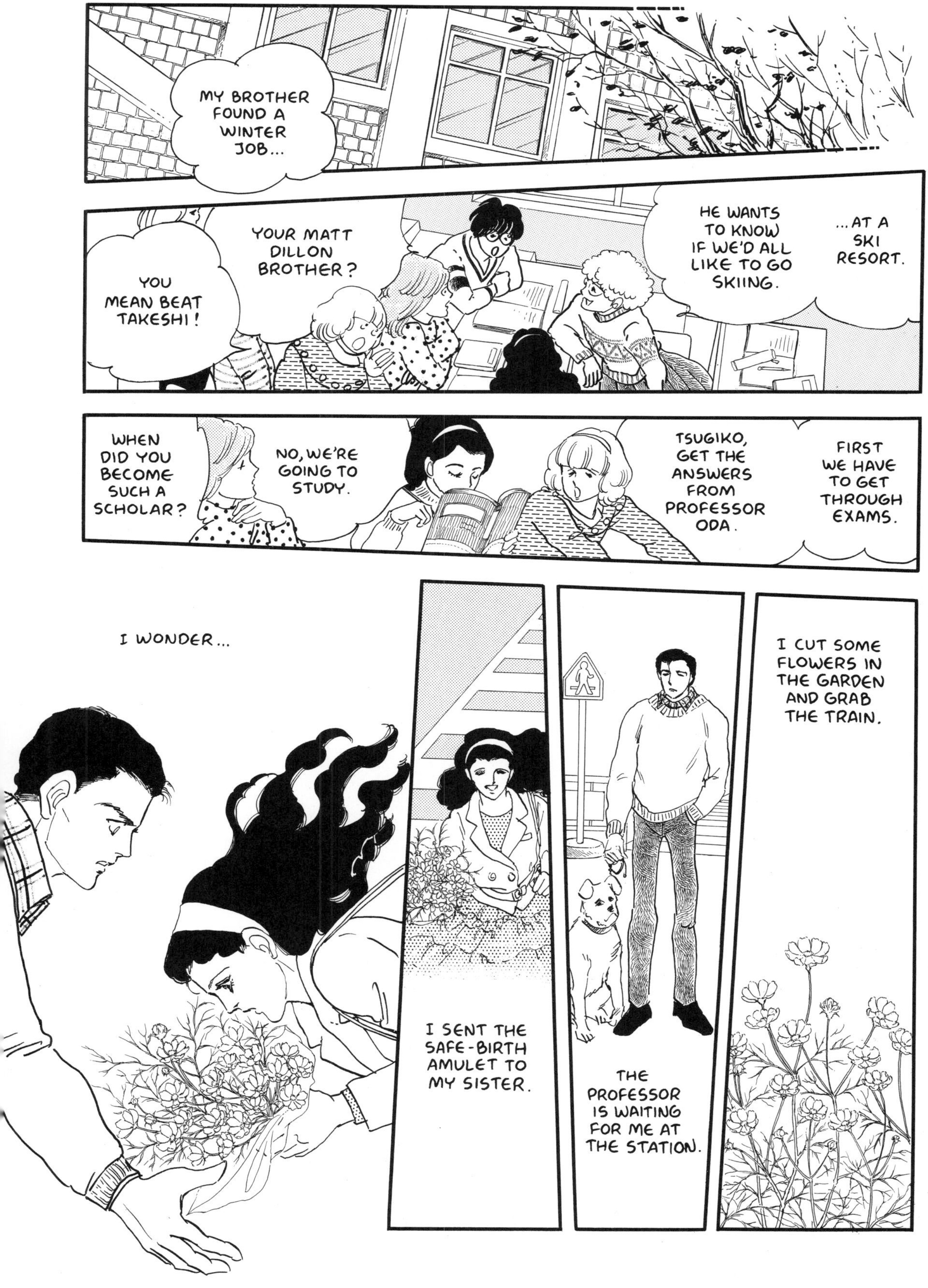
MY BROTHER FOUND A WINTER JOB...
...AT A SKI RESORT.
HE WANTS TO KNOW IF WE'D ALL LIKE TO GO SKIING.
YOUR MATT DILLON BROTHER?
YOU MEAN BEAT TAKESHI!
FIRST WE HAVE TO GET THROUGH EXAMS.
TSUGIKO, GET THE ANSWERS FROM PROFESSOR ODA.
NO, WE'RE GOING TO STUDY.
WHEN DID YOU BECOME SUCH A SCHOLAR?
I CUT SOME FLOWERS IN THE GARDEN AND GRAB THE TRAIN.
THE PROFESSOR IS WAITING FOR ME AT THE STATION.
I SENT THE SAFE-BIRTH AMULET TO MY SISTER.
I WONDER...

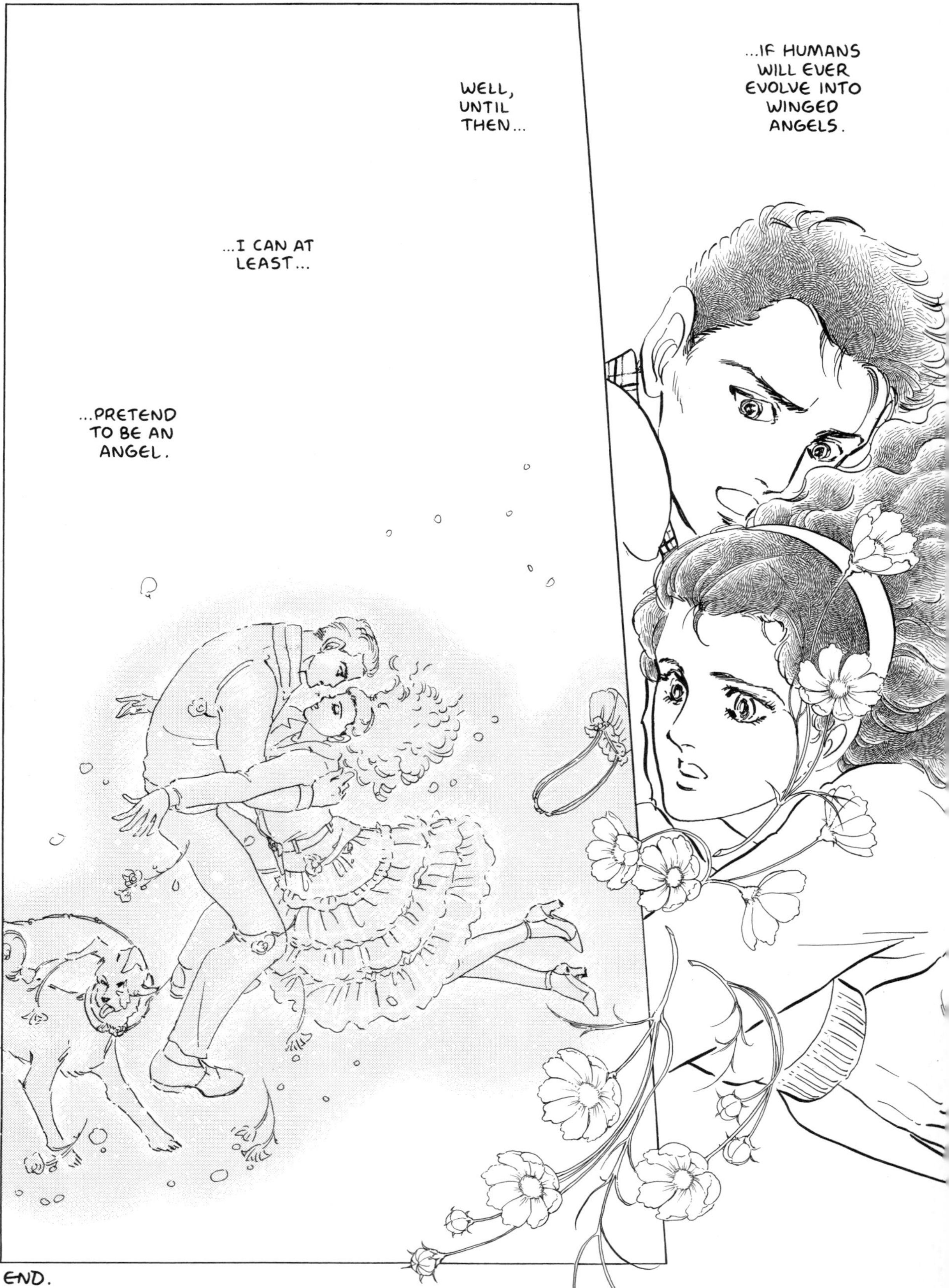
...IF HUMANS WILL EVER EVOLVE INTO WINGED ANGELS.
WELL, UNTIL THEN...
...I CAN AT LEAST...
...PRETEND TO BE AN ANGEL.

END.

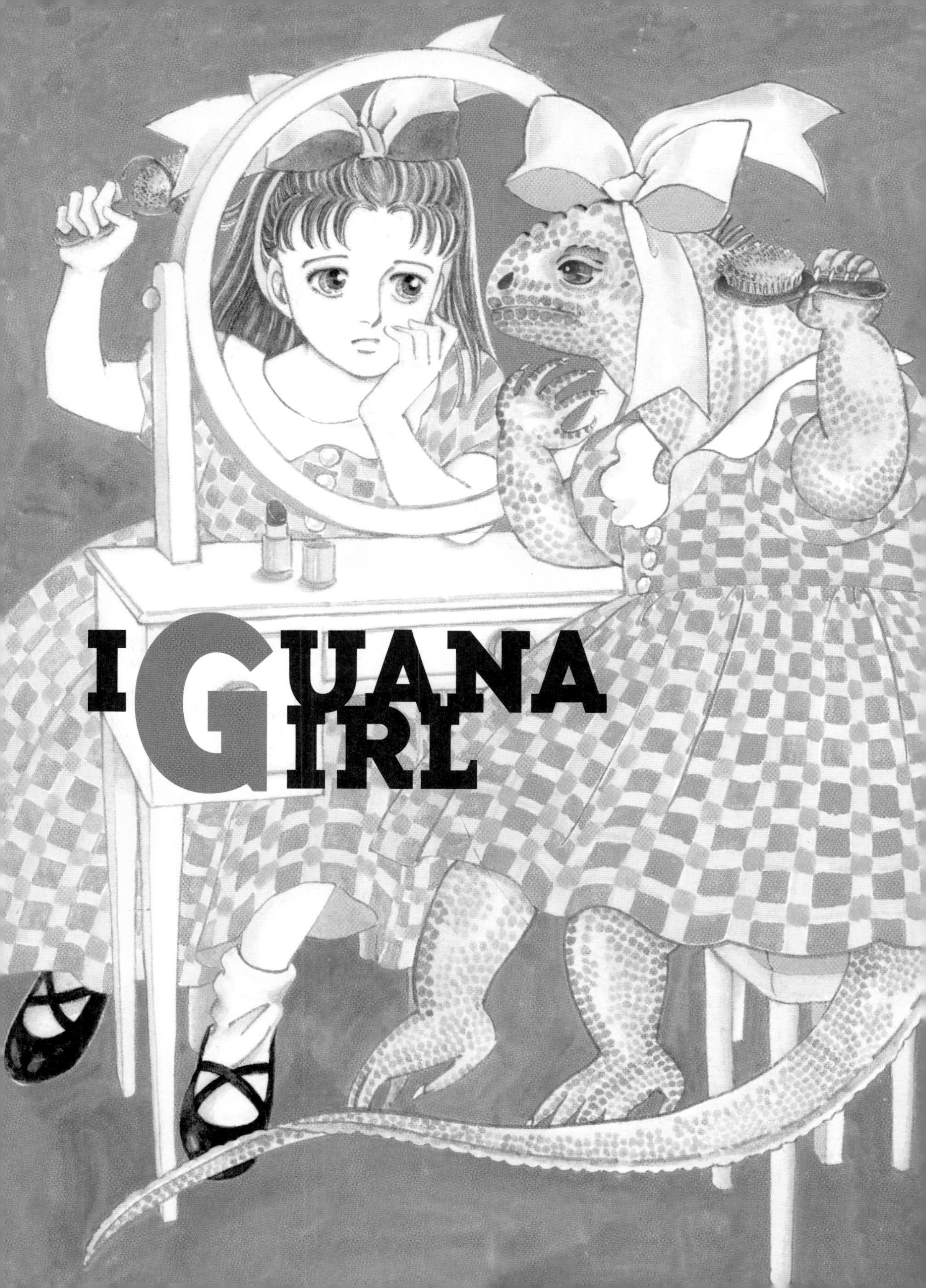
IGUANA
GIRL

THE IGUANA PRINCESS ASKED THE SORCERESS:

"OLD SORCERESS, I HAVE FALLEN IN LOVE WITH A HUMAN PRINCE. PLEASE. MAKE ME A HUMAN GIRL."

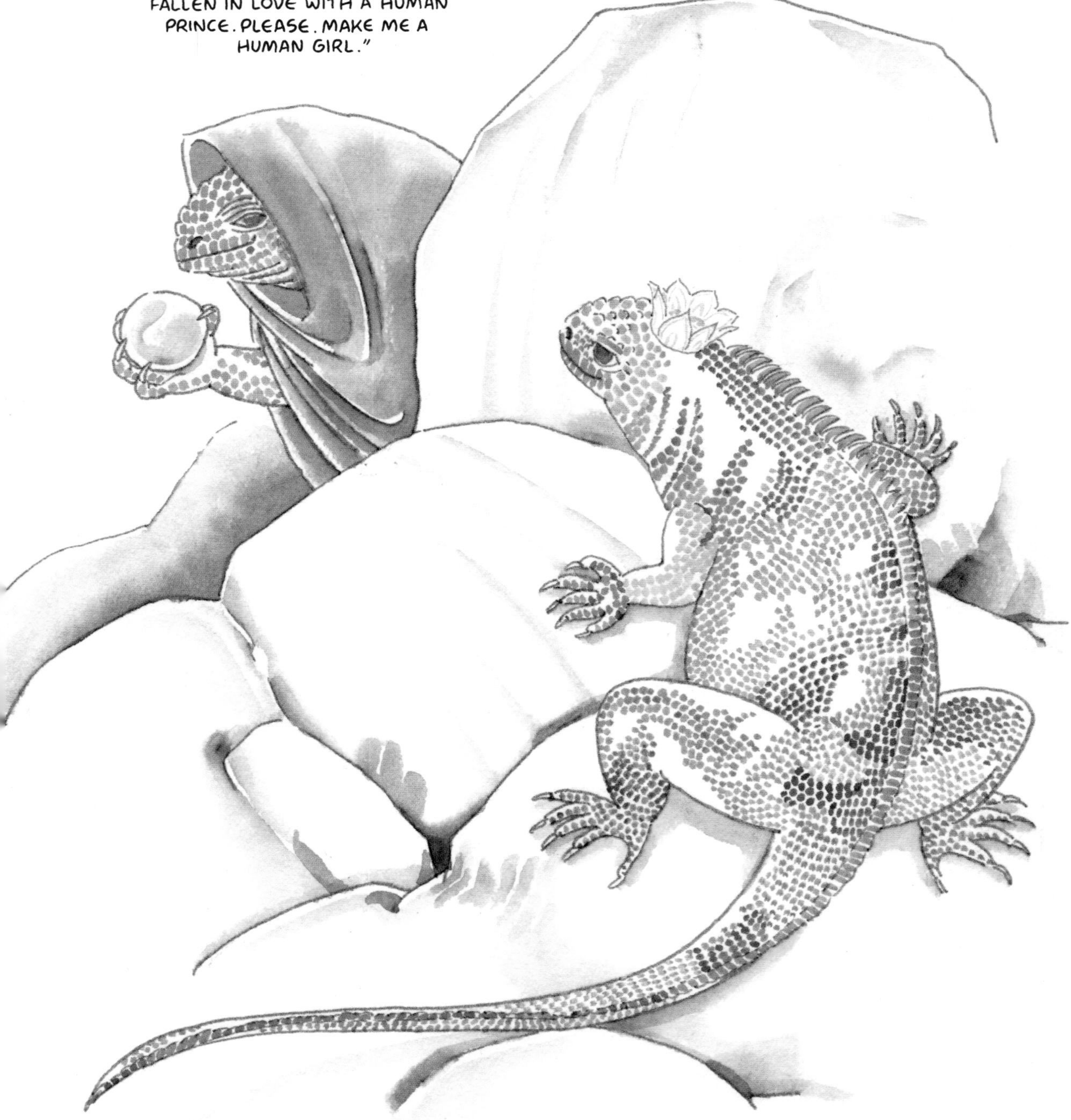

"SO BE IT," SAID THE SORCERESS. "I SHALL MAKE YOU A HUMAN GIRL. BUT IN RETURN..."

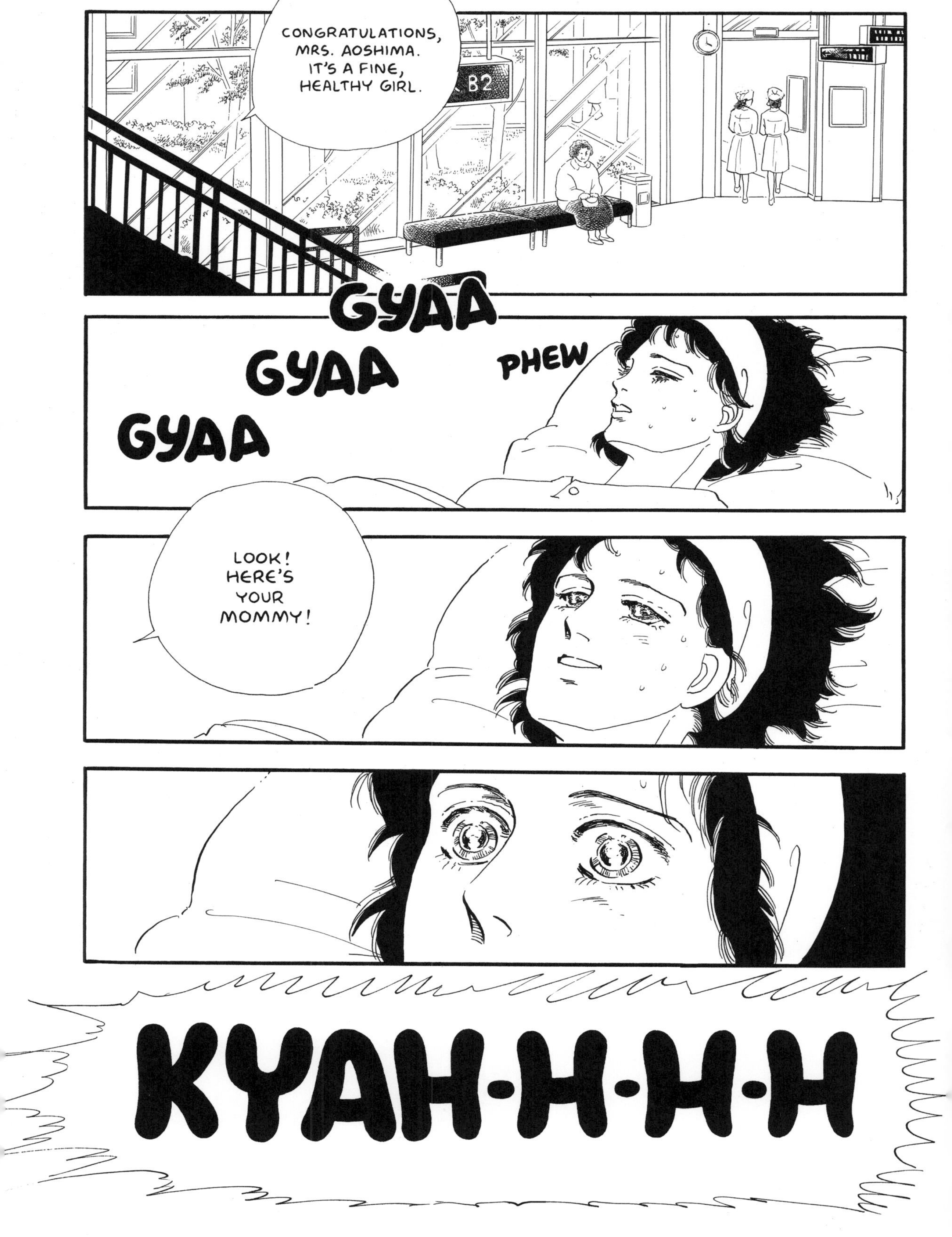
CONGRATULATIONS, MRS. AOSHIMA. IT'S A FINE, HEALTHY GIRL.
GYAA
PHEW
GYAA
GYAA
LOOK! HERE'S YOUR MOMMY!
KYAH-H-H-H

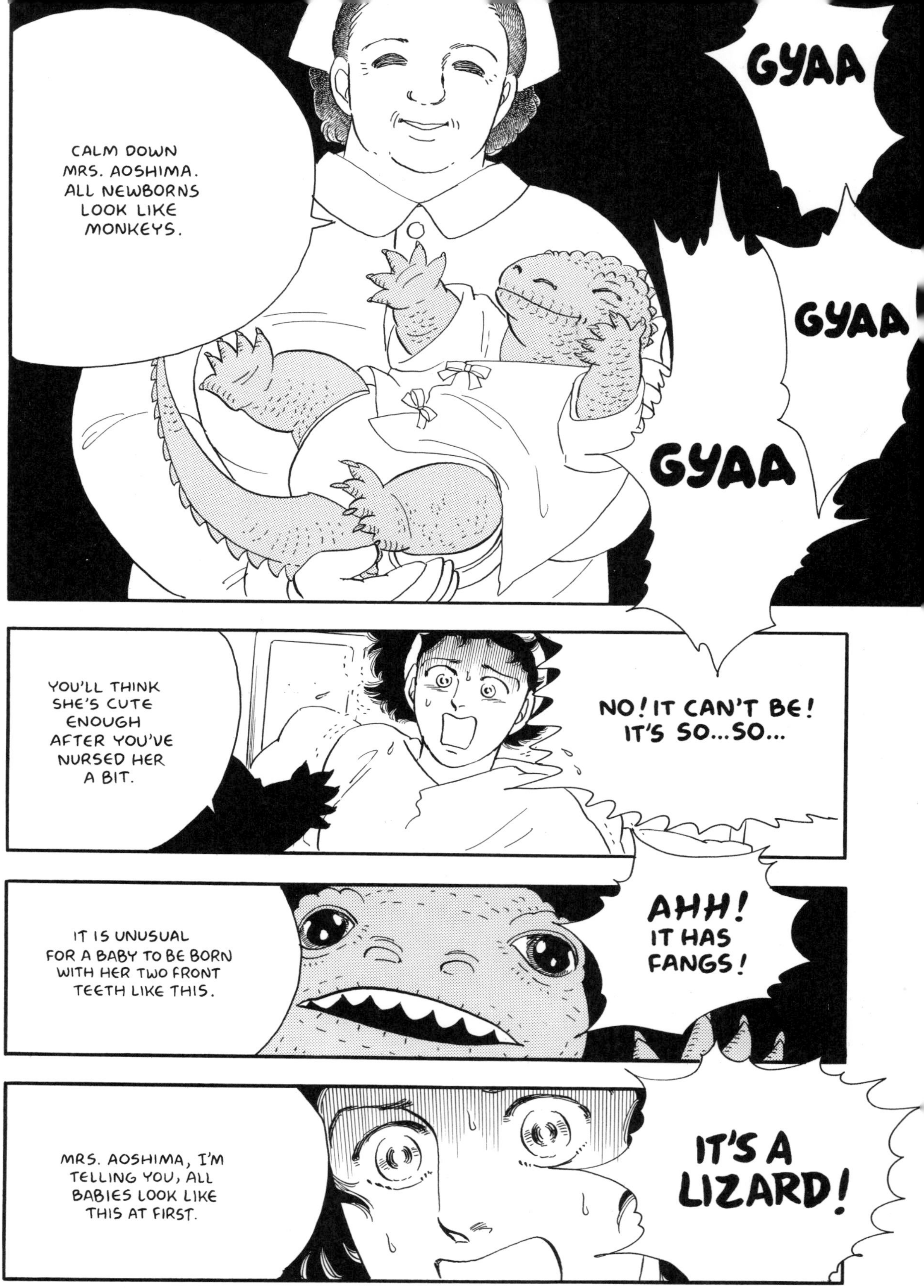
GYAA
GYAA
GYAA
CALM DOWN MRS. AOSHIMA. ALL NEWBORNS LOOK LIKE MONKEYS.
NO! IT CAN'T BE! IT'S SO...SO...
YOU'LL THINK SHE'S CUTE ENOUGH AFTER YOU'VE NURSED HER A BIT.
AHH! IT HAS FANGS!
IT IS UNUSUAL FOR A BABY TO BE BORN WITH HER TWO FRONT TEETH LIKE THIS.
IT'S A LIZARD!
MRS. AOSHIMA, I'M TELLING YOU, ALL BABIES LOOK LIKE THIS AT FIRST.

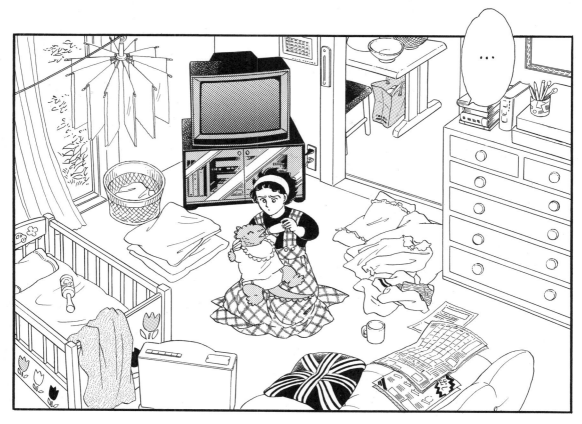

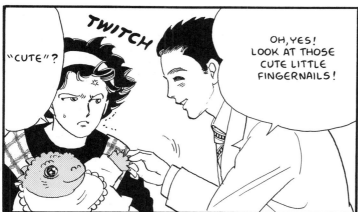

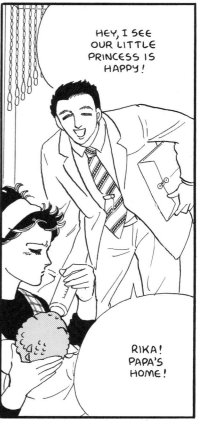

...
HEY, I SEE OUR LITTLE PRINCESS IS HAPPY!
RIKA! PAPA'S HOME!
OH, YES! LOOK AT THOSE CUTE LITTLE FINGERNAILS!
TWITCH
"CUTE"?
D--DOES SHE REALLY LOOK LIKE A HUMAN BABY TO YOU?
TO ME... TO ME...
...

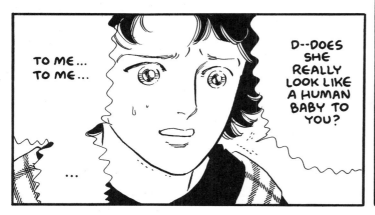

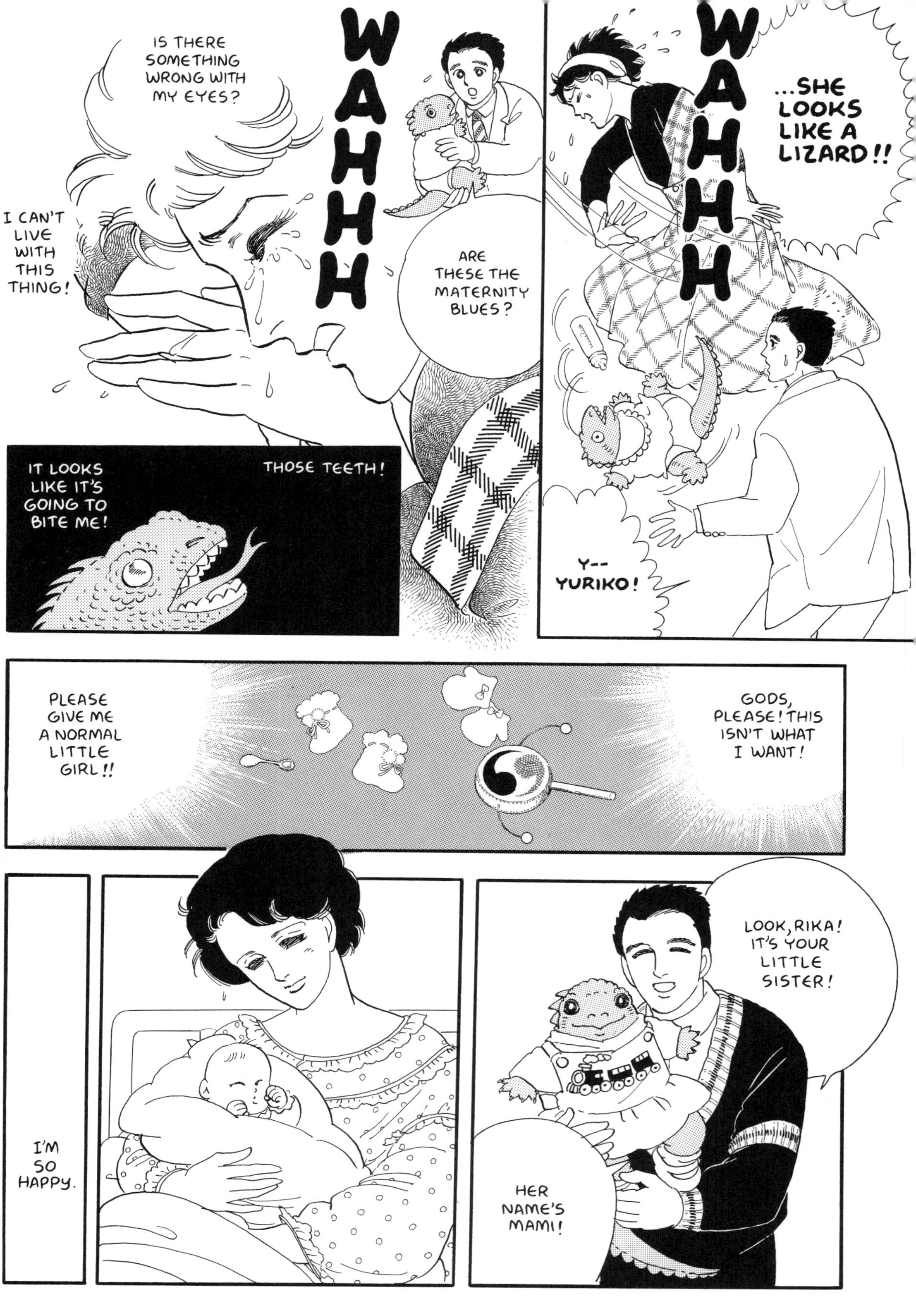
WAHHH
...SHE LOOKS LIKE A LIZARD!!
Y-- YURIKO!
WAHHH
IS THERE SOMETHING WRONG WITH MY EYES?
ARE THESE THE MATERNITY BLUES?
I CAN'T LIVE WITH THIS THING!
THOSE TEETH!
IT LOOKS LIKE IT'S GOING TO BITE ME!
GODS, PLEASE! THIS ISN'T WHAT I WANT!
PLEASE GIVE ME A NORMAL LITTLE GIRL!!
LOOK, RIKA! IT'S YOUR LITTLE SISTER!
HER NAME'S MAMI!
I'M SO HAPPY.

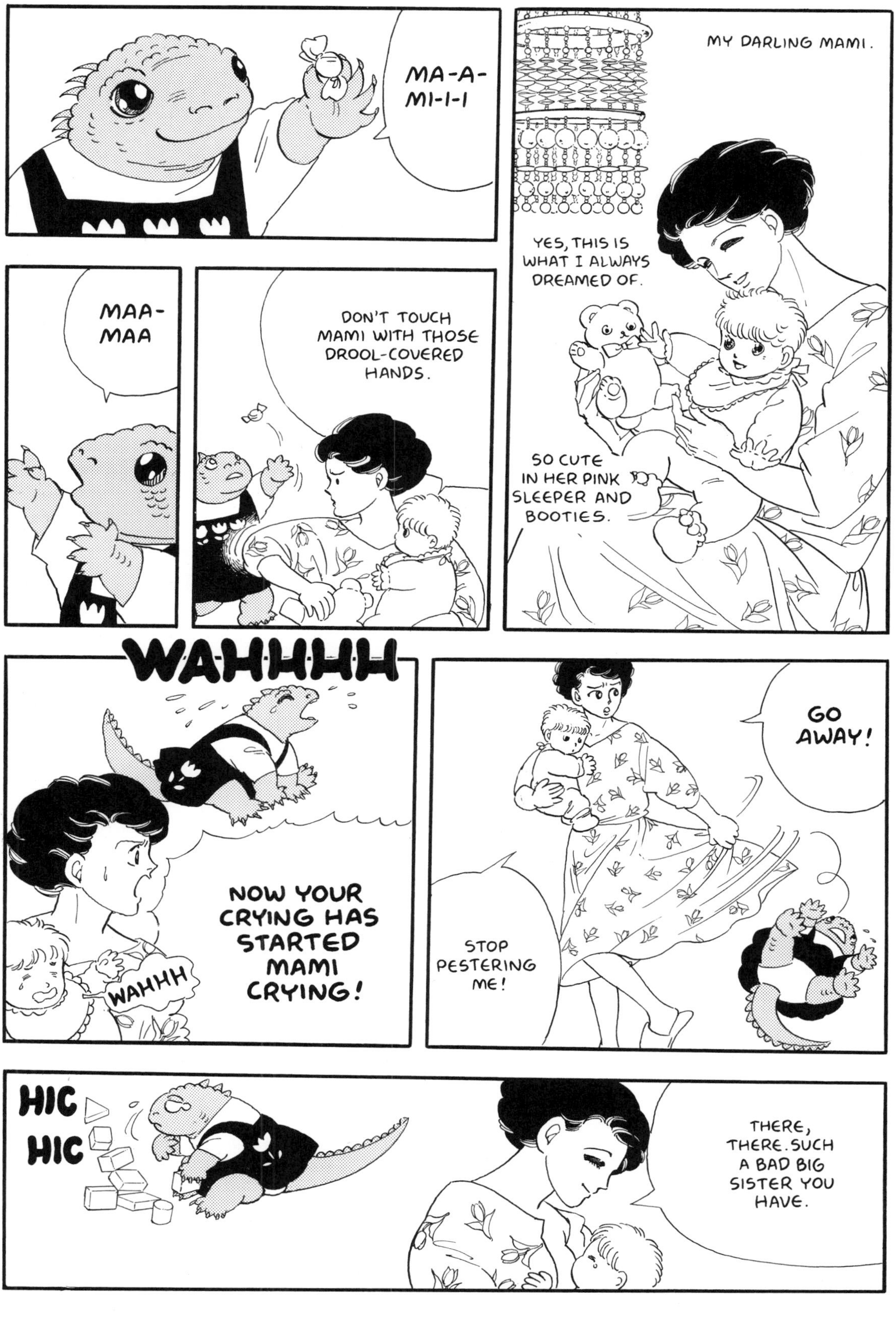
MY DARLING MAMI.
YES, THIS IS WHAT I ALWAYS DREAMED OF.
SO CUTE IN HER PINK SLEEPER AND BOOTIES.
MA-A-MI-I-I
DON'T TOUCH MAMI WITH THOSE DROOL-COVERED HANDS.
MAA-MAA
GO AWAY!
STOP PESTERING ME!
WAHHHH
NOW YOUR CRYING HAS STARTED MAMI CRYING!
WAHHH
THERE, THERE. SUCH A BAD BIG SISTER YOU HAVE.
HIC HIC

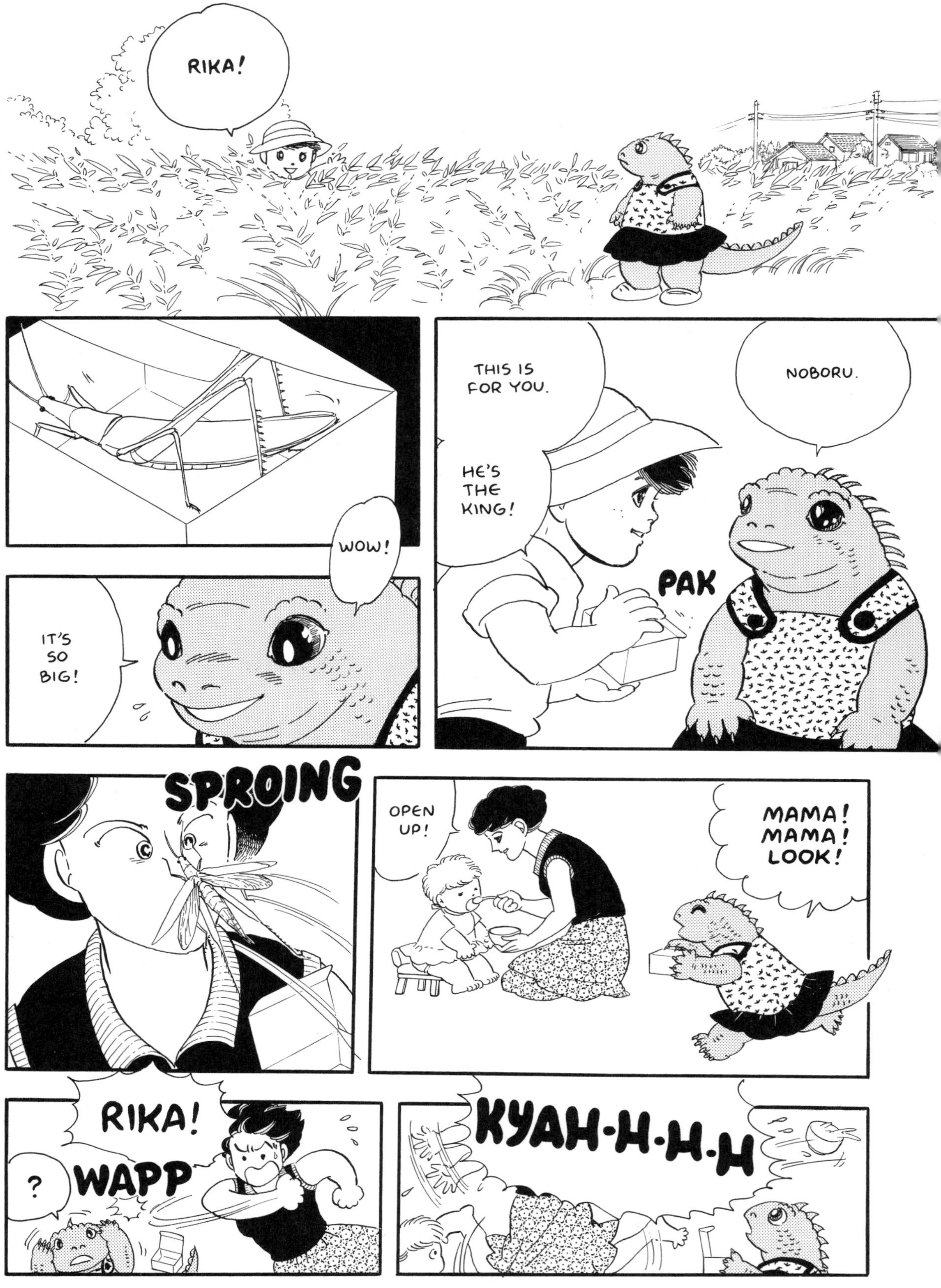
RIKA!
NOBORU.
THIS IS FOR YOU.
HE'S THE KING!
PAK
WOW!
IT'S SO BIG!
MAMA! MAMA! LOOK!
OPEN UP!
SPROING
KYAH-H-H-H
RIKA!
WAPP
?

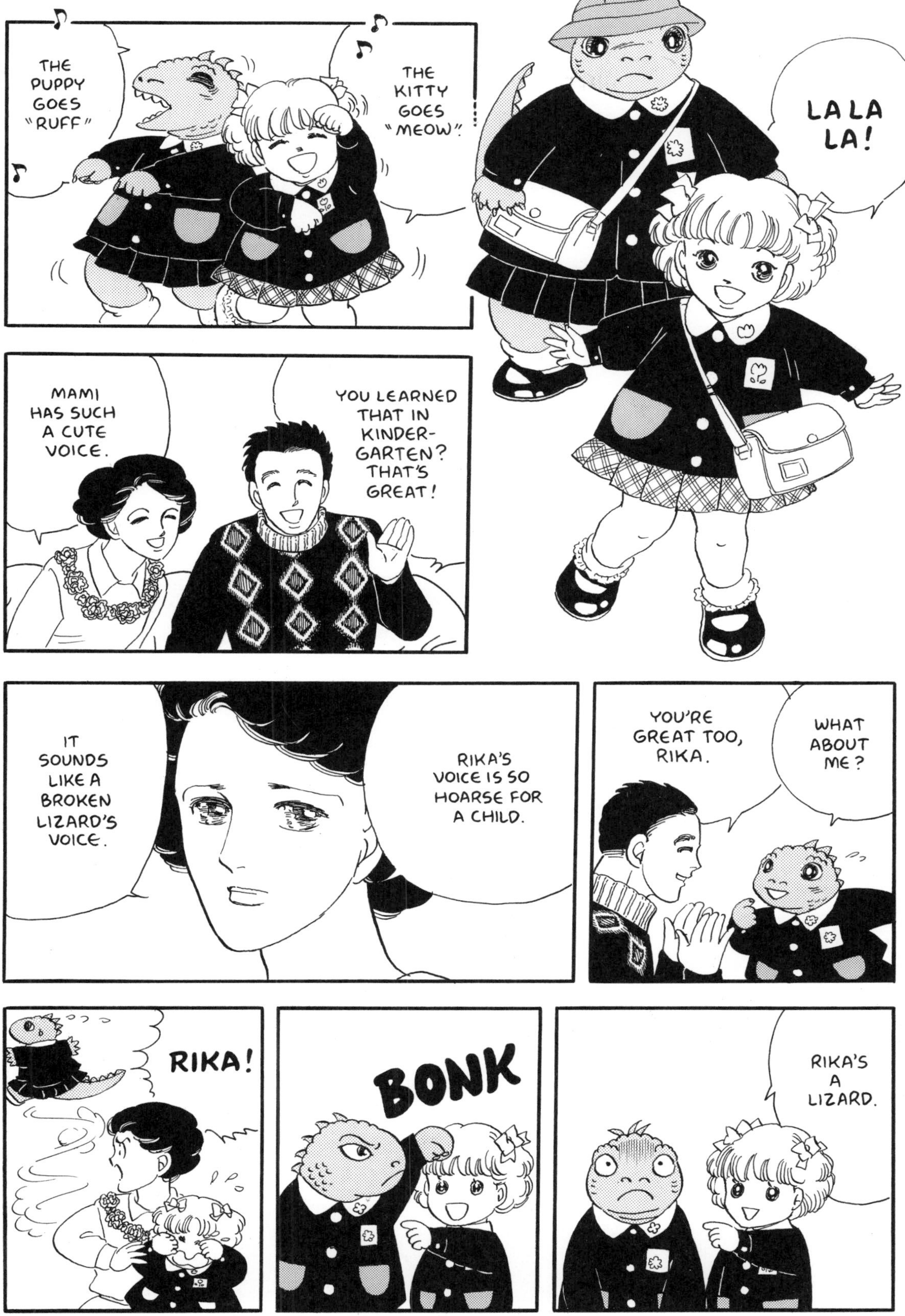
LA LA LA!
THE KITTY GOES "MEOW".
THE PUPPY GOES "RUFF"
YOU LEARNED THAT IN KINDER-GARTEN? THAT'S GREAT!
MAMI HAS SUCH A CUTE VOICE.
WHAT ABOUT ME?
YOU'RE GREAT TOO, RIKA.
RIKA'S VOICE IS SO HOARSE FOR A CHILD.
IT SOUNDS LIKE A BROKEN LIZARD'S VOICE.
RIKA'S A LIZARD.
BONK
RIKA!

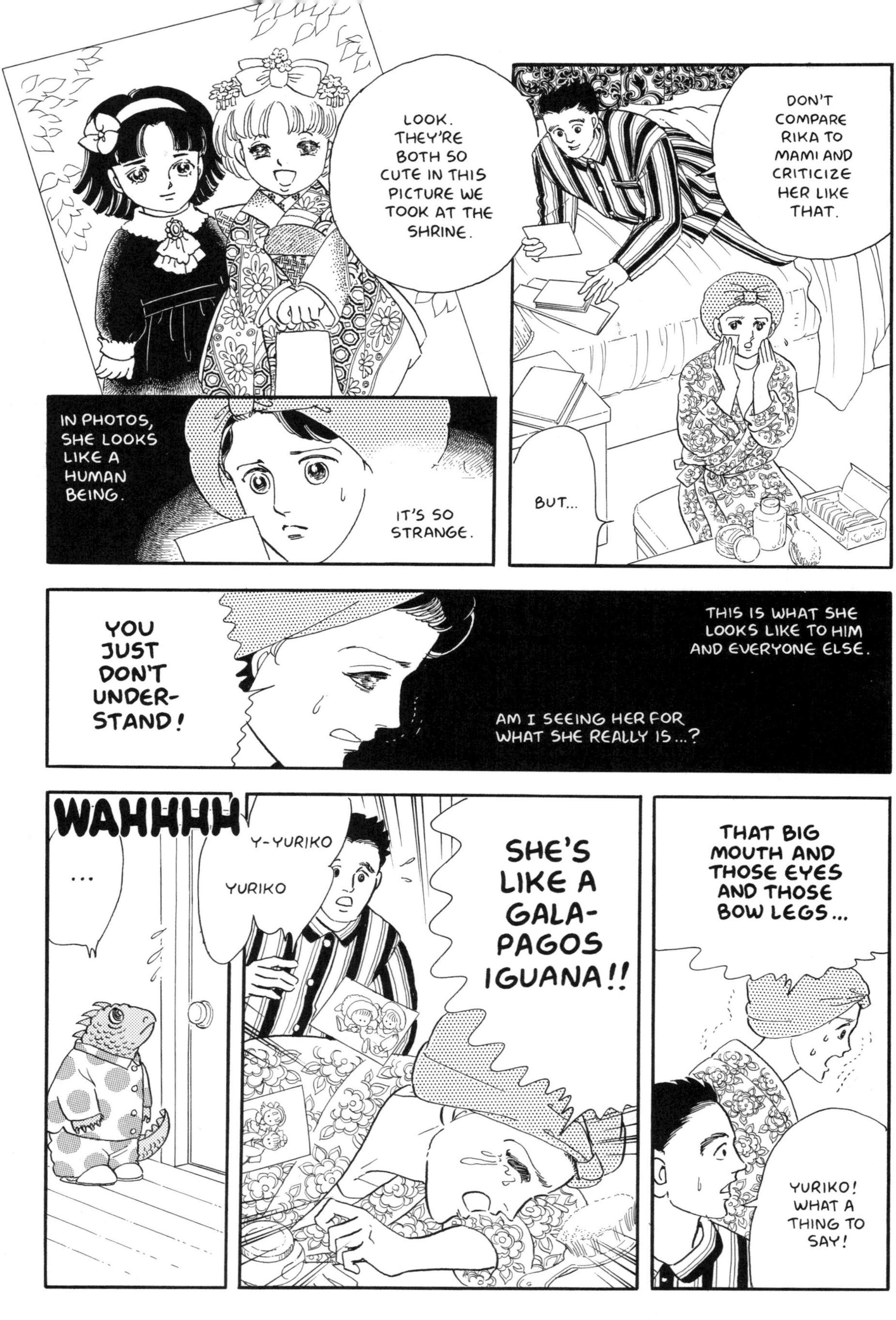
DON'T COMPARE RIKA TO MAMI AND CRITICIZE HER LIKE THAT.
BUT...
LOOK. THEY'RE BOTH SO CUTE IN THIS PICTURE WE TOOK AT THE SHRINE.
IN PHOTOS, SHE LOOKS LIKE A HUMAN BEING.
IT'S SO STRANGE.
THIS IS WHAT SHE LOOKS LIKE TO HIM AND EVERYONE ELSE.
AM I SEEING HER FOR WHAT SHE REALLY IS...?
YOU JUST DON'T UNDER-STAND!
THAT BIG MOUTH AND THOSE EYES AND THOSE BOW LEGS...
YURIKO! WHAT A THING TO SAY!
SHE'S LIKE A GALA-PAGOS IGUANA!!
Y-YURIKO
YURIKO
WAHHHH
...

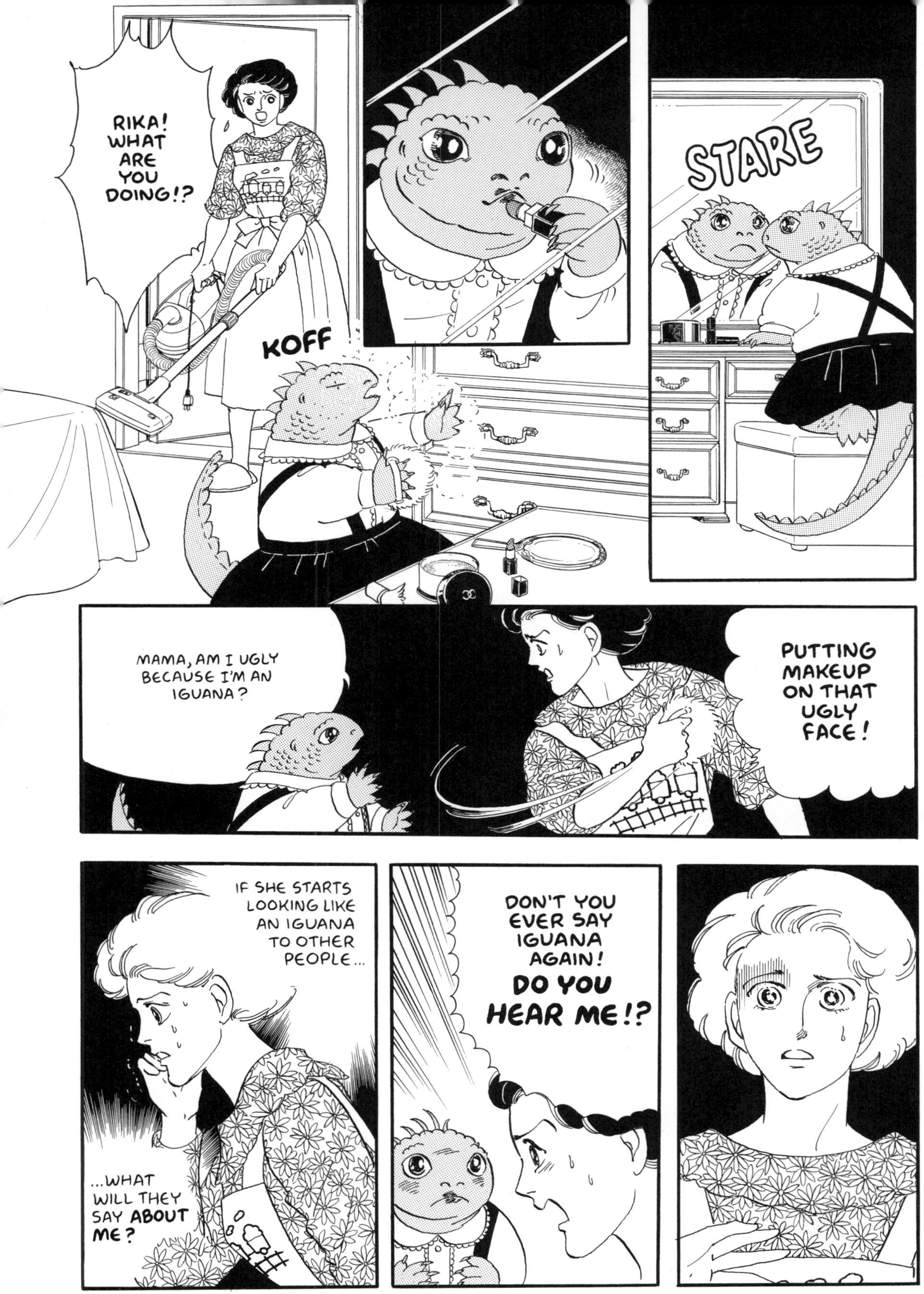
STARE
RIKA! WHAT ARE YOU DOING!?
KOFF
PUTTING MAKEUP ON THAT UGLY FACE!
MAMA, AM I UGLY BECAUSE I'M AN IGUANA?
DON'T YOU EVER SAY IGUANA AGAIN! DO YOU HEAR ME!?
IF SHE STARTS LOOKING LIKE AN IGUANA TO OTHER PEOPLE...
...WHAT WILL THEY SAY ABOUT ME?

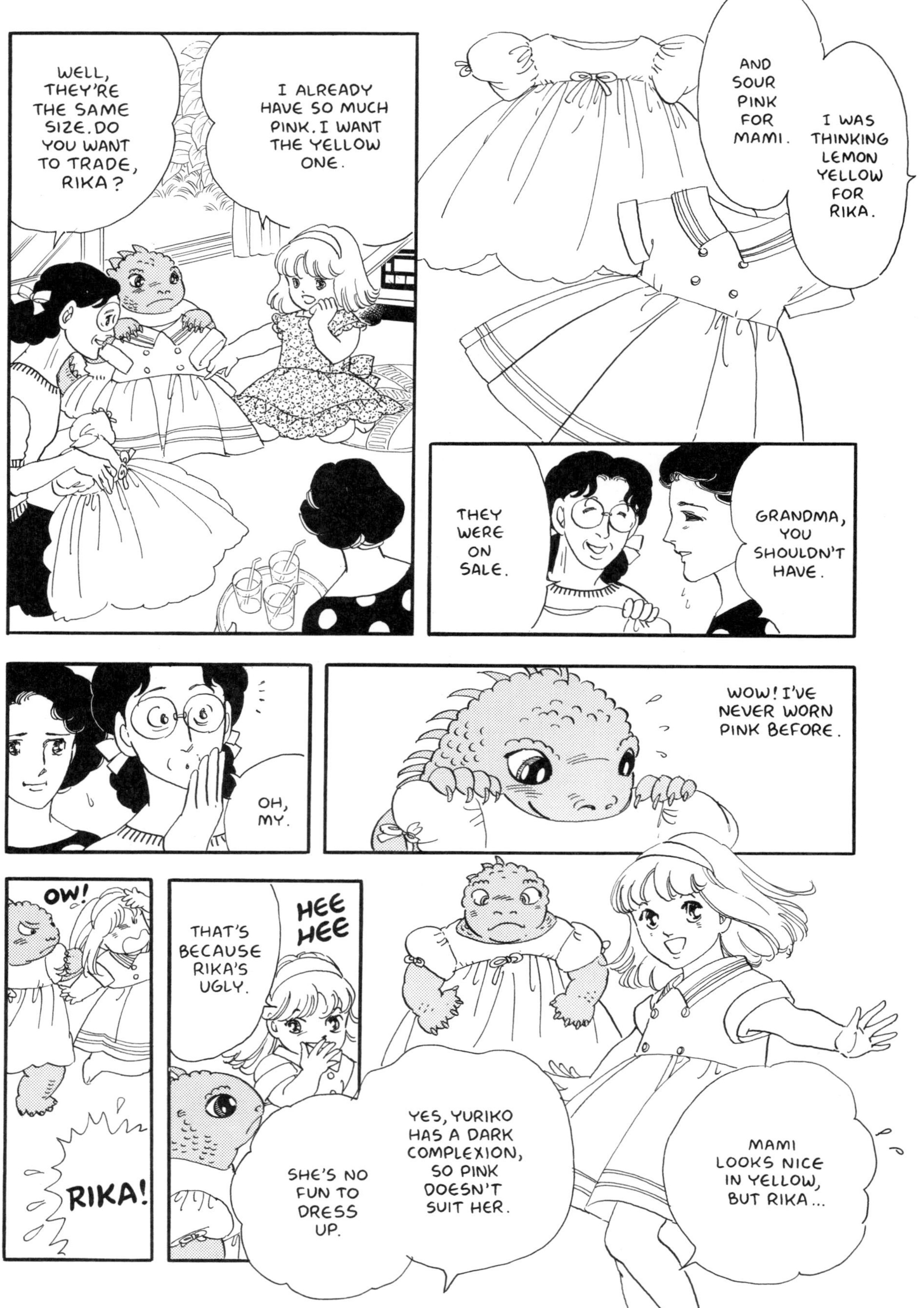
I WAS THINKING LEMON YELLOW FOR RIKA.
AND SOUR PINK FOR MAMI.
GRANDMA, YOU SHOULDN'T HAVE.
THEY WERE ON SALE.
I ALREADY HAVE SO MUCH PINK. I WANT THE YELLOW ONE.
WELL, THEY'RE THE SAME SIZE. DO YOU WANT TO TRADE, RIKA?
WOW! I'VE NEVER WORN PINK BEFORE.
OH, MY.
MAMI LOOKS NICE IN YELLOW, BUT RIKA...
YES, YURIKO HAS A DARK COMPLEXION, SO PINK DOESN'T SUIT HER.
SHE'S NO FUN TO DRESS UP.
HEE HEE
THAT'S BECAUSE RIKA'S UGLY.
OW!
RIKA!

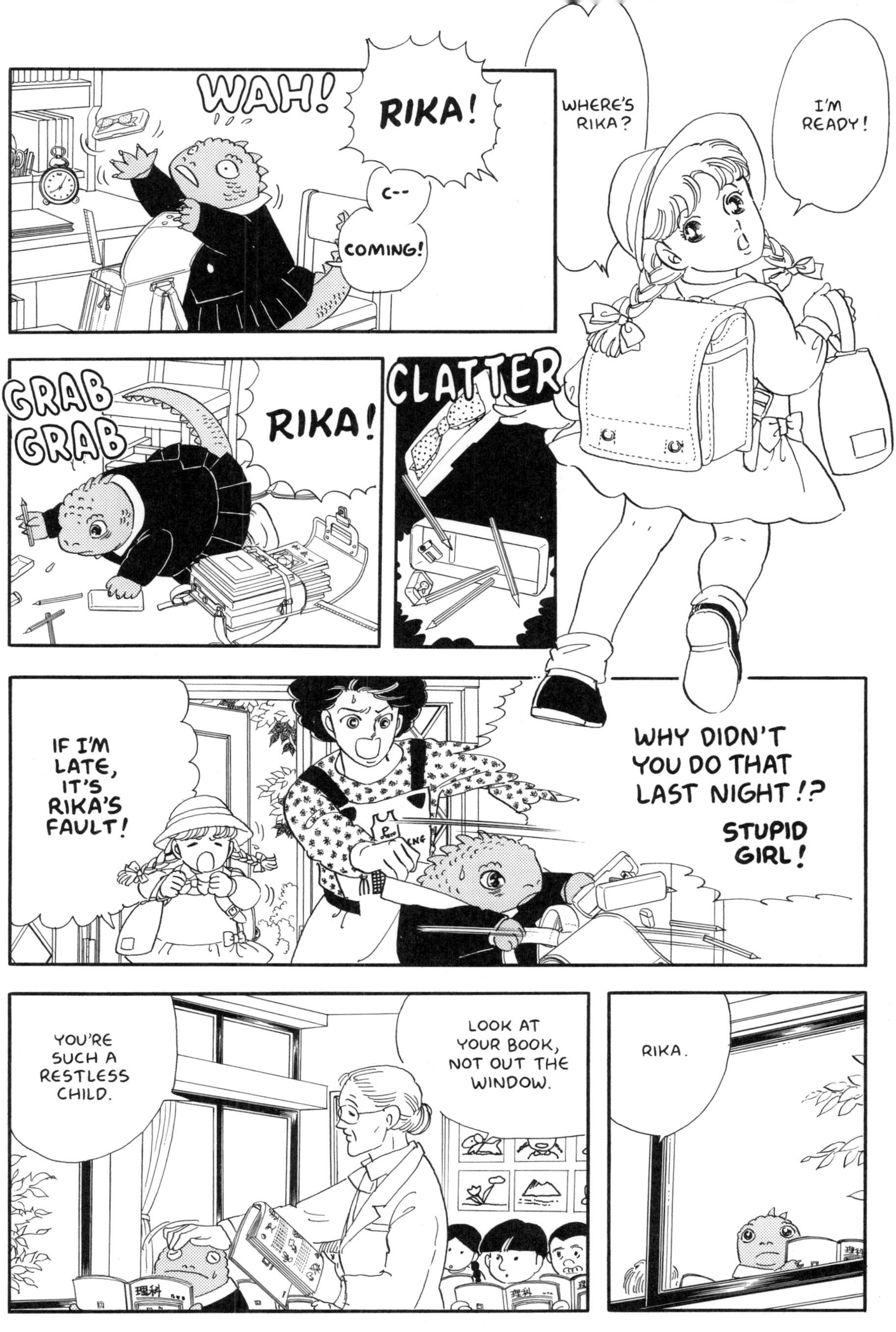
I'M READY!
WHERE'S RIKA?
RIKA!
WAH!
C--
COMING!
CLATTER
RIKA!
GRAB GRAB
WHY DIDN'T YOU DO THAT LAST NIGHT!?
STUPID GIRL!
IF I'M LATE, IT'S RIKA'S FAULT!
RIKA.
LOOK AT YOUR BOOK, NOT OUT THE WINDOW.
YOU'RE SUCH A RESTLESS CHILD.

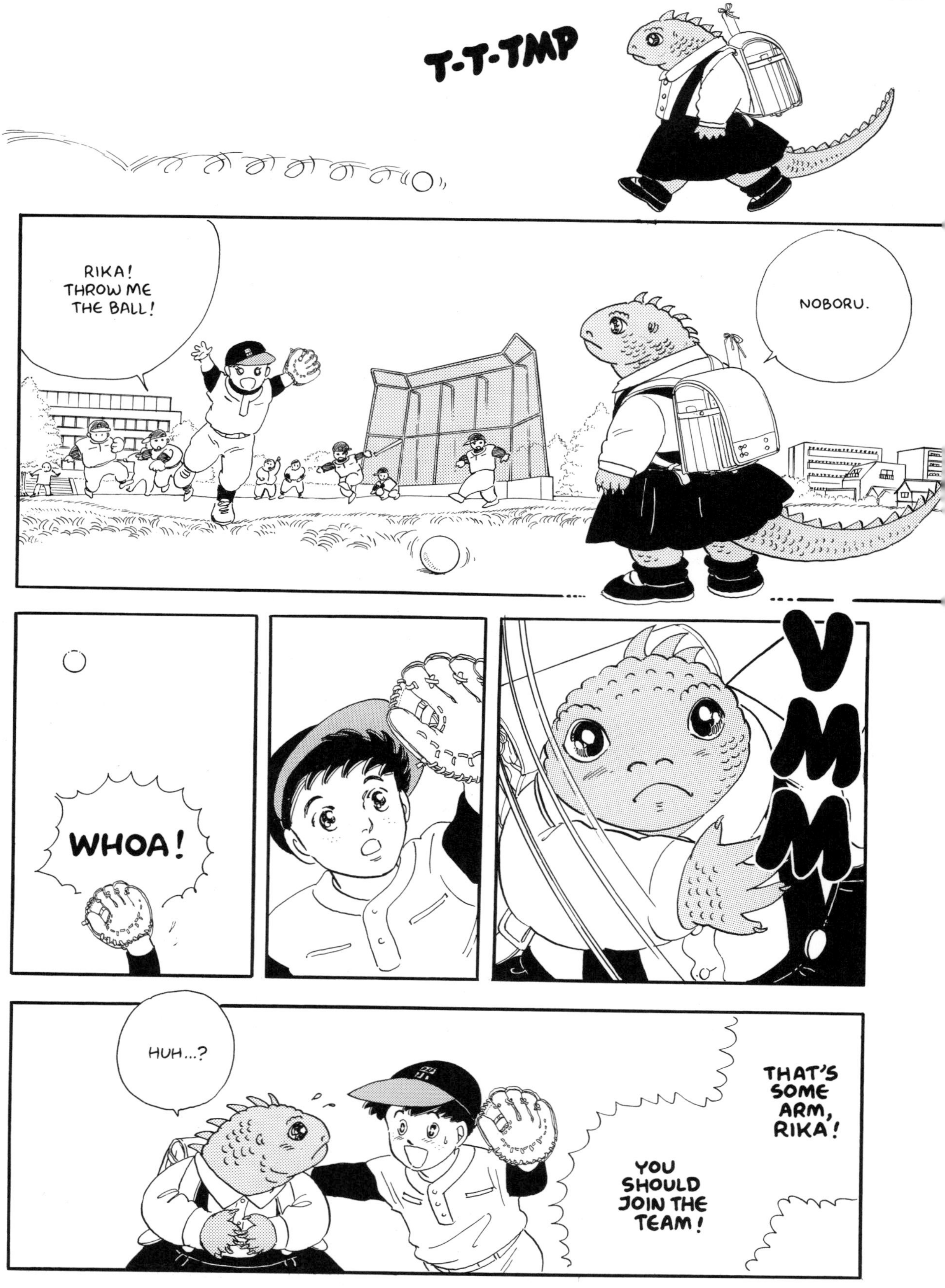
T-T-TMP
NOBORU.
RIKA! THROW ME THE BALL!
VMM
WHOA!
THAT'S SOME ARM, RIKA!
YOU SHOULD JOIN THE TEAM!
HUH...?

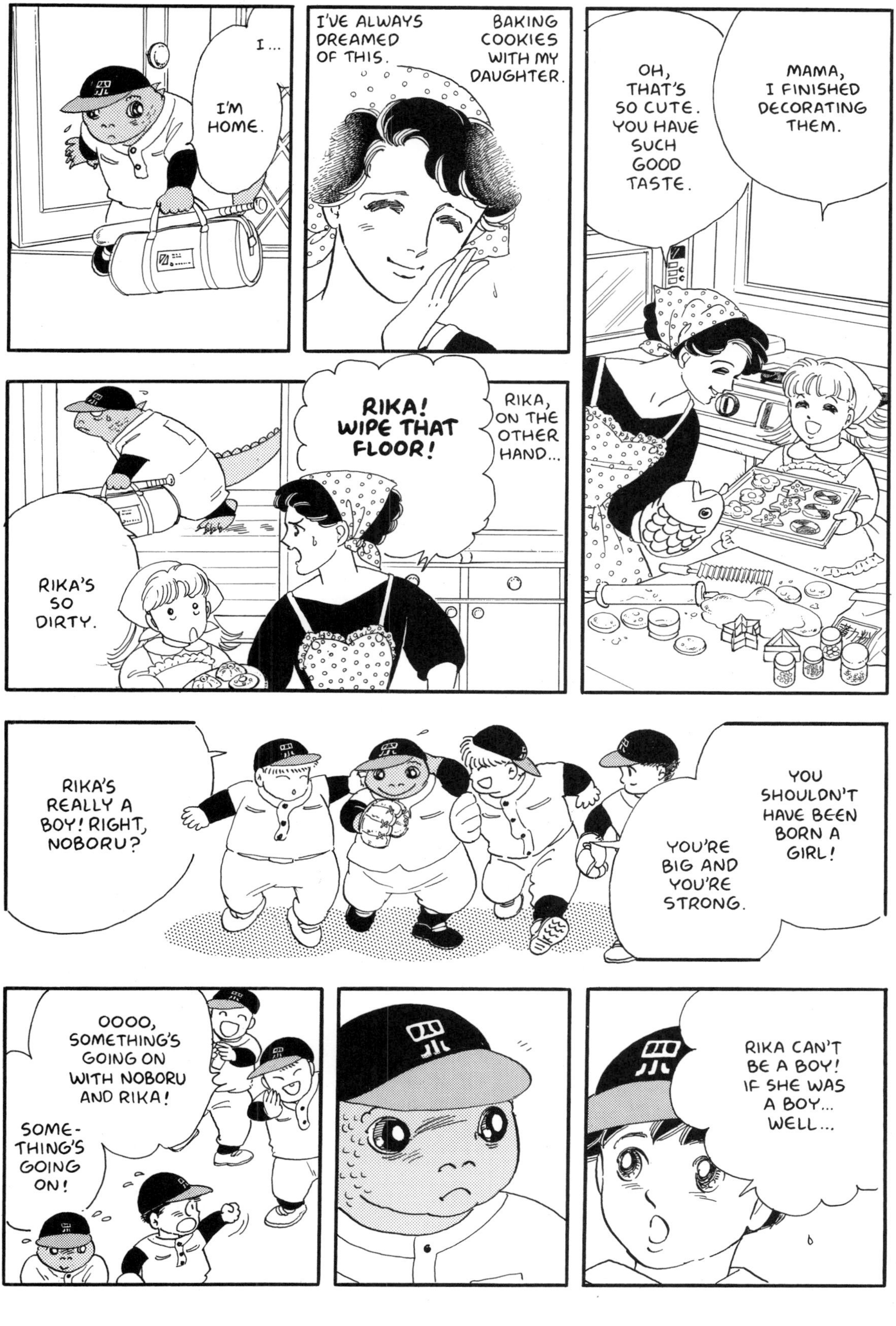
MAMA, I FINISHED DECORATING THEM.
OH, THAT'S SO CUTE. YOU HAVE SUCH GOOD TASTE.
BAKING COOKIES WITH MY DAUGHTER.
I'VE ALWAYS DREAMED OF THIS.
I...
I'M HOME.
RIKA, ON THE OTHER HAND...
RIKA! WIPE THAT FLOOR!
RIKA'S SO DIRTY.
YOU SHOULDN'T HAVE BEEN BORN A GIRL!
YOU'RE BIG AND YOU'RE STRONG.
RIKA'S REALLY A BOY! RIGHT, NOBORU?
RIKA CAN'T BE A BOY! IF SHE WAS A BOY... WELL...
OOOO, SOMETHING'S GOING ON WITH NOBORU AND RIKA!
SOME-THING'S GOING ON!

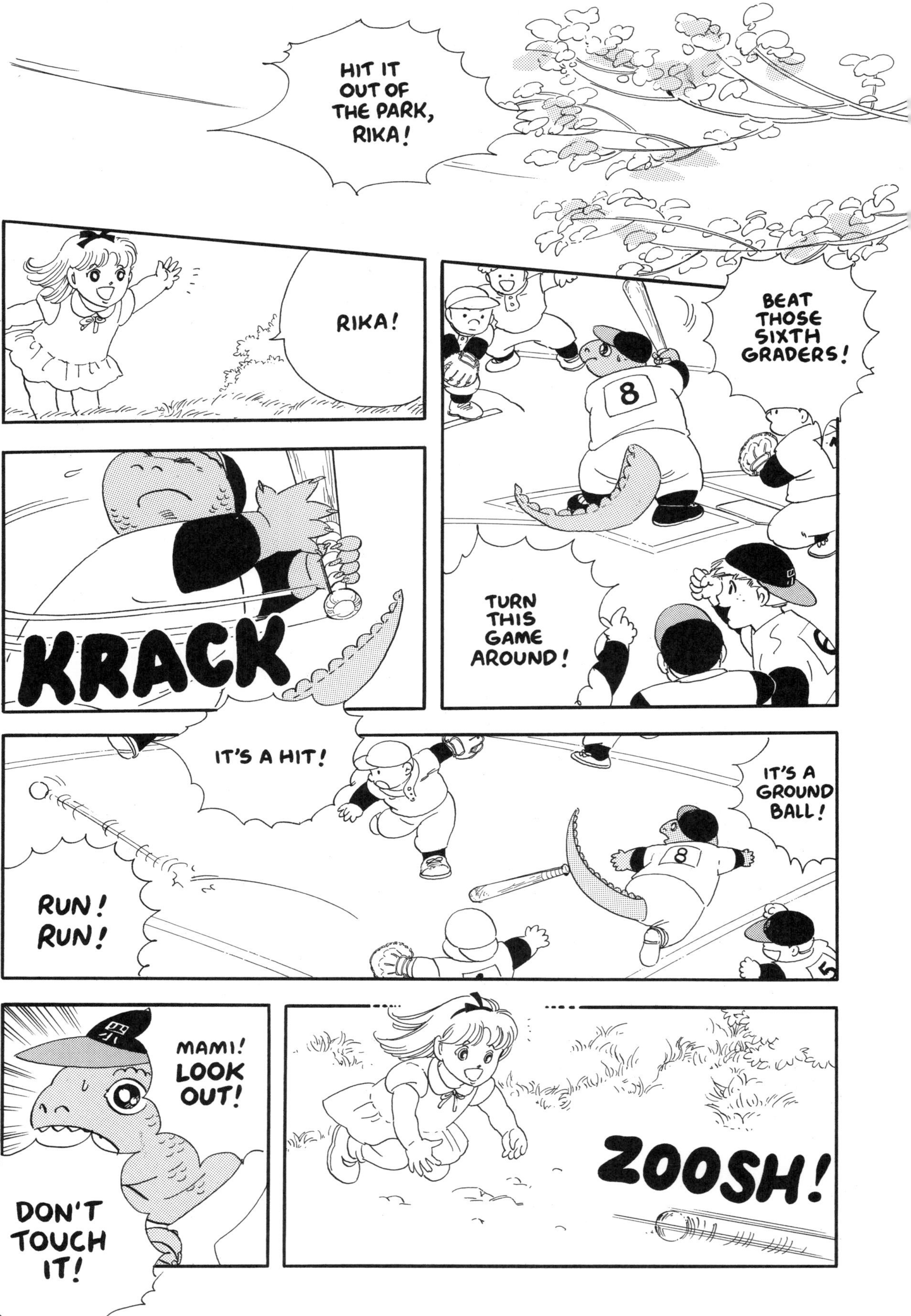
HIT IT OUT OF THE PARK, RIKA!
BEAT THOSE SIXTH GRADERS!
TURN THIS GAME AROUND!
RIKA!
KRACK
IT'S A GROUND BALL!
IT'S A HIT!
RUN! RUN!
ZOOSH!
MAMI! LOOK OUT!
DON'T TOUCH IT!

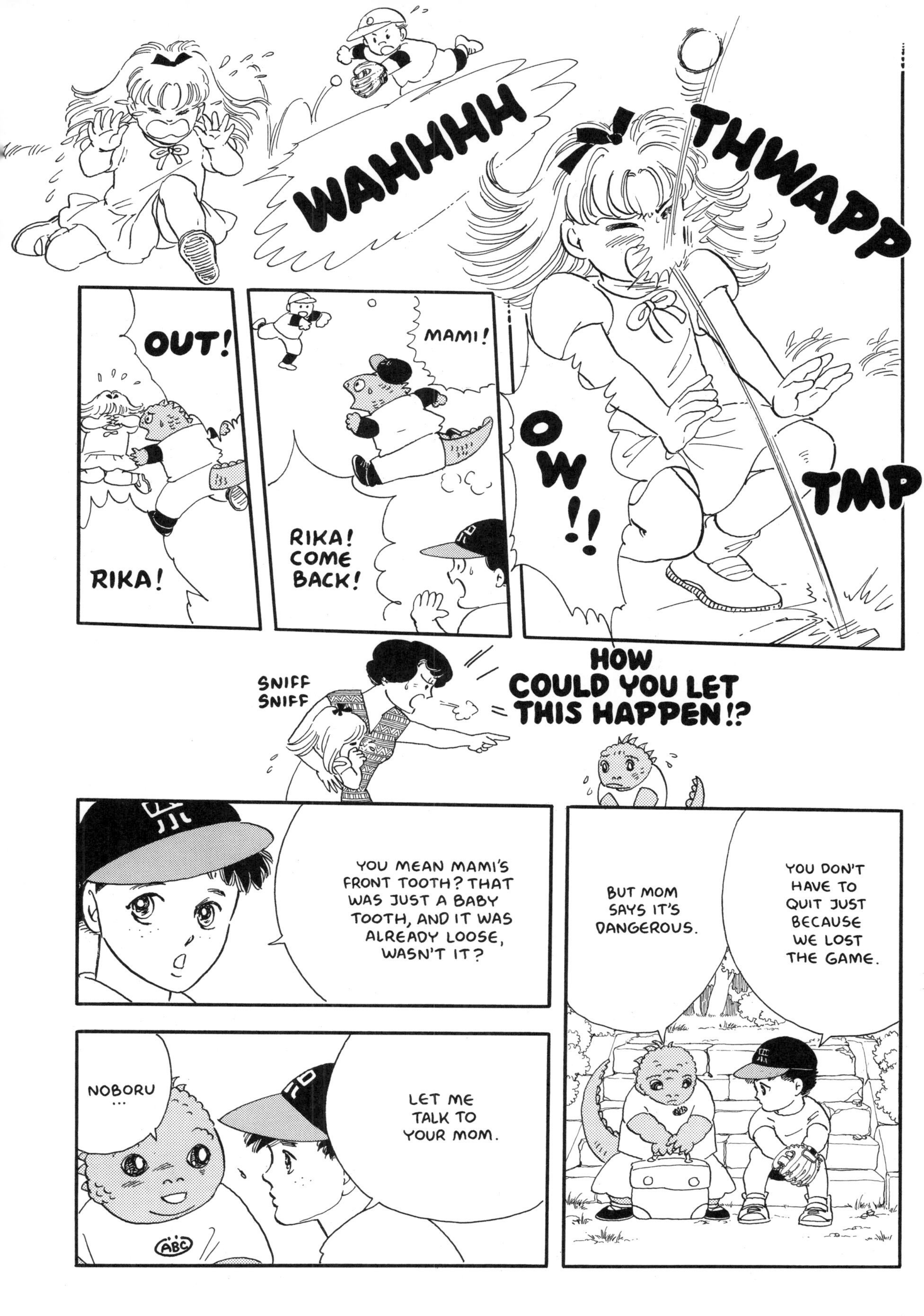
THWAPP
TMP
OW!!
WAHHHH
MAMI!
RIKA! COME BACK!
OUT!
RIKA!
HOW COULD YOU LET THIS HAPPEN!?
SNIFF SNIFF
YOU DON'T HAVE TO QUIT JUST BECAUSE WE LOST THE GAME.
BUT MOM SAYS IT'S DANGEROUS.
YOU MEAN MAMI'S FRONT TOOTH? THAT WAS JUST A BABY TOOTH, AND IT WAS ALREADY LOOSE, WASN'T IT?
LET ME TALK TO YOUR MOM.
NOBORU ...

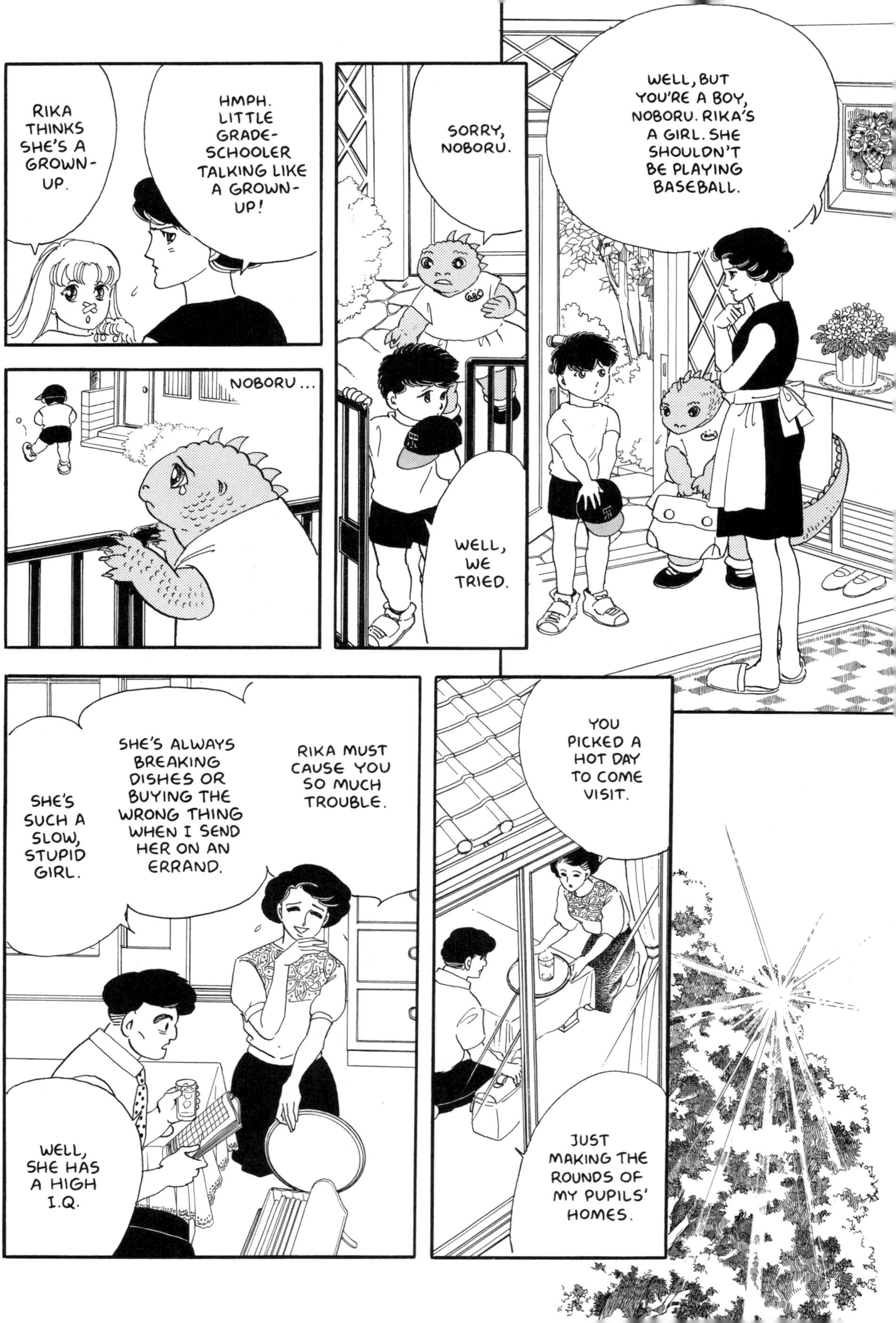
WELL, BUT YOU'RE A BOY, NOBORU. RIKA'S A GIRL. SHE SHOULDN'T BE PLAYING BASEBALL.
SORRY, NOBORU.
WELL, WE TRIED.
HMPH. LITTLE GRADE-SCHOOLER TALKING LIKE A GROWN-UP!
RIKA THINKS SHE'S A GROWN-UP.
NOBORU...
YOU PICKED A HOT DAY TO COME VISIT.
JUST MAKING THE ROUNDS OF MY PUPILS' HOMES.
RIKA MUST CAUSE YOU SO MUCH TROUBLE.
SHE'S ALWAYS BREAKING DISHES OR BUYING THE WRONG THING WHEN I SEND HER ON AN ERRAND.
SHE'S SUCH A SLOW, STUPID GIRL.
WELL, SHE HAS A HIGH I.Q.

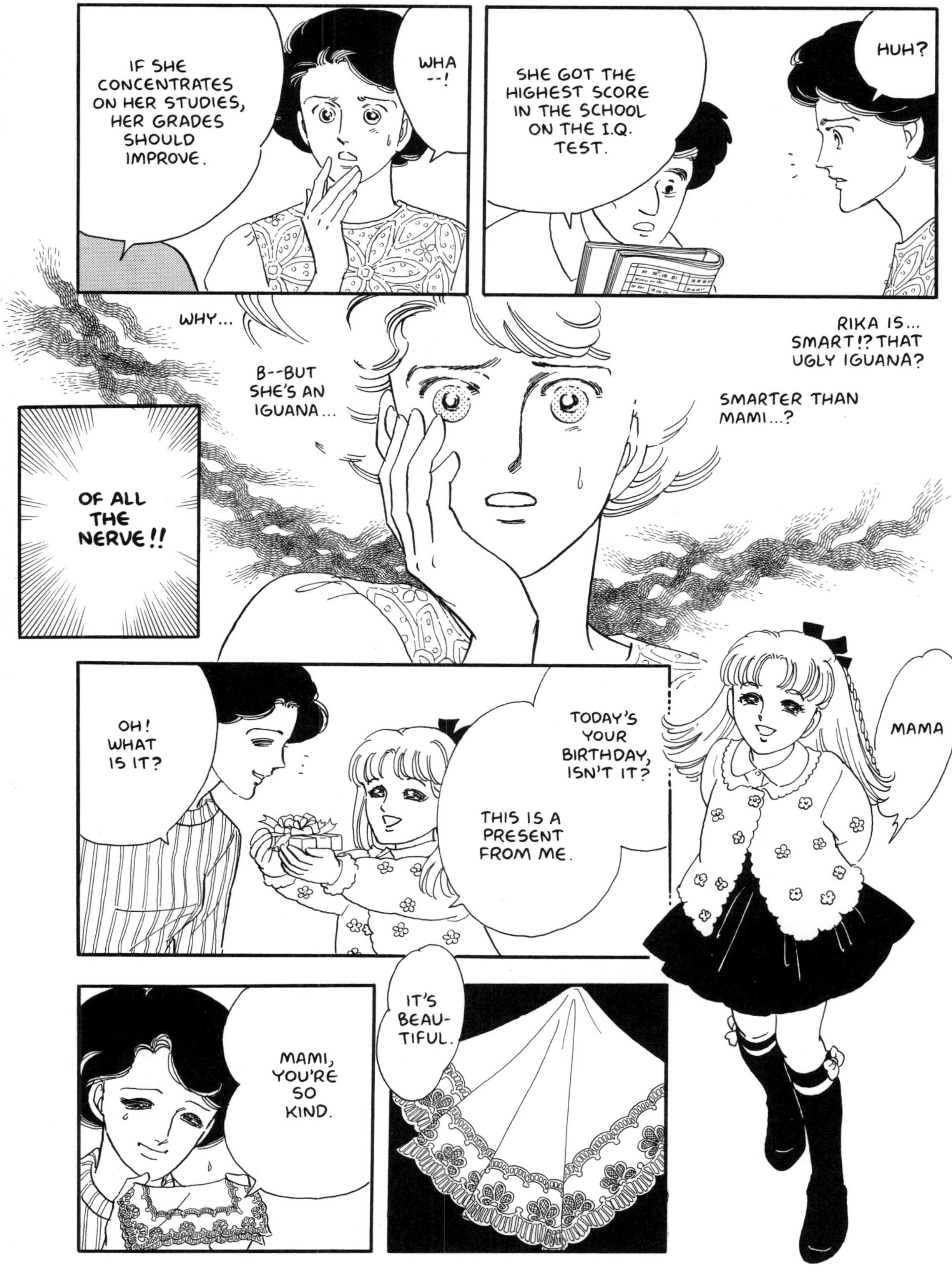
HUH?
SHE GOT THE HIGHEST SCORE IN THE SCHOOL ON THE I.Q. TEST.
WHA --!
IF SHE CONCENTRATES ON HER STUDIES, HER GRADES SHOULD IMPROVE.
RIKA IS... SMART!? THAT UGLY IGUANA?
SMARTER THAN MAMI...?
WHY...
B--BUT SHE'S AN IGUANA...
OF ALL THE NERVE!!
MAMA
TODAY'S YOUR BIRTHDAY, ISN'T IT?
THIS IS A PRESENT FROM ME.
OH! WHAT IS IT?
IT'S BEAU-TIFUL.
MAMI, YOU'RE SO KIND.

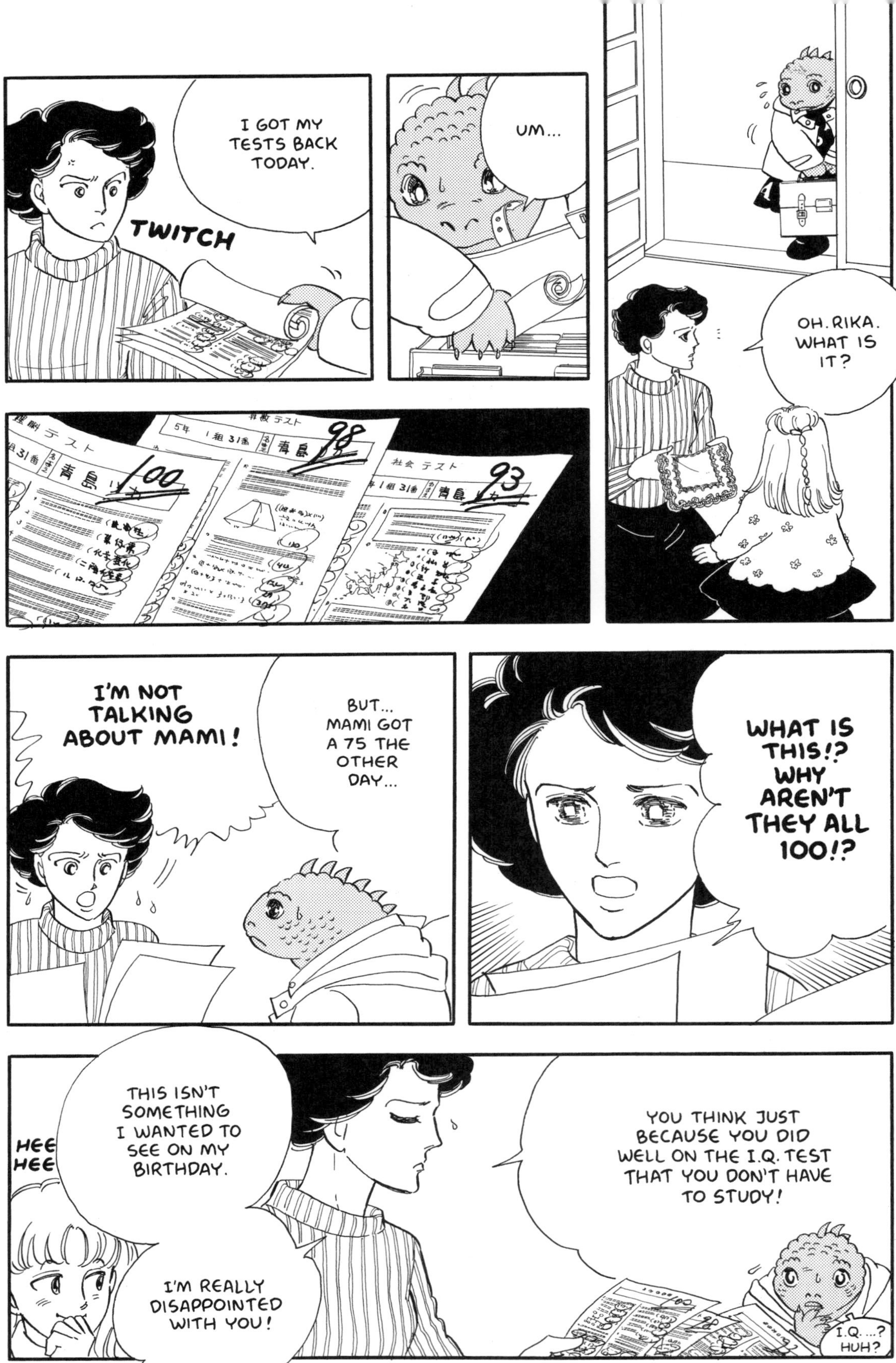
OH. RIKA. WHAT IS IT?
UM...
I GOT MY TESTS BACK TODAY.
TWITCH
算数テスト
5年 1組 31番 青島
98
理科テスト
100
社会テスト
93
WHAT IS THIS!? WHY AREN'T THEY ALL 100!?
BUT... MAMI GOT A 75 THE OTHER DAY...
I'M NOT TALKING ABOUT MAMI!
YOU THINK JUST BECAUSE YOU DID WELL ON THE I.Q. TEST THAT YOU DON'T HAVE TO STUDY!
THIS ISN'T SOMETHING I WANTED TO SEE ON MY BIRTHDAY.
HEE HEE
I'M REALLY DISAPPOINTED WITH YOU!
I.Q....? HUH?

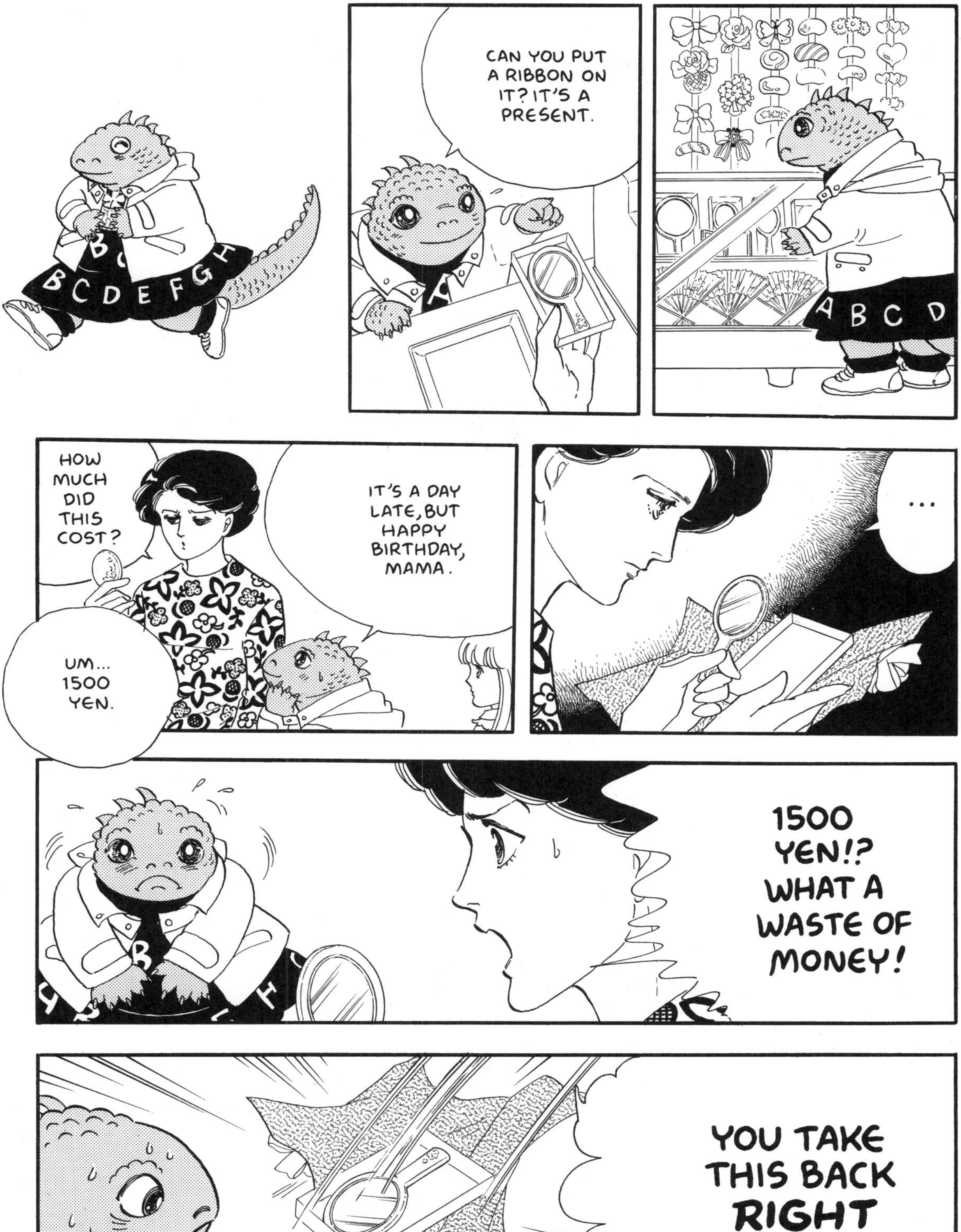
CAN YOU PUT A RIBBON ON IT? IT'S A PRESENT.
...
IT'S A DAY LATE, BUT HAPPY BIRTHDAY, MAMA.
HOW MUCH DID THIS COST?
UM... 1500 YEN.
1500 YEN!? WHAT A WASTE OF MONEY!
YOU TAKE THIS BACK RIGHT NOW!

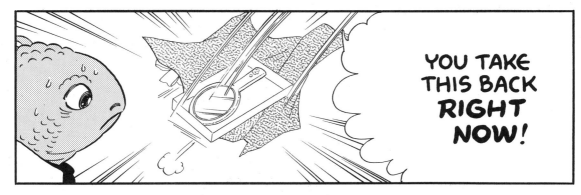

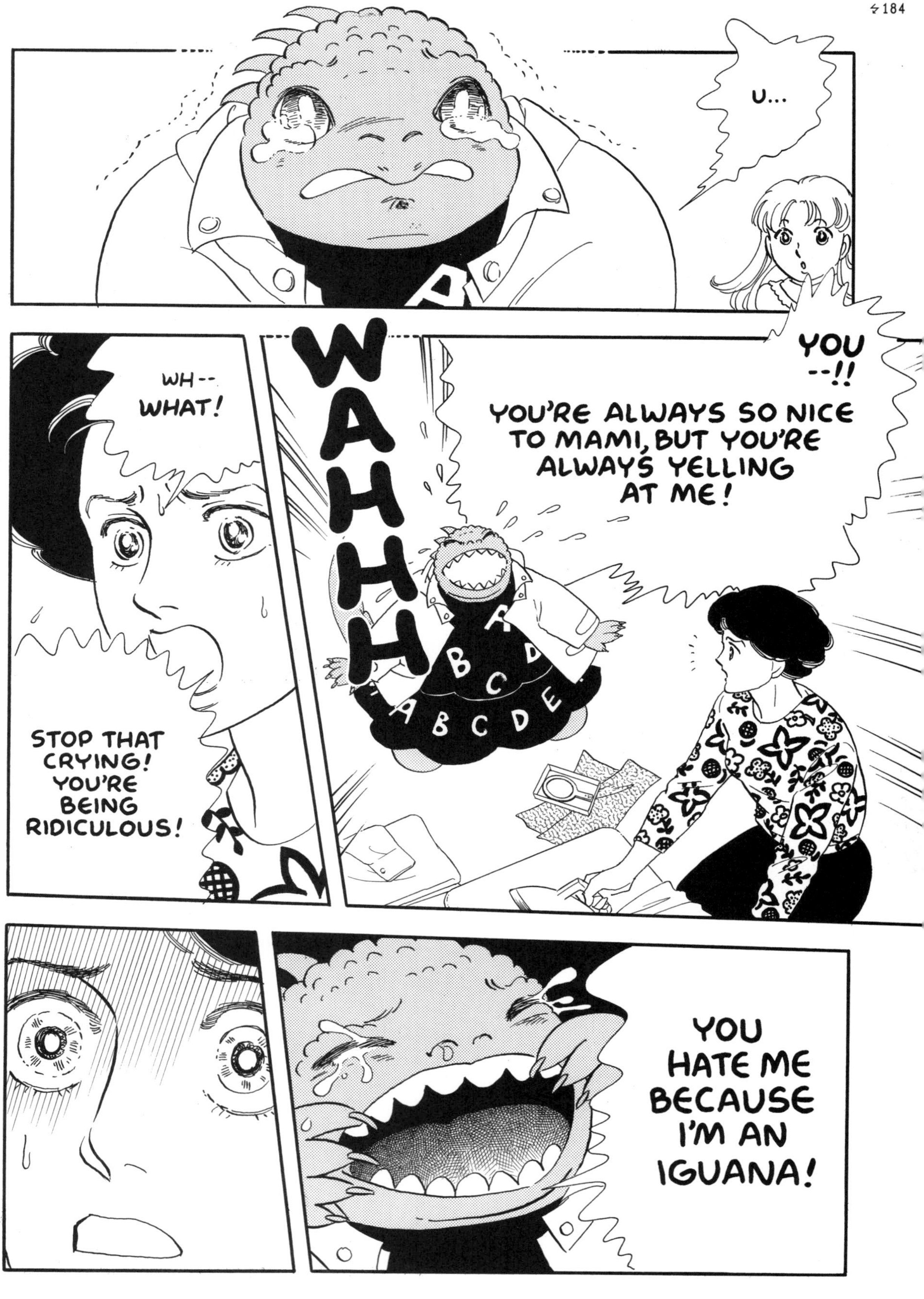
U...
WAHHH
YOU --!!
YOU'RE ALWAYS SO NICE TO MAMI, BUT YOU'RE ALWAYS YELLING AT ME!
WH-- WHAT!
STOP THAT CRYING! YOU'RE BEING RIDICULOUS!
YOU HATE ME BECAUSE I'M AN IGUANA!

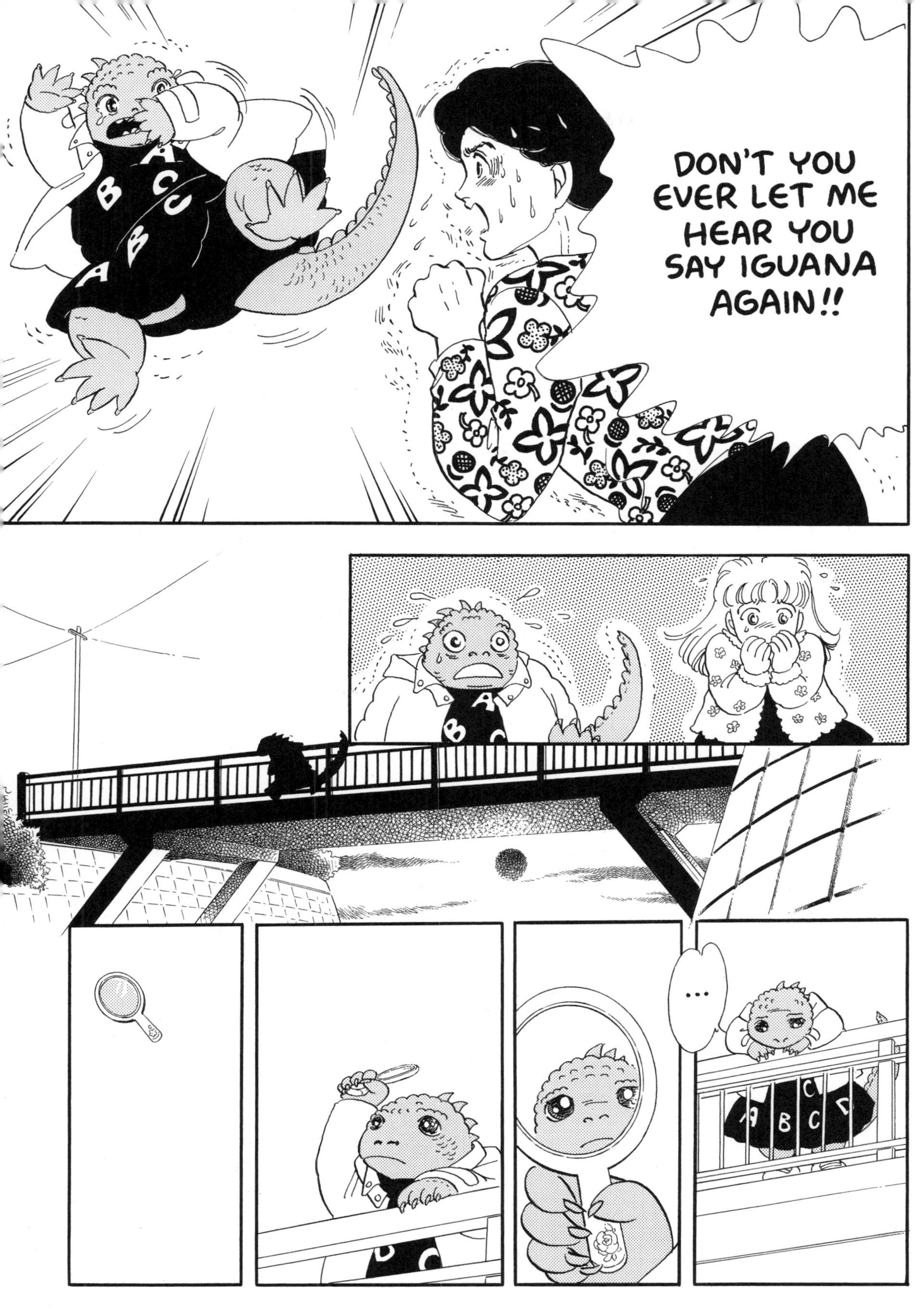
DON'T YOU EVER LET ME HEAR YOU SAY IGUANA AGAIN!!
...

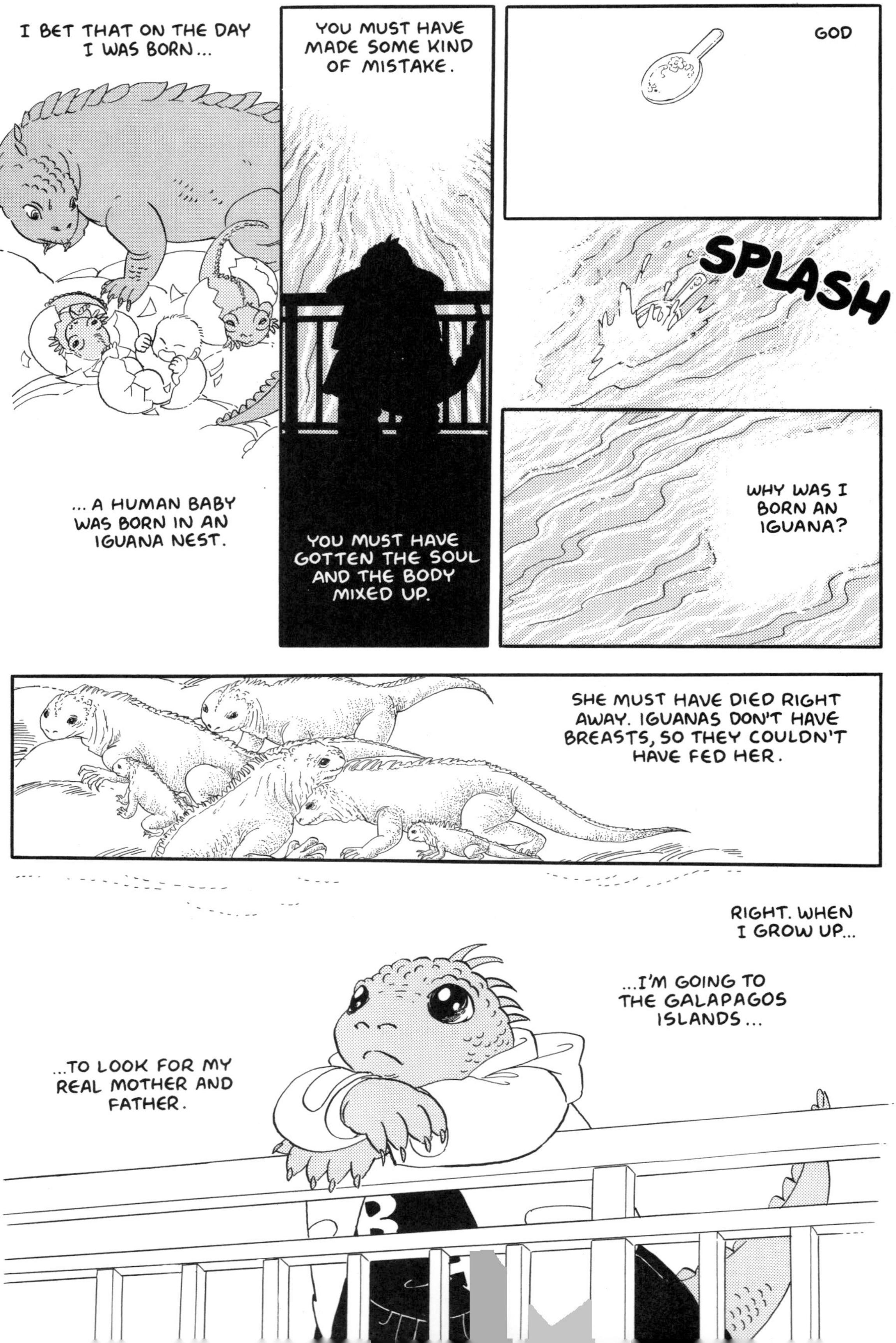
GOD
SPLASH
WHY WAS I BORN AN IGUANA?
YOU MUST HAVE MADE SOME KIND OF MISTAKE.
YOU MUST HAVE GOTTEN THE SOUL AND THE BODY MIXED UP.
I BET THAT ON THE DAY I WAS BORN...
... A HUMAN BABY WAS BORN IN AN IGUANA NEST.
SHE MUST HAVE DIED RIGHT AWAY. IGUANAS DON'T HAVE BREASTS, SO THEY COULDN'T HAVE FED HER.
RIGHT. WHEN I GROW UP...
...I'M GOING TO THE GALAPAGOS ISLANDS...
...TO LOOK FOR MY REAL MOTHER AND FATHER.

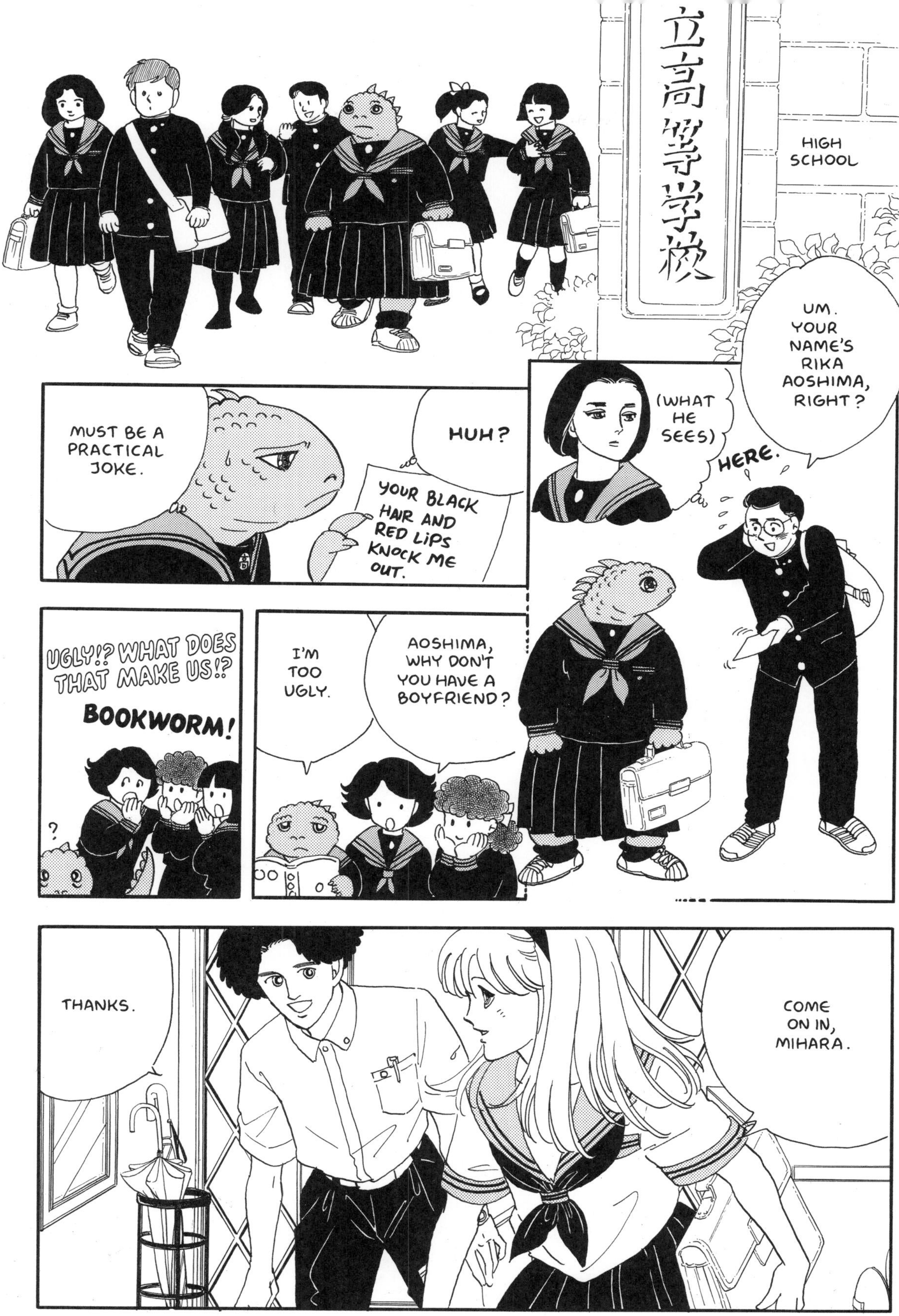
立高等学校
HIGH SCHOOL
UM. YOUR NAME'S RIKA AOSHIMA, RIGHT?
(WHAT HE SEES)
HERE.
HUH?
YOUR BLACK HAIR AND RED LIPS KNOCK ME OUT.
MUST BE A PRACTICAL JOKE.
AOSHIMA, WHY DON'T YOU HAVE A BOYFRIEND?
I'M TOO UGLY.
UGLY!? WHAT DOES THAT MAKE US!?
BOOKWORM!
COME ON IN, MIHARA.
THANKS.

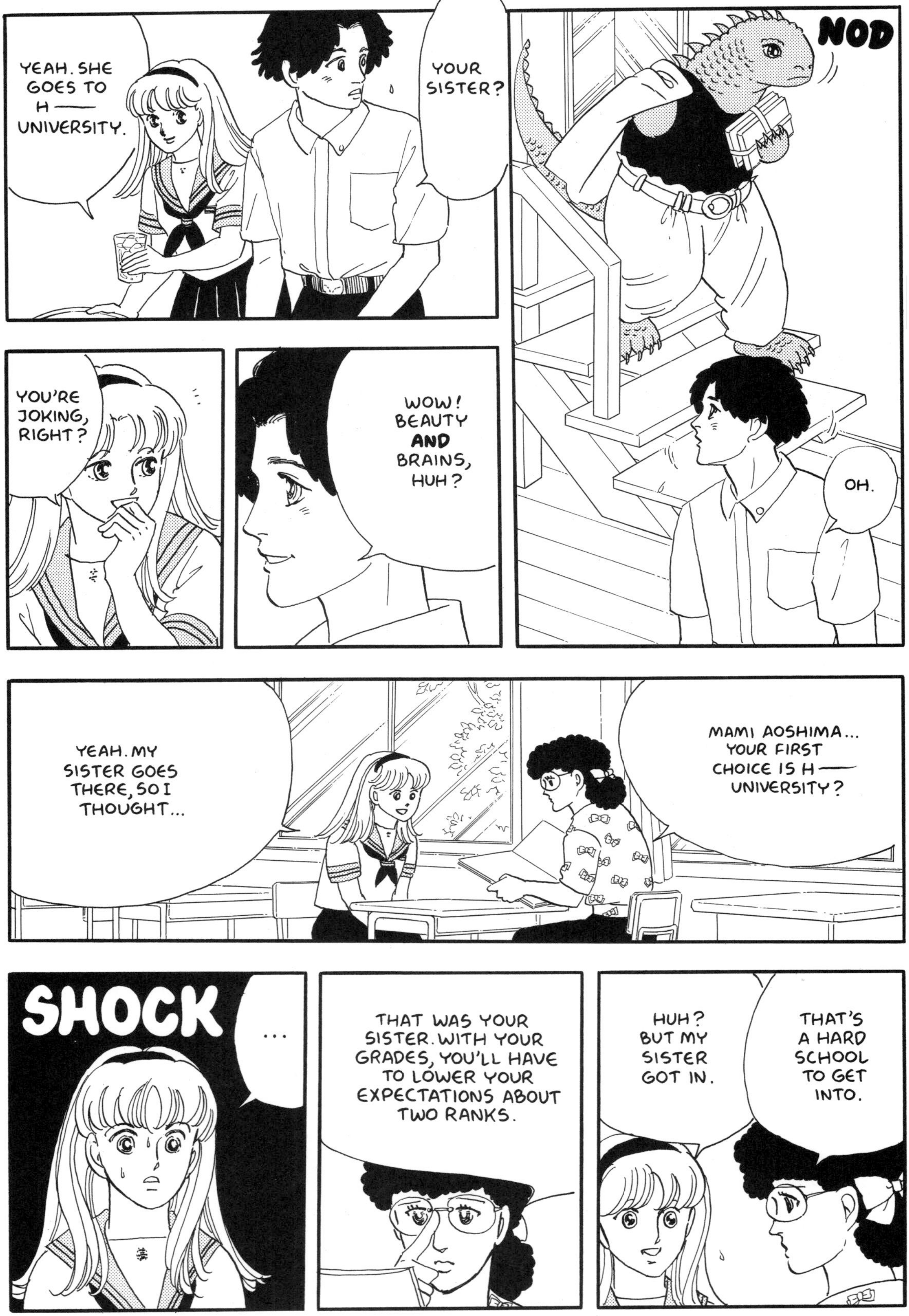
NOD
OH.
YOUR SISTER?
YEAH. SHE GOES TO H—— UNIVERSITY.
WOW! BEAUTY **AND** BRAINS, HUH?
YOU'RE JOKING, RIGHT?
MAMI AOSHIMA... YOUR FIRST CHOICE IS H—— UNIVERSITY?
YEAH. MY SISTER GOES THERE, SO I THOUGHT...
THAT'S A HARD SCHOOL TO GET INTO.
HUH? BUT MY SISTER GOT IN.
THAT WAS YOUR SISTER. WITH YOUR GRADES, YOU'LL HAVE TO LOWER YOUR EXPECTATIONS ABOUT TWO RANKS.
SHOCK
...

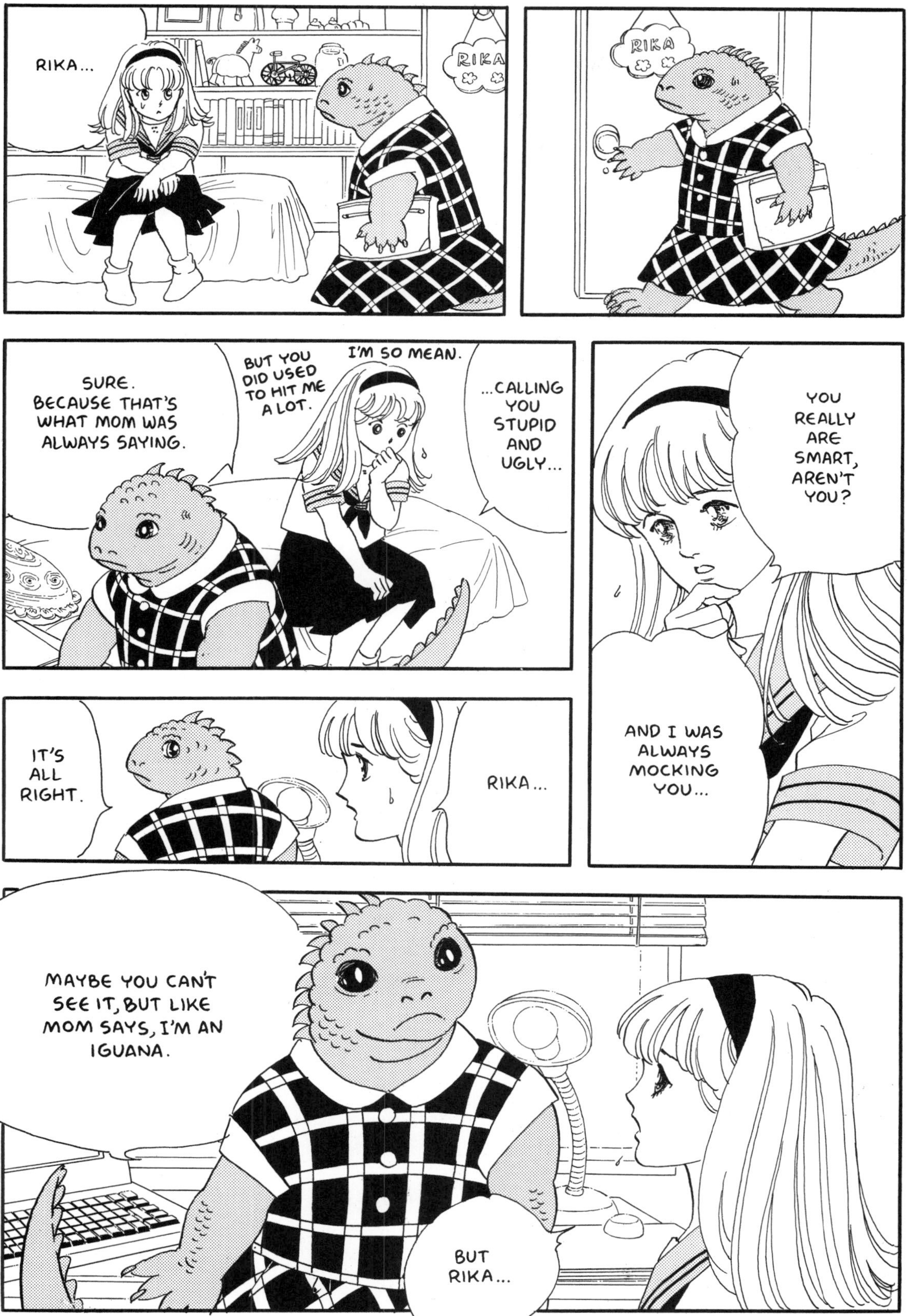
RIKA...
YOU REALLY ARE SMART, AREN'T YOU?
AND I WAS ALWAYS MOCKING YOU...
...CALLING YOU STUPID AND UGLY...
I'M SO MEAN.
BUT YOU DID USED TO HIT ME A LOT.
SURE. BECAUSE THAT'S WHAT MOM WAS ALWAYS SAYING.
RIKA...
IT'S ALL RIGHT.
MAYBE YOU CAN'T SEE IT, BUT LIKE MOM SAYS, I'M AN IGUANA.
BUT RIKA...

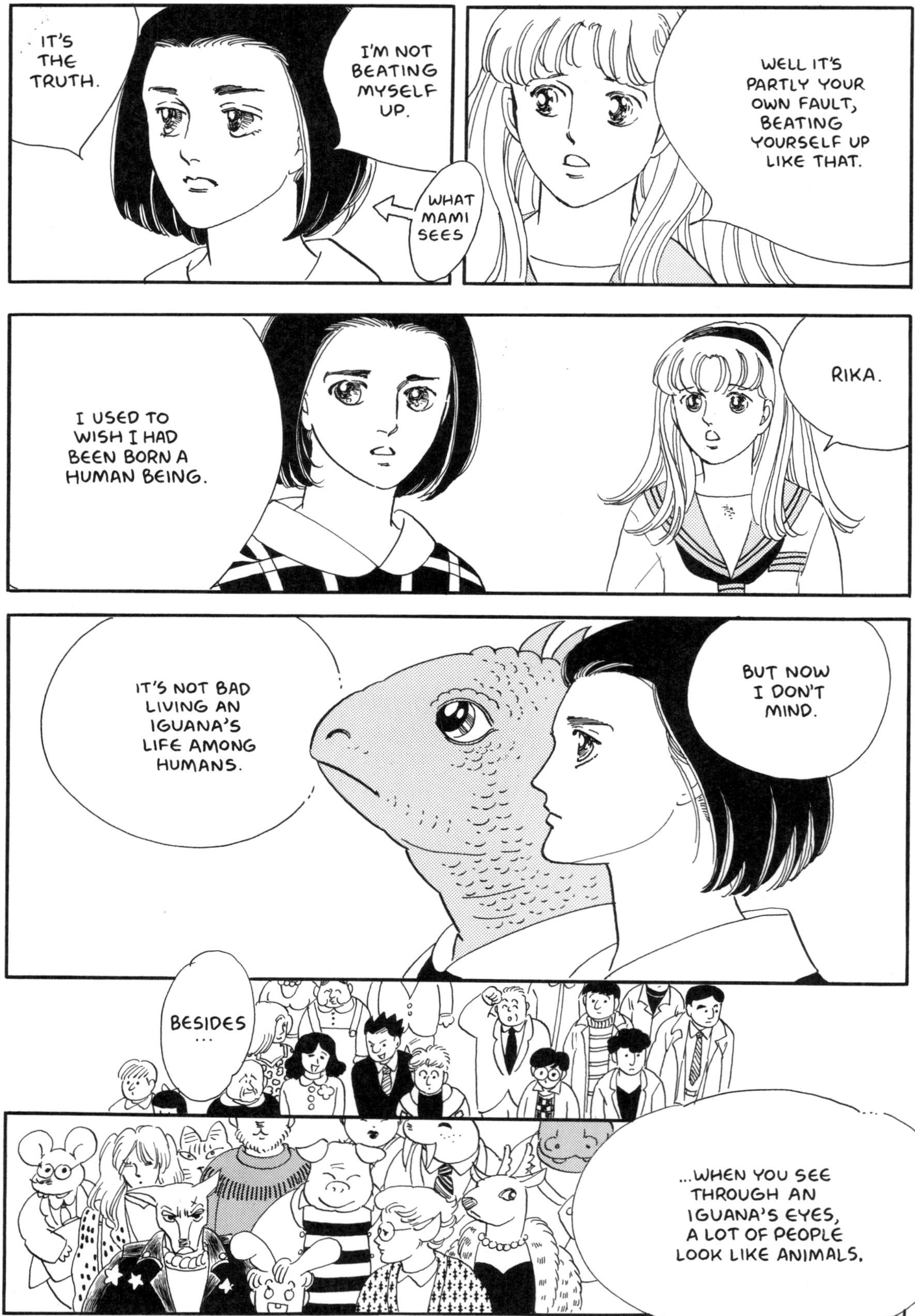
WELL IT'S PARTLY YOUR OWN FAULT, BEATING YOURSELF UP LIKE THAT.
WHAT MAMI SEES
I'M NOT BEATING MYSELF UP.
IT'S THE TRUTH.
RIKA.
I USED TO WISH I HAD BEEN BORN A HUMAN BEING.
BUT NOW I DON'T MIND.
IT'S NOT BAD LIVING AN IGUANA'S LIFE AMONG HUMANS.
BESIDES ...
...WHEN YOU SEE THROUGH AN IGUANA'S EYES, A LOT OF PEOPLE LOOK LIKE ANIMALS.

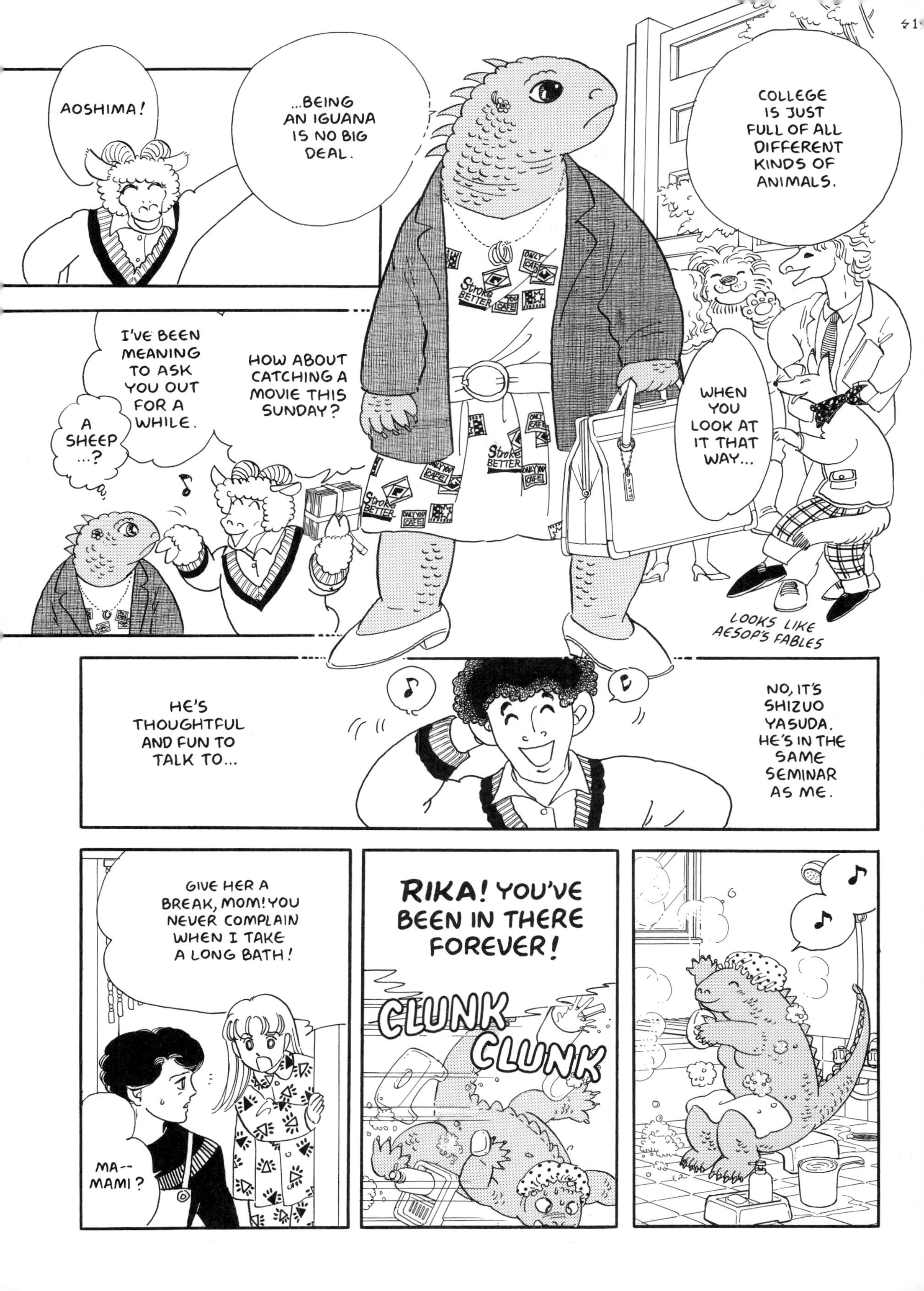
COLLEGE IS JUST FULL OF ALL DIFFERENT KINDS OF ANIMALS.
WHEN YOU LOOK AT IT THAT WAY...
...BEING AN IGUANA IS NO BIG DEAL.
LOOKS LIKE AESOP'S FABLES
AOSHIMA!
I'VE BEEN MEANING TO ASK YOU OUT FOR A WHILE.
HOW ABOUT CATCHING A MOVIE THIS SUNDAY?
A SHEEP ...?
NO, IT'S SHIZUO YASUDA. HE'S IN THE SAME SEMINAR AS ME.
HE'S THOUGHTFUL AND FUN TO TALK TO...
RIKA! YOU'VE BEEN IN THERE FOREVER!
CLUNK
CLUNK
GIVE HER A BREAK, MOM! YOU NEVER COMPLAIN WHEN I TAKE A LONG BATH!
MA-- MAMI?

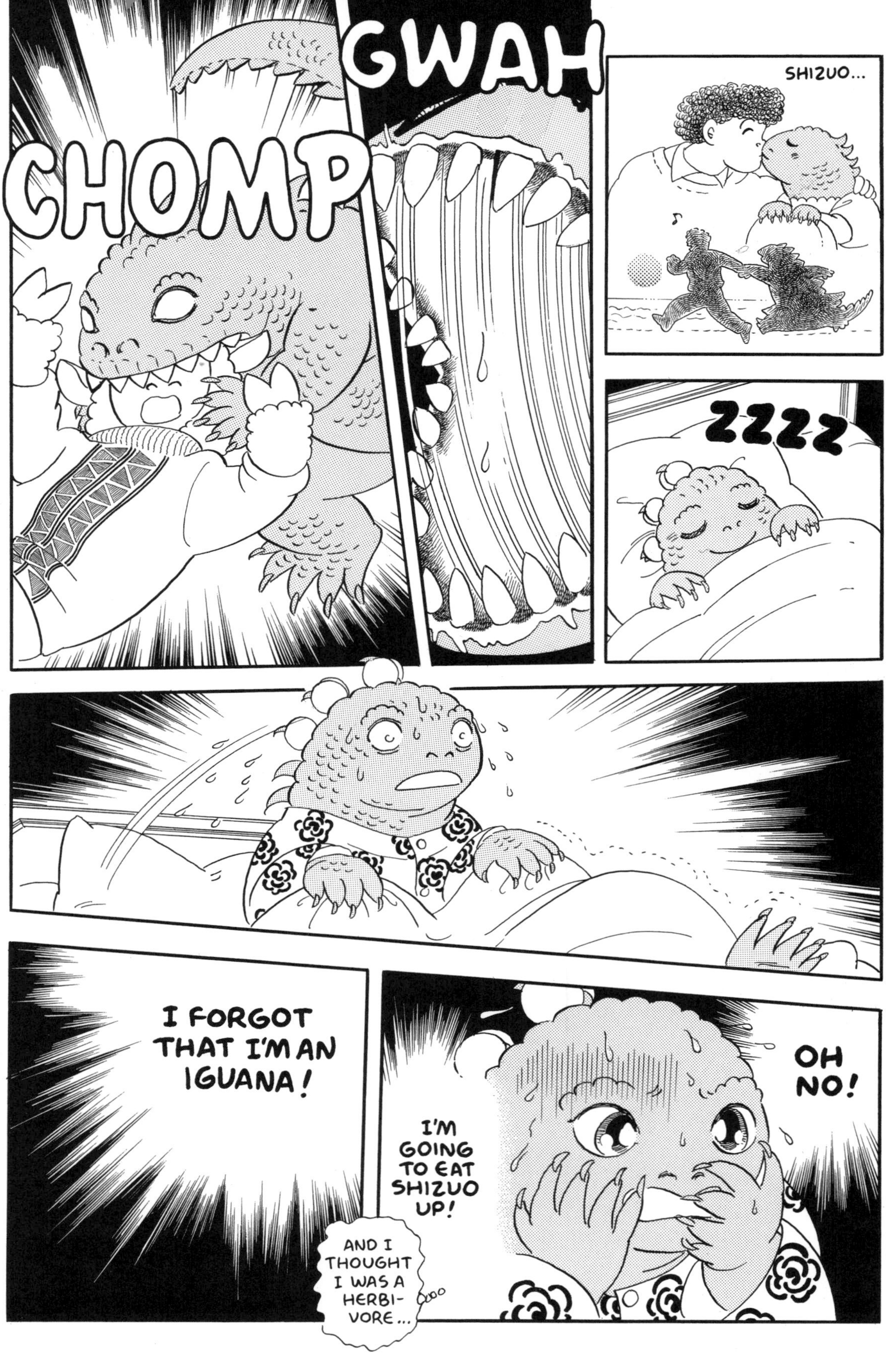
SHIZUO...
ZZZZ
GWAH
CHOMP
OH NO!
I'M GOING TO EAT SHIZUO UP!
AND I THOUGHT I WAS A HERBIVORE...
I FORGOT THAT I'M AN IGUANA!

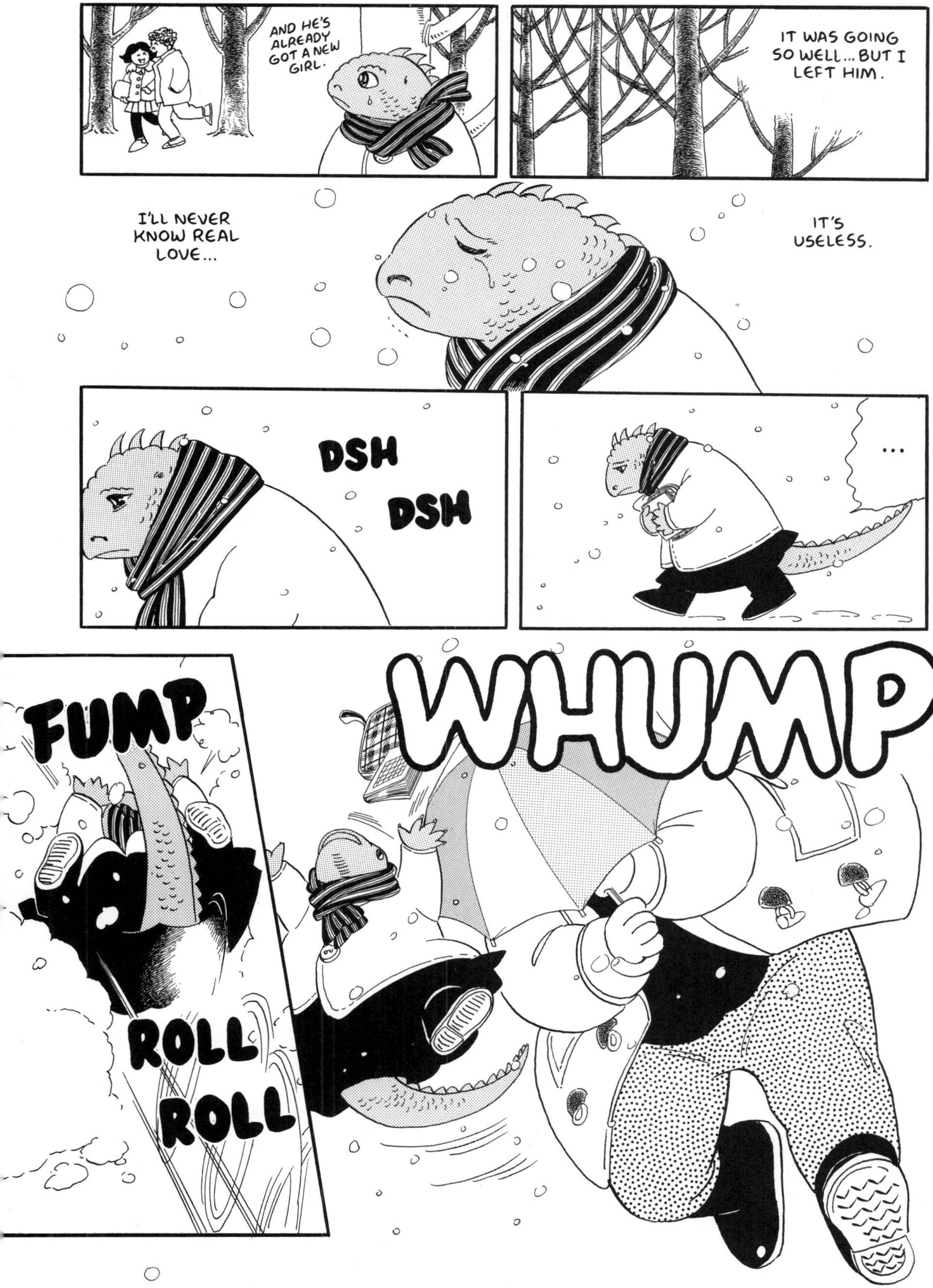
IT WAS GOING SO WELL... BUT I LEFT HIM.
AND HE'S ALREADY GOT A NEW GIRL.
IT'S USELESS.
I'LL NEVER KNOW REAL LOVE...
...
DSH
DSH
WHUMP
FUMP
ROLL
ROLL

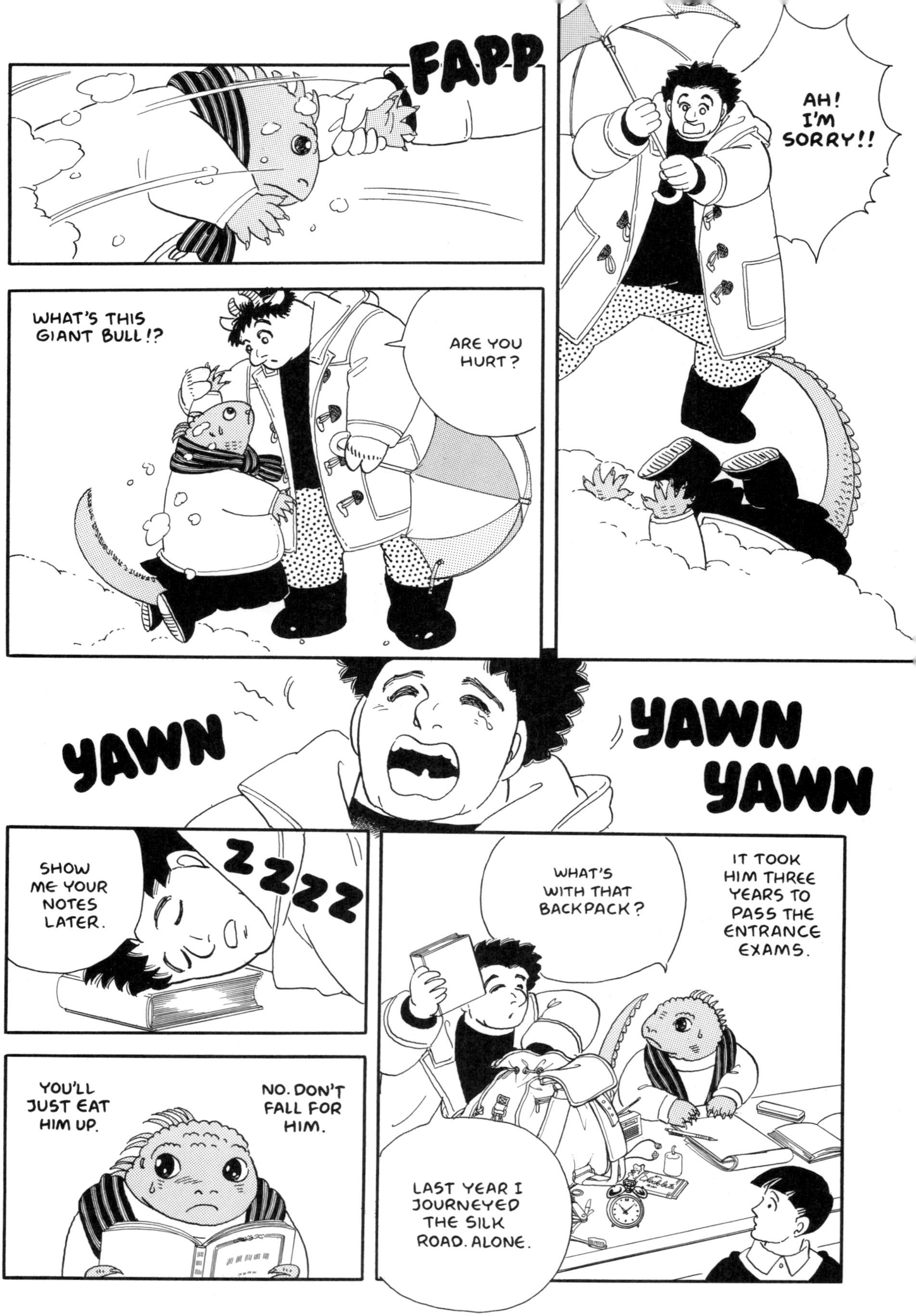
AH! I'M SORRY!!
FAPP
ARE YOU HURT?
WHAT'S THIS GIANT BULL!?
YAWN YAWN
YAWN
IT TOOK HIM THREE YEARS TO PASS THE ENTRANCE EXAMS.
WHAT'S WITH THAT BACKPACK?
LAST YEAR I JOURNEYED THE SILK ROAD. ALONE.
ZZZZ
SHOW ME YOUR NOTES LATER.
NO. DON'T FALL FOR HIM.
YOU'LL JUST EAT HIM UP.

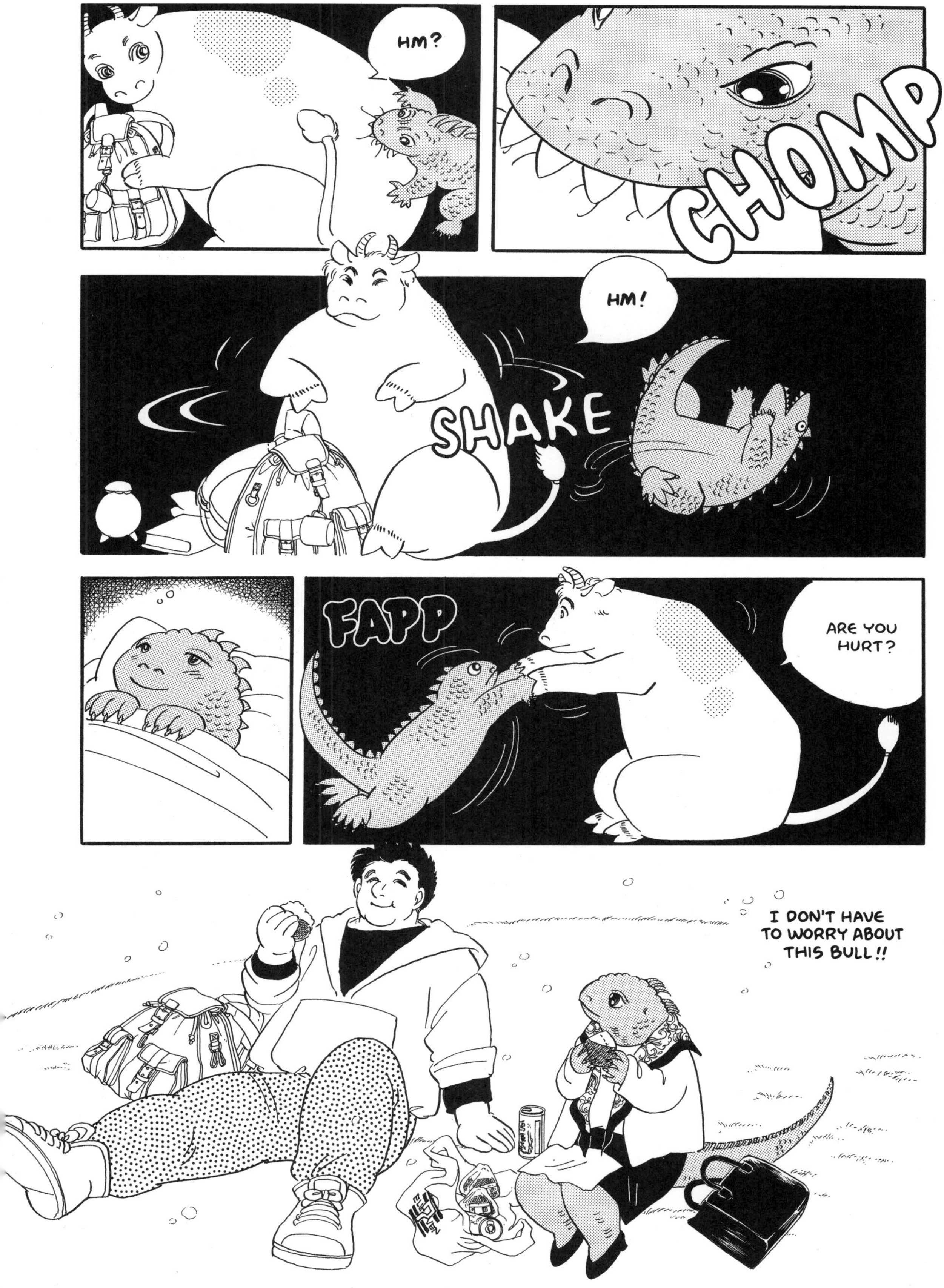
CHOMP
HM?
HM!
SHAKE
ARE YOU HURT?
FAPP
I DON'T HAVE TO WORRY ABOUT THIS BULL!!

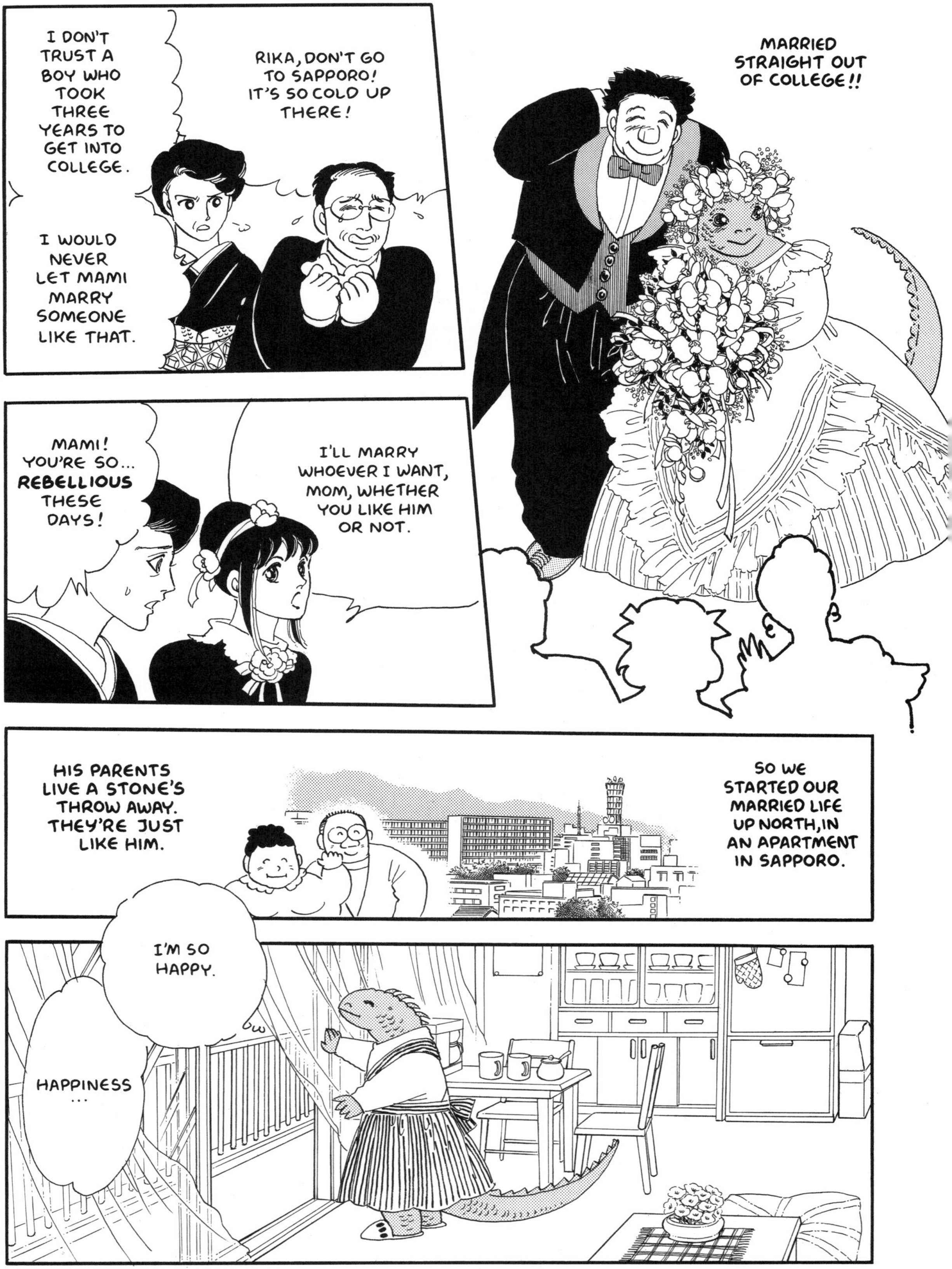
MARRIED STRAIGHT OUT OF COLLEGE!!
RIKA, DON'T GO TO SAPPORO! IT'S SO COLD UP THERE!
I DON'T TRUST A BOY WHO TOOK THREE YEARS TO GET INTO COLLEGE.
I WOULD NEVER LET MAMI MARRY SOMEONE LIKE THAT.
I'LL MARRY WHOEVER I WANT, MOM, WHETHER YOU LIKE HIM OR NOT.
MAMI! YOU'RE SO... REBELLIOUS THESE DAYS!
SO WE STARTED OUR MARRIED LIFE UP NORTH, IN AN APARTMENT IN SAPPORO.
HIS PARENTS LIVE A STONE'S THROW AWAY. THEY'RE JUST LIKE HIM.
I'M SO HAPPY.
HAPPINESS ...

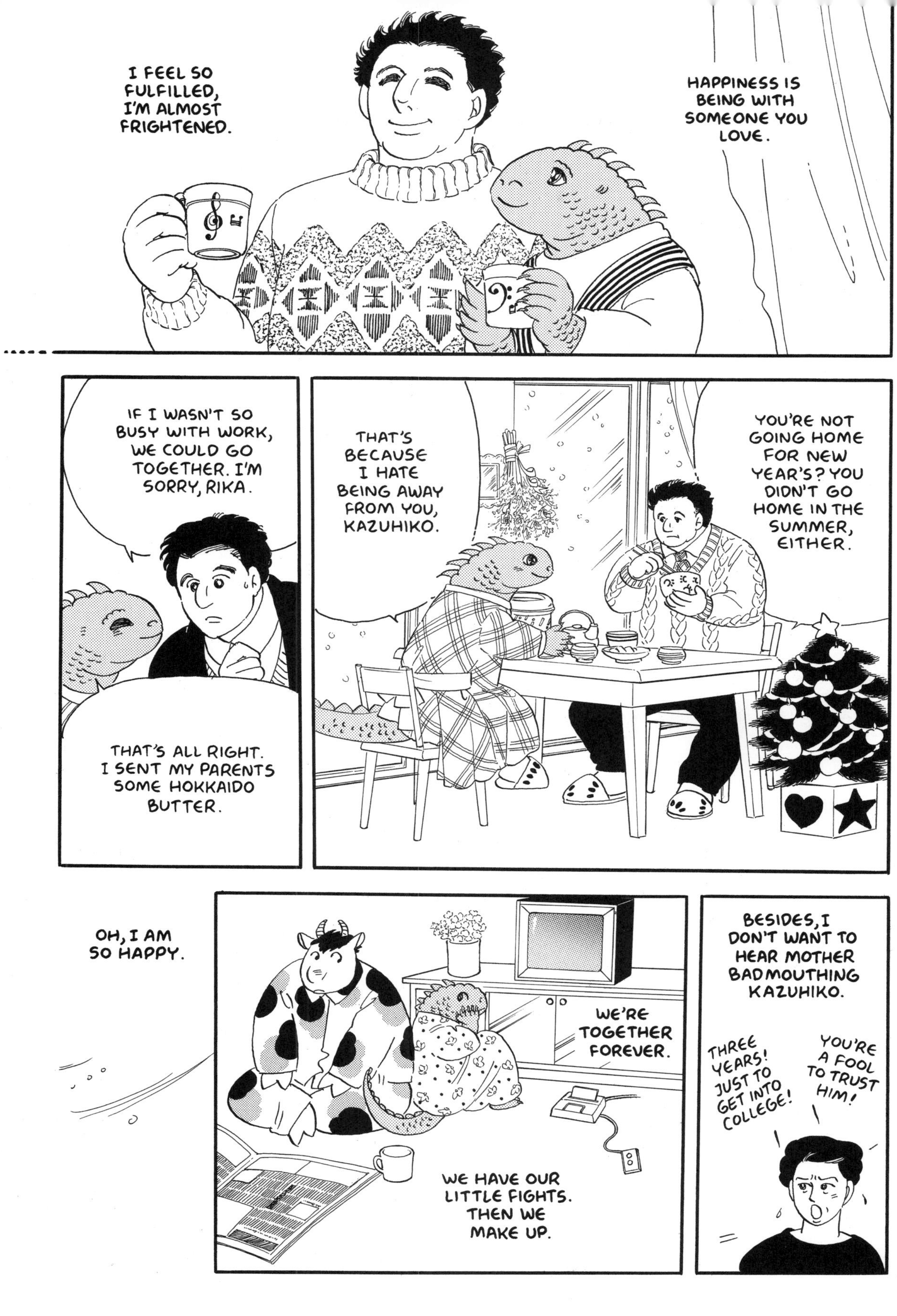
HAPPINESS IS BEING WITH SOMEONE YOU LOVE.
I FEEL SO FULFILLED, I'M ALMOST FRIGHTENED.
YOU'RE NOT GOING HOME FOR NEW YEAR'S? YOU DIDN'T GO HOME IN THE SUMMER, EITHER.
THAT'S BECAUSE I HATE BEING AWAY FROM YOU, KAZUHIKO.
IF I WASN'T SO BUSY WITH WORK, WE COULD GO TOGETHER. I'M SORRY, RIKA.
THAT'S ALL RIGHT. I SENT MY PARENTS SOME HOKKAIDO BUTTER.
BESIDES, I DON'T WANT TO HEAR MOTHER BADMOUTHING KAZUHIKO.
YOU'RE A FOOL TO TRUST HIM!
THREE YEARS! JUST TO GET INTO COLLEGE!
WE'RE TOGETHER FOREVER.
WE HAVE OUR LITTLE FIGHTS. THEN WE MAKE UP.
OH, I AM SO HAPPY.

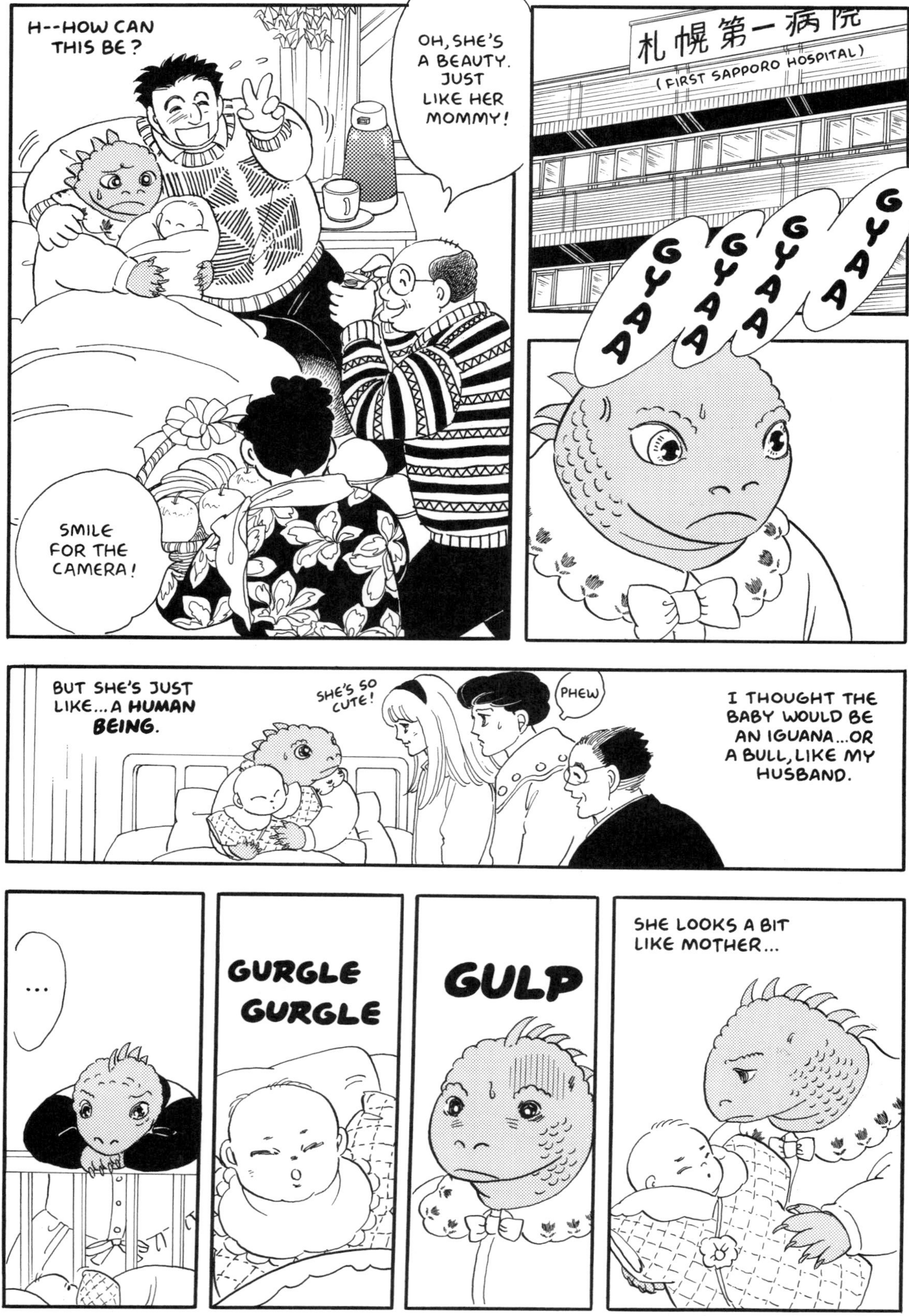
札幌第一病院
(FIRST SAPPORO HOSPITAL)
GYAA GYAA GYAA GYAA
OH, SHE'S A BEAUTY. JUST LIKE HER MOMMY!
H--HOW CAN THIS BE?
SMILE FOR THE CAMERA!
I THOUGHT THE BABY WOULD BE AN IGUANA...OR A BULL, LIKE MY HUSBAND.
PHEW
SHE'S SO CUTE!
BUT SHE'S JUST LIKE... A **HUMAN BEING**.
SHE LOOKS A BIT LIKE MOTHER...
GULP
GURGLE GURGLE
...

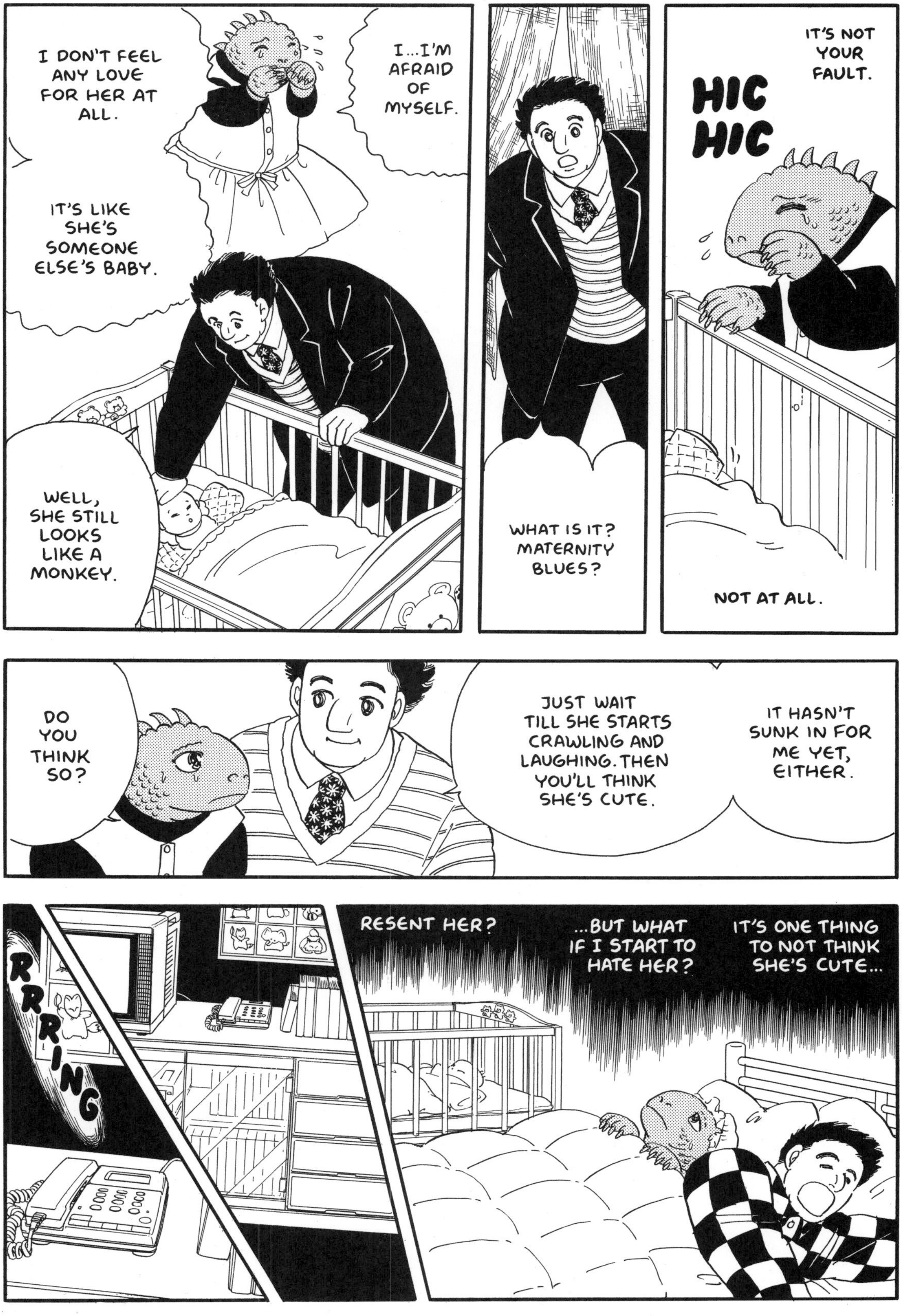
IT'S NOT YOUR FAULT.
HIC HIC
NOT AT ALL.
WHAT IS IT? MATERNITY BLUES?
I...I'M AFRAID OF MYSELF.
I DON'T FEEL ANY LOVE FOR HER AT ALL.
IT'S LIKE SHE'S SOMEONE ELSE'S BABY.
WELL, SHE STILL LOOKS LIKE A MONKEY.
IT HASN'T SUNK IN FOR ME YET, EITHER.
JUST WAIT TILL SHE STARTS CRAWLING AND LAUGHING. THEN YOU'LL THINK SHE'S CUTE.
DO YOU THINK SO?
IT'S ONE THING TO NOT THINK SHE'S CUTE...
...BUT WHAT IF I START TO HATE HER?
RESENT HER?
RRRING

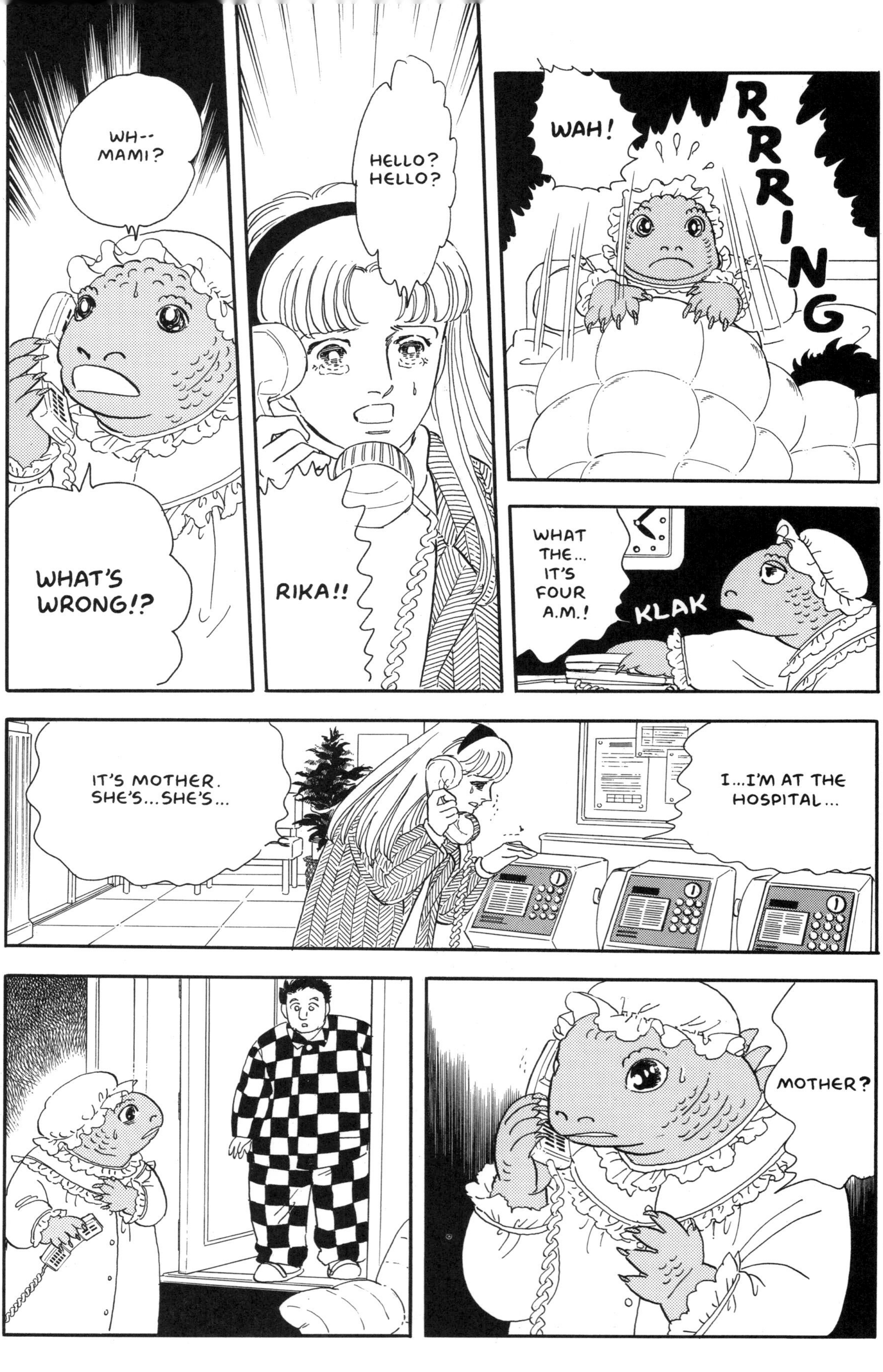
WAH!
RRRING
WHAT THE... IT'S FOUR A.M.!
KLAK
HELLO? HELLO?
RIKA!!
WH-- MAMI?
WHAT'S WRONG!?
I...I'M AT THE HOSPITAL...
IT'S MOTHER. SHE'S...SHE'S...
MOTHER?

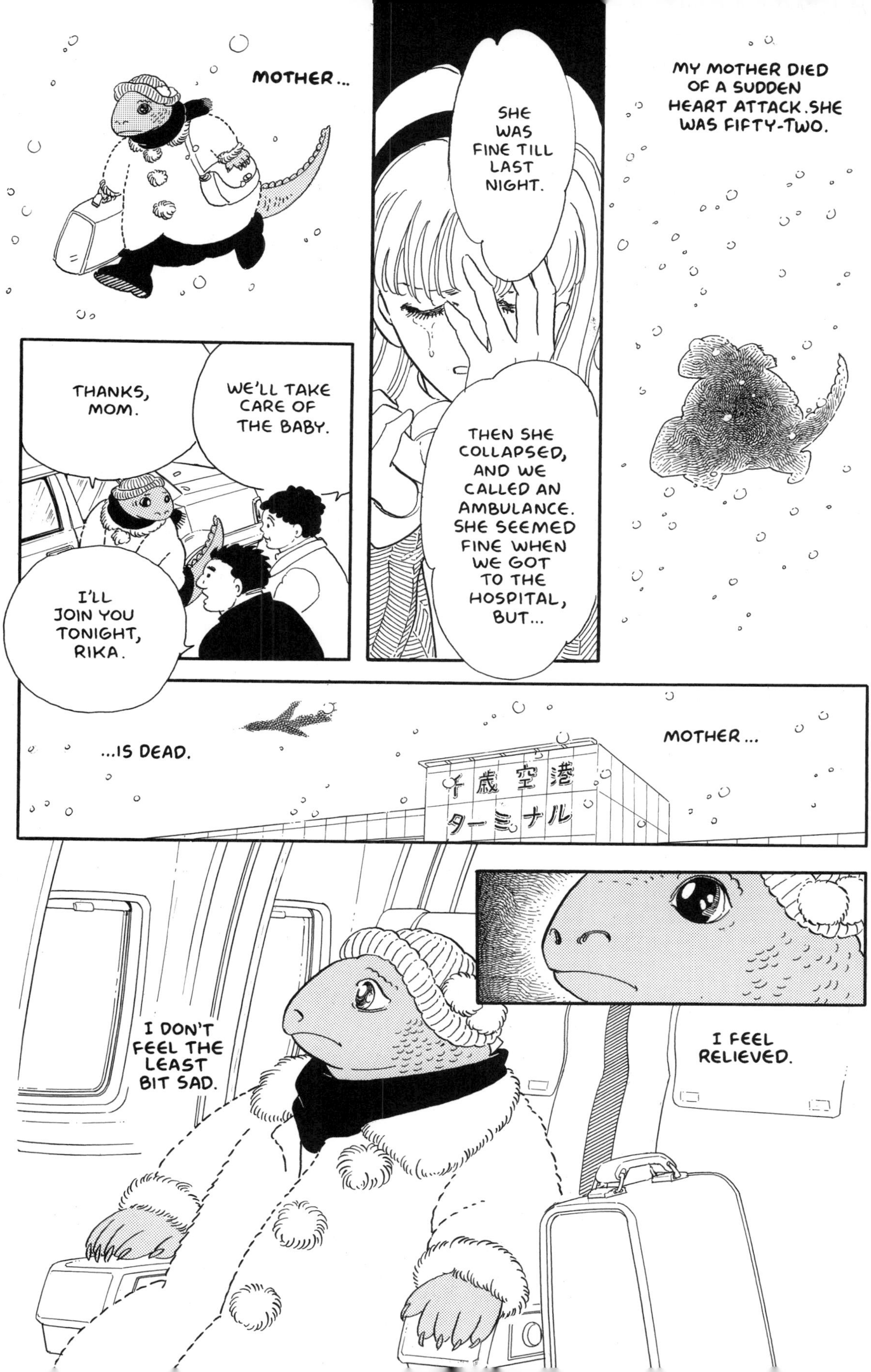
MY MOTHER DIED OF A SUDDEN HEART ATTACK. SHE WAS FIFTY-TWO.
SHE WAS FINE TILL LAST NIGHT.
THEN SHE COLLAPSED, AND WE CALLED AN AMBULANCE. SHE SEEMED FINE WHEN WE GOT TO THE HOSPITAL, BUT...
MOTHER...
WE'LL TAKE CARE OF THE BABY.
THANKS, MOM.
I'LL JOIN YOU TONIGHT, RIKA.
MOTHER...
...IS DEAD.
千歳空港
ターミナル
I FEEL RELIEVED.
I DON'T FEEL THE LEAST BIT SAD.

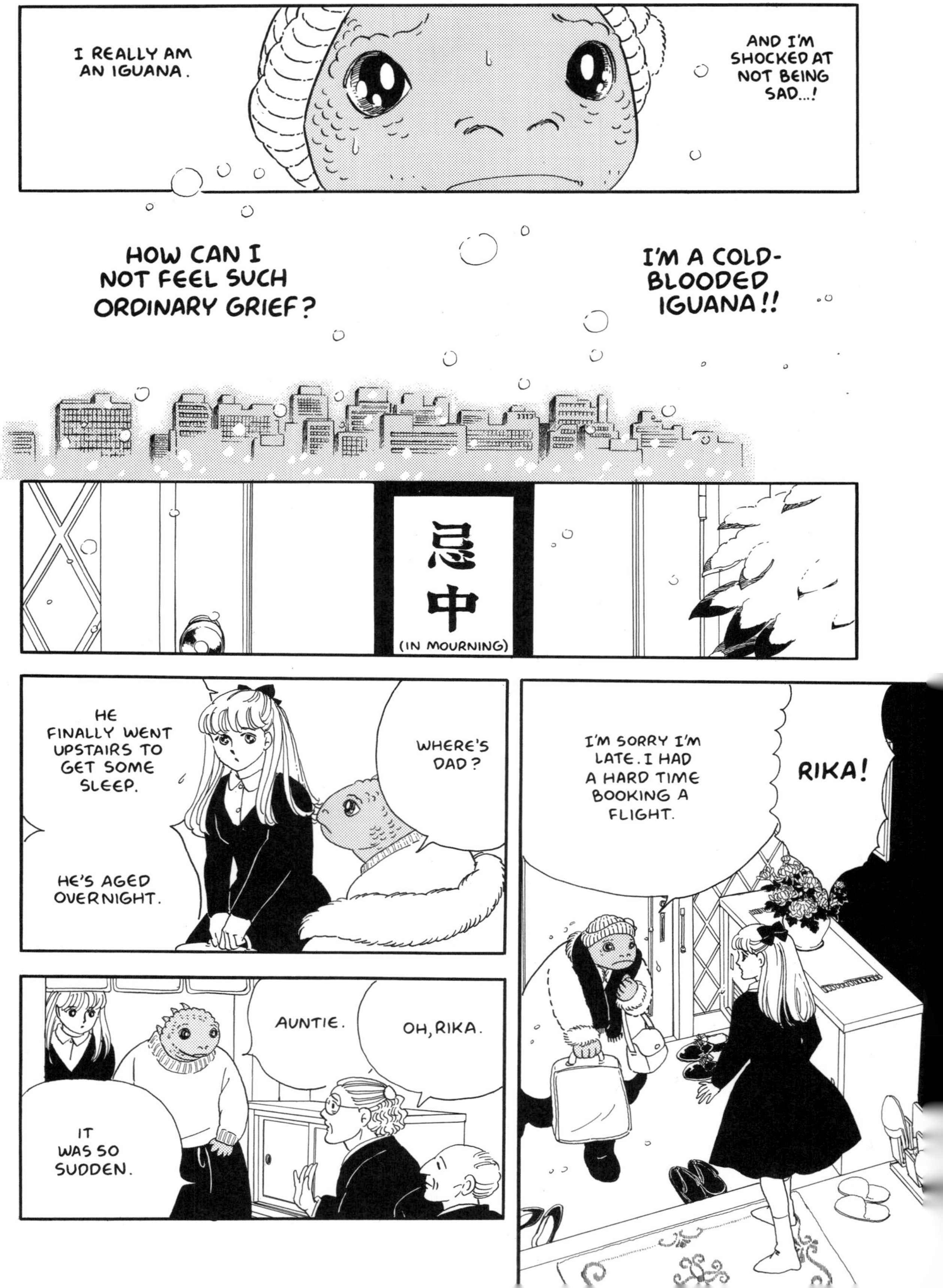
AND I'M SHOCKED AT NOT BEING SAD...!
I REALLY AM AN IGUANA.
I'M A COLD-BLOODED IGUANA!!
HOW CAN I NOT FEEL SUCH ORDINARY GRIEF?
忌中
(IN MOURNING)
RIKA!
I'M SORRY I'M LATE. I HAD A HARD TIME BOOKING A FLIGHT.
WHERE'S DAD?
HE FINALLY WENT UPSTAIRS TO GET SOME SLEEP.
HE'S AGED OVERNIGHT.
OH, RIKA.
AUNTIE.
IT WAS SO SUDDEN.

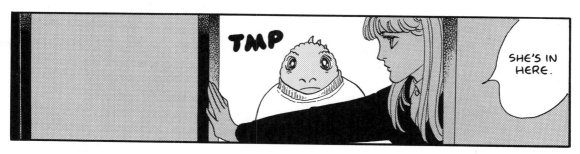

SHE'S IN HERE.
TMP
SHE LOOKS LIKE SHE'S SLEEPING. THEY SAY SHE DIDN'T SUFFER.
LOOK AT HER FACE, RIKA.
MAYBE WHEN I SEE HER FACE...
...I'LL FEEL SOME KIND OF SORROW.
...

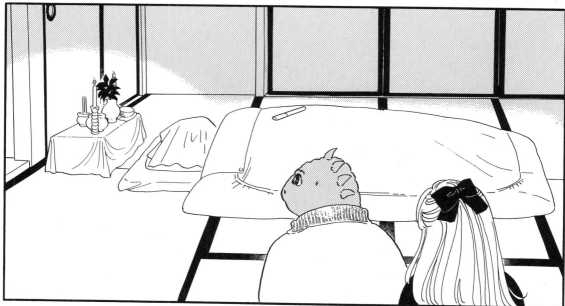

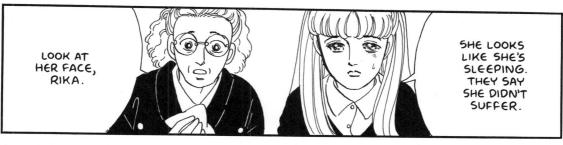

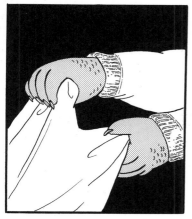

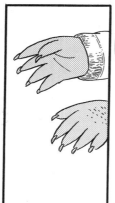

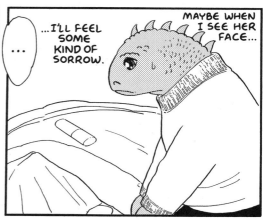

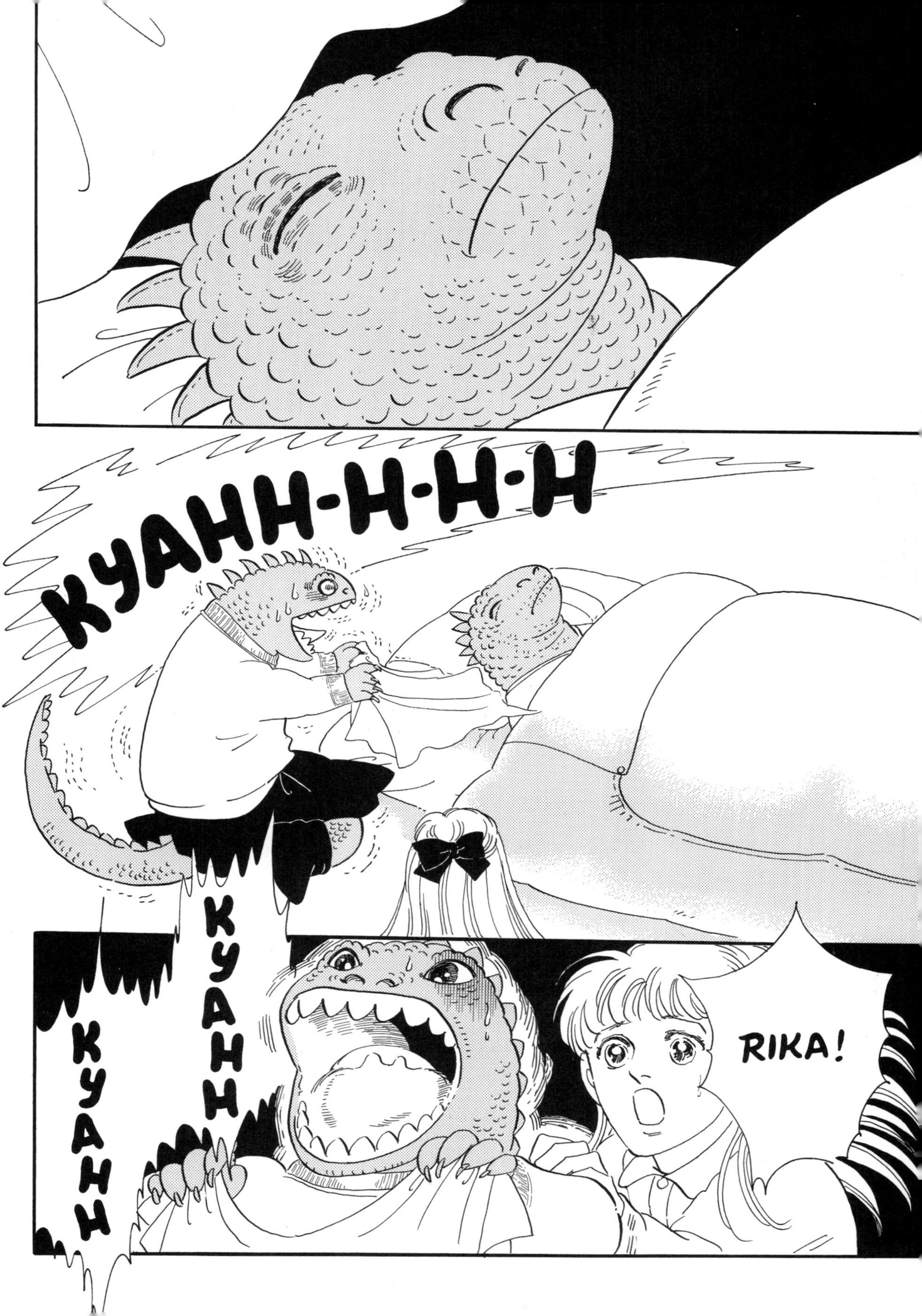
KYAHH-H-H-H
RIKA!
KYAHH
KYAHH

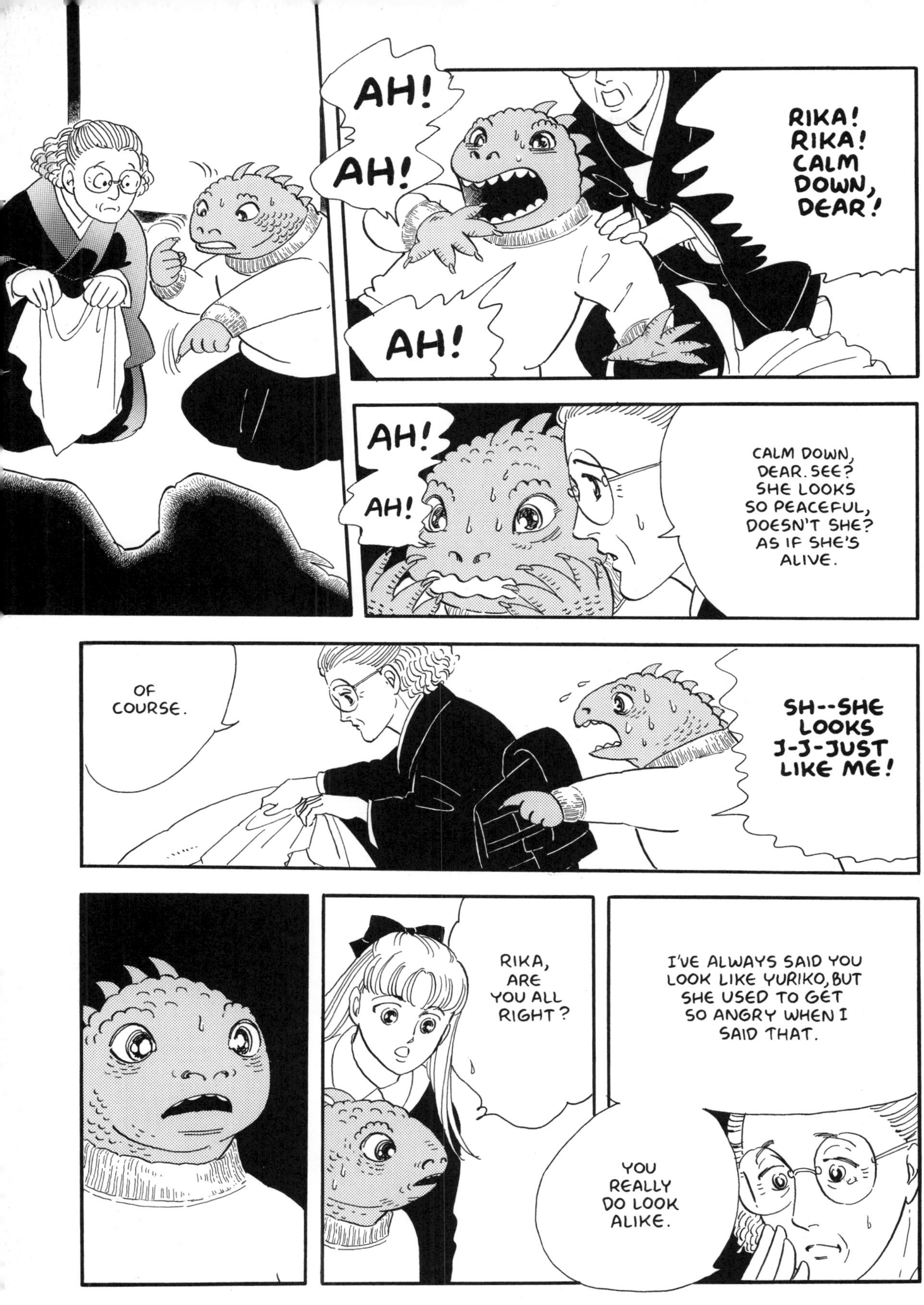
RIKA! RIKA! CALM DOWN, DEAR!
AH!
AH!
AH!
CALM DOWN, DEAR. SEE? SHE LOOKS SO PEACEFUL, DOESN'T SHE? AS IF SHE'S ALIVE.
AH!
AH!
SH--SHE LOOKS J-J-JUST LIKE ME!
OF COURSE.
I'VE ALWAYS SAID YOU LOOK LIKE YURIKO, BUT SHE USED TO GET SO ANGRY WHEN I SAID THAT.
YOU REALLY DO LOOK ALIKE.
RIKA, ARE YOU ALL RIGHT?

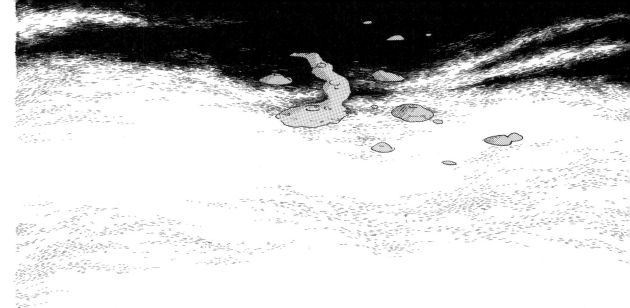

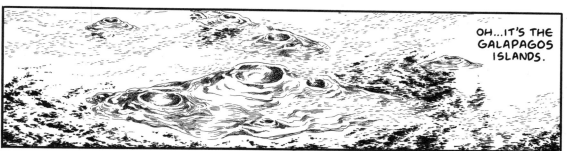

OH...IT'S THE GALAPAGOS ISLANDS.

MY REAL MOTHER AND FATHER MUST BE HERE.

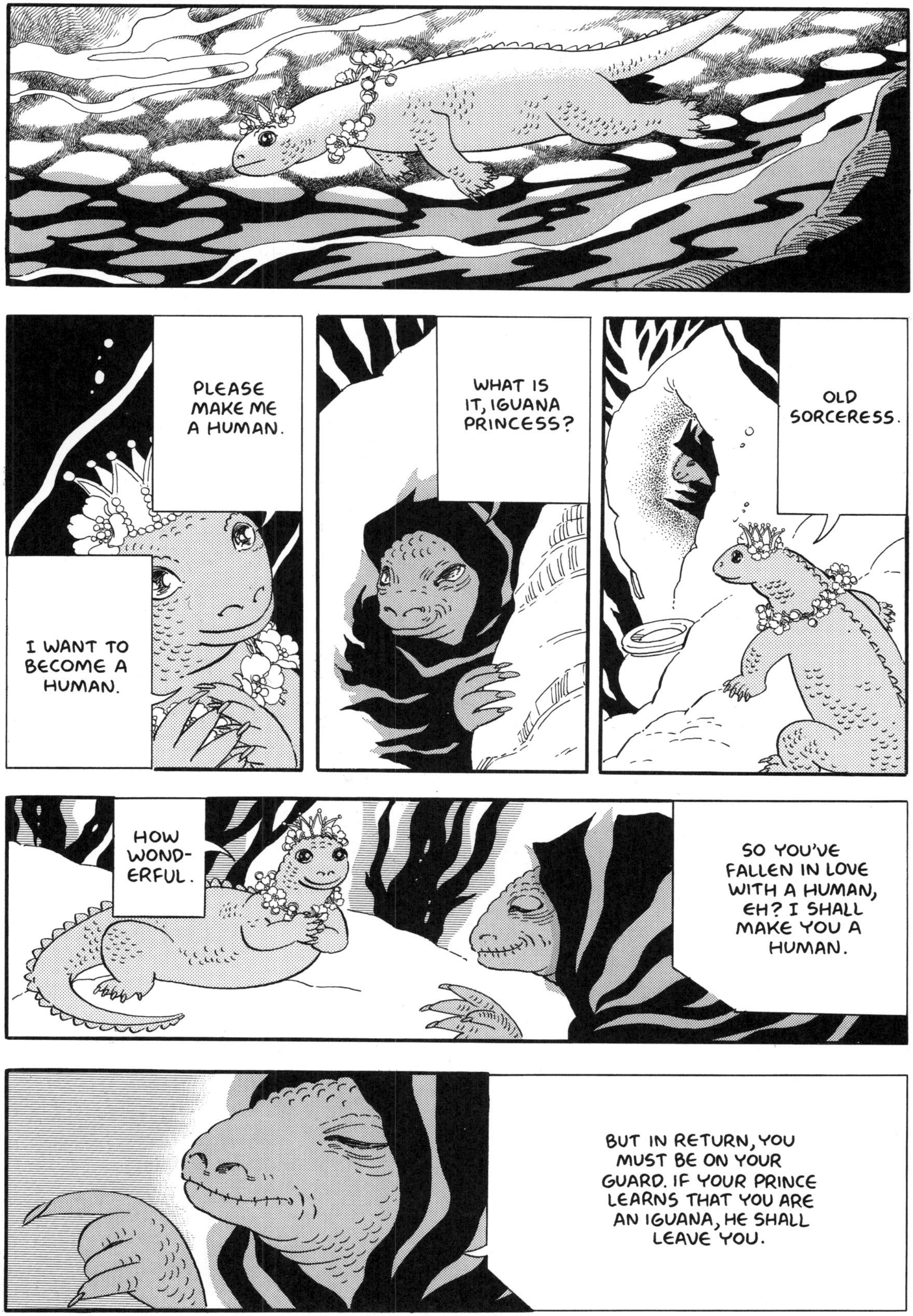
OLD SORCERESS.
WHAT IS IT, IGUANA PRINCESS?
PLEASE MAKE ME A HUMAN.
I WANT TO BECOME A HUMAN.
SO YOU'VE FALLEN IN LOVE WITH A HUMAN, EH? I SHALL MAKE YOU A HUMAN.
HOW WOND-ERFUL.
BUT IN RETURN, YOU MUST BE ON YOUR GUARD. IF YOUR PRINCE LEARNS THAT YOU ARE AN IGUANA, HE SHALL LEAVE YOU.

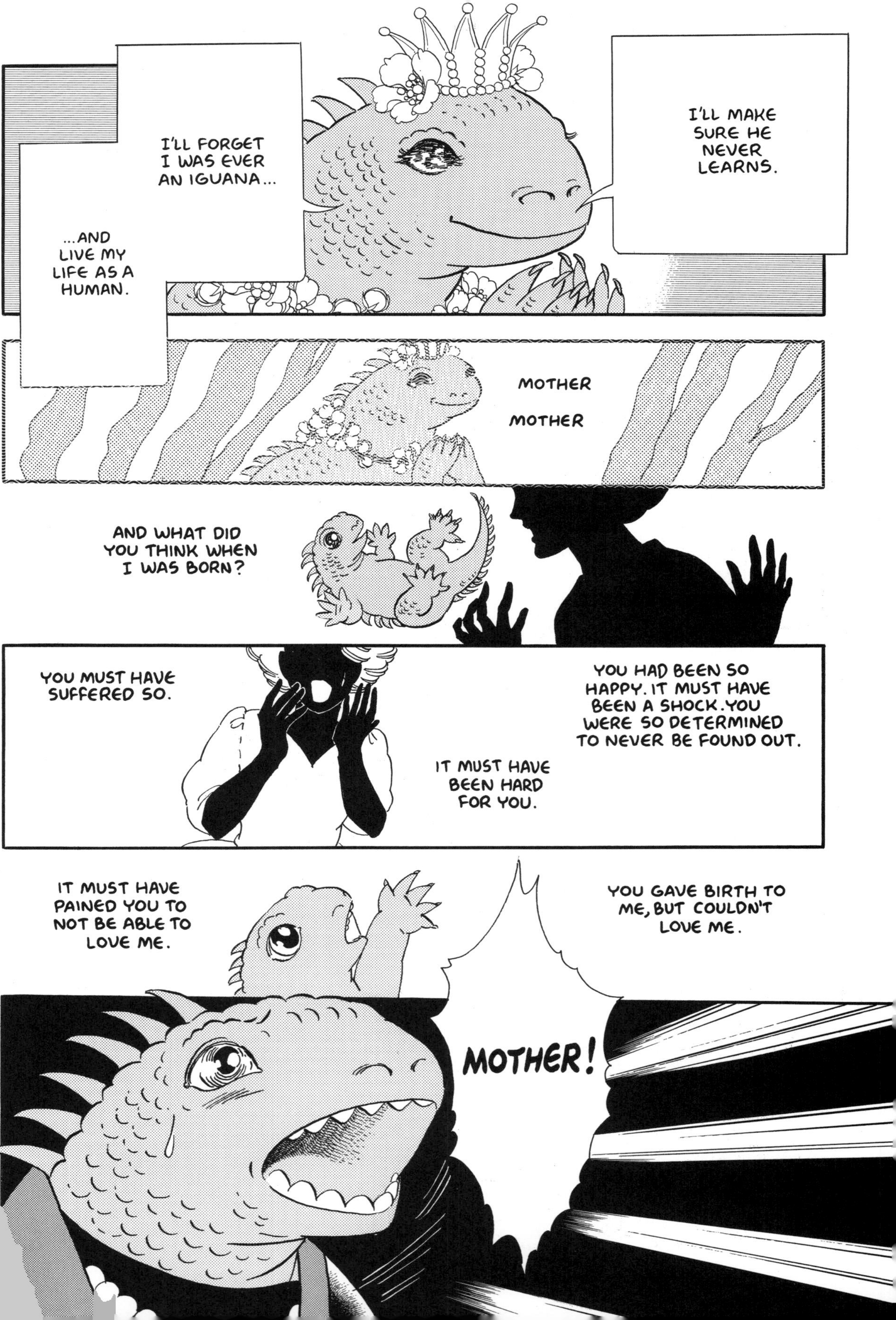
I'LL MAKE SURE HE NEVER LEARNS.
I'LL FORGET I WAS EVER AN IGUANA...
...AND LIVE MY LIFE AS A HUMAN.
MOTHER
MOTHER
AND WHAT DID YOU THINK WHEN I WAS BORN?
YOU HAD BEEN SO HAPPY. IT MUST HAVE BEEN A SHOCK. YOU WERE SO DETERMINED TO NEVER BE FOUND OUT.
IT MUST HAVE BEEN HARD FOR YOU.
YOU MUST HAVE SUFFERED SO.
YOU GAVE BIRTH TO ME, BUT COULDN'T LOVE ME.
IT MUST HAVE PAINED YOU TO NOT BE ABLE TO LOVE ME.
MOTHER!

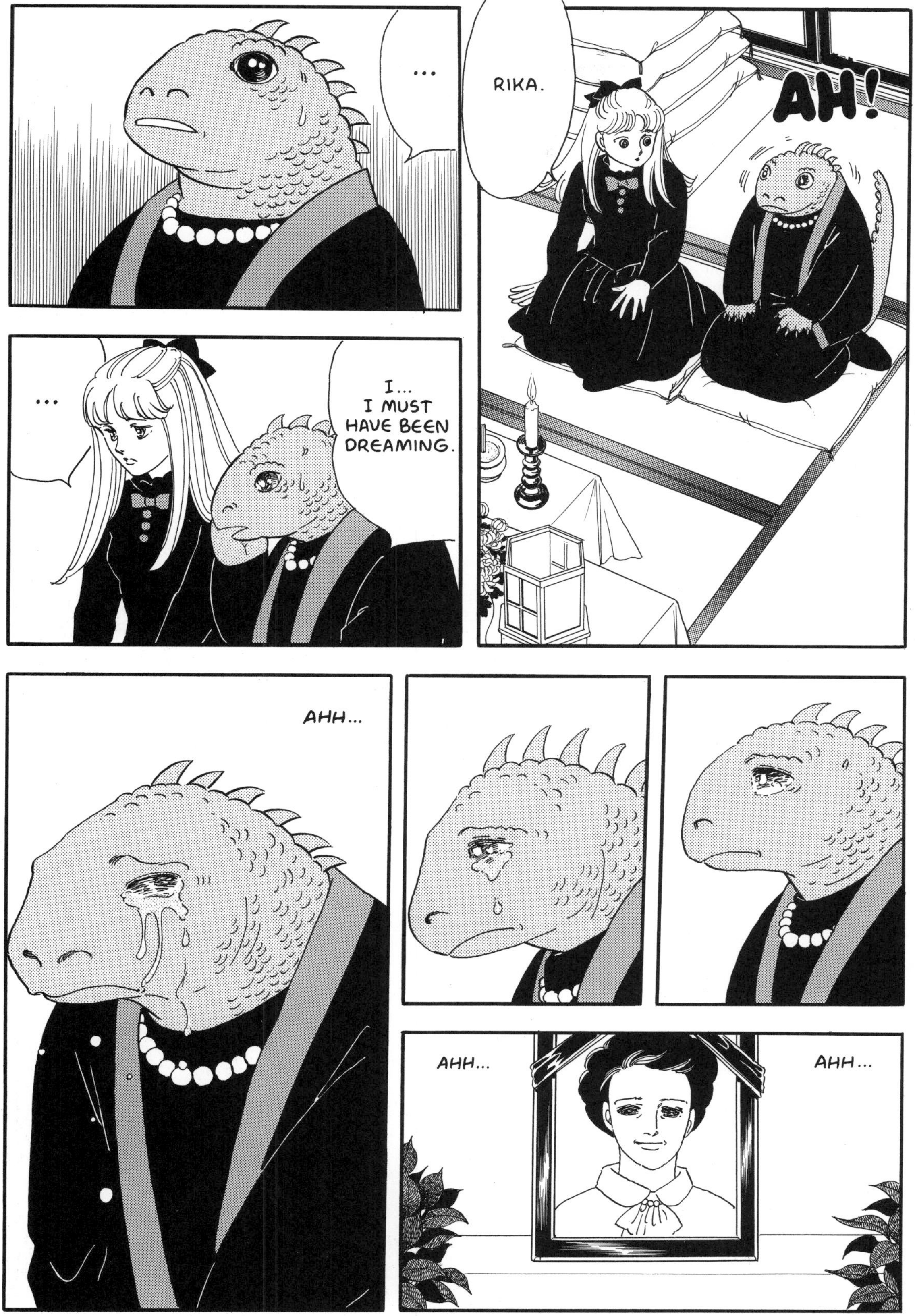
RIKA.
AH!
...
I... I MUST HAVE BEEN DREAMING.
...
AHH...
AHH...
AHH...

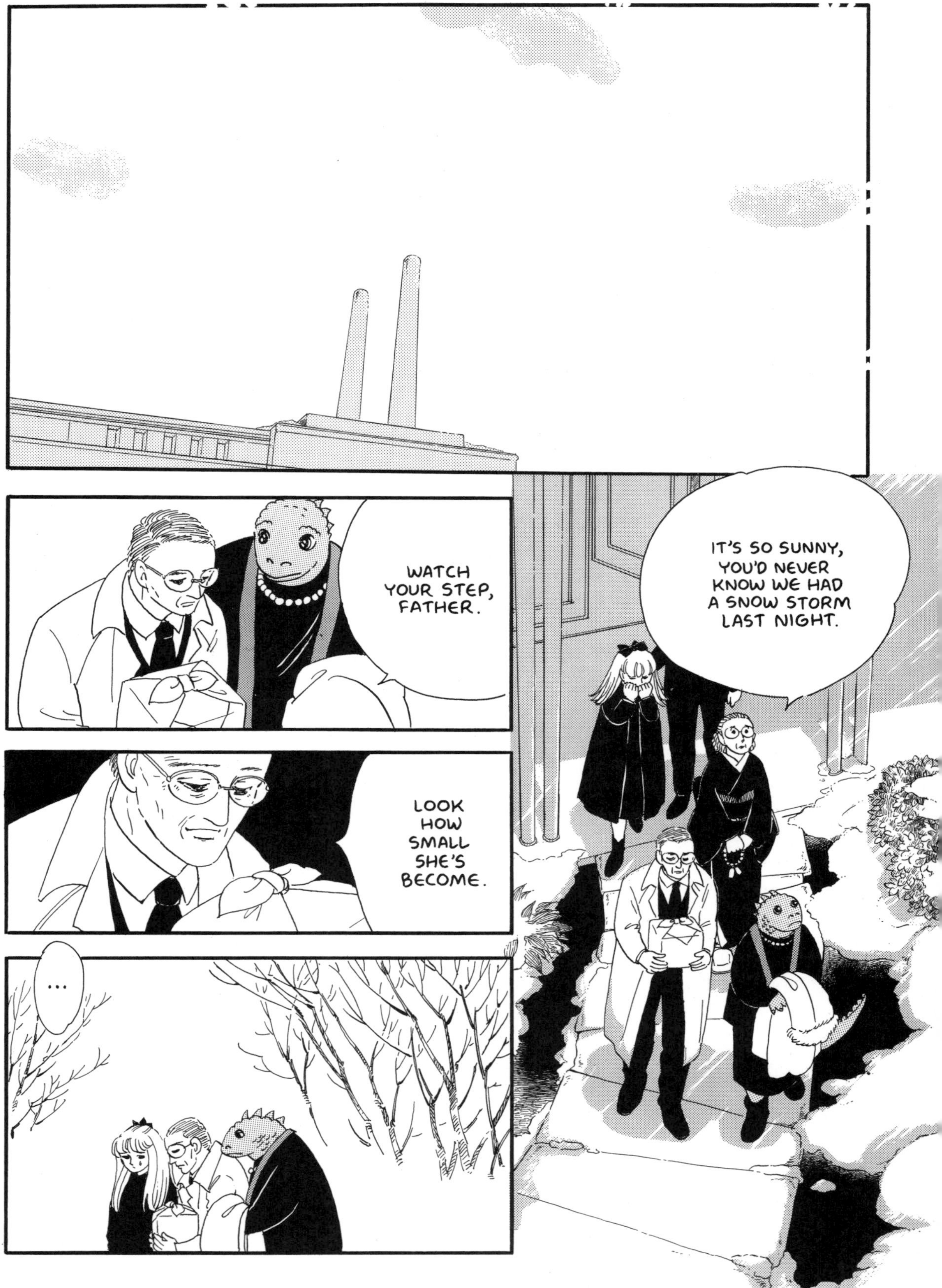
IT'S SO SUNNY, YOU'D NEVER KNOW WE HAD A SNOW STORM LAST NIGHT.
WATCH YOUR STEP, FATHER.
LOOK HOW SMALL SHE'S BECOME.
...

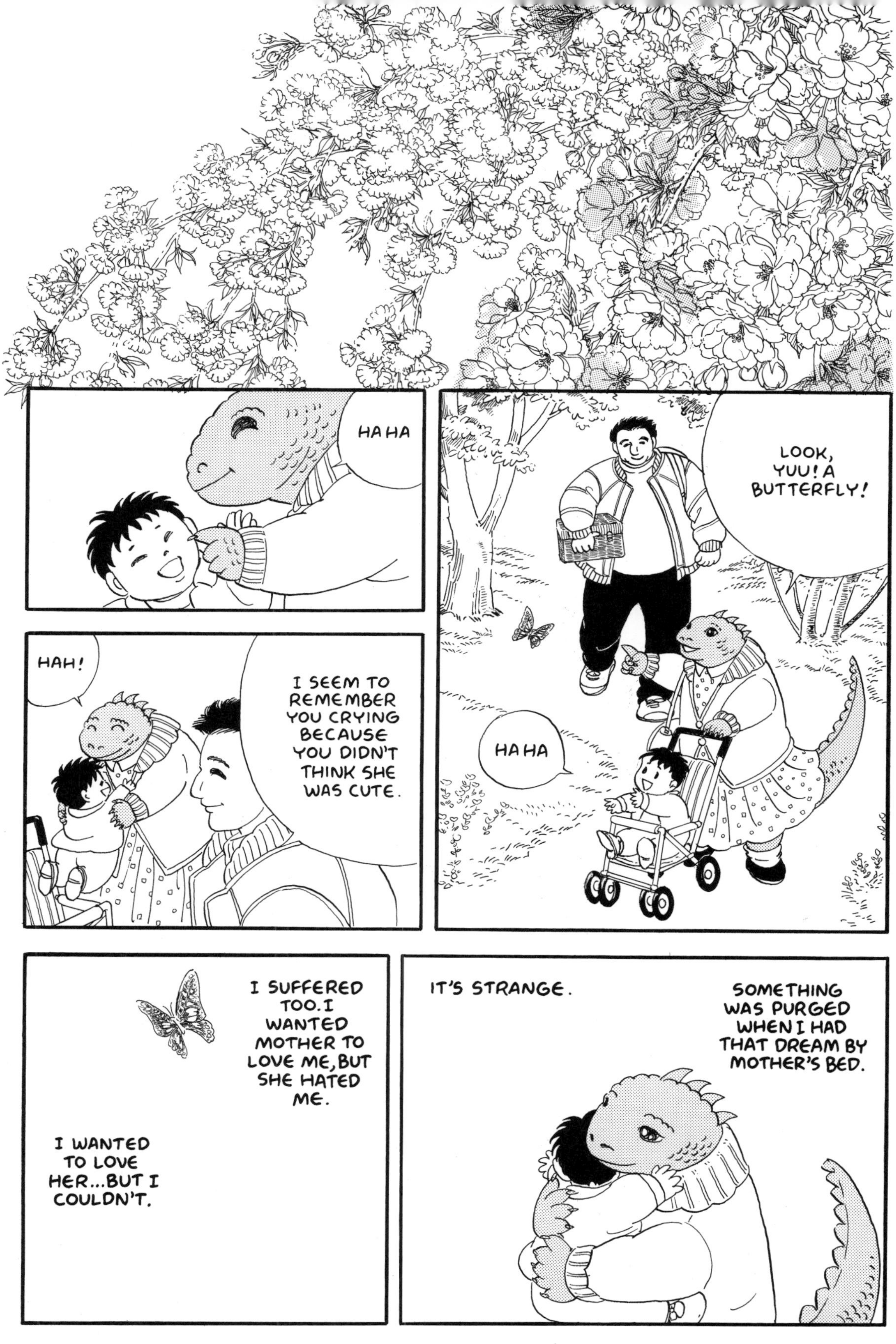
LOOK, YUU! A BUTTERFLY!
HA HA
HA HA
HAH!
I SEEM TO REMEMBER YOU CRYING BECAUSE YOU DIDN'T THINK SHE WAS CUTE.
IT'S STRANGE.
SOMETHING WAS PURGED WHEN I HAD THAT DREAM BY MOTHER'S BED.
I SUFFERED TOO. I WANTED MOTHER TO LOVE ME, BUT SHE HATED ME.
I WANTED TO LOVE HER... BUT I COULDN'T.

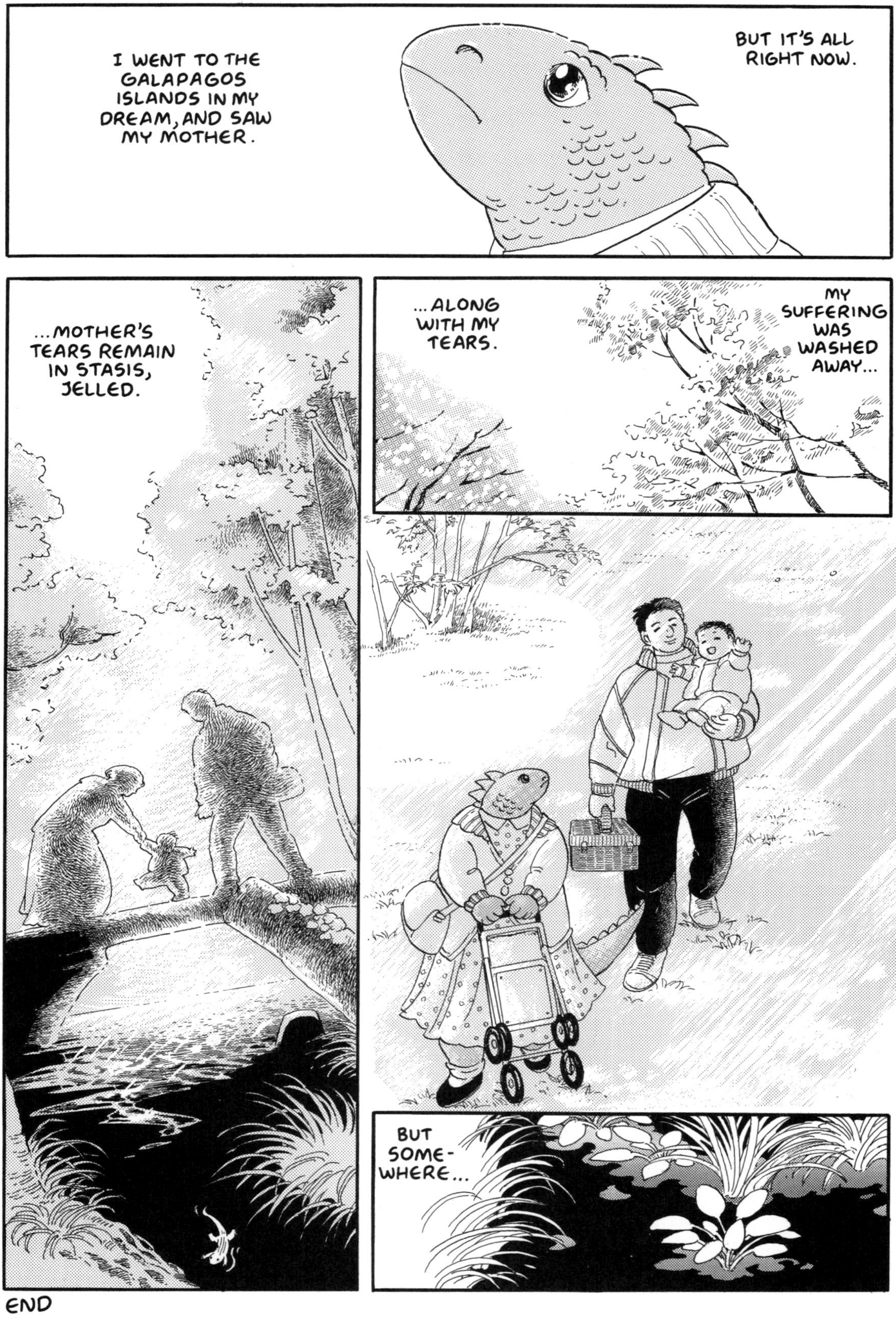
BUT IT'S ALL RIGHT NOW.
I WENT TO THE GALAPAGOS ISLANDS IN MY DREAM, AND SAW MY MOTHER.
MY SUFFERING WAS WASHED AWAY...
...ALONG WITH MY TEARS.
BUT SOME-WHERE...
...MOTHER'S TEARS REMAIN IN STASIS, JELLED.

END

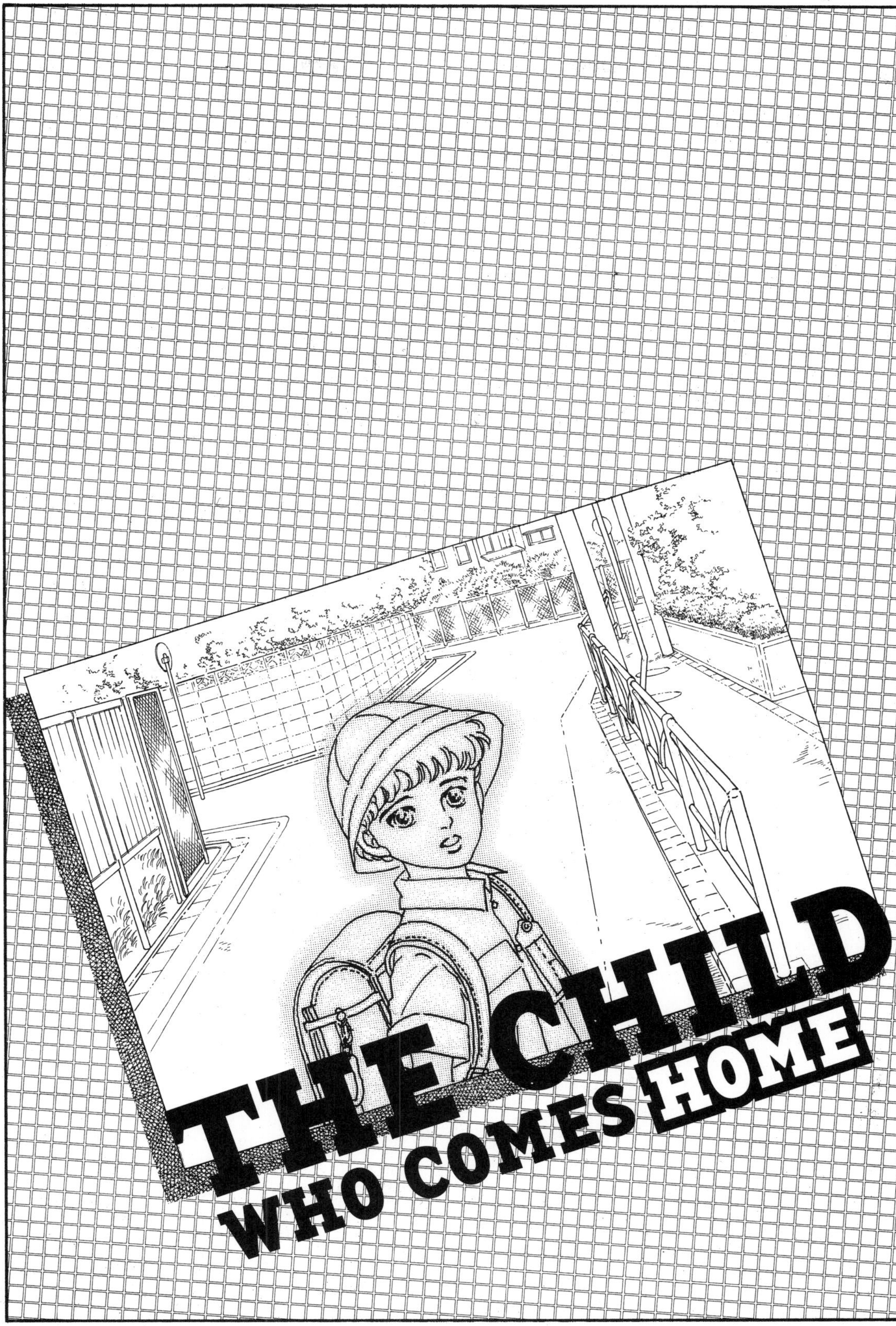
THE CHILD
WHO COMES HOME

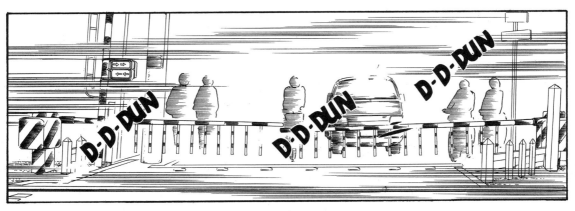

I'M HOME!

WELCOME HOME, YUU.

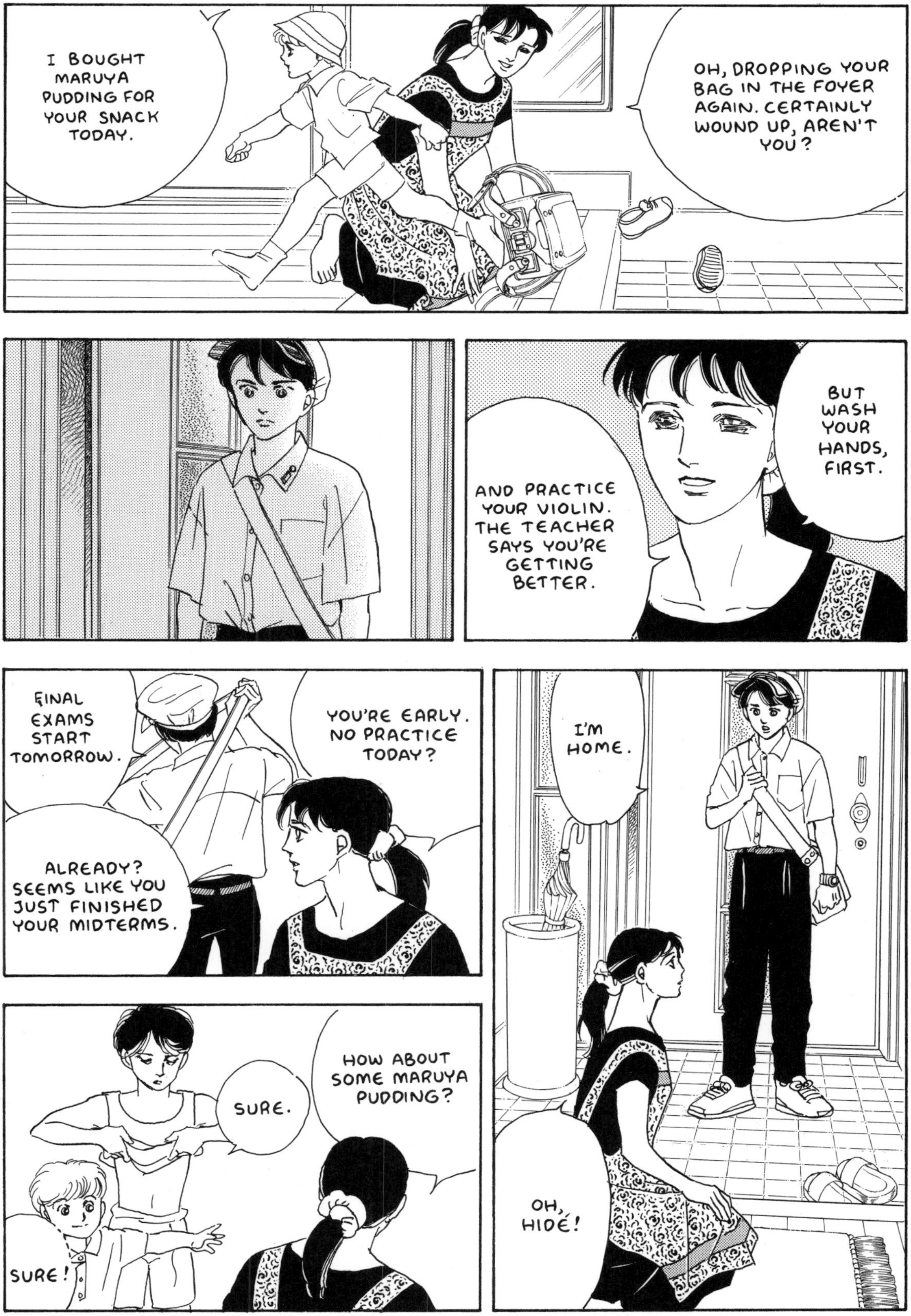
OH, DROPPING YOUR BAG IN THE FOYER AGAIN. CERTAINLY WOUND UP, AREN'T YOU?
I BOUGHT MARUYA PUDDING FOR YOUR SNACK TODAY.
BUT WASH YOUR HANDS, FIRST.
AND PRACTICE YOUR VIOLIN. THE TEACHER SAYS YOU'RE GETTING BETTER.
I'M HOME.
OH, HIDE!
YOU'RE EARLY. NO PRACTICE TODAY?
FINAL EXAMS START TOMORROW.
ALREADY? SEEMS LIKE YOU JUST FINISHED YOUR MIDTERMS.
HOW ABOUT SOME MARUYA PUDDING?
SURE.
SURE!

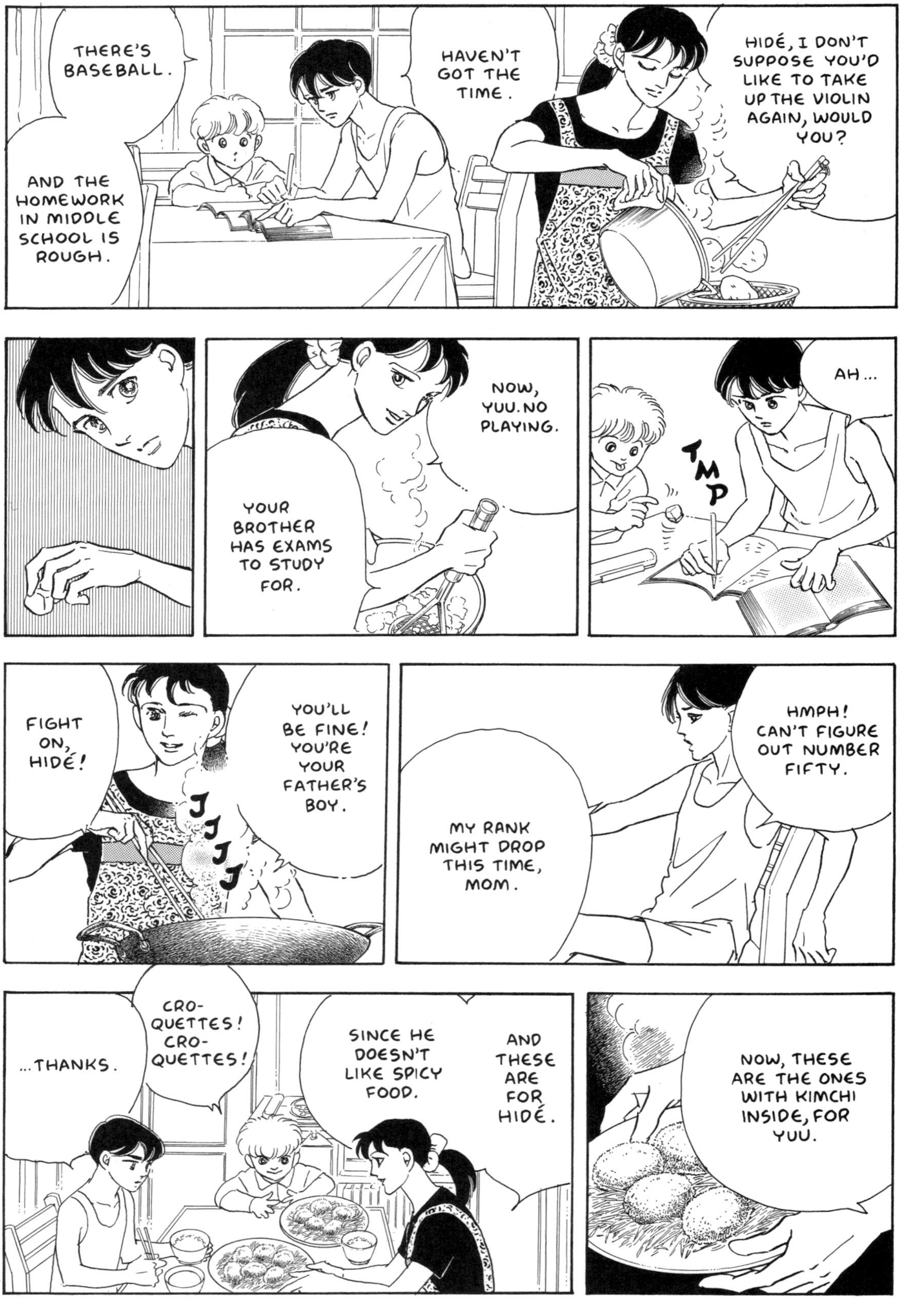
HIDÉ, I DON'T SUPPOSE YOU'D LIKE TO TAKE UP THE VIOLIN AGAIN, WOULD YOU?
HAVEN'T GOT THE TIME.
THERE'S BASEBALL.
AND THE HOMEWORK IN MIDDLE SCHOOL IS ROUGH.
AH...
TMP
NOW, YUU. NO PLAYING.
YOUR BROTHER HAS EXAMS TO STUDY FOR.
HMPH! CAN'T FIGURE OUT NUMBER FIFTY.
MY RANK MIGHT DROP THIS TIME, MOM.
YOU'LL BE FINE! YOU'RE YOUR FATHER'S BOY.
JJJJ
FIGHT ON, HIDÉ!
NOW, THESE ARE THE ONES WITH KIMCHI INSIDE, FOR YUU.
AND THESE ARE FOR HIDÉ.
SINCE HE DOESN'T LIKE SPICY FOOD.
CRO-QUETTES! CRO-QUETTES!
...THANKS.

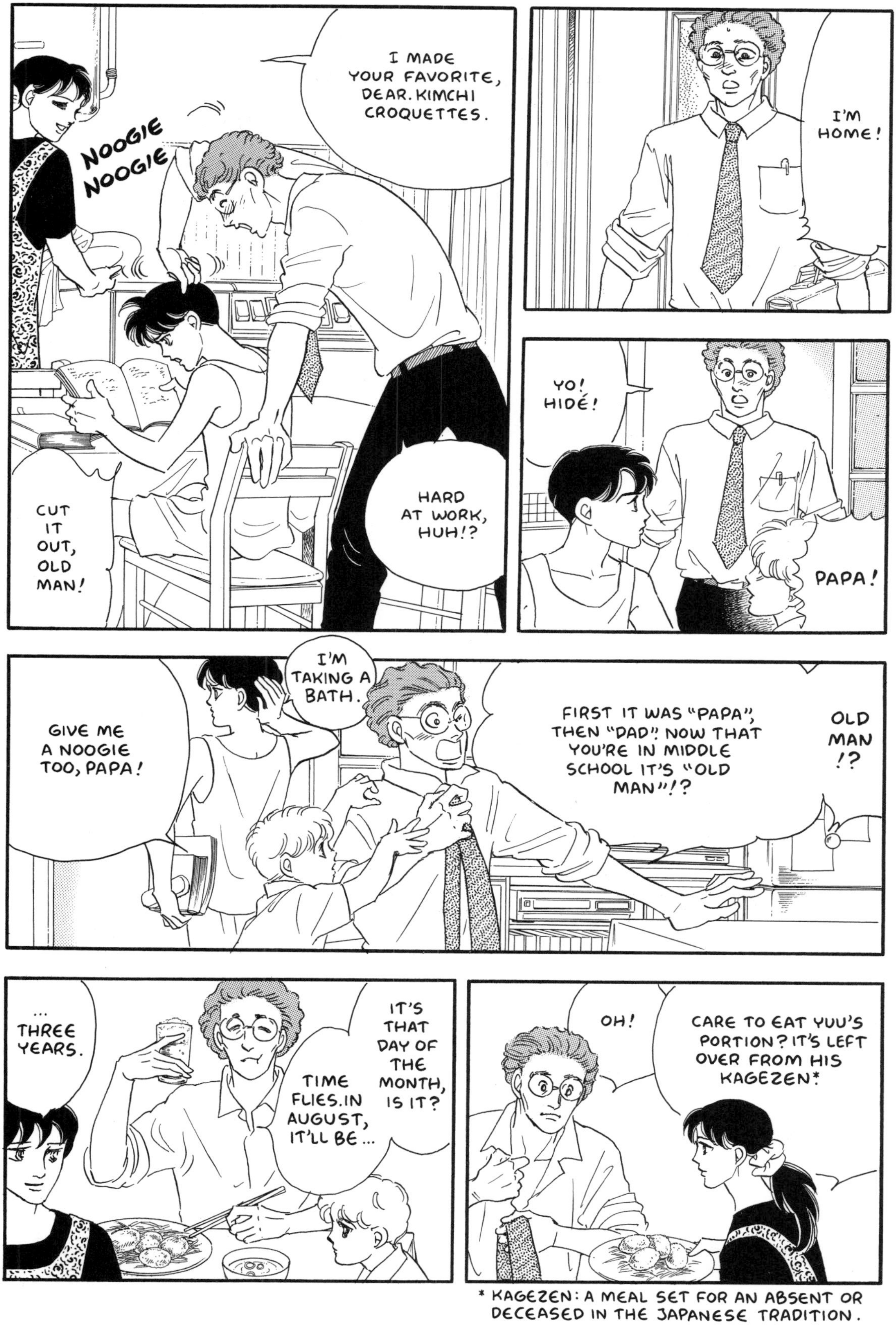
I'M HOME!
YO! HIDÉ!
PAPA!
I MADE YOUR FAVORITE, DEAR. KIMCHI CROQUETTES.
NOOGIE NOOGIE
HARD AT WORK, HUH!?
CUT IT OUT, OLD MAN!
OLD MAN!?
FIRST IT WAS "PAPA", THEN "DAD". NOW THAT YOU'RE IN MIDDLE SCHOOL IT'S "OLD MAN"!?
I'M TAKING A BATH.
GIVE ME A NOOGIE TOO, PAPA!
CARE TO EAT YUU'S PORTION? IT'S LEFT OVER FROM HIS KAGEZEN*
OH!
IT'S THAT DAY OF THE MONTH, IS IT?
TIME FLIES. IN AUGUST, IT'LL BE...
... THREE YEARS.

* KAGEZEN: A MEAL SET FOR AN ABSENT OR DECEASED IN THE JAPANESE TRADITION.

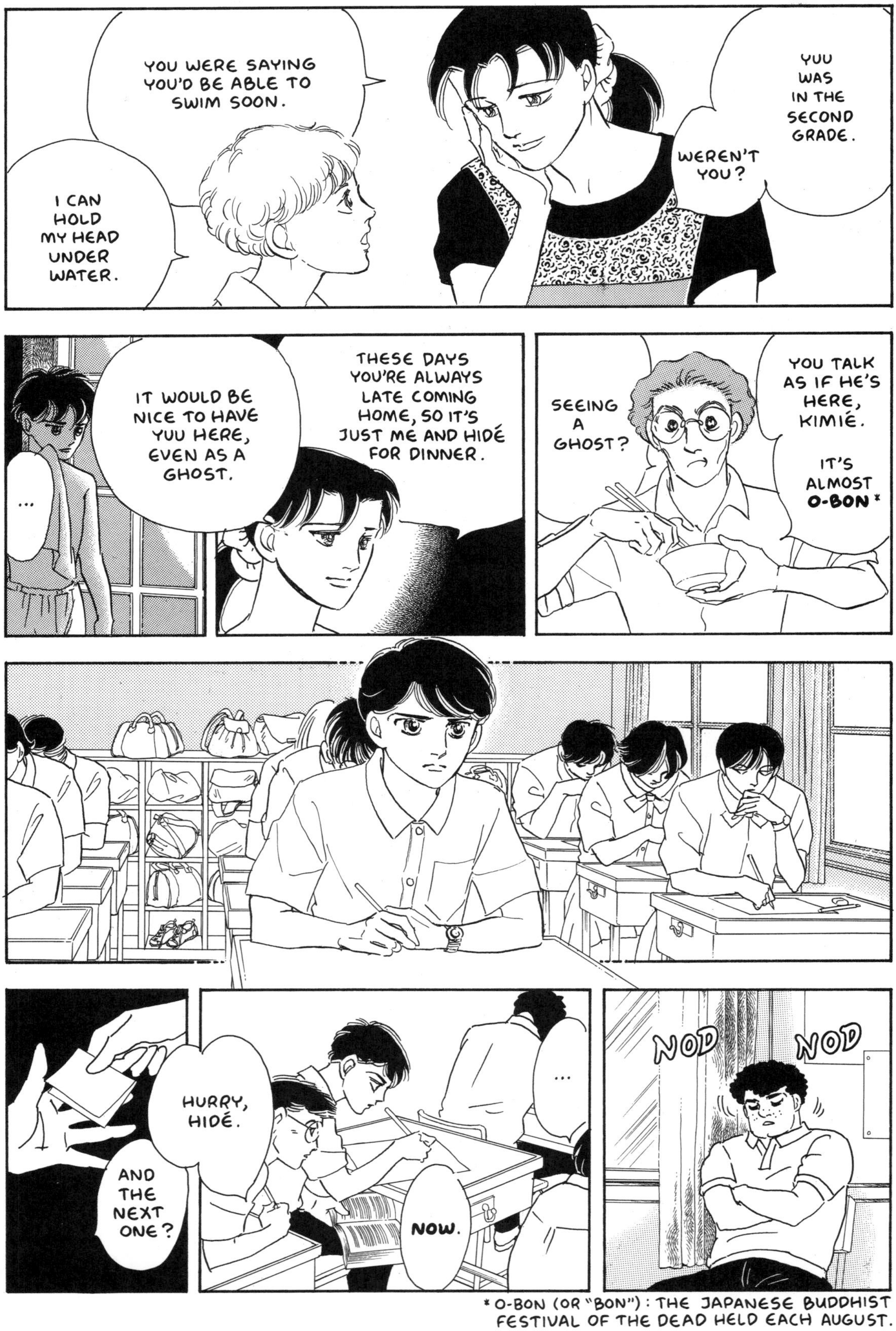
YUU WAS IN THE SECOND GRADE.
WEREN'T YOU?
YOU WERE SAYING YOU'D BE ABLE TO SWIM SOON.
I CAN HOLD MY HEAD UNDER WATER.
YOU TALK AS IF HE'S HERE, KIMIÉ.
IT'S ALMOST O-BON*
SEEING A GHOST?
THESE DAYS YOU'RE ALWAYS LATE COMING HOME, SO IT'S JUST ME AND HIDÉ FOR DINNER.
IT WOULD BE NICE TO HAVE YUU HERE, EVEN AS A GHOST.
...
NOD NOD
...
HURRY, HIDÉ.
NOW.
AND THE NEXT ONE?

* O-BON (OR "BON"): THE JAPANESE BUDDHIST FESTIVAL OF THE DEAD HELD EACH AUGUST.

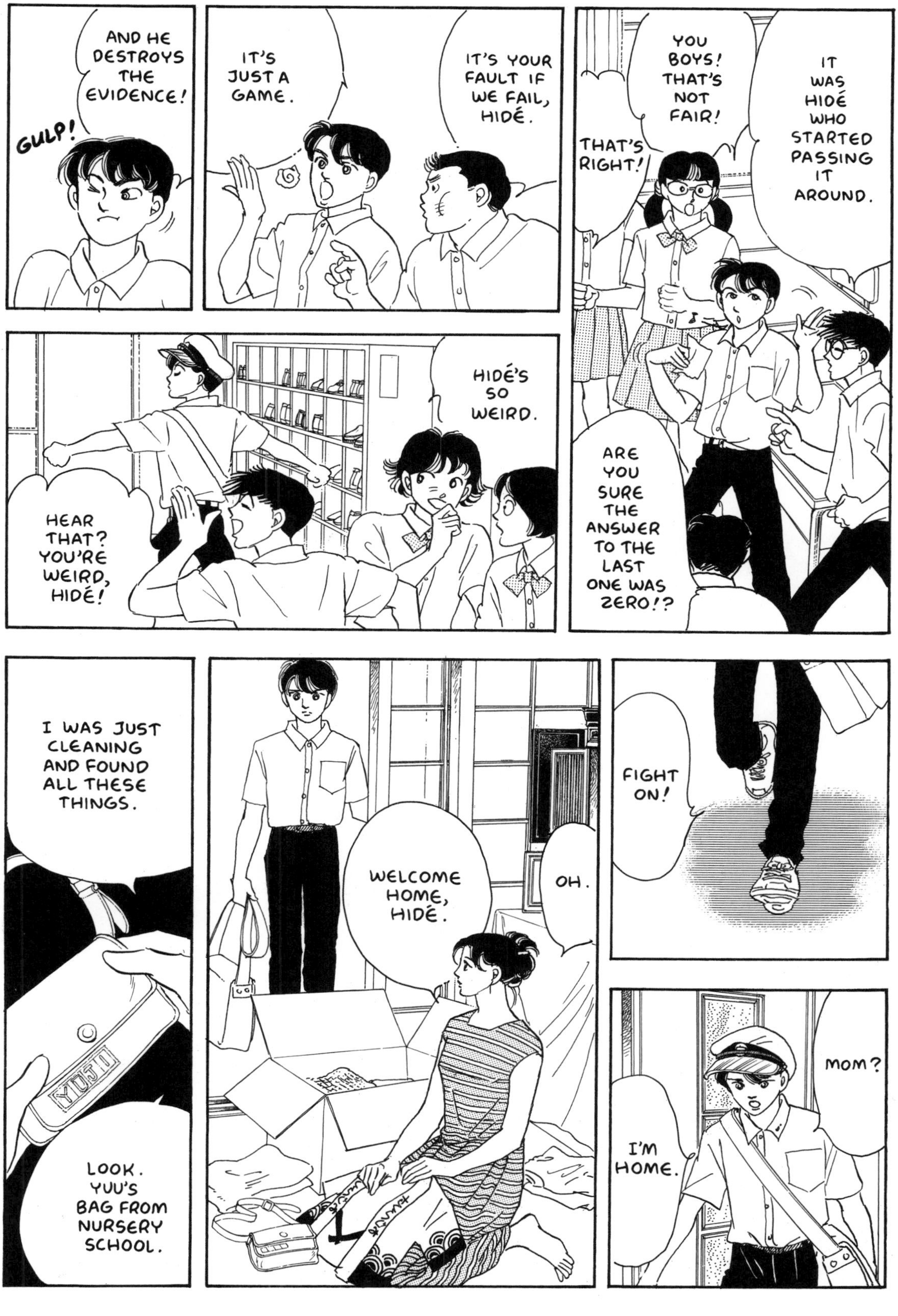
IT WAS HIDÉ WHO STARTED PASSING IT AROUND.
YOU BOYS! THAT'S NOT FAIR!
THAT'S RIGHT!
ARE YOU SURE THE ANSWER TO THE LAST ONE WAS ZERO!?
IT'S YOUR FAULT IF WE FAIL, HIDÉ.
IT'S JUST A GAME.
AND HE DESTROYS THE EVIDENCE!
GULP!
HIDÉ'S SO WEIRD.
HEAR THAT? YOU'RE WEIRD, HIDÉ!
FIGHT ON!
MOM?
I'M HOME.
OH.
WELCOME HOME, HIDÉ.
I WAS JUST CLEANING AND FOUND ALL THESE THINGS.
LOOK. YUU'S BAG FROM NURSERY SCHOOL.

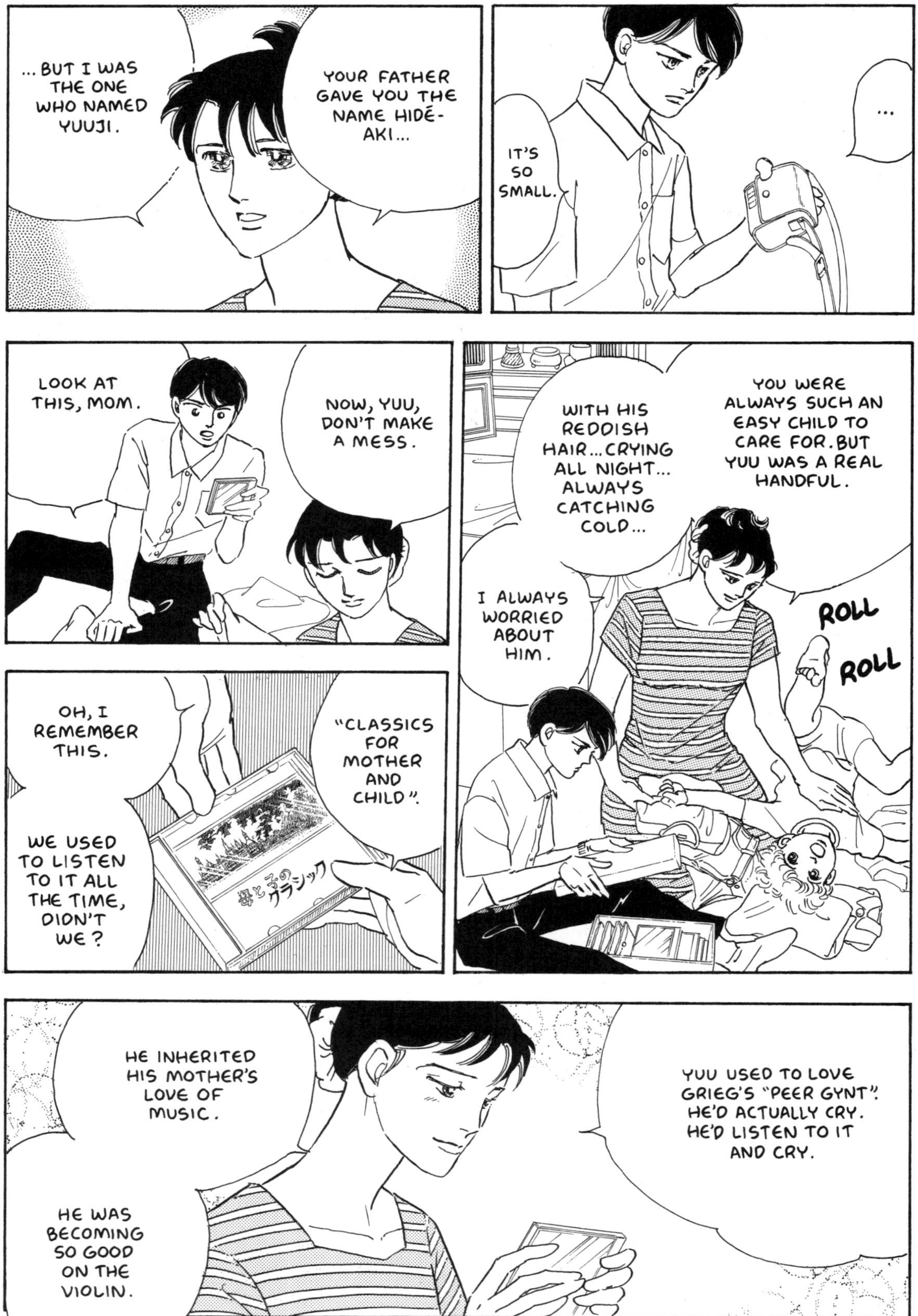
...
IT'S SO SMALL.
YOUR FATHER GAVE YOU THE NAME HIDÉ-AKI...
...BUT I WAS THE ONE WHO NAMED YUUJI.
YOU WERE ALWAYS SUCH AN EASY CHILD TO CARE FOR. BUT YUU WAS A REAL HANDFUL.
WITH HIS REDDISH HAIR... CRYING ALL NIGHT... ALWAYS CATCHING COLD...
I ALWAYS WORRIED ABOUT HIM.
ROLL
ROLL
NOW, YUU, DON'T MAKE A MESS.
LOOK AT THIS, MOM.
"CLASSICS FOR MOTHER AND CHILD".
OH, I REMEMBER THIS.
母と子のクラシック
WE USED TO LISTEN TO IT ALL THE TIME, DIDN'T WE?
YUU USED TO LOVE GRIEG'S "PEER GYNT". HE'D ACTUALLY CRY. HE'D LISTEN TO IT AND CRY.
HE INHERITED HIS MOTHER'S LOVE OF MUSIC.
HE WAS BECOMING SO GOOD ON THE VIOLIN.

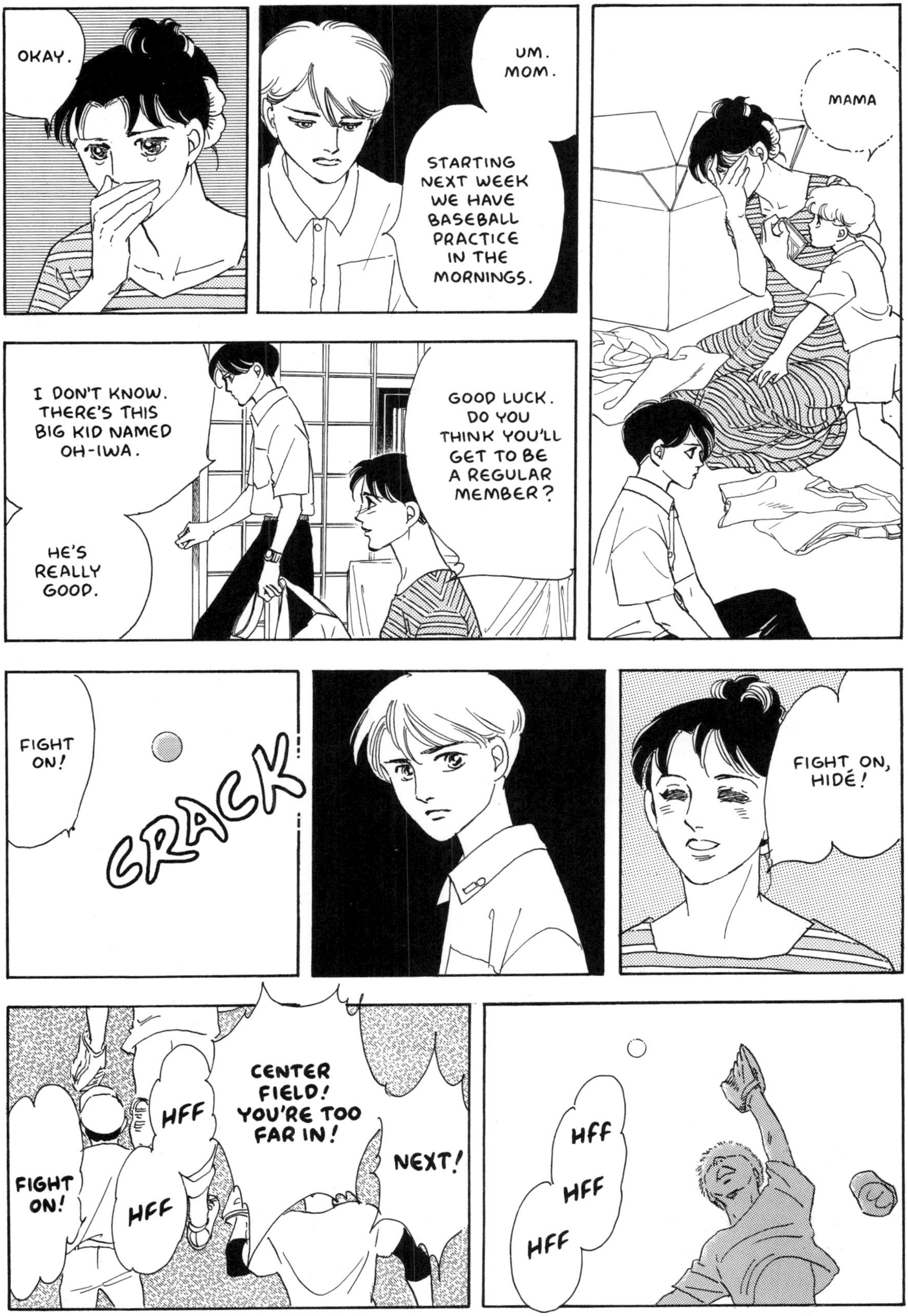
MAMA
UM. MOM.
STARTING NEXT WEEK WE HAVE BASEBALL PRACTICE IN THE MORNINGS.
OKAY.
GOOD LUCK. DO YOU THINK YOU'LL GET TO BE A REGULAR MEMBER?
I DON'T KNOW. THERE'S THIS BIG KID NAMED OH-IWA.
HE'S REALLY GOOD.
FIGHT ON, HIDÉ!
FIGHT ON!
CRACK
HFF
HFF
HFF
CENTER FIELD! YOU'RE TOO FAR IN!
NEXT!
HFF
FIGHT ON!
HFF

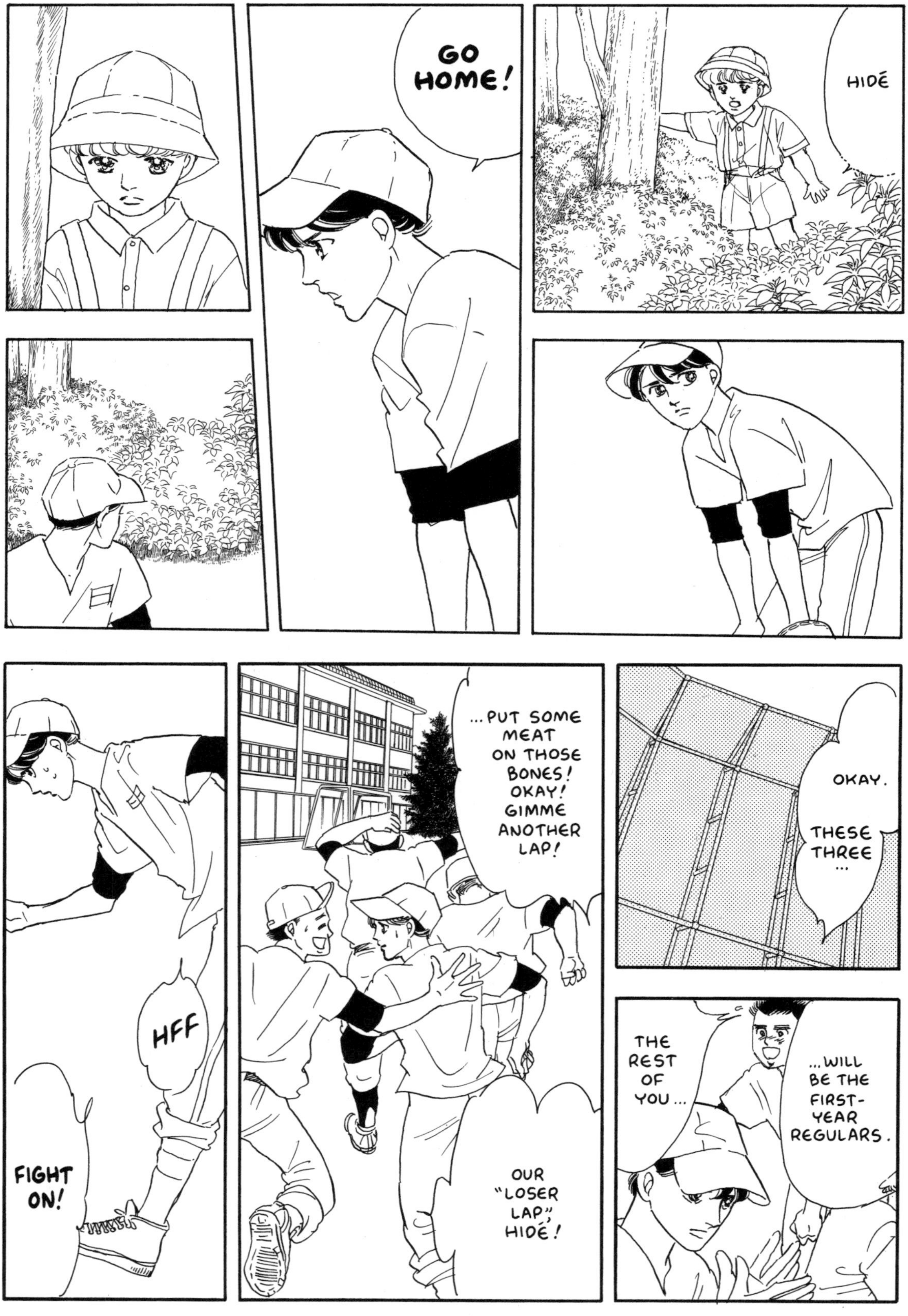
HIDÉ
...
GO HOME!
OKAY.
THESE THREE ...
THE REST OF YOU ...
...WILL BE THE FIRST-YEAR REGULARS.
...PUT SOME MEAT ON THOSE BONES! OKAY! GIMME ANOTHER LAP!
OUR "LOSER LAP," HIDÉ!
HFF
FIGHT ON!

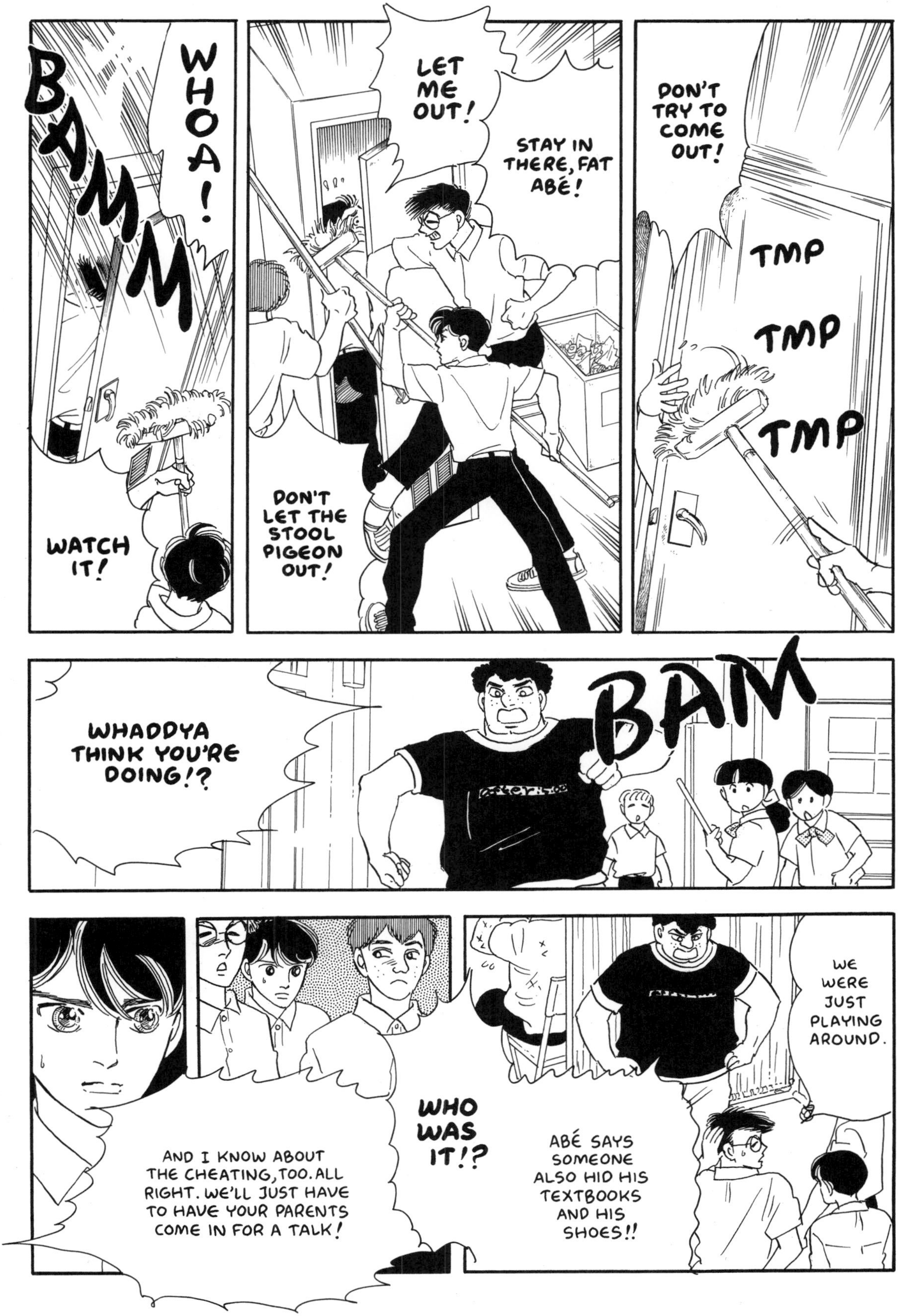
DON'T TRY TO COME OUT!
TMP
TMP
TMP
LET ME OUT!
STAY IN THERE, FAT ABÉ!
DON'T LET THE STOOL PIGEON OUT!
WHOA!
BAMM
WATCH IT!
BAM
WHADDYA THINK YOU'RE DOING!?
WE WERE JUST PLAYING AROUND.
WHO WAS IT!?
ABÉ SAYS SOMEONE ALSO HID HIS TEXTBOOKS AND HIS SHOES!!
AND I KNOW ABOUT THE CHEATING, TOO. ALL RIGHT. WE'LL JUST HAVE TO HAVE YOUR PARENTS COME IN FOR A TALK!

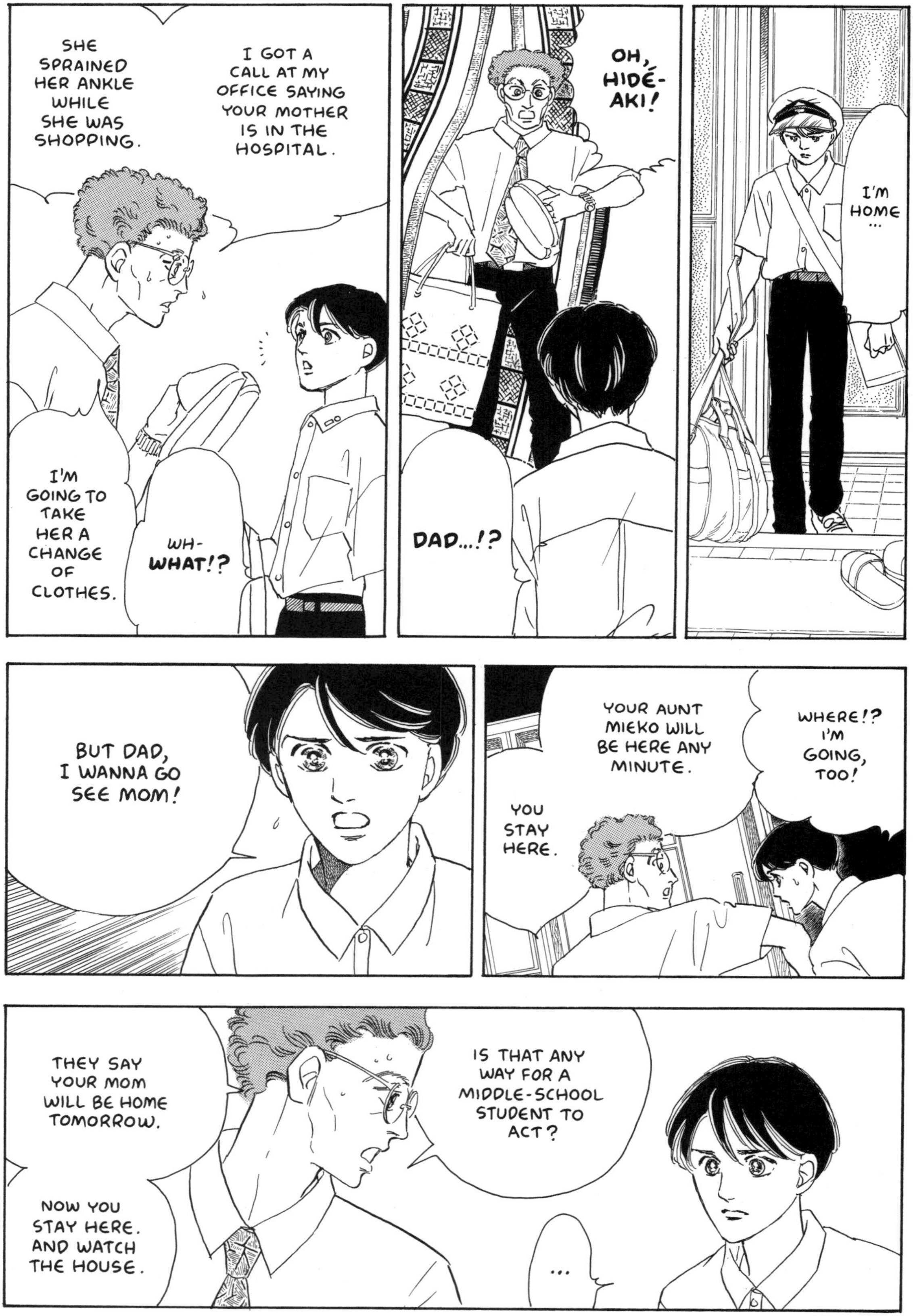
I'M HOME ...
OH, HIDÉ-AKI!
DAD...!?
I GOT A CALL AT MY OFFICE SAYING YOUR MOTHER IS IN THE HOSPITAL.
SHE SPRAINED HER ANKLE WHILE SHE WAS SHOPPING.
WH- WHAT!?
I'M GOING TO TAKE HER A CHANGE OF CLOTHES.
WHERE!? I'M GOING, TOO!
YOUR AUNT MIEKO WILL BE HERE ANY MINUTE.
YOU STAY HERE.
BUT DAD, I WANNA GO SEE MOM!
IS THAT ANY WAY FOR A MIDDLE-SCHOOL STUDENT TO ACT?
THEY SAY YOUR MOM WILL BE HOME TOMORROW.
...
NOW YOU STAY HERE. AND WATCH THE HOUSE.

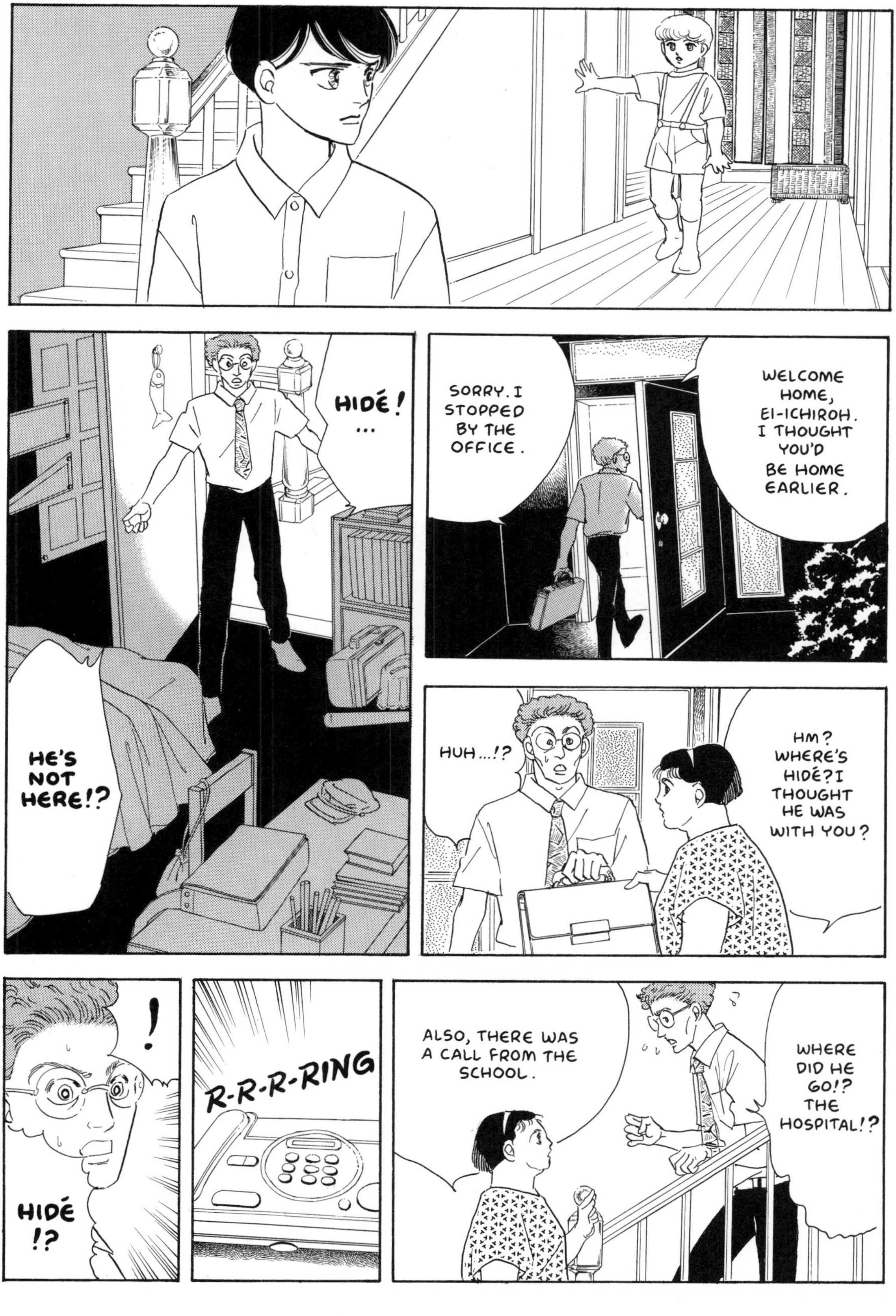
WELCOME HOME, EI-ICHIROH. I THOUGHT YOU'D BE HOME EARLIER.
SORRY. I STOPPED BY THE OFFICE.
HM? WHERE'S HIDÉ? I THOUGHT HE WAS WITH YOU?
HUH...!?
HIDÉ! ...
HE'S NOT HERE!?
WHERE DID HE GO!? THE HOSPITAL!?
ALSO, THERE WAS A CALL FROM THE SCHOOL.
R-R-R-RING
!
HIDÉ !?

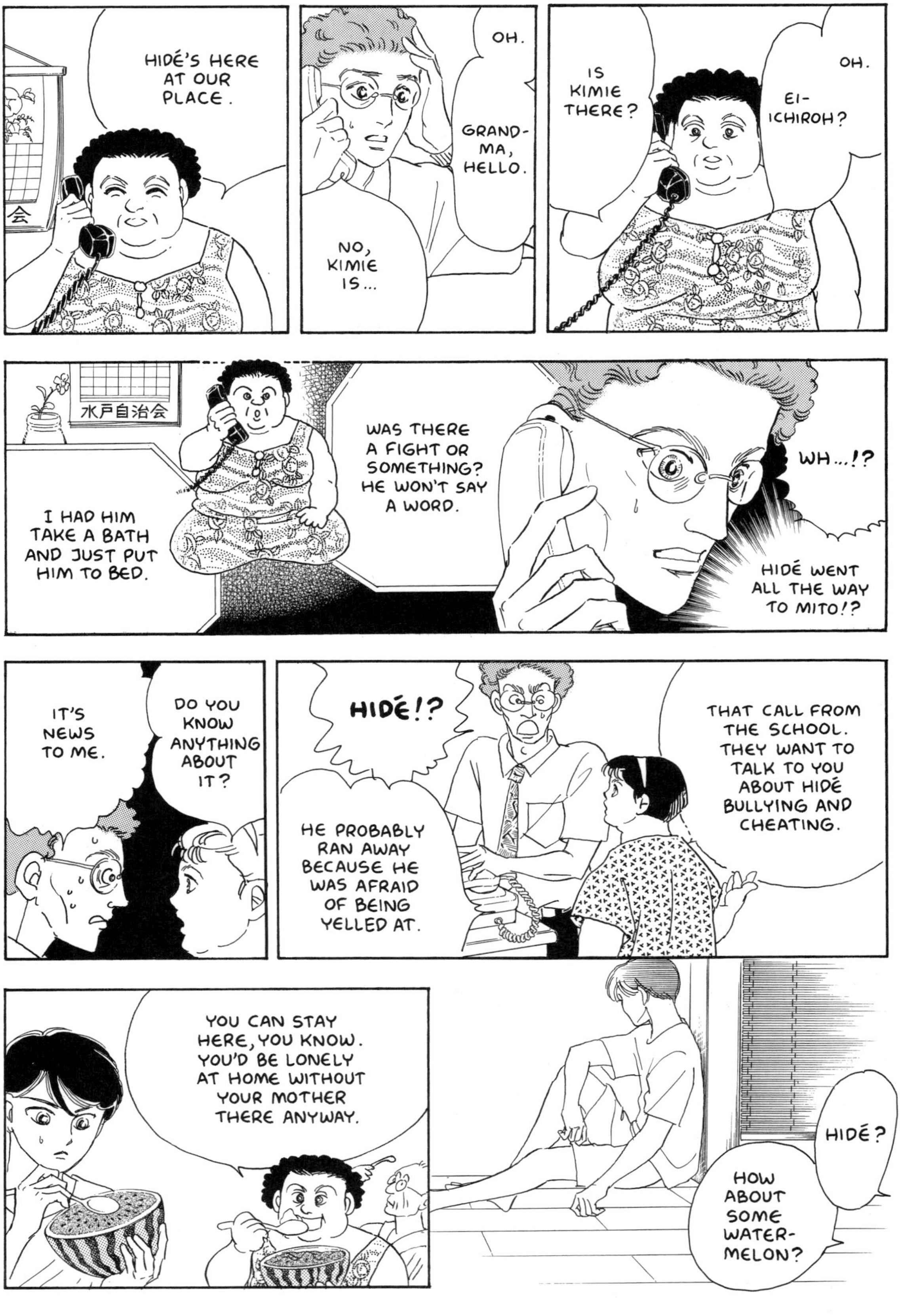
OH.
EI-ICHIROH?
IS KIMIE THERE?
OH.
GRAND-MA, HELLO.
NO, KIMIE IS...
HIDÉ'S HERE AT OUR PLACE.
WH...!?
HIDÉ WENT ALL THE WAY TO MITO!?
WAS THERE A FIGHT OR SOMETHING? HE WON'T SAY A WORD.
I HAD HIM TAKE A BATH AND JUST PUT HIM TO BED.
水戸自治会
THAT CALL FROM THE SCHOOL. THEY WANT TO TALK TO YOU ABOUT HIDÉ BULLYING AND CHEATING.
HIDÉ!?
HE PROBABLY RAN AWAY BECAUSE HE WAS AFRAID OF BEING YELLED AT.
DO YOU KNOW ANYTHING ABOUT IT?
IT'S NEWS TO ME.
HIDÉ?
HOW ABOUT SOME WATER-MELON?
YOU CAN STAY HERE, YOU KNOW. YOU'D BE LONELY AT HOME WITHOUT YOUR MOTHER THERE ANYWAY.

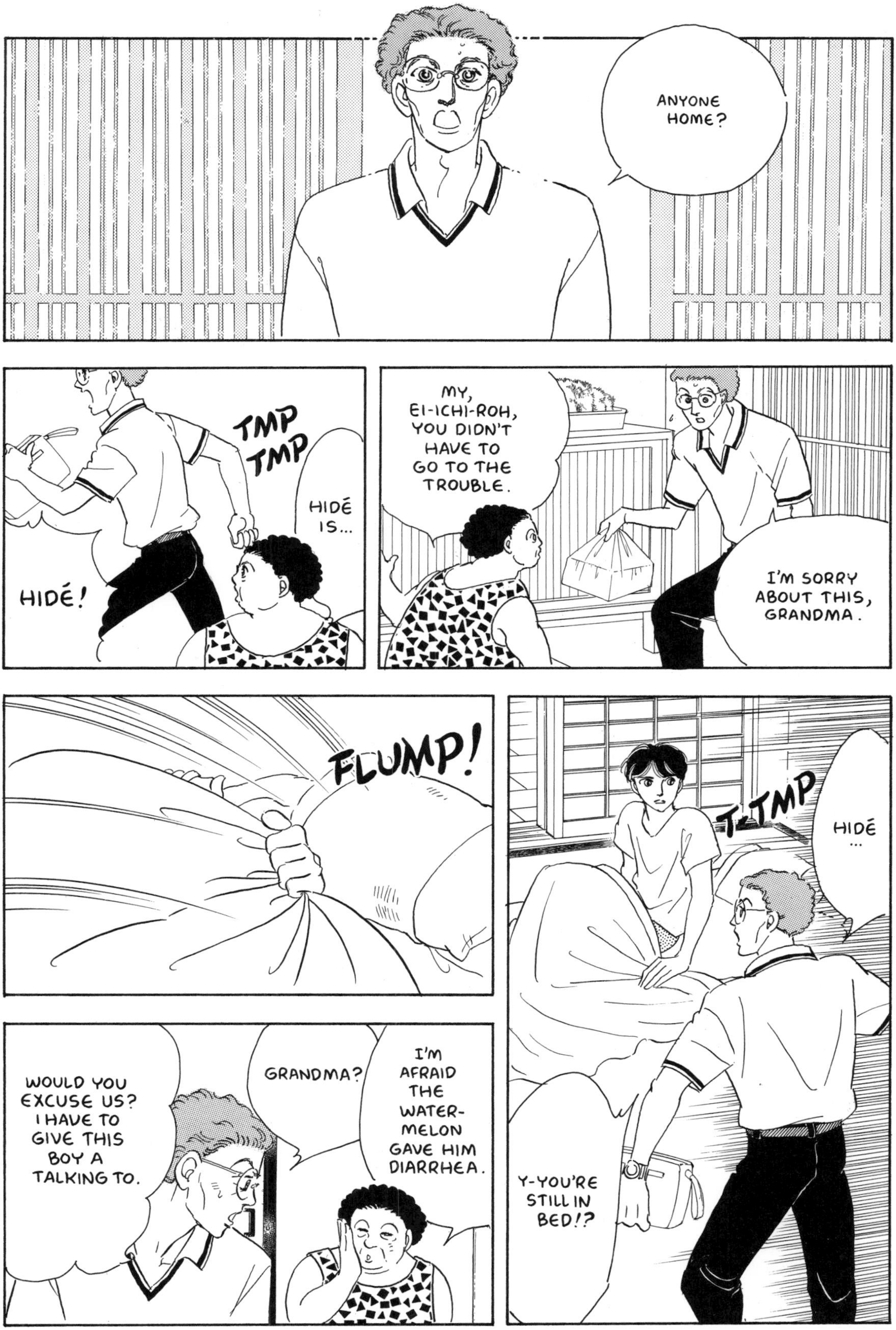
ANYONE HOME?
I'M SORRY ABOUT THIS, GRANDMA.
MY, EI-ICHI-ROH, YOU DIDN'T HAVE TO GO TO THE TROUBLE.
HIDÉ IS...
TMP TMP
HIDÉ!
T-TMP
HIDÉ ...
Y-YOU'RE STILL IN BED!?
FLUMP!
I'M AFRAID THE WATER-MELON GAVE HIM DIARRHEA.
GRANDMA?
WOULD YOU EXCUSE US? I HAVE TO GIVE THIS BOY A TALKING TO.

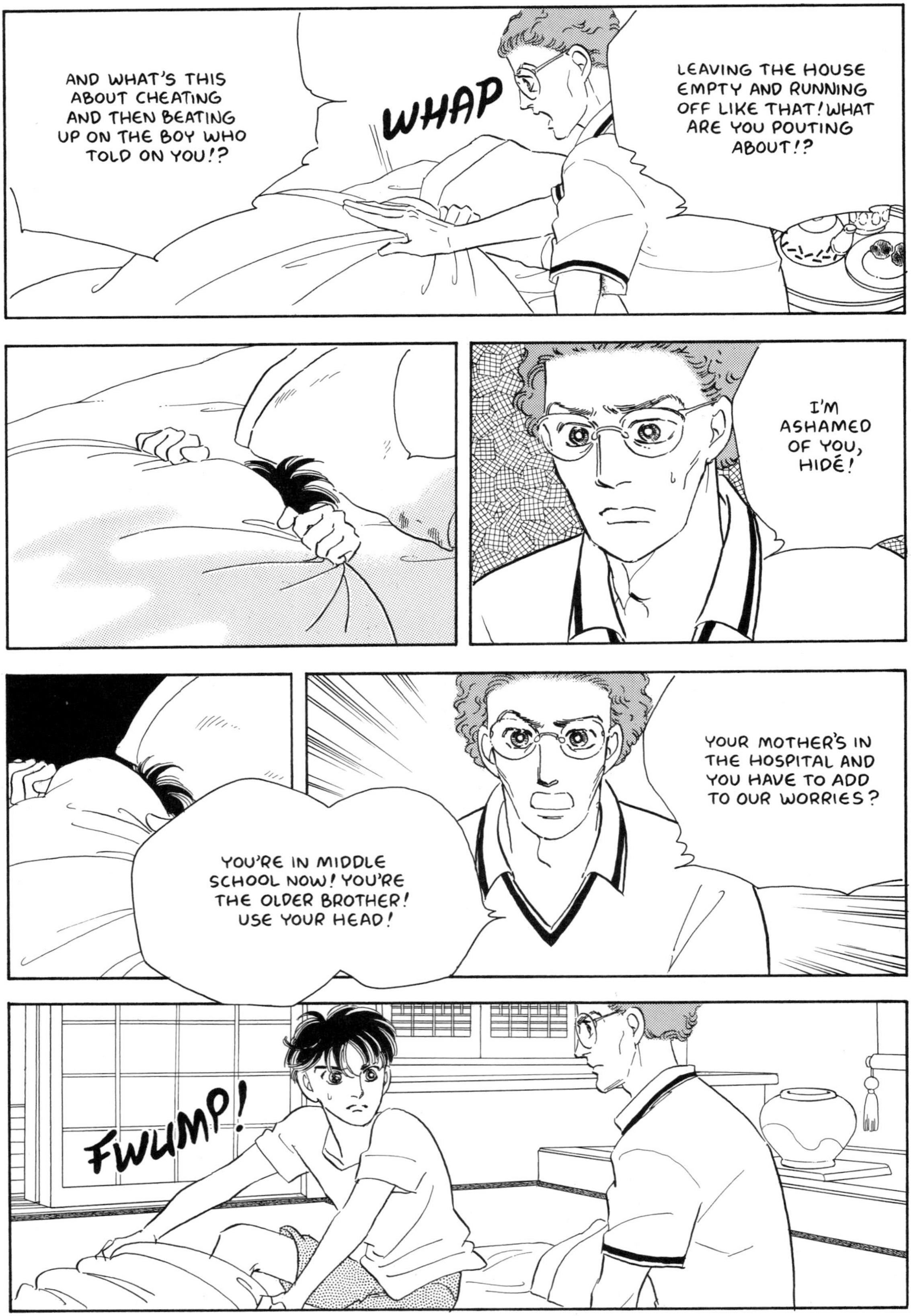
LEAVING THE HOUSE EMPTY AND RUNNING OFF LIKE THAT! WHAT ARE YOU POUTING ABOUT!?
WHAP
AND WHAT'S THIS ABOUT CHEATING AND THEN BEATING UP ON THE BOY WHO TOLD ON YOU!?
I'M ASHAMED OF YOU, HIDÉ!
YOUR MOTHER'S IN THE HOSPITAL AND YOU HAVE TO ADD TO OUR WORRIES?
YOU'RE IN MIDDLE SCHOOL NOW! YOU'RE THE OLDER BROTHER! USE YOUR HEAD!
FWUMP!

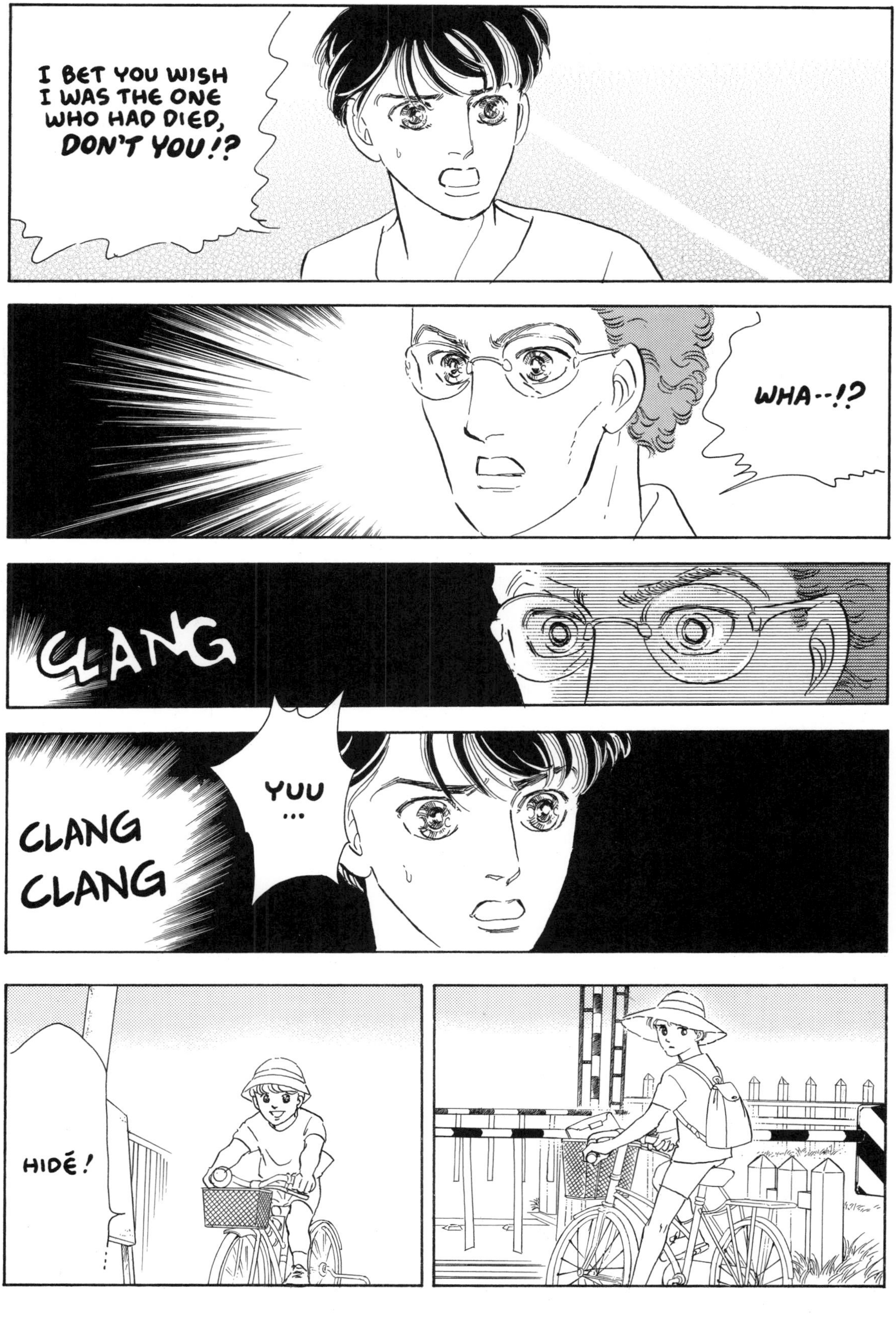
I BET YOU WISH I WAS THE ONE WHO HAD DIED, DON'T YOU!?
WHA--!?
CLANG
YUU ...
CLANG CLANG
HIDÉ!
...

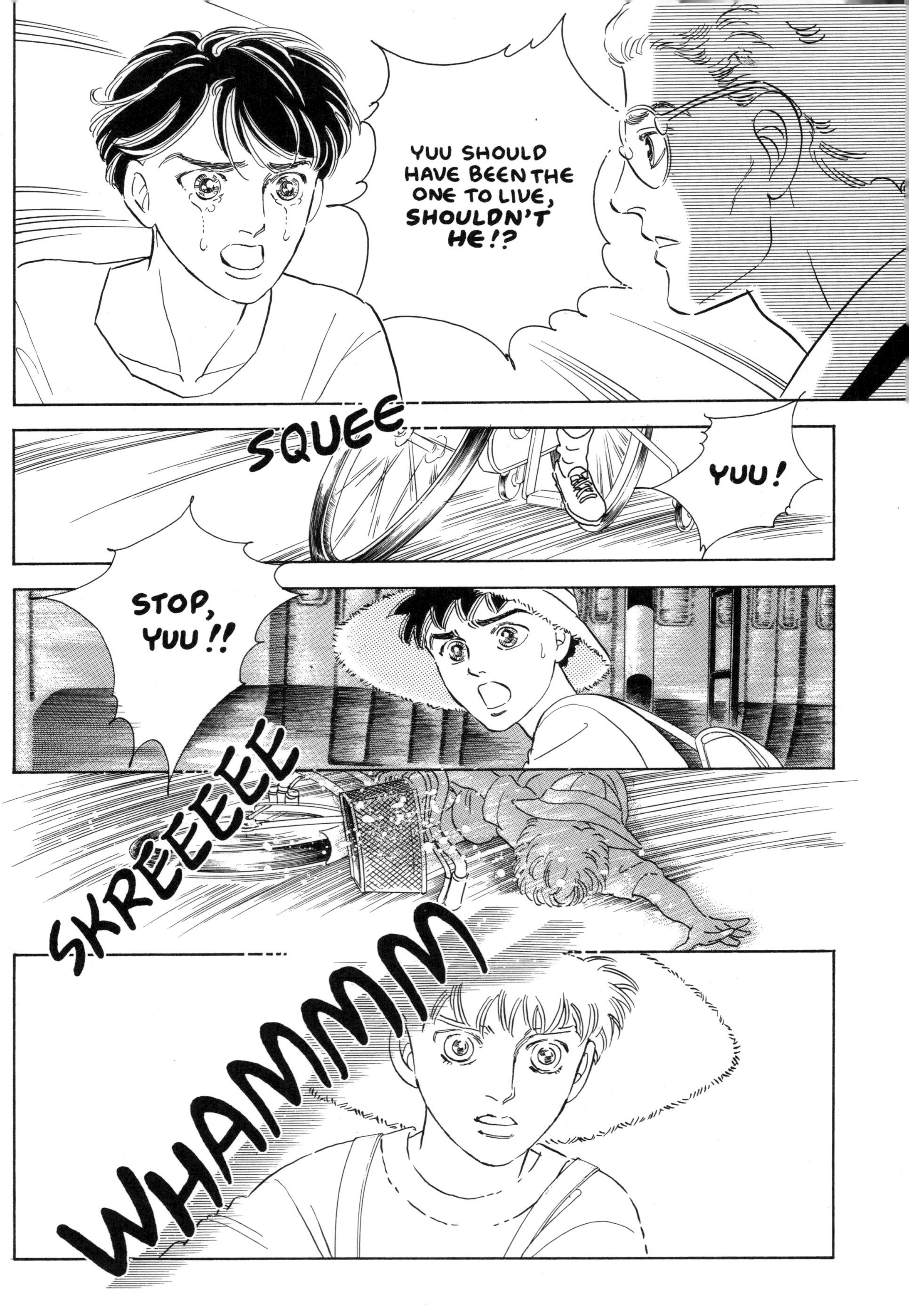
YUU SHOULD HAVE BEEN THE ONE TO LIVE, SHOULDN'T HE!?
YUU!
SQUEE
STOP, YUU!!
SKREEEEEE
WHAMMMM

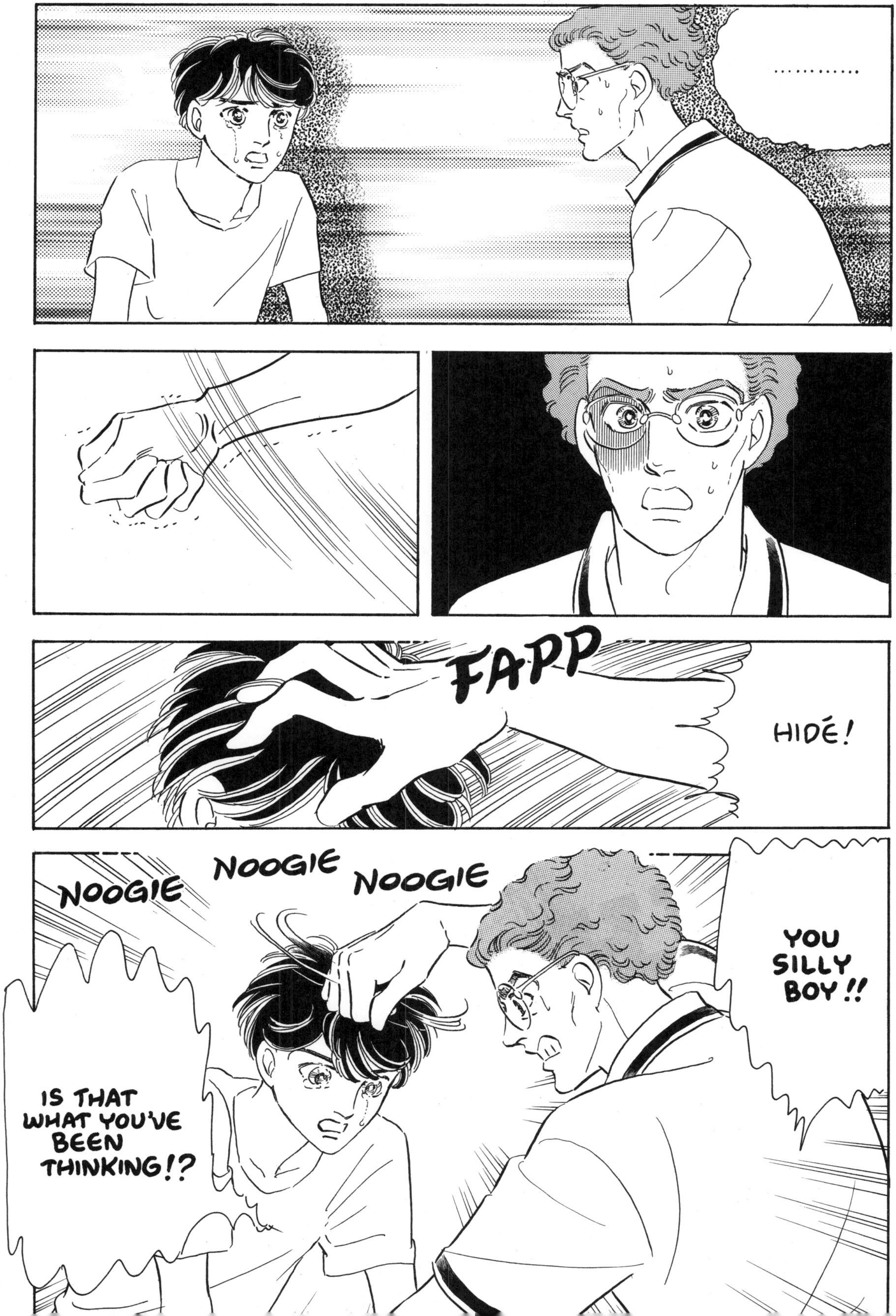
....
HIDÉ!
FAPP
YOU SILLY BOY!!
NOOGIE NOOGIE NOOGIE
IS THAT WHAT YOU'VE BEEN THINKING!?

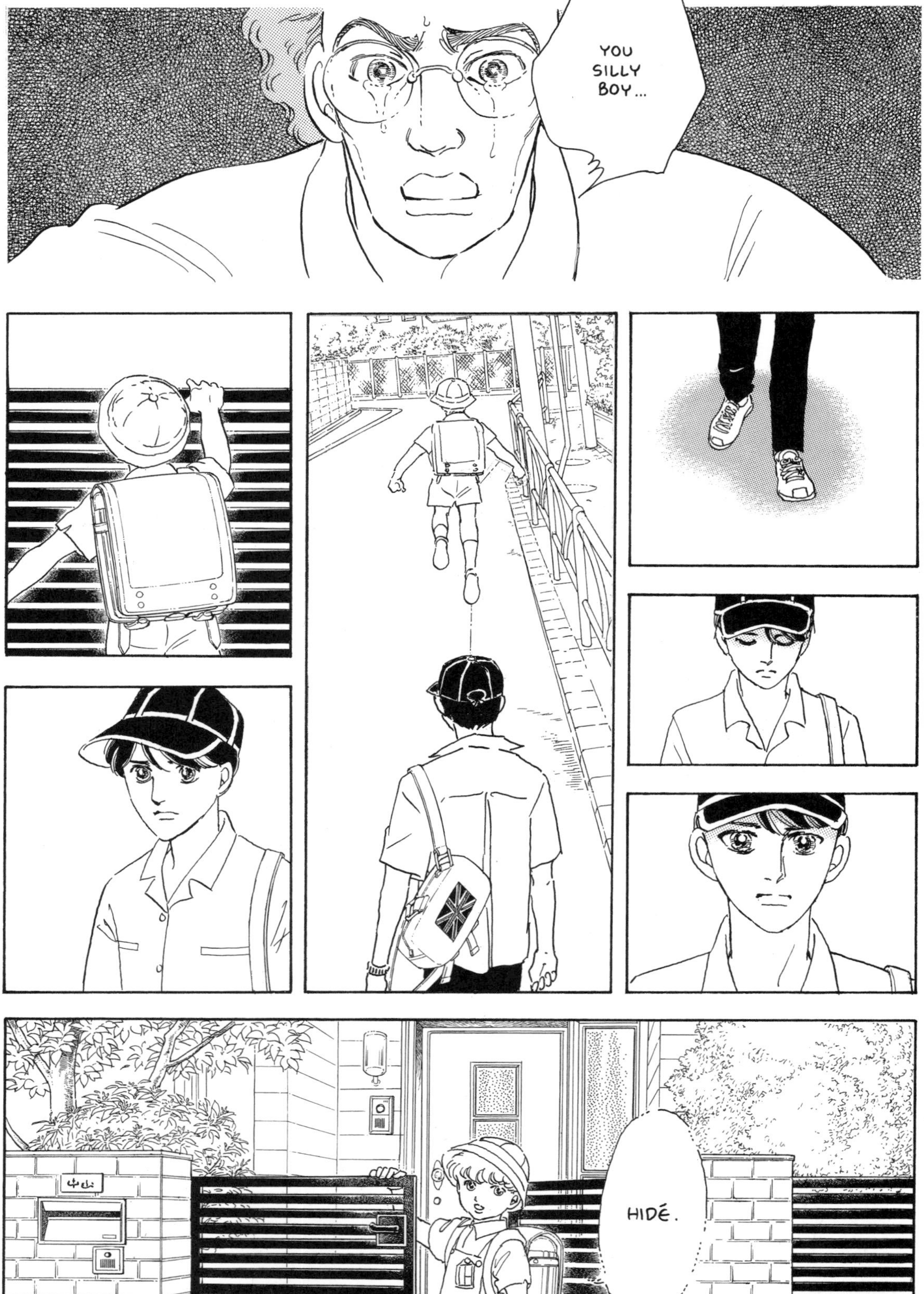
YOU SILLY BOY...
HIDÉ.

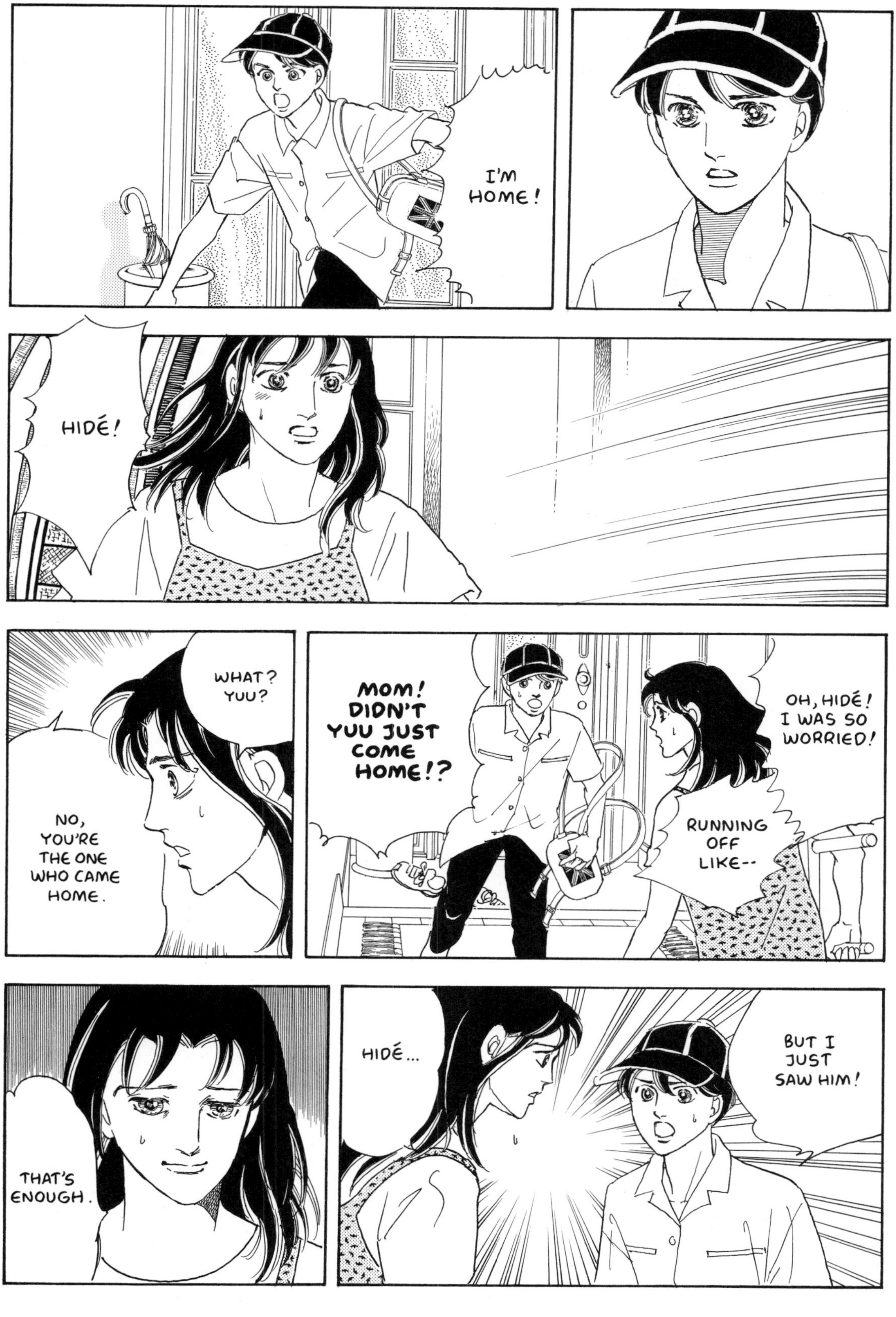
I'M HOME!
HIDÉ!
OH, HIDÉ! I WAS SO WORRIED!
RUNNING OFF LIKE--
MOM! DIDN'T YUU JUST COME HOME!?
WHAT? YUU?
NO, YOU'RE THE ONE WHO CAME HOME.
BUT I JUST SAW HIM!
HIDÉ...
THAT'S ENOUGH.

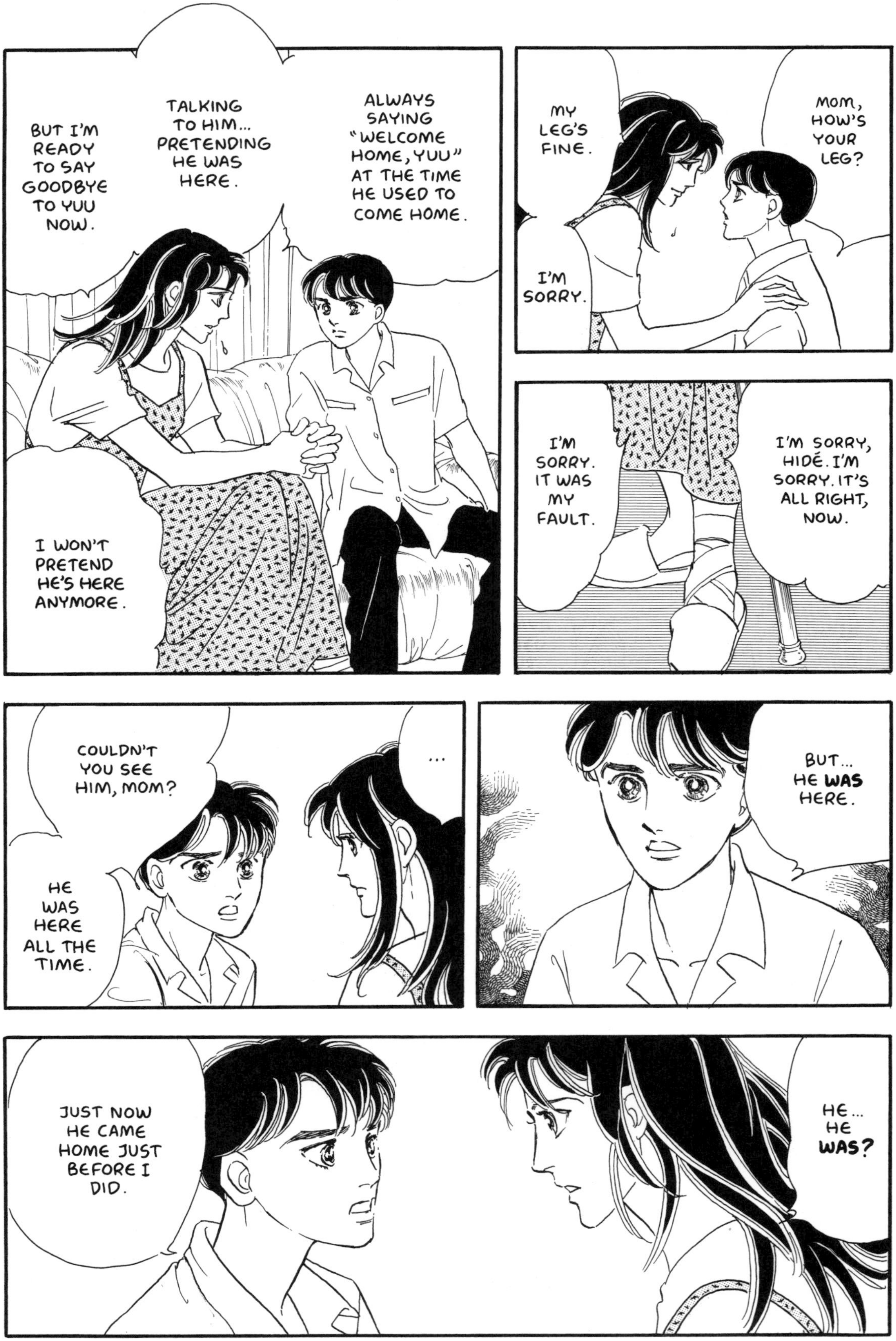
MOM, HOW'S YOUR LEG?
MY LEG'S FINE.
I'M SORRY.
I'M SORRY, HIDÉ. I'M SORRY. IT'S ALL RIGHT, NOW.
I'M SORRY. IT WAS MY FAULT.
ALWAYS SAYING "WELCOME HOME, YUU" AT THE TIME HE USED TO COME HOME.
TALKING TO HIM... PRETENDING HE WAS HERE.
BUT I'M READY TO SAY GOODBYE TO YUU NOW.
I WON'T PRETEND HE'S HERE ANYMORE.
BUT... HE **WAS** HERE.
...
COULDN'T YOU SEE HIM, MOM?
HE WAS HERE ALL THE TIME.
HE... HE **WAS?**
JUST NOW HE CAME HOME JUST BEFORE I DID.

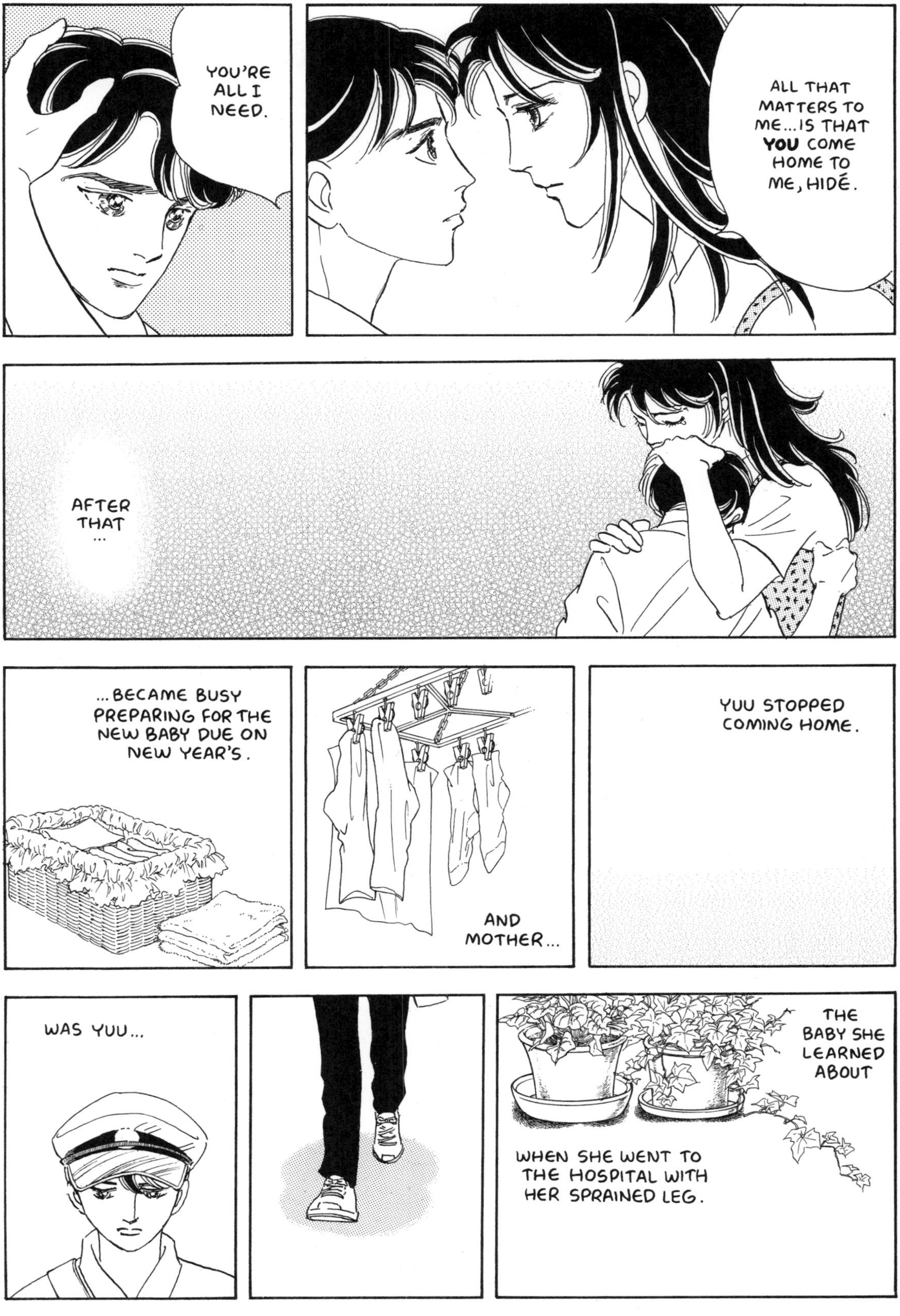
ALL THAT MATTERS TO ME...IS THAT **YOU** COME HOME TO ME, HIDÉ.
YOU'RE ALL I NEED.
AFTER THAT ...
YUU STOPPED COMING HOME.
AND MOTHER...
...BECAME BUSY PREPARING FOR THE NEW BABY DUE ON NEW YEAR'S.
THE BABY SHE LEARNED ABOUT
WHEN SHE WENT TO THE HOSPITAL WITH HER SPRAINED LEG.
WAS YUU...

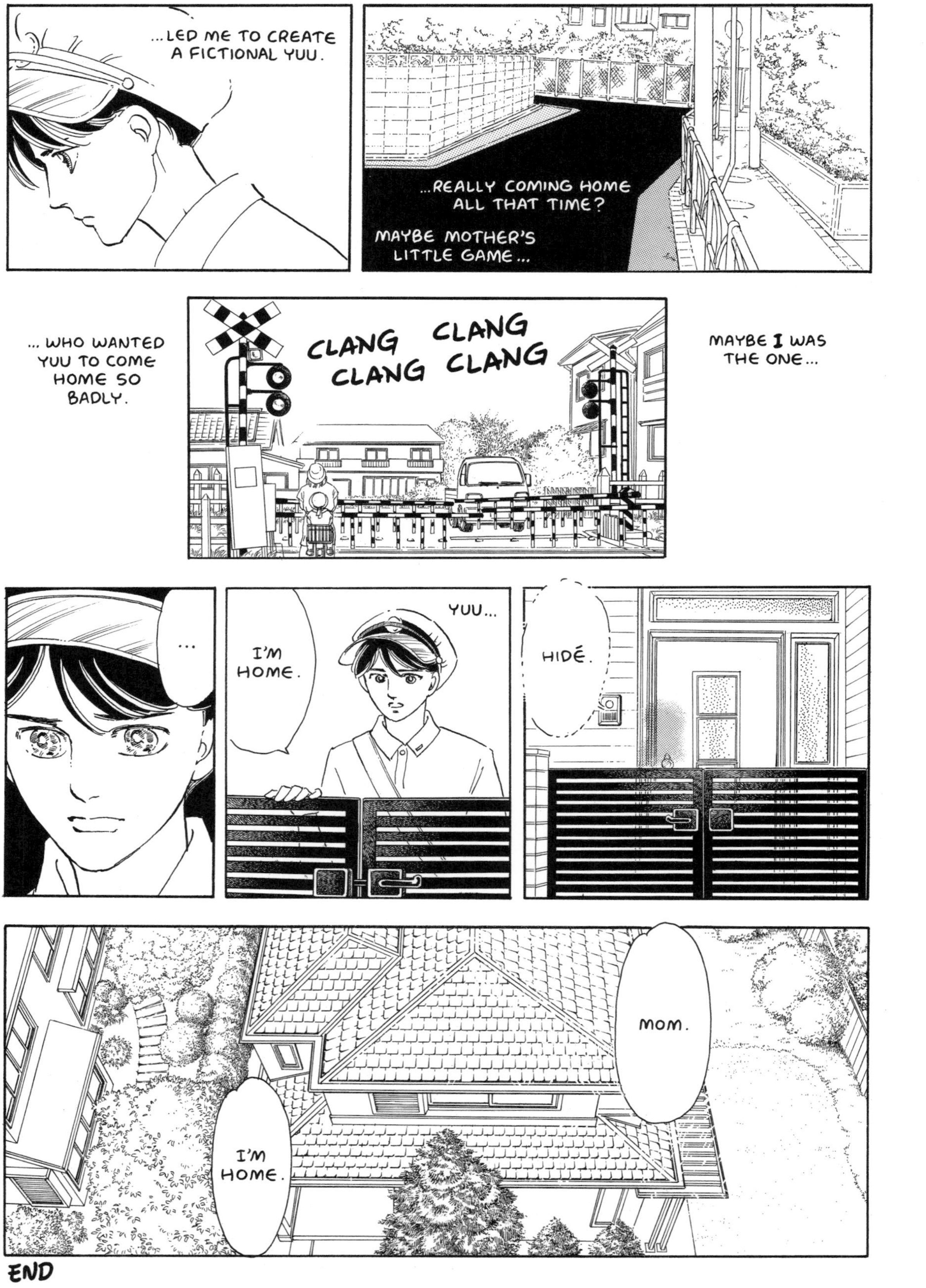
...REALLY COMING HOME ALL THAT TIME?
MAYBE MOTHER'S LITTLE GAME...
...LED ME TO CREATE A FICTIONAL YUU.
MAYBE I WAS THE ONE...
CLANG CLANG CLANG CLANG
... WHO WANTED YUU TO COME HOME SO BADLY.
HIDÉ.
YUU...
I'M HOME.
...
MOM.
I'M HOME.

END

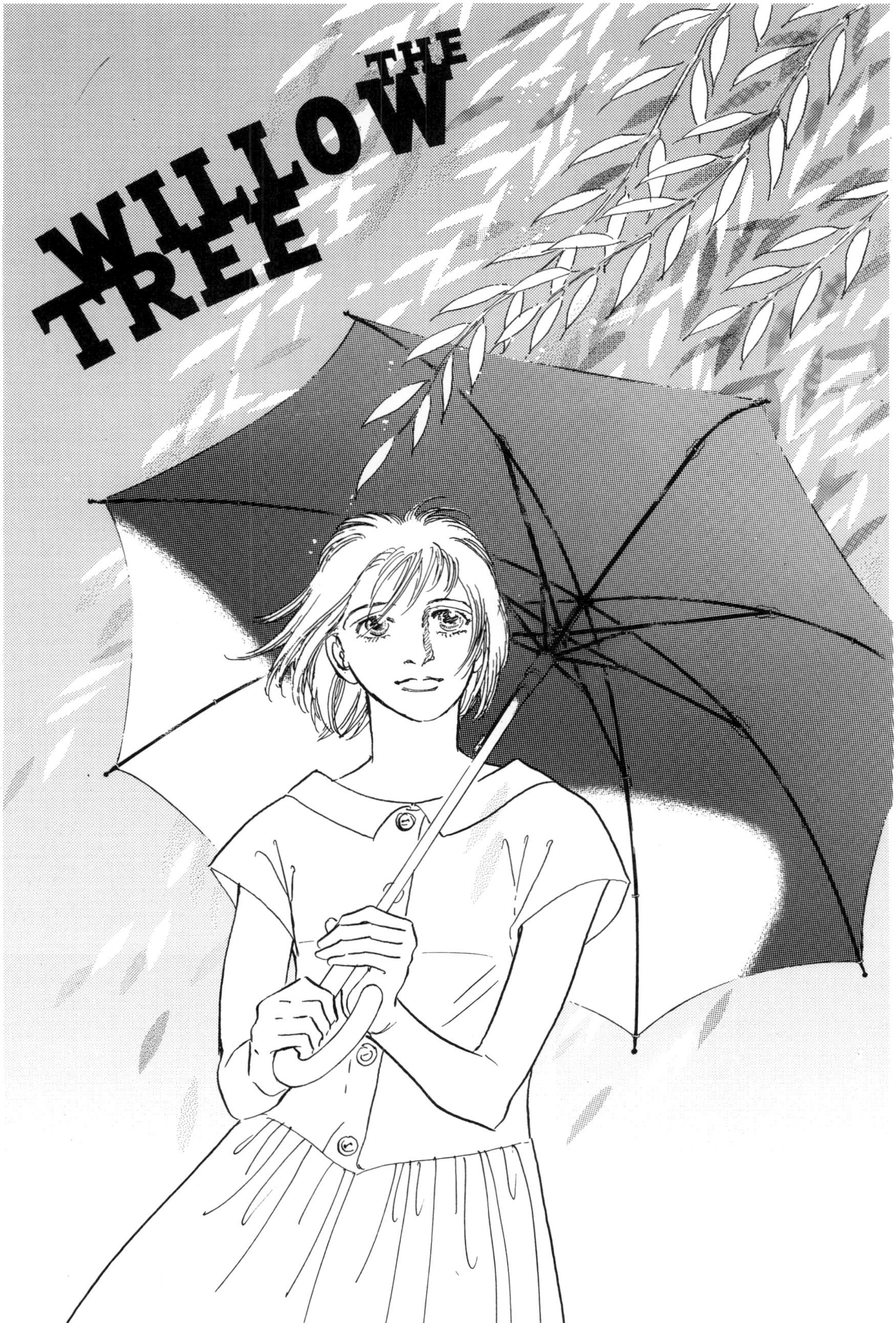
THE
WILLOW
TREE

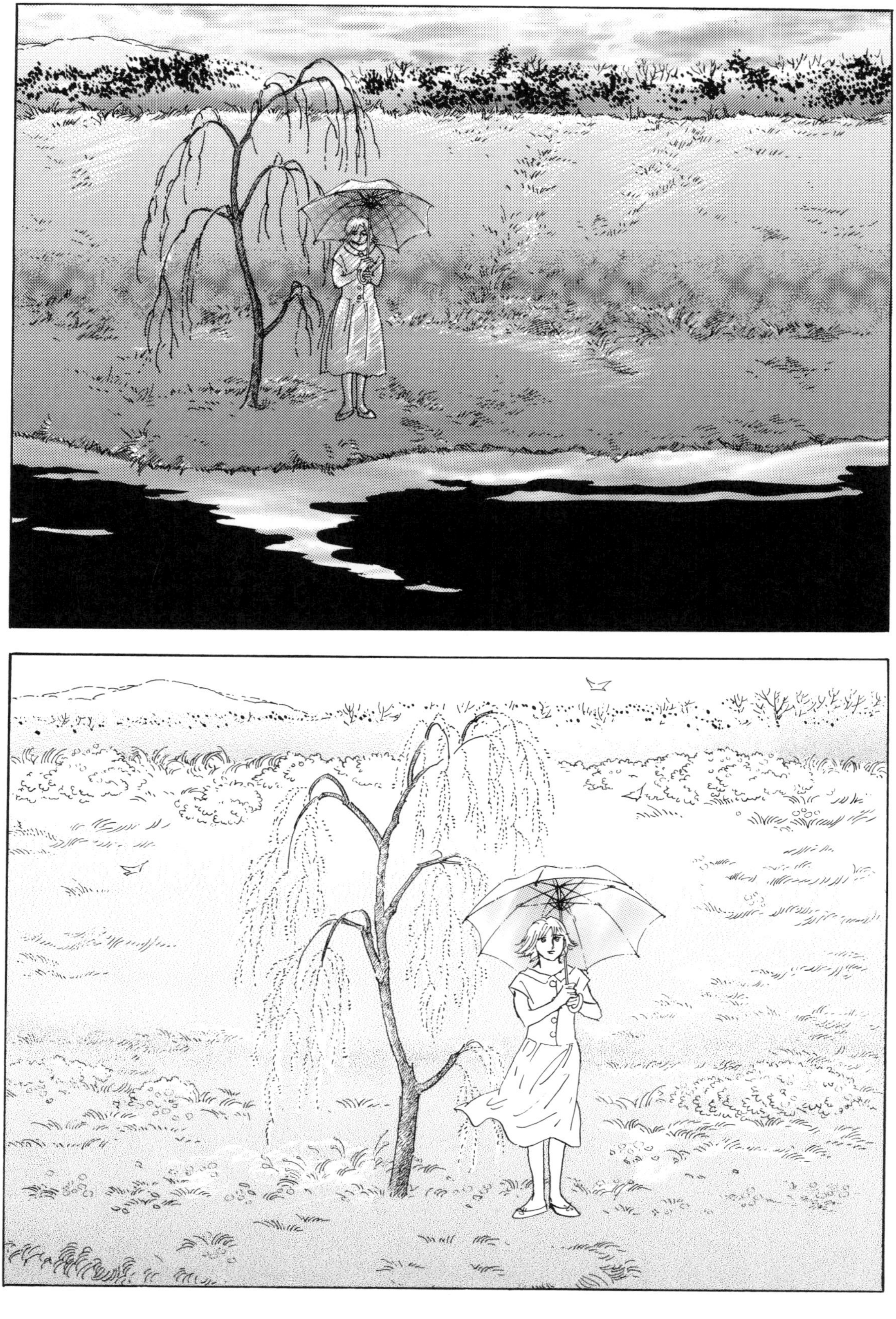

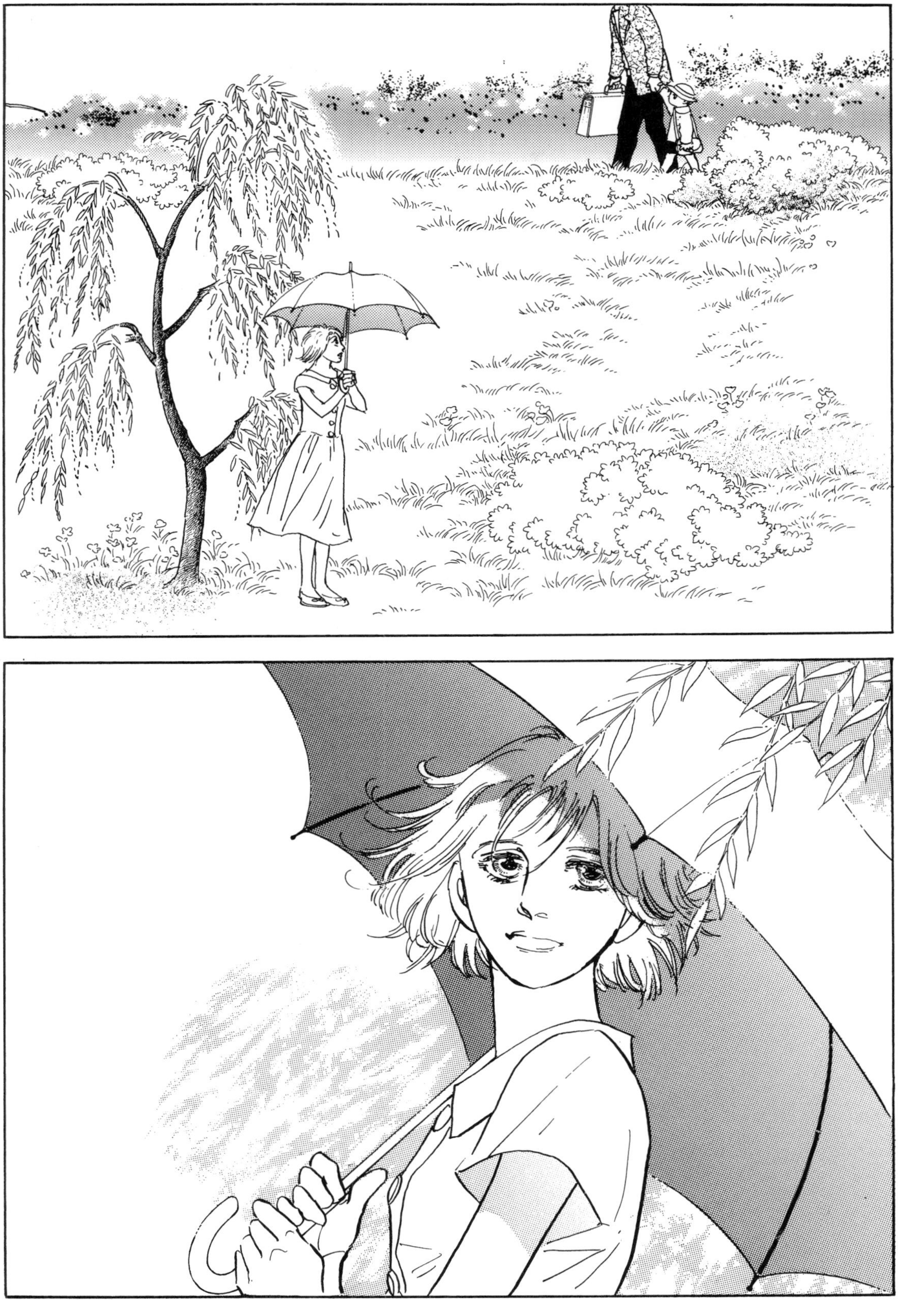

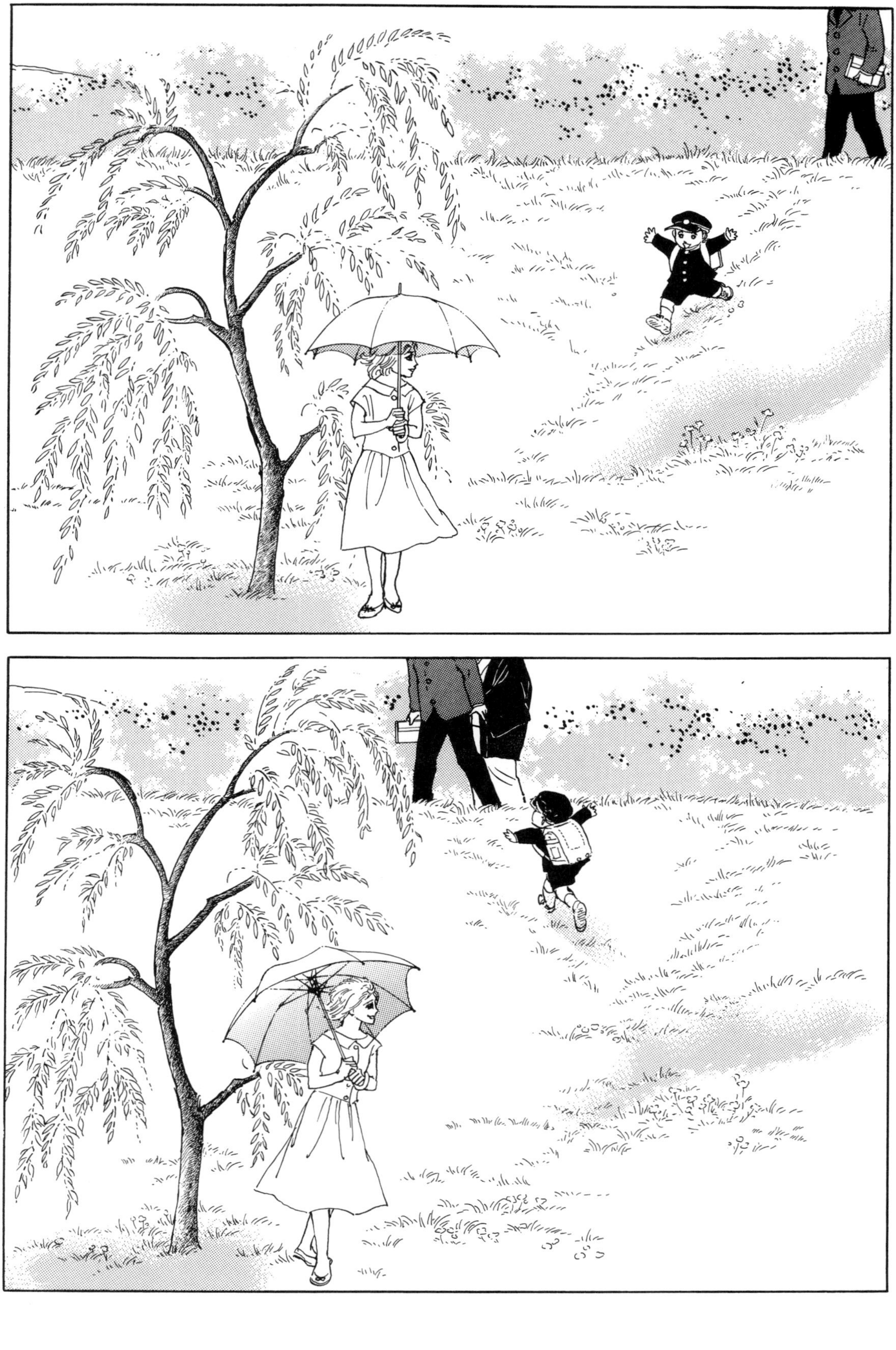

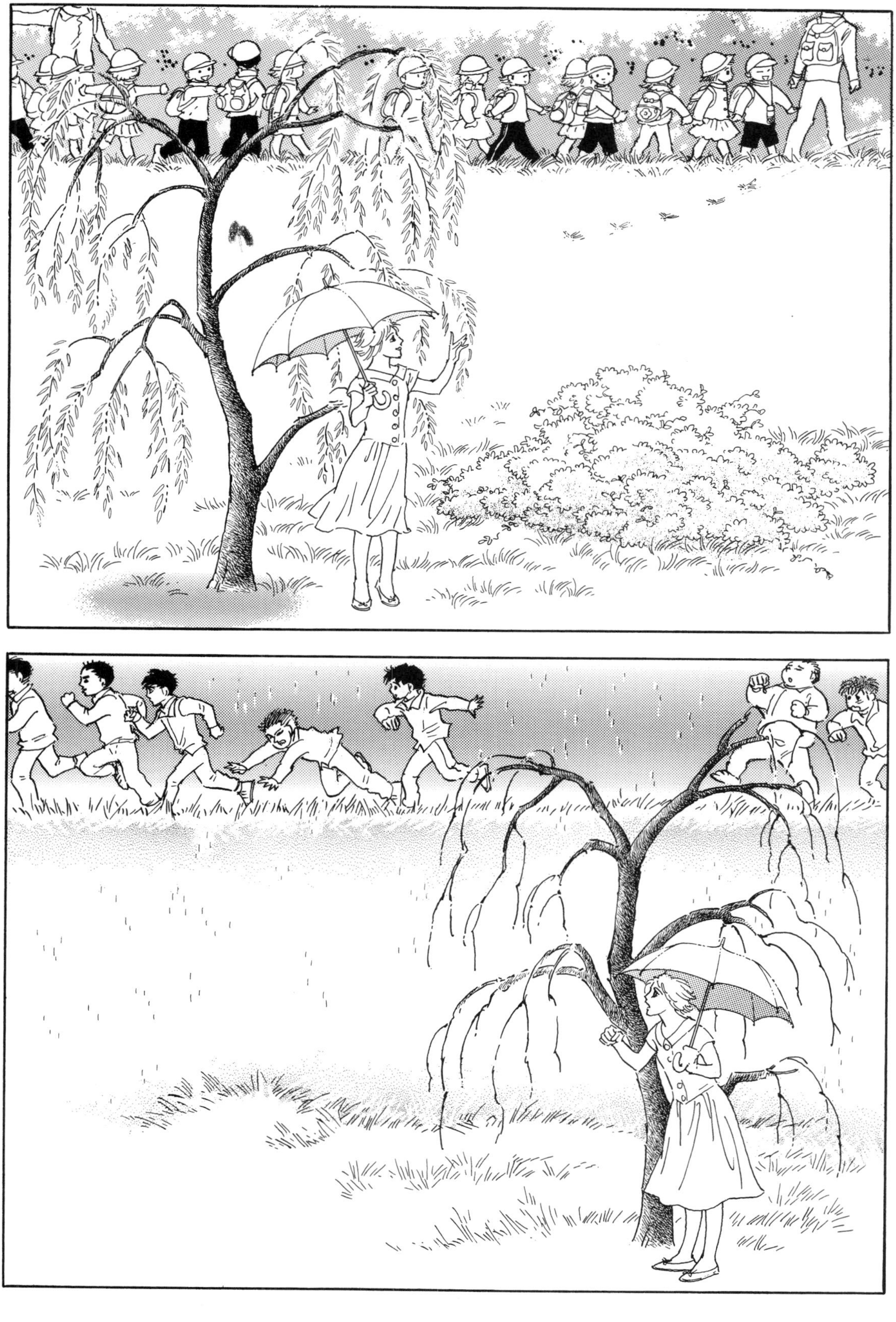

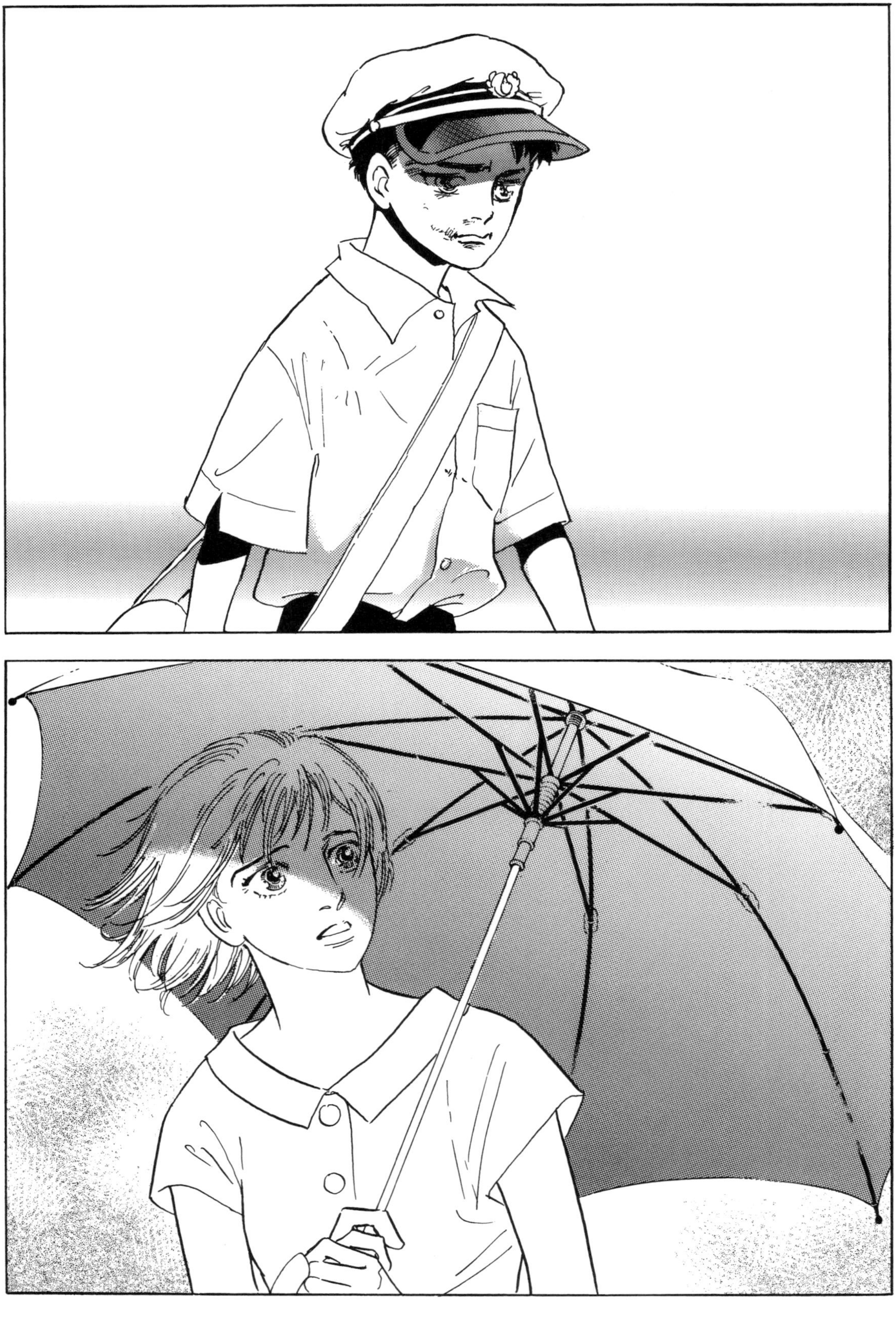

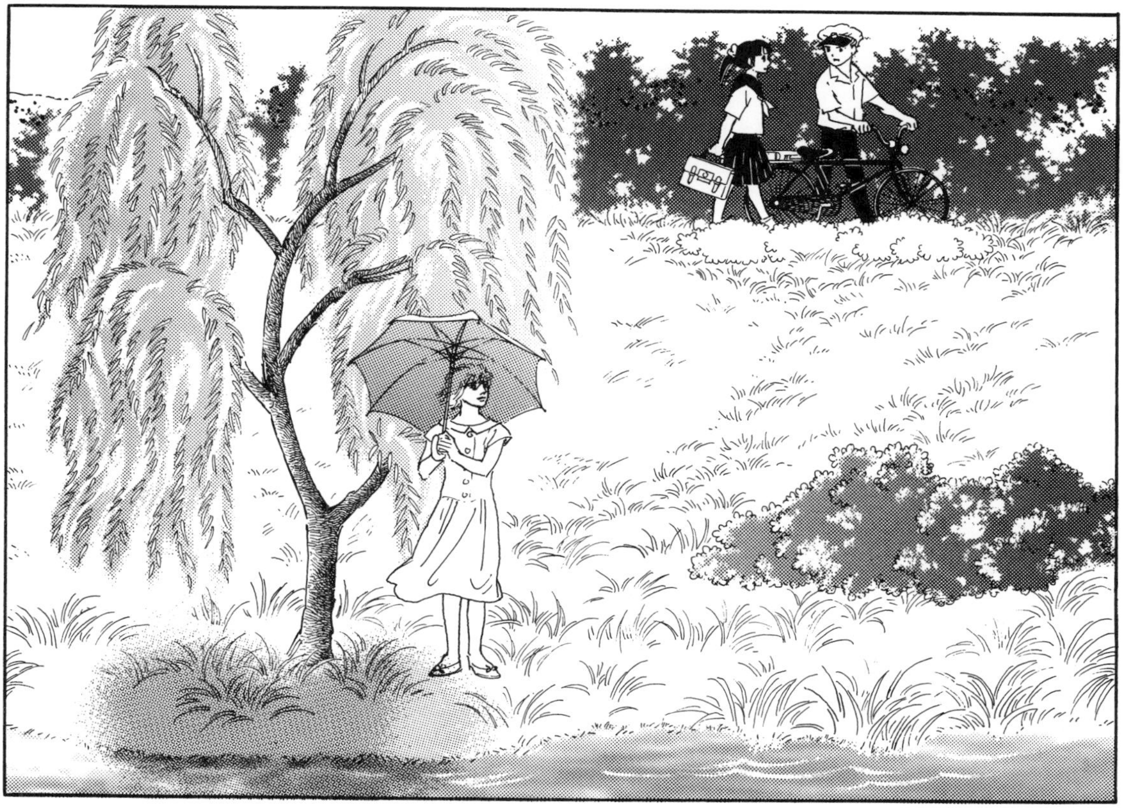

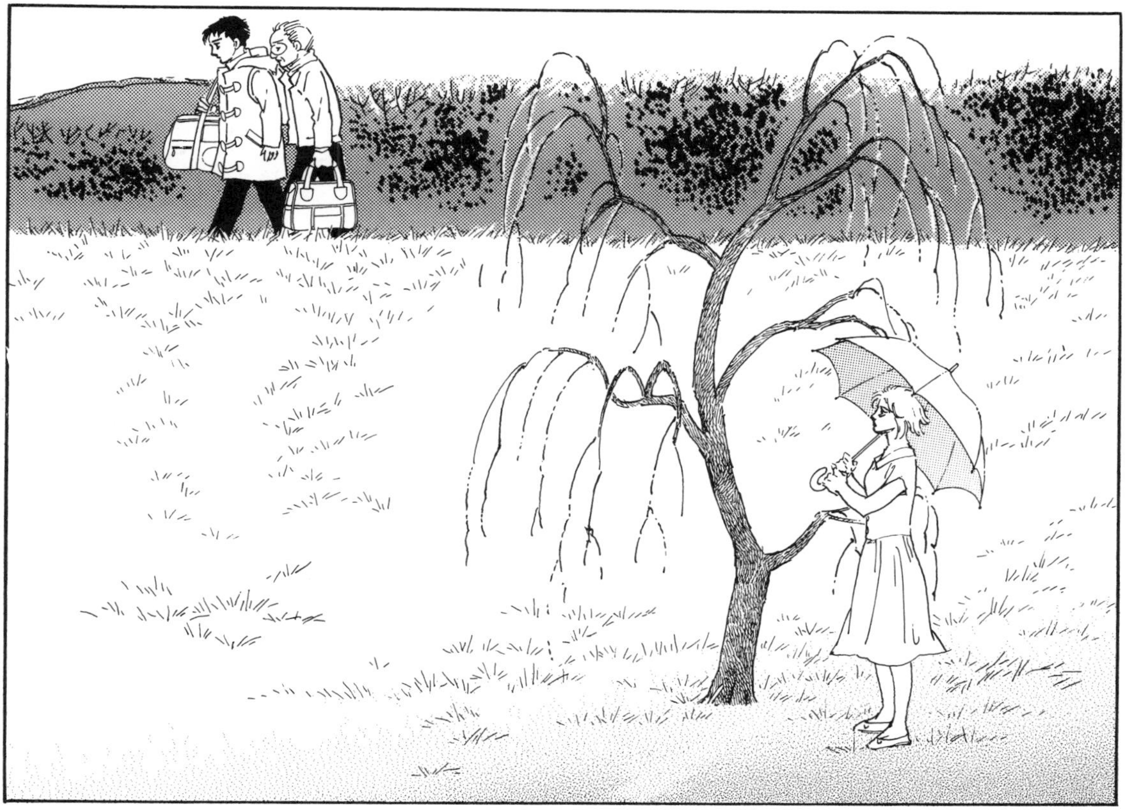

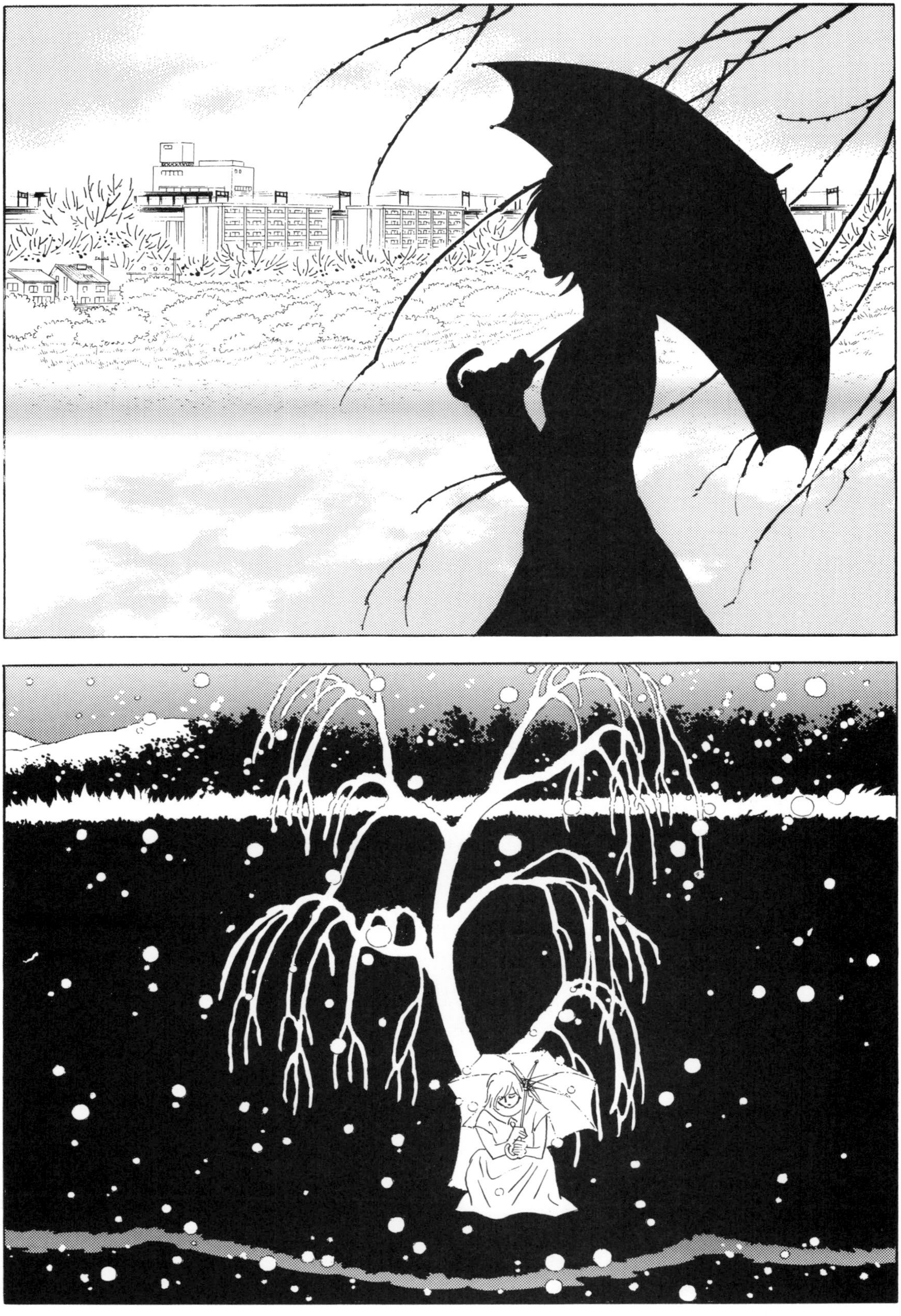

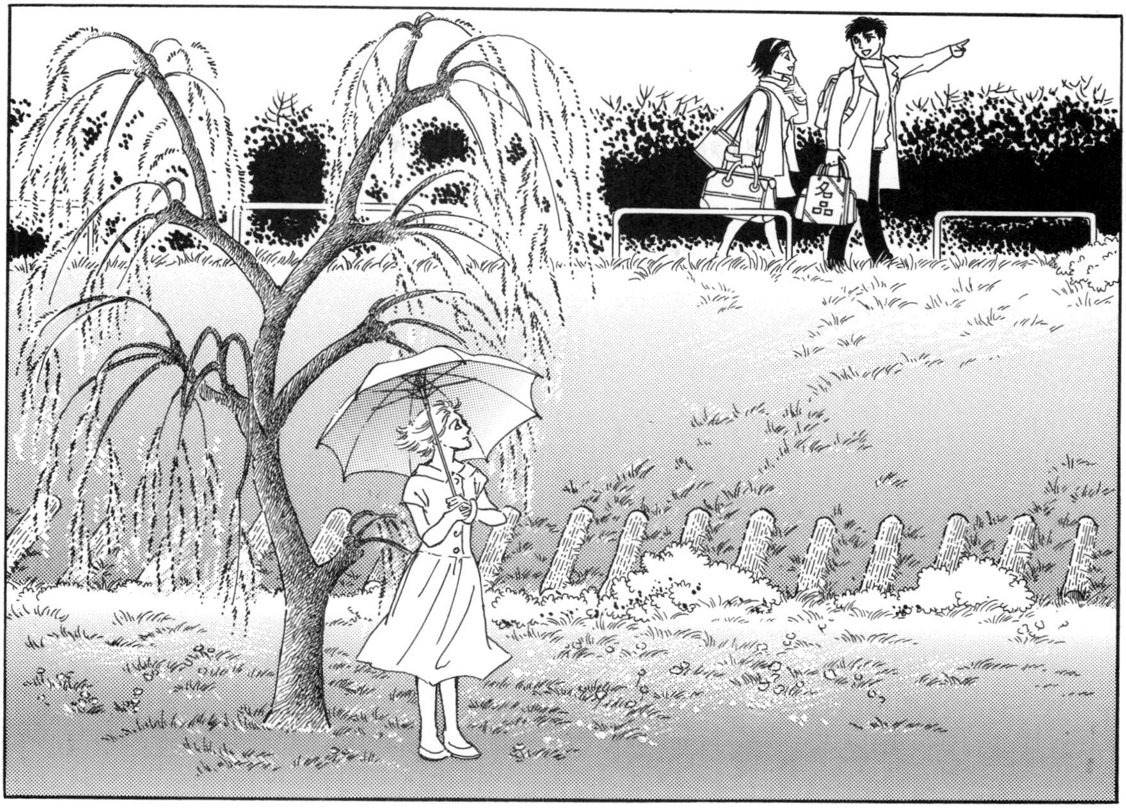
名品

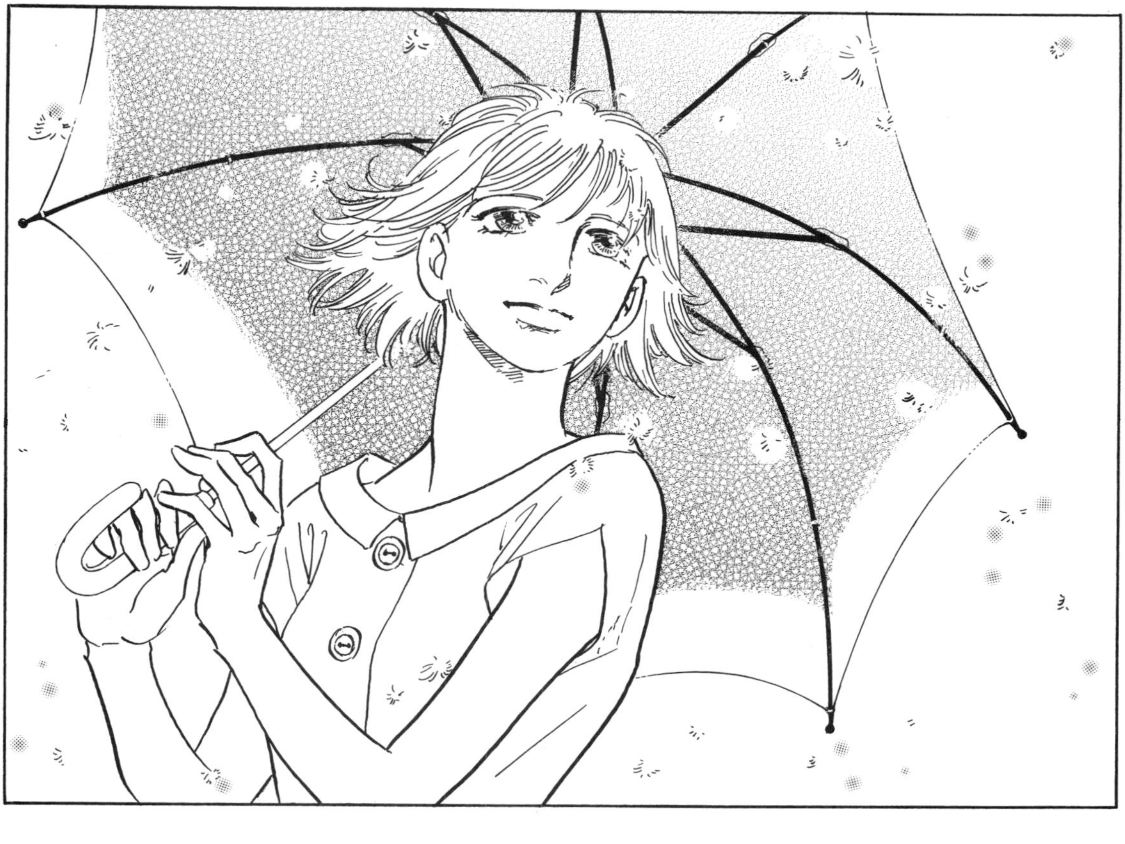

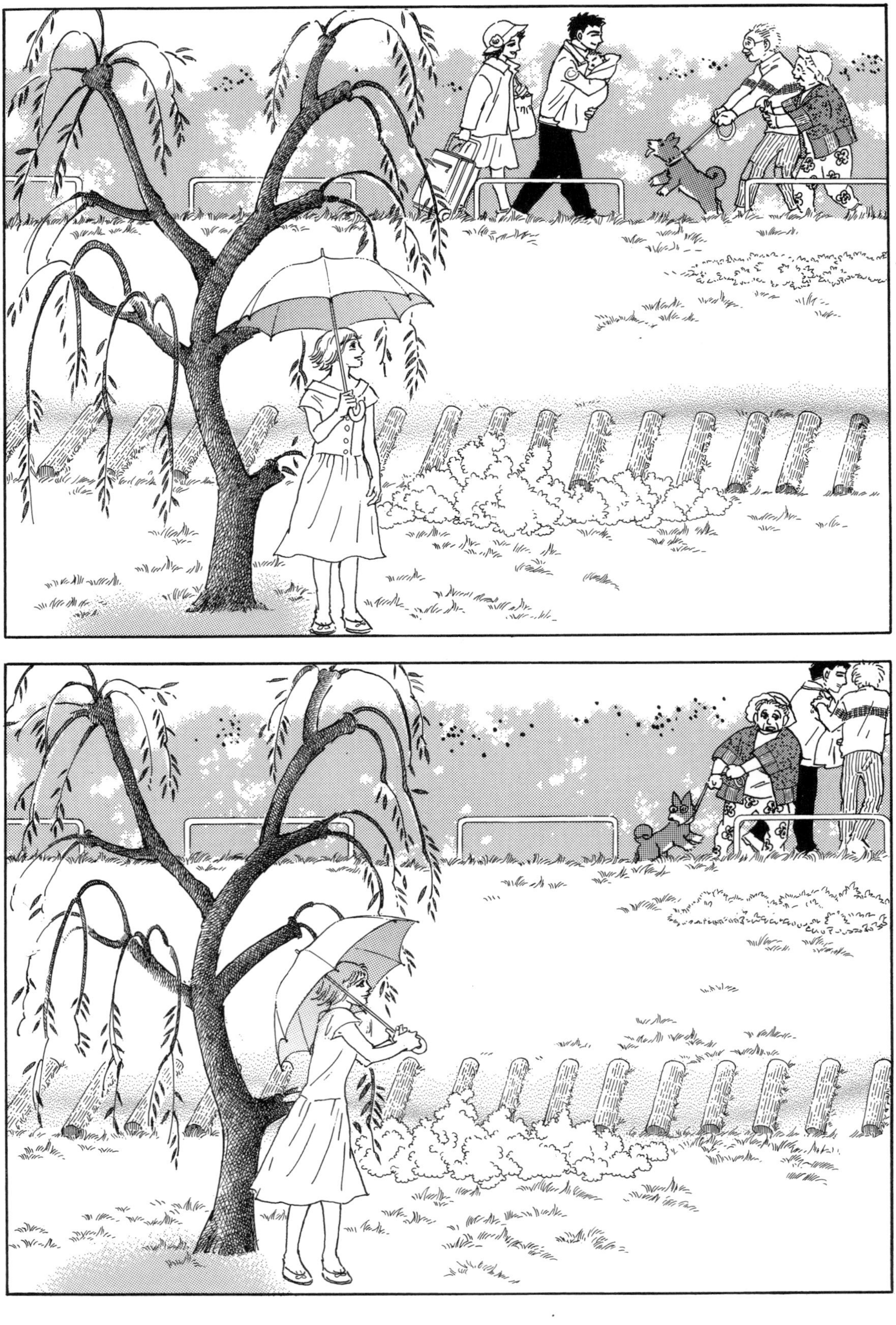

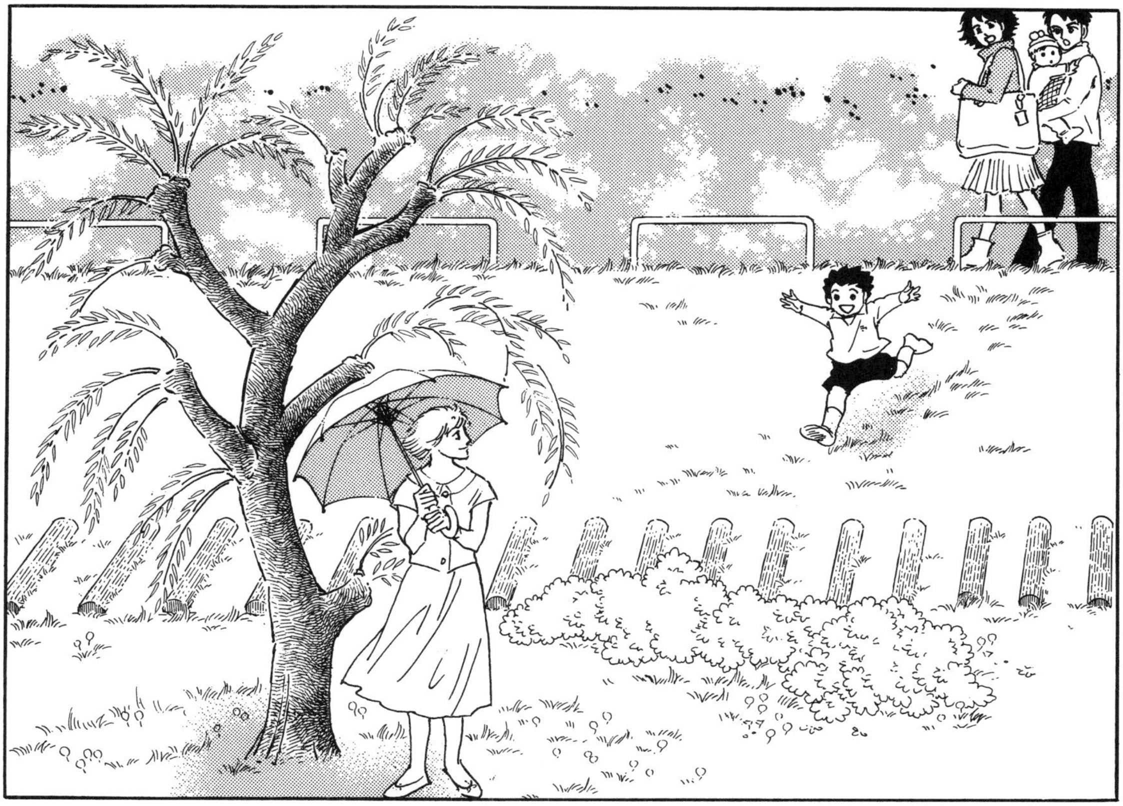

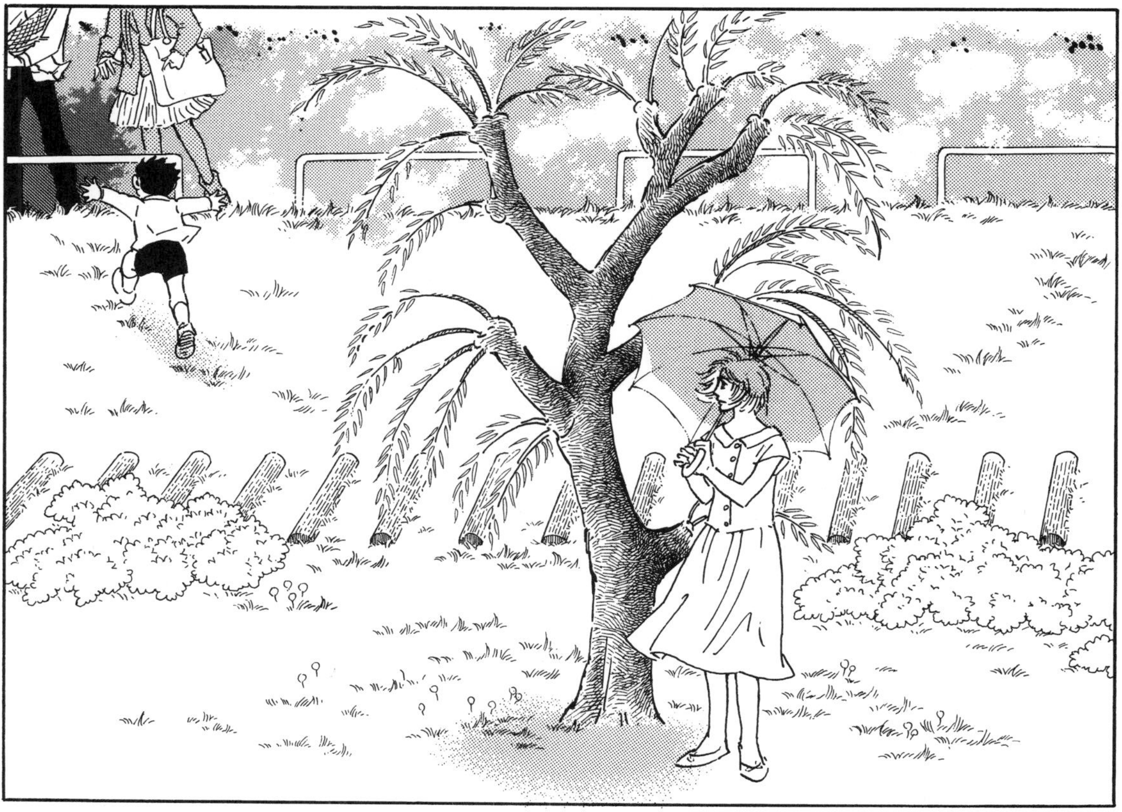

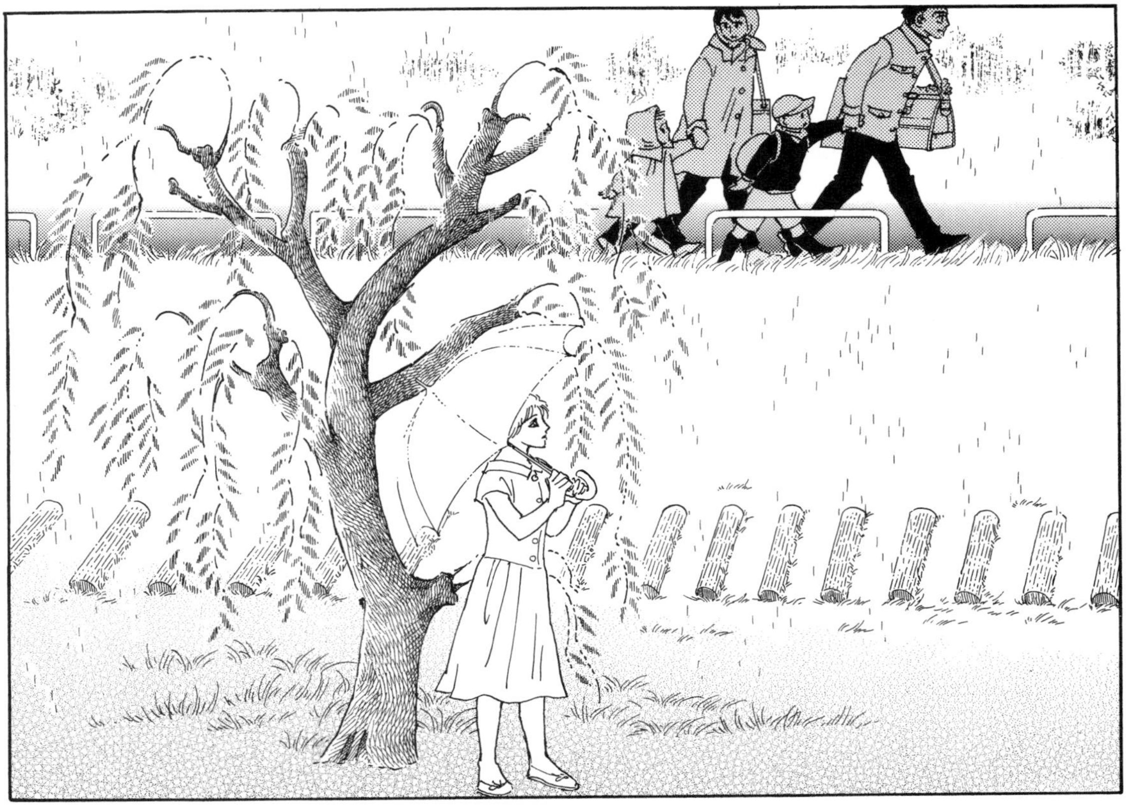

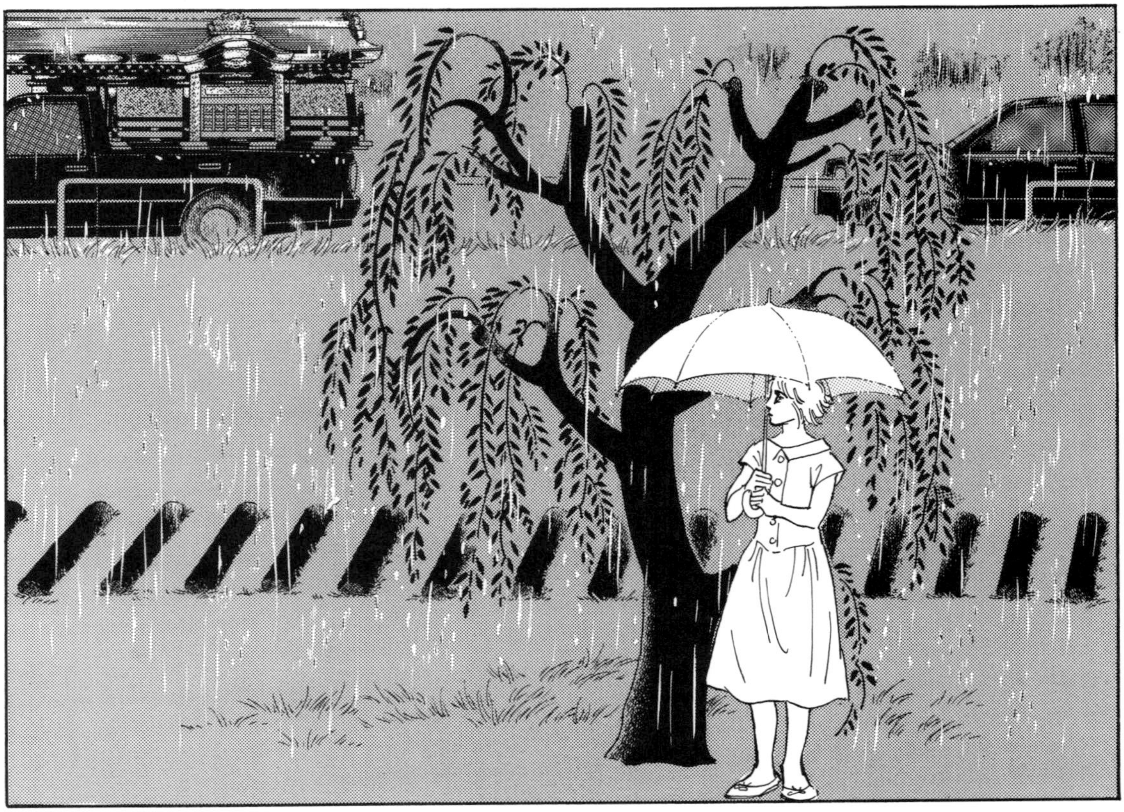

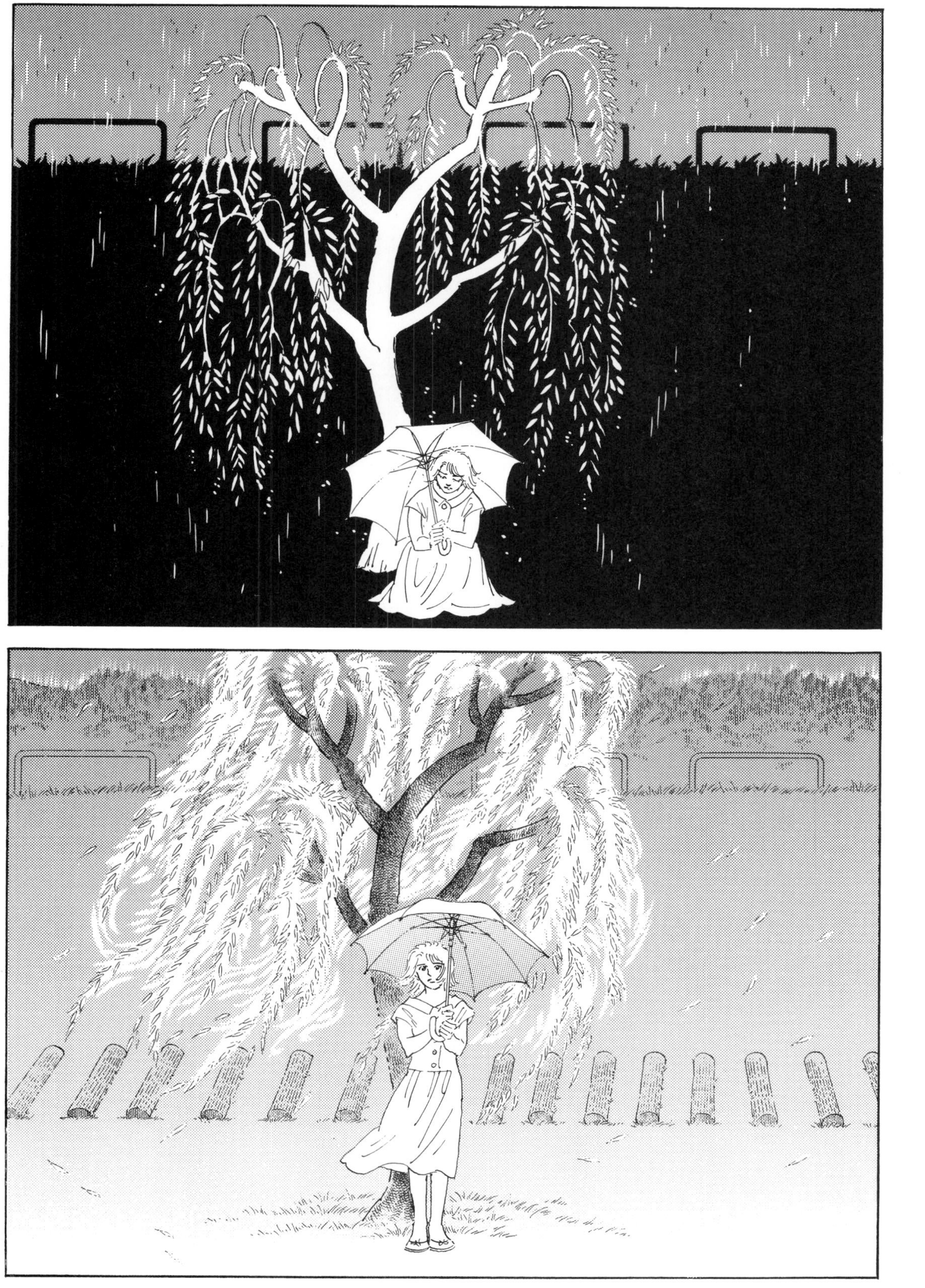

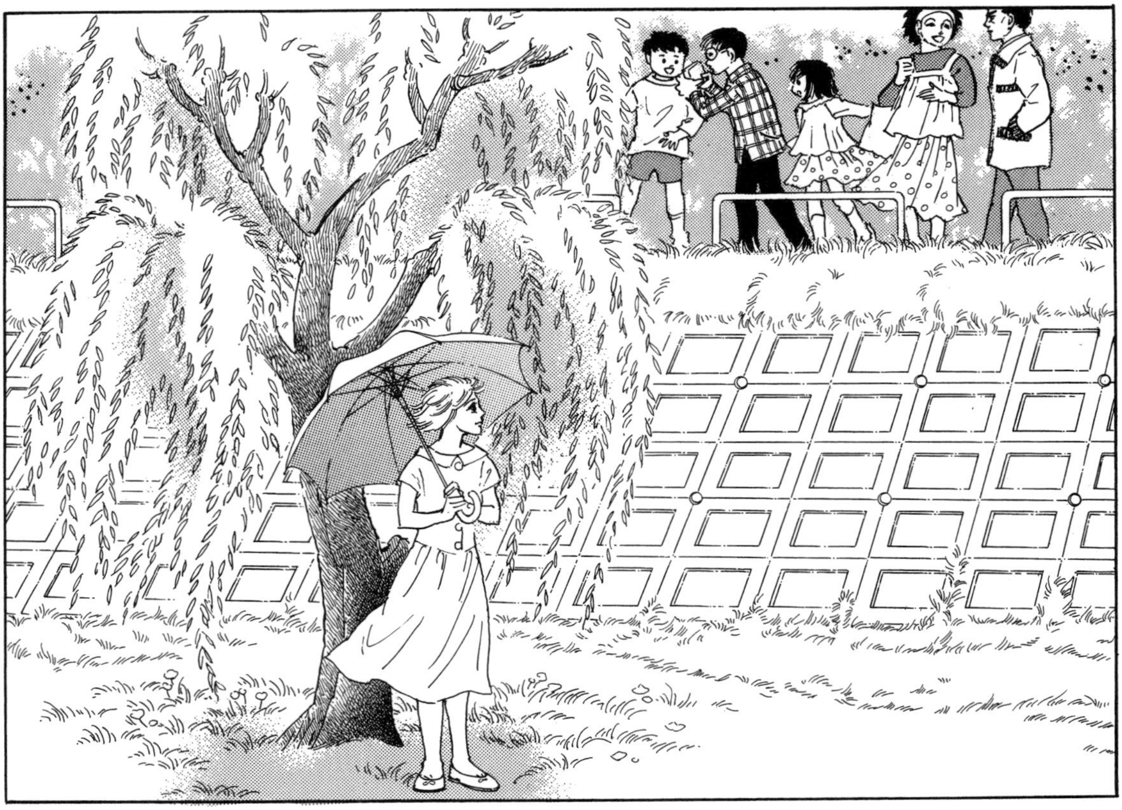

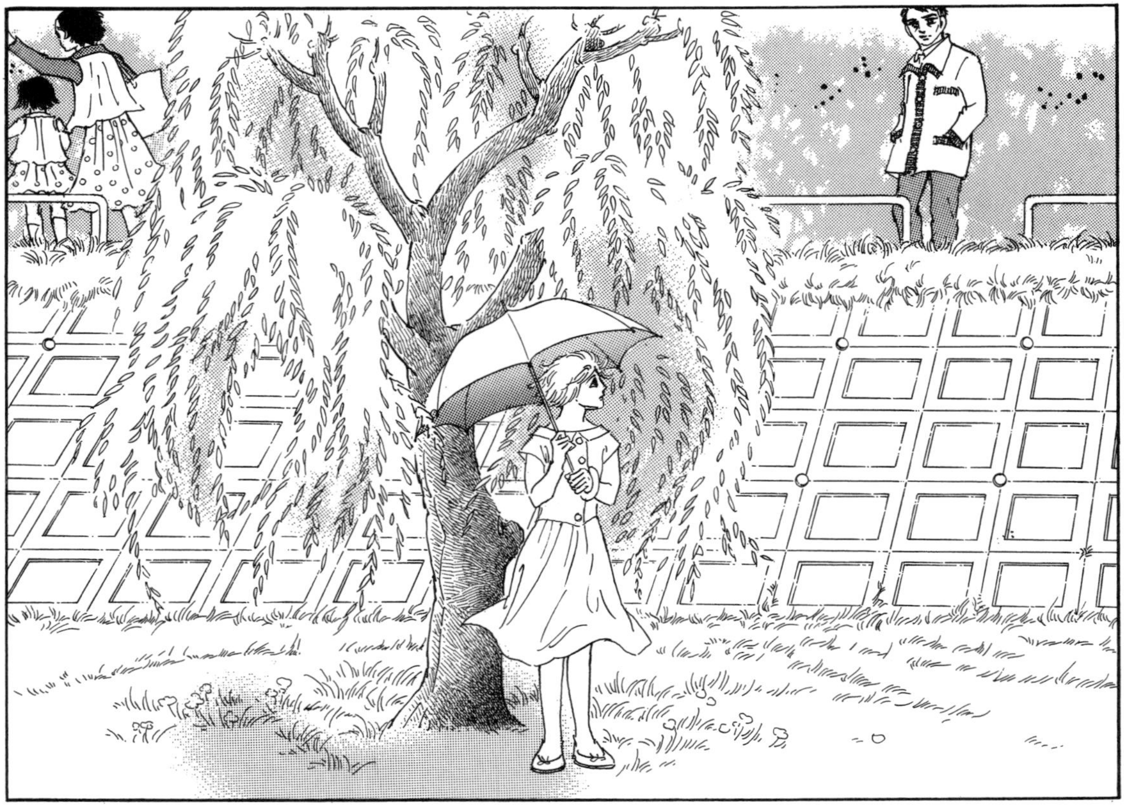

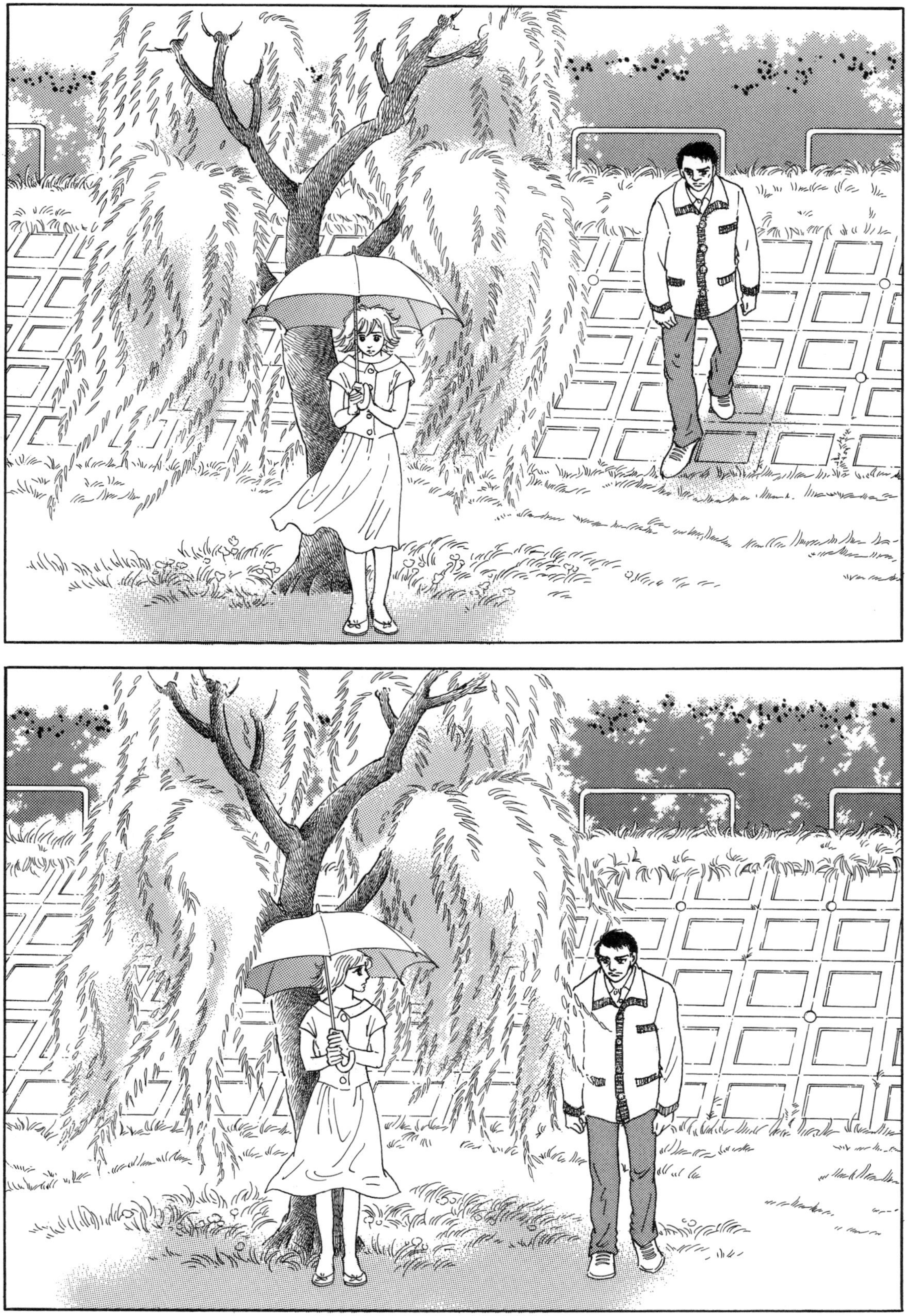

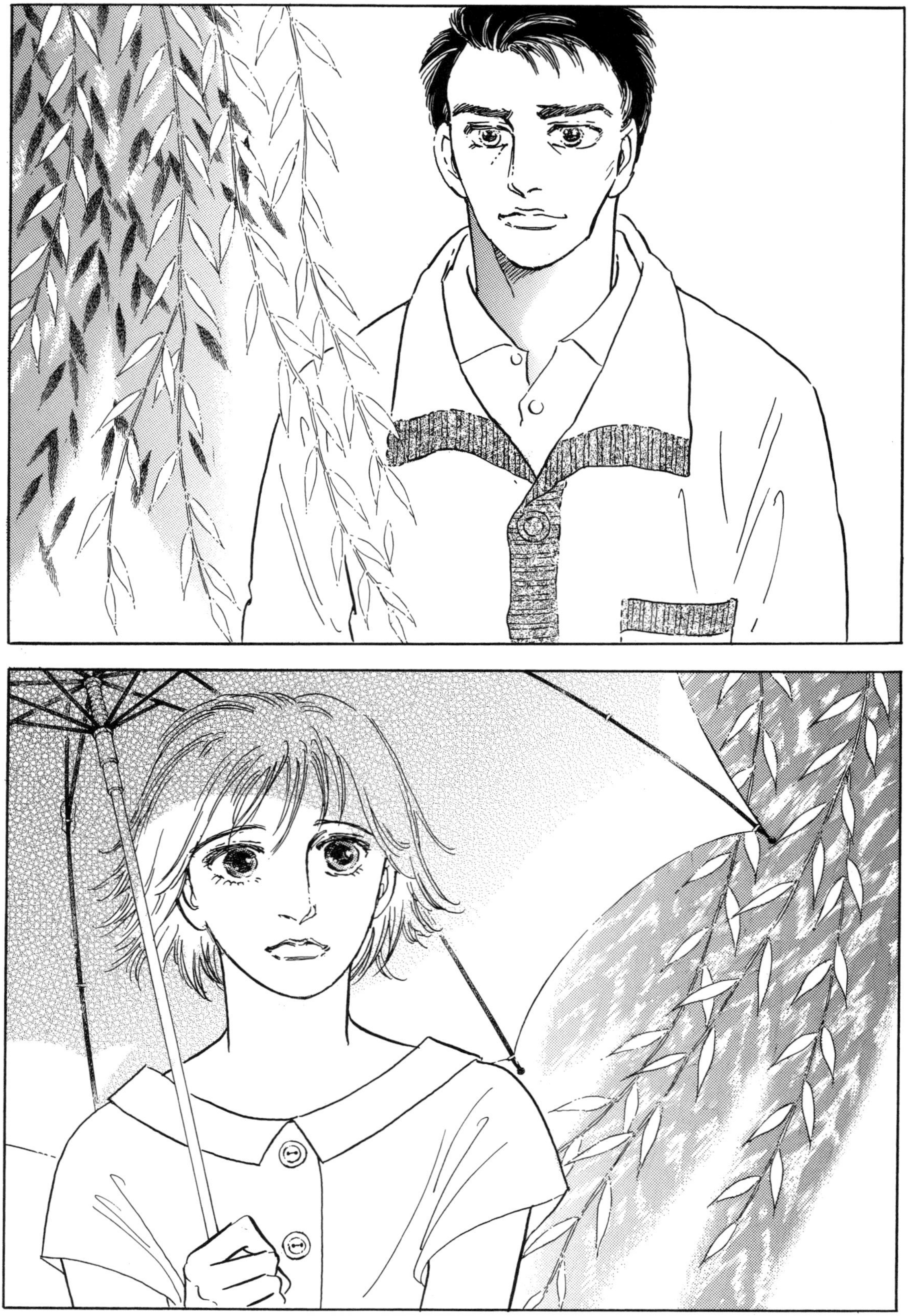

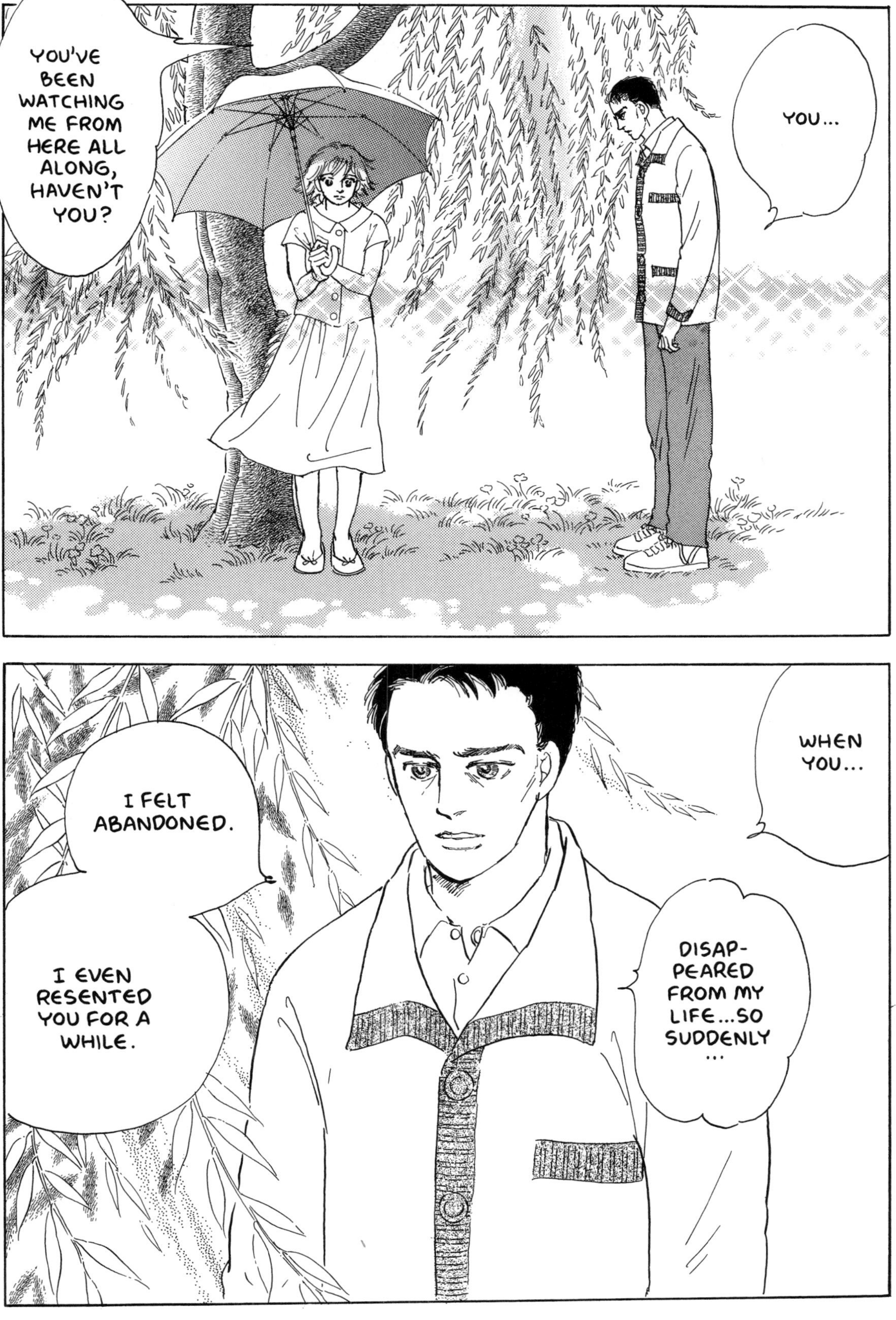
YOU...
YOU'VE BEEN WATCHING ME FROM HERE ALL ALONG, HAVEN'T YOU?
WHEN YOU...
DISAP-PEARED FROM MY LIFE...SO SUDDENLY...
I FELT ABANDONED.
I EVEN RESENTED YOU FOR A WHILE.

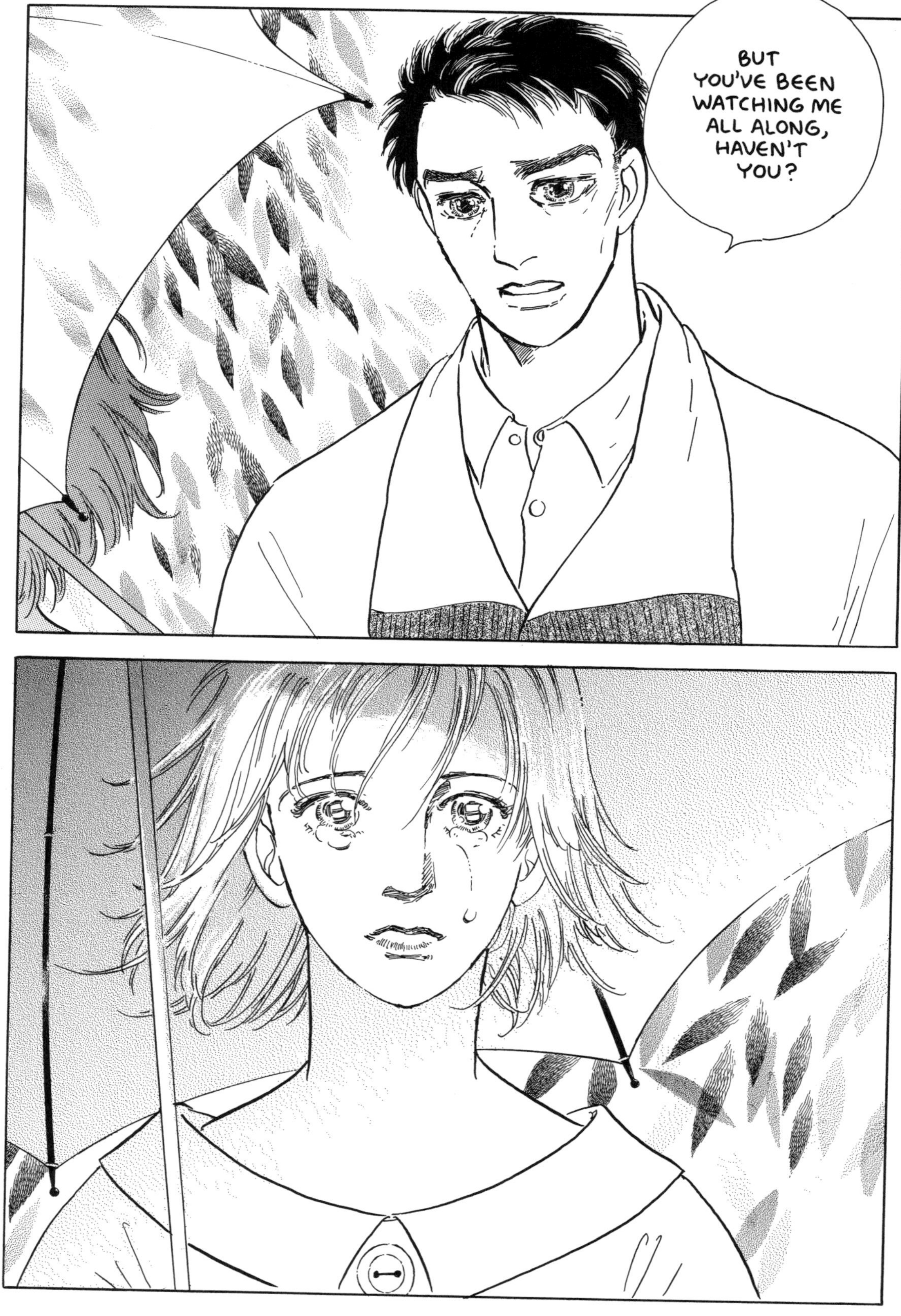
BUT YOU'VE BEEN WATCHING ME ALL ALONG, HAVEN'T YOU?

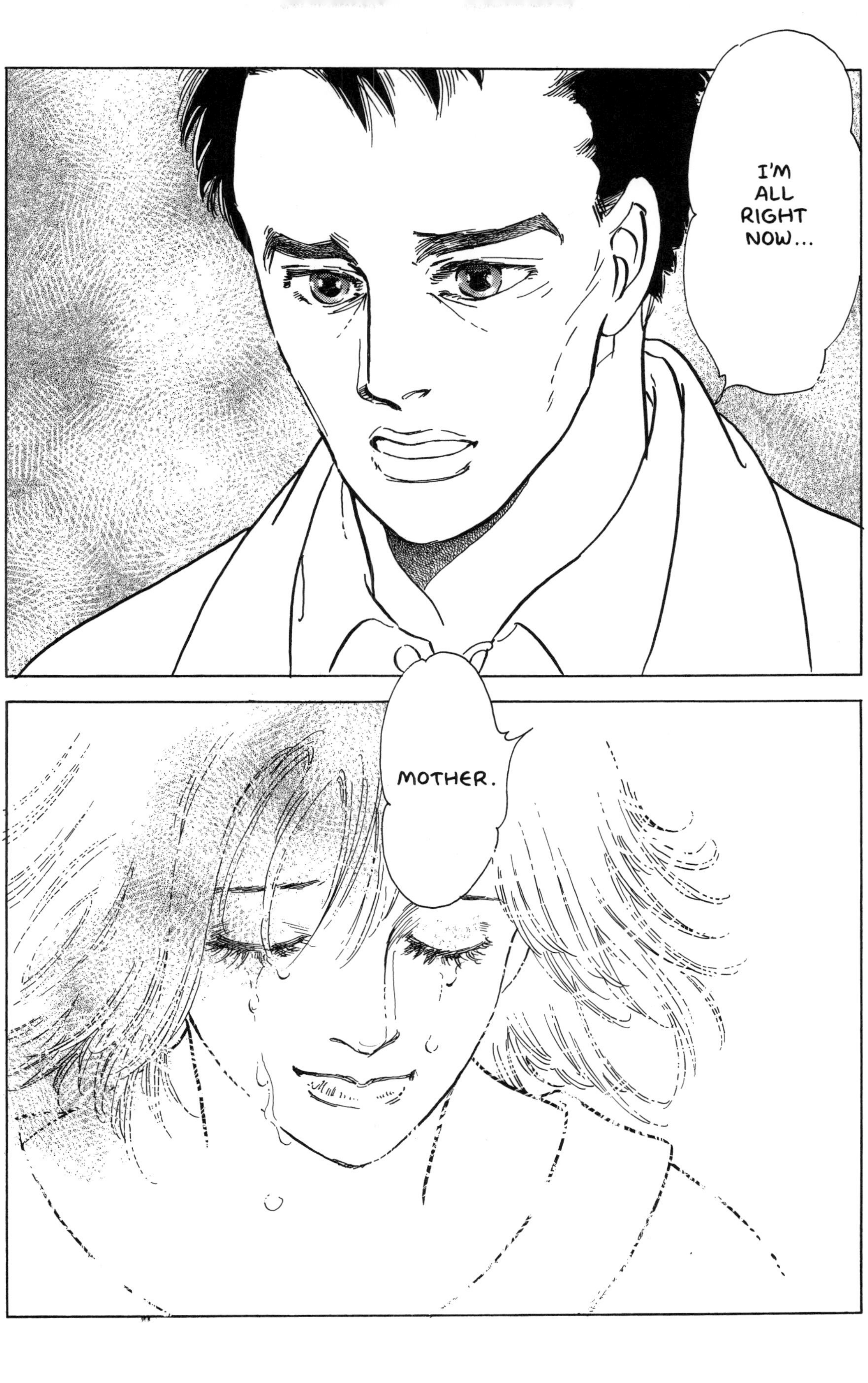
I'M ALL RIGHT NOW...
MOTHER.

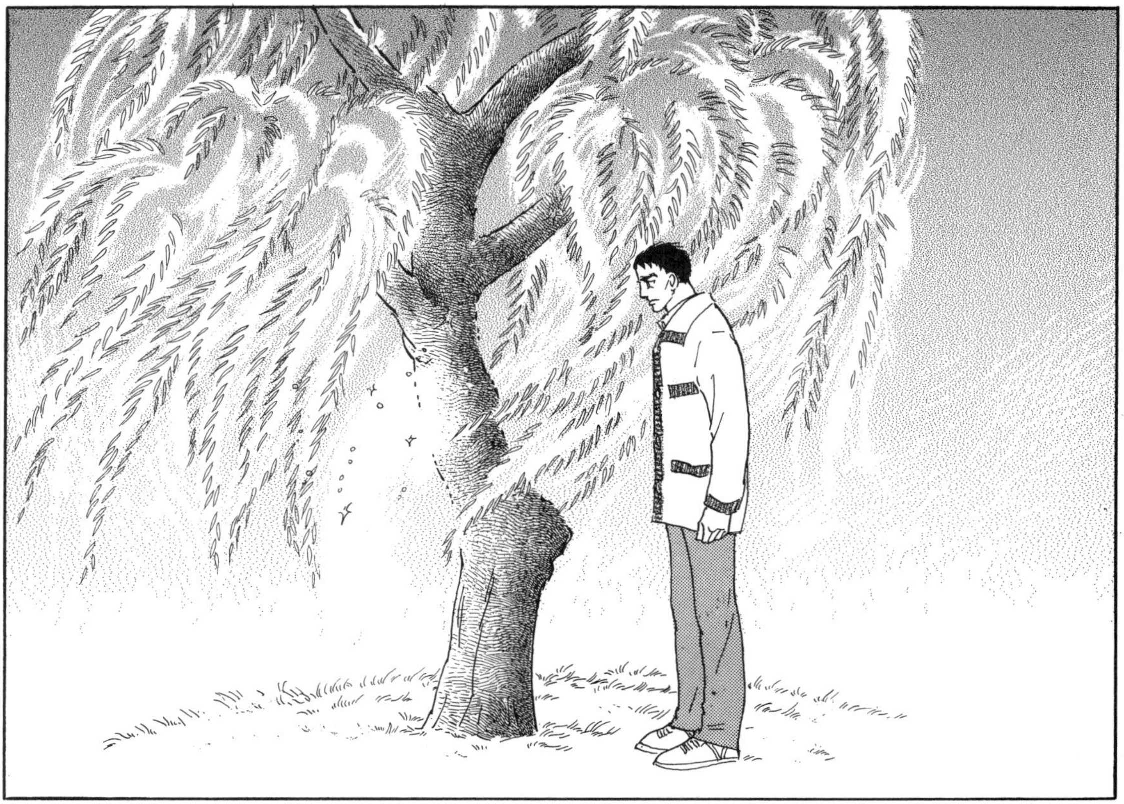

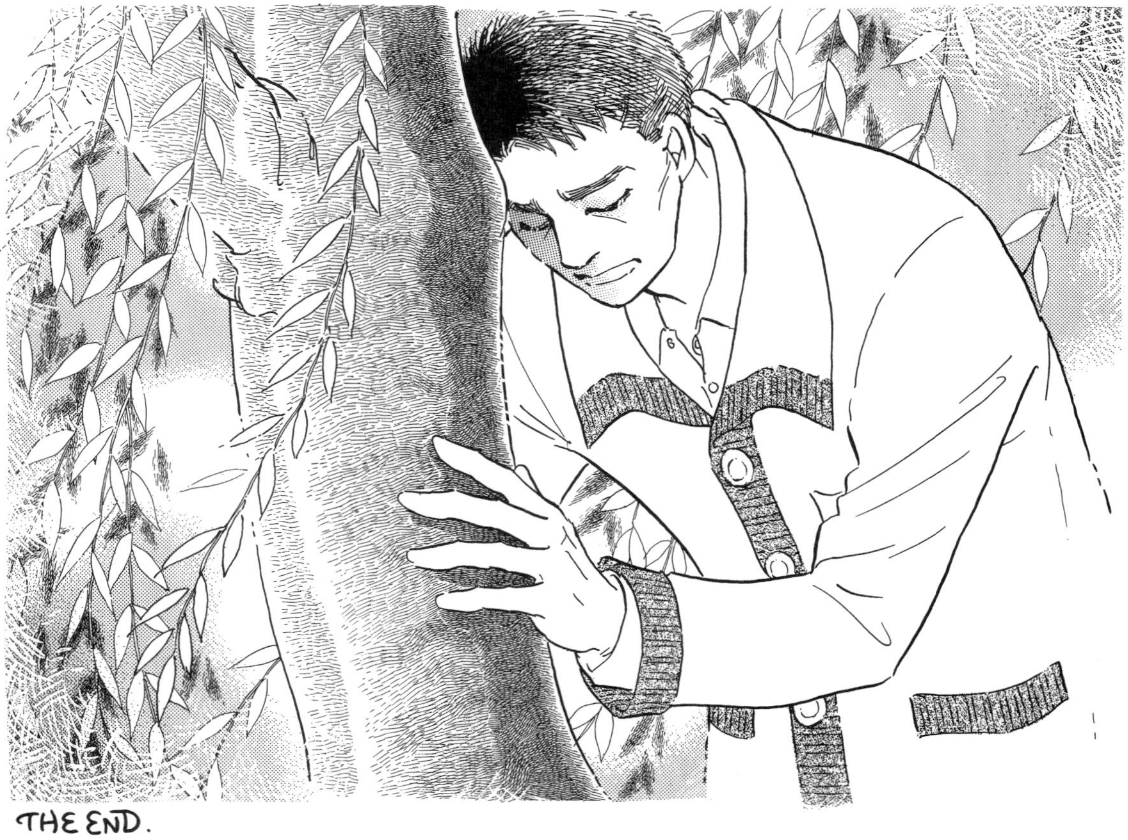

THE END.

STOP!

FANTAGRAPHICS
BOOKS MANGA
2010

THE MANGA IN THIS BOOK IS "UNFLIPPED," MEANING PAGES RUN BACK-TO-FRONT AND PANELS START AT THE TOP-RIGHT AND END IN THE BOTTOM-LEFT. TURN THIS PAGE AND YOU'LL BE AT THE END OF THE STORY. FLIP THE BOOK AROUND FOR A MUCH MORE SATISFYING READING EXPERIENCE.

24. Yasuko Sakata (born 1953) is often categorized as a member of the "Post Forty-Niners." She began working professionally in 1975, and remains active today. She is one of a very small number of Japanese cartoonists who, despite specializing in short works, has maintained high name-recognition throughout her career. Akiko Hatsu is the younger sister of the late Yukiko Kai, another member of the "Post Forty-Niners" whose brief but impressive career came to an end when she died of stomach cancer in 1980. Hatsu was also a popular adjunct instructor in Kyoto Seika University's Department of Comic Art until health problems forced her to resign that post this year.

25. Aiko Itoh (probably born around 1949) was fairly active in the 1970s, and though she has kept a low profile, she continues to work professionally in the genre of "ladies' comics."

26. *Clan of the Rose* was founded in 1971 by the remarkable Bungaku Itoh, and was Japan's first serious gay magazine. It continues to this day, but in response to declining sales, and also in response to a rapidly aging society, it has narrowed its target audience to older gay men.

27. Machiko Satonaka (born 1948) began her professional career in 1964, when she was in her junior year of high school. After a long and successful career, she is now something of a manga ambassador, involved in a wide variety of organizations and activities.

28. The first girls' weekly anthologies, Kodansha Publishing's *Weekly Girls' Friend* and Shueisha's *Margaret*, appeared in 1963, four years after the first boys' weeklies were founded.

29. Actually, Shogakukan Publishing's *Girls' Comic* was founded as a monthly anthology in 1968, and became *Weekly Girls' Comic* in 1970, at the same time that the monthly Special Edition *Girls' Comic* was founded.

30. Yumiko Oshima (born 1947) — see the article on the Magnificent Forty-Niners.

31. With few exceptions, comics anthology magazines in Japan today are not intended to make a profit. They are printed on cheap paper and sold almost at cost in order to generate interest in works that are then sold for a profit in paperback form. But while magazines do not directly generate profit, they are extremely important in promoting the paperbacks, so publishers are acutely sensitive to fluctuations in magazine sales.

End Notes

1. Miyako Maki (born 1935) and Masako Watanabe (born 1929) were two of a handful of female artists working in comics in Japan in the 1950s and early 1960s, and were both enormously popular among girls of the day. The illustrious career of Tetsuya Chiba (born 1939) spans nearly half a century and includes a great many hits, such as the boxing classic *Tomorrow's Joe*, which he co-created with writer Ikki Kajiwara. Mitsuteru Yokoyama (born 1934) is another of the most successful cartoonists of the 1950s and 1960s, in both girls' and boys' comics.

2. Kazuo Umezu (born 1936) is the best-known horror cartoonist in the history of Japanese comics. Among his classics are the terrifying *Snake Girl* (1968), and the deeply disturbing *Floating Classroom* (1972-1974), which can be seen as a harsh and heart-rending critique of the Japanese education system of the day.

3. Shogakukan Publishing's "grade" magazines (*First Grader, Second Grader*, etc.) have been standard reading for Japanese children for decades.

4. Hagio received the 1975 Shogakukan Comics Award for *They Were Eleven!* and *The Poe Clan*. She also received the first ever Tezuka Osamu Culture Award in 1997 for *A Savage God Reigns*. She now serves as a judge for the latter award (as does Matt Thorn).

5. Enka is a genre of sentimental Japanese folk song that is popular with working-class and elderly Japanese, and in some ways parallels American Country & Western music.

6. One version of this tale has been translated by Helen C. McCullough as *The Tale of the Heike*.

7. This is in reference to a famous scene in the tale, which would of course be meaningless to child with no background knowledge of the characters and events.

8. Kenji Miyazawa (1896-1933) is Japan's most famous creator of so-called "children's literature." His best-known work, *Milky Way Railroad* (also translated as *Night of the Milky Way Railway*), was made into a brilliant feature-length animation by director Gisaburo Sugii, available in English under the title *Night on the Galactic Railroad*.

9. Shotaro Ishimori (1938-1998), known to some English readers as the creator of Japan, Inc., is best known for such "hero" works as *Cyborg 009* (1964), *Mutant Sub* (1965), *Masked Rider* (1971), and *Kikaider* (1972), as well as his experimental *Fantasy World Jun* (1967). The famous Power Rangers are direct (and authorized) descendants of his *Go Ranger* (1975). Very early in his career, he did a lot of work in girls' magazines, and was one of the first cartoonists to create science fiction stories for girls. He changed his pen-name to Shotaro Ishinomori in 1980.

10. Hideko Mizuno (born 1939), herself a tomboy, disliked the melodramatic "mother" stories described earlier, and instead pursued fantasy (*Harp of the Stars*, 1960), Westerns ("Red Pony," 1956), and comedy (*Honey-Honey's Wonderful Adventure*, 1966). She was also the only woman cartoonist to live (in 1958) in the now-famous Tokiwaso Apartments that became a (literally) low-rent Mecca for struggling young artists who would go on to define the style of the modern manga. The more famous residents included Ishimori, Hiroshi Fujimoto (1933-1996) & Motoh Abiko (born 1934) — a pair better known by the pen name "Fujiko Fujio," Fujio Akatsuka (born 1935), and Jiro Tsunoda (born 1936), as well as animator Shinichi Suzuki (born 1933).

11. *SF Magazine* was and remains Japan's leading science fiction magazine, and has introduced countless science fiction authors from around the world to Japanese readers.

12. Two of the most famous postwar Japanese novelists, the former a man, the latter a woman. Ariyoshi's *The Twilight Years* is available in English. Shiba's works available in English include *Drunk as a Lord: Samurai Stories* and *The Last Shogun: The Life of Tokugawa Yoshinobu*.

13. Shinsengumi was a group of samurai, all skilled swordsmen, dedicated to the defense of the embattled Shogunate in the middle of the 19th century. For more information, see http://en.wikipedia.org/wiki/Shinsengumi.

14. *COM* was Osamu Tezuka's anthology "Magazine for the Comics Elite" (according to the copy on the cover) and ran from 1967 to 1972. It was begun partly as a forum for Tezuka's now-classic *Phoenix* series, but became a forum for young artists eager to break free of the limitations of the children's magazines. Ishimori's *Fantasy World Jun* was serialized in *COM*.

15. *COM* had a lively letters column, and occasionally included an extra volume that was a collection of work by young, unknown amateurs. In addition to the comics, there were essays and articles, and roundtable discussions about various topics in comics.

16. Sanpei Shirato (born 1932) is best known for the Marxist-inspired *Legend of Kamui* and *The Ninja Book of Martial Arts*. The former was the centerpiece of the anthology *GARO* throughout the magazine's early years, but Yoshiharu Tsuge's short classic "Screw-Style" is more representative of the underground flavor the magazine is famous for.

17. Japanese anthology magazines have a number of editors, and each artist is assigned an editor. The editor-in-chief can change the editor at any time, and in a big publishing house, editors are regularly moved from one magazine to another, the idea being that they can get a variety of experience within the company, making them more useful when they are eventually (if ever) promoted to positions of greater authority.

18. *Star of the Giants* (1966, Ikki Kajiwara and Noboru Kawasaki) was a hugely popular (and in retrospect, comically over-the-top) boys' baseball story, and *Viva! Volleyball* (1968, Chikae Ide) was a girls' comics by an artist famous for drawing eyes that were dazzling even by the standards of girls' comics of the day.

19. Junya Yamamoto (born 1938) — see the article on the Magnificent Forty-Niners.

20. A tatami mat is about 6' x 3', so the rooms would be 9' x 9', 9' x 6', and 9' x 12', respectively.

21. Nanae Sasaya (born 1950) — see the article on the Magnificent Forty-Niners.

22. Mineko Yamada (year of birth not known, but probably around 1950) — see the article on the Magnificent Forty-Niners.

23. Ryoko Yamagishi (born 1947) — see the article on the Magnificent Forty-Niners. Jun Morita (born 1948) was famous for romantic comedies, and for her unusually sexy female characters. Drawing characters with hourglass figures in a genre where "test-tube figures" were and are the norm garnered Morita a good many male fans. In recent years she has worked mainly in the genre of "ladies' comics."

Thorn: *I see. And what kind of image was that?*

Hagio: Whatever it is, we were far from it. We children fought amongst ourselves, we would forget our homework, we didn't get straight A's.

Joh: Your father never lived with his siblings.

Hagio: That's right. And my mother wanted to make a home that was as close to Father's image as possible. Her own childhood was hardly ideal, so she wanted to create such a home and get revenge in that way. She had that burning in her, so there was no room for relaxation in our home, not emotionally. And of course children have energy, so they become unruly sometimes, right? The tension was hard to bear, so I escaped into the world of comics, the world of stories. *[Laughs.]*

Thorn: *Is your brother's depression connected to this in any way?*

Hagio: He was fine while he was succeeding in his job, but at one point he was transferred to some obscure post, and that's when his depression started. He felt that he wasn't needed in his company any more. Ever since he was small, he was very bright. He got into the best private junior high school in the area, and went on to the best high school in the area. So to my parents, he was the ideal child of an ideal home. *[Laughter.]*

Thorn: *It's a pretty simple-minded ideal, isn't it?*

Hagio: Isn't it? Isn't it just? And they even carefully selected his friends. When he was in junior high, my mother went to the school and said, "I hear my son is in a mountain-climbing club, but I want him taken out because it's interfering with his studies." And his teacher said, "Your son is extremely quiet in class, but in the club he has friends and he's talking, so please let him stay in the club." My mother came back extremely disappointed. That was a rare case of her backing down, but normally she would never back down.

Thorn: *So your mother wanted to provide your father with this ideal family?*

Hagio: Right. So, for example, I have an argument with my mother. Well, I don't argue with her these days, but when I did, I would at least be able to understand her reasoning. She has this certain idea of how she wants to do things, and to achieve that I have to get good grades or whatever. But my father is like an eel. There's nothing to grab onto.

Thorn: *So your mother had it hardest.*

Hagio: Maybe, yes.

Thorn: *She wants to make your father happy, but if it fails, it comes back to her.*

Hagio: Yes.

Thorn: *So she becomes neurotic.*

Hagio: I think so, yes. But she would say, "I don't know about men, and I don't know about the company," so she was at least able to avoid all that. So it seems like things were pretty hard for a few years when the children had all grown up and left the house and it was just my mother and father left at home. Before, in trying to build the perfect home, she would take out all her frustration on the children, but when the children left that all landed on my father.

There's a psychiatrist named Judith Herman who wrote a big book titled *Trauma and Recovery*. In it she talks a great deal about sexual abuse. She talks about what happens when a family hides such abuse, and what happens when it is revealed. She talks about cases in which the father shows sexual interest in his daughter but the mother is too strong and won't let him. She talks about all different variations. It was so interesting, and I really got into it. Or rather I learned a lot from it. I really can understand the mindset of a family or daughter who feels pushed to the brink, and loses faith in humanity, or runs away from home, or becomes bulimic or anorexic or just becomes crazy. So we had no sexual abuse in our family, but the tension that was in our family was very much like what she describes.

Thorn: *From a child's point of view, one might be as bad as the other.*

Hagio: Yes. ⚡

Postscript

The day after our interview, I received the following e-mail from Hagio:

During the course of yesterday's interview, I came to a fresh realization. My father and mother, in an attempt to create the ideal family, disciplined us in various ways. Accepting us as we were was out of the question. In their minds, the proper way was to force the children into the form the parents desired. In fact, I accepted my parents' way of disciplining us and forcing us into a mold as reality. But now I wonder if that discipline itself was not un-reality, was not a fiction. I can't explain myself well, but I wonder if my parents, too, did not mistake the fiction of "creating the ideal family" for reality? Would you call such a situation a "self-contained domestic illusion"? And I, in order to escape from this "self-contained domestic illusion," fled to the worlds of science fiction and fantasy. Hmm ... ⚡

express what I wanted to better without clear panel divisions. In those days, in girls' comics, too, you wouldn't use standard panel divisions in the first or last pages. I think this was a variation on or extension of that. You could also use, say, the bottom half of a two-page spread as a single panel, and divide up the upper half normally. It changed gradually.

Thorn: *In the old girls' comics, back in the 1950s, the artist would sometimes use, say, the left one-third or so of a page for a head-to-toe portrait of a character that had nothing to do with the scene on the page. What's the word for that?*

Hagio: It was a sort of picture for the reader to color in if she wanted to, I think.

Thorn: *Did this grow as an extension of that sort of thing?*

Hagio: No, when I was young, I found those coloring pictures quite jarring. You'd be absorbed in the story and all of a sudden here's this big picture that has nothing to do with anything. It was quite annoying. *[Laughter.]* I mean, I liked the pictures, but I wanted them to put them somewhere else.

Thorn: *As I said earlier, we recently had Hideko Mizuno at our university, along with Akira Mochizuki and Sato Tomoe, and the three of them were talking about the early days of postwar girls' comics. One interesting thing Mizuno said was that she would always work that coloring picture into the scene portrayed on the page.*

Hagio: Oh, that's right. Her comics weren't jarring in that way. The heroine would be standing there in a dress, maybe with flowers, but it was part of the scene.

Thorn: *Was that an influence?*

Hagio: Yes, I think it was, because it showed us how to use a large image effectively in a scene.

Phantoms in the Brain

Thorn: *When you came to Seika three years ago, you gave a talk about differences between the left and right brain, and how you believe these related to the reading of comics. Is there any subject you're particularly interested in these days?*

Hagio: I'm interested in the development of language in the human race, when human beings first began to develop a consciousness of words. For example, cats call to their own offspring, and birds sing mating calls, right? I was thinking about at what point humans went beyond that and developed conscious language, when I discovered a book by Noam Chomsky titled *The Generative Enterprise Revisited*. In this book, he argues that abstract thinking, language, and mathematical thinking all developed together as a set. I'm not finished reading it yet, but it's very interesting.

Joh: And then there's the thing about food.

Hagio: *Right. Depending on a species' eating practices, its brain can grow dramatically over time.*

Joh: In other words, they learn how to divide food evenly. It was only recently in human history that food became plentiful.

Hagio: Right. And there's a scholar named Kenichiro Mogi who studies the relationship between the brain and how humans perceive God. Every human society throughout history has had some concept of a god or gods, and the notion that when you die, you go to heaven or you go to some different world. And it seems to me that this is something distinctive to the human brain. What got me interested in this was a book titled *Phantoms in the Brain*, by V.S. Ramachandran. He talks about a variety of brain disorders. It's quite interesting.

Thorn: *May I ask a very personal question?*

Hagio: Certainly.

Thorn: *In* The Heart of Thomas, A Savage God Reigns *and some other works, the theme of sexual abuse comes up again and again. Is that based on your experience?*

Hagio: Hmm … No, I don't have any experience like that … but I do understand very well what it's like to be subjected to psychological abuse to a degree that leads to a collapse of one's personality.

Thorn: *Because of your own childhood experiences?*

Hagio: Yes, I think so. My parents aren't bad people … but I wonder if something bad didn't happen to them. For example, my father's parents died when he was very young, and he was raised by his uncle and grandfather. So he had a home, and didn't want for anything, and yet he was not raised with a family's love. So my father had this ideal of creating a warm family life. But he had never known such a family life, so all he had was an image. And we spent every day trying to live up to Father's image.

Thorn: *But in the end, you did put your plans into action.*

Hagio: Yes, I suppose I finally did, didn't I? I always wanted to portray my frustration towards my mother in comics form, and I tried to think of all different kinds of situations, but the problem is, in real life I am frustrated with my mother, so if I were to portray it straightforwardly, it would just end up as nothing but an expression of resentment. So I would think of a story, then decide it was too ugly and scrap it. And I did this over and over, until I hit upon the idea of the Iguana Girl. I thought, now this I can write, and can make interesting.

Thorn: *Oh! So you came up with that idea quite a long time ago?*

Hagio: The idea of making the daughter an iguana, yes, I came up with it a long time ago. When you don't like someone, you can come up with all kinds of reasons, right? The mother is so responsible but the daughter is so irresponsible, so she hates her daughter. Something like that. I wanted to try to make things work with my parents for so long, I read all sorts of psychology books, but could never find a solution, so I finally turned to a book on fortunetelling, and according to the book, we are just incompatible. *[Laughs.]* "Oh, so we're just incompatible!" Redeemed by fortunetelling. *[Laughter.]*

Thorn: *I see. So, going back to* The Poe Clan*…*

Hagio: When I started making *The Poe Clan*, I found that the boy characters could say what I wanted to say so easily. They were standing in for me. It went very smoothly. It was so easy to make *Poe*. But once I had done that, I found that when I created a female character, I would put myself into her, and I was told that I was imposing my own notions of what a woman is on the character. I thought, "Ouch!" I was surprised at myself. *[Laughter.]*

It made me realize that I'm still bound by stereotypes.

Thorn: *Why do you suppose that's the case?*

Hagio: That's a good question.

Joh: We complain about discrimination, and then we do it ourselves. *[Laughter.]*

Hagio: That's true. I suppose we all have a powerful desire to not be hated by society or those around us, so even though I'd love to create a completely selfish female character, I don't think that's what the readers really want.

Thorn: *Is there a particular reason you made the protagonist a young boy? I mean, I think it's perfect myself. He's not a child, he's a not an adult, he can never become an adult.*

Hagio: First of all, I wanted to make him non-sexual, so I thought it would be best to have a character whose body had not yet changed in that way. But also, that was just about the average age of the readers at the time, so it seemed just right. Long afterwards, it occurred to me that if I had made him slightly older, I could have had more story options available to me.

Joh: But then again, you didn't know anything about men. *[Laughter.]*

Hagio: Well, I knew about middle-aged men. *[Laughter.]*

Thorn: *But then it would have become an adult comic. There would be sex involved.*

Hagio: That's true. There's the difficulty.

Craft

Thorn: *Forgive me for suddenly changing the subject again, but I'd like to ask you about page layouts, about how you use a page.*

Hagio: All right.

Thorn: *The kind of page layouts you and Takemiya did back in those days was very different from anything that came before, wasn't it? Was that a conscious thing?*

Hagio: When you say, "anything that came before," what do you mean?

Thorn: *Well, this is an obvious example, but [Suiho Tagawa's]* Norakuro *(1931) always had three panels per page, stacked, and each was the same size. Tezuka, and particularly Ishimori, introduced more interesting and dramatic page layouts, but in your early works, each page is composed almost like a single painting.*

Hagio: Do you mean a page that consists of a single large panel?

Thorn: *Well, for example, this page here.*

Hagio: Oh, I see what you mean.

Thorn: *In an ordinary boys' comic, the focus is on the action, and the page is laid out to show the flow of the action. "First this happens, then this happens." But in a page like this, the flow of the panels has nothing to do with action, does it?*

Hagio: Right, it's the atmosphere that's important.

Thorn: *It's about the atmosphere and the relationships between the characters. Did you consciously choose this sort of unconventional layout?*

Hagio: That's a good question. Now that you mention it … *[Thorn laughs.]* I suppose, as I was drawing, I found that bigger images worked better, and I could

Opposite: Illustration based on the Mother Goose rhyme "The Death and Burial of Cock Robin." *©1976 Moto HAGIO*

Body and Soul

Thorn: *If I can go back to an earlier subject ...*

Hagio: Please.

Thorn: *About "boys' love." We lump these together as "boys' love," but it seems to me, reading your* The Heart of Thomas *and Takemiya's* The Song of the Wind and the Trees *that they are completely different. The* Heart of Thomas *seems to me to be about spiritual or mental love.*

Hagio: That's right.

Thorn: *The body has little to do with anything. But Takemiya's work, on the contrary, is specifically about physical love.*

Hagio: Yes.

Thorn: *Even in the case of* A Savage God Reigns, *the body obviously plays an important role* [laughter], *but it's still basically about the mind.*

Hagio: Yes.

Thorn: *You said that as a child, you were drawn to the fantastic or the ideal. Do you think that is still reflected in your work today? Is that at the core?*

Hagio: Yes, you could say it's the result of an internal fantasy. As I write these kinds of stories, I'm sometimes asked why I don't make more realistic stories. "Aren't you just running away from reality?" they ask. They suggest that I go off in that direction because I cannot face reality. The genre of fiction itself is that way. The genre of science fiction itself is that way. The genre of fantasy itself is that way. This is the kind of thing people say. How can I put this? I wonder if what they call "reality" is actually reality. *[Laughs.]*

From my point of view, I'm not avoiding reality. What I'm trying to do — and this sounds so pretentious — is trying to get at the truth, at what is real. That's why I prefer those kinds of situations and settings.

The Poe Clan

Thorn: The Poe Clan — *pardon me for suddenly changing the topic* — but The Poe Clan *is of course a fantastic story, but it explores fundamental questions of human existence.*

Hagio: Right.

Thorn: *What kind of theme were you pursuing there?*

Hagio: Stories about monsters, about vampires, whether they're movies or comics, portray vampires as zombies, as villains who attack human beings. And when I read stories like that [as a child], I was afraid of the vampires and didn't like them at all, but then I read a story by Shotaro Ishimori titled "Mist, Roses and Stars."

It's just 40 pages or so, but it's a sort of omnibus that follows the life of a vampire girl from the past to the present and into the future, a science-fiction future. It was quite beautiful. The heroine is of course a vampire, so, for example, if she falls in love with someone, she worries that he'll hate her if he finds out she's a vampire. In other words, she thinks in a very human way.

It seemed very beautiful to me, and around that time I was thinking I wanted to draw something that involved costumes, so I put the two together and decided to draw a beautiful vampire story. So I put myself in the shoes of a vampire and tried to see from a vampire's eyes. A vampire doesn't ask to become a vampire. He may long to return to a normal human existence, but he's rejected by humanity. He is hated unconditionally by all, and told he should not exist. But he does exist, so what is he supposed to do? In my own case, I was told by my mother that comics were utterly unacceptable, and yet I had drawn comics. So what am I supposed to do? *[Laughter.]*

Joh: Run away from home. *[Laughter.]*

Hagio: That's what it comes down to, yes. Ever since the third grade, I had planned on how to run away from home, but I never put my plans into action.

Hagio: Right.

Thorn: *Is that right?*

Hagio: Yes it is. When I was conceptualizing *A Savage God*, the characters kept overlapping [with the characters in *Thomas*], which was a problem, so I had to always consciously strive for a different image. In the beginning, I just couldn't get Julian [the older stepbrother of the sexually abused protagonist] to come to life. I really struggled with that one.

Thorn: *It's interesting, because even the names are similar: "Juli" [pronounced "Yuli," as in the German] and "Julian."*

Hagio: I suppose so.

Thorn: *The root is the same.*

Hagio: Oh! Now that you mention it, that's true! *[Laughter.]*

Thorn: *"The seventh month." Anyway, that's how I read it.*

Hagio: Right.

Twins and Mothers

Thorn: *I see some recurring themes in your work. One is this theme of an abused character that has to come to terms with and overcome that experience. Another is the motif of twins, which comes up so often in your work. Can you talk about the twins? Is this related to the fact that your sister had twins?* [Laughter.]

Hagio: Well, she had the twins after the fact. *[Laughs.]* When I was in elementary school, there was a set of twin girls in the next class. They wore the same clothes and had the same hairstyle, and you couldn't tell them apart. I thought that was so neat. What I thought at the time, in the first grade, was that to have a twin was to have another of yourself, someone who would understand you perfectly and take seriously everything you said; she would be a sibling you could really have fun with. So I dreamed of having a twin. Masako Watanabe drew a lot of stories about twins, and I think that was an influence on me, too. Anyway, there was something enormously appealing to me about twins. Of course, when I got older, I realized that twins are not truly identical. *[Laughs.]*

I suppose it's a variation of the idea of narcissism, but when you explore the question of what it means to love, you run into various problems. For example, you fall in love with someone who is not yourself, but just how much difference can be accepted? I think there are certain points or aspects you love. The idea of loving a thing completely seems unnatural. But what degree of difference can you accept? It's a difficult question. Cats or dogs are lovable because you love them

specifically for being cats or dogs. It's focused. It's not as if they make themselves useful by, say, locking up the house at night or making dinner. *[Laughter.]* You love them in a specific way and don't ask anything more of them. But when it's another human you're in love with, you can't help having a selfish desire for that person to be as much like yourself as possible. And that's where the difficulties arise. So that's why I always come back to twins. *[Laughs.]*

Thorn: *Of your works that involve twins, I think the one that is … how to put it? … most highly regarded? … is probably "Hanshin."*

Hagio: Right.

Thorn: *It seems to me that "Hanshin" is very different from what you were just talking about.*

Hagio: You're right. "Hanshin" is the other side of the coin. It's the idea that love and hate are in a sense the same. The thing you hate is actually the thing you desire. So after the operation, the protagonist ends up becoming the very thing she had said was the one thing she wanted to destroy. It's an exploration of that feeling.

Thorn: *So is it really one character in the end?*

Hagio: Yes, maybe it's one person looking first one way and then another. But to express that in a single character is difficult, so I tried separating out the two elements.

Thorn: *The one is intelligent, yet by society's standards, ugly. The other is basically empty-headed* [laughter] *… and yet loved by everyone. It's an encapsulation of the irrational pressure women are subjected to in society today, isn't it?*

Hagio: Yes.

Thorn: *Another motif that comes up often is that of "mother."*

Hagio: Yes.

Thorn: *Is that your own mother?* [Laughter.]

Hagio: Yes, it is. Once I was working on a story and someone watching commented, "There are always mothers dying in your stories." *[Laughter.]* Scary mothers. And I thought, "Come to think of it, that's true." Basically, I'm afraid of my mother. *[Laughs.]*

Thorn: *A lot of your mothers seem incapable of loving their own children in the ordinary way.*

Hagio: Yes. The mother in "Iguana Girl" [1991] is a typical case. I had various faults when I was a child, so I suppose our relationship when I was small couldn't be helped, but as an adult I tried in various ways to make peace with her. All different ways. And every one failed. *[Laughs.]*

Thorn: *Oh, my. But you see the same themes in Yumiko Oshima's works.* [Hagio laughs.] *Maybe she had the same kind of problems?*

Hagio: Maybe.

Opposite: Illustration based on the Mother Goose rhyme "The Death and Burial of Cock Robin." ©*1976 Moto HAGIO*

ぼくの空に
あこがれ 昔は
待ちあけるくる
好き きらきだ

そんな けたら 二十年のねゆ
よとも ちがまに

Hagio: That's right. So I went to talk with them about putting out the paperback, and they told me the first print run would be 30,000. I said, "Huh!? Do you really think you can sell that many copies?" and they said, "We don't know. But we should be able to sell them a bit at a time over one or two years." *[Laughs.]* And I said, "Really!? But what if it doesn't sell?" And Yamamoto joked, "Your page rate will be paid by the paperback sales, so you'll just have to go to Ikebukuro and hawk them on the corner." *[Laughter.]*

The Heart of Thomas

Thorn: *I'd like to ask about* The Heart of Thomas *in some detail if I may. You said that the idea came from the film* Les Amitiés Particulières, *but it seems to me the theme is very different, and I'd like to ask about that theme.*

Hagio: Yes. The theme is ... hmm ... "When does a person learn love? When does one awake to love?" Something like that. *[Laughs.]* So the whole crazy premise — a boy leaving a letter and dying right at the start of the story — is something I could only have come up with when I was so young. *[Laughter.]*

Thorn: *The title character dies on page 2. [Laughter.]*

Hagio: Yeah. If I had written it after the age of 30, I probably would have worked out some logical reason for the character to die, but at the time I thought, "He doesn't need a reason to die." *[Laughs.]* I could have said that he died because he was sick and didn't have long to live anyway, or something like that. At the time, I thought, how one lives is important, but how one dies might be important, too, and so that's how I wrote it. In a sense, that mystery of why he had to die is never solved, and I think that unsolved mystery is what sustains the work.

Thorn: *It was read by girls ranging from elementary to high school.*

Hagio: In actuality, yes, but on paper the magazine was supposed to be for elementary-school girls, so the editors always told me to make the stories easier to understand. And after it started, it was unpopular with readers, so they asked me to cut it short. *[Laughter.]*

Thorn: *So you originally planned to make it longer?*

Hagio: Yes, at first I had in mind a serial that would run for at least a year. Thirty-three episodes. But midway through the run, the paperback of *The Poe Clan* came out and was selling well, so the editors decided to take a risk and let me finish *The Heart of Thomas*. So it was spared the axe.

Thorn: *So, from the start you had the whole story plotted out?*

Hagio: Yes. The overall arc of the story was planned out, but I only had planned the details of each episode for the first half of the story. When I was first asked to do a weekly serial, they said they wanted a long story, so I told them that the only things I had that could be sustained through a long serial were science fiction *[laughs]* or *Thomas*, so they asked me to do *Thomas*. So I took these episodes I had drawn for myself and used what I could.

Thorn: *You had already penned them?*

Hagio: Only partially. The rest was pencils. So there are penciled episodes that I never used. *[Laughter.]* Really, my earlier drawings were not well-proportioned, so I only used the better portions for the serial.

Thorn: *I first read* Thomas *at the age of, I think, 22. And when I read the scene where Juli is explaining how he lost his figurative "wings," I just naturally interpreted it to mean that he had been sexually abused.*

Hagio: Yes.

Thorn: *When I read* A Savage God Reigns *[1992], I thought, "Oh, this is the adult version of* Thomas."

I've always read boys' comics, too, so I understand their appeal. But if you put a boys' comic and a girls' comic in front of me and ask which one I'll read first, I'll choose the girls' comic, because it's closer to my own sensibilities. Men are going to make smug comments, and that's all there is to it. I knew what they said wasn't true, so I didn't let it bother me.

Thorn: *If girls' comics were 10 years behind, wasn't it the fault of those middle-aged men?* [Laughter.] *I mean, they [the male editors] insisted for years that they knew what girls wanted to read.*

Hagio: I think there is that, but it also goes both ways. For example, the male characters that appear in girls' comics are a girls' ideal, right? There aren't any boys like that in real life. *[Laughs.]* In the same way, the female characters who appear in boys' comics are completely unrealistic. *[Laughter.]* There are no such girls.

You know, serving as a judge for the Tezuka Awards, I find myself thinking, "Men just are incapable of reading girls' comics." *[Laughter.]* It's the same when I'm judging the Shogakukan Awards. They have four categories: children's, boys', girls' and adult, or rather "general." In the children's, boys' and general categories, there aren't any major divisions in opinion, but as soon as discussion turns to the girls' comics, more than half of the men say, "I just don't get it. I'll have one of my [female] assistants read them." *[Laughs.]* "I didn't get it, so I asked my wife for her opinion."

Thorn: *Yes, the Tezuka Awards are pretty dominated by middle-aged men.*

Hagio: Yeah, there's no helping that. But I'm talking about the Shogakukan Awards, where I've been through this year after year. In a sense, that makes it easier for the women to impose their opinions [in the girls' comics category]. *[Laughs.]* You can't force people to like something they have an aversion to. But it makes me think that our brains are really structured in different ways.

Thorn: *But Yamamoto wasn't like that, was he?*

Hagio: Oh, he was. His favorite comics were the *GARO* type. But even so, he believed that girls' comics had something special to offer. What I admire about him is that he went to the trouble to ask a lot of different people about the genre, and tried to understand just what girls' comics are about. He did a lot of homework.

Thorn: *So do you think that Yamamoto was a major factor in the sudden appearance at that time of what is commonly called the Magnificent 24-Year Group, and the kind of, for want of a better word, "literary" girls' comics associated with those artists?*

Hagio: Oh, I think he was a major factor, yes. I think it was really Yumiko Oshima[30] who blazed that trail, though. She had been working for [Shueisha's] *Margaret*, but she moved over to Shogakukan, where she did *You Can Hear the Rain* [1972] and all those short stories. They were a real shock.

Thorn: *Stories like* Birth! *[1970]?*

Hagio: Yes, well, *Birth!* was one she did for Margaret, and it was incredible, but she appeared in Margaret so irregularly, you never knew when she was going to show up. But when she came to *Special Edition Girls' Comic*, you knew you could read her every month. The whole "Yumiko Oshima World" just unfolded in an amazing way. Very poetic. Very philosophical.

Thorn: *So you were stunned by her work?*

Hagio: I was. It was beautiful.

Waiting for the Trade

Thorn: *Speaking of comics reprints, in the old days, instead of the smaller trade paperbacks we have now, reprints were in the same format as the magazines, right?*

Hagio: Hmm? Oh, oh, I see what you mean. Yes, in the old days they were like that.

Thorn: *Did the kind of paperback we have now first appear in the late 1960s?*

Hagio: I think so. I wonder when exactly that started. I think it was actually in girls' comics that they began to put them out regularly in that format. [Riyoko Ikeda's] *The Rose of Versailles* [1972] came out in paperback, and it sold very well, and I think that was the impetus for them to begin to systematically put out paperbacks of every serialized work. When I was in junior high and high school, Asahi Sonorama Publishing put out a lot of trade paperbacks. But none of the other publishers thought that paperback reprints would sell well. It all changed in just a few short years, but before that they rarely put out reprints.

Thorn: *Today, the magazines are essentially advertisements for the paperbacks.*[31]

Hagio: That's right. So when I was growing, I had no idea what might be reprinted, so I clipped and kept every story I liked. *[Laughs.]*

Thorn: *I heard from Yamamoto that your* Poe Clan *[1972] was the first girls' trade paperback Shogakukan ever published [in 1974].*

Opposite: Illustration based on the Mother Goose rhyme "The Death and Burial of Cock Robin." *©1976 Moto HAGIO*

Masuyama used to ask me, "Why doesn't this interest you? Why doesn't this turn you on?" and I would say, "No, thanks" and keep my distance. But one movie changed all that. *[Laughter.]*

So Takemiya may wish she had never told me about it. *[Laughter.]*

Thorn: *So "November Gymnasium" was the first story you did that reflected that influence?*

Hagio: Well…

Thorn: *But you actually came up with the story for* The Heart of Thomas *first?*

Hagio: Yes. After seeing *Les Amitiés Particulières*, I began doing *The Heart of Thomas* on an impulse. You see, I did a lot of stories that I never published.

Thorn: *Really?*

Hagio: These days I suppose they'd be called *doujinshi*. *[Laughs.]* So I started doing *The Heart of Thomas* for myself, really. And as I was fiddling with this, it occurred to me that I could make another story using these two characters, and that became "November Gymnasium." *[Laughs.]* So I made "November Gymnasium" for publication. And the idea in that story was that they were attracted to each other because they were actually brothers, which Masuyama, who loves boys' love stories, thought was terrible. "How could you draw something like this?" *[Laughter.]* So the idea of actually publishing *The Heart of Thomas* came some time later.

Thorn: *Did you see it as problem at the time to do a story for a girls' magazine in which all the characters are boys?*

Hagio: Yes. It had never occurred to me to do an all-boy story unless it was science fiction, so I was concerned. I considered doing it as an all-girl story. When it came to writing the plot, I did two versions: a boys' version — heavily influenced by *Les Amitiés Particulières* — and a girls' version. So I thought about it, but I was in for a surprise. When I wrote it as a boys' school story, everything fell into place smoothly. But when I wrote the girls' school version, it came out sort of giggly. Maybe it's because I was a girl myself, but that sort of nastiness distinctive to girls worked its way into the story. So I decided the boys' school version was better. "November Gymnasium: The Boys' School Version." *[Laughter.]*

Thorn: *And it was [Special Edition Girls' Comic Editor-in-Chief] Junya Yamamoto who gave "November Gymnasium" the go ahead.*

Hagio: Right. He told me my next story would be 40 pages, so I decided to go with this. So he ran the teaser for "November Gymnasium," and he also gave me five more pages, which was a big help.

Thorn: *Didn't he say anything about the fact that the characters were all boys?*

Hagio: Nothing. After I moved to Shogakukan, and Yamamoto became my editor, he only checked the roughs of my first two or three stories, and after that he would just accept the finished piece.

Thorn: *[Laughs.] Really? No discussion, no checking?*

Hagio: Only with much longer works would he ask the artists what they were planning to do.

Thorn: *In other words, he trusted you that much.*

Hagio: I don't know. He seemed to look forward to seeing what I would come up with. Maybe he found my work interesting. So I would take him the finished piece, and he would read it on the spot, but he wouldn't say much about it. And I was so nervous. I would watch every expression on his face, the way he moved his eyebrows *[laughs]*, and think, "Is he thinking this is no good? Is he thinking it's fine?" And he wouldn't say anything when he was done, so I would think "Phew! This one was all right, too." I had to rely on telepathy. *[Laughter.]*

Thorn: *But Yamamoto was unique, wasn't he?*

Hagio: Yes, he was. And after he had looked at my piece, he would start talking about movies and books and other artists' comics. But he wouldn't talk about my piece. *[Laughter.]* But you can tell a person's mood by the way they talk, right?

The Forty-Niners and the Shōjo Manga Renaissance

Thorn: *Around that time, the number of female cartoonists grew quite suddenly, didn't it? Right around 1970?*

Hagio: That's right. Around the late 1960s. Machiko Satonaka made her debut.[27] Well, the weekly anthology magazines had been around for a few years before that, but the number increased.[28] Then *Girls' Comic* was founded around 1970, which meant one more place for artists to find work.[29] It's sort of like the creation of a new baseball team. *[Laughs.]* So new artists came into the field.

Thorn: *Was there an atmosphere of male chauvinism at the time? Actually, I suppose there often still is today.*

Hagio: I used to go to Shogakukan's offices and be told, "Girls' comics are 10 years behind boys' comics." They would ask, "Why don't girls' comics artists draw backgrounds properly?" The implication being that they didn't draw them because they lacked the skill. All kinds of stuff. Oh, you know how you lay out a page, and a close-up of a character will spill out over into the next panel? They would say you can't do that sort of thing. So I had to listen to that all the time, but I just became inured to it. I would just think, "I don't care what these old farts think." *[Laughter.]*

Hagio: But then again, I once visited Sasaya in Hokkaido and stayed for a month. *[Laughs.]* She would draw her stories for [Shueisha Publishing's magazine] *Ribbon* at O-izumi. She did "The Boy from Dartmoor" there. Mineko Yamada[22] came to help her out with that work. Ryoko Yamagishi and Jun Morita used to hang out, too.[23]

Thorn: *What about Yasuko Sakata?*

Hagio: Oh, that's right. Yasuko Sakata used to come from Kanazawa City [in Ishikawa Prefecture]. And so did Akiko Hatsu.[24] They came a lot. This was before they became pros. I think they were still college students.

Thorn: *And Shio Satoh?*

Hagio: Right, she came as an assistant. Well, actually I got a fan letter from her, and it was so interesting I invited her to come visit us. She said she was hoping to become a professional cartoonist, so I asked her to help me. And there was a woman named Ikumi Ikeda who later moved back to Hokkaido. And then there was Aiko Itoh.[25] It was always lively.

Thorn: *Were you interested in European literature at the time?*

Hagio: At that time, I was into [Hermann] Hesse. I read everything I could find by Hesse. I was also into [Ray] Bradbury for a long time.

Thorn: *And [Jean] Cocteau?*

Hagio: Cocteau was a shock. If you think about it, his is a pretty sick world. *[Laughter.]* The protagonist does nothing at all, and everything's so dark.

Thorn: *But that's what made it appealing, right?*

Hagio: Exactly. *[Laughs.]*

Thorn: *How about movies?*

Hagio: There was A *Death in Venice. [Laughs.]* 2001: *A Space Odyssey* came along, too, so I went to see that. The price of a movie suddenly went up to 700 yen, so deciding to see a film was a serious business. *[Laughter.]*

Boys' Love

Thorn: *Now, I may get in trouble for asking about this ...* [Laughter.] *... about the whole "boys' love" thing ...*

Hagio: Oh! *[Laughs.]* Go ahead.

Thorn: *Some people say it was started by the woman who occupies the office next to mine [Keiko Takemiya] ... others say it was started by you.* [Laughter.]

Hagio: Oh, it was Takemiya. The woman who lived across the way, Masuyama, was something of an expert on homosexuality. She brought a copy of the magazine *Clan of the Rose* to show us.

Thorn: *Was this a European magazine?*

Hagio: No, it was Japanese.[26] It had plenty of personal ads and such. I'm not sure if it's still around. There were two kinds of publications about gay men. One was for men who are serious about loving other men, and the other was for women who found the idea of men in love to be intriguing. *Clan of the Rose* was the former, and, I'm sorry, but it didn't do a thing for me. *[Laughter.]*

So Masuyama introduced us to this stuff, and Takemiya was crazy about it. What was her first story along those lines? "In the Sunroom"? And I was just looking on in puzzlement. *[Laughs.]* Then one day they invited me to go see *Les Amitiés Particulières* [1964, directed by Jean Delannoy, known in English as "Particular Friendships" or "The Special Friendship"]. It was playing in Kichijoji. It stars Didier Haudepin, and is a love story set in a boys' boarding school. It's the kind of story women get excited by. *[Laughs.]* I thought it was so beautiful. I'm a sucker for anything beautiful. *Clan of the Rose,* on the other hand, seemed ugly to me. *[Laughs.]* Maybe "coarse" is a better word. But this movie was beautiful. That's when I got into this. Until then, Takemiya and

Below: Illustration based on the Mother Goose rhyme "The Death and Burial of Cock Robin." ©1976 Moto HAGIO

Thorn: *In those days [Kodansha's girls' magazine] Nakayoshi didn't carry that sort of thing. Or rather, no girls' magazines back then carried that sort of thing, right?*

Hagio: Right. At the time, the hot genre was sports stories. *[Sighs.]* I liked reading those stories, stuff like *Star of the Giants* and *Viva! Volleyball*,[18] but I didn't think I could do such a fast-paced story myself. *[Laughter.]*

Thorn: *No, I don't think you could.*

Hagio: So I would send them story ideas that I wanted to do, and every idea was rejected, every finished story I sent was rejected. *[Laughter.]* So I thought, "How am I going to eat?" *[Laughs.]* And there's a big gap between what I want to do and what they want me to do. And I thought, "There's no way I can become a pro this way." So I wondered if I should change my direction. But I want to draw what I want to draw, right?

Thorn: *Right.*

Hagio: So I wondered if I should give up trying to be a pro and just be satisfied doing amateur, self-published work. This was about two years that I was in this situation.

The O-izumi Salon

Thorn: *You were in Fukuoka during this time?*

Hagio: Right. So I would have maybe 10 stories I wanted to do, and I would think, "Of these 10, this one might be accepted," so I'd work on that one. And I thought it would just be that way indefinitely. So during this time, when school was out, I went to Tokyo to give them a piece, and the editor told me that Keiko Takemiya was holed up trying to meet a deadline, and asked if I wouldn't go and help her out. Takemiya had been published in *COM*, and I think she had also been published in *Margaret*, or was it *Special Edition Margaret*? But she was also in *Nakayoshi*. Anyway, she was all over the place, and was quite a famous rookie.

Thorn: *So Takemiya's pro debut preceded your own?*

Hagio: Oh, of course. I told the editor, "Yes, I'm familiar with her work," and he said, "She's familiar with your work, too." So I went and assisted her.

Takemiya asked me if I was planning to move to Tokyo. I told her that my parents were worried about sending me off to the city by myself, and that first I would have to convince them. I also told her I was having trouble selling my work, and was worried that I wouldn't be able to make a living if I came to Tokyo. So — even though we were both there doing work for Kodansha — she said, "I know an editor at Shogakukan. Would you like me to introduce you?"

Thorn: *And that was Junya Yamamoto.*[19]

Hagio: That was Junya Yamamoto. So I sent the roughs of the stories that had been rejected by Kodansha

to Takemiya's apartment, and asked if she could show them to Yamamoto. The stories I sent were "Holy Night on Sailor Hill," "The Fife of the White Boy in the White Forest," "Maudlin" and I think there was one other.

Thorn: *One of these? [Matt shows her a list of her earliest published works.] Maybe "Bianca"?*

Hagio: No, I did "Bianca" for Kodansha. Was it "Poor Mama"? Yes, that was it. I had drawn it as a 16-page story, but Yamamoto said he would publish it, so I turned it into a 32-page story. Anyway, I sent these, and Yamamoto said, "I'll buy them all." And I thought, "Great! Now I can eat." *[Laughter.]*

And then Takemiya contacted me and said, "I'm thinking of moving. Would you like to share an apartment with me?"

Thorn: *So you were still in Fukuoka?*

Hagio: Right. So I thought, "I can use this to convince my parents to let me go."

Thorn: *And it worked?*

Hagio: It worked.

Thorn: *Did you have a hard time convincing them?*

Hagio: They thought I'd be back after about a year. *[Laughter.]* So I took my savings, and my parents gave me 10,000 yen as a going-away present, and I moved to Tokyo. We lived together for about two years in a place called O-izumi. Living catty-corner to us was a woman named Norie Masuyama who really loved comics.

Thorn: *But she wasn't a cartoonist herself?*

Hagio: No, she wasn't. For a while I think she worked as what you might call Takemiya's "brain staff." We had so many different people hanging out there. It was a very interesting two years.

Thorn: *This was the famous "O-izumi Salon."*

Hagio: *[Laughs.]* It was more like "O-izumi Row-house." When I first heard that name, I thought, "Huh? Who came up with that one?" *[Laughter.]* It's pretty embarrassing, really.

Thorn: *Was it an apartment?*

Hagio: No, it really was an old row-house.

Thorn: *Did it have a name?*

Hagio: No, no name. It was one building divided into two houses. I can't remember who lived on the house to the left, but we lived on the right. There was a four-and-a-half tatami mat room on the first, and a three-mat room and six-mat room on the second.[20] It was very small.

Thorn: *And who were some of the people who hung out there during those two years?*

Hagio: Oh, there were a lot of them. The one who came the most was Nanae Sasaya.[21] She once came and stayed over for six months. *[Laughter.]*

Thorn: *That's not "staying over." I think the common term for such a person is "freeloader."* [Laughter.]

Thorn: *Am I right in thinking that it was serious comics fans that were the core readers of* COM?

Hagio: Yes. I remember being excited to see so many comics lovers in one place.[15] There was another magazine at the time called *GARO*. It featured Sanpei Shirato.[16] I suppose you could say it represented the "hardcore." But frankly I never really liked it. I read it, and I thought Shirato's work was great.

Thorn: *Other than Shirato's work, what were the comics in* GARO *like in those days?*

Hagio: I must have read a lot of them, but all I have left is a really dark impression. *[Laughs.]*

Thorn: Gekiga, *that sort of thing?*

Hagio: *Gekiga,* psycho mysteries, that sort of thing. Mostly stories about youthful anguish from a male perspective.

Anyway, I was raised in a home where comics were completely disparaged. I was so grateful to be able to become a girls' comics artist, and to get to the point where I could do comics professionally. I couldn't have cared less that male cartoonists were saying girls' comics were drivel, because anything they could say would be preferable to what my parents were saying. *[Laughter.]*

Thorn: *I see. At least you were both cartoonists.*

Hagio: Right. In a perverse sense, my parents taught me a lot in that respect. *[Laughs.]*

Thorn: *So your debut piece was the short story "Lulu and Mimi." [1969]*

Hagio: Yes. When I was in my senior year of high school, I moved back to Ohmuta from Osaka, and I heard that there was a cartoonist living in Ohmuta, and I went to visit her. She was a girl named Makiko Hirata. She was being published by Kodansha, and she was the same age as me. She was doing pro work while she was still in high school. After graduation, she moved to Tokyo, and she told me that if I were interested, she would introduce me to her editor. After I graduated, I entered a design school back home, and after I had drawn a few stories, I went to Tokyo and Makiko Hirata took me to Kodansha. The editor there told me to send him something before the end of the month. It was just 15 days or so.

Thorn: *How many pages?*

Hagio: I think he told me between 20 and 25 pages.

Thorn: *All of a sudden.* [Laughter.] *"Finish it in two weeks."*

Hagio: Right. He didn't tell me they'd actually publish it, but since I said "Yes," I had to do it. *[Laughs.]* So I did.

Thorn: *And that was "Lulu and Mimi"?*

Hagio: Right.

Thorn: *So you didn't really hit it off with the editors at Kodansha?*

Hagio: I think I did about seven stories for them. During that time they gave me a new editor,[17] but both editors followed company policy, which was not to let artists do whatever they want, but to have artists do something that fits the theme of whatever project they are currently doing. Their idea was that a magazine without such projects or featured themes was no magazine at all. I can understand that as a concept for creating a magazine, but their themes did not fit the kind of thing I wanted to do. *[Laughs.]* I wanted to do sci-fi, that sort of thing.

Right: From *Aria of the Sea (Umi no Aria)*. ©1989 Moto HAGIO

works. I think the reason was that I grew up in a coal-mining town. At the time, there were these fierce labor disputes, so there were often these fights among the grownups. Children were never hurt in these fights, but they saw these people screaming into microphones and running. And they were not spewing abstractions, like the fascists do in their sound-trucks. It was rough, raw stuff. It was terrifying.

Thorn: *So that reality was just too ...*

Hagio: Yes, it was a reality of violence and poverty, and I wanted to escape from it. I wanted to move toward something more beautiful.

Thorn: *So you were pursuing an ideal.*

Hagio: No, just pursuing an escape. *[Laughs.]* But, yes.

Breaking In

Thorn: *You said you were drawn to the way Tezuka portrayed his characters' psychology?*

Hagio: You may remember that the last time I visited Kyoto Seika University, I talked about Tezuka's *Shinsengumi* in my lecture.[13] It was this comic that made me decide to become a cartoonist. The protagonist joins the Shinsengumi, and there he becomes very close friends with another young man, called Oka-chan. But Oka-chan turns out to be a spy, and the protagonist is obliged to kill him. He has to choose between loyalty to his group, or rescuing his friend. I sympathized so much with the situation of the hero, that I found myself reading the book as if I were him. I completely synchronized with him. When that happens, you become emotionally involved with the story in a strange way that is beyond words. "I know how you feel. I know exactly how you feel!" *[Laughs.]*

I was surprised at myself, and I realized for the first time that comics were capable of having such an impact on a reader, and I thought, "If you can affect someone in this way, I'd like to take a serious stab at it myself." Before that, I had really liked comics, and I would talk with my friend about how to present work to a publisher and things like that, but I also worried about not being able to sell my work, or even how to go to the publisher's offices. *[Laughs.]* If I couldn't sell my work, how could I make a living? In other words, I was fretting about things not having directly to do with the comics themselves. And I would think, "I can't really become a pro cartoonist." I was finding reasons to run away from it. "I'll just have to make it a hobby."

Thorn: *This was in high school?*

Hagio: Right. In my first and second year of high school, when I was beginning to think about my future. And it was just around that time that Ishimori came out with *An Introduction to Cartooning* and *An Introduction to Cartooning, Continued* [1965 and 1966]. In those books he talks about how he got to be a cartoonist, and how poor he was when he was younger. He would buy a single daikon radish, and live on that for a week. *[Laughs.]* Stories like that. And I would think, "Living for a week on daikon!? I hate daikon!" *[Laughs.]* But after I read Tezuka's *Shinsengumi*, I thought, "I'll try it even if I have to live on daikon for a week." I became serious about cartooning. I started looking for publishers and submitting work. I submitted for about two years. About 10 different pieces I sent here and there.

Thorn: *"Here and there"?*

Hagio: I sent to Kodansha, and once I sent a piece to *COM. COM* was —

Thorn: *— the magazine Tezuka was putting out.*

Hagio: Right.[14] And then there was Shueisha. Shueisha had its annual comics awards, but each month on the pages of *Special Edition Margaret*, they invited submissions of 16-page stories, so I sent several stories to them.

Hideko Mizuno did *Harp of the Stars* [1960], and then *Hello, Teacher* [1964] and *The White Troika* [1964]. She worked with legends and famous historical figures, and looked to other countries [for inspiration]. The lines of the dresses she drew were just so beautiful. I tried so hard to copy the way she drew dresses, but was never able to do it as well as she did. *[Laughter.]* "How does she do it!?"

Asimov in High School

Thorn: *I hear that you moved a lot as a child.*

Hagio: That's right.

Thorn: *You moved back and forth between Suita City [in Osaka Prefecture] and Ohmuta City several times.*

Hagio: Right.

Thorn: *Did that have to do with your father's work?*

Hagio: That's right. So I went to two elementary schools, two junior high schools, and two high schools.

Thorn: *That must have been hard.*

Hagio: Yes, because your environment changes so abruptly. In a way, it was interesting. In particular, moving from Ohmuta to Osaka, the language was so different. You know, the Osaka dialect.

Thorn: *Right.*

Hagio: It was startling. But the most startling thing was the boys in Osaka. They were so stylish. *[Laughter.]*

One time, my mother asked me to go to my little brother's elementary school to deliver something to him. And these boys come over and ask me where I'm going, so I tell them, and one of them immediately takes my bag and says, "Let me carry that for you," like a real gentleman. *[Laughs.]* I was bowled over. "So this is what city boys are like!" *[Laughter.]*

Thorn: *So, were you able to make friends in Suita?*

Hagio: Yes. I became friends with a girl who had just transferred to the school three days before me. It was because of her that I was able to make it through my second year of junior high school. You see, there were these group divisions in the class, and you couldn't just jump right into one of them. Actually, that itself was a surprise to me. Back in the country, the parents of all the kids worked in the same place, and you could become friends with just about anybody quite easily. But in Osaka, the kids divided up into groups of four or five, and wouldn't say hello to or play with the kids of other groups. They wouldn't invite anyone else to play. It took me a while to get used to that. But in my third year in junior high, our school changed. I mean, it was the same school, but we moved from an old school into a new one. The old school was in the hills, and was an old place with real character. But one Monday we went to school, and found that the ceiling in the hallway of the second floor had fallen in. *[Laughs.]* There was a huge hole in the ceiling. That's how old the place was. The teachers were very upset, and saying, "What if this had happened on a school day?" So we moved to a new school, and all the classes were rearranged. There were two kids from my previous class, and though they had never spoken a word to me before, we suddenly became good friends. And once we became friends I realized they were really nice kids. *[Laughs.]* Strange, isn't it?

Thorn: *Going back to something we were talking about earlier, was it that reading corner in elementary school that got you interested in science fiction?*

Hagio: No. In my second year of junior high, I read Isaac Asimov's *The Currents of Space*. It's set on a completely alien planet, and you don't find out who the protagonist is until the end of the book. Oh yeah, this is another amnesia story. *[Laughter.]* When he finally gets back his memory at the end, he remembers that he's from Earth. He's a scientist from Earth studying the currents of space. But the nobles from this advanced planet say, "Earth? We've never heard of such a planet." So he's treated as an outlaw, as a foreigner. So I had first assumed this was a story about the Earth, but my assumption turned out to be completely wrong. This was quite a shock to my brain at the time, and it occurred to me for the first time that there could be a future in which the Earth is all but unknown.

So I became fascinated with this genre, and wanted to read more. You know *SF Magazine*?[11] I would occasionally find copies in used bookstores. Every story interested me. And then these sci-fi paperbacks began to be published, and I just got in deeper and deeper.

Thorn: *I also became interested in sci-fi in junior high school, and I particularly liked Robert Heinlein. But then in high school, I began to understand Heinlein's political perspective, and I got to the point where I couldn't read him any more.* [Laughter.]

Hagio: There is that about Heinlein. It's when you have no idea what he's talking about that you can enjoy him the most. *[Laughs.]*

Thorn: *He was famous for saying that it shouldn't be against the law to shoot pacifists or anarchists, but you have to watch out for the anarchists because they might shoot back.* [Laughter.]

So you basically preferred fantastic stories to more mundane dramas?

Hagio: Yes. How should I put it? The only authors of realistic stories I could read were Ryotaro Shiba and Sawako Ariyoshi.[12] Of course, these days I read all kinds of more realistic novels. But when I was in my teens and 20s, I just had no patience at all for realistic

Opposite: Illustration based on the Mother Goose rhyme "The Death and Burial of Cock Robin." ©1976 Moto HAGIO

Hagio: Right. When I remember my parents and comics, my only memories are of being scolded. *[Laughs.]* The only exception was when I first won a prize, and the magazine published a panel from the winning work and sent me a check. I showed it to my mother, and she was taken by surprise and said, "You mean your comics can earn money?" Until then, I had been lectured so many times. "At your age you shouldn't be doing such nonsense."

"But I want to become a cartoonist."

"Well, you can't make a living just doing whatever you want." She would say, "These cartoonists get paid just one hundred yen a page; you can't live on that." *[Laughter.]* Where did she get that figure? I once heard in an interview someone say that long ago the page rate was one hundred yen. So I suppose my mother must have heard that, too, way back then. *[Laughter.]*

Girl Books and Beyond

Thorn: *I understand that you read a lot of literature when you were young.*

Hagio: Yes, I would read anything and everything. I started with the books in school. There was a little reading corner in the school. There was a movement at the time to get children to read literature. There were biographies of famous people, like Florence Nightingale and Thomas Edison, as well as Japanese folk tales. These could be read pretty quickly, so I'd finish one and start another right away. Then, when I was in the fifth grade, our school got a proper library. I was so happy. I went every day.

Thorn: *What kind of books did you like?*

Hagio: American writers like Gene Stratton-Porter and Louisa May Alcott, and then there was Lucy Maud Montgomery. *The Secret Garden*, *Anne of Green Gables*, *Rebecca of Sunnybrook Farm*, *Little Women*... all those typical "girl books," in which the protagonist is a girl and has all sorts of adventures. There was a series of all those books, and I read them all. And then there were the Greek and Roman myths. Yeah, there was a series titled *Myths From Around the World*, and I particularly liked the volumes on Greek and Roman myths. And for some reason there was a science-fiction corner, too. A dozen or so books geared at boys and girls.

Thorn: *Wasn't that unusual for an elementary school library in those days?*

Hagio: It was. There was also a Japanese classics corner, but the only thing I read from there was Ikku Jippensha's *Shanks Mare*. Nothing there really grabbed me. *[Laughs.]*

Thorn: *Why was that?*

Hagio: First of all, there weren't many stories that featured women. And I just didn't find the situations in the stories interesting. For example, there was The Battle of the Minamoto and the Taira.[6] This can be quite interesting if you know the history, but if you don't, and all of a sudden some guy named Kiyomori appears and he's trying to hide his armor beneath his robes...[7] *[Laughter.]*

I preferred stories that I could dive right into without any prior knowledge.

Thorn: *So it was mostly Western literature you were attracted to?*

Hagio: Yes. I read some Japanese children's literature, but all I remember of it was that it was preachy. *[Laughs.]* I think there were a lot of books like that back then, books with moral lessons.

Thorn: *And you were attracted to Western literature because...?*

Hagio: I think because it allowed you to use your imagination more. Oh, come to think of it, I really liked Kenji Miyazawa.[8]

Thorn: *I see. So you preferred stories that were more fantastic.*

Hagio: Yes, I think so.

Thorn: *And as for comics, you liked Tezuka?*

Hagio: Osamu Tezuka, Shotaro Ishimori,[9] Hideko Mizuno.[10] I was crazy about them. I copied them constantly.

Thorn: *Was there any one work in particular that blew you away?*

Hagio: They all did. In particular, everything by Tezuka blew me away when I was in elementary school. Every story I read, I would think, "Wow! So this is what happens? This is what the character thinks?" Particularly the near-future science fiction stories, such as *Astro Boy*. They were just so imaginative. And I also would think, "So this how you make a story?" It was because the stories were so carefully crafted that it was so easy for me to understand them. Ishimori was more sensually rich. His drawings were beautiful. But his stories weren't as solid. He would jump from one episode to another indiscriminately, and you'd be left wondering, "Whatever happened to that character?" or, "Huh? You mean the story's over?" *[Laughter.]* A lot of his stories were like that. But they still carried impact.

Thorn: *My own impression is that Ishimori liked playing with form.*

Hagio: With technique.

Thorn: *Right, playing with technique, and theme was a secondary consideration.*

Hagio: Yes. I think so. So he knew how to make a scene look cool, and could draw fight scenes that had real impact. He was good at stunning the reader.

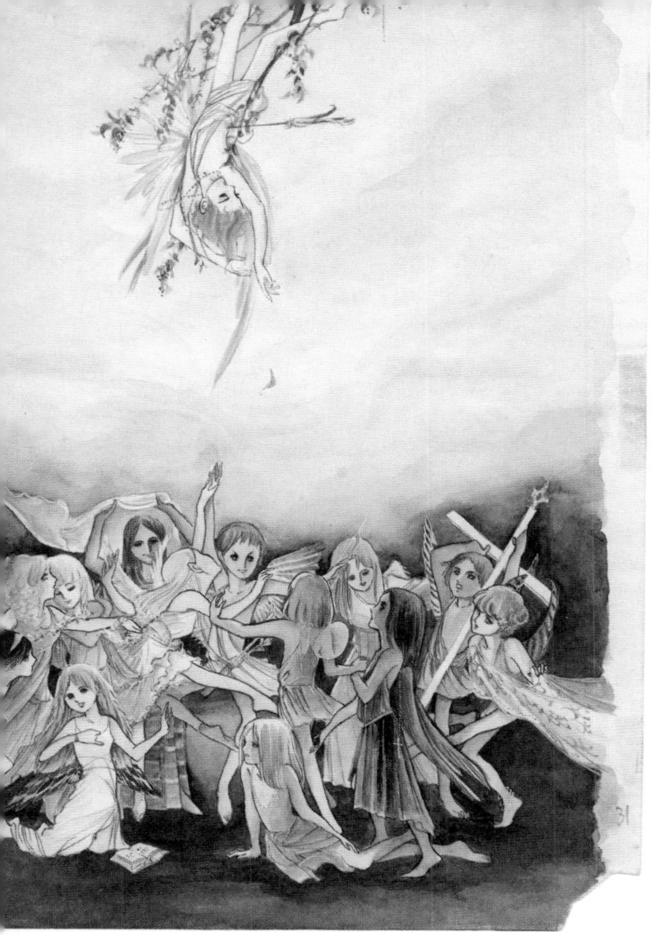

Hagio: Oh, she's seen it, but she seems incapable of comprehending the notion of cartooning as a profession. *[Thorn laughs.]* She's come with me to the editorial offices, she's been to Shogakakun's End-of-the-Year Party with me, she's seen my books, and she's even seen me working, but ... she just doesn't seem to get it.

Thorn: *Wow. That must be hard for you.*

Hagio: Yes. Until I was about 30 years old, she constantly told me to stop doing such work.

Thorn: *Really?* [Laughs.] *Until you were 30?*

Hagio: *[Laughs.]* And the reason she stopped was that we had a huge fight about it.

Thorn: *Is that so? When you were in your 30s? And had received the [Shogakukan Comics] Award?* [4]

Hagio: Oh, that made no difference at all.

Thorn: *That didn't matter?*

Hagio: Not at all. Oh, when I won that award, she bragged to all her neighbors that her daughter had won an award. But then she turned around and told me to quit. *[Laughs.]*

Thorn: *Quit and do what? What did she want you to do?*

Hagio: Something with a higher status. For example, she said, "If you like making stories, why not write children's literature?" Or "Why don't you appear on television?" *[Laughter.]* Because I had been interviewed on TV a few times. In the minds of my mother and father, cartooning was the most pathetic and sleazy sort of work, and they apparently thought I would eventually give it up.

Thorn: *Is your mother still alive?*

Hagio: Alive and well.

Thorn: *How old is she?*

Hagio: She's about 77.

Thorn: *And your father?*

Hagio: He's about 83. When he was young, he wanted to be a violinist, and studied with local teachers for many years. He then joined the company orchestra, where he played and even took on students of his own. So in his mind, classical is the peak of beauty. Any other kind of music is worthless, be it enka,[5] folk, or The Beatles. *[Laughter.]* So my parents have very clear ideas of what is good and what is bad. And comics are bad.

Thorn: *So your parents have never accepted your career?*

Hagio: That's right.

Thorn: *That must be very difficult for you.*

Hagio: Yes. But everyone has their own likes and dislikes, right? There's nothing I can do about that, but I at least want them to keep their mouths shut about my work. *[Laughs.]* So we now maintain a certain distance on that subject.

Thorn: *It must have been very difficult when you first began cartooning.*

Hagio: Yes. So I kept it a secret from them for a long time. I would draw comics with a friend at school, and then hide what I had drawn. I think they had an inkling of what was going on, but they never confronted me about it. But I hid it all along.

One day my father ran into my friend, and she told him that she and I were working hard to become professional cartoonists. Then he came home and, teasingly, told me what she had said. If I had said, "That's true," a lengthy lecture would be sure to follow, so I lied and said, "That's her own idea, not mine." I betrayed my friend. *[Laughs.]*

Any comics-related mail would be a problem if it came directly to my house, so I had it all sent to my friend's house and she would give it to me. *[Laughs.]*

Thorn: *So that's what you did when you first began submitting work to publishers?*

Above: Illustration based on the Mother Goose rhyme "The Death and Burial of Cock Robin." *©1976 Moto HAGIO*

Anyway, as I continued to draw, I found a "comics friend," and one day she said, "Let's make a proper comic." But we were just in our first year of junior high school, and we had no information, no idea how to go about it. Comics are of course printed on both sides of the paper, but one of us had heard that you mustn't draw on both sides of the paper. *[Laughter.]* And after we had already drawn it, we learned that you're supposed to use a ruler when you draw the panel frame. *[Laughter.]* We had drawn them freehand.

Thorn: *At the time, there weren't many books available on cartooning, were there?*

Hagio: No, there weren't.

Thorn: *I think there was Osamu Tezuka's akahon (children's illustrated booklets) "Cartoon College."*

Hagio: Yes, in fact it was in an akahon that included a solicitation for original work that we learned a lot of the basics. You know, "Use India ink and opaque white. Draw with a crow quill pen; pencil drawings can't be used." *[Laughs.]* That sort of thing.

Thorn: *So that's where you learned.*

Hagio: Yes. We had never seen a page of original art, so we wondered what one should look like. *[Laughter.]*

Thorn: *So you read a lot of akahon comics?*

Hagio: At the time, in addition to regular bookstores, there were also a lot of book-rental shops. You could borrow a book for about five yen. So I would help around the house, get five yen, and sometimes use that to rent a book. The scariest were the ones by Kazuo Umezu.[2] *[Laughter.]* Seriously. Somebody told me he was good, so I borrowed something, but it was so incredibly scary. The book I borrowed contained serialized stories by various artists, so I never read the rest of the continuation, but most of the stories created this feeling of dread that something creepy was coming.

Thorn: *And how old were you then?*

Hagio: This was from elementary school to the beginning of junior high school.

Thorn: *So you encountered comics rather early in elementary school?*

Hagio: My older sister — Well, I started renting comics in about the third grade. And there was a space in the classroom for kids to put old books they had finished reading, and some of them were comics. My sister bought the "grade" magazines, which contained some comics.[3] And I knew a woman — she was apparently a distant relative — who had a bookstore, so I would visit her shop on the day a comic was released and ask her to let me read it. Maybe once or twice a year, I would actually buy a comic.

Thorn: *Really? So you didn't buy many comics?*

Hagio: No. My mother hated comics, so I needed special permission: for example, if my grades went up, some special event, like that. My mother and father both saw comics as something for children not old enough to read. They firmly believed — and still believe — that comics are an impediment to studying.

Thorn: *You mean they still believe that even now?*

Hagio: Yes. I think human beings cannot easily shake off an idea once it's planted in their head.

Thorn: *So what does your mother think of the fact that you became a cartoonist?*

Hagio: You know, she seems to think I'm some kind of art teacher. *[Laughs.]*

Thorn: *An art teacher?*

Hagio: You know how there are some people who teach art privately to children? She seems to think that's what I do, like someone who is teaching tea ceremony or flower arrangement.

Thorn: *[Laughs.] All these years? Hasn't she seen your work?*

Thorn: *So you're married to comics.*

Hagio: That's right. Oh, and I have a few cats. *[Laughter.]*

Thorn: *And you started drawing at a very young age?*

Hagio: Yes. I really loved drawing. If there was a piece of paper around, I'd draw on it. I'd draw on the back of advertising fliers, wrapping paper, and for some reason we had this thin, B4-sized paper (ca. 10" x 14") in our house. My mother would give me one of those if I asked her. At the time one sheet of that cost half a yen. *[Laughs.]* So I would play at drawing picture stories.

Thorn: *What do you think the act of drawing meant to you at the time?*

Hagio: Well, all children like to draw. But I was more passionate about it than most. There's something interesting about watching a picture take shape before your eyes as you draw it — a world of pictures drawn in lines, a world of comics. When I started reading comics, I would grow to like the characters, they were interesting to me, so I would draw them myself, making them move in my own way, creating my own stories. It was a game. But I would come up with one story after another. So when I entered elementary school, I bought a notebook for drawing comics in, and proceeded to fill it up with all kinds of stories.

Thorn: *What kind of stories?*

Hagio: You have to understand the situation in [Japanese] comics in those days. In the girls' comics, you would have stories in which the woman you thought was the mother turns out not to be the mother *[laughs]*, and the real mother is actually somewhere else. There were a variety of settings. For example, the poor child in the story turns out to actually come from a rich family, or the child of a rich family turns out to have been adopted from a poor family. And one of the standard devices was amnesia. *[Laughs.]* There's a popular Korean drama that's using the same device. It appeared so often, it makes me think that what with the war and the harsh social conditions, people had an unconscious desire to forget everything. So the heroine goes off in search of her real mother, but along the way she develops amnesia, and ends up being taken care of by a string of kind strangers.

Another popular motif was ballet. There was quite a boom in girls' comics about ballet for a while. For example, the heroine would be a girl from a poor family who's really good at ballet, but she loses the lead to an untalented girl from a rich family. *[Laughter.]* In the standard story, there would be a mean girl and a kind-hearted heroine, and there would be a very clear-cut struggle between good and evil. *[Laughter.]* They were

very simplistic stories. But the good artists would draw these standard stories with an interesting twist; for example, Miyako Maki and Masako Watanabe. There were only about seven artists drawing girls' comics in those days. Women, I mean; there were plenty of male artists drawing girls' comics then. Tetsuya Chiba's girls' comics were particularly good.[1]

Thorn: *Chiba's first serial,* Mama's Violin, *was a story like that. The heroine is looking for her mother, who is suffering from amnesia.*

Hagio: Right, and the mother regains her memory when she hears her daughter's violin.

Thorn: *And of course the heroine goes through all kinds of troubles and is eventually reunited with her mother.*

Hagio: Right. Mitsuteru Yokohama also did a story titled *Tomboy Angel*, which featured a tomboy as the heroine. I really liked stories like that, in which the heroine was lively.

Above: A sequence from the second volume of Hagio's fantasy epic, *Marginal.* ©1986 Moto HAGIO created remains in print today in Japan, in some cases in multiple editions, and her works have been analyzed and written about by dozens of scholars and critics. To quantify Hagio's popularity in globally meaningful terms, on June 4, 2005, the third volume of *Otherworld Barbara* was ranked 1,699 on Amazon.co.jp, and the current edition of her 1974 classic *The Heart of Thomas* was ranked 4,690. (*Batman: Year One Deluxe Edition* was ranked 1,469 and *Blankets* was ranked 6,729 on Amazon.com on the same day.)

This interview was conducted on December 6, 2004, at Hagio's spacious home in the sleepy sub-suburb of Tokyo known as Hanno City. Also present was Hagio's housemate and manager of many years, Akiko Joh, who was herself a cartoonist for a brief time in the early 1970s. Hagio had just woken up when I arrived at 3:00 p.m., and I stayed till after 8:00 p.m., just barely catching the last bullet train back to Kyoto.

Matt Thorn: *Let's begin with the beginning, shall we? You were born on May 12, 1949, so you and I share a birthday.*

Moto Hagio: That's right. Florence Nightingale was also born on May 12.

Thorn: *This was in Ohmuta City, Fukuoka Prefecture. Can I start by asking about your childhood? Your father worked for a mining company?*

Hagio: Yes. Ohmuta is a mining town, and there are some chemical companies, too. My father worked at the port from which they shipped coal as well as timber products, so the kids in the elementary school were all either children of local shop owners or of mine workers. Our Baby Boom generation was of course very large, so each class in the elementary school had more than 50 children, and I think there were five or six classes in each grade.

Thorn: *So it was a pretty big school.*

Hagio: Yes. It was a two-story wood-frame school, but they kept adding new buildings to accommodate our generation.

Thorn: *And you were one of four children?*

Hagio: That's right. My older sister, me, my younger sister and then my brother came last.

Thorn: *And what are your siblings doing now?* [Hagio laughs.] *May I ask?*

Hagio: Sure. Ours was something of a matrilineal family. Practically every child born is a girl. My older sister married and gave birth to twins, a boy and a girl. Her husband is from a town in Fukuoka called Yanagawa. They live there now with his mother. My younger sister is married and living ... where is it? Off on the edge of Saitama Prefecture. They have three girls. The youngest is married, but the older two girls are still single and working. And my little brother was working for a computer company, but suffers from depression and quit about two or three years ago. Now he just takes it easy, photographing birds and going to hot-spring resorts.

And I never married and have done nothing but make comics. *[Laughs.]*

everyone else, and who is periodically reborn, phoenix style. Hagio portrays a rich and convincing culture (strongly reminiscent of Arab culture) in which men take post-pubescent boys to be both their lovers and apprentices. As it turns out, though, there is far more to this planet than meets the eye. "Mother" produces fewer and fewer babies each year, and the population is dwindling. When two nomad men, with the beautiful, confused boy they find and adopt, go in search of an answer to the mystery, they find more than they could ever have imagined, and they also find that the boy, Kira, is the key to the future of the planet.

By now, a clear pattern had begun to emerge in Hagio's works. The story will center on a remarkable and strange character who, for one reason or another, seems incapable of so-called "normal" human interaction (and who is usually small, beautiful, and androgynous). But we see this character through the eyes of an unremarkable (but invariably handsome, and often long-haired) young man, unsure of his place in the world, and just trying to muddle through. This "straight man," usually through arbitrary coincidence, forms a unique bond with the "eccentric."

We also see the coalescing of certain motifs. One, of course, is childhood trauma — including sexual abuse — and dysfunctional families. Another, related motif is genetics (and genetic engineering), heredity, and environmental factors in psychological growth. Also related is the notion of synchronicity, in this case meaning a powerful resonance between two or more characters who often seem to be extremely different from one another. And while the ostensible genre may be science fiction or "realism," almost all of Hagio's major works take the form of a mystery.

In her shorter works, though, Hagio pursues every idea and theme that catches her fancy, and in the late '80s, music was one such theme. Hagio, using music by rock musician Yoshihiro Kai, created in 1988 what may be the world's only "musical graphic novel" (or should that be "graphic novel musical"?), *The Perfect Crime: Faerie*. It was also around this time that Hagio fell in love with ballet, and began a series of short stories revolving around ballet, most notably the somewhat longer *An Ungrateful Man*.

Between 1989 and 1993, Hagio created two "psychological sci-fi mysteries," both of which featured an alien or aliens appearing in unexpected places in contemporary Japan: *Aria of the Sea* and *House on a Dangerous Hill*. While Hagio is characteristically careful in her use of science, these tales, like most of Hagio's, are ultimately more about psychological issues, and individuals overcoming trauma, fear, and insecurity in the process of forming bonds with each other.

But Hagio's career in the 1990s is dominated by her longest (3000-plus pages) and most serious work to date, *A Savage God Reigns*. The title comes from A. Alvarez' *The Savage God: A Study of Suicide* (which in turn, although Hagio did not know it, comes from a diary entry by William Butler Yeats lamenting the rise of what would come to be known as "Modernism"). Beautifully executed, yet brutal in its frankness and often painful to read, *A Savage God Reigns* is the story of a teenage boy, Jeremy, who is sexually and psychologically abused by his stepfather, Greg. Although the abusive stepfather dies early in the story, Jeremy is all but incapacitated by his trauma, and also wracked with guilt, since his mother died along with his stepfather in the car crash Jeremy himself orchestrated. The straight man in this story is Jeremy's blissfully ignorant stepbrother, Ian, who must come to terms with the reality that his father was not the man he had always thought him to be. Ian becomes Jeremy's *de facto* guardian, and struggles awkwardly to help Jeremy regain some semblance of sanity and self-esteem, while simultaneously struggling with his own unexpected and frightening feelings of lust for Jeremy. Although the psychological scars of sexual abuse can never be completely healed, Ian and Jeremy manage in the end, after literally coming to the very brink (of a very real cliff), to end the downward spiral and begin to crawl back up again. This amazing contribution to graphic literature was recognized in 1997 when it was awarded the first Osamu Tezuka Cultural Prize.

Hagio had time for very little else during the 1990s, and after finishing *A Savage God Reigns* in 2001, she took a well-earned, year-long vacation. In 2002, understandably wanting to turn to less emotionally draining material, began her most ambitious science fiction work since Marginal. *Otherworld Barbara* (and no, "Barbara" is not a woman's name in this story) contains many of the themes and motifs I discussed earlier, as well as Hagio's most current interests, which she describes in detail in the interview. Though it will probably end up to be fewer than 600 pages, it is one of Hagio's most complex stories.

Hagio's influence is not limited to the world of comics. Hagio's works have been turned into an animated feature-length film (*They Were Eleven!*), a movie (*Summer Vacation 1999*, based loosely on *The Heart of Thomas*), several plays (*Hanshin*, *The Heart of Thomas*, *The Visitor*, *They Were Eleven!*, *Mesh*), radio dramas (*The Poe Clan*, *Marginal*), and televisions dramas (*They Were Eleven!*, *Iguana Girl*). She has even written a musical for children, *Curdken's Hat: A Jigsaw Puzzle of the Land of Grimm*, based loosely on the Grimm Brothers' story, "The Goose-Girl." Almost every comic she has ever

Opposite: Early sketch for *The Heart of Thomas*. *©1971 Moto HAGIO*

The Moto Hagio INTERVIEW

CONDUCTED BY
MATT THORN

Originally published in The Comics Journal #269 (July, 2005).

As I type this, in the bullet train that is taking me back from Hagio's home in Saitama Prefecture to my own home in Kyoto, I find myself pondering the nature of fate and the place of Hagio's work in contemporary Japanese culture, insofar as the artist occupies a very prominent position in the pantheon of postwar Japanese comics.

For the past 36 years, Hagio has produced one masterpiece after another. Her first hit series, *The Poe Clan* (1972-1976, 800-plus pages), explored the nature of life and death, growth and aging, joy and grief, all through the eyes of a vampire trapped for eternity in the body of a 14-year-old boy. It also earned Hagio the Shogakukan Manga Award in 1976. In 1975, she published the gender-bending science-fiction mystery *They Were Eleven!* (which I translated years ago), and the next year she came out with its sequel, *Horizon of the East, Eternity of the West*. In the late 1970s, in addition to a string of original short pieces, Hagio drew three major "covers": the first, Ray Bradbury's "R is for Rocket" and other short stories; the second, Japanese novelist Ryu Mitsuse's mind-blowing sci-fi epic, *Ten Billion Days and One Hundred Billion Nights*; and the third, Jean Cocteau's disturbing *Les Enfants Terribles*.

As the 1980s dawned, Hagio returned to her own original work with zeal, launching what was to become one of the major series (at 700-plus pages) of her career, *Mesh*. Portraying a turbulent few months in the life of a teenage boy determined to kill his drug-dealer father, *Mesh* became a vehicle for Hagio to purge her own familial demons. In *Mesh*, as in virtually all Hagio's works, there are no "normal" families, no "normal" relationships. Human relationships are intense, yet fragile. Trust is hard-earned, and subject to renegotiation at any moment. Catharsis, redemption, revelation and reconciliation are never cut and dried. Nowhere is this more elegantly captured than in the last scene of the last chapter (titled "The Realistic Death of a Surrealistic Love"), in which the protagonist suddenly finds himself stranded, by his own choice, watching two trains pull away in opposite directions, and then, utterly alone, turns to set off on a new path.

In the meantime, Hagio continued to pursue serious science fiction, such as *A, A'* (again, translated by me for Viz), as well more fantastic, dreamlike short works. In the latter 1980s, after *Mesh*, Hagio occupied herself with another major project, her first long (1000-plus pages) science-fiction series, *Marginal*. Set on a planet where everyone is male except, it seems, for the one "Mother," who is said to give birth to literally

地球へ…
こ…ここは!?
いったい——
……

仏教を擁護する立場にある大王が 神になど頼ったから
仏のご加護は得られなかった
ひいては今の大王に仏のご加護を得る徳はないのだ……と
この大王が在位するかぎり 天地の恩恵はない！

フィレンツェのダビダおけしようしないデビッドボウイモロー描くオーフェースベニスに死すのアンドレセンみんなたして四で割る森蘭丸とは彼のこと!!

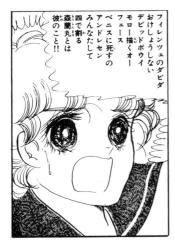

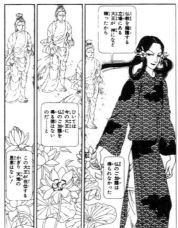

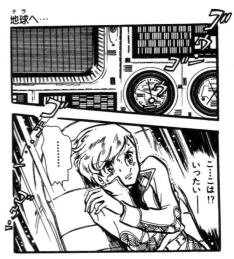

took the staid, semi-legendary Japanese historical figure, Prince Shotoku, and portrayed him as a brilliant, beautifully androgynous homosexual with supernatural powers. Her more recent *Dancing Girl: Terpsichore* won the Tezuka Osamu Cultural Prize in 2007.

Toshie Kihara: Though she started off doing ordinary teen love stories, she made her mark with something completely different, *Mari and Shingo* (1977), a story of the bond between two handsome, talented and charismatic boys coming of age in the days leading up to World War I. Though Mari's love for Shingo is never fully requited, their friendship is never diminished by time or distance. Kihara has declared *A Staff and Wings* — a tale of the French Revolution starring Robespierre, the beautiful Louis-Antoine de Saint-Just, and a fictitious woman with strange powers — to be her final long work.

Minori Kimura: Actually born in 1949, Kimura made her pro debut in 1964 at the tender age of 15. Preferring realistic, contemporary settings to the fantastic, and understatement to melodrama, she reveals the profound in the mundane through characters whose warmth and humanity seem to spill off the page. For the last decade and a half, she has passionately pursued issues of interest to women, including sexuality, work and health. Since commercial publishers have an aversion to anything potentially controversial, she has created her own one-woman publishing house, and has also been commissioned by various non-government organizations.

Nanae Sasaya: Though lacking the name recognition of Hagio or Takemiya, she is widely admired by those familiar with girls' comics of the 1970s. Her occult and horror stories are truly terrifying. Her recent work includes the acclaimed *Eyes of Ice*, a documentary graphic novel about child abuse. She is still active today, though she has changed her pen name from "Nanae" to "Nanaeko."

Mineko Yamada: A pioneer in the genres of science fiction and fantasy in female-oriented comics, she got her start in the rental comics market around 1969, then worked for various commercial girls' magazines through the mid-1980s, when she shifted her focus to self-publication. She remains a big name in the field of Japanese science-fiction fandom.

Junya Yamamoto: Neither a cartoonist nor a woman, Yamamoto, former Editor in Chief of *Special Edition Girls' Comic* and *Petit Flower*, is the invisible member of the 24-Year Group, because it was he who brought so much of their work to the light of day. What any other editor of the day would have seen as flaws in these young artists, Yamamoto saw as enormous potential. In the face of pressure from above, he published one unconventional, controversial story after another, for no other reason than that they were interesting and well-executed. Although his contribution to the girls' comics revolution was long known only to industry insiders, in 2004 he was awarded the Special Achievement Prize of the Japan Media Arts Festival. He served as Professor in Kyoto Seika University's Department of Cartoon and Comic Art for the first four years of that program's existence, from 2000 to 2004. ϟ

Enter the "Magnificent 24-Year Group" ("Hana no nijuuyo nen gumi"), otherwise known as the Magnificent Forty-Niners. Incubated in the radical youth culture of the late 1960s and inspired not only by the best work of older girls' comics artists, but also by European cinema and literature (not to mention American and British rock 'n' roll), a number of talented, innovative, young female artists made their debut at more or less the same time. Who were the Magnificent Forty-Niners? It depends who you ask. If you ask the women who are said to be members — Moto Hagio, Keiko Takemiya, Yumiko Oshima — they will tell you that there is no such group: It is an invention of critics and fans. The name itself refers to the fact that the members are supposed to have been born in the 24th year of the Showa Era (1949 by Western reckoning), but, ironically, of the three whose names come up in anyone's list (the three I listed above), only Hagio was actually born in that year. Some people include in the Forty-Niners any very popular female cartoonist of that generation, such as *Rose of Versailles* creator Riyoko Ikeda, or Sumika Yamamoto, creator of the tennis hit *Aim for the Ace!*. Others include just about anyone who hung out in the apartment shared by Hagio and Takemiya from 1970 to 1972 — even women who were not cartoonists! But most will agree that the Magnificent Forty-Niners are "all those artists who revolutionized girls' comics back in the 1970s."

Using this vague definition, it's easy to see why Hagio, Takemiya, and Oshima are at the top of every list.

Takemiya, who had strongly hinted at homoeroticism in her 1970 short story "In the Sunroom," shocked the nation in 1976 when she dropped the innuendo and portrayed — tastefully, but unambiguously — sex (as well as sexual abuse) between boys and young men in her devastating *The Song of the Wind and the Trees*. She also pioneered the genres of science fiction and fantasy, and even created a sci-fi romantic comedy, *Fly Me to the Moon!*, about a spaceship pilot and his 9-year-old fiancée who has supernatural powers (1980). The most accessible of the three, she has tried her hand at practically every conceivable genre, and continues to cartoon today, though her responsibilities as Professor in Kyoto Seika University's Department of Comic and Cartoon Art leave her little time to do so.

Yumiko Oshima is something of an enigma. Her drawing style is extremely spare when compared with her contemporaries, and on the surface her stories (almost all short stories) seem lighthearted, cute and mundane. But at their heart, they are profound, terrifying and fantastic. Just to give you a taste, her mind-blowing *Banana Bread Pudding* features a young girl slipping into madness because her older sister is to be married, and won't be able to accompany her to the bathroom after 10 PM and stand outside singing "Twinkle, Twinkle, Little Star." Without this protection, she believes, a beautiful, androgynous clown will take her and run her through a meat grinder. Since her dream is to marry a closeted gay man and help him to accept his sexuality, her best friend convinces her playboy brother to play gay. As it turns out, the boy this best friend is in love with is an uncloseted gay who is in love with her brother. And, in turn, this boy is sexually abused secretly by a middle-aged teacher who is a closeted gay man. Are you still with me? It may sound comical (and it often is), but I've had to swear off reading Oshima's stories in public because I've never gotten through one without crying. The novelist Banana Yoshimoto considers Oshima to be her greatest influence.

Here are some other artists often counted among the Forty-Niners.

Ryoko Yamagishi: Amongst her other accomplishments, she was the first artist to portray lesbianism in girls' comics, with her short story "Two in a White Room" (1971). She is best known for her ballet classic *Arabesque* (1971), in which she took the tired genre of ballet (which had been a standard since the '50s) and turned it into a laboratory for complex and erotically charged psychological explorations. In *The Son of Heaven in the Land of the Rising Sun* (1980), she

...the Magnificent Forty-Niners are "all those artists who revolutionized girls' comics back in the 1970s."

Opposite, left: From Yumiko Oshima's "F Shiki Ranmaru." © *Yumiko OSHIMA*
Opposite, center: From Ryoko Yamagishi's *The Son of Heaven in the Land of the Rising Sun.* © *1980 Ryoko YAMAGISHI*
Opposite, right: From Keiko Takemiya's *Toward the Terra.* © *1980 Keiko TAKEMIYA*

The Magnificent Forty-Niners

BY MATT THORN

Originally published in The Comics Journal #269 *(July, 2005).*

From the dawn of the dynamic Tezuka-style "story manga" in the early 1950s through the pre-hippy 1960s, the genre of Japanese girls' comics — shōjo manga — was a backwater in which mostly male artists, unable to find better work, drew either light humor strips that were cute-but-forgettable, or sappy, formulaic melodramas about some pretty, passive little girl tossed by fate from one abusive circumstance to another, until some handsome, kind young man shows up to rescue her and reunite her with her mother (who would have looked for her earlier, but had amnesia until yesterday). Girls' comics were of little interest to anyone other than their artists and editors and the elementary-school girls who were their readers.

Good work was being done by good artists, including two of the handful of women cartoonists working at the time: *Fuichin-san* creator Toshiko Ueda and *Harp of the Stars* creator Hideko Mizuno. Some men, too, such as *Joh of Tomorrow* creator Tetsuya Chiba, did work of lasting value in girls' comics. But the genre was still bound by extremely narrow notions of what girls' comics could or should be. In the mid-1960s, a young woman named Yoshiko Nishitani defied convention by creating girls' comics whose heroines were neither little girls nor faraway princesses, but contemporary Japanese teenagers whose interests included (gasp!) boys. This was a reflection of the gradual rise in age of readers, as well as the increasing prominence of baby-boomer teens in popular culture. But it was also a reaching out to teen girls who may have dismissed comics as "kid stuff."

In the early 1960s, children's magazines responded to the threat from the new medium of television by introducing a weekly format and increasing the amount of photos, illustrations, and comics in their pages. In doing so, they created Japan's first generation of comics addicts, reluctant to "grow out of" comics. This in turn triggered the comics boom of the 1960s, creating a sudden demand for talent to work in the many new magazines (which were rapidly transforming from general children's magazines into comics magazines). This coincided with changes in societal views of the "proper roles" of women. If women could be elected to the National Diet of Japan, why couldn't they draw comics? Publishers opened the spigot, and what had been a trickle of young women artists became a cascade. Almost overnight, the male artists who had been creating girls' comics moved over to the new boys' magazines, and a generation of young women took over. (Considering that Americans tend to think of Japan as horribly backwards in terms of gender equity, it is ironic that this gender revolution took place 30-odd years ago in Japan, but has yet to happen in the U.S.)

Despite the influx of women, however, most shōjo manga remained formulaic and unremarkable. What was needed was a revolution in the mindset of artists, editors and readers alike — a revolution in the concept of what was possible in the genre of female-targeted comics.

V   "THE MAGNIFICENT FORTY-NINERS"   By Matt THORN

IX   "THE MOTO HAGIO INTERVIEW"   Conducted by Matt THORN

⚡007   BIANCA   BIANKA © 1977 Moto HAGIO

⚡023   GIRL ON PORCH WITH PUPPY   PORCH DE SHOJO GA KOINUTO © 1977 Moto HAGIO

⚡035   AUTUMN JOURNEY   AKI NO TABI © 1977 Moto HAGIO

⚡059   MARIÉ, TEN YEARS LATER   JUNENME NO MARIE © 1985 Moto HAGIO

⚡075   A DRUNKEN DREAM   SUIMU © 1985 Moto HAGIO

⚡097   HANSHIN: HALF-GOD   HANSHIN © 1985 Moto HAGIO

⚡113   ANGEL MIMIC   TENSHI NO GITAI © 2008 Moto HAGIO

⚡163   IGUANA GIRL   IGUANA NO MUSUME © 2008 Moto HAGIO

⚡213   THE CHILD WHO COMES HOME   KAETTEKURU KO © 2008 Moto HAGIO

⚡237   THE WILLOW TREE   YANAGI NO KI © 2007 Moto HAGIO

FANTAGRAPHICS BOOKS
7563 Lake City Way NE, Seattle, WA 98115

Translation: Matt THORN
Editorial Liaison: Gary GROTH
Design: Adam GRANO
Lettering: Rich TOMMASO
Production: Paul BARESH
Associate Publisher: Eric REYNOLDS
Publishers: Gary GROTH and Kim THOMPSON

To receive a free full-color catalog of comics, graphic novels, and other manga, call 1-800-657-1100,
or visit www.fantagraphics.com. You may order books at our web site or by phone.

Distributed in the U.S. by W.W. Norton and Company, Inc. (212-354-5500)
Distributed in Canada by the Canadian Manda Group (416-516-0911)
Distributed in the United Kingdom by Turnaround Distribution (108-829-3009)

First Fantagraphics printing: September, 2010
ISBN: 978-1-60699-377-4
Printed in China

If you enjoy the graphic design of this book, please read: HTTP://EN.WIKIPEDIA.ORG/WIKI/WABI-SABI

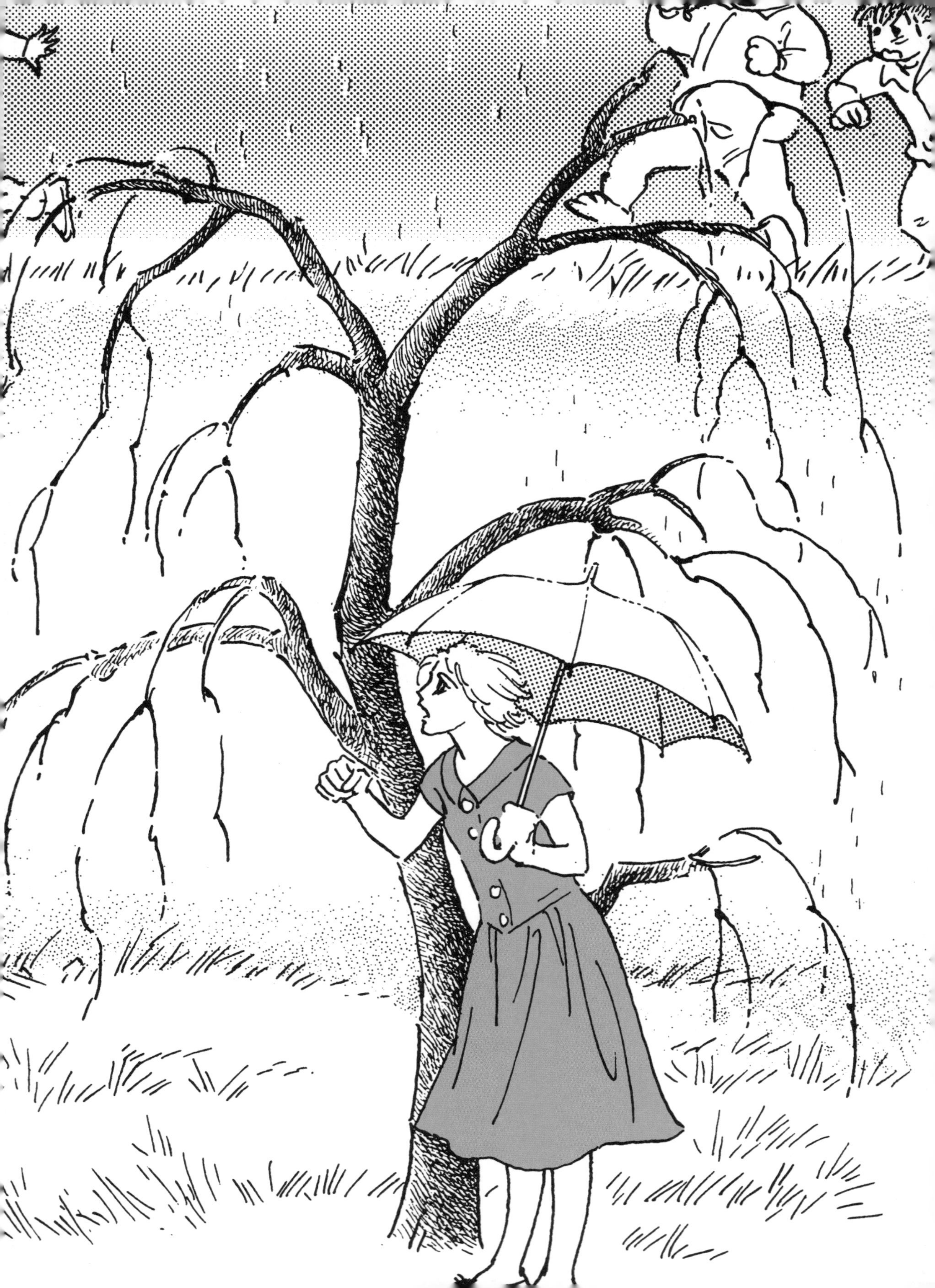

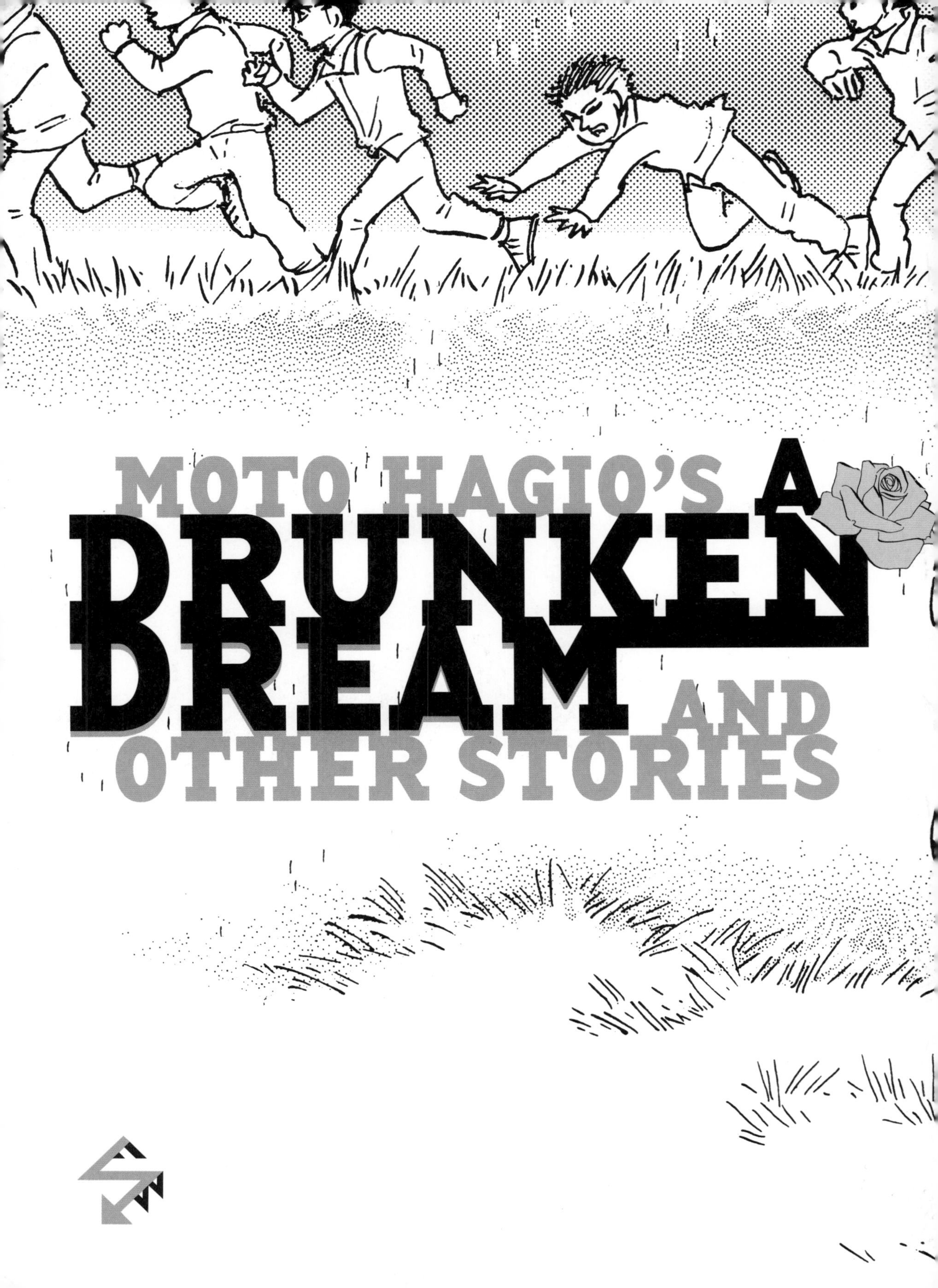

MOTO HAGIO'S A DRUNKEN DREAM AND OTHER STORIES

OMUTA CITY, FUKUOKA PREFECTURE. SHE IS A WRITERS OF JAPAN AND THE JAPAN CARTOONISTS *THE POE CLAN, THEY WERE ELEVEN, THE HEART GIRL," MARGINAL,* AND *MESH*. IN 1976, SHE FOR *THE POE CLAN* AND *THEY WERE ELEVEN*. IN THE OSAMU TEZUKA CULTURE AWARD GRAND WAS AWARDED THE 27TH JAPAN SF GRAND PRIZE CREATING A MANGA ABOUT A CAT NAMED *FLOWERS*.

LANSDALE, PENNSYLVANIA. HE IS A CULTURAL AND TEACHER. HE IS BEST KNOWN IN THE EVANGELIST, A CALLING HE WAS INSPIRED TO *THOMAS* AT THE AGE OF 21. HIS TRANSLATIONS *A,A',* HAYAO MIYAZAKI'S *NAUSICAÄ OF THE* AND AKIMI YOSHIDA'S *BANANA FISH*.